VIKTOR KALVACHEV'S

# BLUE ESTATE®

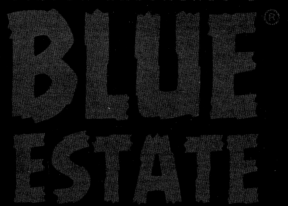

**IMAGE COMICS, INC.**
Robert Kirkman – Chief Operating Officer
Erik Larsen – Chief Financial Officer
Todd McFarlane – President
Marc Silvestri – Chief Executive Officer
Jim Valentino – Vice-President

Eric Stephenson – Publisher
Ron Richards – Director of Business Development
Jennifer de Guzman – Director of Trade Book Sales
Kat Salazar – Director of PR & Marketing
Jeremy Sullivan – Director of Digital Sales
Emilio Bautista – Sales Assistant
Branwyn Bigglestone – Senior Accounts Manager
Emily Miller – Accounts Manager
Jessica Ambriz – Administrative Assistant
Tyler Shainline – Events Coordinator
David Brothers – Content Manager
Jonathan Chan – Production Manager
Drew Gill – Art Director
Meredith Wallace – Print Manager
Monica Garcia – Senior Production Artist
Jenna Savage – Production Artist
Addison Duke – Production Artist
Tricia Ramos – Production Assistant
IMAGECOMICS.COM

# BLUE™
# ESTATE

CREATED BY
## VIKTOR KALVACHEV

AND
## KOSTA YANEV

Books like Blue Estate don't work for me. They never have.

How can a reader, particularly me, enjoy a story where the art continually changes every few pages? It's difficult and always disappointing. There's always one or two artists that must have slept with the editor to have been included. Hell, maybe it was an orgy. Disgusting. I'm not even a big fan of individual artists that use multiple styles to tell stories. Generally you get a few exceptional panels and a bunch of cheat panels in an unfinished style. They don't mesh. They don't gel. I sound finicky, don't I? But you probably feel the same way, right? ....I knew we had something in common. Good.

Somehow, I don't know how, but somehow, Blue Estate works. It works perfectly. It works so well that you and I probably can't pick our favorite artists from the series and say [ preferably on a blog or Tumblr page ], "I wish so and so was drawing the entire series!" Nope. There's a lot of gelling. So much so that it gets as messy as most of the situations that unfold page after page in the book you're about to enjoy. It's disturbing how well all of the diverse talents seamlessly connect with the story. There has to be someone involved that should take the blame and I don't want to accuse Andrew Osborne of anything. With the amount of sex and violence in this book - I don't want to upset a guy like him.

Oh yeah, Viktor. Of course! He's an incredibly annoying artist. Before ever meeting him I thought I had him pegged. He was a talented black and white European interior artist. His pages were powerful stark and graphic. Thank goodness there wasn't any color. But there was – I turned away for a second and discovered Viktor illustrated in color too. And that black and white style of his I loved so much? Well, that was just one of the many styles he excelled at. Viktor is so adapt at so many styles it must be difficult to decide which one to use from one project to the next. Like my wife with 100 shoes to cross examine with her closet full of countless dresses and outfits [ that example probably helps you understand what I mean a little better ]. I don't know how either of them do it but let's concentrate on Viktor for now.

So I guess it would make sense that an artist capable of so many varied art styles would excel at picking out such a talented and cohesive group of artists. He's like Yul Brenner in The Magnificent Seven gathering a band of toughs to tame the West – except Viktor doesn't allow for casualties. They're all top notch, highly acclaimed talents and they all do one thing exceptionally well. All of them approach graphic storytelling from unique and fresh angles. None of them are cookie cutter artists. They all bring something different. So, technically, how on Earth does Blue Estate work? How is that cohesive? Remember I used the word "gel"? How does that gel? It's a legitimate question.

Like most questions, I rarely have the answer. This is no exception. Andrew Osborne and Viktor have done the seemingly impossible. Blue Estate just works. Accept it. I have.

I'm lying again and I apologize. I haven't accepted it. I'm going to figure it out. But that doesn't mean you have to as well. You can just enjoy the juicy fruits of their labor. You lucky bastard! I envy you.

**~Dan Panosian, downtown Los Angeles, California 2014**

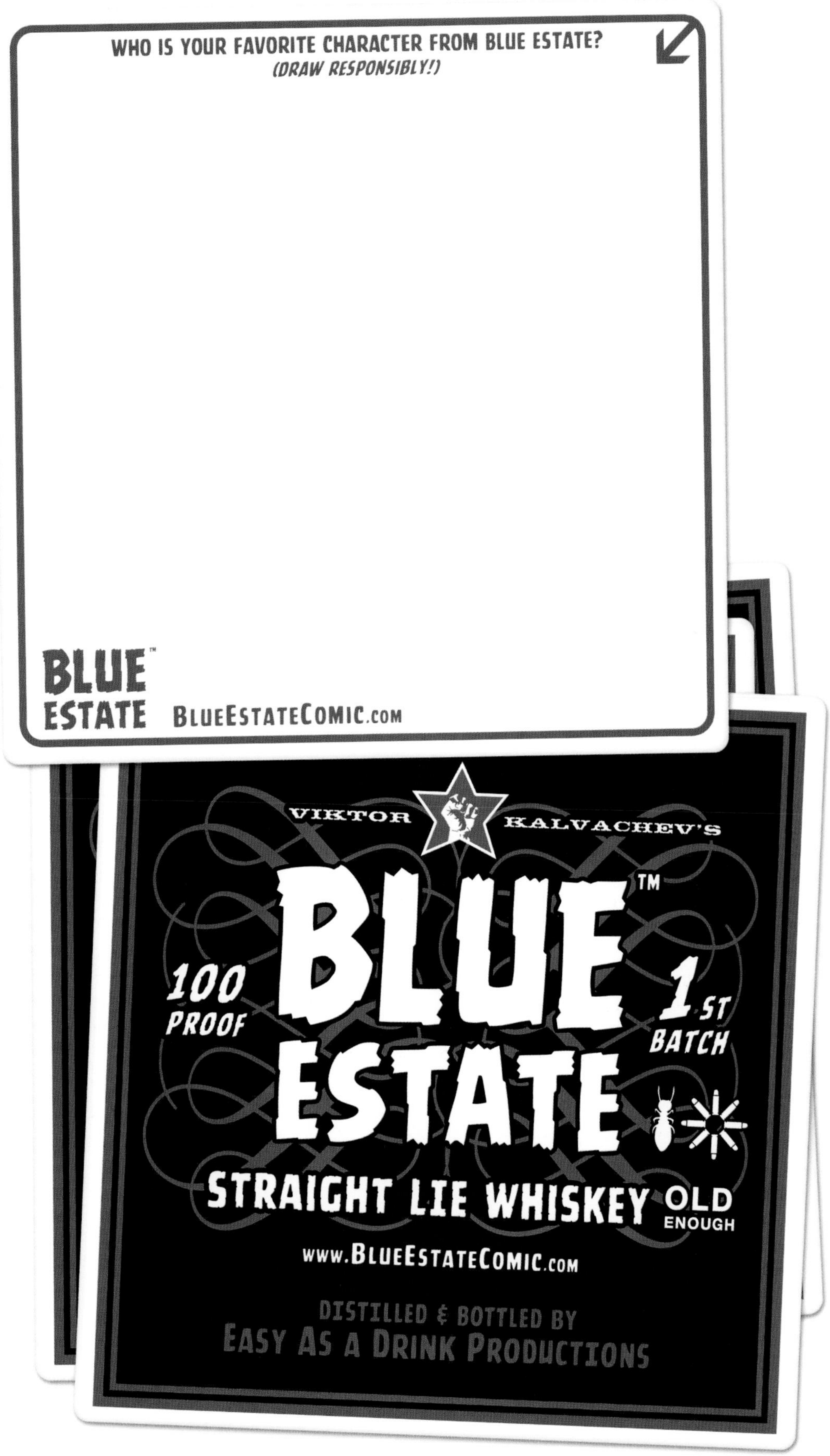
WHO IS YOUR FAVORITE CHARACTER FROM BLUE ESTATE?
(DRAW RESPONSIBLY!)
BLUE ESTATE™
BLUEESTATECOMIC.COM
VIKTOR KALVACHEV'S
BLUE ESTATE™
100 PROOF
1ST BATCH
STRAIGHT LIE WHISKEY
OLD ENOUGH
www.BLUEESTATECOMIC.com
DISTILLED & BOTTLED BY
EASY AS A DRINK PRODUCTIONS

# BLUE
## ESTATE

Tony Livárno!

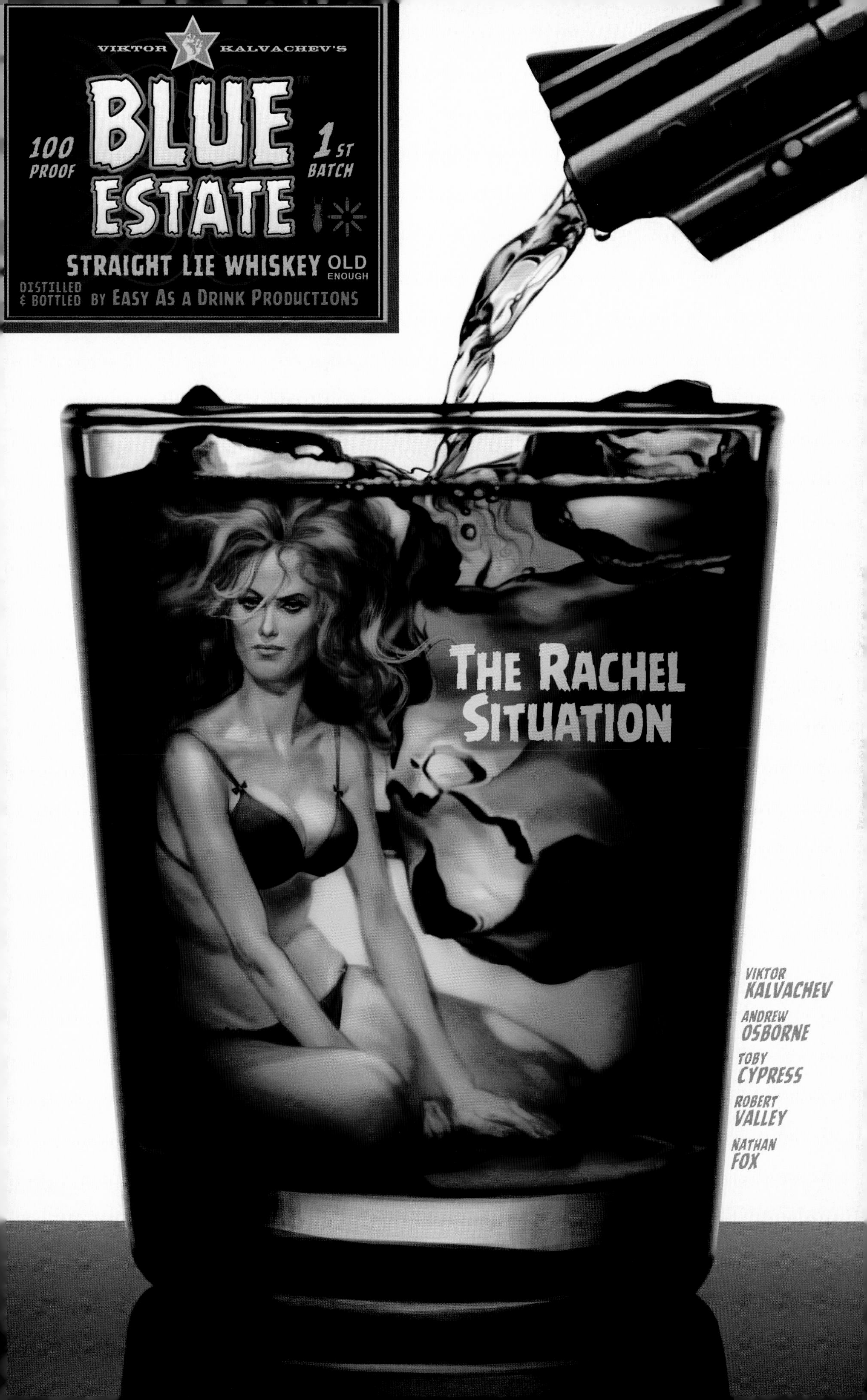
VIKTOR KALVACHEV'S
BLUE ESTATE
100 PROOF
1 ST BATCH
STRAIGHT LIE WHISKEY OLD ENOUGH
DISTILLED & BOTTLED BY EASY AS A DRINK PRODUCTIONS
THE RACHEL SITUATION
VIKTOR KALVACHEV
ANDREW OSBORNE
TOBY CYPRESS
ROBERT VALLEY
NATHAN FOX

# BLUE ESTATE ™

## ESTATE

### EPISODE ONE:
## THE RACHEL SITUATION

ORIGINAL STORY:
**VIKTOR KALVACHEV** AND **KOSTA YANEV**

SCRIPT BY **ANDREW OSBORNE**

ARTISTS:
**VIKTOR KALVACHEV**
**TOBY CYPRESS**
**NATHAN FOX**
**ROBERT VALLEY**

ART DIRECTION BY **VIKTOR KALVACHEV**

COVER, COLORS & DESIGN:
**VIKTOR KALVACHEV**

CONTRIBUTING EDITOR:
**PHILO NORTHRUP**

### WWW.BlueEstateComic.com

EZD ™
PRODUCTIONS

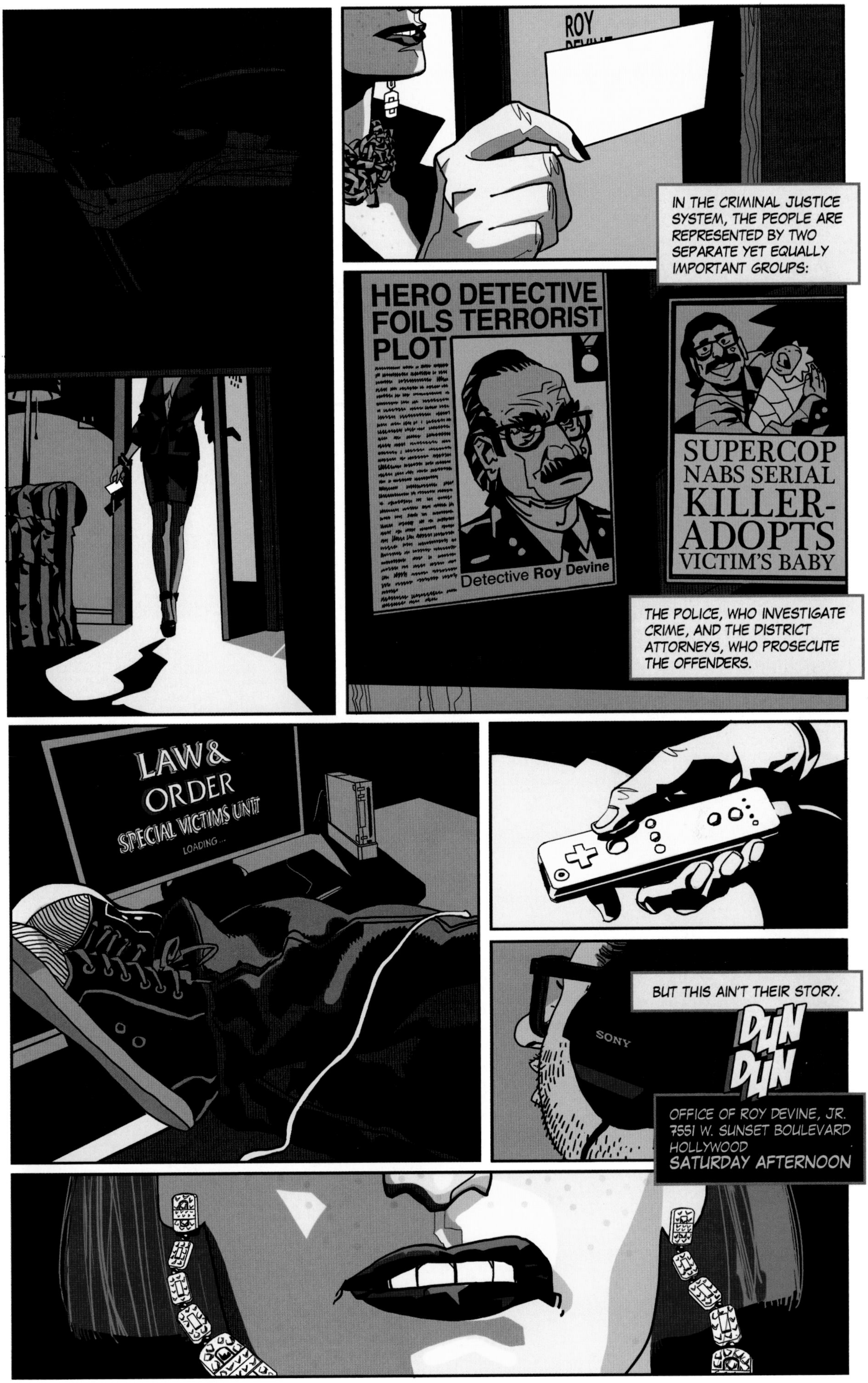
ROY
IN THE CRIMINAL JUSTICE SYSTEM, THE PEOPLE ARE REPRESENTED BY TWO SEPARATE YET EQUALLY IMPORTANT GROUPS:
HERO DETECTIVE FOILS TERRORIST PLOT
Detective Roy Devine
SUPERCOP NABS SERIAL KILLER-ADOPTS VICTIM'S BABY
THE POLICE, WHO INVESTIGATE CRIME, AND THE DISTRICT ATTORNEYS, WHO PROSECUTE THE OFFENDERS.
LAW & ORDER
SPECIAL VICTIMS UNIT
LOADING...
BUT THIS AIN'T THEIR STORY.
SONY
DUN DUN
OFFICE OF ROY DEVINE, JR.
7551 W. SUNSET BOULEVARD
HOLLYWOOD
SATURDAY AFTERNOON

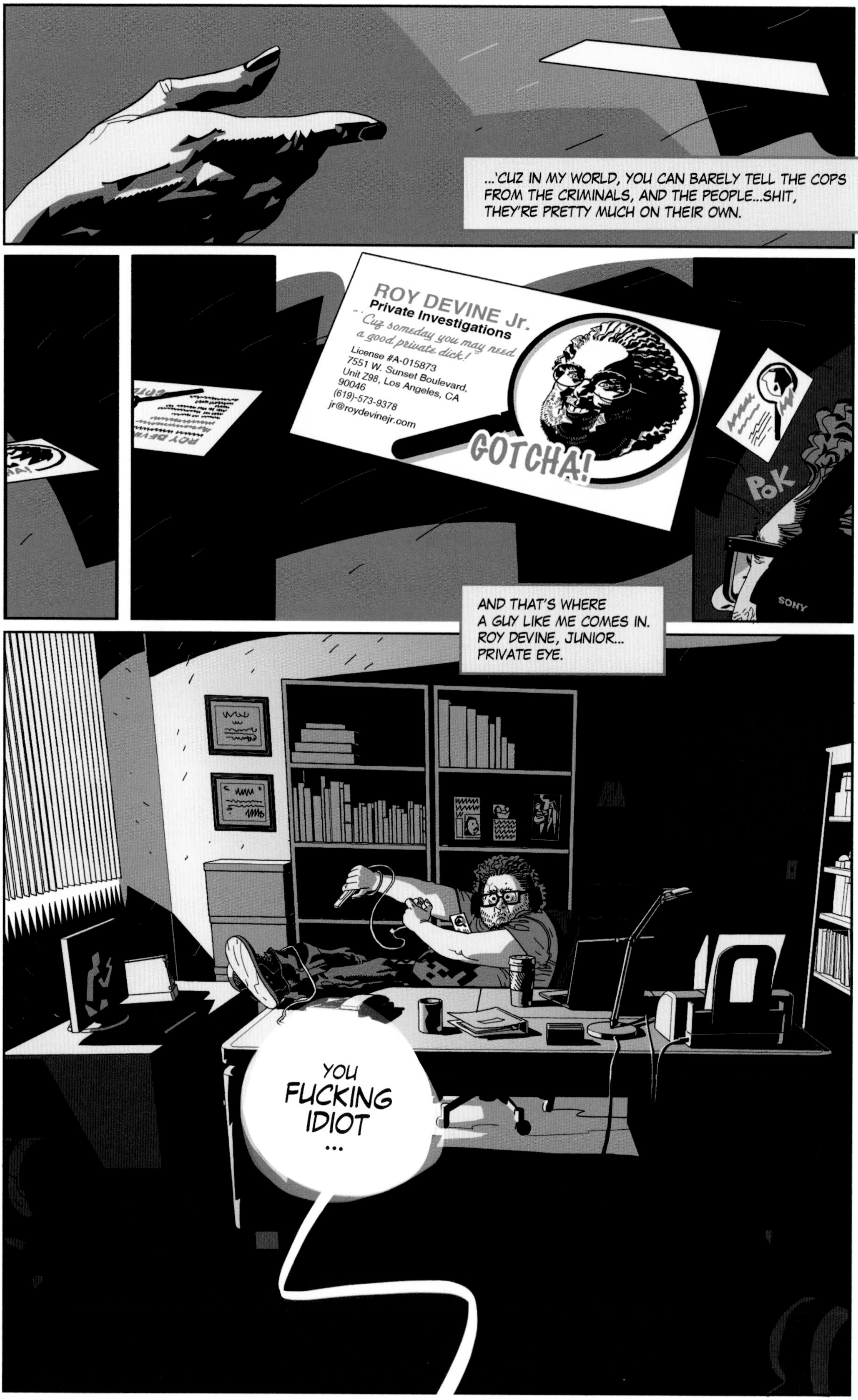
...'CUZ IN MY WORLD, YOU CAN BARELY TELL THE COPS FROM THE CRIMINALS, AND THE PEOPLE...SHIT, THEY'RE PRETTY MUCH ON THEIR OWN.
ROY DEVINE Jr.
Private Investigations
"'Cuz someday you may need a good private dick!"
License #A-015873
7551 W. Sunset Boulevard,
Unit Z98, Los Angeles, CA
90046
(619)-573-9378
jr@roydevinejr.com
GOTCHA!
POK
SONY
AND THAT'S WHERE A GUY LIKE ME COMES IN. ROY DEVINE, JUNIOR... PRIVATE EYE.
YOU FUCKING IDIOT ...

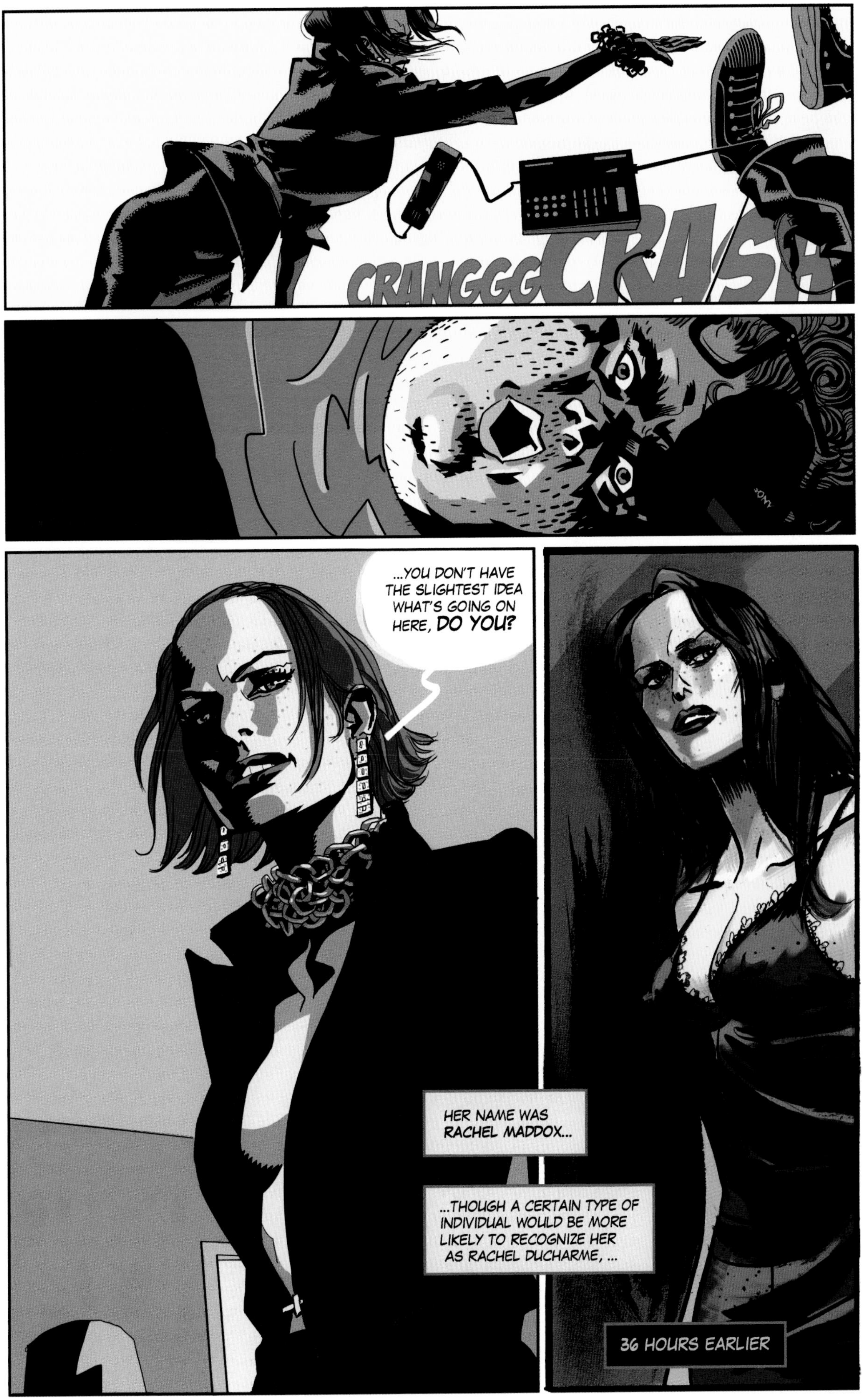
CRANGGG CRASH
...YOU DON'T HAVE THE SLIGHTEST IDEA WHAT'S GOING ON HERE, DO YOU?
HER NAME WAS RACHEL MADDOX...
...THOUGH A CERTAIN TYPE OF INDIVIDUAL WOULD BE MORE LIKELY TO RECOGNIZE HER AS RACHEL DUCHARME, ...
36 HOURS EARLIER

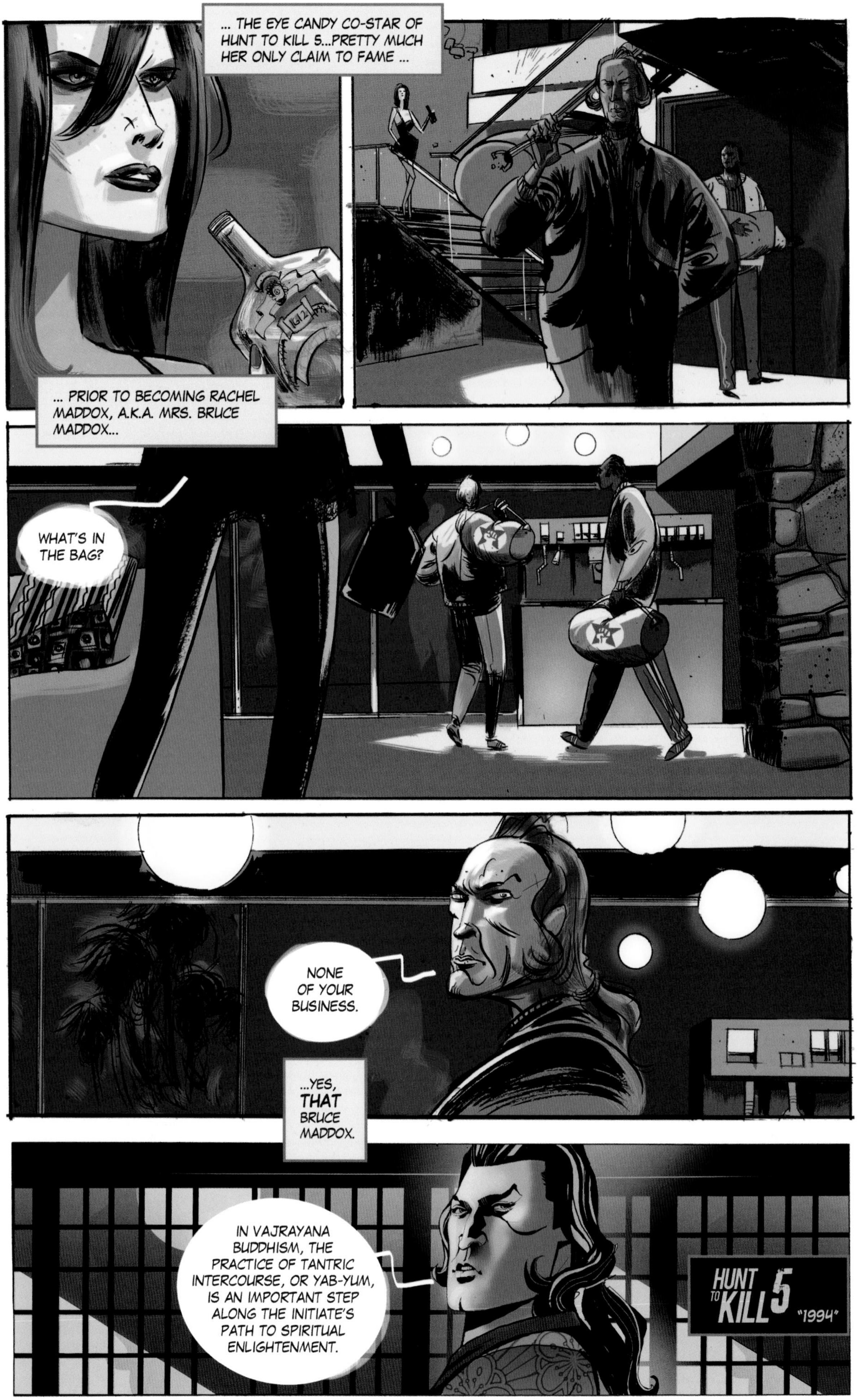
... THE EYE CANDY CO-STAR OF HUNT TO KILL 5...PRETTY MUCH HER ONLY CLAIM TO FAME ...
... PRIOR TO BECOMING RACHEL MADDOX, A.K.A. MRS. BRUCE MADDOX...
WHAT'S IN THE BAG?
NONE OF YOUR BUSINESS.
...YES, THAT BRUCE MADDOX.
IN VAJRAYANA BUDDHISM, THE PRACTICE OF TANTRIC INTERCOURSE, OR YAB-YUM, IS AN IMPORTANT STEP ALONG THE INITIATE'S PATH TO SPIRITUAL ENLIGHTENMENT.
HUNT TO KILL 5 "1994"

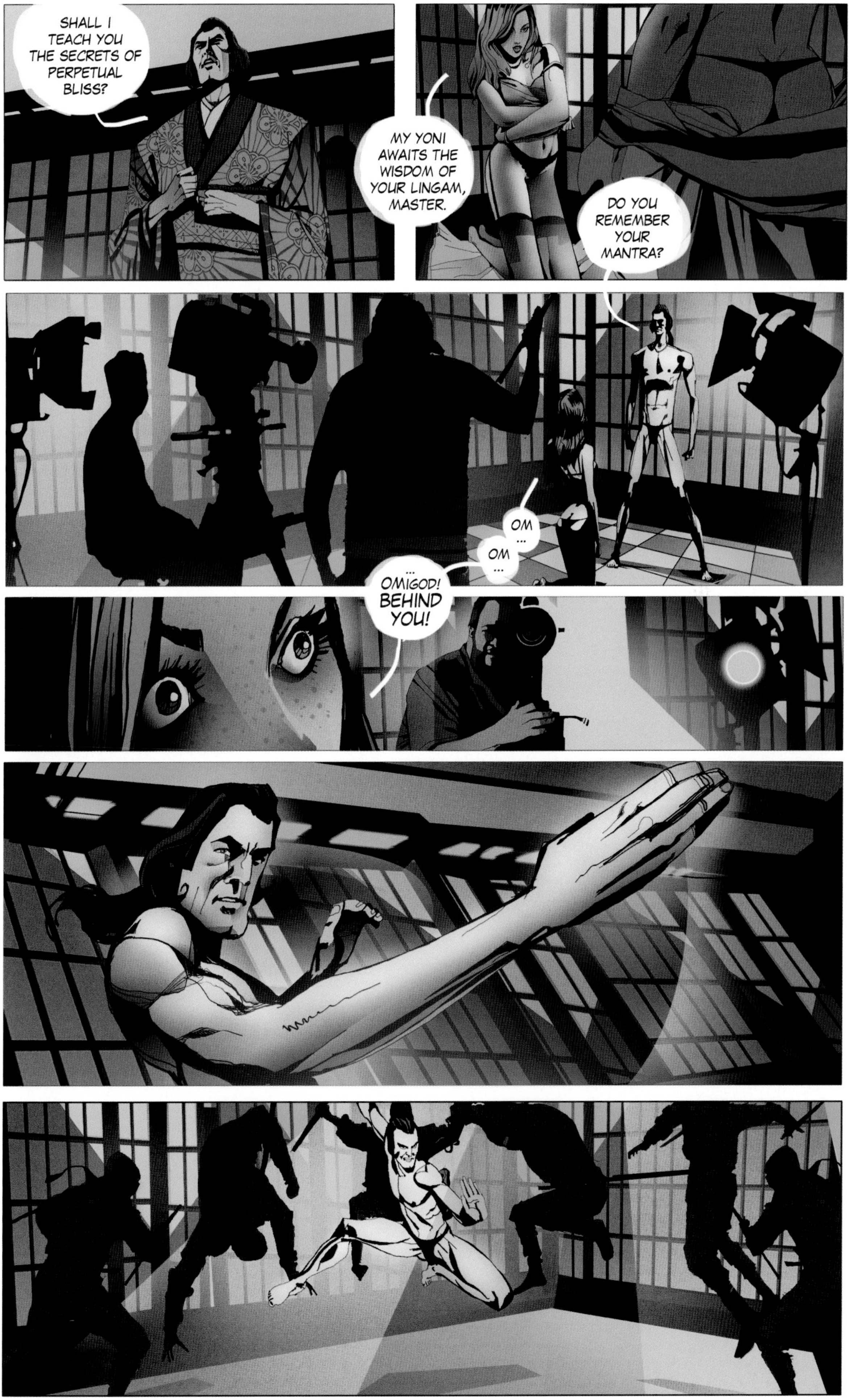
SHALL I TEACH YOU THE SECRETS OF PERPETUAL BLISS?
MY YONI AWAITS THE WISDOM OF YOUR LINGAM, MASTER.
DO YOU REMEMBER YOUR MANTRA?
OM ...
OM ...
... OMIGOD! BEHIND YOU!

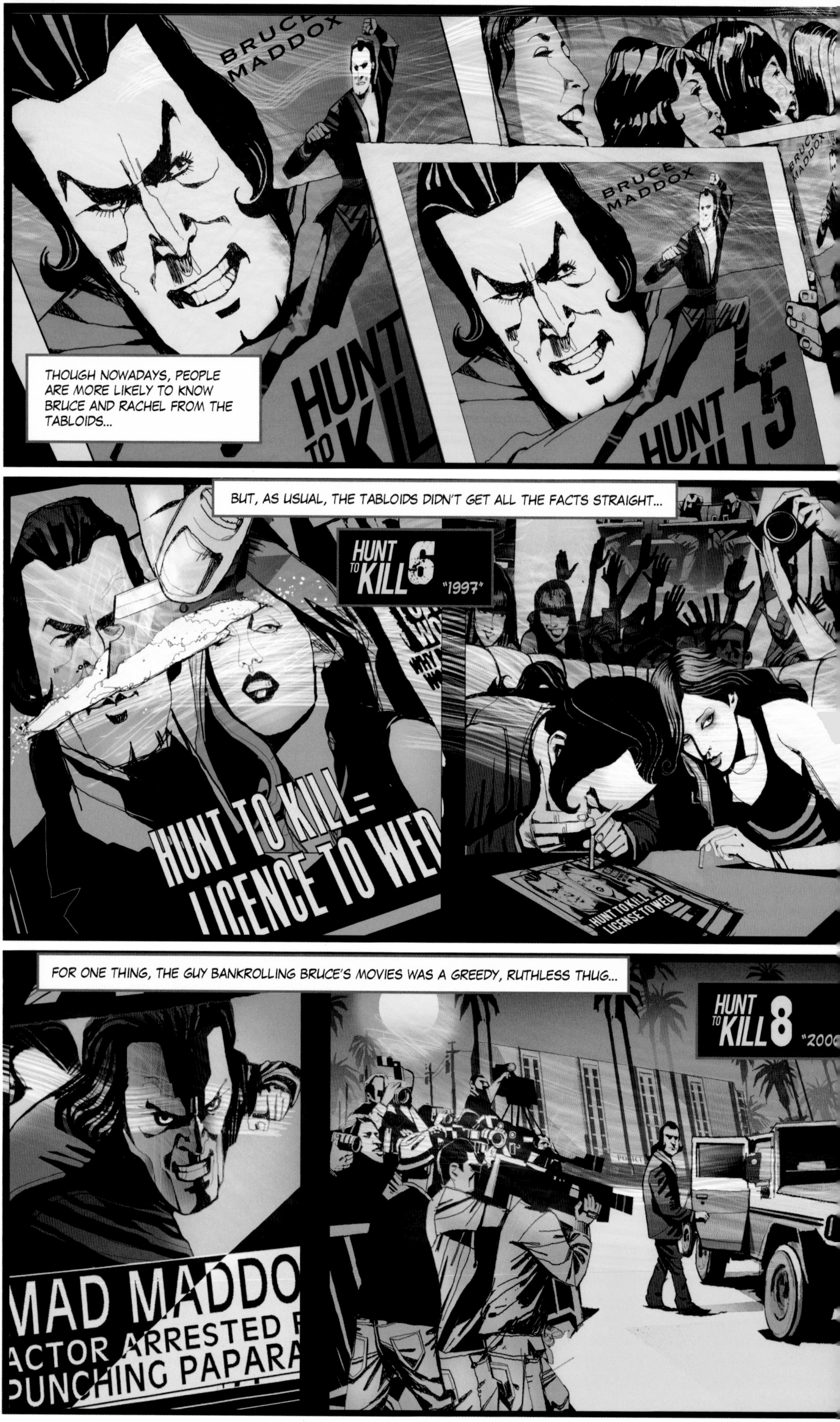
BRUCE MADDOX
HUNT TO KIL
BRUCE MADDOX
HUNT
5
THOUGH NOWADAYS, PEOPLE ARE MORE LIKELY TO KNOW BRUCE AND RACHEL FROM THE TABLOIDS...
BUT, AS USUAL, THE TABLOIDS DIDN'T GET ALL THE FACTS STRAIGHT...
HUNT TO KILL 6
"1997"
HUNT TO KILL=
LICENCE TO WED
HUNT TO KILL
LICENSE TO WED
FOR ONE THING, THE GUY BANKROLLING BRUCE'S MOVIES WAS A GREEDY, RUTHLESS THUG...
HUNT TO KILL 8
MAD MADDO
ACTOR ARRESTED
PUNCHING PAPARA

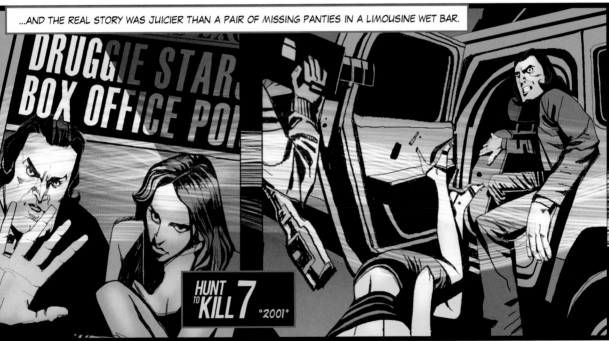

...AND THE REAL STORY WAS JUICIER THAN A PAIR OF MISSING PANTIES IN A LIMOUSINE WET BAR.

DRUGGIE STARS
BOX OFFICE POI

HUNT TO KILL 7 "2001"

...BUT UNLIKE MOST *OTHER* HOLLYWOOD PRODUCERS, HE WAS ALSO AN *ACTUAL CRIMINAL!*

VADIM PETROVICH RAZOV...

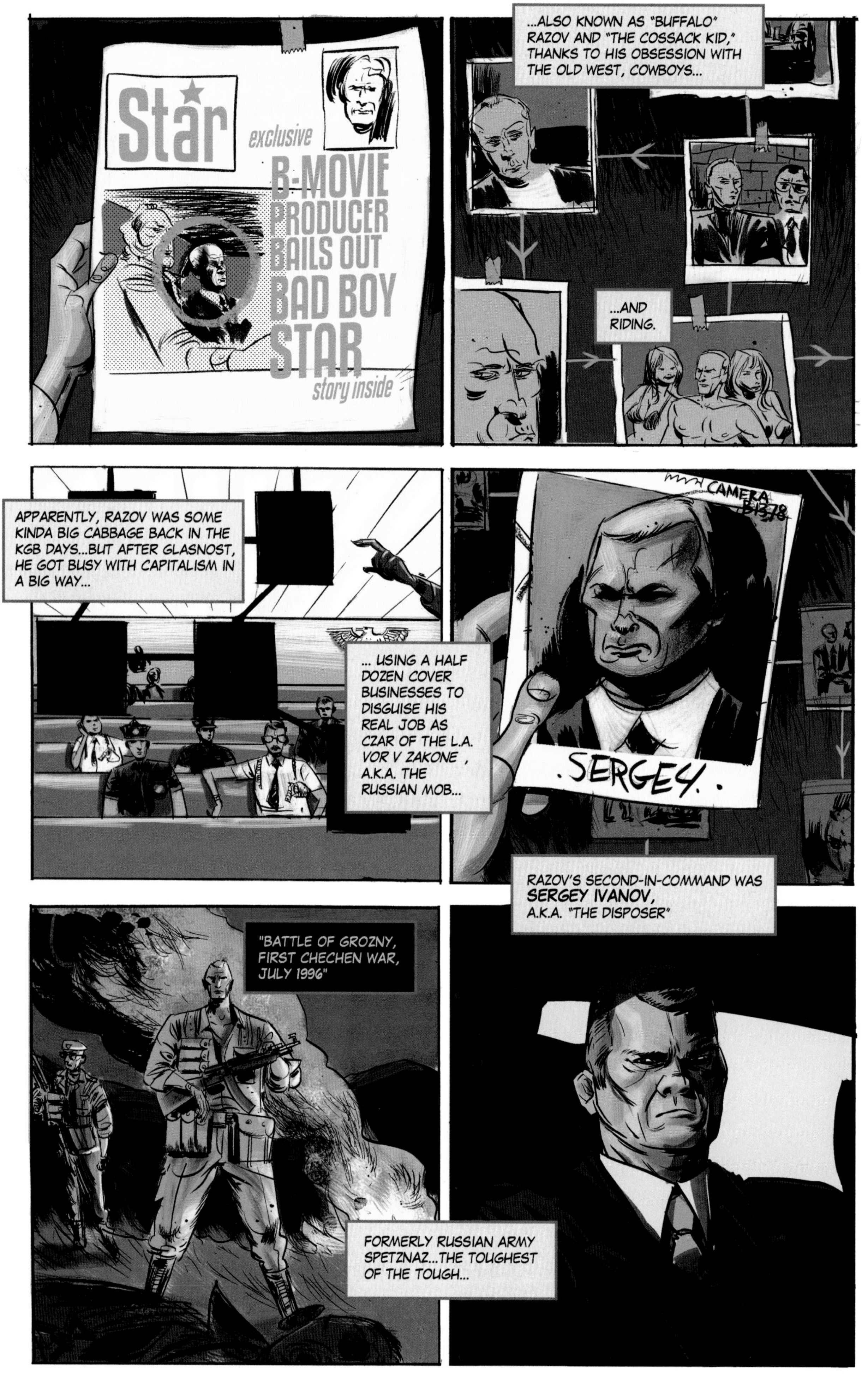
Star
exclusive
B-MOVIE PRODUCER BAILS OUT BAD BOY STAR
story inside
...ALSO KNOWN AS "BUFFALO" RAZOV AND "THE COSSACK KID," THANKS TO HIS OBSESSION WITH THE OLD WEST, COWBOYS...
...AND RIDING.
APPARENTLY, RAZOV WAS SOME KINDA BIG CABBAGE BACK IN THE KGB DAYS...BUT AFTER GLASNOST, HE GOT BUSY WITH CAPITALISM IN A BIG WAY...
... USING A HALF DOZEN COVER BUSINESSES TO DISGUISE HIS REAL JOB AS CZAR OF THE L.A. VOR V ZAKONE , A.K.A. THE RUSSIAN MOB...
CAMERA
SERGEY.
RAZOV'S SECOND-IN-COMMAND WAS SERGEY IVANOV, A.K.A. "THE DISPOSER"
"BATTLE OF GROZNY, FIRST CHECHEN WAR, JULY 1996"
FORMERLY RUSSIAN ARMY SPETZNAZ...THE TOUGHEST OF THE TOUGH...

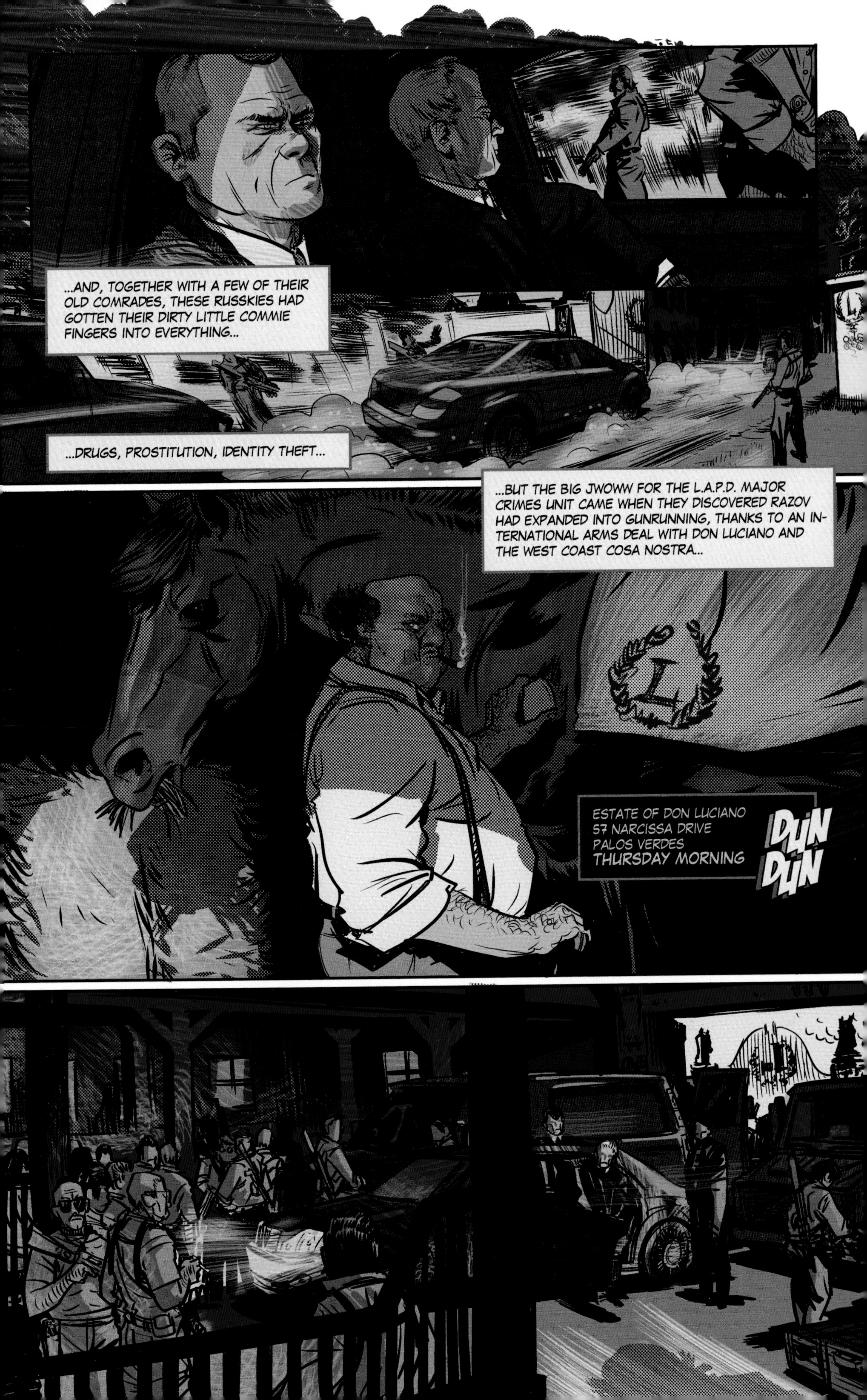
...AND, TOGETHER WITH A FEW OF THEIR OLD COMRADES, THESE RUSSKIES HAD GOTTEN THEIR DIRTY LITTLE COMMIE FINGERS INTO EVERYTHING...
...DRUGS, PROSTITUTION, IDENTITY THEFT...
...BUT THE BIG JWOWW FOR THE L.A.P.D. MAJOR CRIMES UNIT CAME WHEN THEY DISCOVERED RAZOV HAD EXPANDED INTO GUNRUNNING, THANKS TO AN INTERNATIONAL ARMS DEAL WITH DON LUCIANO AND THE WEST COAST COSA NOSTRA...
ESTATE OF DON LUCIANO
57 NARCISSA DRIVE
PALOS VERDES
THURSDAY MORNING
DUN DUN

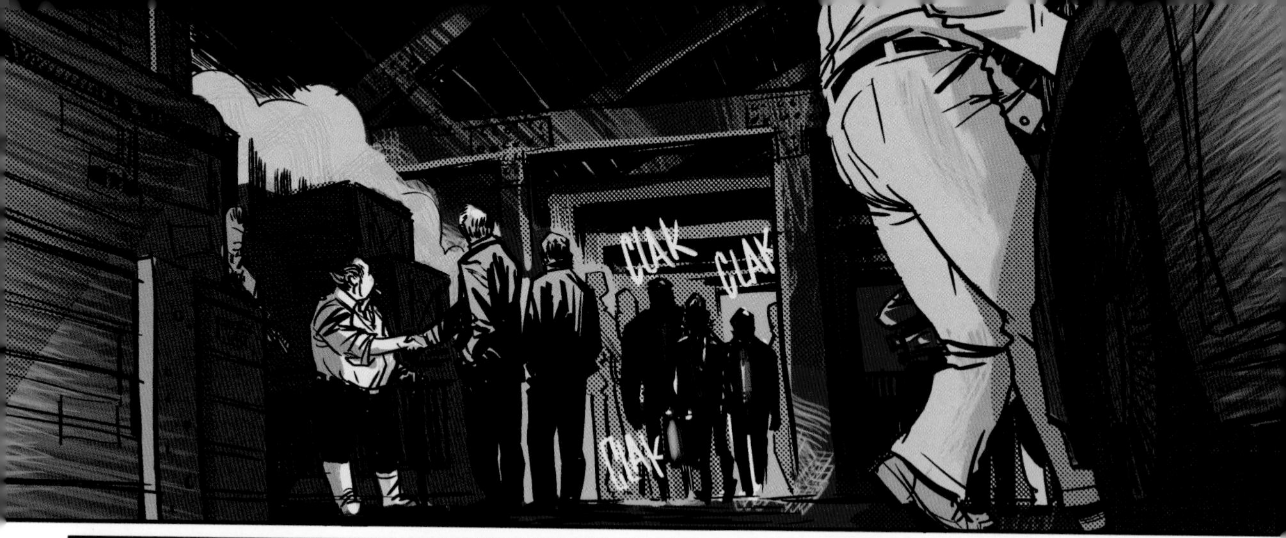
CLAK
CLAK
CLAK

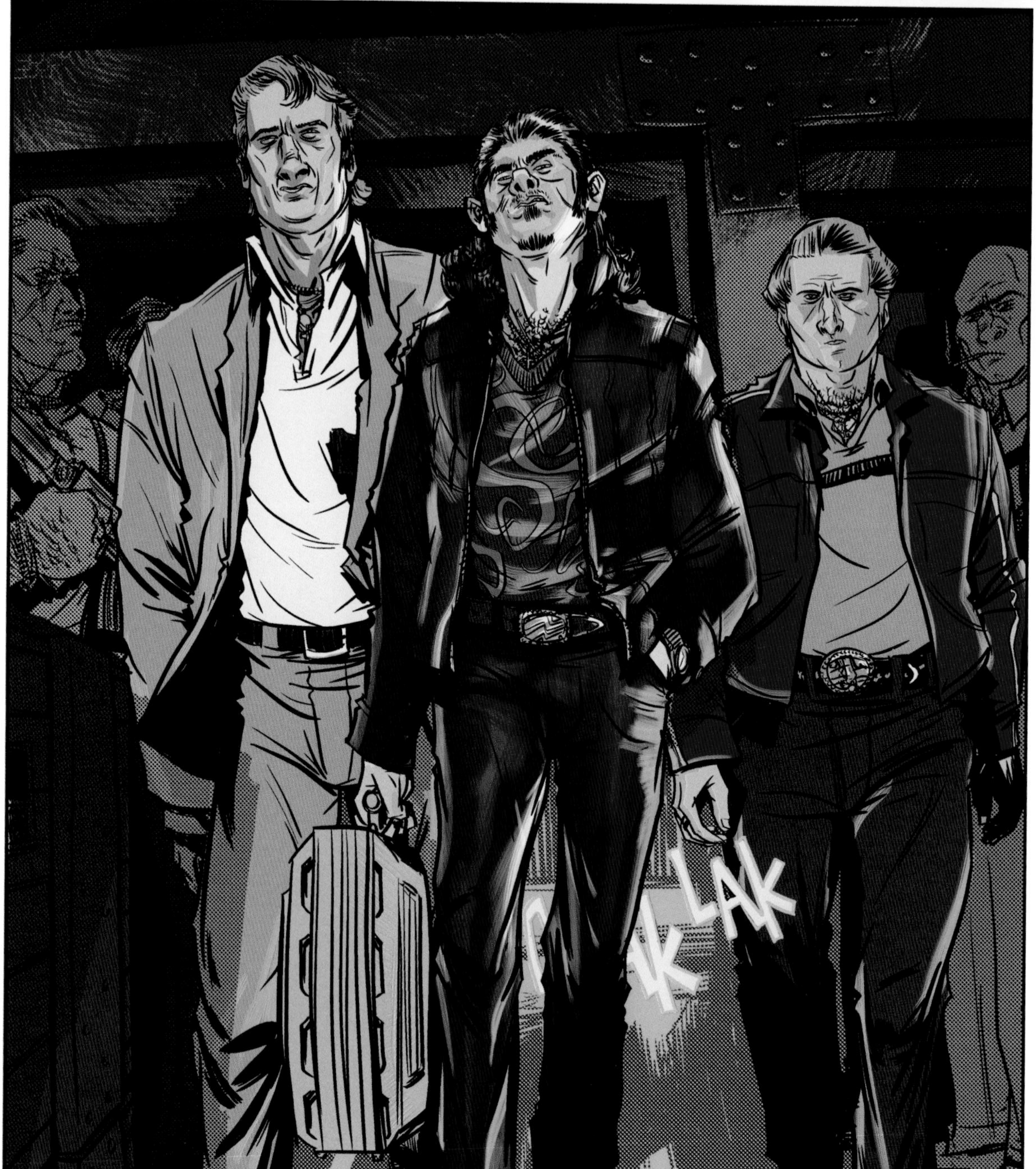
LAK

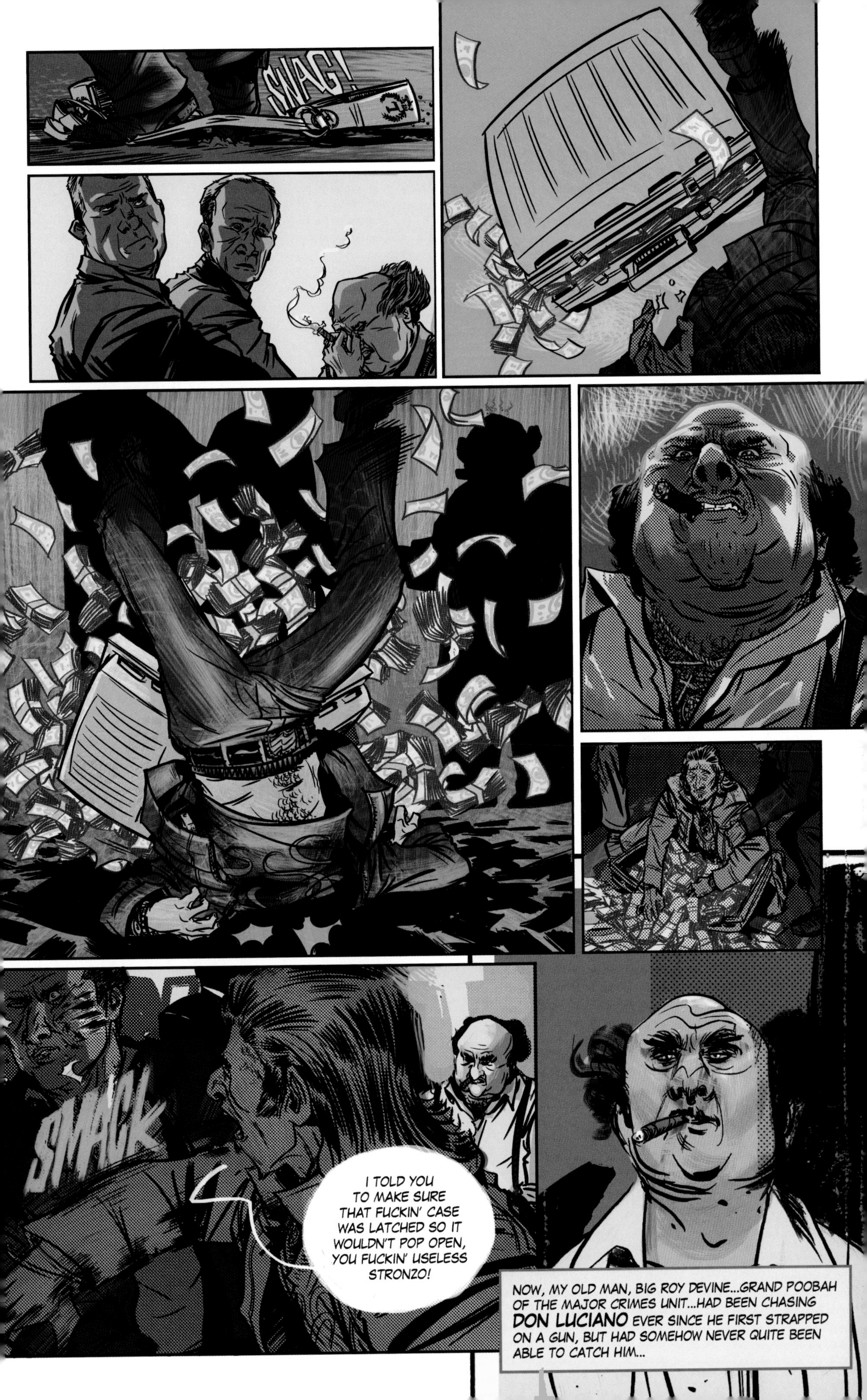
SNAG!
SMACK
I TOLD YOU TO MAKE SURE THAT FUCKIN' CASE WAS LATCHED SO IT WOULDN'T POP OPEN, YOU FUCKIN' USELESS STRONZO!
NOW, MY OLD MAN, BIG ROY DEVINE...GRAND POOBAH OF THE MAJOR CRIMES UNIT...HAD BEEN CHASING DON LUCIANO EVER SINCE HE FIRST STRAPPED ON A GUN, BUT HAD SOMEHOW NEVER QUITE BEEN ABLE TO CATCH HIM...

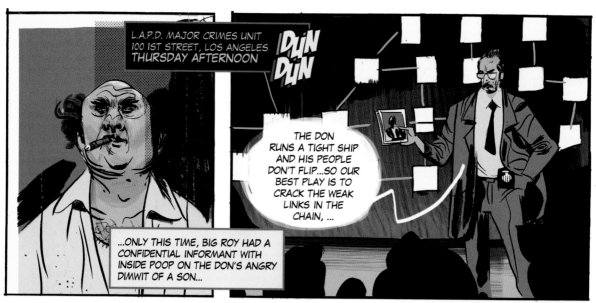

L.A.P.D. MAJOR CRIMES UNIT
100 1ST STREET, LOS ANGELES
**THURSDAY AFTERNOON**

DUN DUN

THE DON RUNS A TIGHT SHIP AND HIS PEOPLE DON'T FLIP...SO OUR BEST PLAY IS TO CRACK THE WEAK LINKS IN THE CHAIN, ...

...ONLY THIS TIME, BIG ROY HAD A CONFIDENTIAL INFORMANT WITH INSIDE POOP ON THE DON'S ANGRY DIMWIT OF A SON...

... LIKE HIS IDIOT KID AND WHOEVER THE RUSSIANS ARE USING TO LAUNDER THEIR MONEY.

... A.K.A. **TONY LUCIANO**...

ANY QUESTIONS?

YEAH... WHO'S THE INFORMANT?

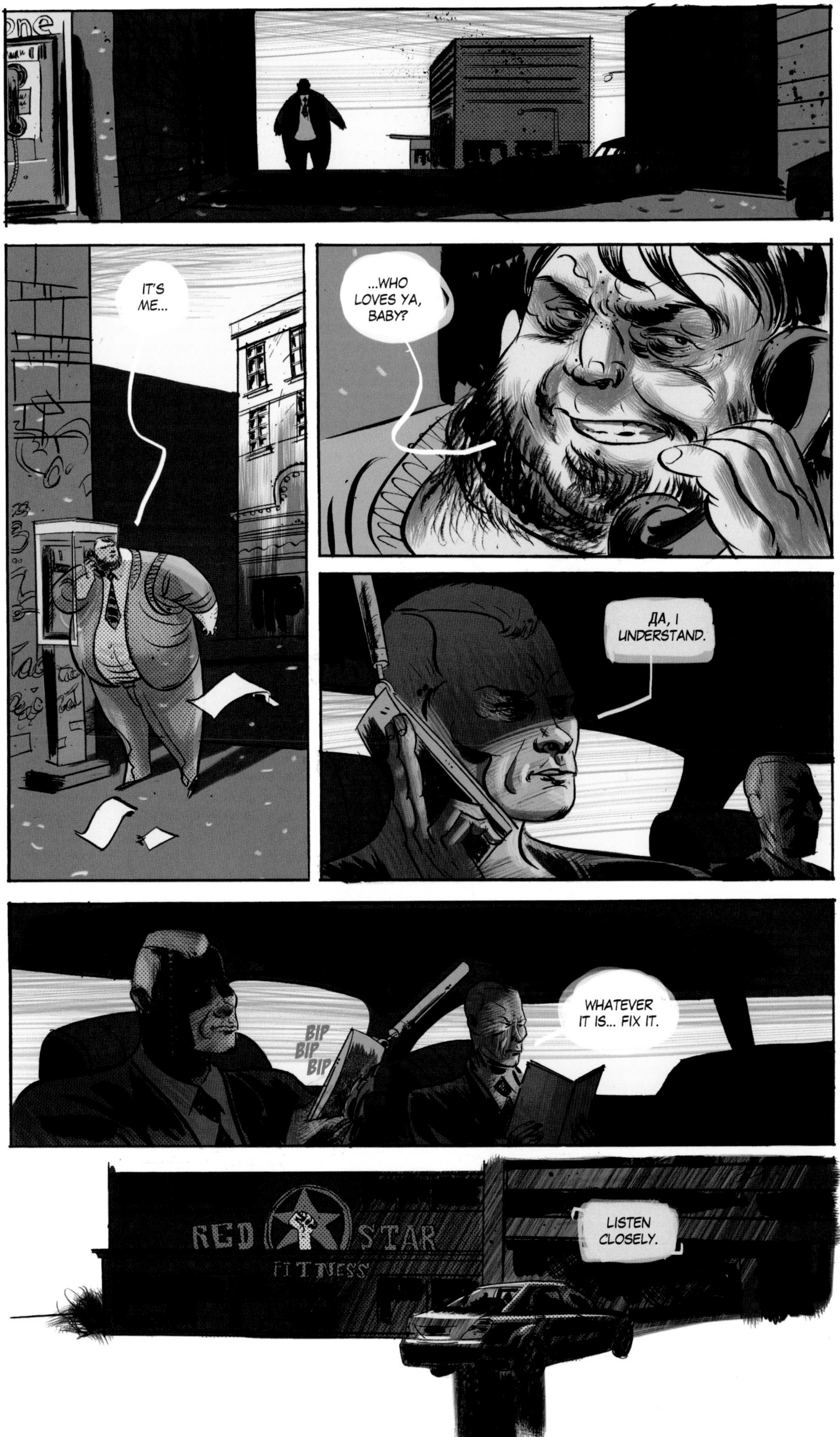
IT'S ME...
...WHO LOVES YA, BABY?
ДА, I UNDERSTAND.
BIP BIP BIP
WHATEVER IT IS... FIX IT.
RED STAR FITNESS
LISTEN CLOSELY.

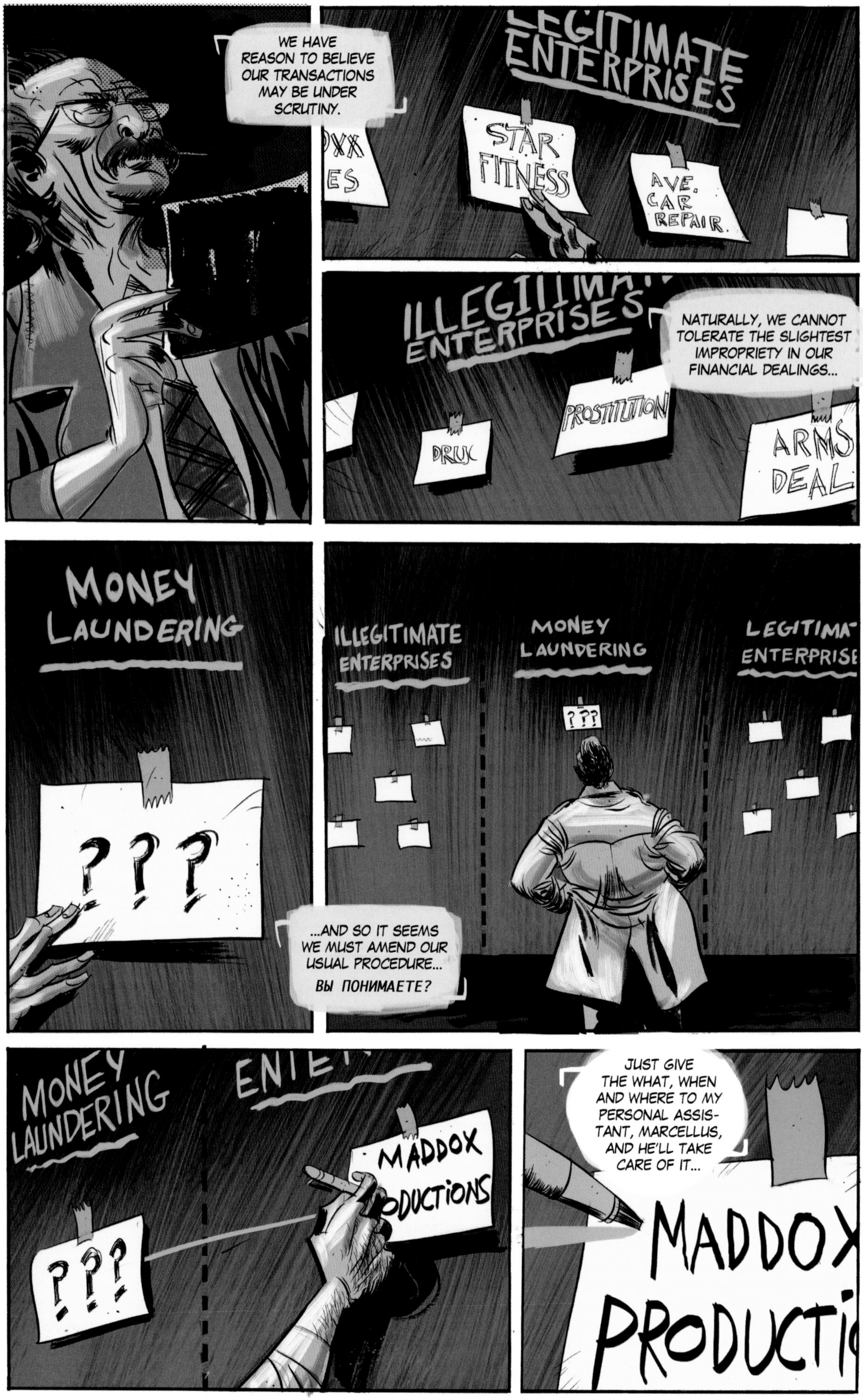
WE HAVE REASON TO BELIEVE OUR TRANSACTIONS MAY BE UNDER SCRUTINY.
LEGITIMATE ENTERPRISES
STAR FITNESS
AVE. CAR REPAIR
ILLEGITIMATE ENTERPRISES
NATURALLY, WE CANNOT TOLERATE THE SLIGHTEST IMPROPRIETY IN OUR FINANCIAL DEALINGS...
PROSTITUTION
DRUG
ARMS DEAL
MONEY LAUNDERING
???
ILLEGITIMATE ENTERPRISES
MONEY LAUNDERING
???
...AND SO IT SEEMS WE MUST AMEND OUR USUAL PROCEDURE...
ВЫ ПОНИМАЕТЕ?
MONEY LAUNDERING
???
MADDOX PRODUCTIONS
JUST GIVE THE WHAT, WHEN AND WHERE TO MY PERSONAL ASSIS-TANT, MARCELLUS, AND HE'LL TAKE CARE OF IT...
MADDOX PRODUCTI

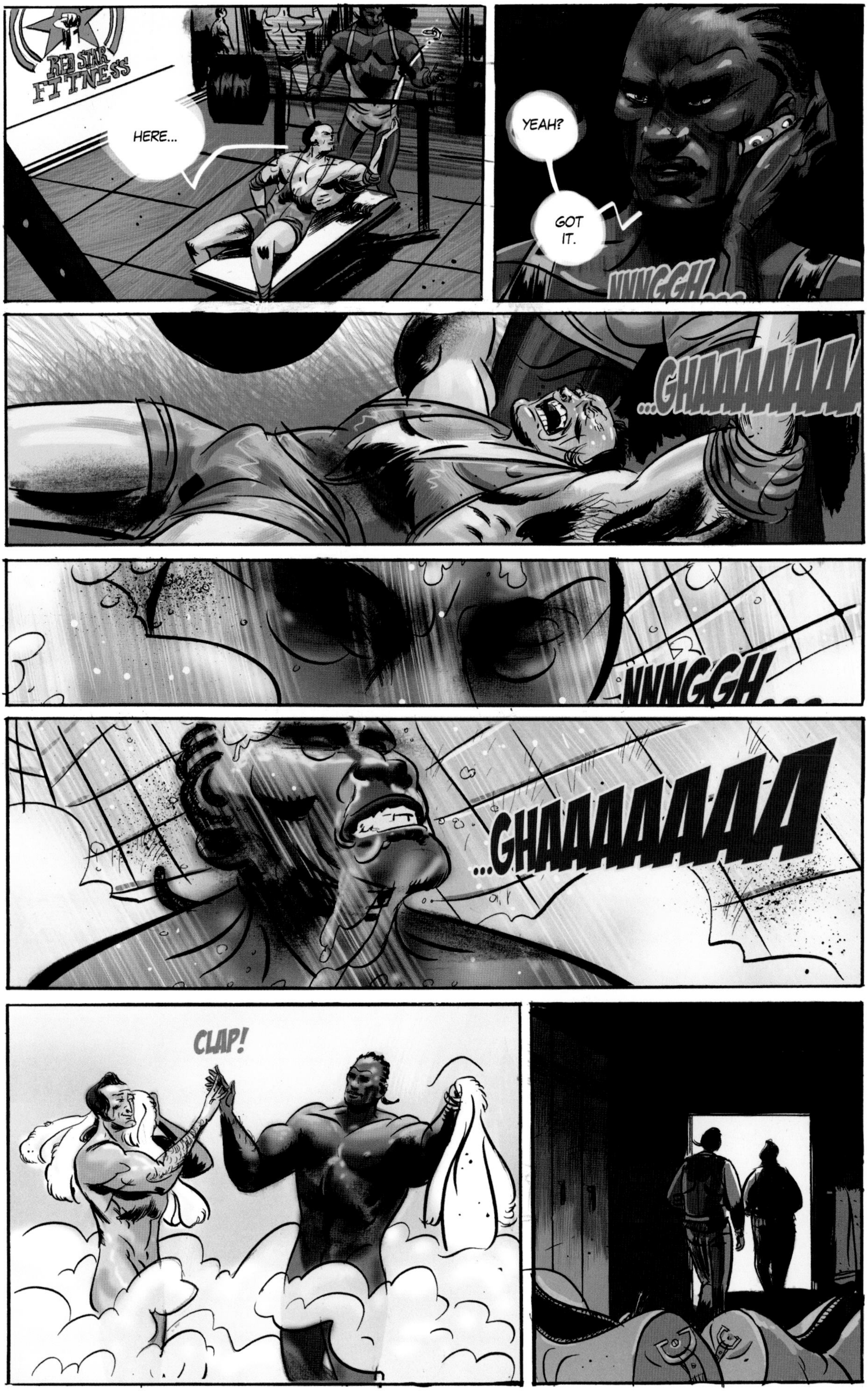
RED STAR FITNESS
HERE...
YEAH?
GOT IT.
NNNGGH...
...GHAAAAAA
NNNGGH...
...GHAAAAAAA
CLAP!

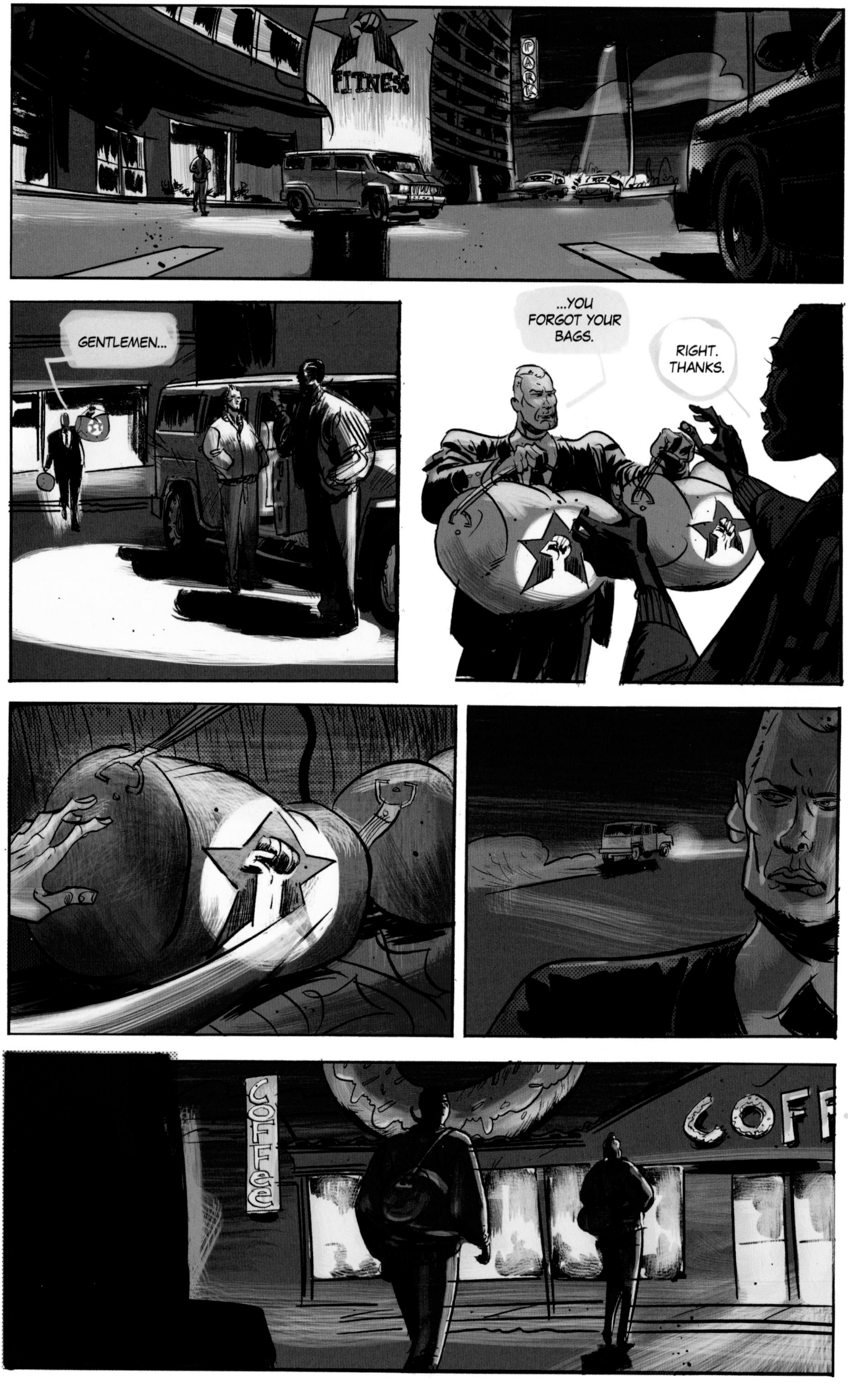
FITNESS
PARK
GENTLEMEN...
...YOU FORGOT YOUR BAGS.
RIGHT. THANKS.
COFFEE
COFF

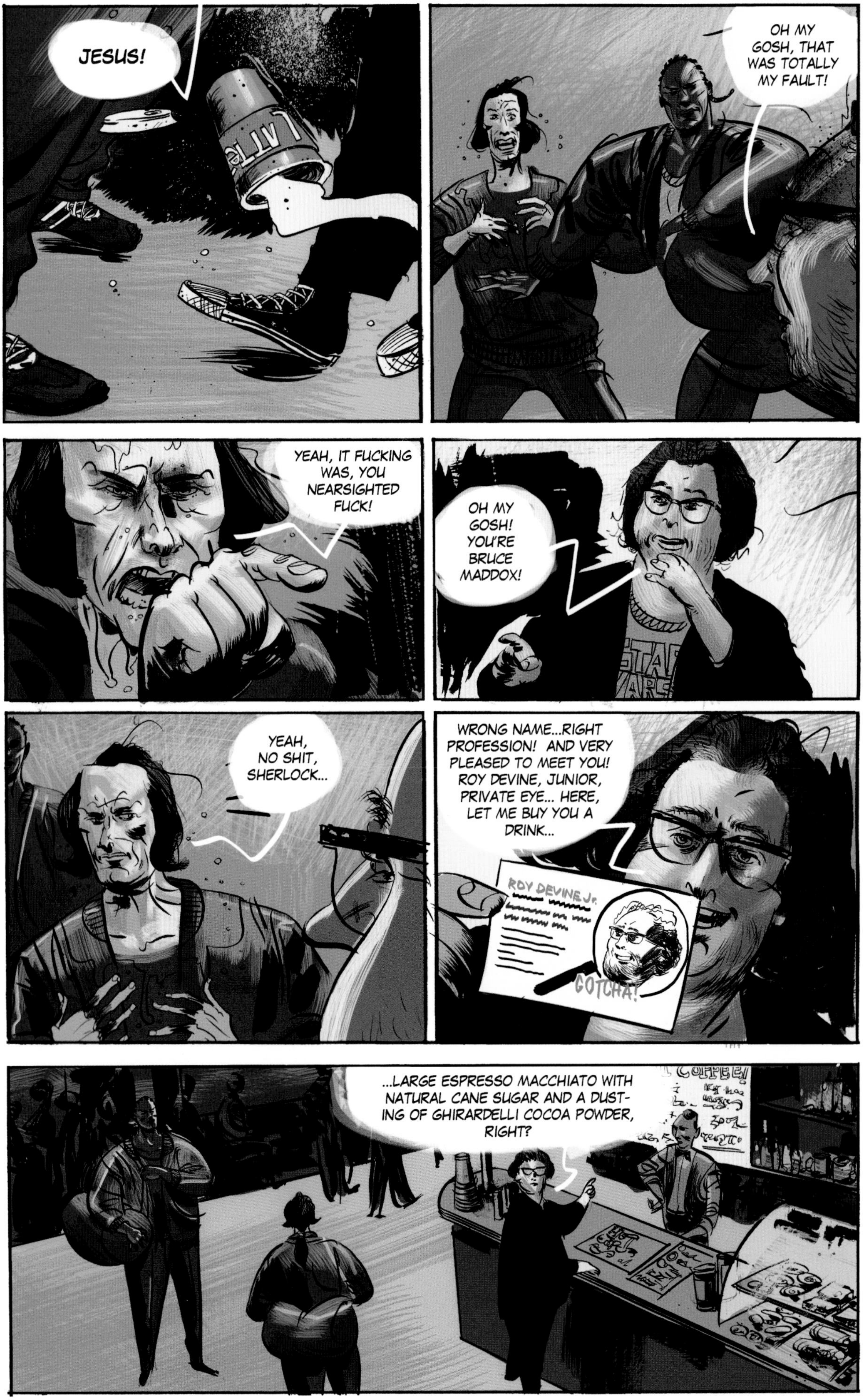
JESUS!
OH MY GOSH, THAT WAS TOTALLY MY FAULT!
YEAH, IT FUCKING WAS, YOU NEARSIGHTED FUCK!
OH MY GOSH! YOU'RE BRUCE MADDOX!
YEAH, NO SHIT, SHERLOCK...
WRONG NAME...RIGHT PROFESSION! AND VERY PLEASED TO MEET YOU! ROY DEVINE, JUNIOR, PRIVATE EYE... HERE, LET ME BUY YOU A DRINK...
ROY DEVINE Jr.
GOTCHA!
...LARGE ESPRESSO MACCHIATO WITH NATURAL CANE SUGAR AND A DUSTING OF GHIRARDELLI COCOA POWDER, RIGHT?

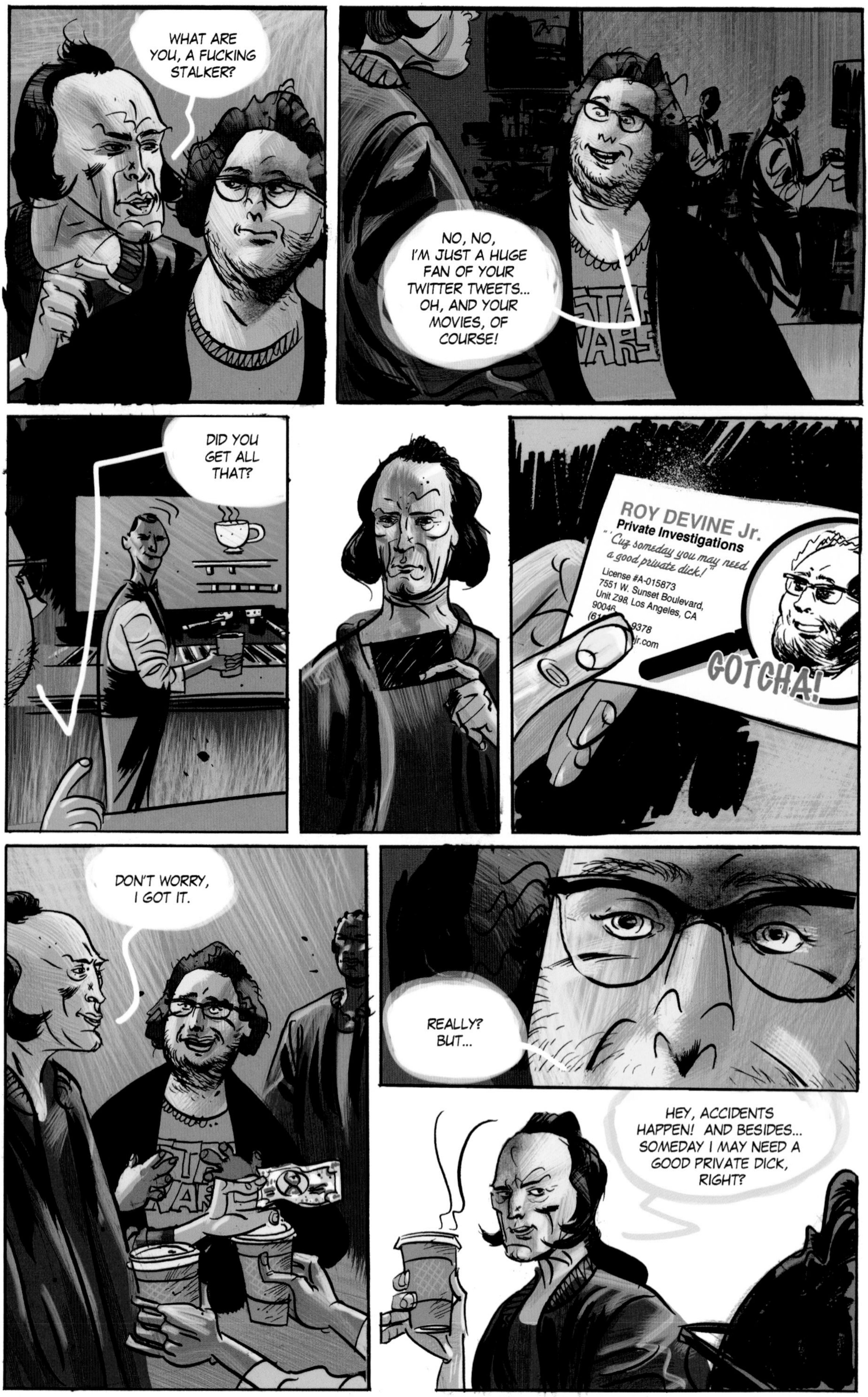
WHAT ARE YOU, A FUCKING STALKER?
NO, NO, I'M JUST A HUGE FAN OF YOUR TWITTER TWEETS... OH, AND YOUR MOVIES, OF COURSE!
DID YOU GET ALL THAT?
ROY DEVINE Jr.
Private Investigations
"'Cuz someday you may need a good private dick!"
License #A-015873
7551 W. Sunset Boulevard,
Unit Z98, Los Angeles, CA
GOTCHA!
DON'T WORRY, I GOT IT.
REALLY? BUT...
HEY, ACCIDENTS HAPPEN! AND BESIDES... SOMEDAY I MAY NEED A GOOD PRIVATE DICK, RIGHT?

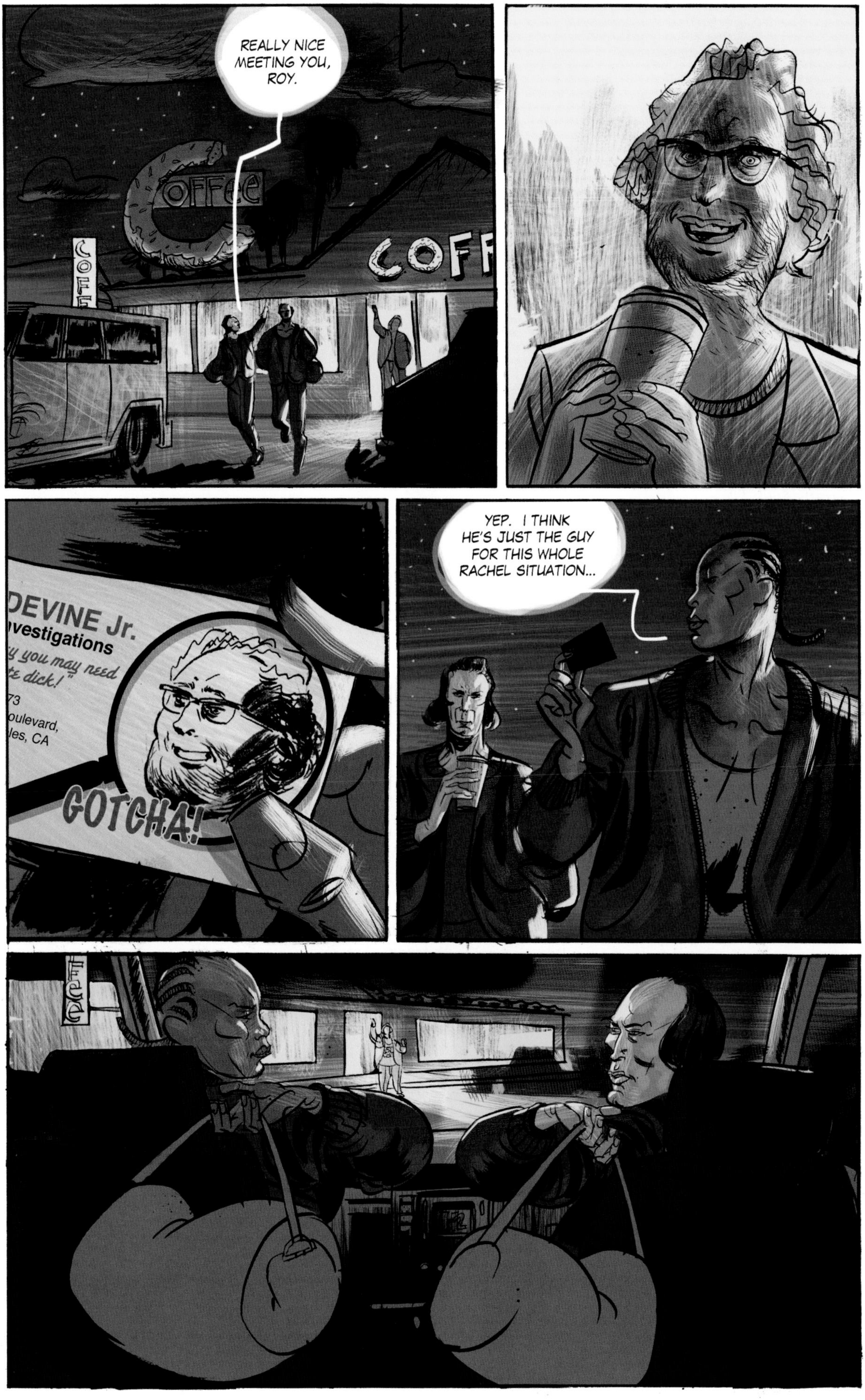
REALLY NICE MEETING YOU, ROY.
COFFEE
COFF
COFF
DEVINE Jr.
nvestigations
y you may need
te dick!"
73
oulevard,
les, CA
GOTCHA!
YEP. I THINK HE'S JUST THE GUY FOR THIS WHOLE RACHEL SITUATION...

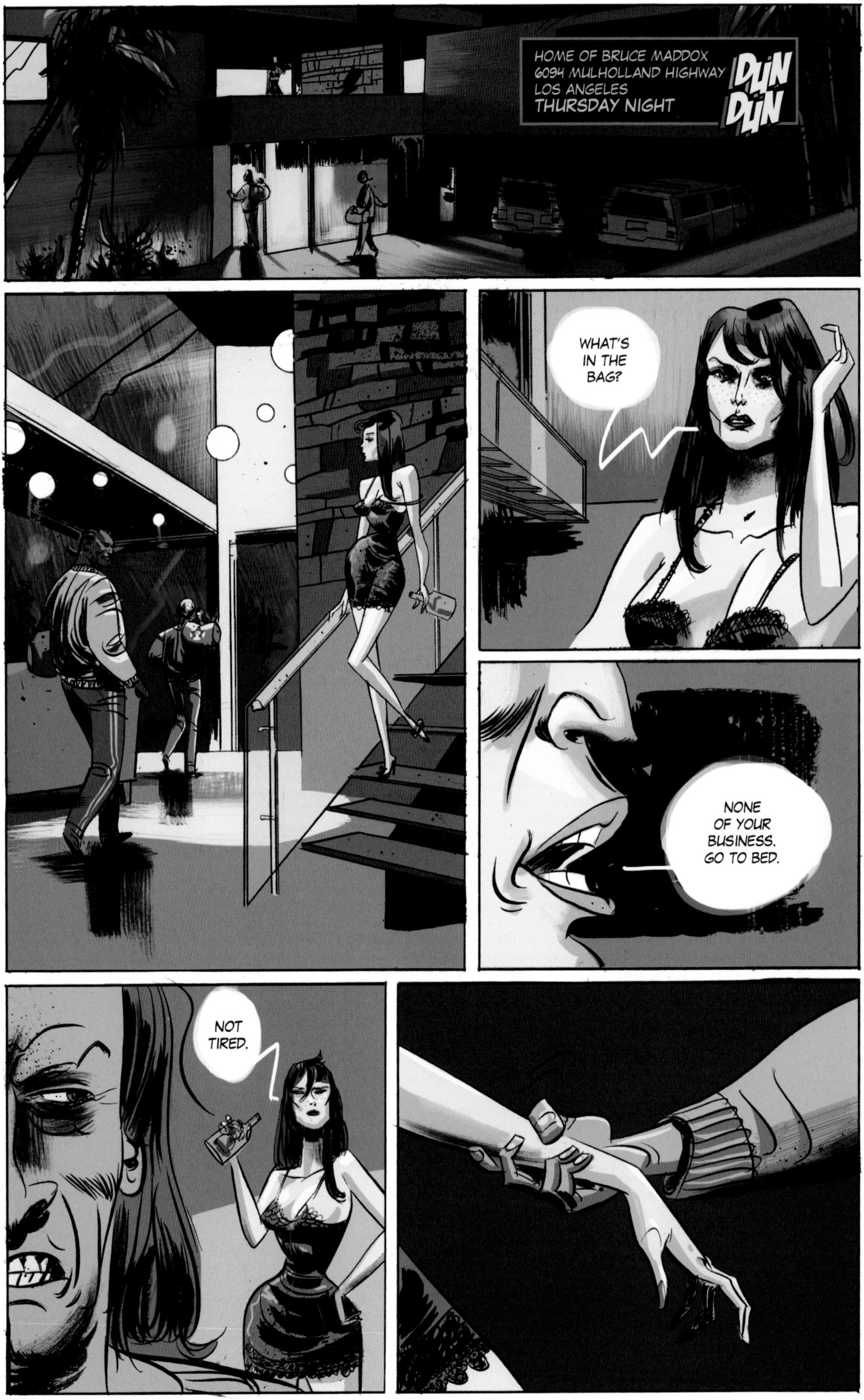
HOME OF BRUCE MADDOX
6094 MULHOLLAND HIGHWAY
LOS ANGELES
THURSDAY NIGHT
DUN DUN
WHAT'S IN THE BAG?
NONE OF YOUR BUSINESS. GO TO BED.
NOT TIRED.

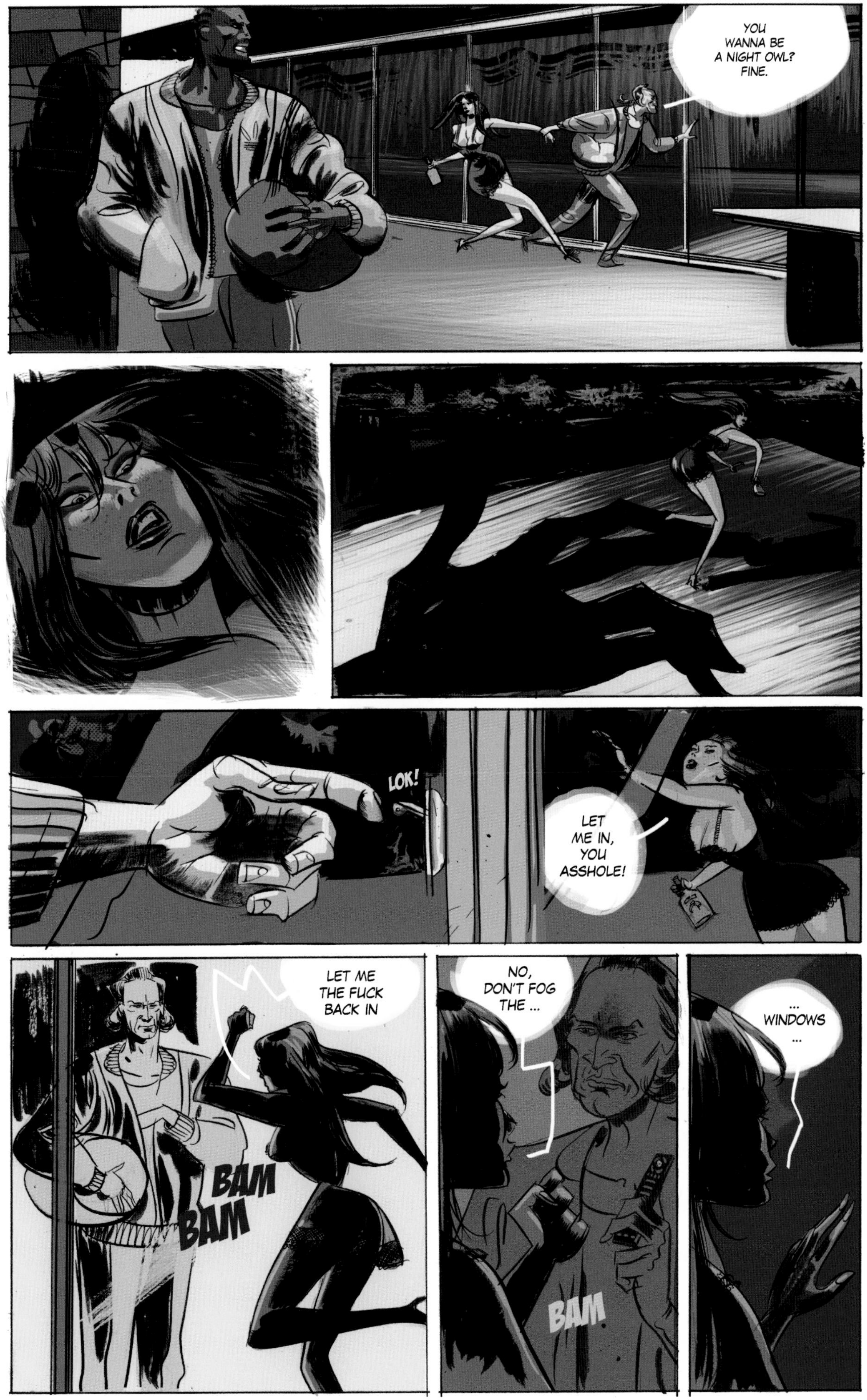

YOU WANNA BE A NIGHT OWL? FINE.
LOK!
LET ME IN, YOU ASSHOLE!
LET ME THE FUCK BACK IN
BAM
BAM
NO, DON'T FOG THE ...
BAM
... WINDOWS ...

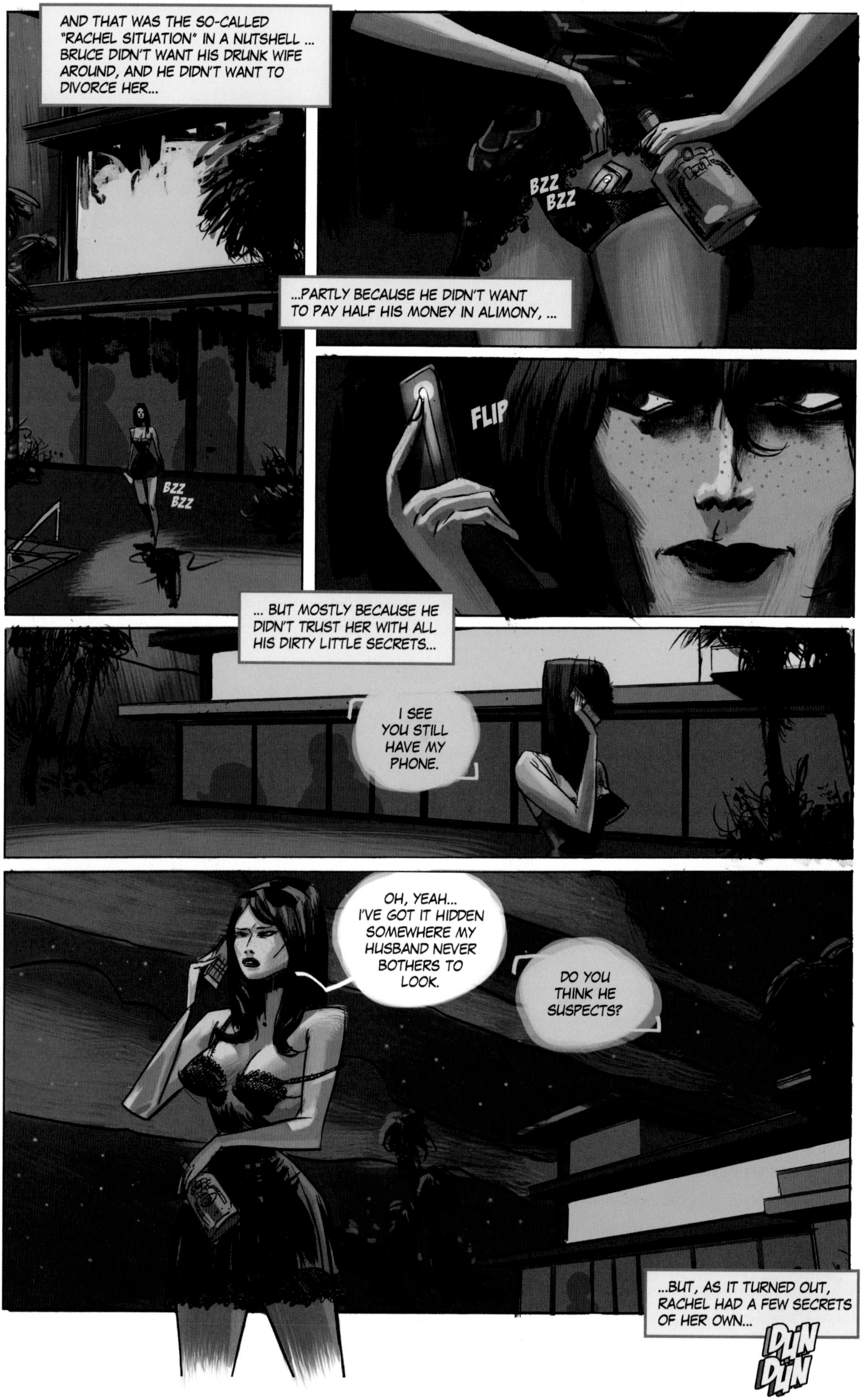
AND THAT WAS THE SO-CALLED "RACHEL SITUATION" IN A NUTSHELL ... BRUCE DIDN'T WANT HIS DRUNK WIFE AROUND, AND HE DIDN'T WANT TO DIVORCE HER...
BZZ BZZ
BZZ BZZ
...PARTLY BECAUSE HE DIDN'T WANT TO PAY HALF HIS MONEY IN ALIMONY, ...
FLIP
... BUT MOSTLY BECAUSE HE DIDN'T TRUST HER WITH ALL HIS DIRTY LITTLE SECRETS...
I SEE YOU STILL HAVE MY PHONE.
OH, YEAH... I'VE GOT IT HIDDEN SOMEWHERE MY HUSBAND NEVER BOTHERS TO LOOK.
DO YOU THINK HE SUSPECTS?
...BUT, AS IT TURNED OUT, RACHEL HAD A FEW SECRETS OF HER OWN...
DUN DUN

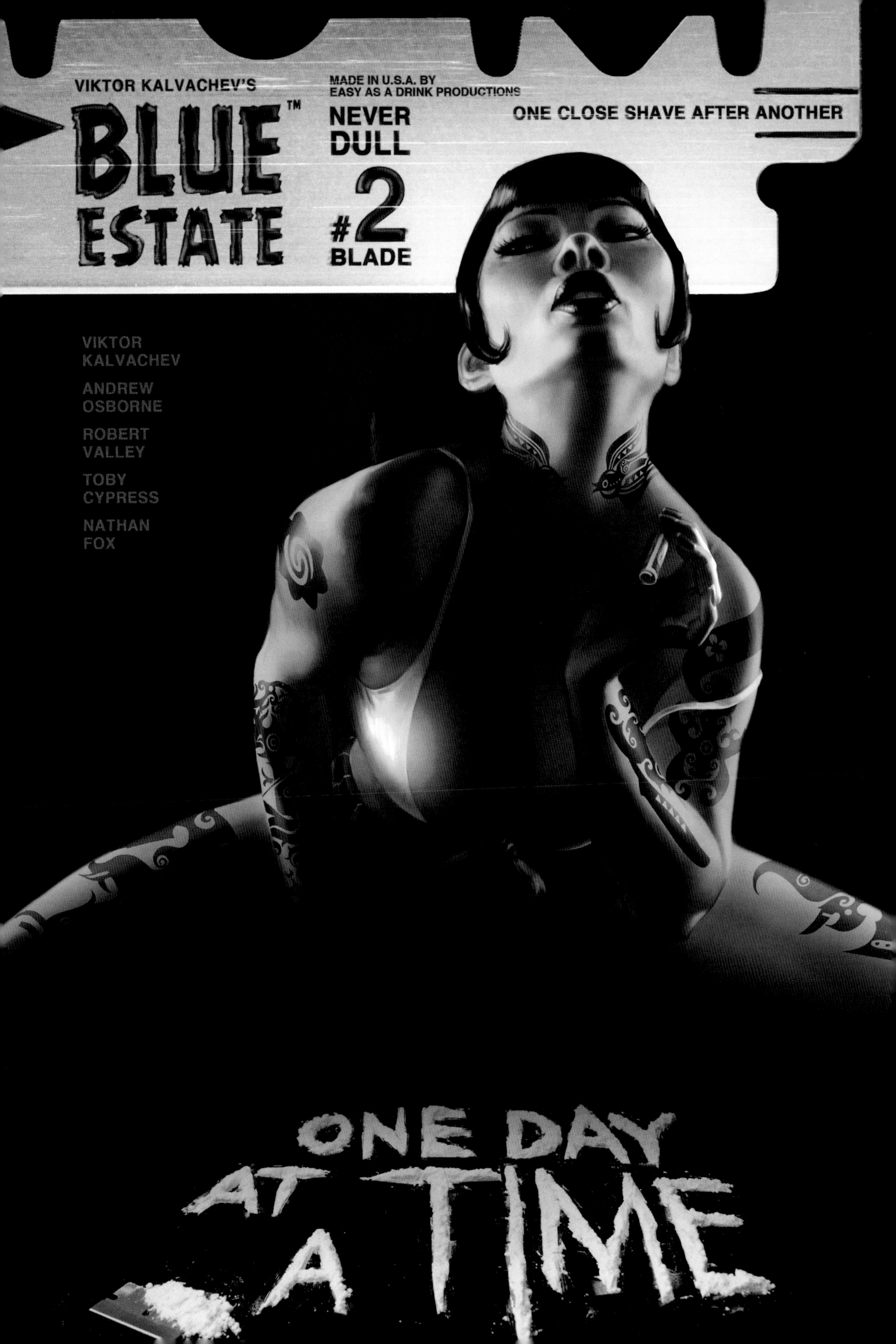
VIKTOR KALVACHEV'S
BLUE™ ESTATE
MADE IN U.S.A. BY
EASY AS A DRINK PRODUCTIONS
NEVER DULL
#2 BLADE
ONE CLOSE SHAVE AFTER ANOTHER
VIKTOR KALVACHEV
ANDREW OSBORNE
ROBERT VALLEY
TOBY CYPRESS
NATHAN FOX
ONE DAY AT A TIME

# BLUE ESTATE ™

## EPISODE TWO:
## ONE DAY AT A TIME

ORIGINAL STORY:
**VIKTOR KALVACHEV** and **KOSTA YANEV**

SCRIPT BY **ANDREW OSBORNE**

ARTISTS:
**VIKTOR KALVACHEV**
**TOBY CYPRESS**
**NATHAN FOX**
**ROBERT VALLEY**

ART DIRECTION BY **VIKTOR KALVACHEV**

COVER, COLORS & DESIGN:
**VIKTOR KALVACHEV**

CONTRIBUTING EDITOR:
**PHILO NORTHRUP**

WWW.BLUEESTATECOMIC.COM

EZD ™
PRODUCTIONS

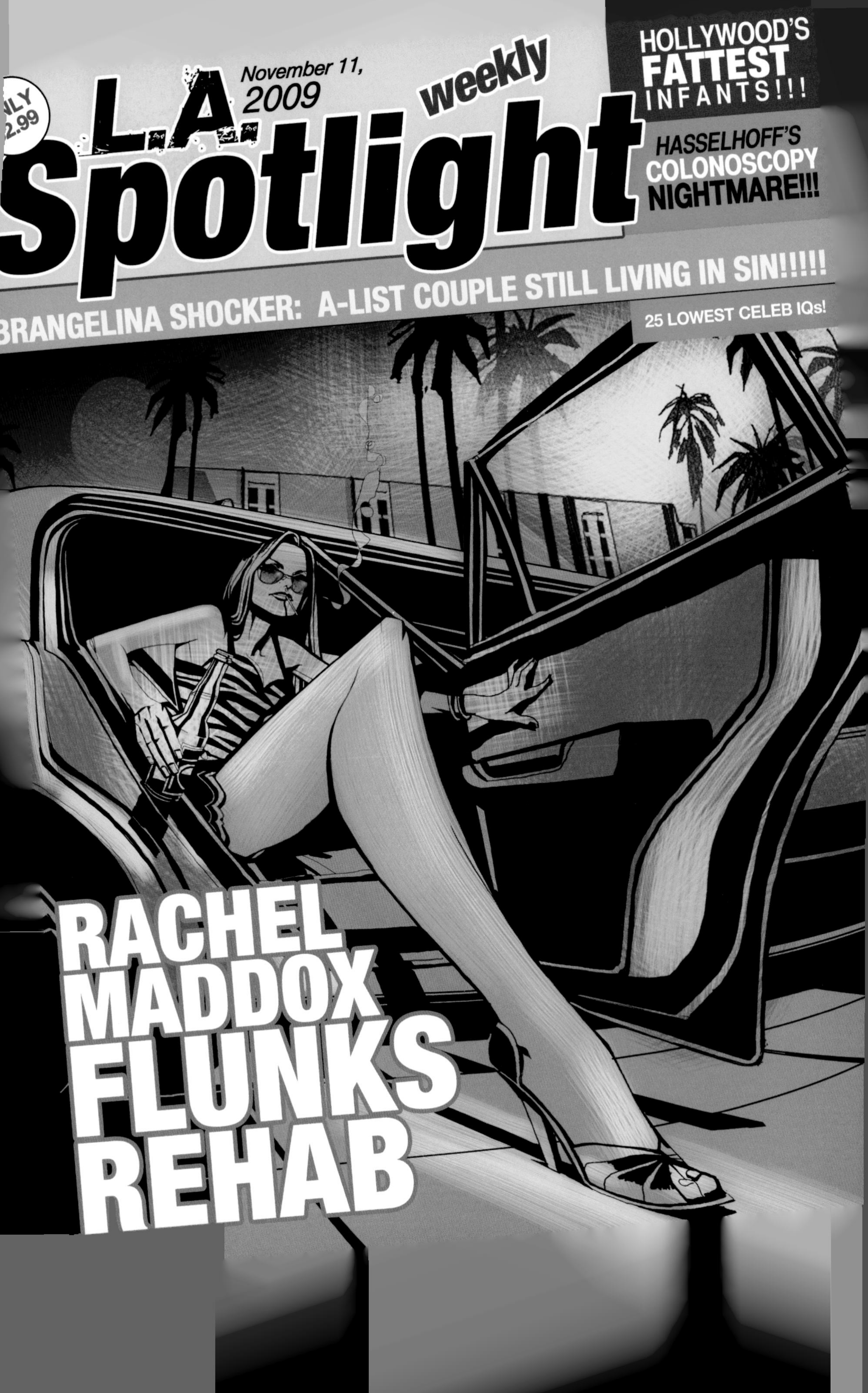
ONLY $2.99
L.A. Spotlight weekly
November 11, 2009
HOLLYWOOD'S FATTEST INFANTS!!!
HASSELHOFF'S COLONOSCOPY NIGHTMARE!!!
BRANGELINA SHOCKER: A-LIST COUPLE STILL LIVING IN SIN!!!!!
25 LOWEST CELEB IQs!
RACHEL MADDOX FLUNKS REHAB

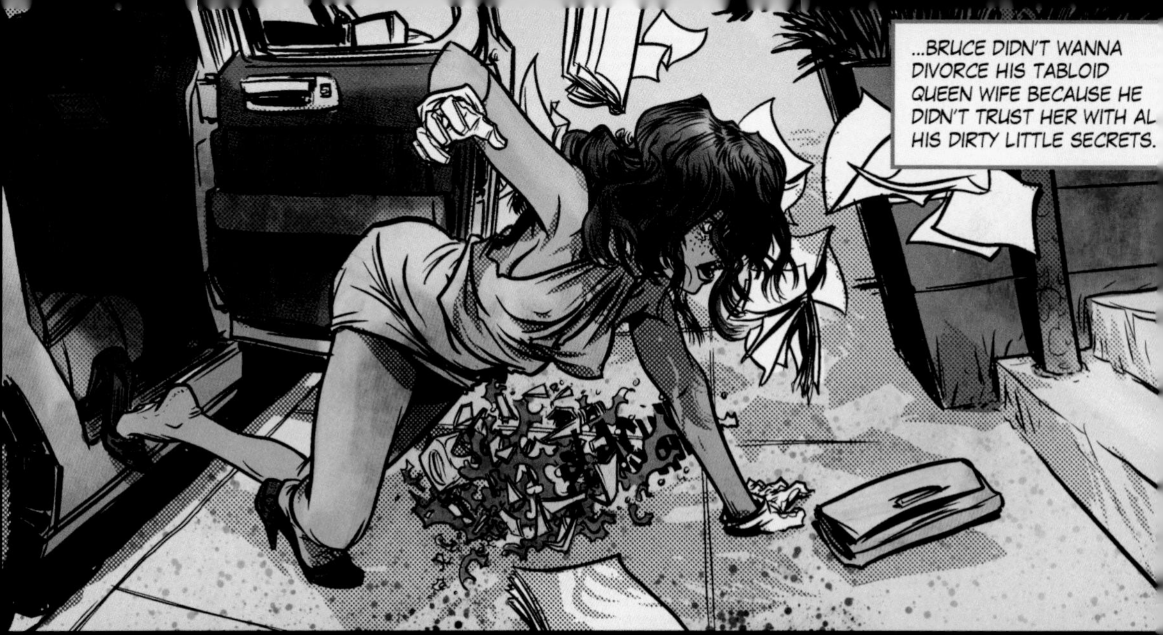
...BRUCE DIDN'T WANNA DIVORCE HIS TABLOID QUEEN WIFE BECAUSE HE DIDN'T TRUST HER WITH AL HIS DIRTY LITTLE SECRETS.

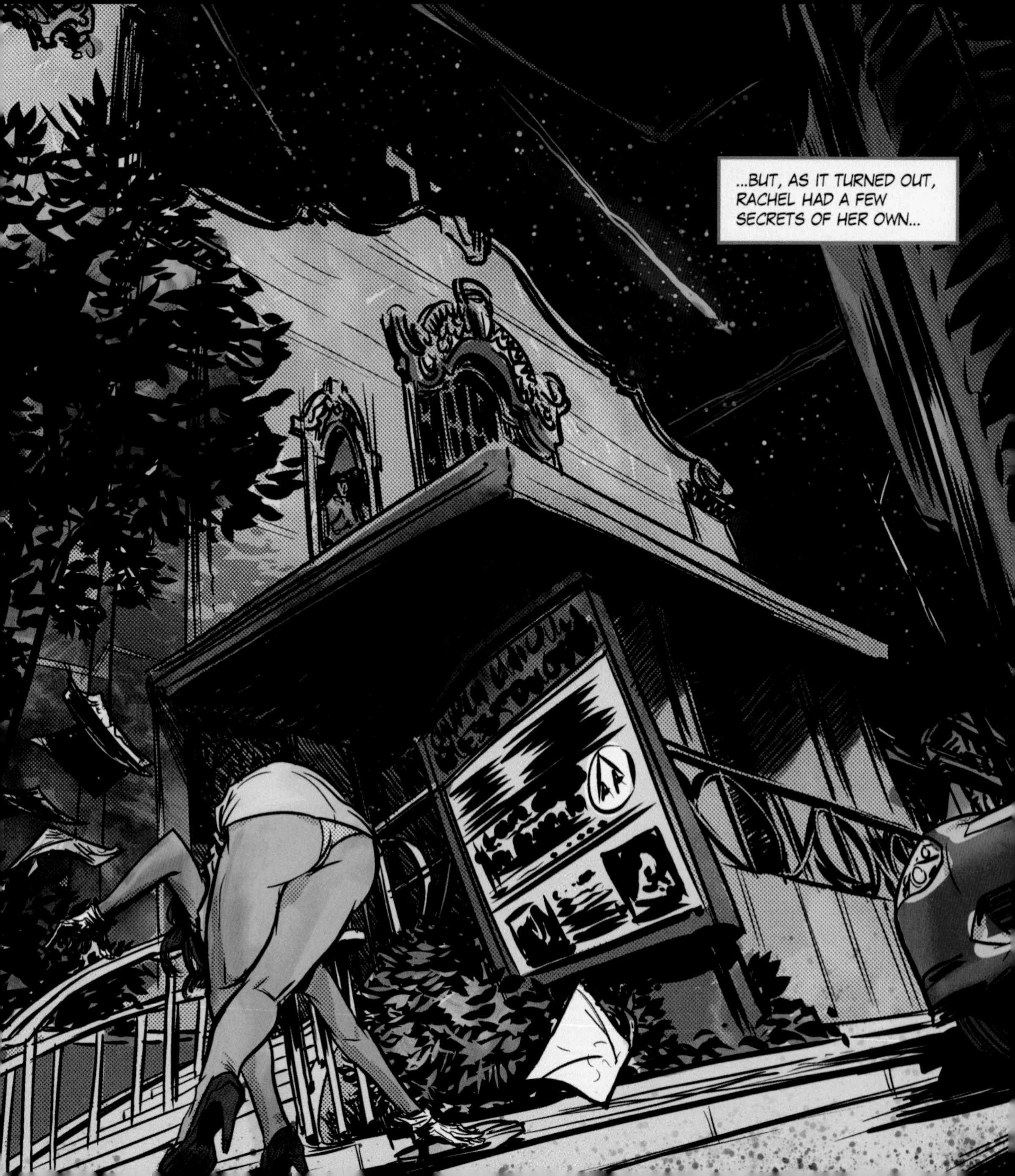
...BUT, AS IT TURNED OUT, RACHEL HAD A FEW SECRETS OF HER OWN...

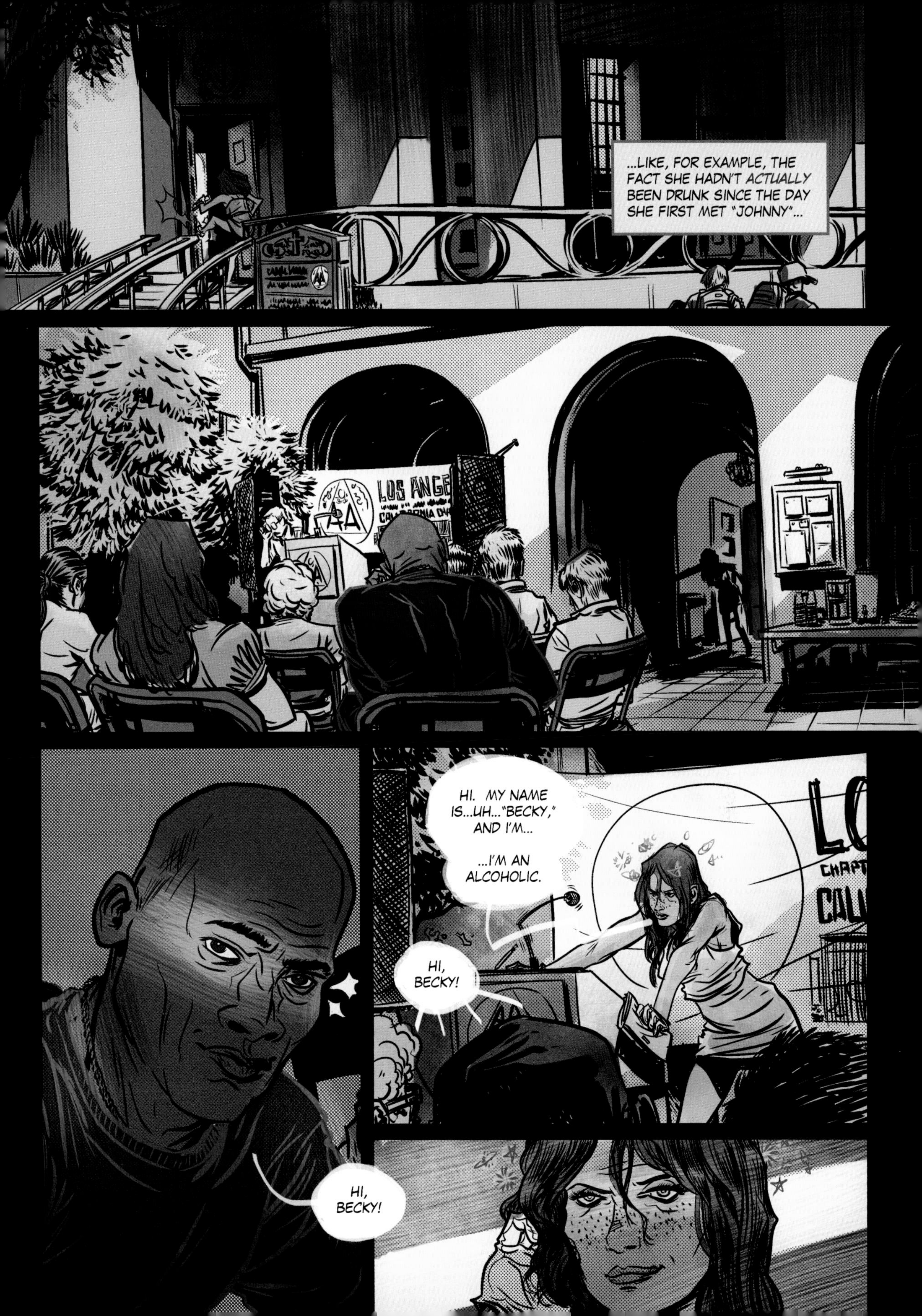
...LIKE, FOR EXAMPLE, THE FACT SHE HADN'T *ACTUALLY* BEEN DRUNK SINCE THE DAY SHE FIRST MET "JOHNNY"...
HI. MY NAME IS...UH..."BECKY," AND I'M...
...I'M AN ALCOHOLIC.
HI, BECKY!
HI, BECKY!

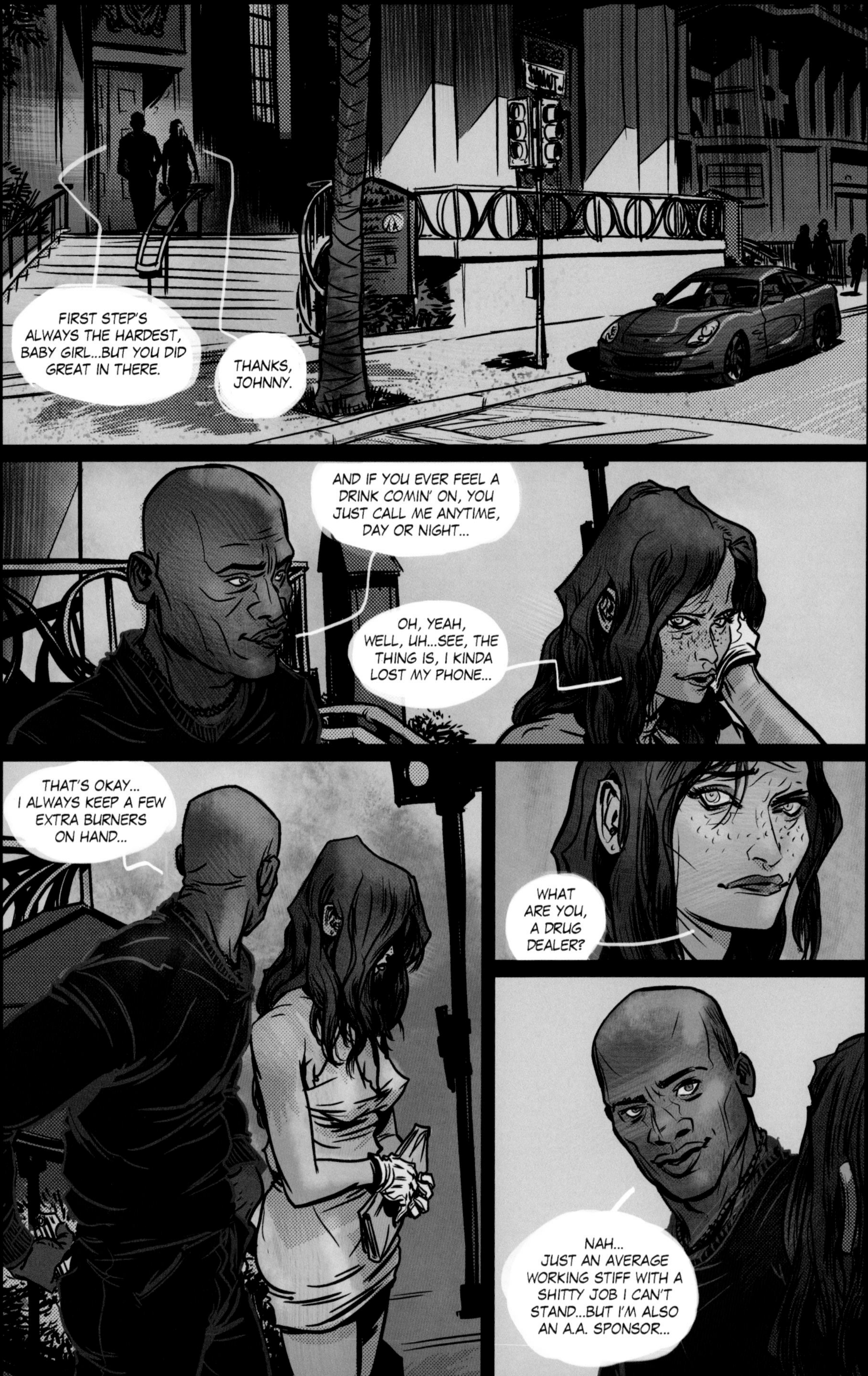
FIRST STEP'S ALWAYS THE HARDEST, BABY GIRL...BUT YOU DID GREAT IN THERE.
THANKS, JOHNNY.
AND IF YOU EVER FEEL A DRINK COMIN' ON, YOU JUST CALL ME ANYTIME, DAY OR NIGHT...
OH, YEAH, WELL, UH...SEE, THE THING IS, I KINDA LOST MY PHONE...
THAT'S OKAY... I ALWAYS KEEP A FEW EXTRA BURNERS ON HAND...
WHAT ARE YOU, A DRUG DEALER?
NAH... JUST AN AVERAGE WORKING STIFF WITH A SHITTY JOB I CAN'T STAND...BUT I'M ALSO AN A.A. SPONSOR...

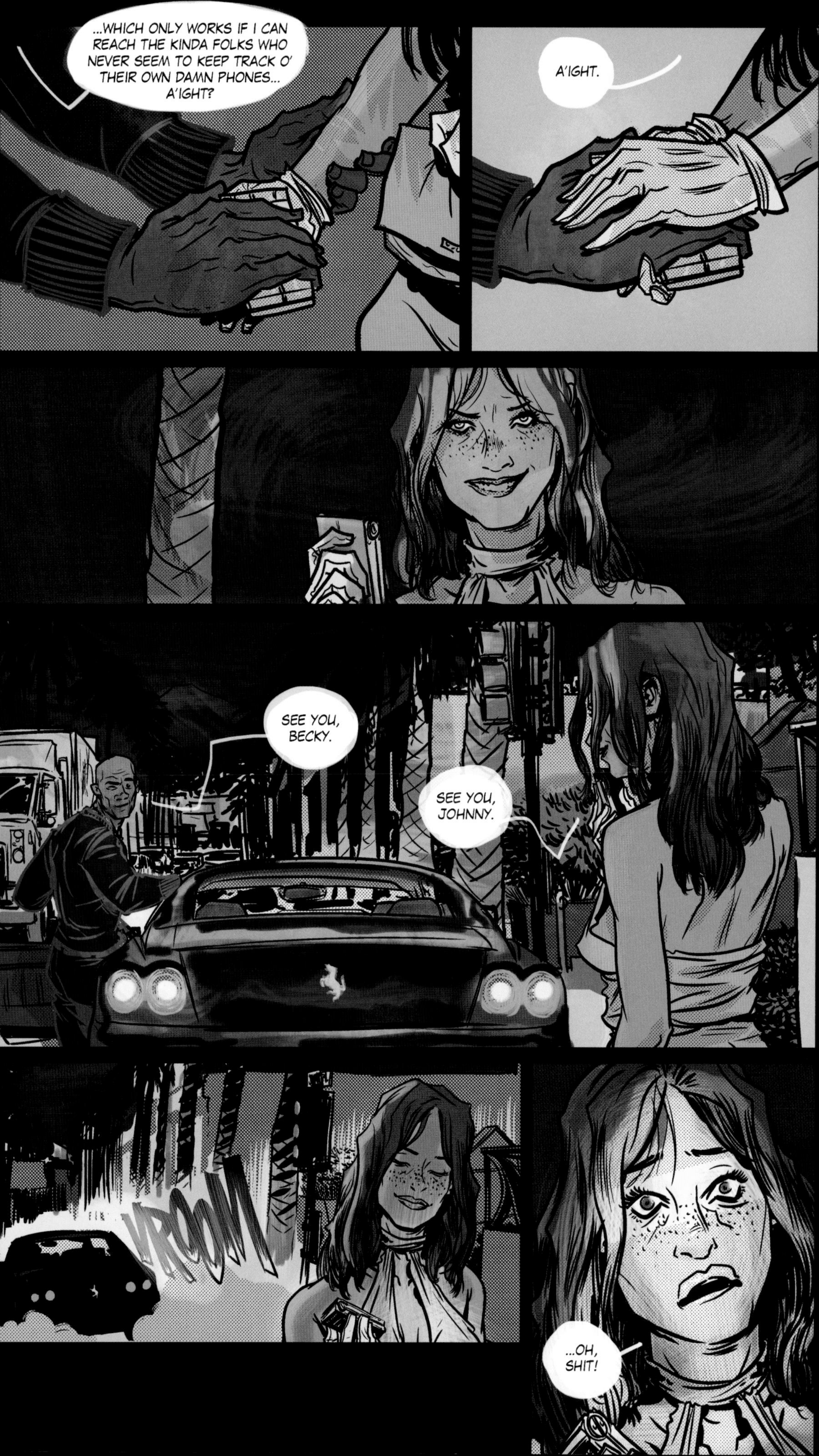
...WHICH ONLY WORKS IF I CAN REACH THE KINDA FOLKS WHO NEVER SEEM TO KEEP TRACK O' THEIR OWN DAMN PHONES... A'IGHT?
A'IGHT.
SEE YOU, BECKY.
SEE YOU, JOHNNY.
VROOM
...OH, SHIT!

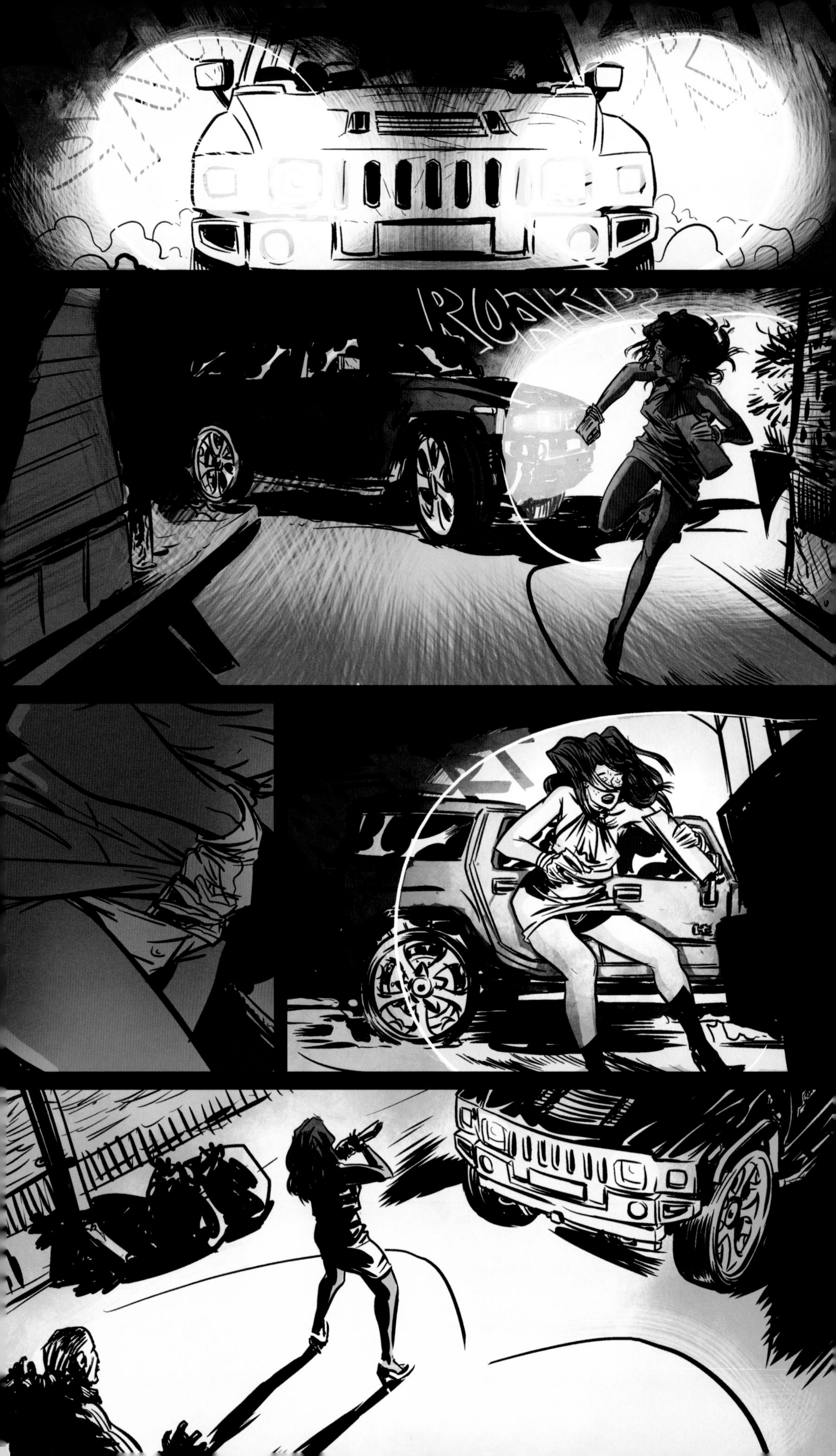
ROARR

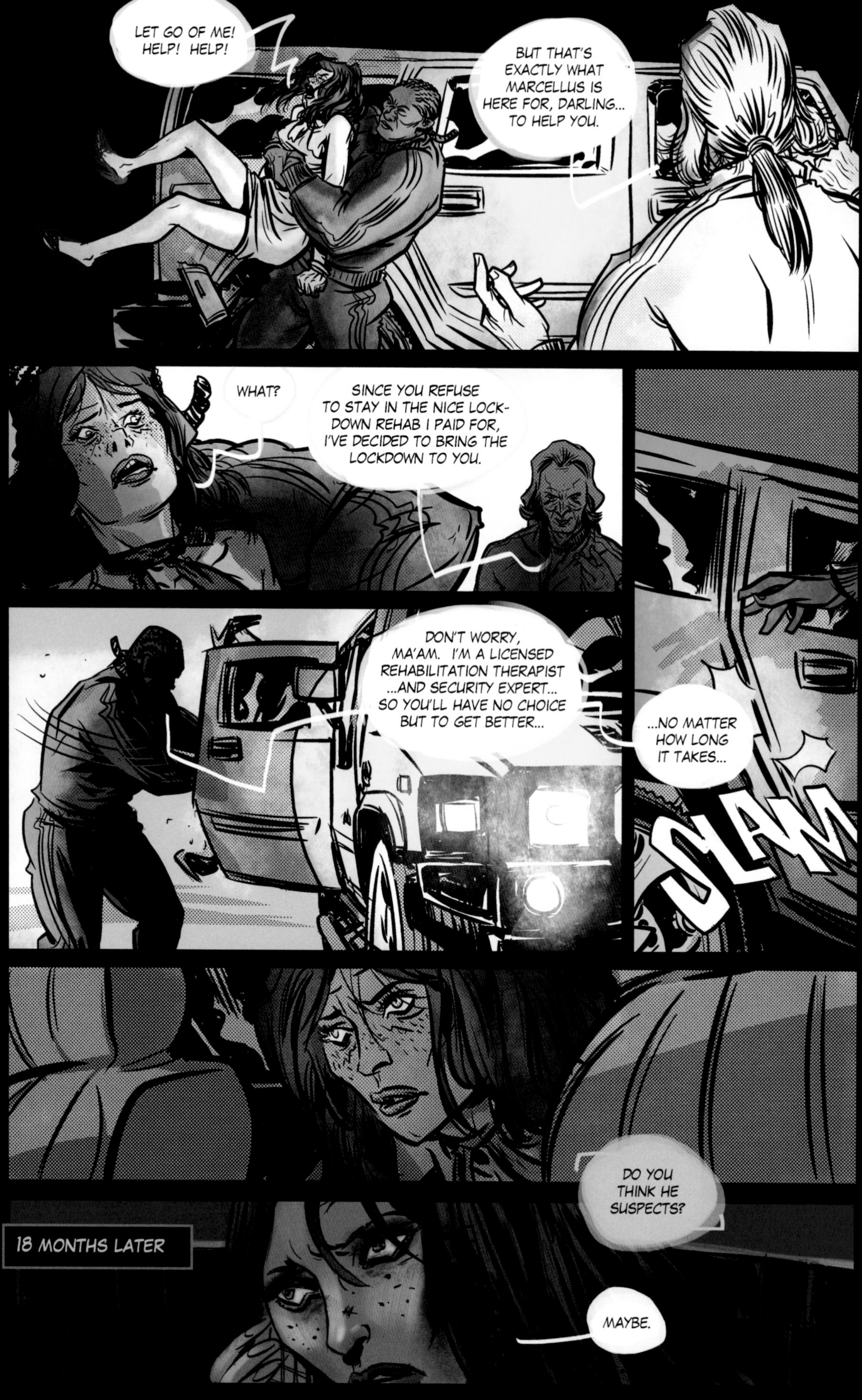
LET GO OF ME! HELP! HELP!
BUT THAT'S EXACTLY WHAT MARCELLUS IS HERE FOR, DARLING... TO HELP YOU.
WHAT?
SINCE YOU REFUSE TO STAY IN THE NICE LOCK-DOWN REHAB I PAID FOR, I'VE DECIDED TO BRING THE LOCKDOWN TO YOU.
DON'T WORRY, MA'AM. I'M A LICENSED REHABILITATION THERAPIST ...AND SECURITY EXPERT... SO YOU'LL HAVE NO CHOICE BUT TO GET BETTER...
...NO MATTER HOW LONG IT TAKES...
SLAM
18 MONTHS LATER
DO YOU THINK HE SUSPECTS?
MAYBE.

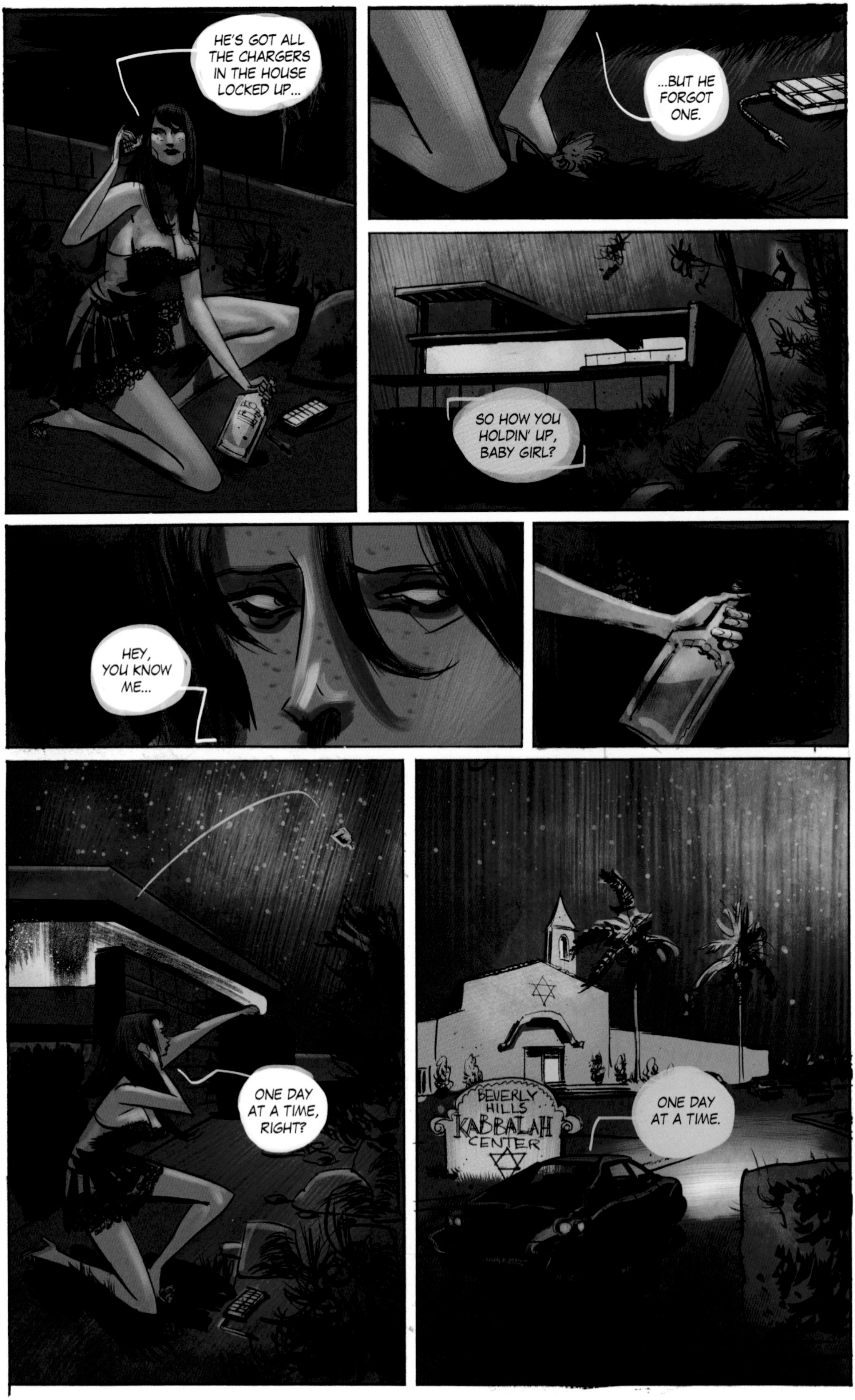
HE'S GOT ALL THE CHARGERS IN THE HOUSE LOCKED UP...
...BUT HE FORGOT ONE.
SO HOW YOU HOLDIN' UP, BABY GIRL?
HEY, YOU KNOW ME...
ONE DAY AT A TIME, RIGHT?
BEVERLY HILLS KABBALAH CENTER
ONE DAY AT A TIME.

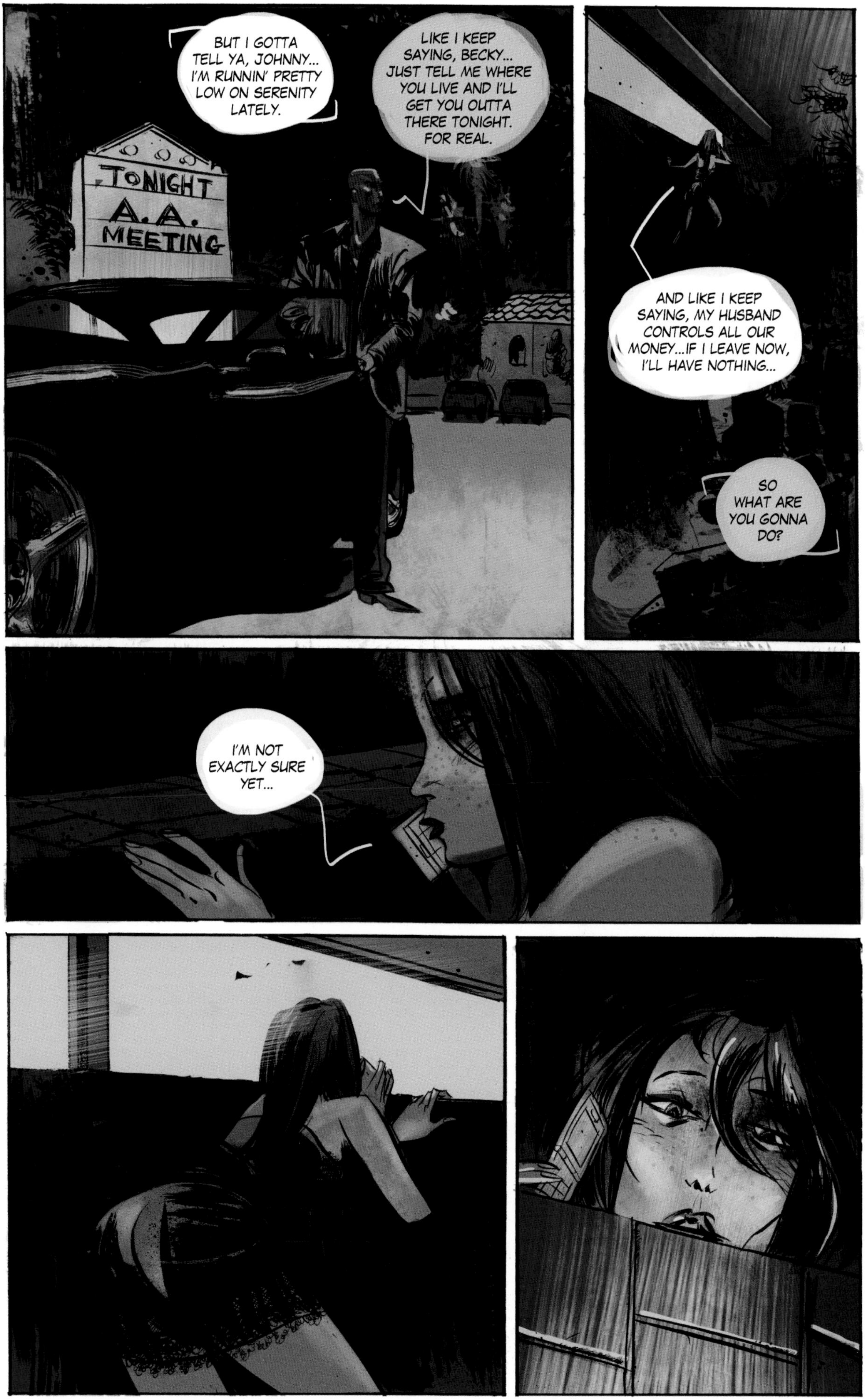
BUT I GOTTA TELL YA, JOHNNY... I'M RUNNIN' PRETTY LOW ON SERENITY LATELY.
TONIGHT A.A. MEETING
LIKE I KEEP SAYING, BECKY... JUST TELL ME WHERE YOU LIVE AND I'LL GET YOU OUTTA THERE TONIGHT. FOR REAL.
AND LIKE I KEEP SAYING, MY HUSBAND CONTROLS ALL OUR MONEY...IF I LEAVE NOW, I'LL HAVE NOTHING...
SO WHAT ARE YOU GONNA DO?
I'M NOT EXACTLY SURE YET...

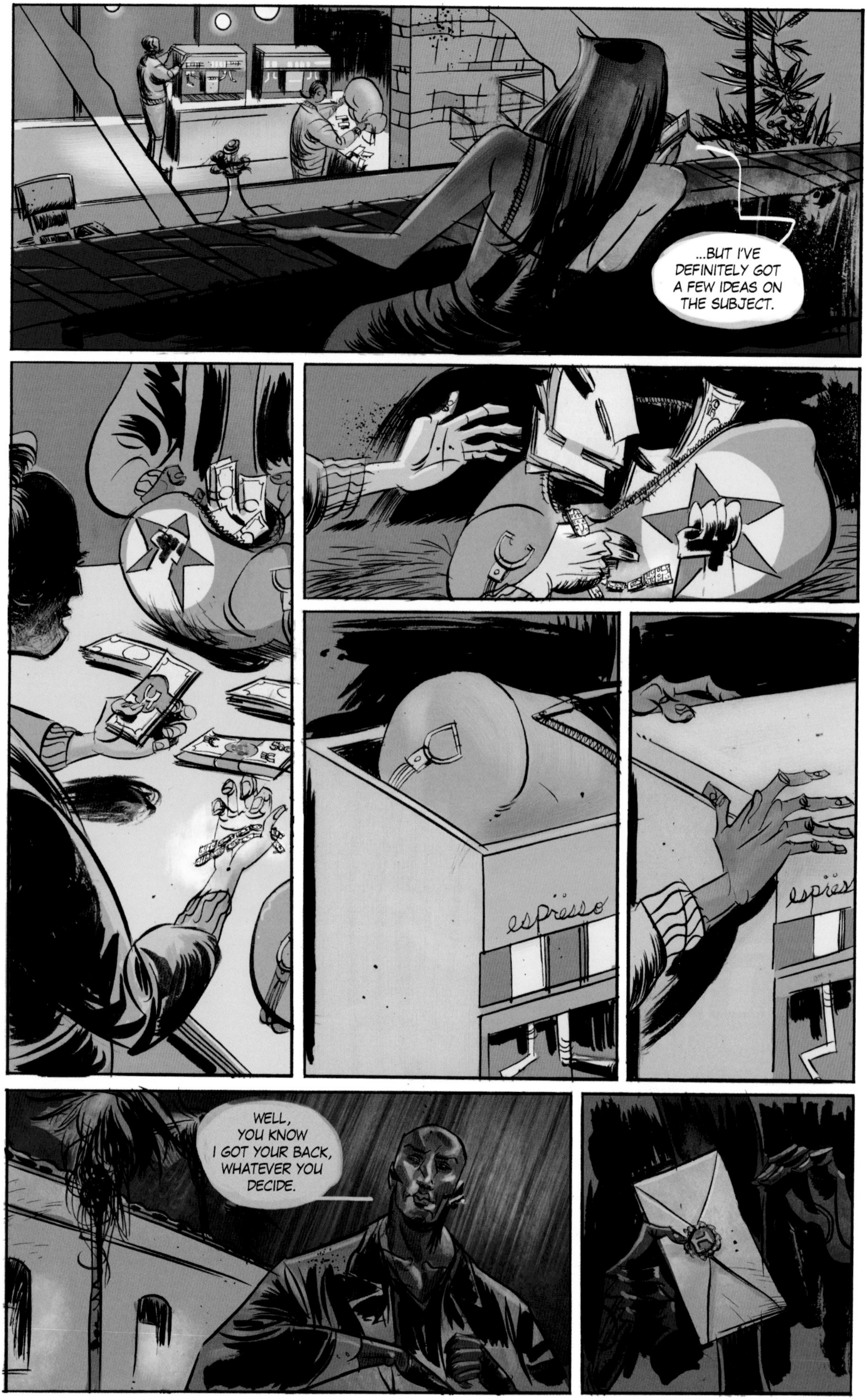
...BUT I'VE DEFINITELY GOT A FEW IDEAS ON THE SUBJECT.
espresso
espresso
WELL, YOU KNOW I GOT YOUR BACK, WHATEVER YOU DECIDE.

INVESTMENT BANKER **WALDO JOHNSON** SCAMS WEST COAST **MOB**

on stock is an equity, usually trading on the
k Market, OTC Bulletin Board or Pink
es, that is purchased at pennies
culous stock brokers to

LIKE I SAID, I AM SICK TO DEATH OF MY JOB...

...AND I'D LOVE A CLEAN BREAK...

THAT'S EXACTLY WHAT I WANT, JOHNNY! A FRESH START... WITH YOU...

**WELCOME**
ALCOHOLICS
ANONYMOUS.
① ②

LOOK, I HAVEN'T GOT ALL NIGHT FOR THIS COURT-APPOINTED BULLSHIT, SO...

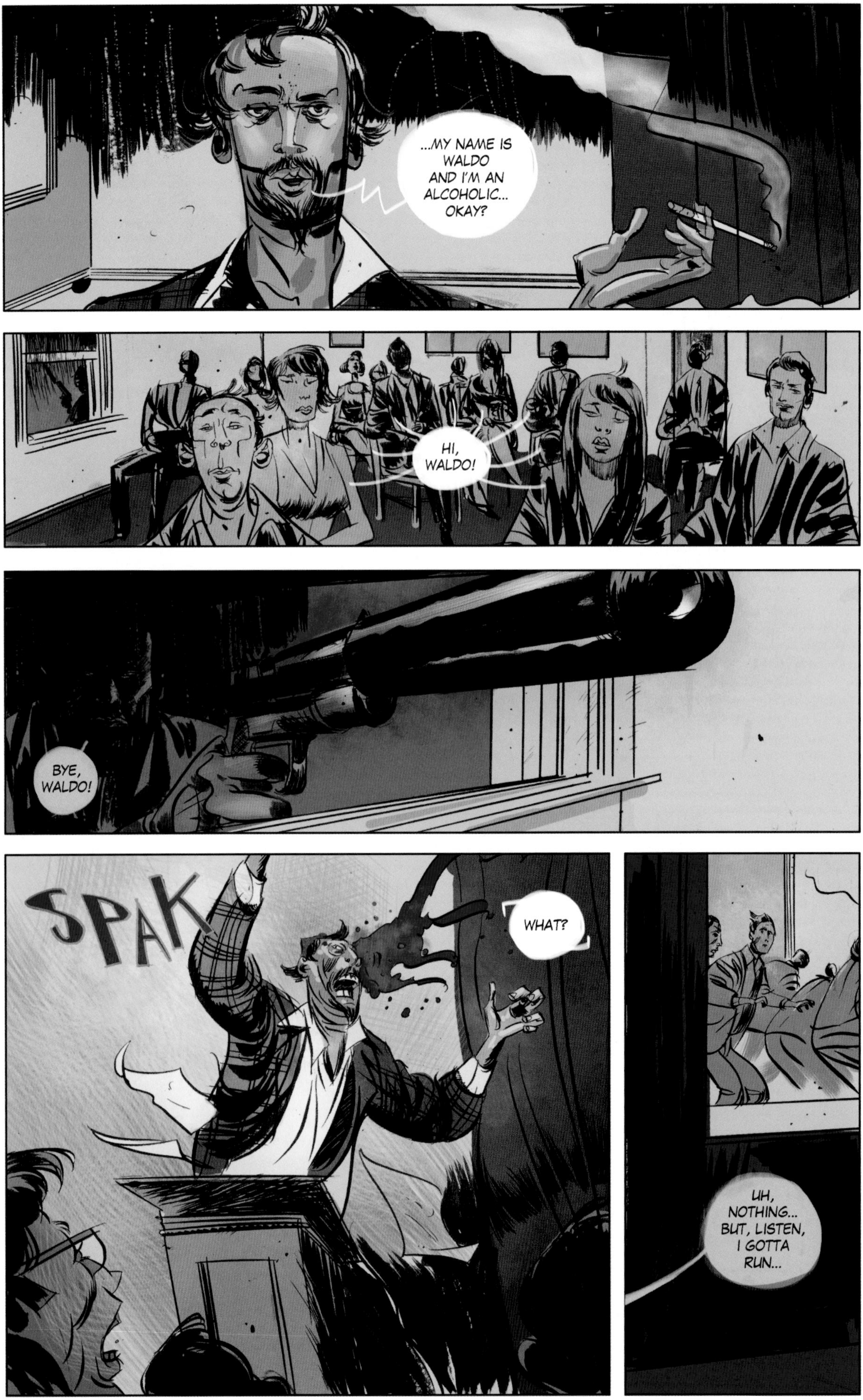
...MY NAME IS WALDO AND I'M AN ALCOHOLIC... OKAY?
HI, WALDO!
BYE, WALDO!
SPAK
WHAT?
UH, NOTHING... BUT, LISTEN, I GOTTA RUN...

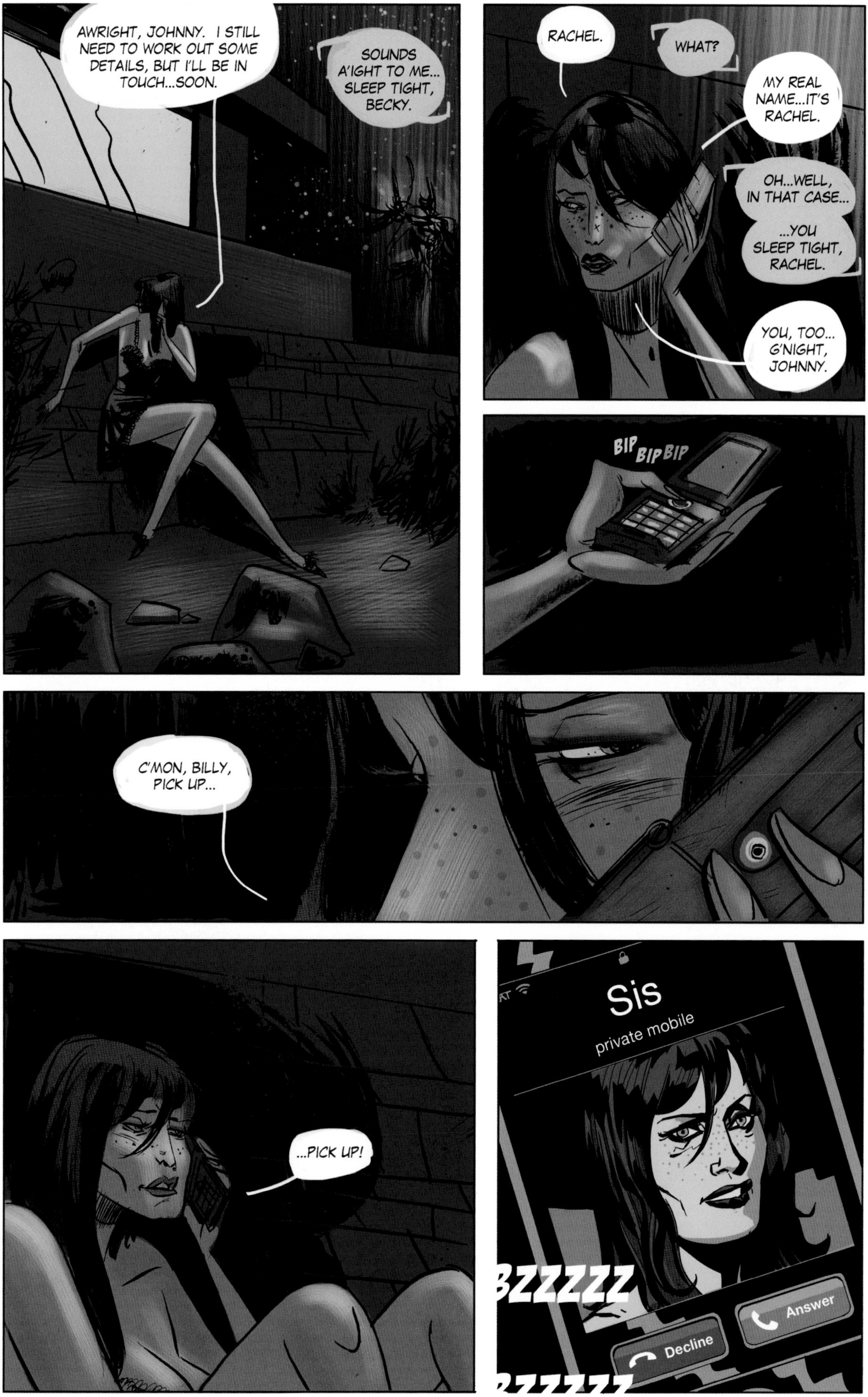
AWRIGHT, JOHNNY. I STILL NEED TO WORK OUT SOME DETAILS, BUT I'LL BE IN TOUCH...SOON.
SOUNDS A'IGHT TO ME... SLEEP TIGHT, BECKY.
RACHEL.
WHAT?
MY REAL NAME...IT'S RACHEL.
OH...WELL, IN THAT CASE...
...YOU SLEEP TIGHT, RACHEL.
YOU, TOO... G'NIGHT, JOHNNY.
BIP BIP BIP
C'MON, BILLY, PICK UP...
...PICK UP!
Sis
private mobile
BZZZZZ
Decline
Answer
ZZZZZZ

OOOOH SWEEEEEET CHIIIILD O' MINE!

TONY' LUCIANO'S CLUB... *THE SMOKING BARREL*

BZZZZZ BZZZZ

BZZZZZ BZZZZZ

PAT

HEY, DUMMY!

PAY ATTENTION! I'M ASKING YOU A QUESTION! IS THE DEAL A DONE FUCKIN' DEAL OR ISN'T IT?

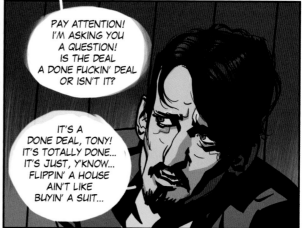

IT'S A DONE DEAL, TONY! IT'S TOTALLY DONE... IT'S JUST, Y'KNOW... FLIPPIN' A HOUSE AIN'T LIKE BUYIN' A SUIT...

WHAT AM I, FUCKIN' STUPID? YOU THINK I DON'T KNOW THAT? LIKE I'M TOO FUCKIN' DUMB TO UNDERSTAND REAL ESTATE 'CUZ I DIDN'T TAKE SOME FUCKIN' LEARNING ANNEX COURSE LIKE YOU?

NO, TONY! NOT AT ALL! I'M JUST SAYIN' THERE'S A LOTTA FUCKIN' PAPERWORK, Y'KNOW?

NO, I DON'T KNOW, BILLY...THAT'S WHY I'M FUCKIN' ASKING! DO I OWN THE HOUSE OR NOT, YOU STAMMERING MOTHER-FUCKER?

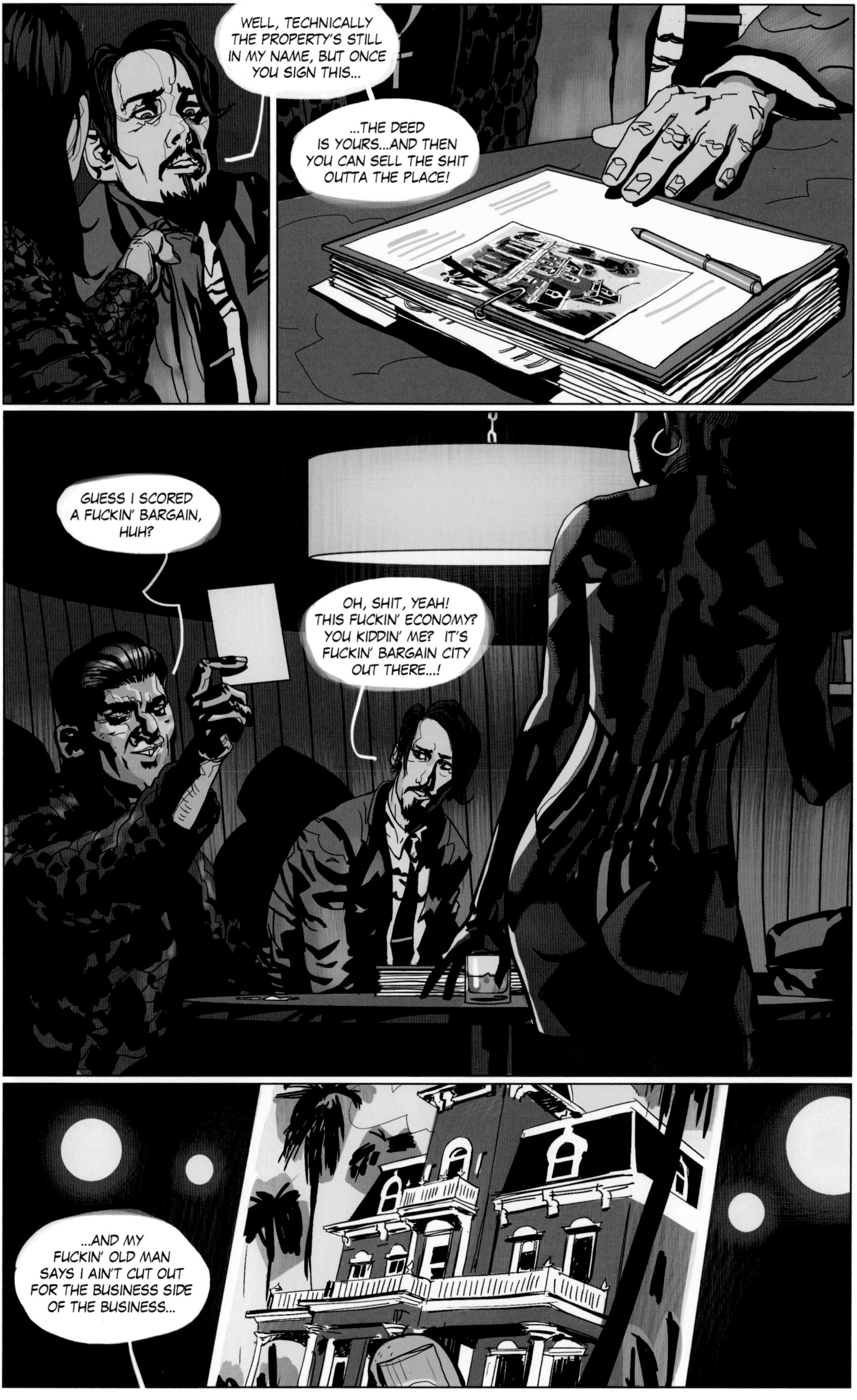
WELL, TECHNICALLY THE PROPERTY'S STILL IN MY NAME, BUT ONCE YOU SIGN THIS...
...THE DEED IS YOURS...AND THEN YOU CAN SELL THE SHIT OUTTA THE PLACE!
GUESS I SCORED A FUCKIN' BARGAIN, HUH?
OH, SHIT, YEAH! THIS FUCKIN' ECONOMY? YOU KIDDIN' ME? IT'S FUCKIN' BARGAIN CITY OUT THERE...!
...AND MY FUCKIN' OLD MAN SAYS I AIN'T CUT OUT FOR THE BUSINESS SIDE OF THE BUSINESS...

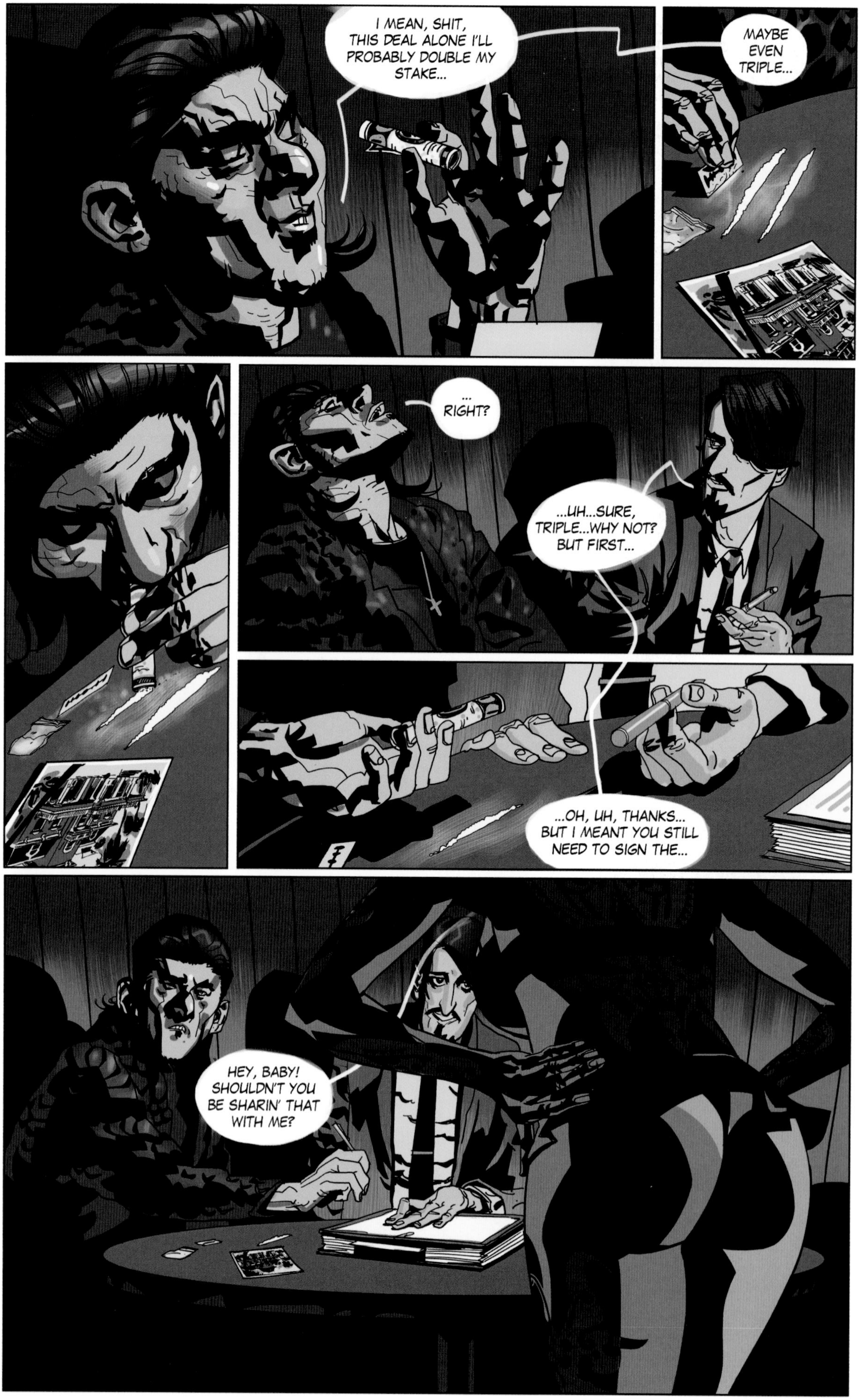
I MEAN, SHIT, THIS DEAL ALONE I'LL PROBABLY DOUBLE MY STAKE...
MAYBE EVEN TRIPLE...
... RIGHT?
...UH...SURE, TRIPLE...WHY NOT? BUT FIRST...
...OH, UH, THANKS... BUT I MEANT YOU STILL NEED TO SIGN THE...
HEY, BABY! SHOULDN'T YOU BE SHARIN' THAT WITH ME?

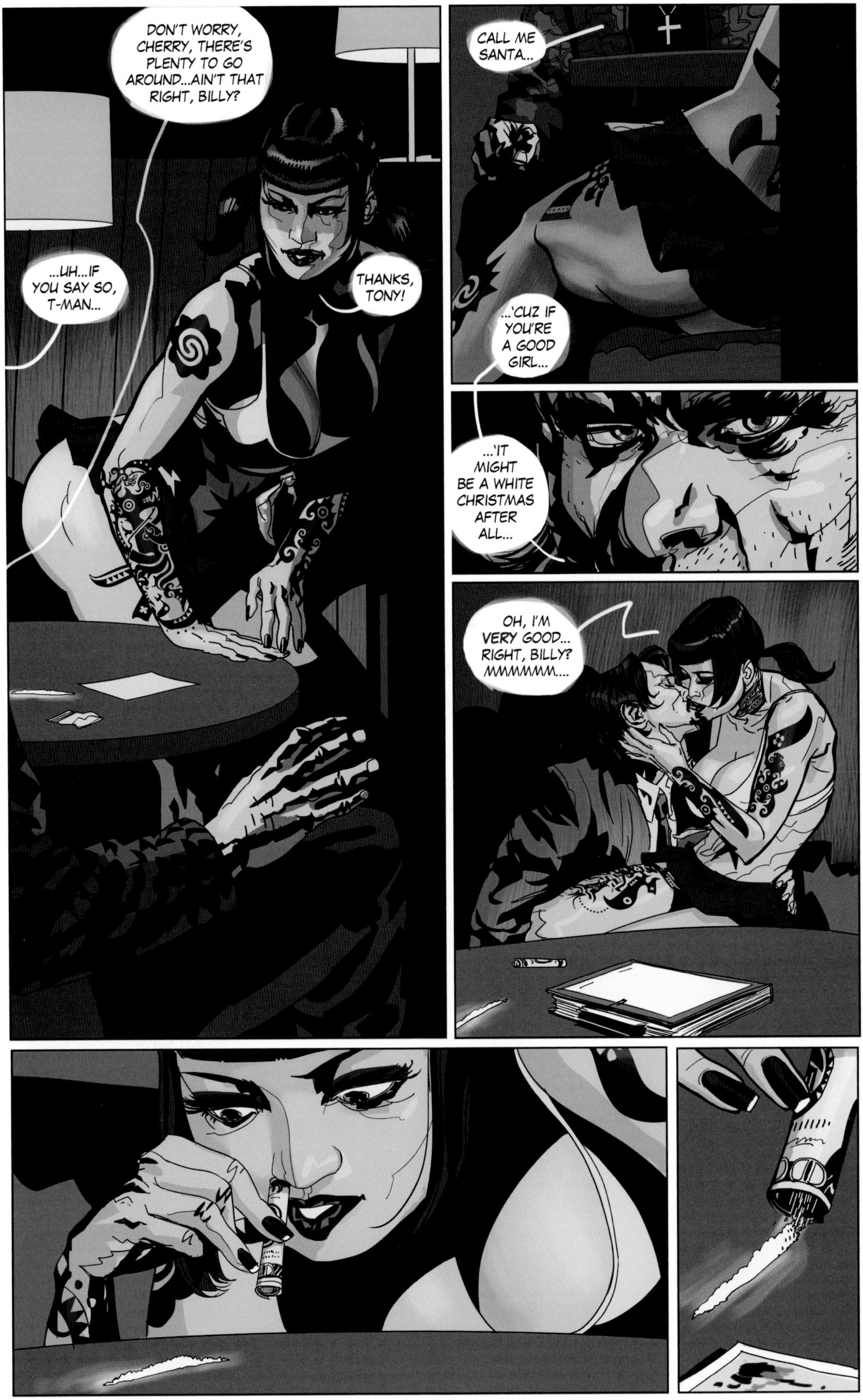
DON'T WORRY, CHERRY, THERE'S PLENTY TO GO AROUND...AIN'T THAT RIGHT, BILLY?
...UH...IF YOU SAY SO, T-MAN...
THANKS, TONY!
CALL ME SANTA...
...'CUZ IF YOU'RE A GOOD GIRL...
...'IT MIGHT BE A WHITE CHRISTMAS AFTER ALL...
OH, I'M VERY GOOD... RIGHT, BILLY? MMMMMM....

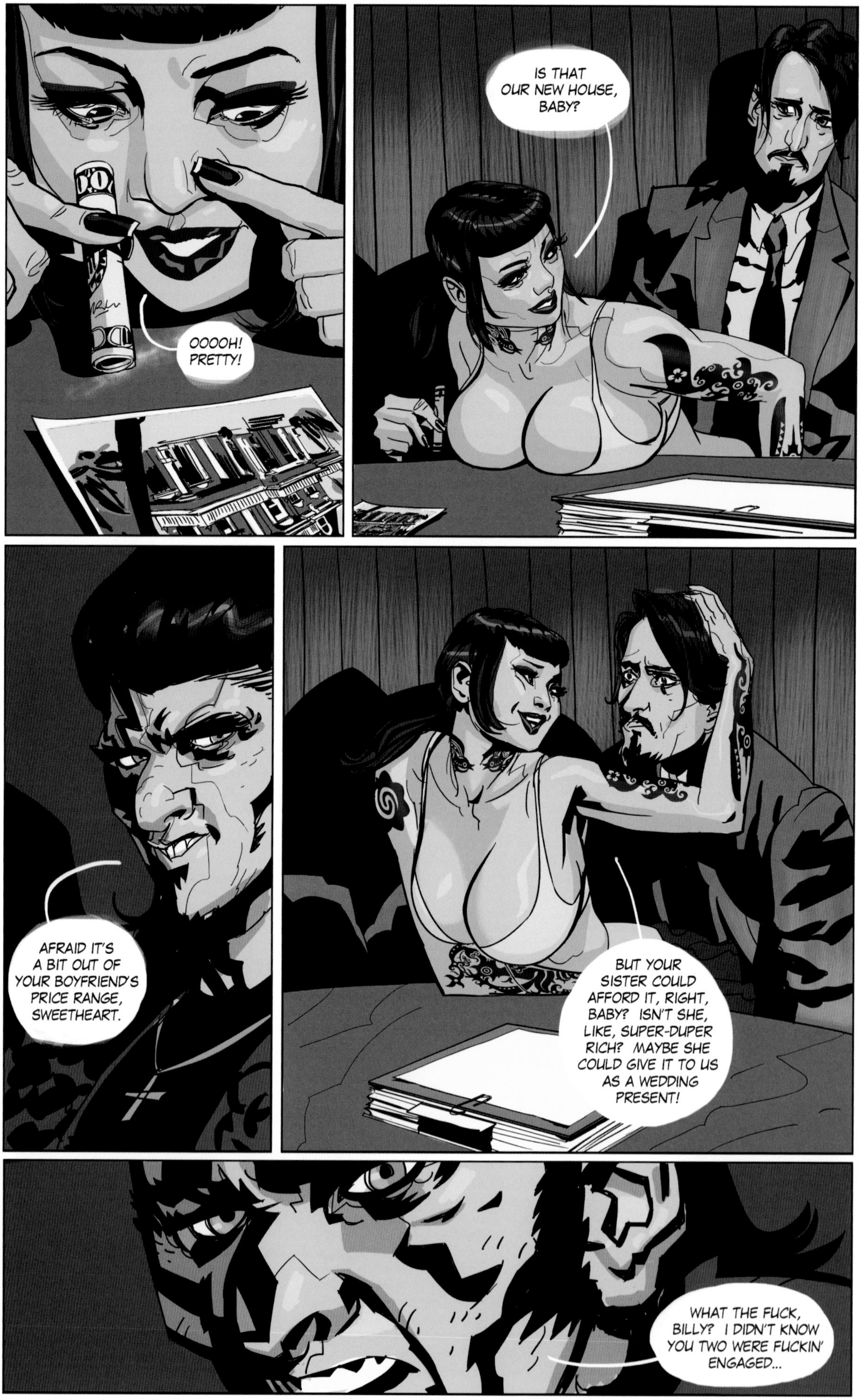
OOOOH! PRETTY!
IS THAT OUR NEW HOUSE, BABY?
AFRAID IT'S A BIT OUT OF YOUR BOYFRIEND'S PRICE RANGE, SWEETHEART.
BUT YOUR SISTER COULD AFFORD IT, RIGHT, BABY? ISN'T SHE, LIKE, SUPER-DUPER RICH? MAYBE SHE COULD GIVE IT TO US AS A WEDDING PRESENT!
WHAT THE FUCK, BILLY? I DIDN'T KNOW YOU TWO WERE FUCKIN' ENGAGED...

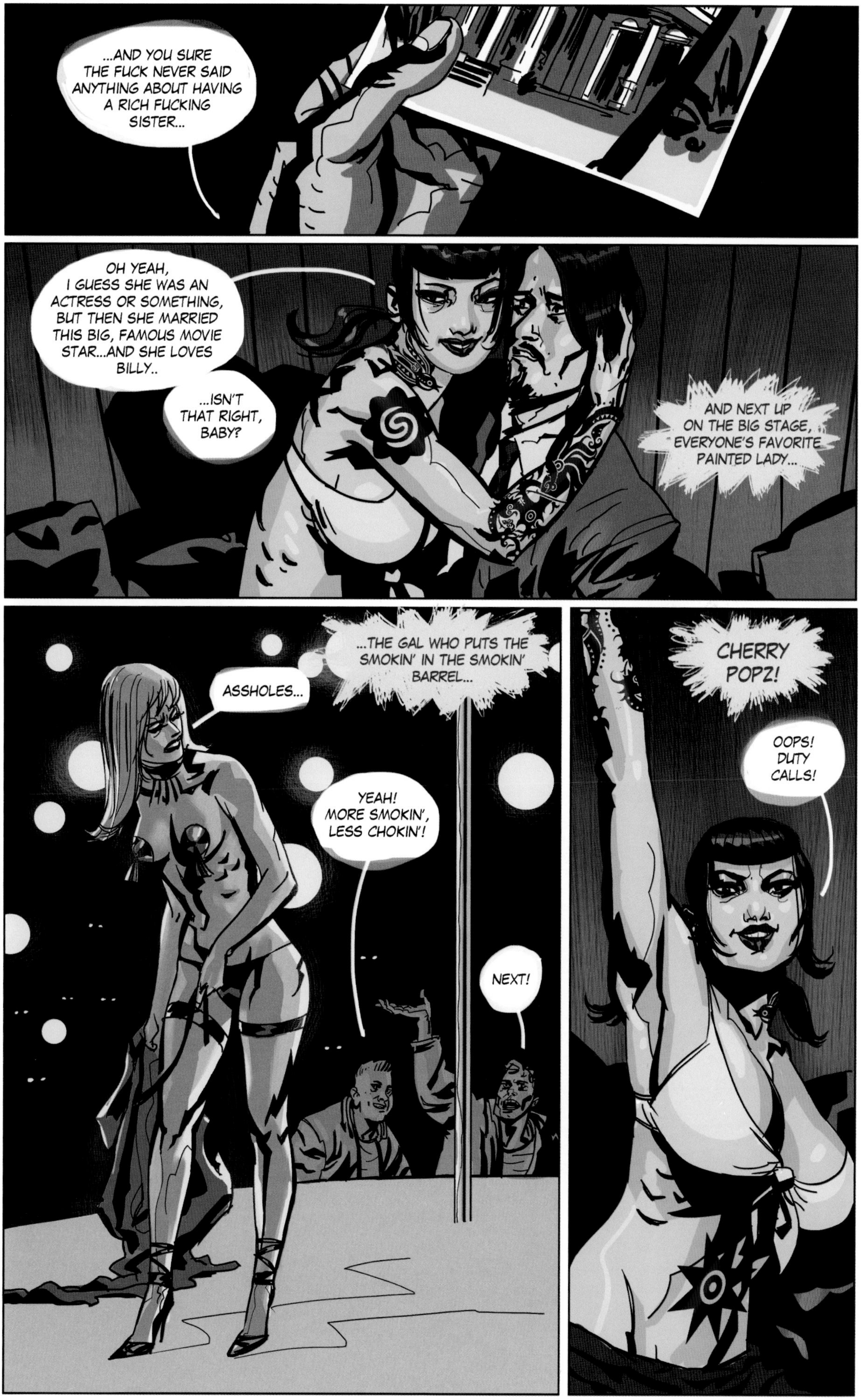
...AND YOU SURE THE FUCK NEVER SAID ANYTHING ABOUT HAVING A RICH FUCKING SISTER...
OH YEAH, I GUESS SHE WAS AN ACTRESS OR SOMETHING, BUT THEN SHE MARRIED THIS BIG, FAMOUS MOVIE STAR...AND SHE LOVES BILLY..
...ISN'T THAT RIGHT, BABY?
AND NEXT UP ON THE BIG STAGE, EVERYONE'S FAVORITE PAINTED LADY...
...THE GAL WHO PUTS THE SMOKIN' IN THE SMOKIN' BARREL...
ASSHOLES...
YEAH! MORE SMOKIN', LESS CHOKIN'!
NEXT!
CHERRY POPZ!
OOPS! DUTY CALLS!

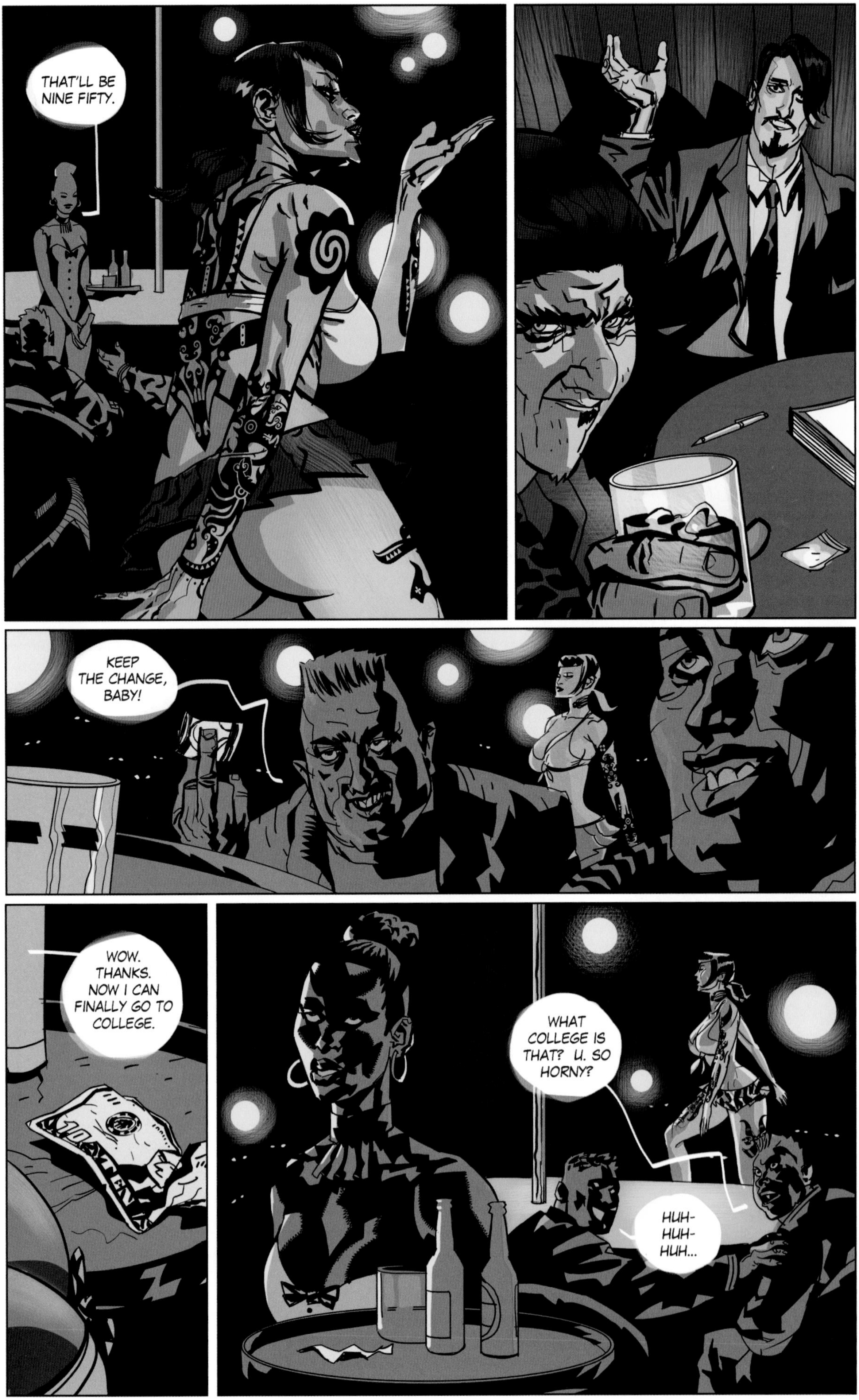
THAT'LL BE NINE FIFTY.
KEEP THE CHANGE, BABY!
WOW. THANKS. NOW I CAN FINALLY GO TO COLLEGE.
WHAT COLLEGE IS THAT? U. SO HORNY?
HUH-HUH-HUH...

WHO LET THE DOGS OUT

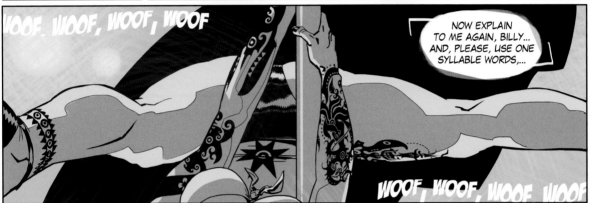

WOOF, WOOF, WOOF, WOOF

NOW EXPLAIN TO ME AGAIN, BILLY... AND, PLEASE, USE ONE SYLLABLE WORDS,...

WOOF, WOOF, WOOF, WOOF

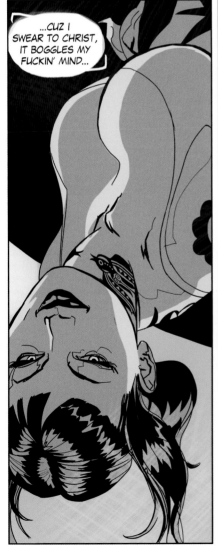

...CUZ I SWEAR TO CHRIST, IT BOGGLES MY FUCKIN' MIND...

...HOW A WORTHLESS MOOK LIKE YOU SCORES A FUCKIN' KNOCKOUT LIKE HER.

JUST LUCKY, I GUESS...

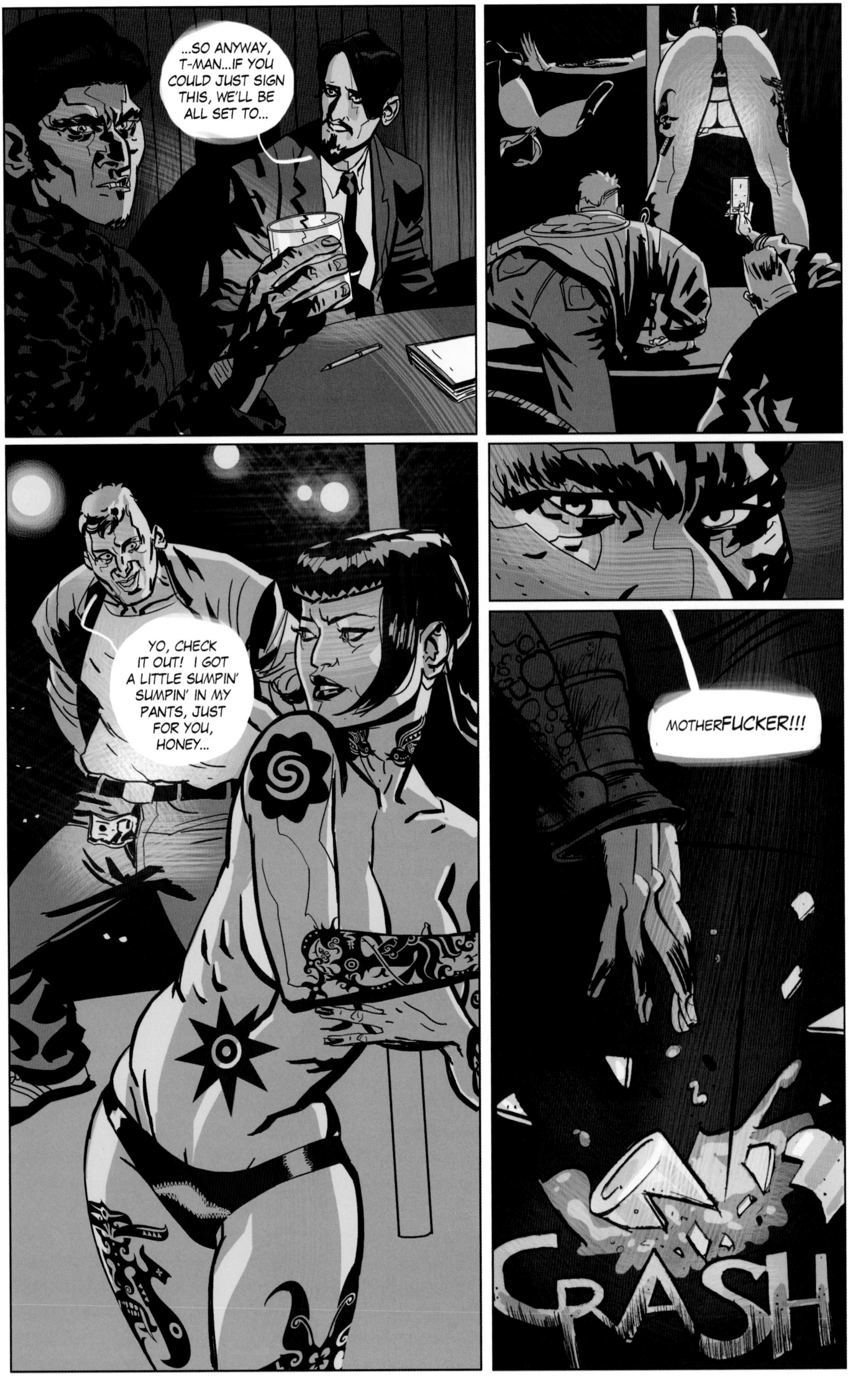
...SO ANYWAY, T-MAN...IF YOU COULD JUST SIGN THIS, WE'LL BE ALL SET TO...
YO, CHECK IT OUT! I GOT A LITTLE SUMPIN' SUMPIN' IN MY PANTS, JUST FOR YOU, HONEY...
MOTHERFUCKER!!!
CRASH

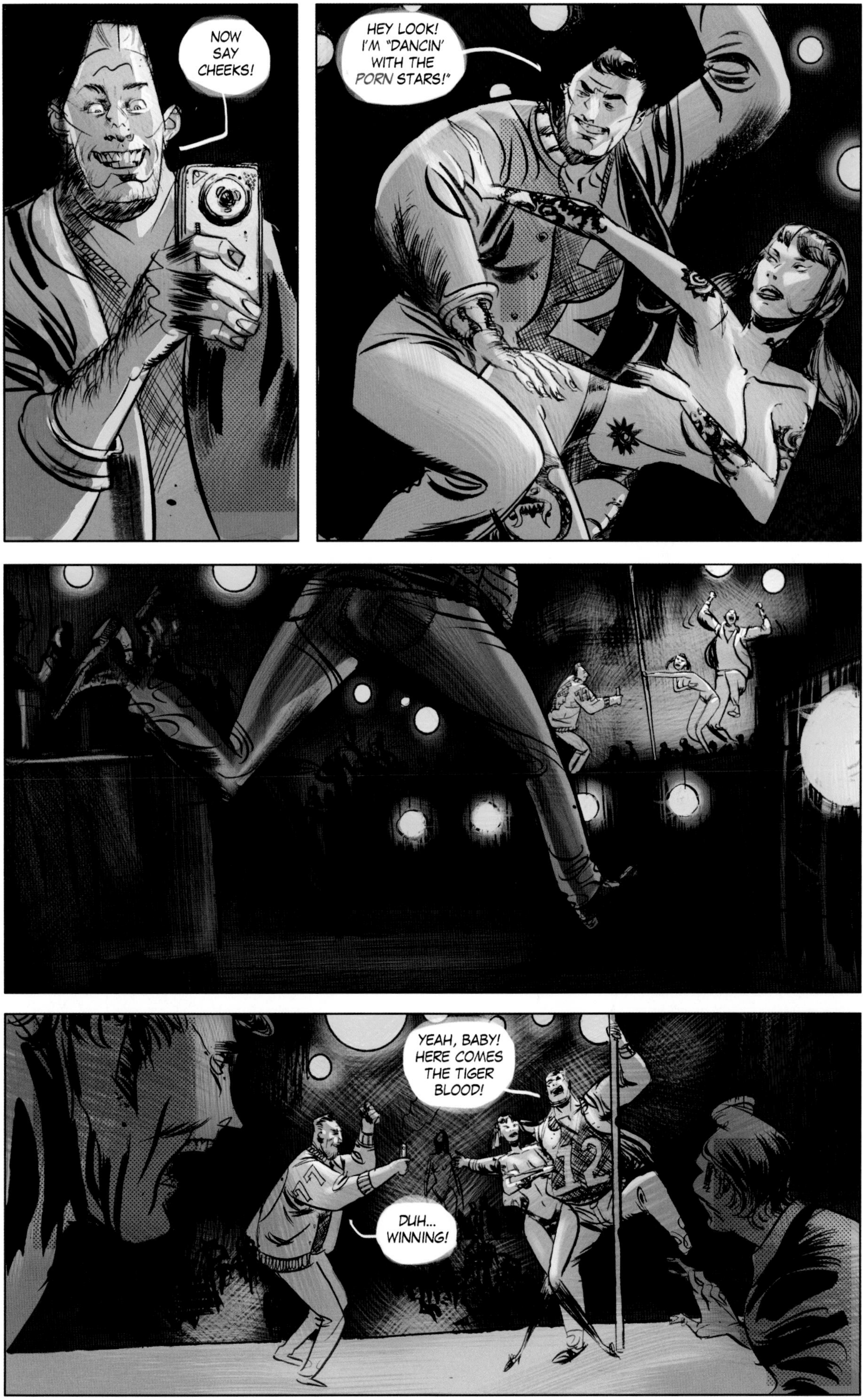
NOW SAY CHEEKS!
HEY LOOK! I'M "DANCIN' WITH THE PORN STARS!"
YEAH, BABY! HERE COMES THE TIGER BLOOD!
DUH... WINNING!

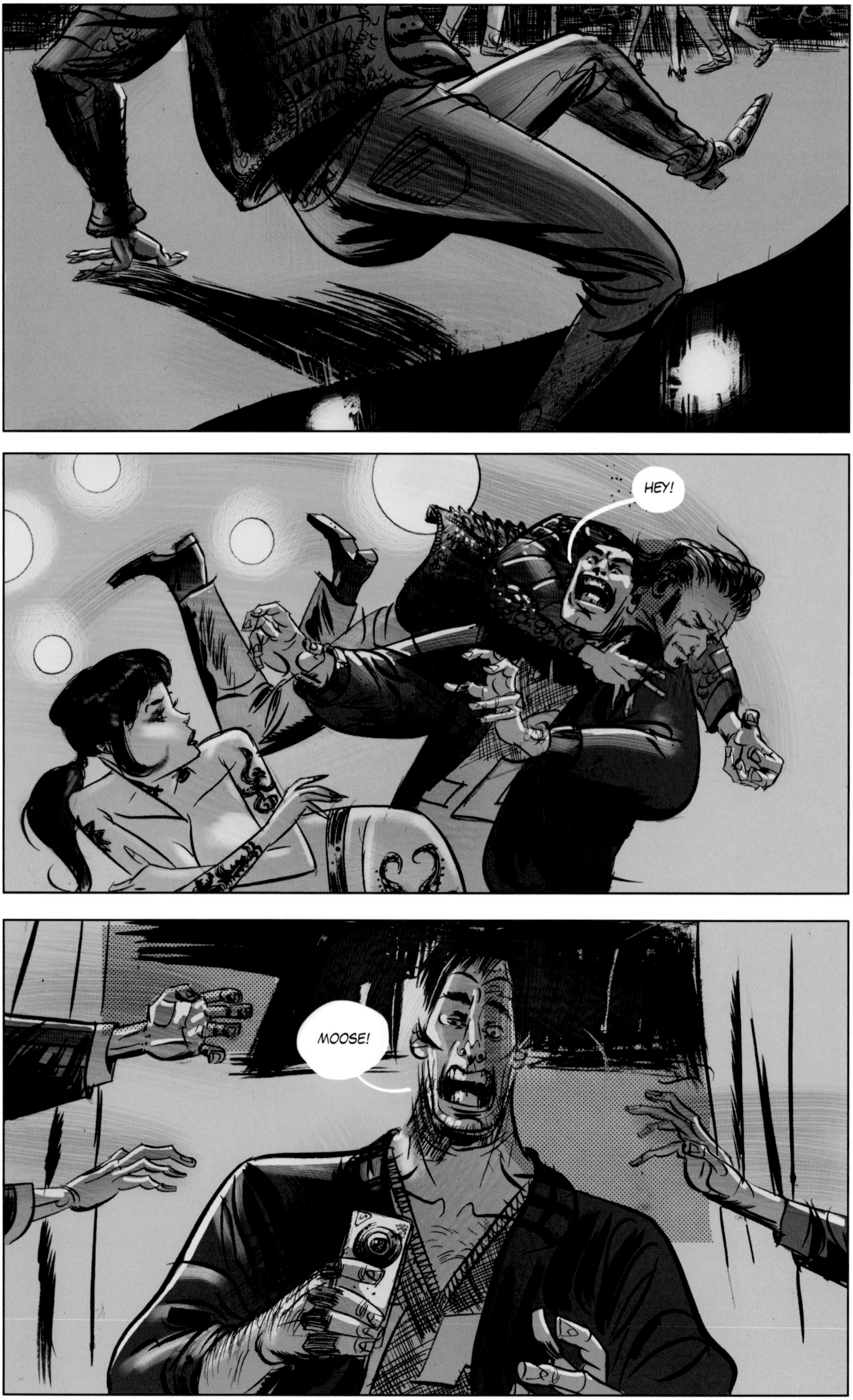
HEY!
MOOSE!

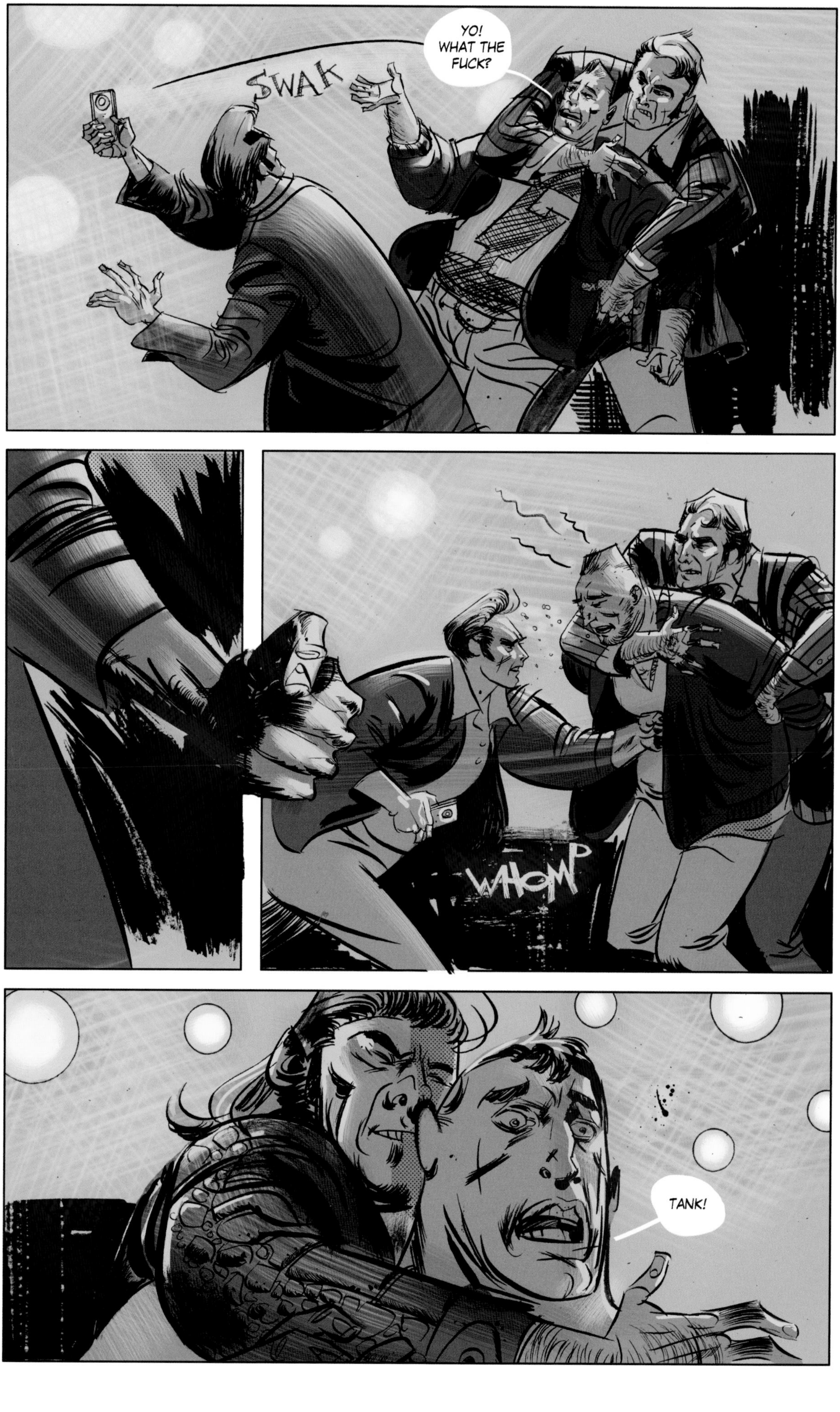
YO! WHAT THE FUCK?
SWAK
WHOMP
TANK!

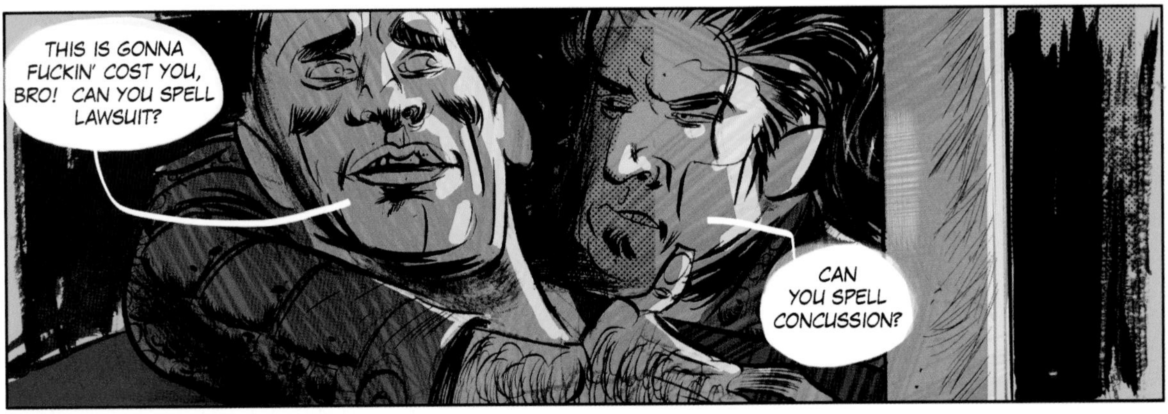
THIS IS GONNA FUCKIN' COST YOU, BRO! CAN YOU SPELL LAWSUIT?
CAN YOU SPELL CONCUSSION?

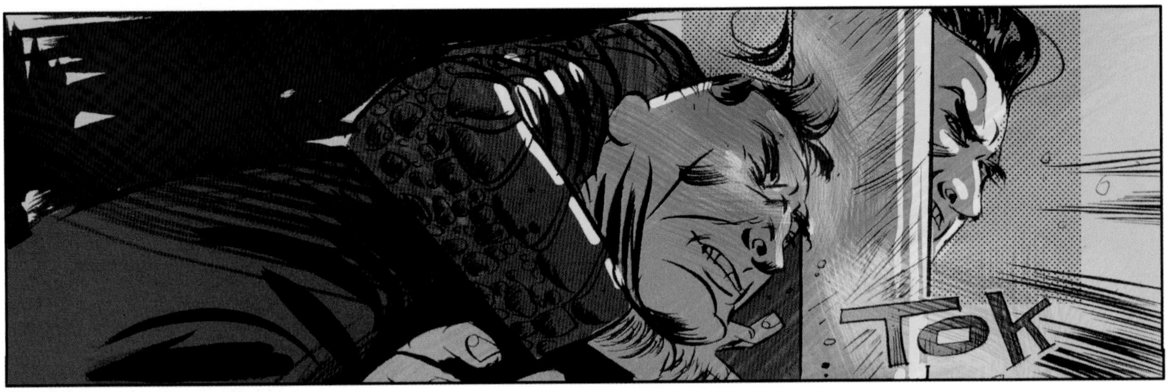
TOK

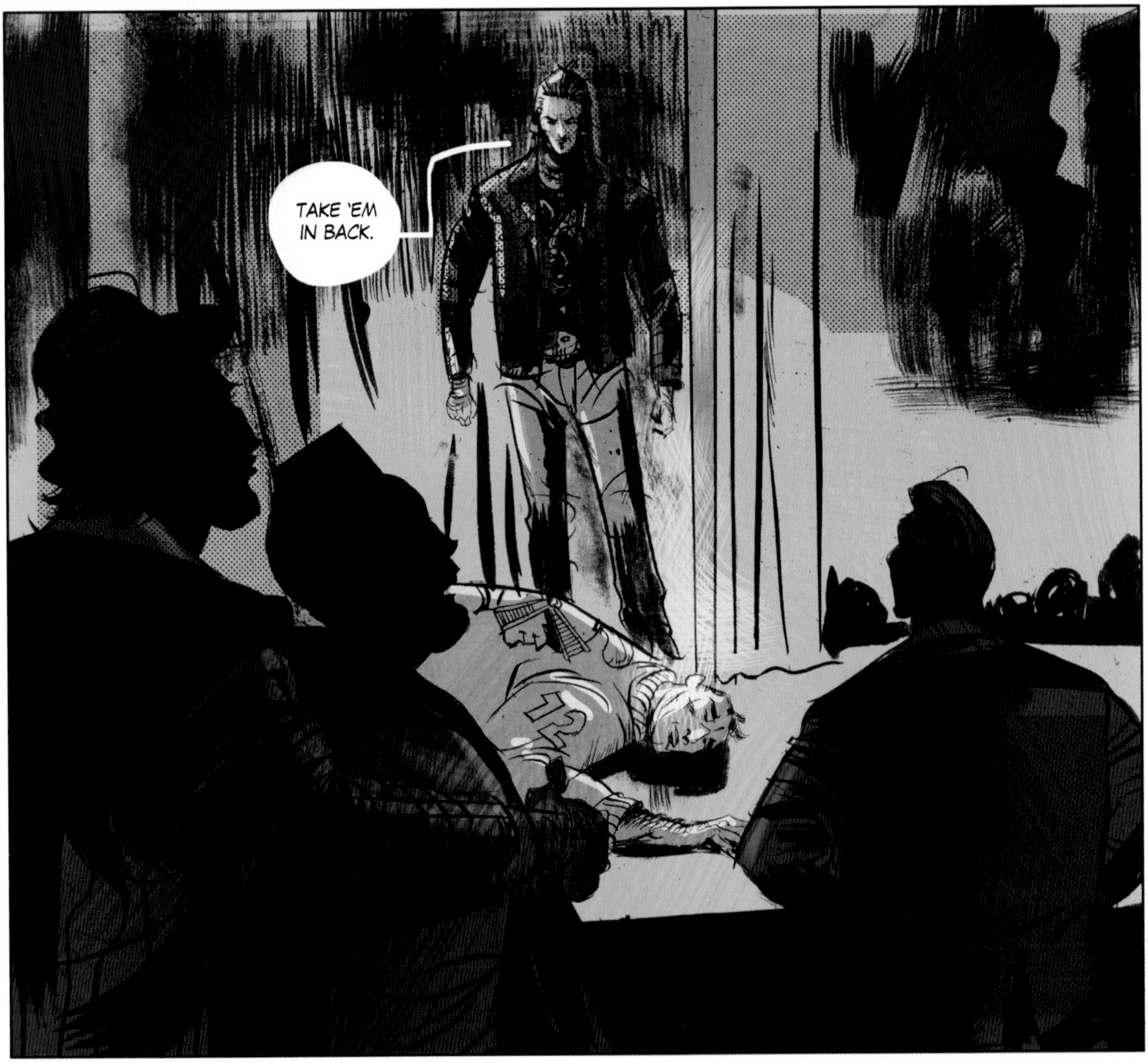
TAKE 'EM IN BACK.

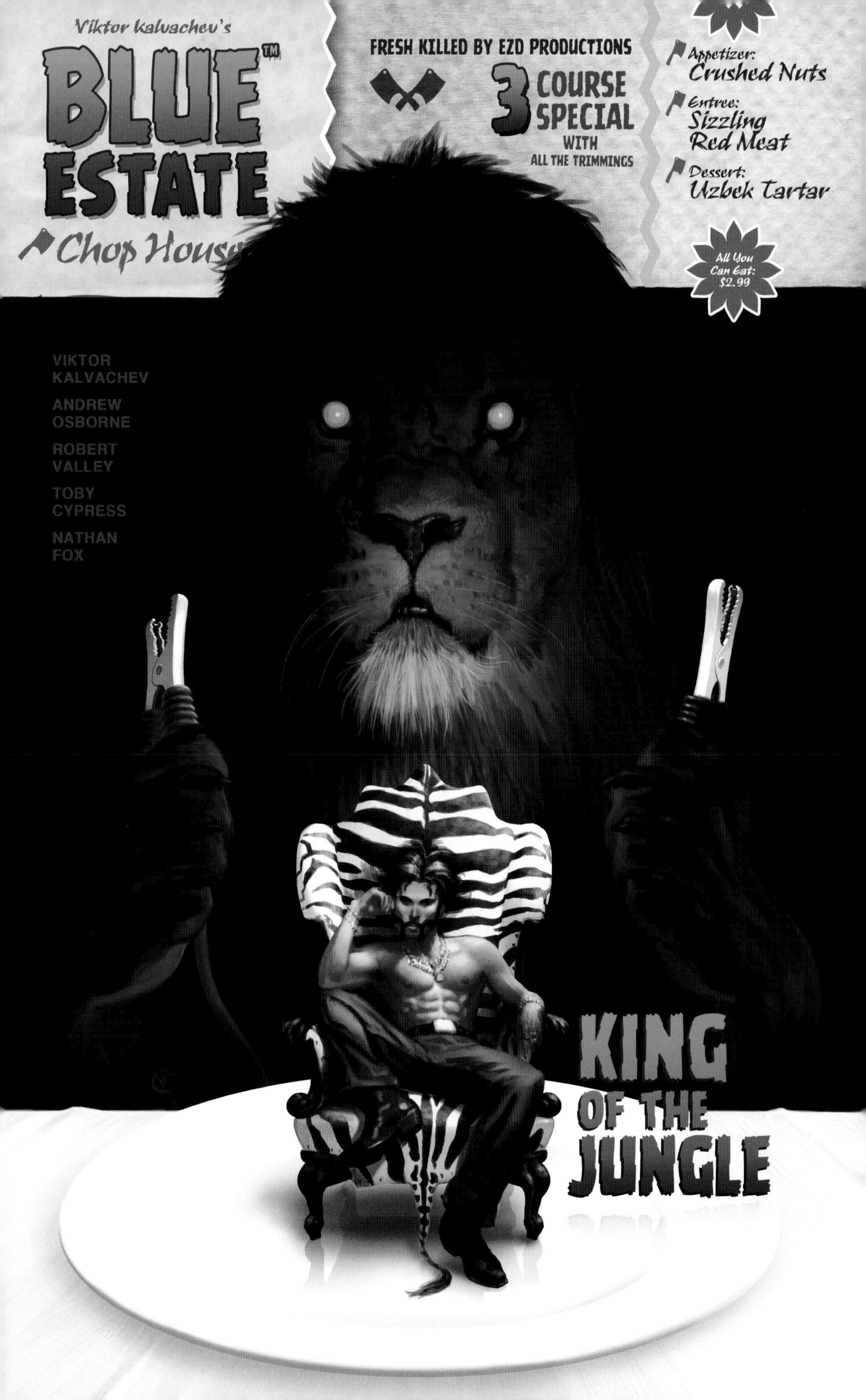

Viktor Kalvachev's
BLUE ESTATE™
Chop House
FRESH KILLED BY EZD PRODUCTIONS
3 COURSE SPECIAL
WITH
ALL THE TRIMMINGS
Appetizer:
Crushed Nuts
Entree:
Sizzling
Red Meat
Dessert:
Uzbek Tartar
All You Can Eat:
$2.99
VIKTOR KALVACHEV
ANDREW OSBORNE
ROBERT VALLEY
TOBY CYPRESS
NATHAN FOX
KING OF THE JUNGLE

# BLUE ESTATE ™

EPISODE THREE:
## KING OF THE JUNGLE

ORIGINAL STORY:
**VIKTOR KALVACHEV** AND **KOSTA YANEV**

SCRIPT BY **ANDREW OSBORNE**

ARTISTS:
**VIKTOR KALVACHEV**
**TOBY CYPRESS**
**NATHAN FOX**
**ROBERT VALLEY**

ART DIRECTION BY **VIKTOR KALVACHEV**

COVER, COLORS & DESIGN:
**VIKTOR KALVACHEV**

CONTRIBUTING EDITOR:
**PHILO NORTHRUP**

www.BlueEstateComic.com

EZD ™
PRODUCTIONS

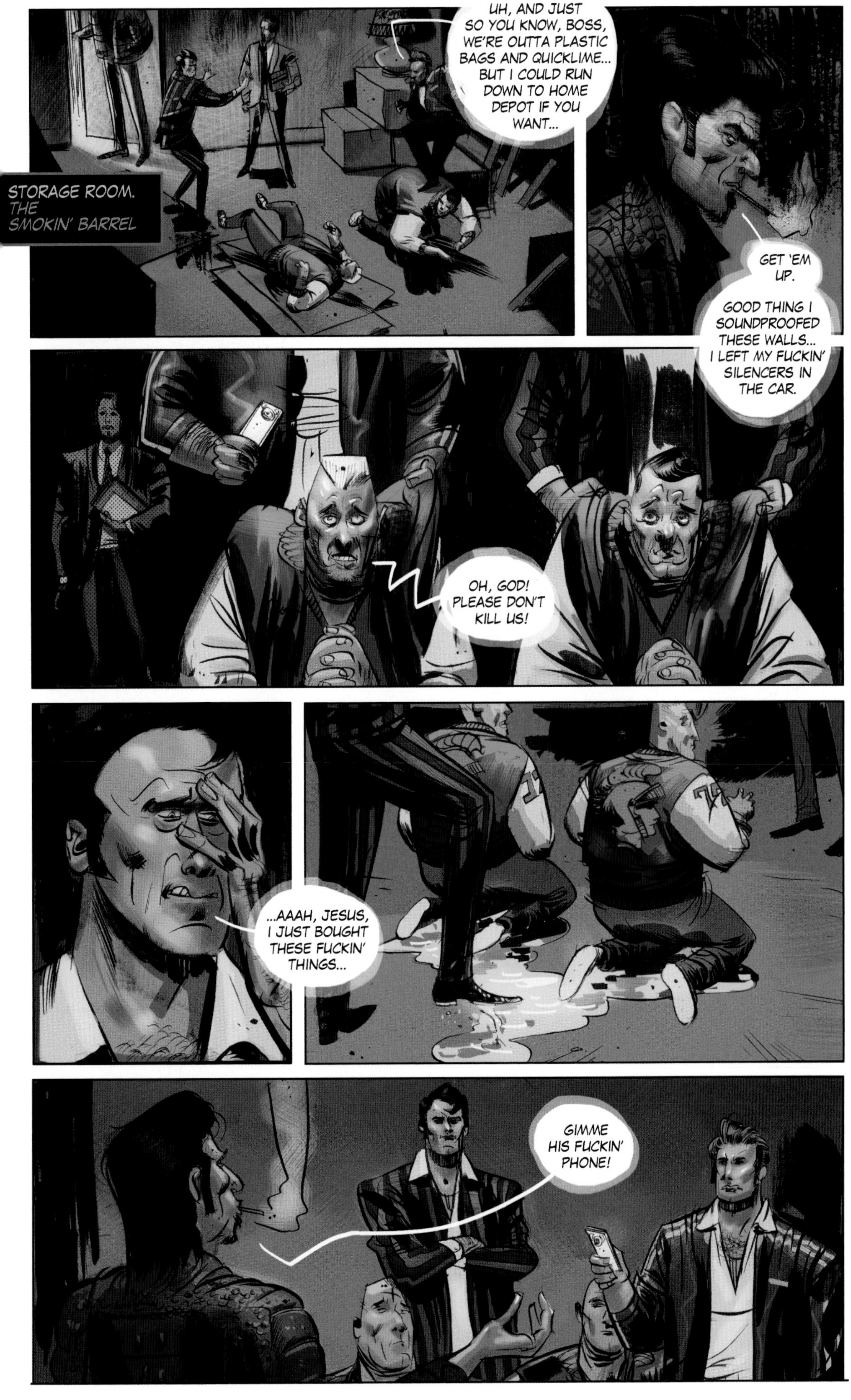
STORAGE ROOM.
THE SMOKIN' BARREL
UH, AND JUST SO YOU KNOW, BOSS, WE'RE OUTTA PLASTIC BAGS AND QUICKLIME... BUT I COULD RUN DOWN TO HOME DEPOT IF YOU WANT...
GET 'EM UP.
GOOD THING I SOUNDPROOFED THESE WALLS... I LEFT MY FUCKIN' SILENCERS IN THE CAR.
OH, GOD! PLEASE DON'T KILL US!
...AAAH, JESUS, I JUST BOUGHT THESE FUCKIN' THINGS...
GIMME HIS FUCKIN' PHONE!

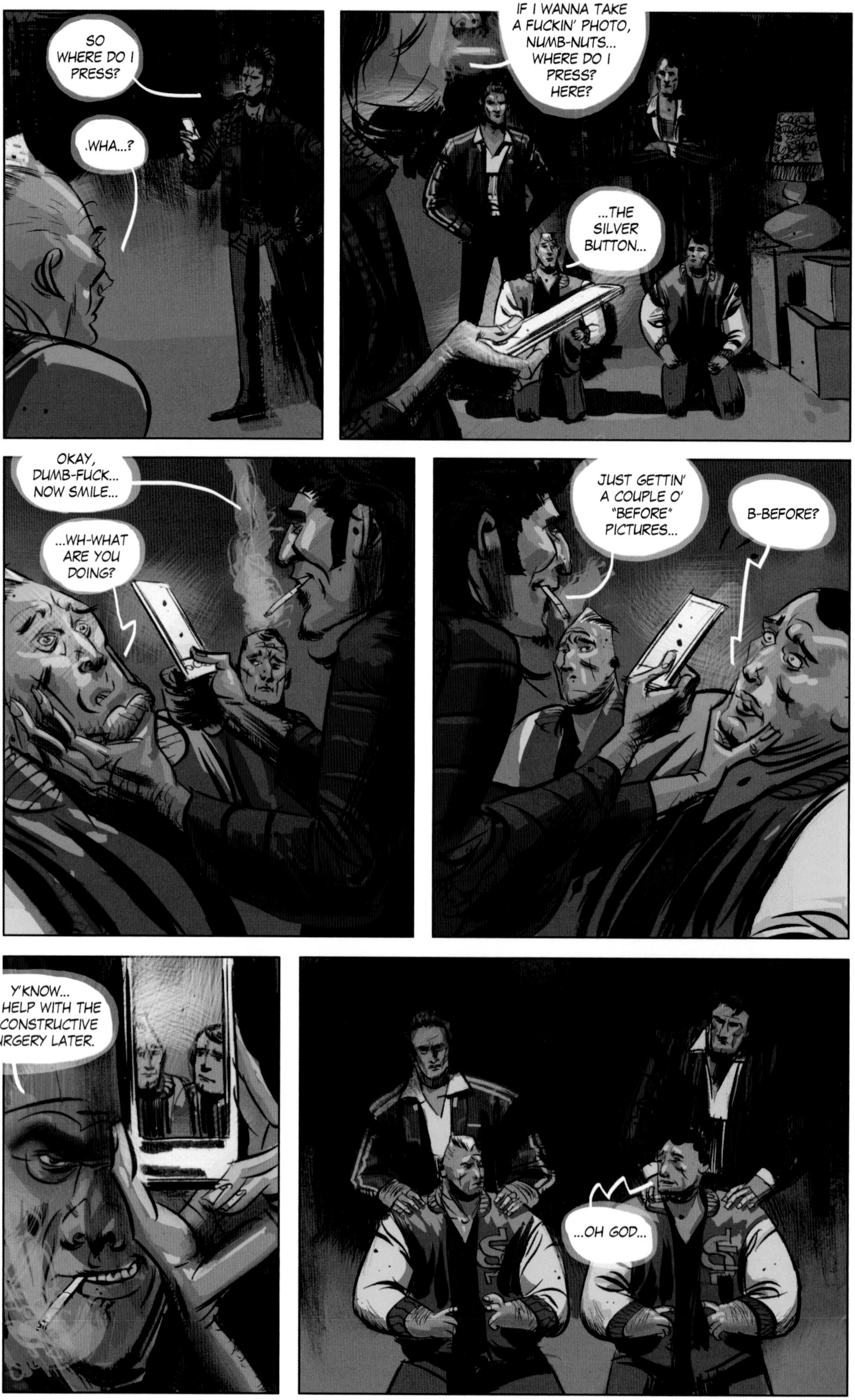
SO WHERE DO I PRESS?
.WHA...?
IF I WANNA TAKE A FUCKIN' PHOTO, NUMB-NUTS... WHERE DO I PRESS? HERE?
...THE SILVER BUTTON...
OKAY, DUMB-FUCK... NOW SMILE...
...WH-WHAT ARE YOU DOING?
JUST GETTIN' A COUPLE O' "BEFORE" PICTURES...
B-BEFORE?
Y'KNOW... TO HELP WITH THE RECONSTRUCTIVE SURGERY LATER.
...OH GOD...

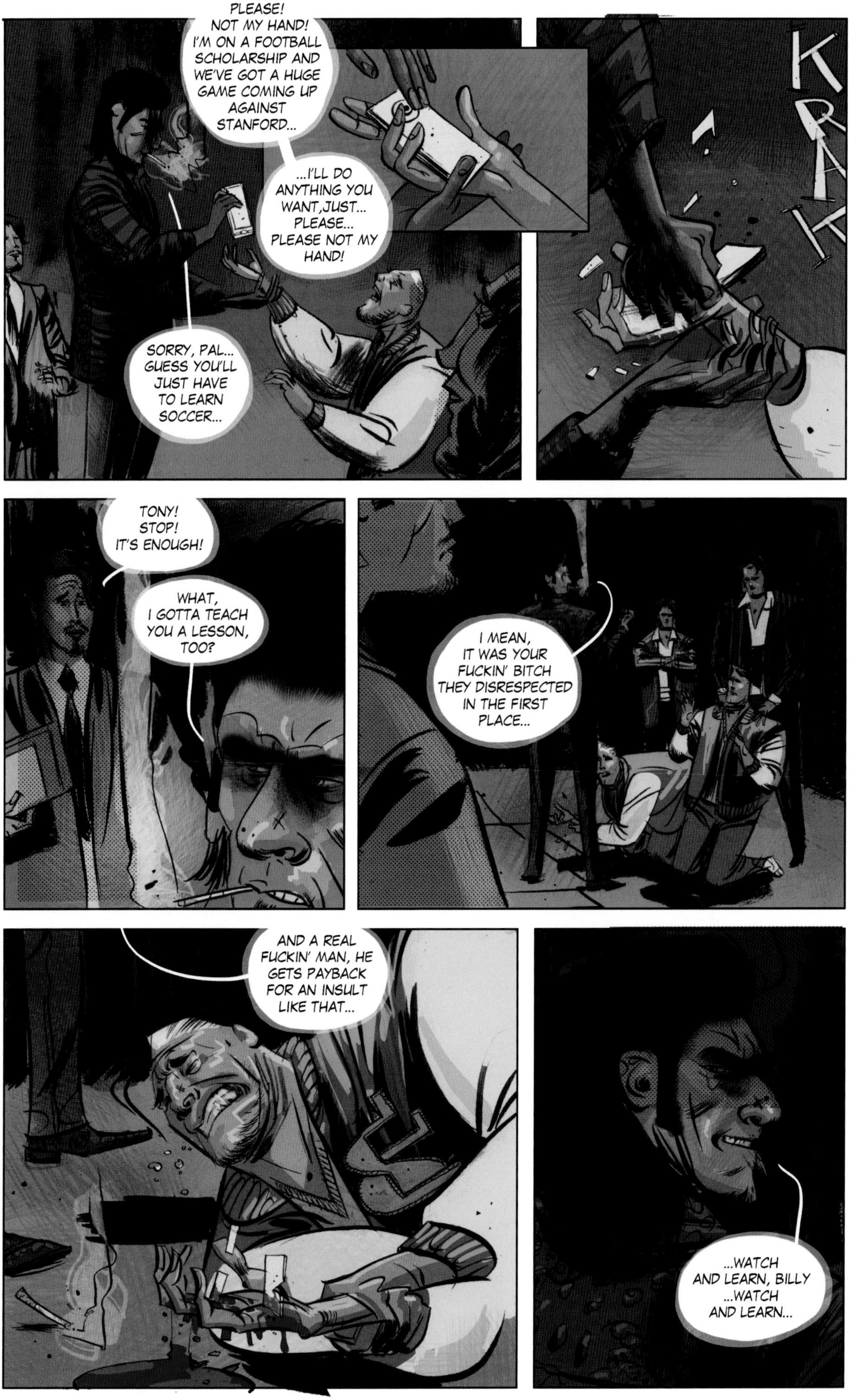
PLEASE! NOT MY HAND! I'M ON A FOOTBALL SCHOLARSHIP AND WE'VE GOT A HUGE GAME COMING UP AGAINST STANFORD...
...I'LL DO ANYTHING YOU WANT, JUST... PLEASE... PLEASE NOT MY HAND!
SORRY, PAL... GUESS YOU'LL JUST HAVE TO LEARN SOCCER...
KRAK
TONY! STOP! IT'S ENOUGH!
WHAT, I GOTTA TEACH YOU A LESSON, TOO?
I MEAN, IT WAS YOUR FUCKIN' BITCH THEY DISRESPECTED IN THE FIRST PLACE...
AND A REAL FUCKIN' MAN, HE GETS PAYBACK FOR AN INSULT LIKE THAT...
...WATCH AND LEARN, BILLY ...WATCH AND LEARN...

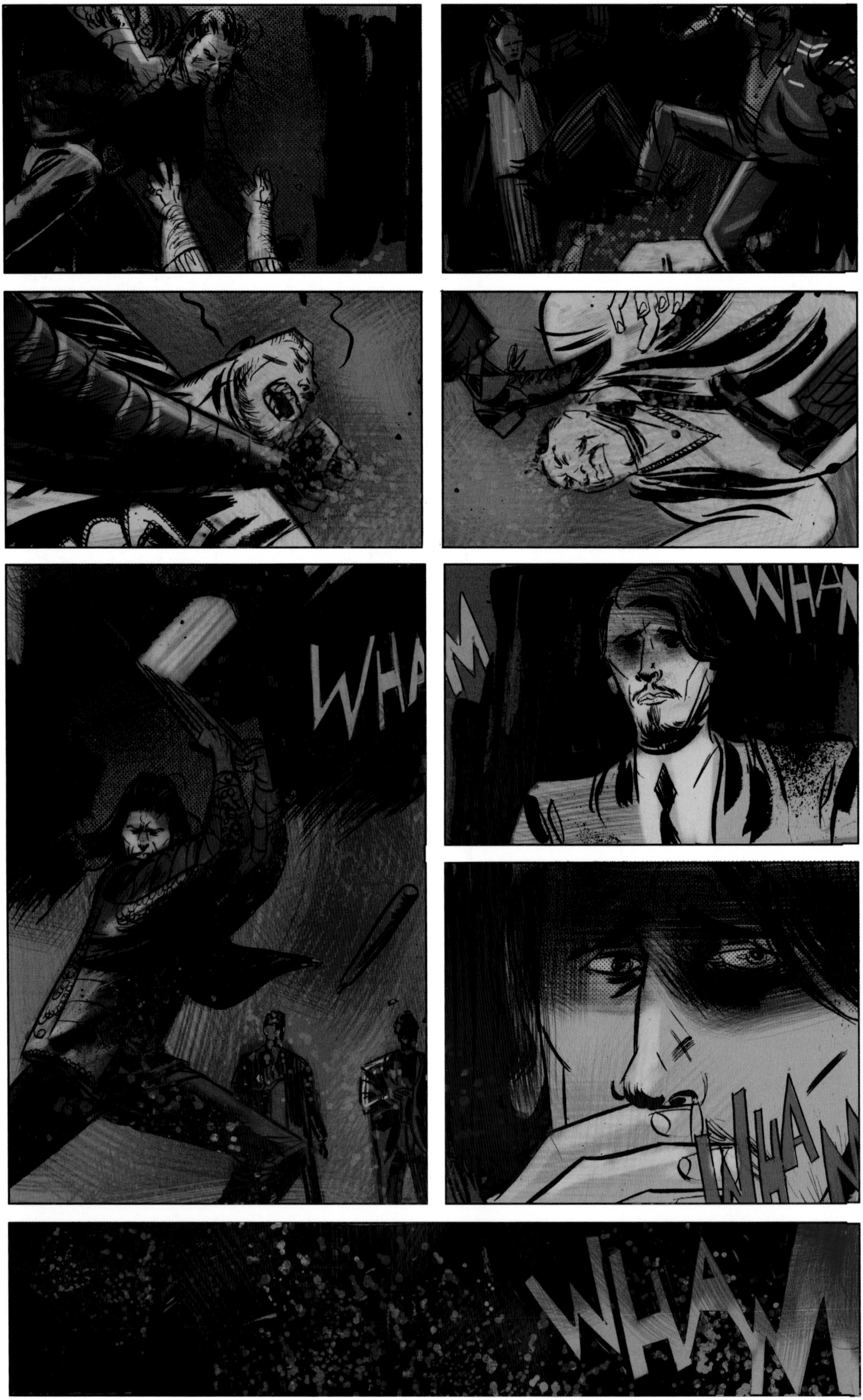

WHA
WHAM
WHA
WHAM
WHAM

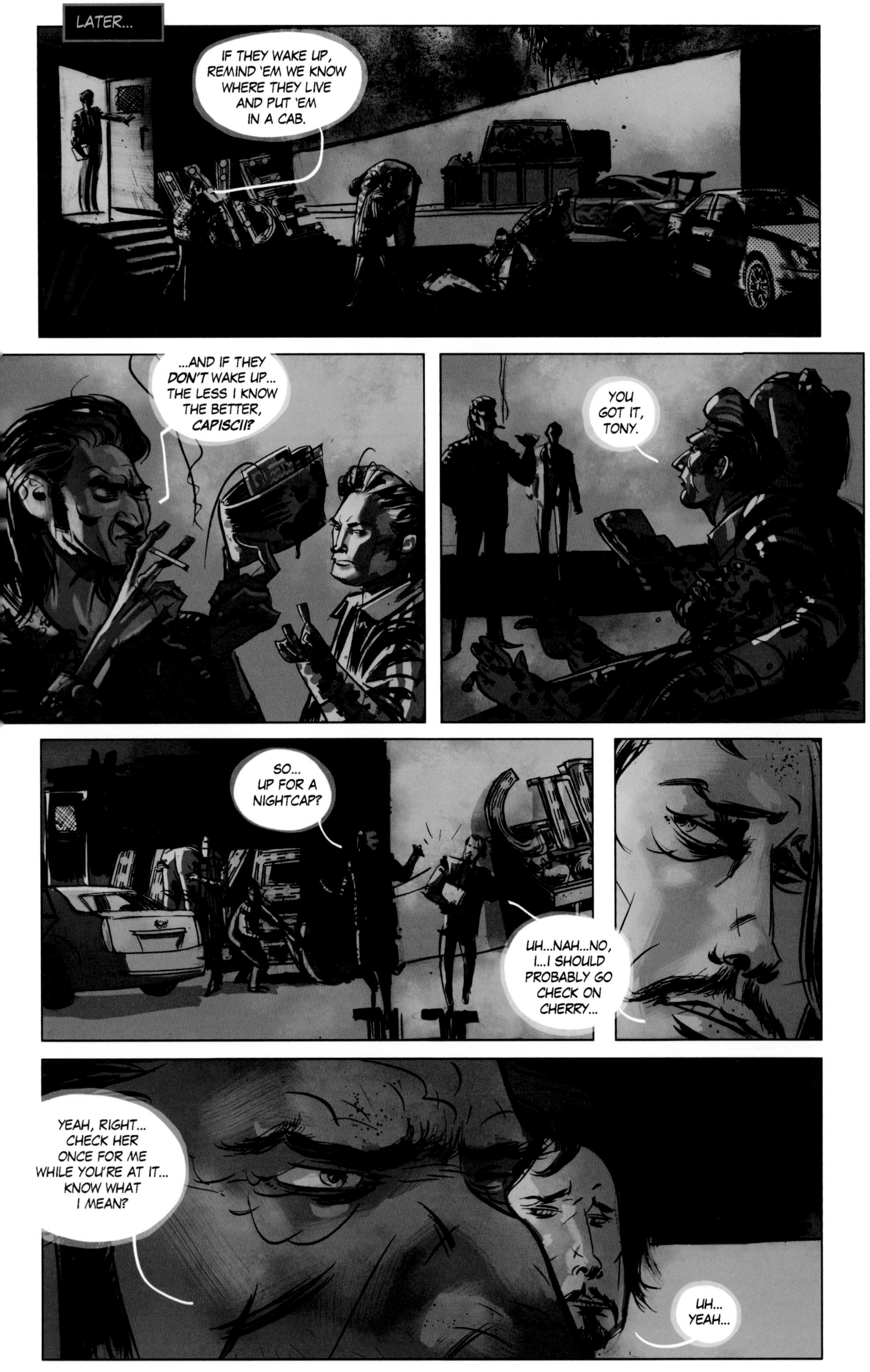
LATER...
IF THEY WAKE UP, REMIND 'EM WE KNOW WHERE THEY LIVE AND PUT 'EM IN A CAB.
...AND IF THEY *DON'T* WAKE UP... THE LESS I KNOW THE BETTER, *CAPISCI!?*
YOU GOT IT, TONY.
SO... UP FOR A NIGHTCAP?
UH...NAH...NO, I...I SHOULD PROBABLY GO CHECK ON CHERRY...
YEAH, RIGHT... CHECK HER ONCE FOR ME WHILE YOU'RE AT IT... KNOW WHAT I MEAN?
UH... YEAH...

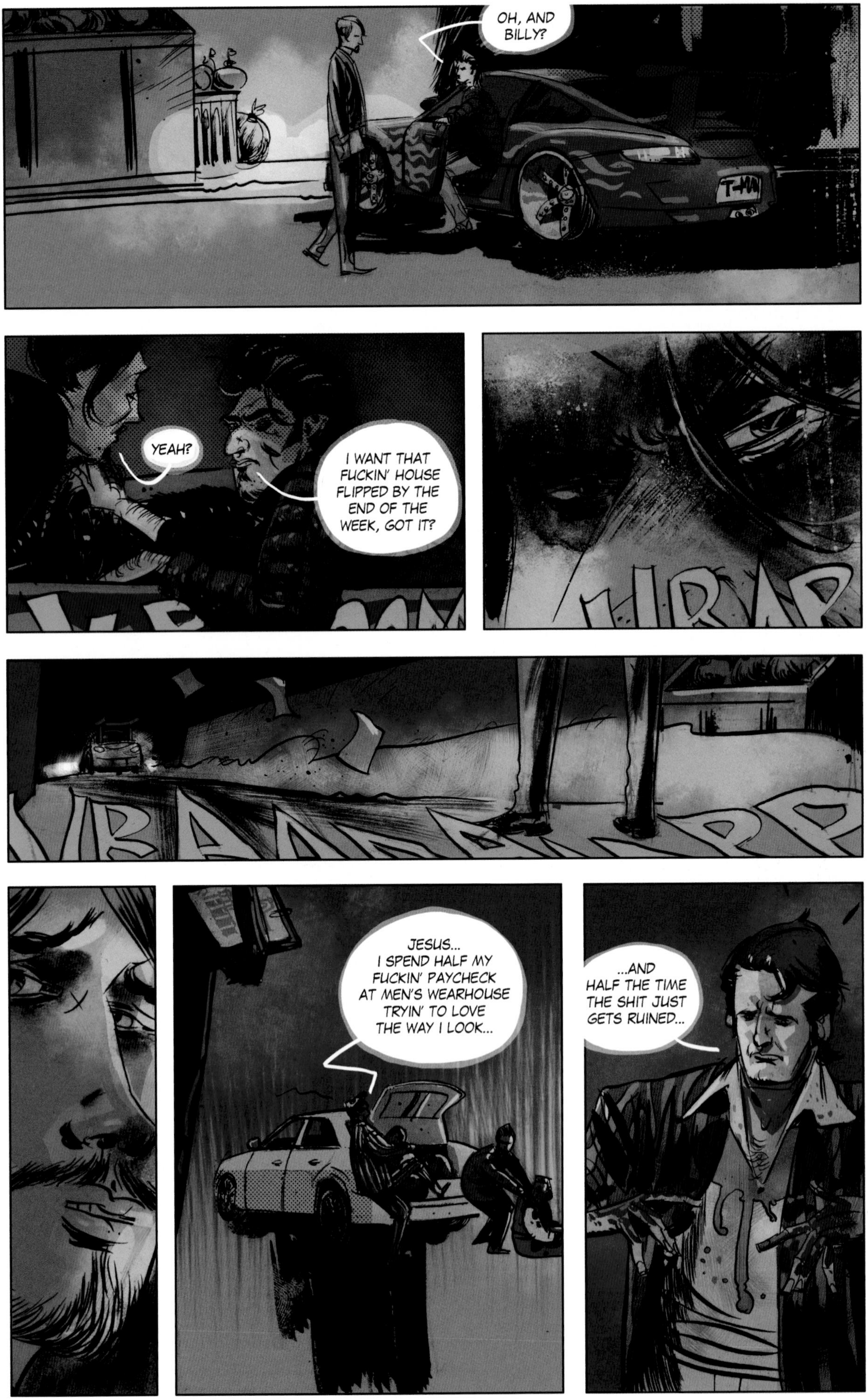

OH, AND BILLY?
YEAH?
I WANT THAT FUCKIN' HOUSE FLIPPED BY THE END OF THE WEEK, GOT IT?
JESUS... I SPEND HALF MY FUCKIN' PAYCHECK AT MEN'S WEARHOUSE TRYIN' TO LOVE THE WAY I LOOK...
...AND HALF THE TIME THE SHIT JUST GETS RUINED...

YOU NEED TO RELAX, MAN...
...I MEAN, YOU NEVER SEE
THE HOFF GETTIN' UPTIGHT
OVER CLOTHES...NOT EVEN
ON BAYWATCH NIGHTS.

NUMBER ONE,
JUST 'CUZ YOU'RE
STONED ALL THE TIME
DOESN'T EXACTLY MAKE
YOU THE KING OF
FUCKIN' RELAXATION...

NGHT RDR

...IN FACT, IF YOU ASK ME,
THAT FUCKIN' SKUNKWEED OF
YOURS MAKES YOU *MORE*
UPTIGHT, NOT LESS...

HEY!

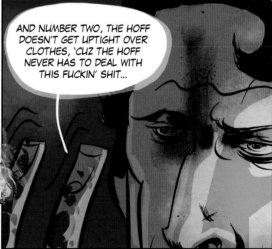

AND NUMBER TWO, THE HOFF
DOESN'T GET UPTIGHT OVER
CLOTHES, 'CUZ THE HOFF
NEVER HAS TO DEAL WITH
THIS FUCKIN' SHIT...

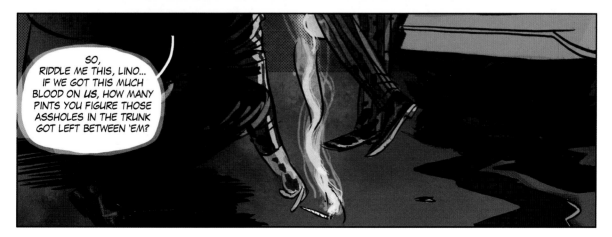

SO,
RIDDLE ME THIS, LINO...
IF WE GOT THIS MUCH
BLOOD ON *US*, HOW MANY
PINTS YOU FIGURE THOSE
ASSHOLES IN THE TRUNK
GOT LEFT BETWEEN 'EM?

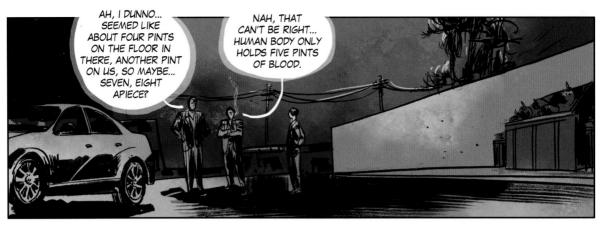

AH, I DUNNO... SEEMED LIKE ABOUT FOUR PINTS ON THE FLOOR IN THERE, ANOTHER PINT ON US, SO MAYBE... SEVEN, EIGHT APIECE?

NAH, THAT CAN'T BE RIGHT... HUMAN BODY ONLY HOLDS FIVE PINTS OF BLOOD.

LITERS.

WHAT?

THE AVERAGE HUMAN BODY HOLDS FIVE LITERS OF BLOOD.

SO WHAT'S THAT IN PINTS?

I DUNNO...

...TEN?

WHAT'S WITH HIM?

GUESS HE DON'T KNOW MUCH ABOUT BLOOD.

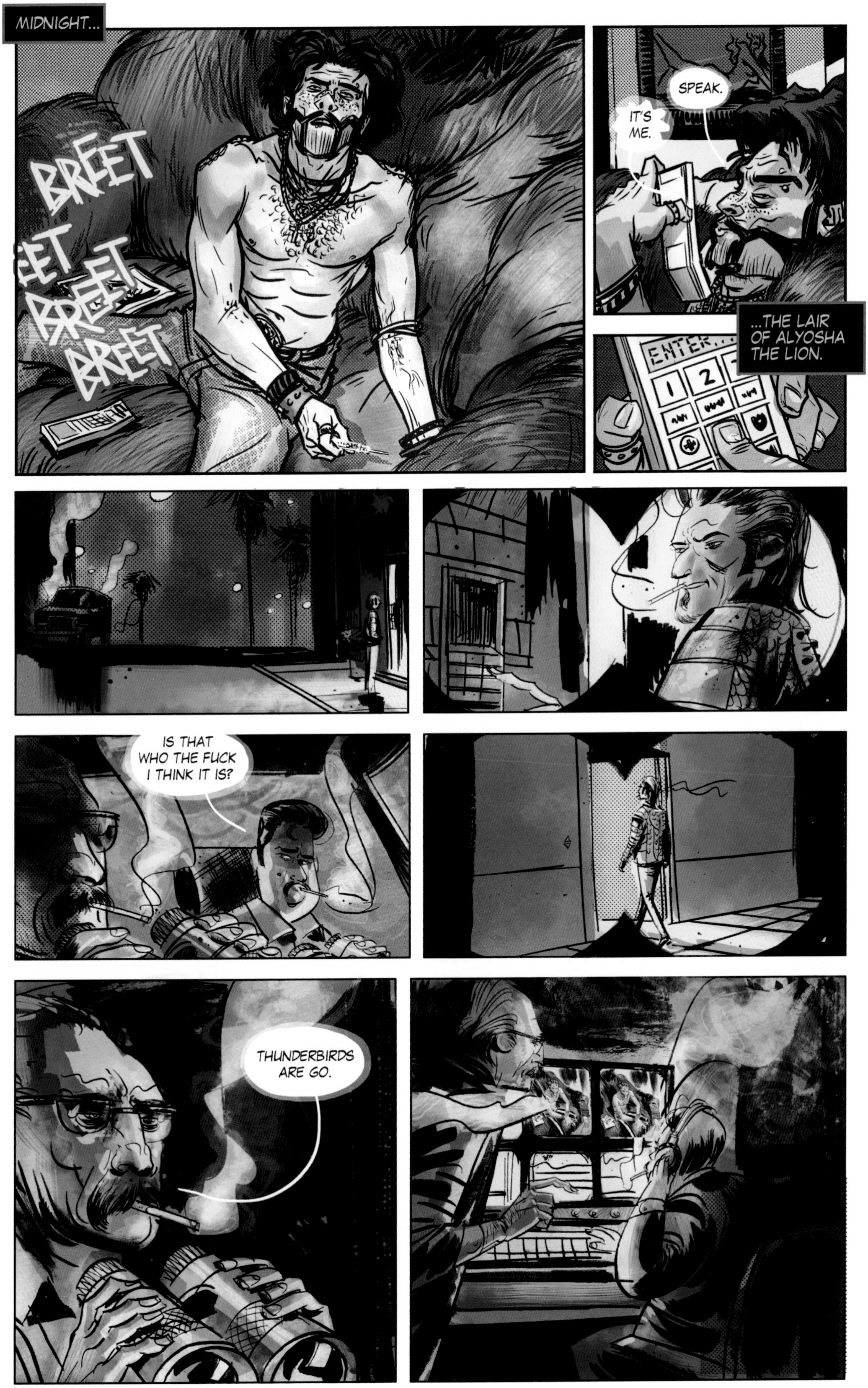
MIDNIGHT...
BREET
EET BREET
BREET
BREET
SPEAK.
IT'S ME.
...THE LAIR OF ALYOSHA THE LION.
ENTER...
IS THAT WHO THE FUCK I THINK IT IS?
THUNDERBIRDS ARE GO.

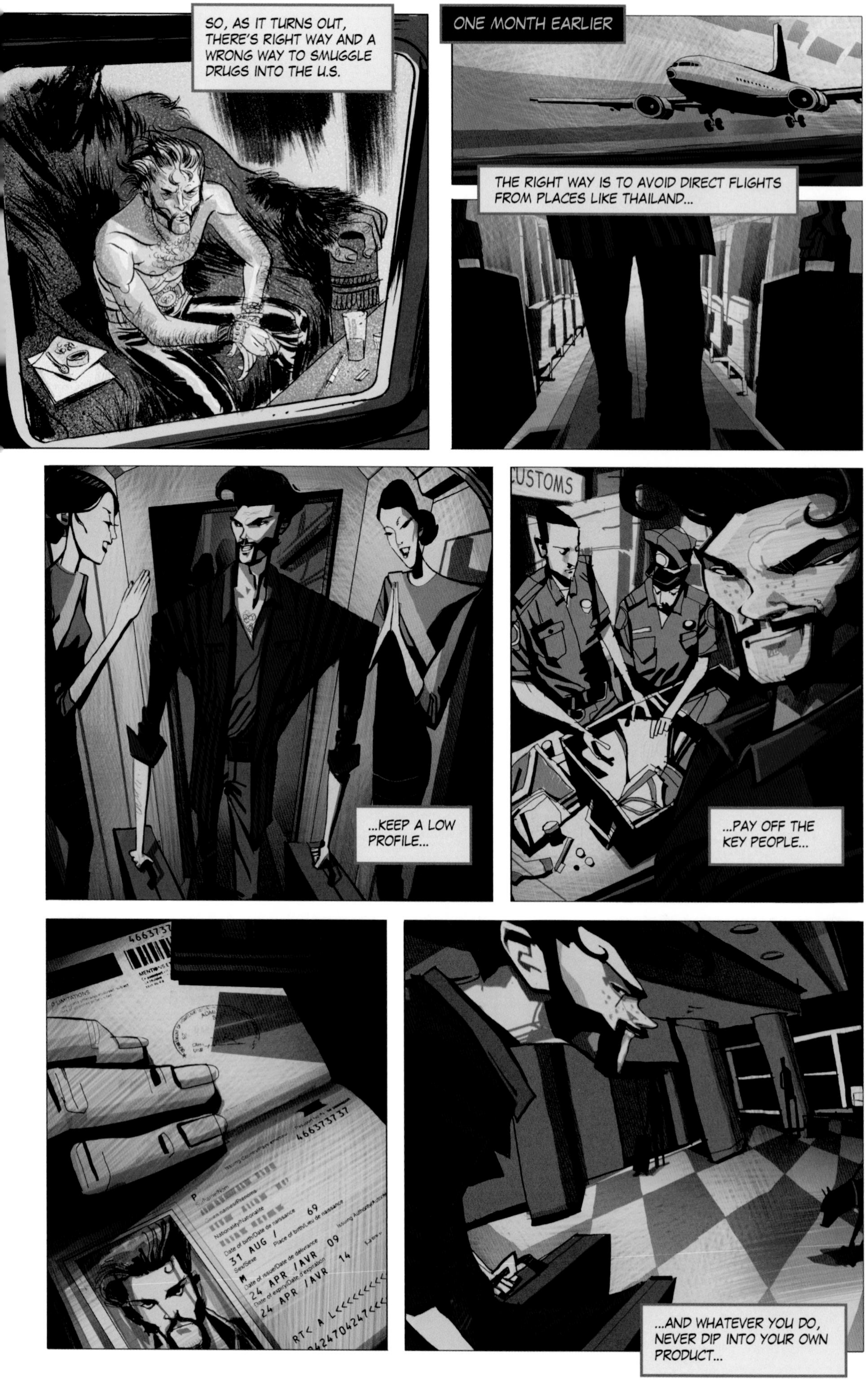
SO, AS IT TURNS OUT, THERE'S RIGHT WAY AND A WRONG WAY TO SMUGGLE DRUGS INTO THE U.S.
ONE MONTH EARLIER
THE RIGHT WAY IS TO AVOID DIRECT FLIGHTS FROM PLACES LIKE THAILAND...
...KEEP A LOW PROFILE...
CUSTOMS
...PAY OFF THE KEY PEOPLE...
...AND WHATEVER YOU DO, NEVER DIP INTO YOUR OWN PRODUCT...

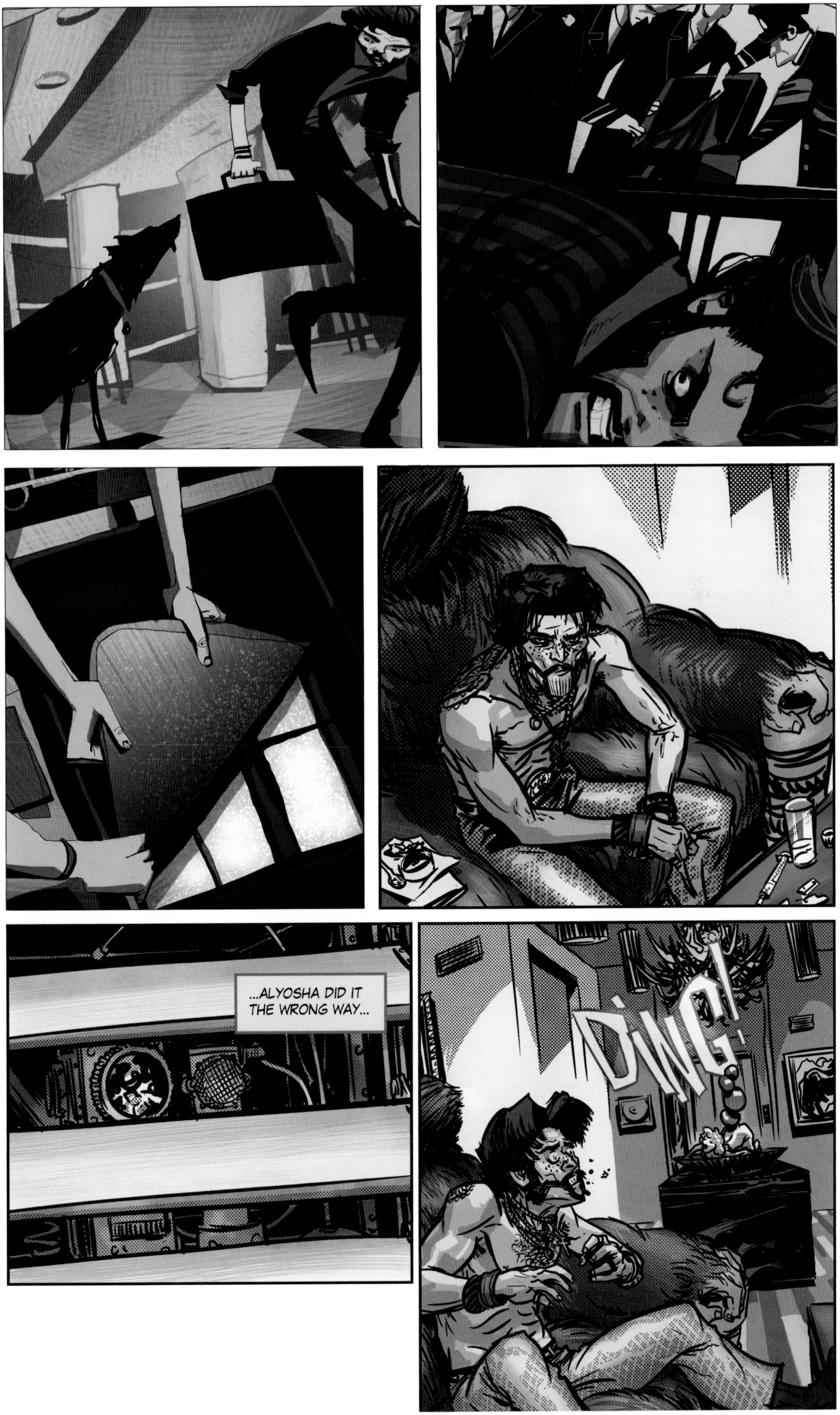
...ALYOSHA DID IT
THE WRONG WAY...
DING!

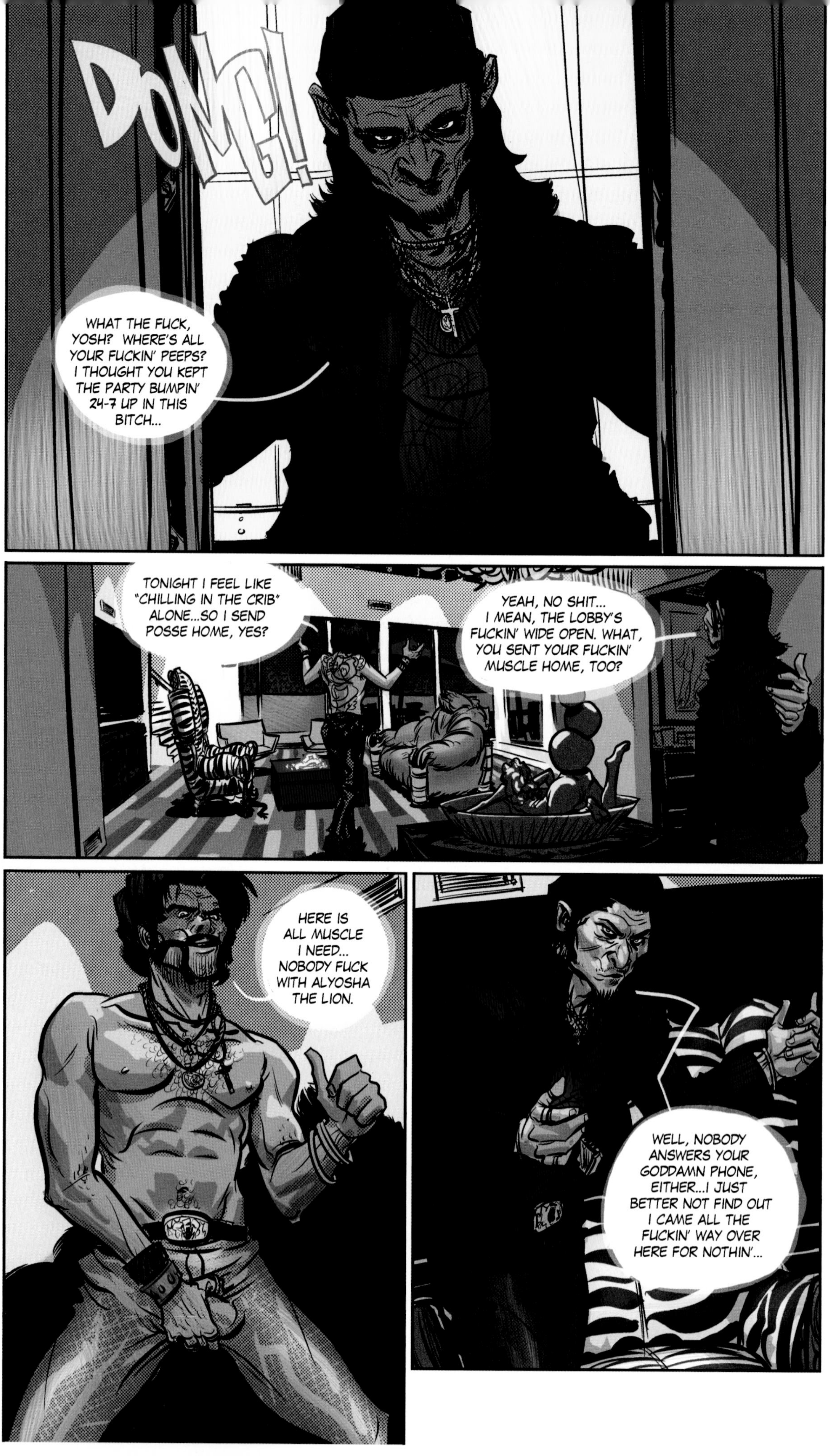
DONG!
WHAT THE FUCK, YOSH? WHERE'S ALL YOUR FUCKIN' PEEPS? I THOUGHT YOU KEPT THE PARTY BUMPIN' 24-7 UP IN THIS BITCH...
TONIGHT I FEEL LIKE "CHILLING IN THE CRIB" ALONE...SO I SEND POSSE HOME, YES?
YEAH, NO SHIT... I MEAN, THE LOBBY'S FUCKIN' WIDE OPEN. WHAT, YOU SENT YOUR FUCKIN' MUSCLE HOME, TOO?
HERE IS ALL MUSCLE I NEED... NOBODY FUCK WITH ALYOSHA THE LION.
WELL, NOBODY ANSWERS YOUR GODDAMN PHONE, EITHER...I JUST BETTER NOT FIND OUT I CAME ALL THE FUCKIN' WAY OVER HERE FOR NOTHIN'...

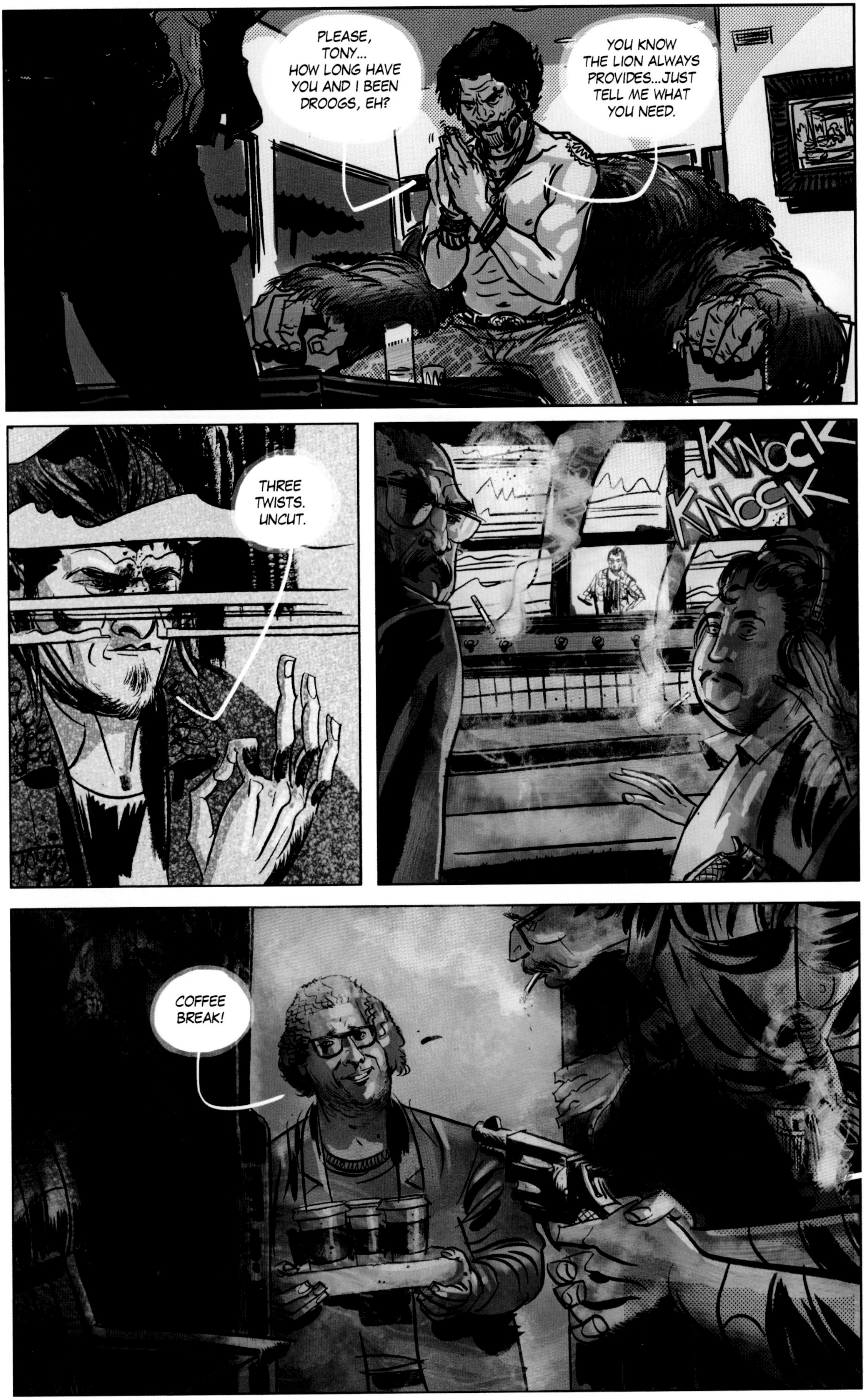
PLEASE, TONY... HOW LONG HAVE YOU AND I BEEN DROOGS, EH?
YOU KNOW THE LION ALWAYS PROVIDES...JUST TELL ME WHAT YOU NEED.
THREE TWISTS. UNCUT.
KNOCK KNOCK
COFFEE BREAK!

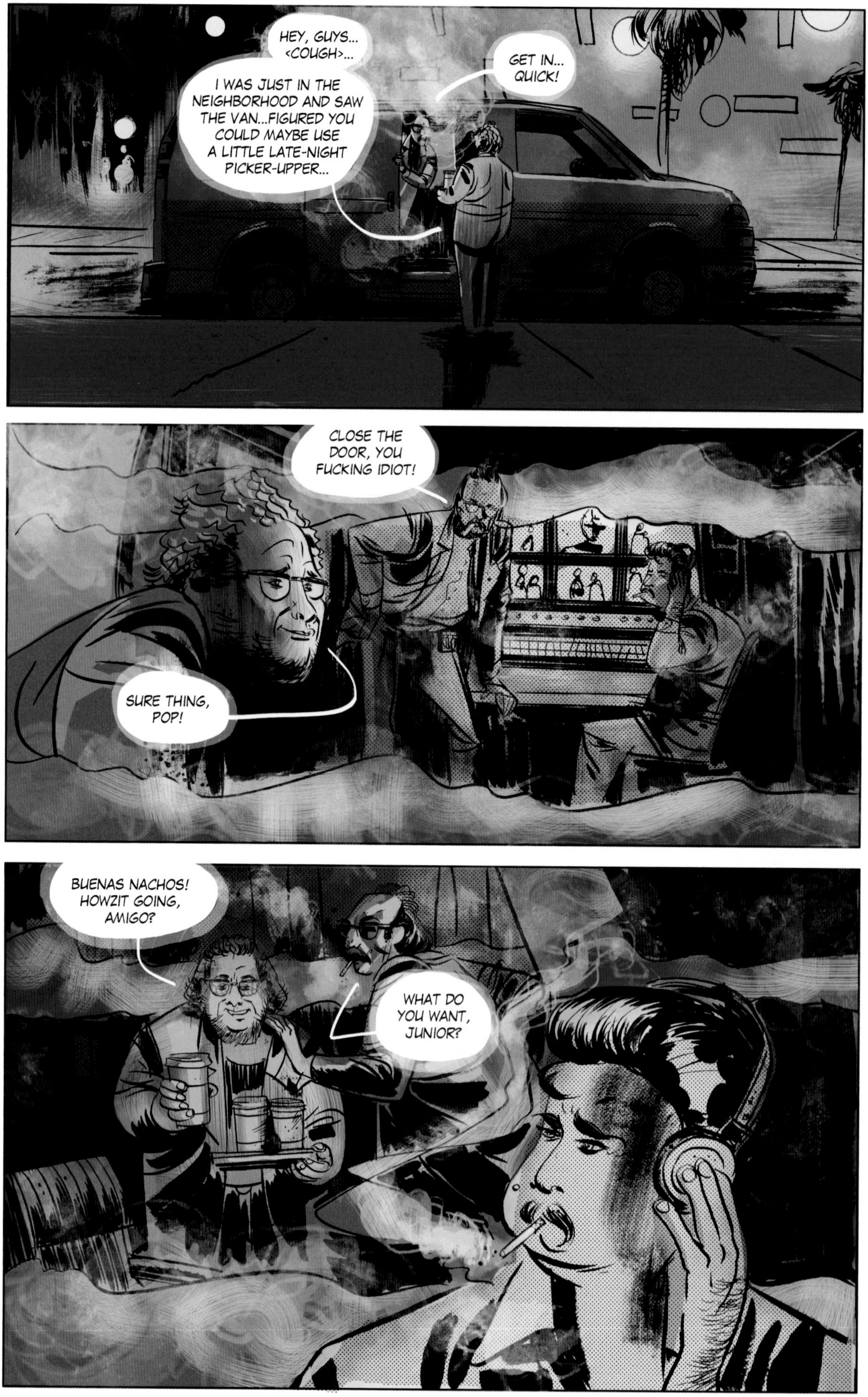
HEY, GUYS... <COUGH>...
I WAS JUST IN THE NEIGHBORHOOD AND SAW THE VAN...FIGURED YOU COULD MAYBE USE A LITTLE LATE-NIGHT PICKER-UPPER...
GET IN... QUICK!
CLOSE THE DOOR, YOU FUCKING IDIOT!
SURE THING, POP!
BUENAS NACHOS! HOWZIT GOING, AMIGO?
WHAT DO YOU WANT, JUNIOR?

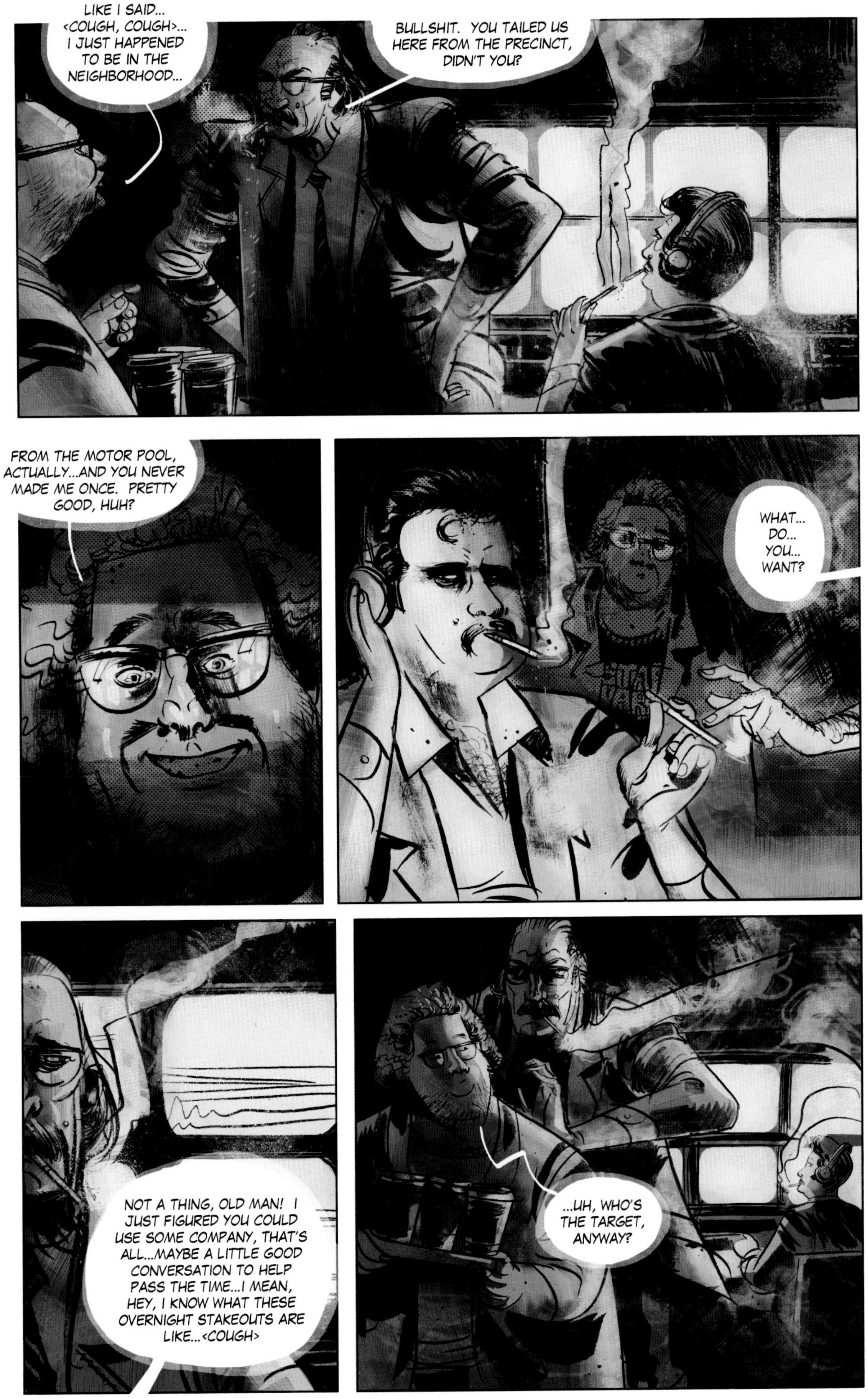
LIKE I SAID... <COUGH, COUGH>... I JUST HAPPENED TO BE IN THE NEIGHBORHOOD...
BULLSHIT. YOU TAILED US HERE FROM THE PRECINCT, DIDN'T YOU?
FROM THE MOTOR POOL, ACTUALLY...AND YOU NEVER MADE ME ONCE. PRETTY GOOD, HUH?
WHAT... DO... YOU... WANT?
NOT A THING, OLD MAN! I JUST FIGURED YOU COULD USE SOME COMPANY, THAT'S ALL...MAYBE A LITTLE GOOD CONVERSATION TO HELP PASS THE TIME...I MEAN, HEY, I KNOW WHAT THESE OVERNIGHT STAKEOUTS ARE LIKE...<COUGH>
...UH, WHO'S THE TARGET, ANYWAY?

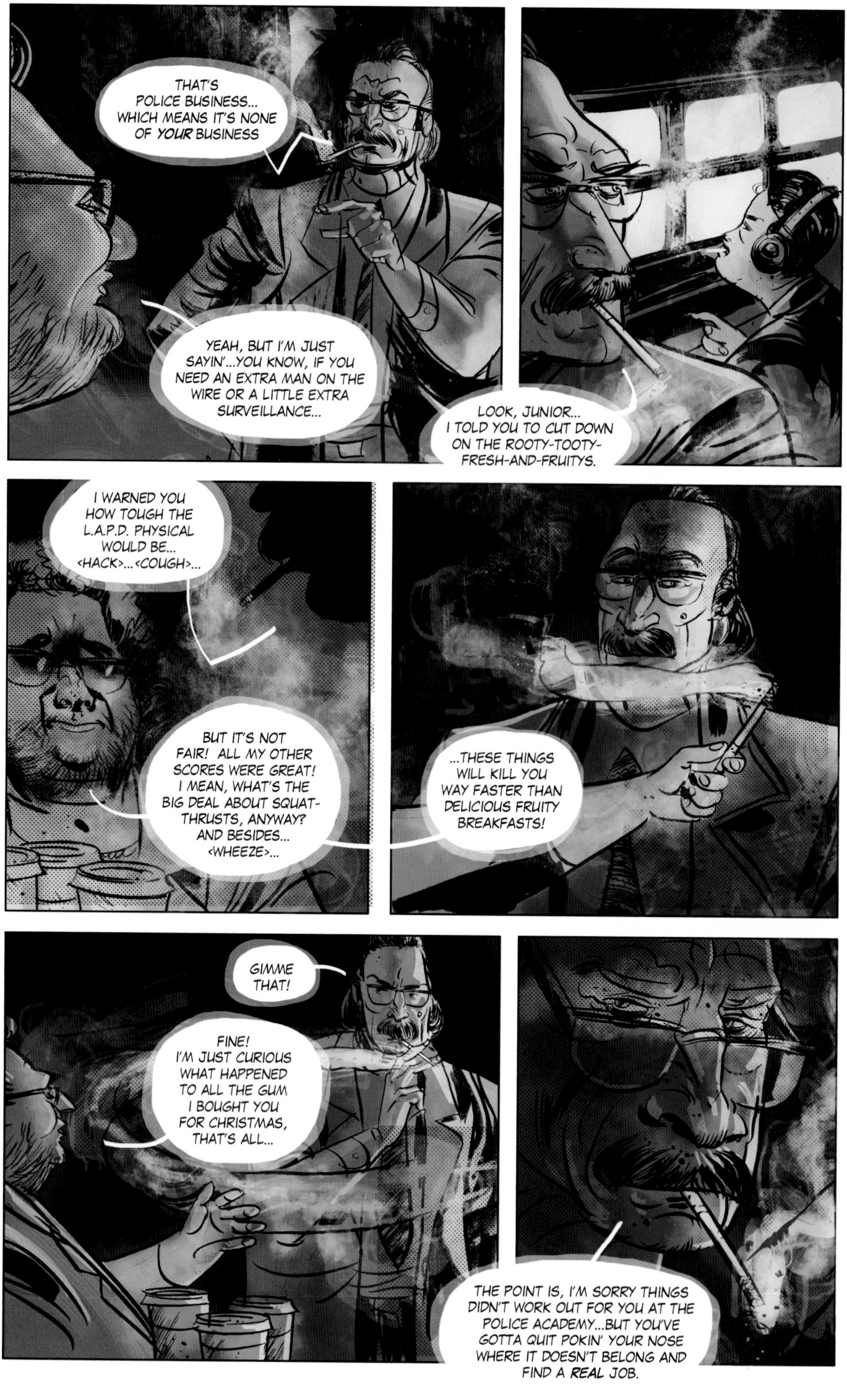
THAT'S POLICE BUSINESS... WHICH MEANS IT'S NONE OF *YOUR* BUSINESS
YEAH, BUT I'M JUST SAYIN'...YOU KNOW, IF YOU NEED AN EXTRA MAN ON THE WIRE OR A LITTLE EXTRA SURVEILLANCE...
LOOK, JUNIOR... I TOLD YOU TO CUT DOWN ON THE ROOTY-TOOTY-FRESH-AND-FRUITYS.
I WARNED YOU HOW TOUGH THE L.A.P.D. PHYSICAL WOULD BE... <HACK>...<COUGH>...
BUT IT'S NOT FAIR! ALL MY OTHER SCORES WERE GREAT! I MEAN, WHAT'S THE BIG DEAL ABOUT SQUAT-THRUSTS, ANYWAY? AND BESIDES... <WHEEZE>...
...THESE THINGS WILL KILL YOU WAY FASTER THAN DELICIOUS FRUITY BREAKFASTS!
GIMME THAT!
FINE! I'M JUST CURIOUS WHAT HAPPENED TO ALL THE GUM I BOUGHT YOU FOR CHRISTMAS, THAT'S ALL...
THE POINT IS, I'M SORRY THINGS DIDN'T WORK OUT FOR YOU AT THE POLICE ACADEMY...BUT YOU'VE GOTTA QUIT POKIN' YOUR NOSE WHERE IT DOESN'T BELONG AND FIND A *REAL* JOB.

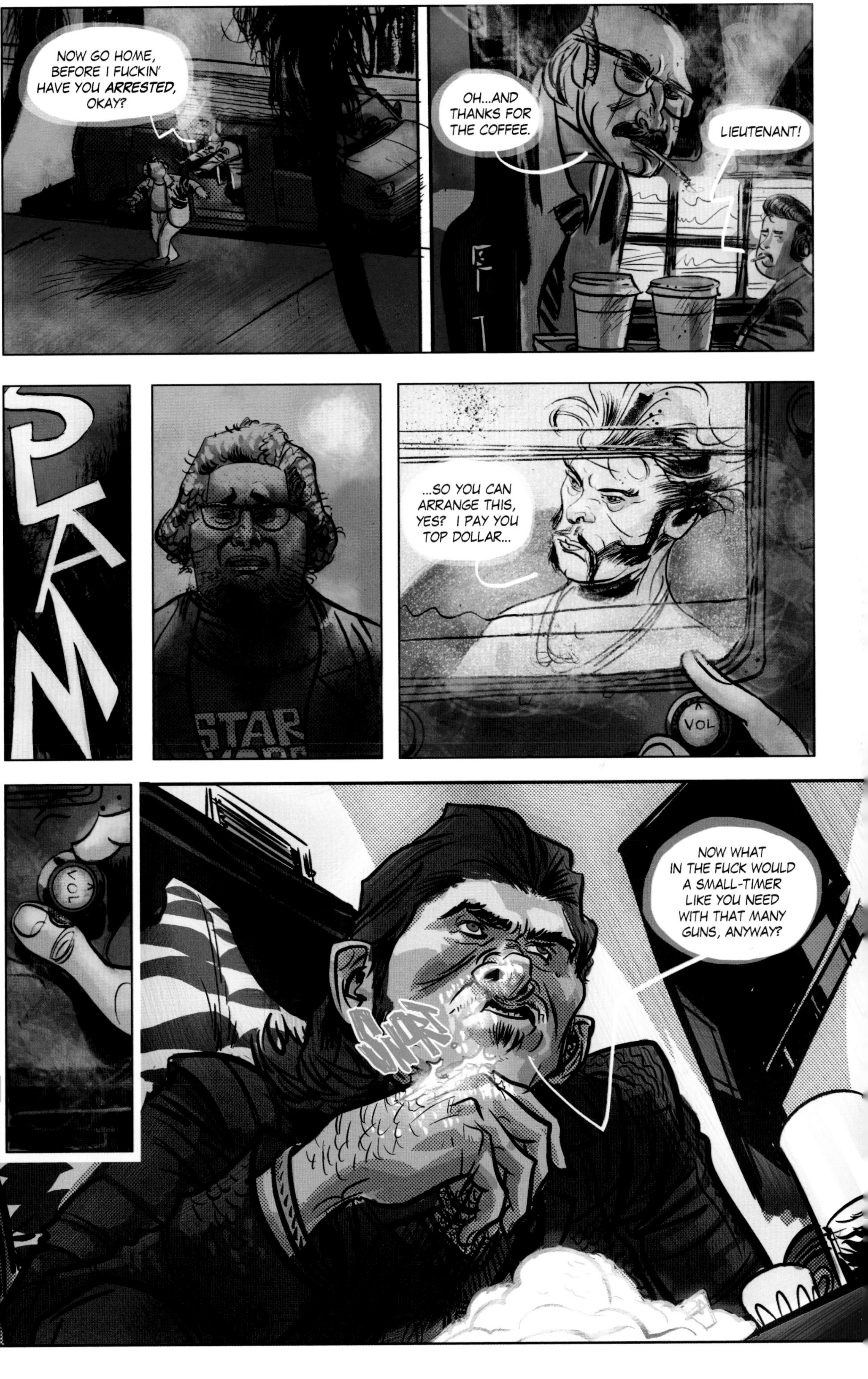
NOW GO HOME, BEFORE I FUCKIN' HAVE YOU ARRESTED, OKAY?
OH...AND THANKS FOR THE COFFEE.
LIEUTENANT!
SLAM
...SO YOU CAN ARRANGE THIS, YES? I PAY YOU TOP DOLLAR...
VOL
NOW WHAT IN THE FUCK WOULD A SMALL-TIMER LIKE YOU NEED WITH THAT MANY GUNS, ANYWAY?

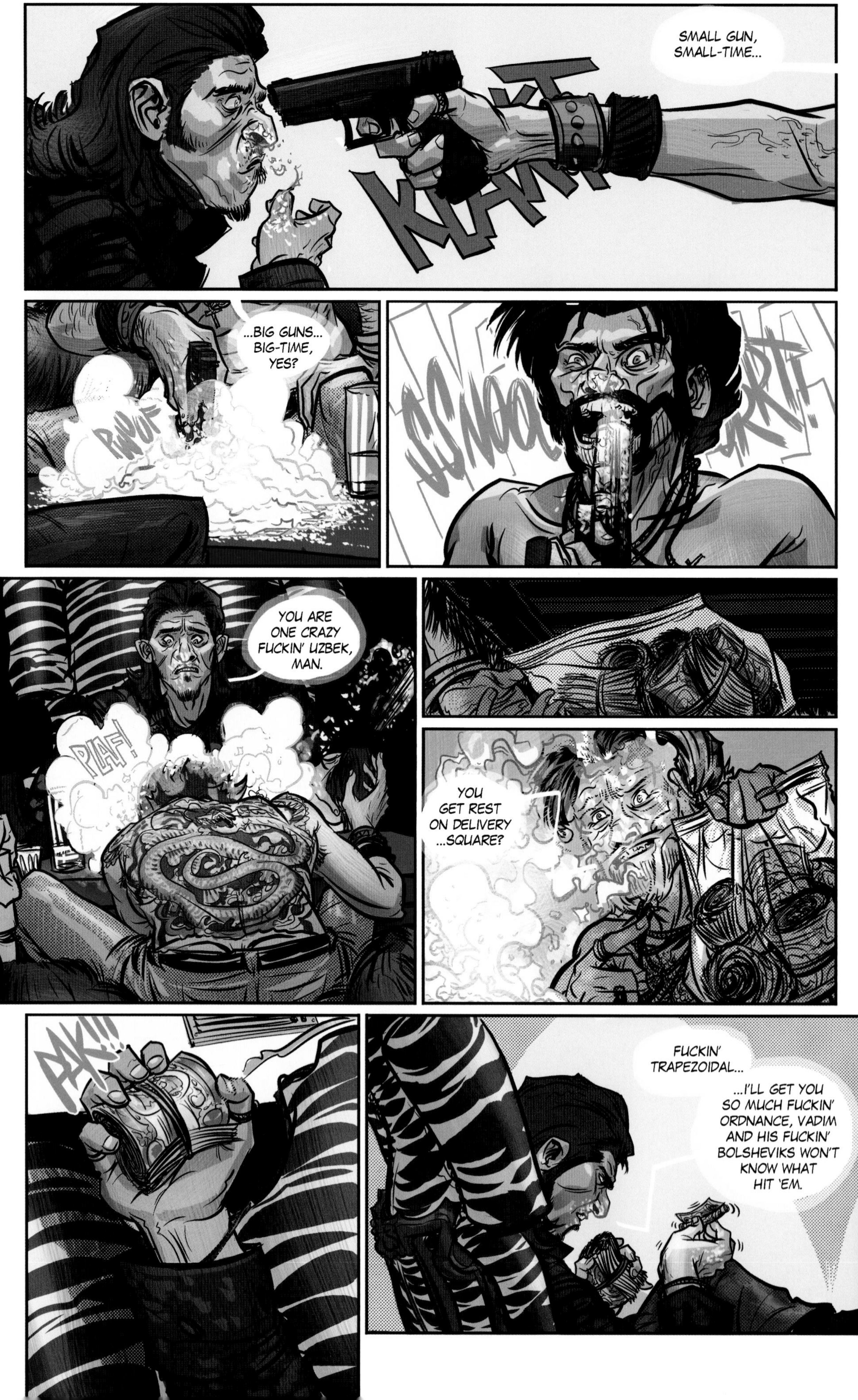
SMALL GUN, SMALL-TIME...
...BIG GUNS... BIG-TIME, YES?
YOU ARE ONE CRAZY FUCKIN' UZBEK, MAN.
PLAF!
YOU GET REST ON DELIVERY ...SQUARE?
PAK!!
FUCKIN' TRAPEZOIDAL...
...I'LL GET YOU SO MUCH FUCKIN' ORDNANCE, VADIM AND HIS FUCKIN' BOLSHEVIKS WON'T KNOW WHAT HIT 'EM.

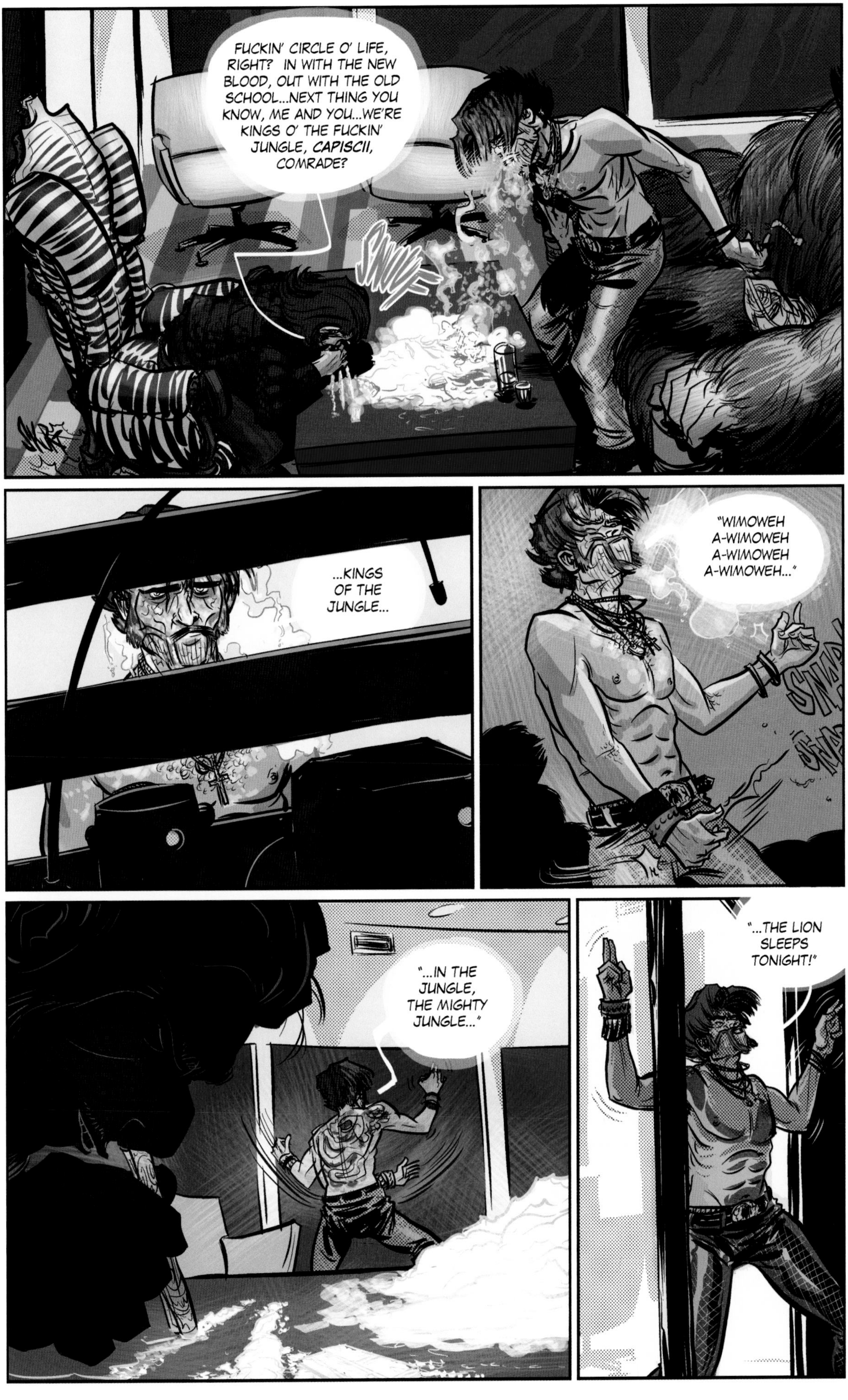
FUCKIN' CIRCLE O' LIFE, RIGHT? IN WITH THE NEW BLOOD, OUT WITH THE OLD SCHOOL...NEXT THING YOU KNOW, ME AND YOU...WE'RE KINGS O' THE FUCKIN' JUNGLE, *CAPISCII*, COMRADE?
...KINGS OF THE JUNGLE...
"WIMOWEH A-WIMOWEH A-WIMOWEH A-WIMOWEH..."
"...IN THE JUNGLE, THE MIGHTY JUNGLE..."
"...THE LION SLEEPS TONIGHT!"

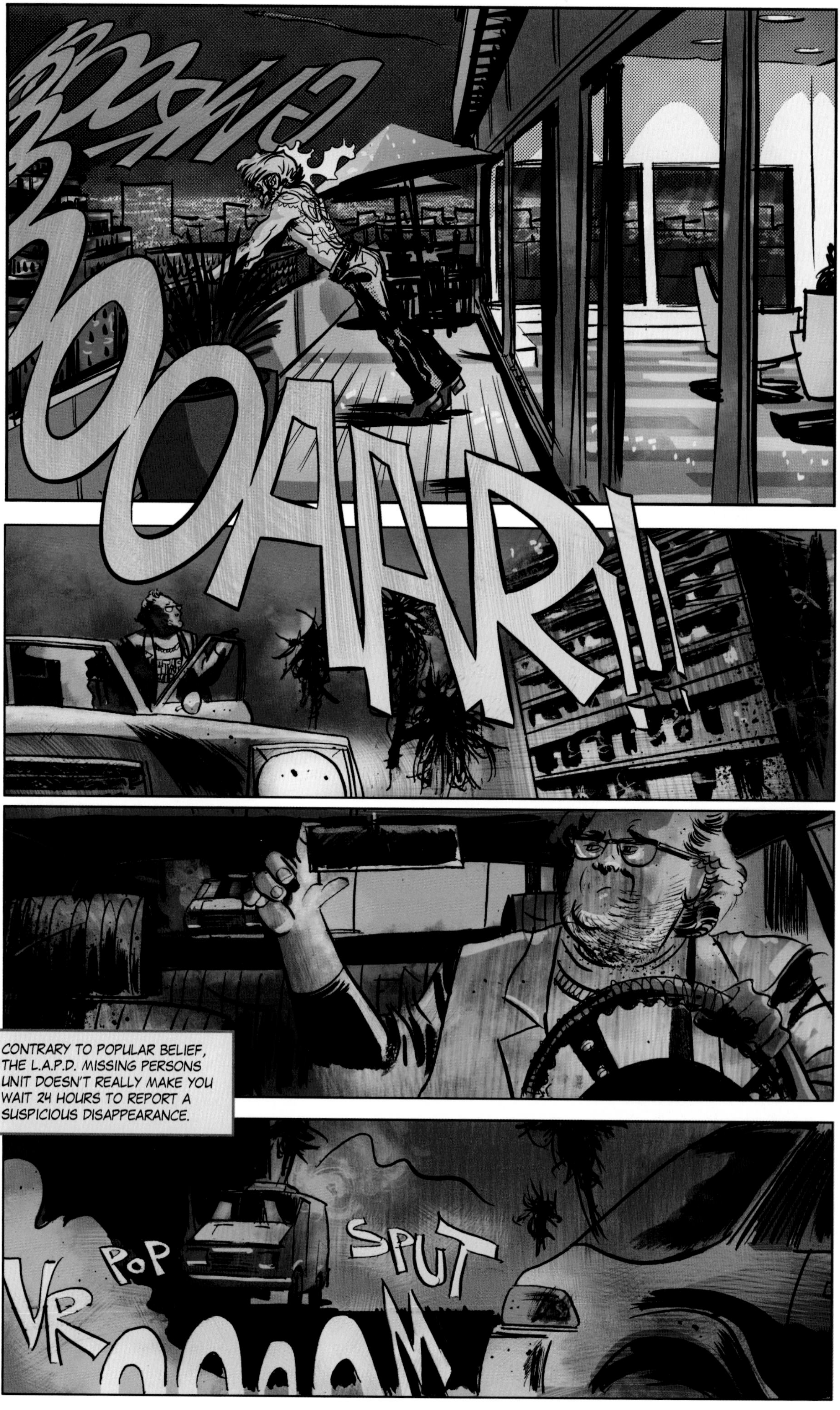
CONTRARY TO POPULAR BELIEF, THE L.A.P.D. MISSING PERSONS UNIT DOESN'T REALLY MAKE YOU WAIT 24 HOURS TO REPORT A SUSPICIOUS DISAPPEARANCE.
VR
POP
SPUT

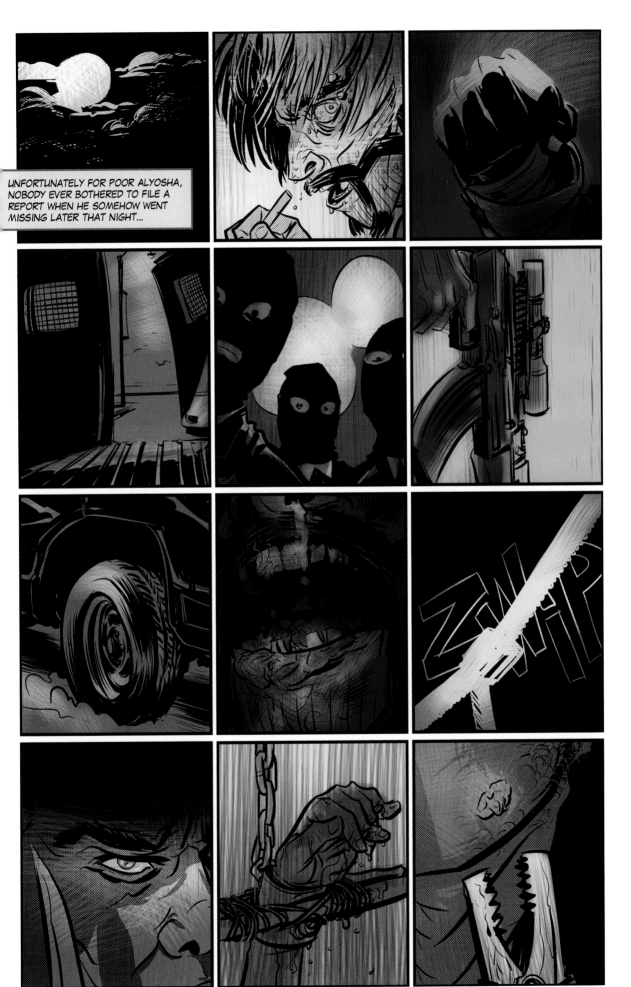

UNFORTUNATELY FOR POOR ALYOSHA, NOBODY EVER BOTHERED TO FILE A REPORT WHEN HE SOMEHOW WENT MISSING LATER THAT NIGHT...

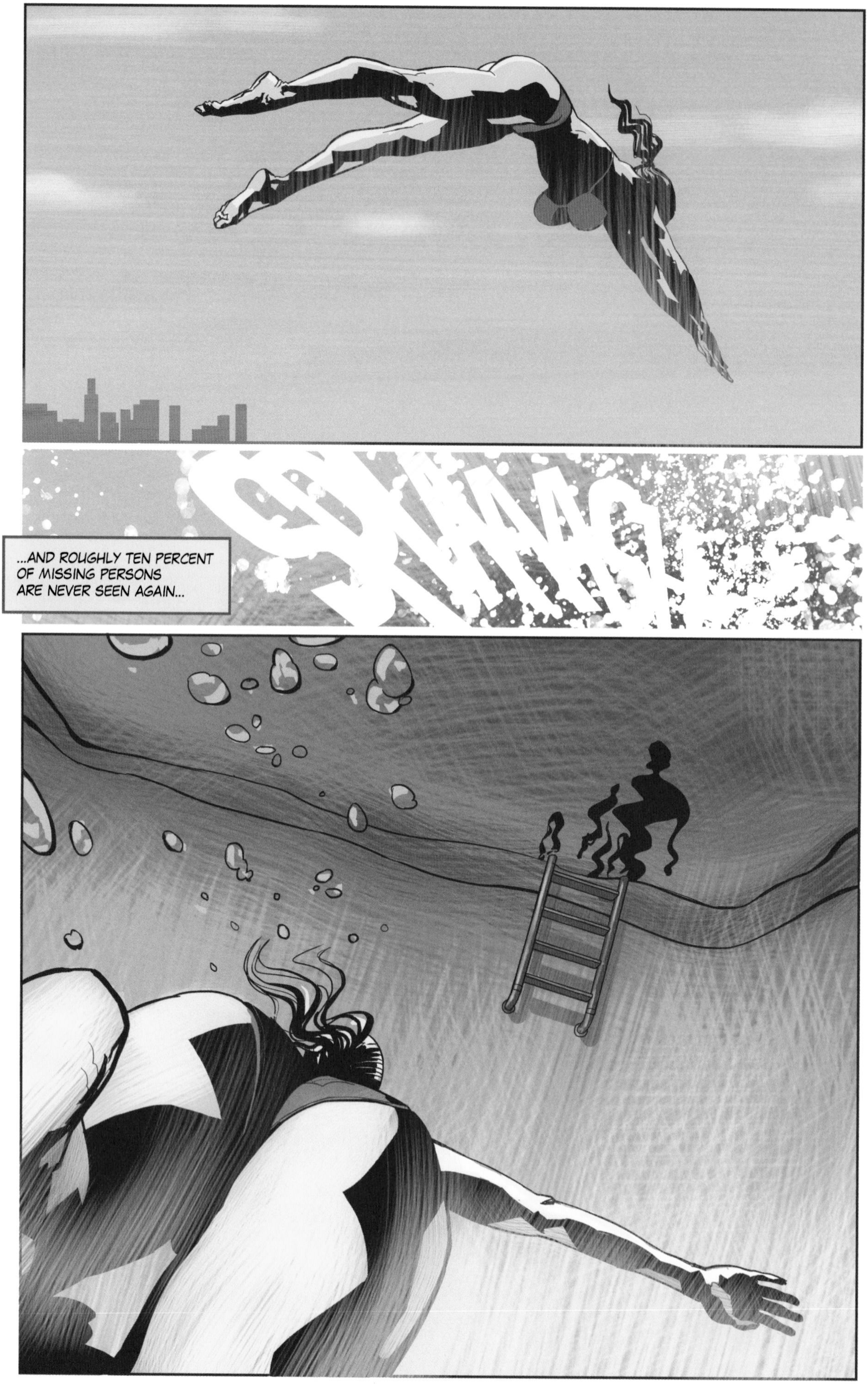
...AND ROUGHLY TEN PERCENT OF MISSING PERSONS ARE NEVER SEEN AGAIN...

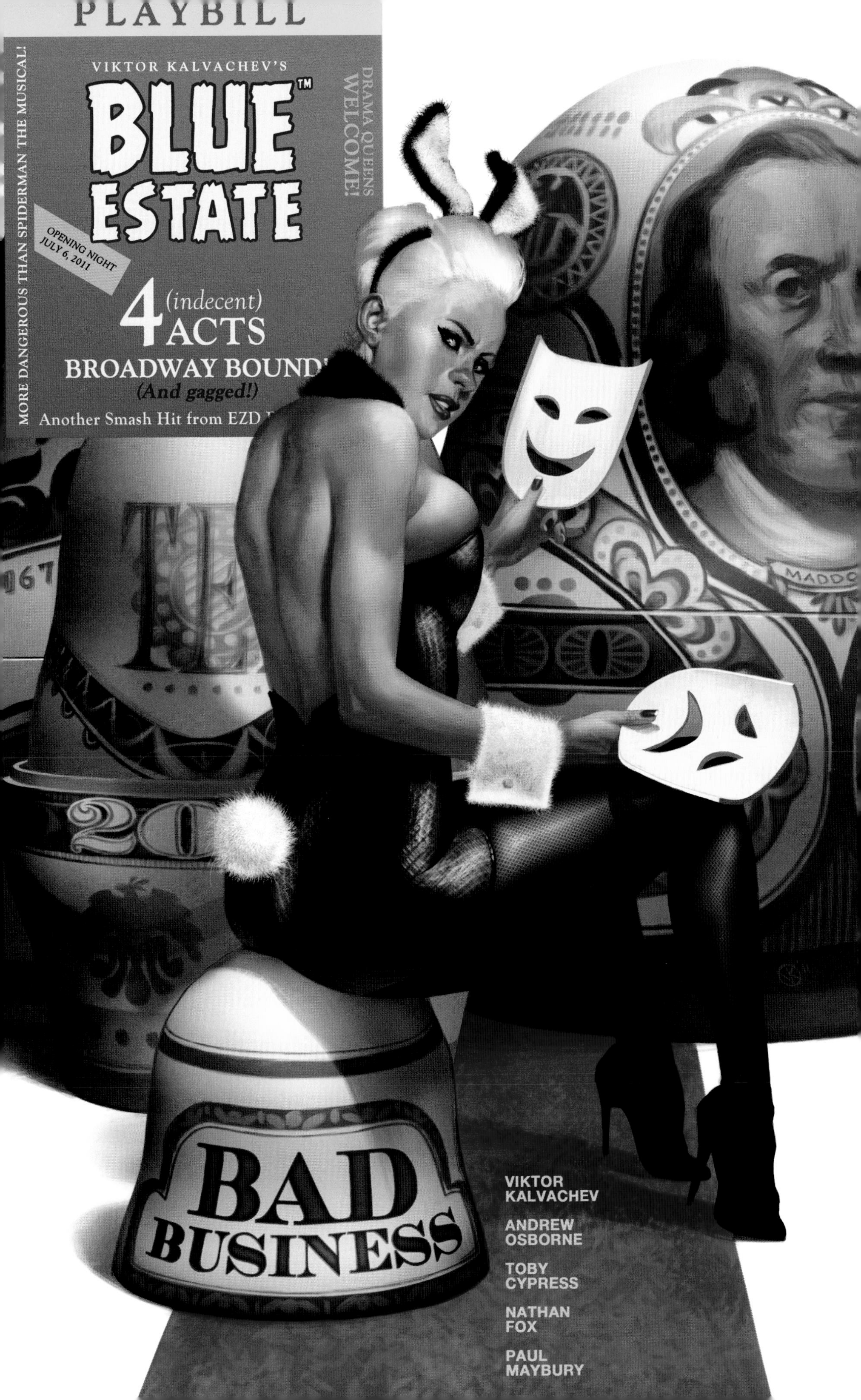

PLAYBILL
VIKTOR KALVACHEV'S
BLUE™ ESTATE
MORE DANGEROUS THAN SPIDERMAN THE MUSICAL!
DRAMA QUEENS WELCOME!
OPENING NIGHT JULY 6, 2011
4 (indecent) ACTS
BROADWAY BOUND
(And gagged!)
Another Smash Hit from EZD
BAD BUSINESS
VIKTOR KALVACHEV
ANDREW OSBORNE
TOBY CYPRESS
NATHAN FOX
PAUL MAYBURY

# BLUE ESTATE™

EPISODE FOUR:
## BAD BUSINESS

ORIGINAL STORY:
**VIKTOR KALVACHEV** AND **KOSTA YANEV**

SCRIPT BY **ANDREW OSBORNE**

ARTISTS:
**VIKTOR KALVACHEV**
**TOBY CYPRESS**
**NATHAN FOX**
**PAUL MAYBURY**

ART DIRECTION BY **VIKTOR KALVACHEV**

COVER, COLORS & DESIGN:
**VIKTOR KALVACHEV**

CONTRIBUTING EDITOR:
**PHILO NORTHRUP**

www.BlueEstateComic.com

EZD
PRODUCTIONS

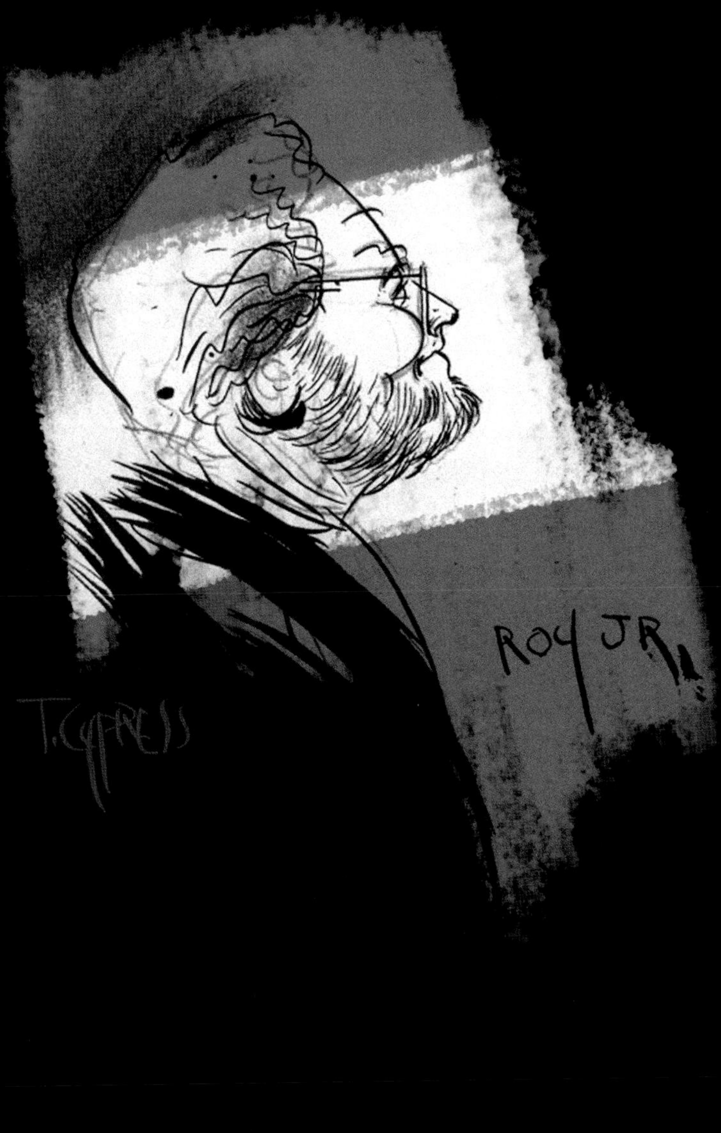
ROY JR.
T. CYPRESS

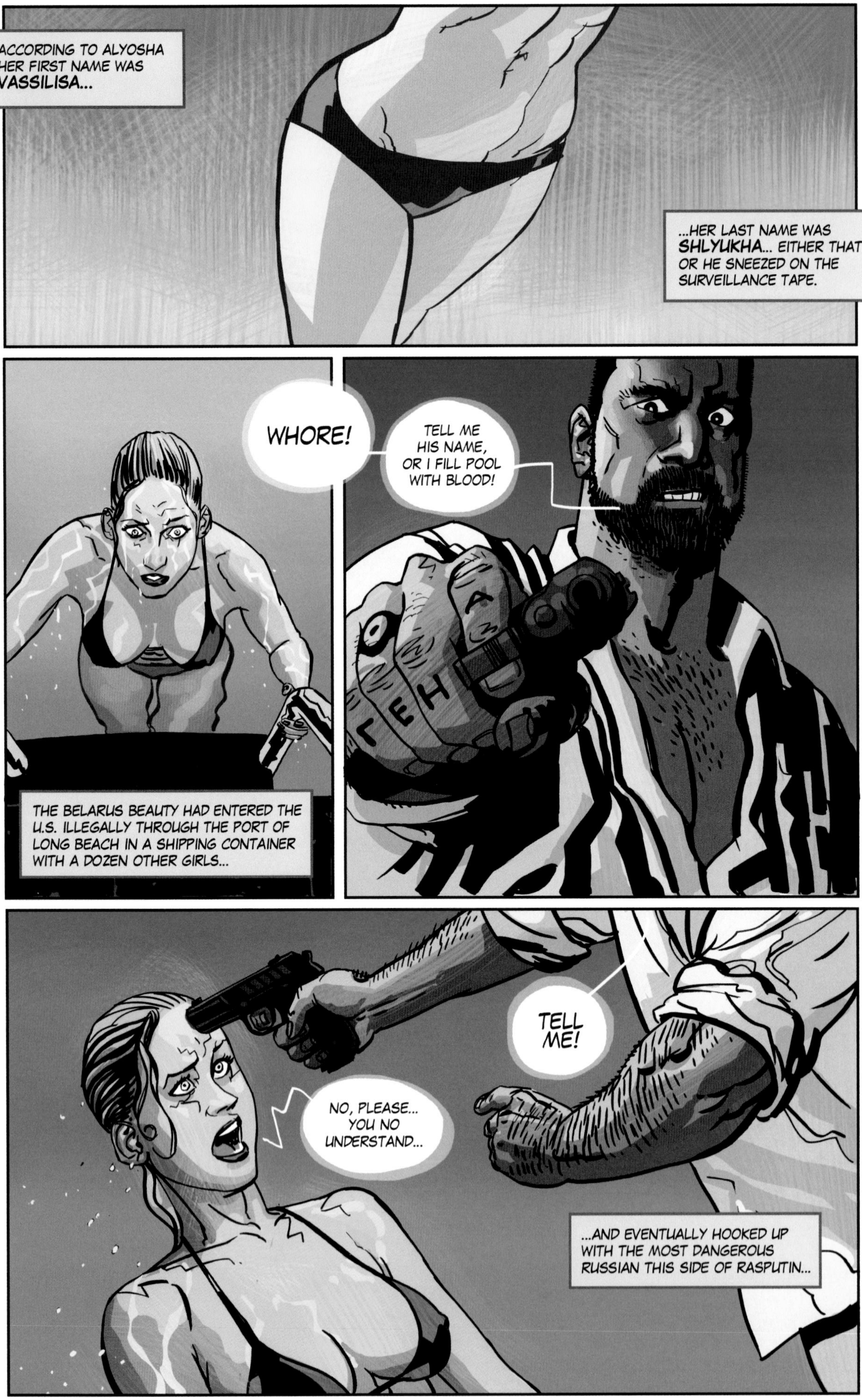

ACCORDING TO ALYOSHA HER FIRST NAME WAS VASSILISA...
...HER LAST NAME WAS SHLYUKHA... EITHER THAT, OR HE SNEEZED ON THE SURVEILLANCE TAPE.
THE BELARUS BEAUTY HAD ENTERED THE U.S. ILLEGALLY THROUGH THE PORT OF LONG BEACH IN A SHIPPING CONTAINER WITH A DOZEN OTHER GIRLS...
WHORE!
TELL ME HIS NAME, OR I FILL POOL WITH BLOOD!
TELL ME!
NO, PLEASE... YOU NO UNDERSTAND...
...AND EVENTUALLY HOOKED UP WITH THE MOST DANGEROUS RUSSIAN THIS SIDE OF RASPUTIN...

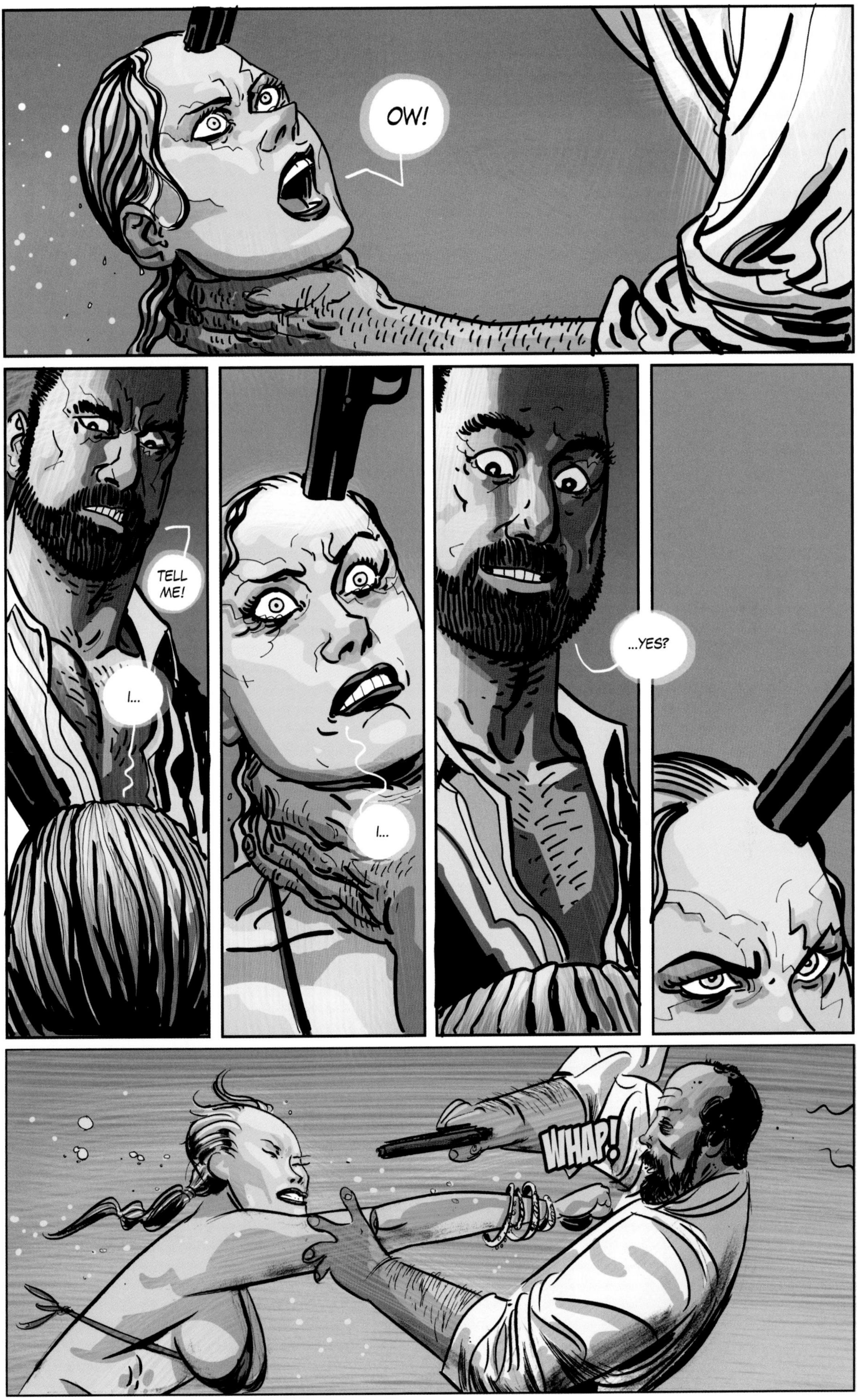
OW!
TELL ME!
I...
I...
...YES?
WHAP!

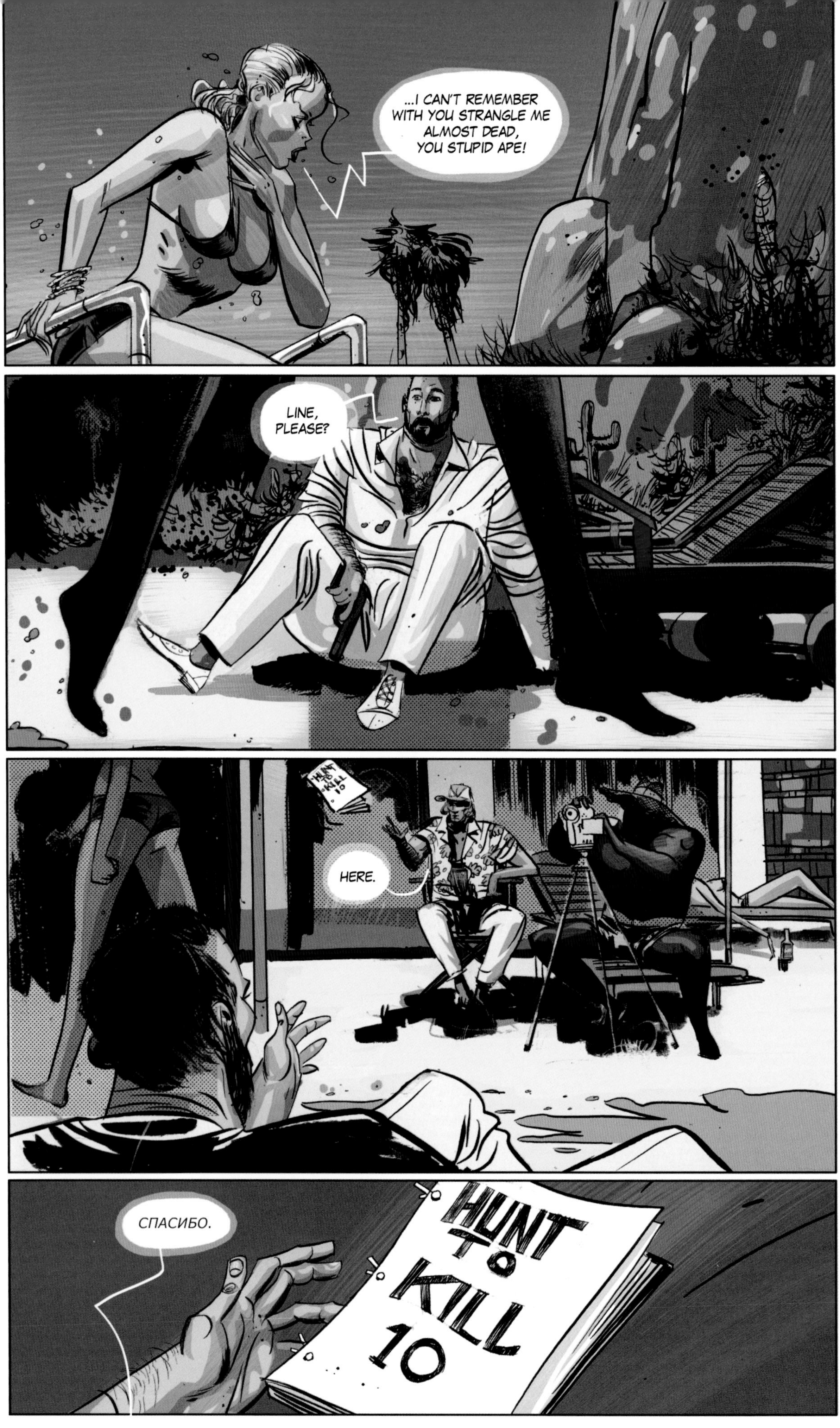
...I CAN'T REMEMBER WITH YOU STRANGLE ME ALMOST DEAD, YOU STUPID APE!
LINE, PLEASE?
HERE.
HUNT TO KILL 10
СПАСИБО.
HUNT TO KILL 10

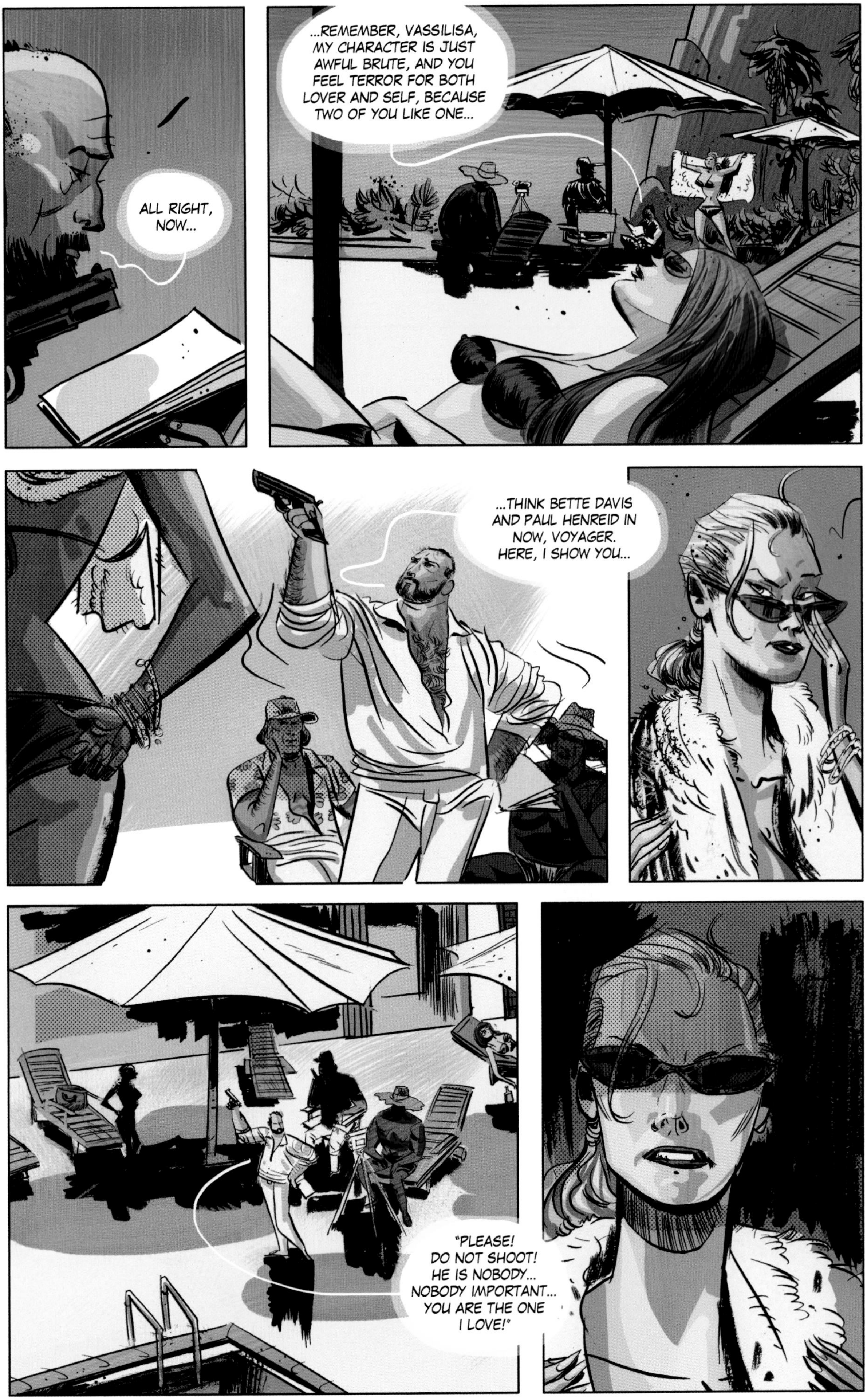
ALL RIGHT, NOW...
...REMEMBER, VASSILISA, MY CHARACTER IS JUST AWFUL BRUTE, AND YOU FEEL TERROR FOR BOTH LOVER AND SELF, BECAUSE TWO OF YOU LIKE ONE...
...THINK BETTE DAVIS AND PAUL HENREID IN NOW, VOYAGER. HERE, I SHOW YOU...
"PLEASE! DO NOT SHOOT! HE IS NOBODY... NOBODY IMPORTANT... YOU ARE THE ONE I LOVE!"

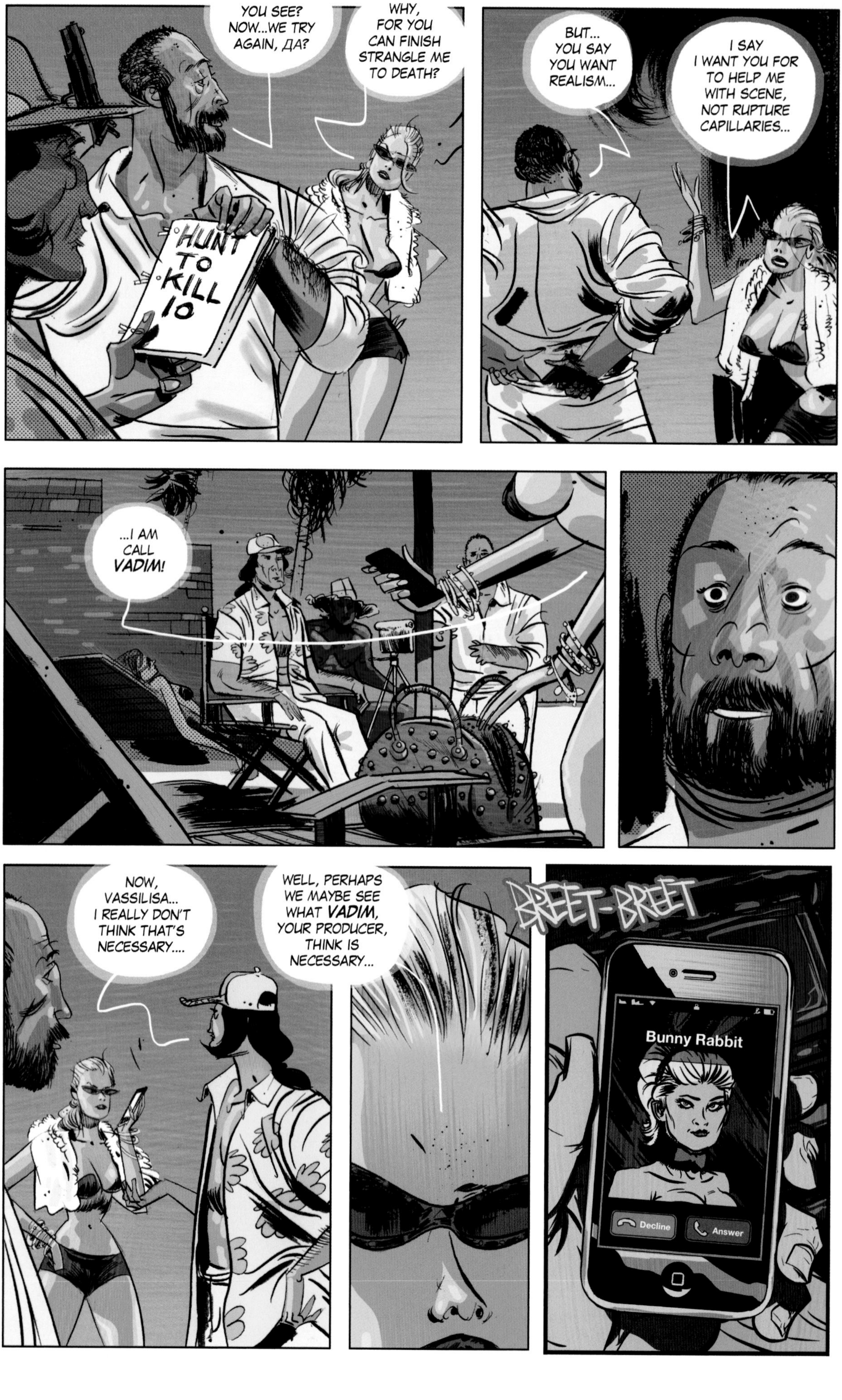
YOU SEE? NOW...WE TRY AGAIN, ДА?
WHY, FOR YOU CAN FINISH STRANGLE ME TO DEATH?
HUNT TO KILL 10
BUT... YOU SAY YOU WANT REALISM...
I SAY I WANT YOU FOR TO HELP ME WITH SCENE, NOT RUPTURE CAPILLARIES...
...I AM CALL VADIM!
NOW, VASSILISA... I REALLY DON'T THINK THAT'S NECESSARY....
WELL, PERHAPS WE MAYBE SEE WHAT VADIM, YOUR PRODUCER, THINK IS NECESSARY...
BREET-BREET
Bunny Rabbit
Decline
Answer

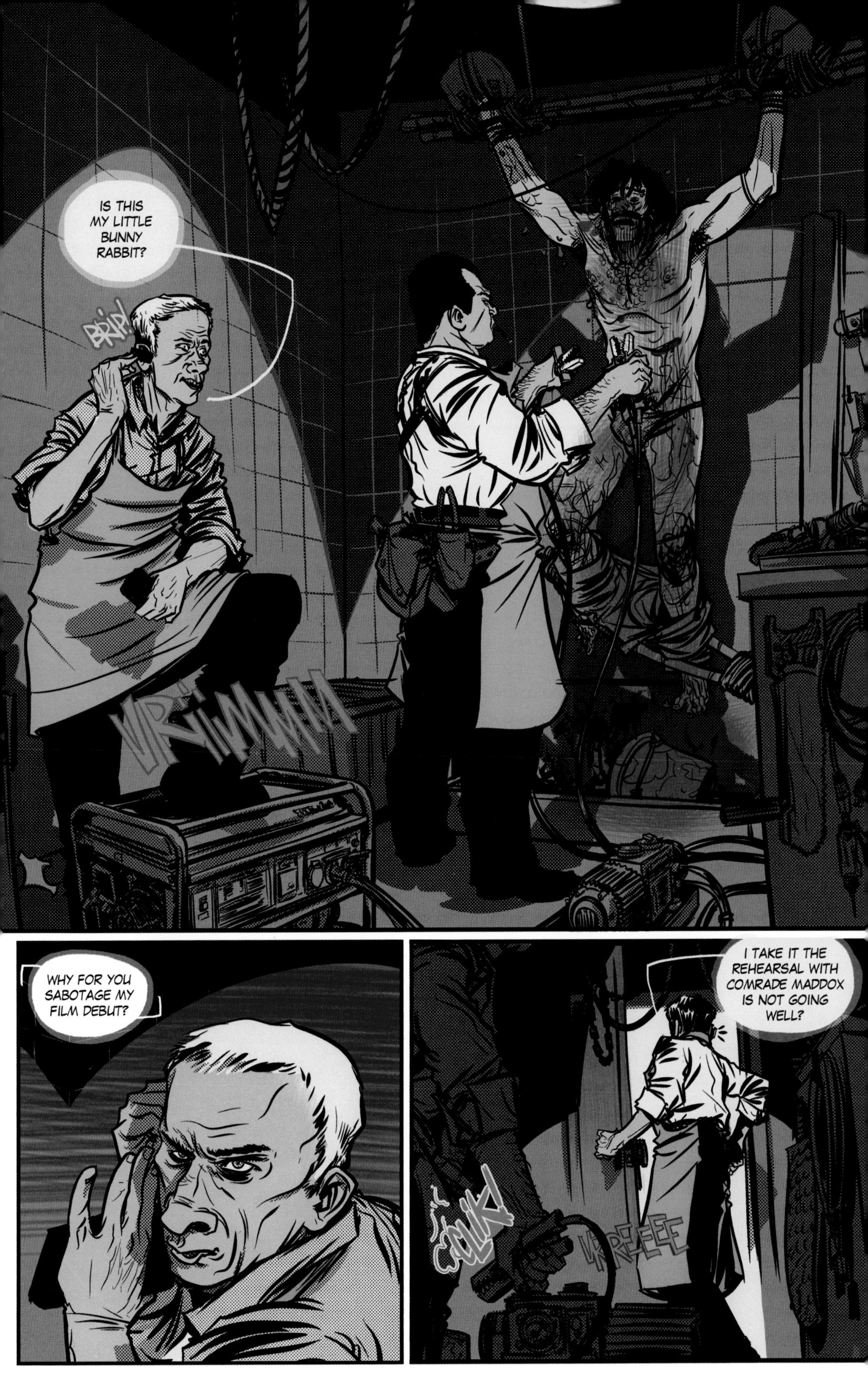
IS THIS MY LITTLE BUNNY RABBIT?
BRIP!
WHY FOR YOU SABOTAGE MY FILM DEBUT?
I TAKE IT THE REHEARSAL WITH COMRADE MADDOX IS NOT GOING WELL?

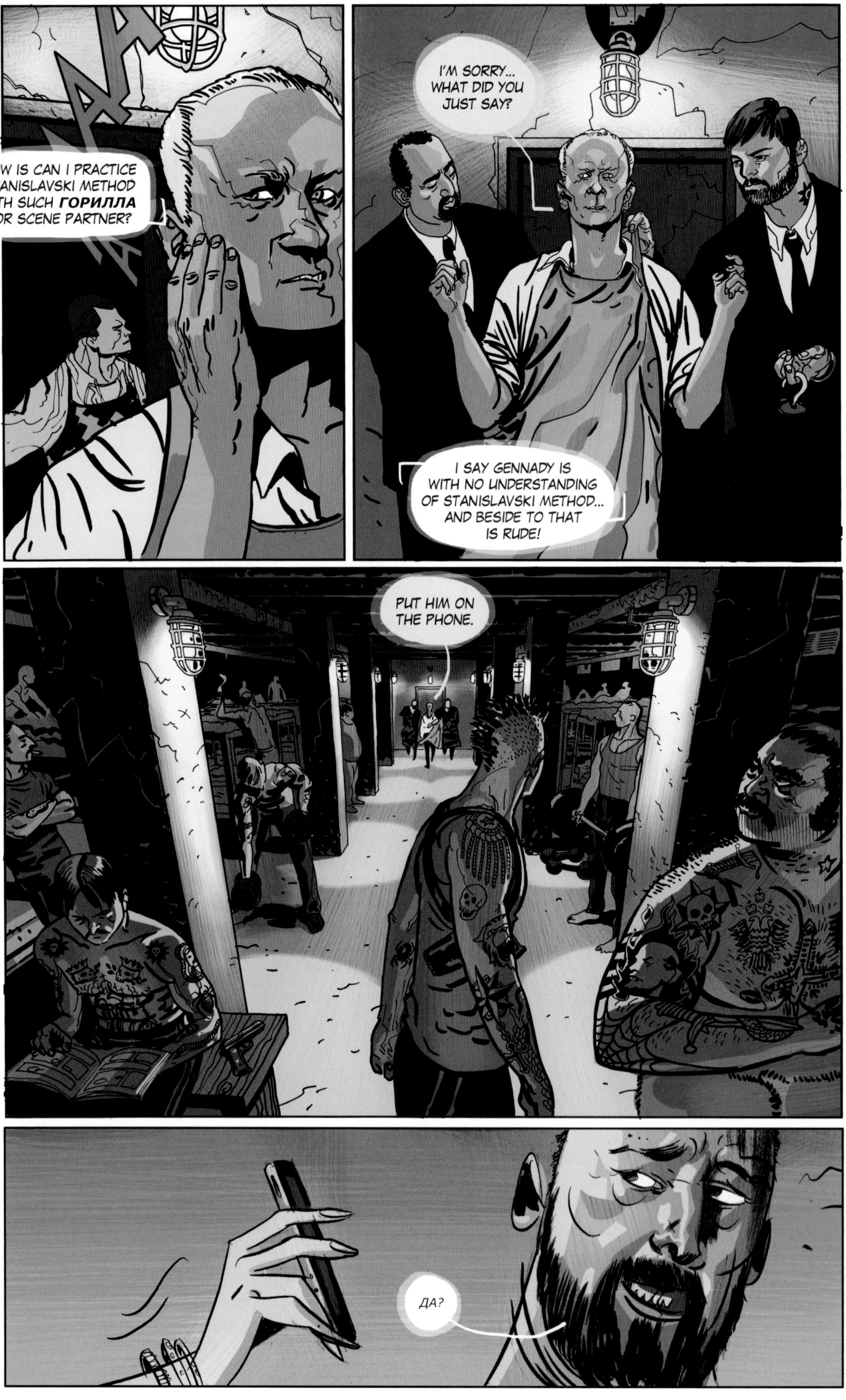
HOW IS CAN I PRACTICE STANISLAVSKI METHOD WITH SUCH **ГОРИЛЛА** FOR SCENE PARTNER?
I'M SORRY... WHAT DID YOU JUST SAY?
I SAY GENNADY IS WITH NO UNDERSTANDING OF STANISLAVSKI METHOD... AND BESIDE TO THAT IS RUDE!
PUT HIM ON THE PHONE.
ДА?

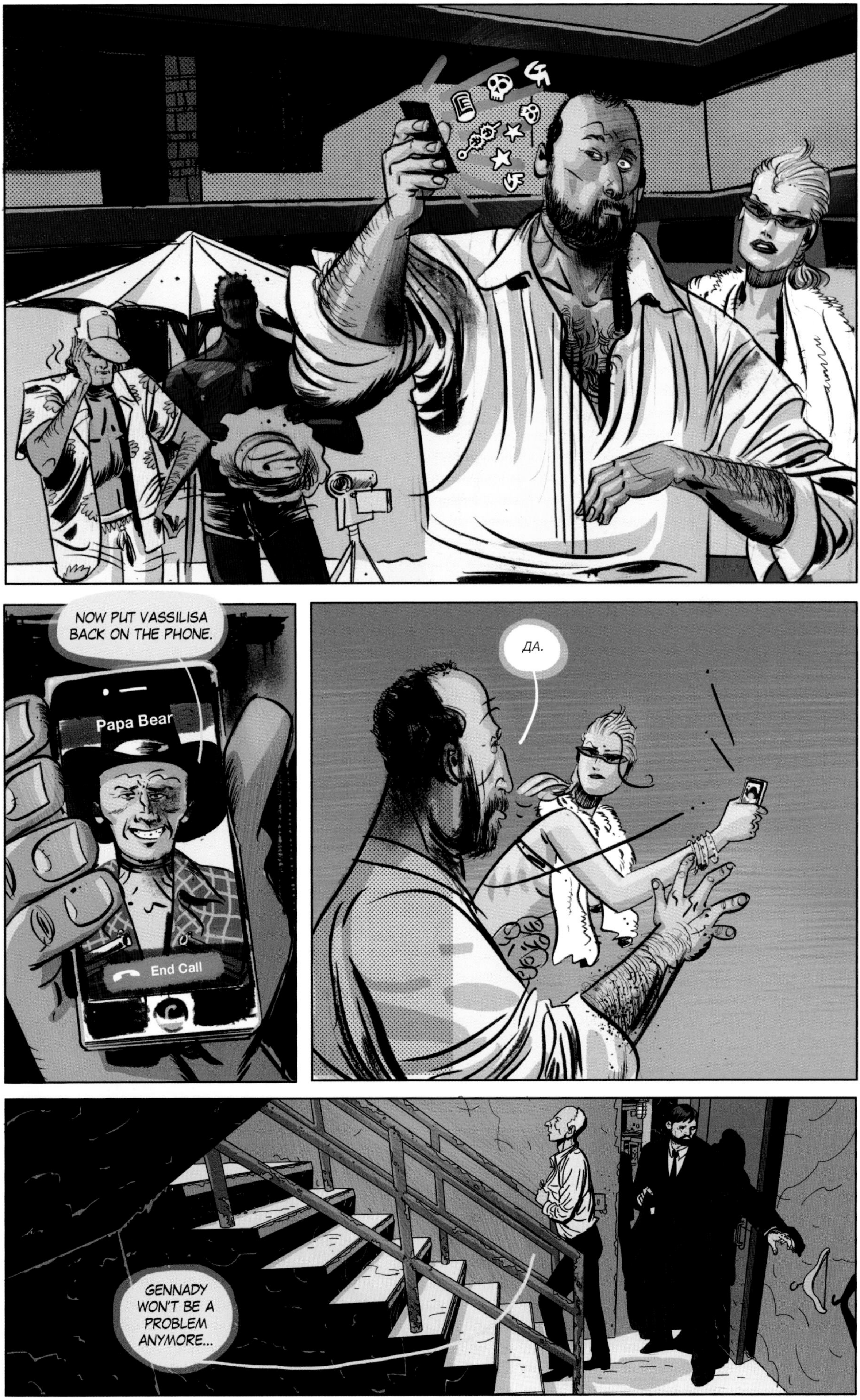
NOW PUT VASSILISA BACK ON THE PHONE.
Papa Bear
End Call
ДА.
GENNADY WON'T BE A PROBLEM ANYMORE...

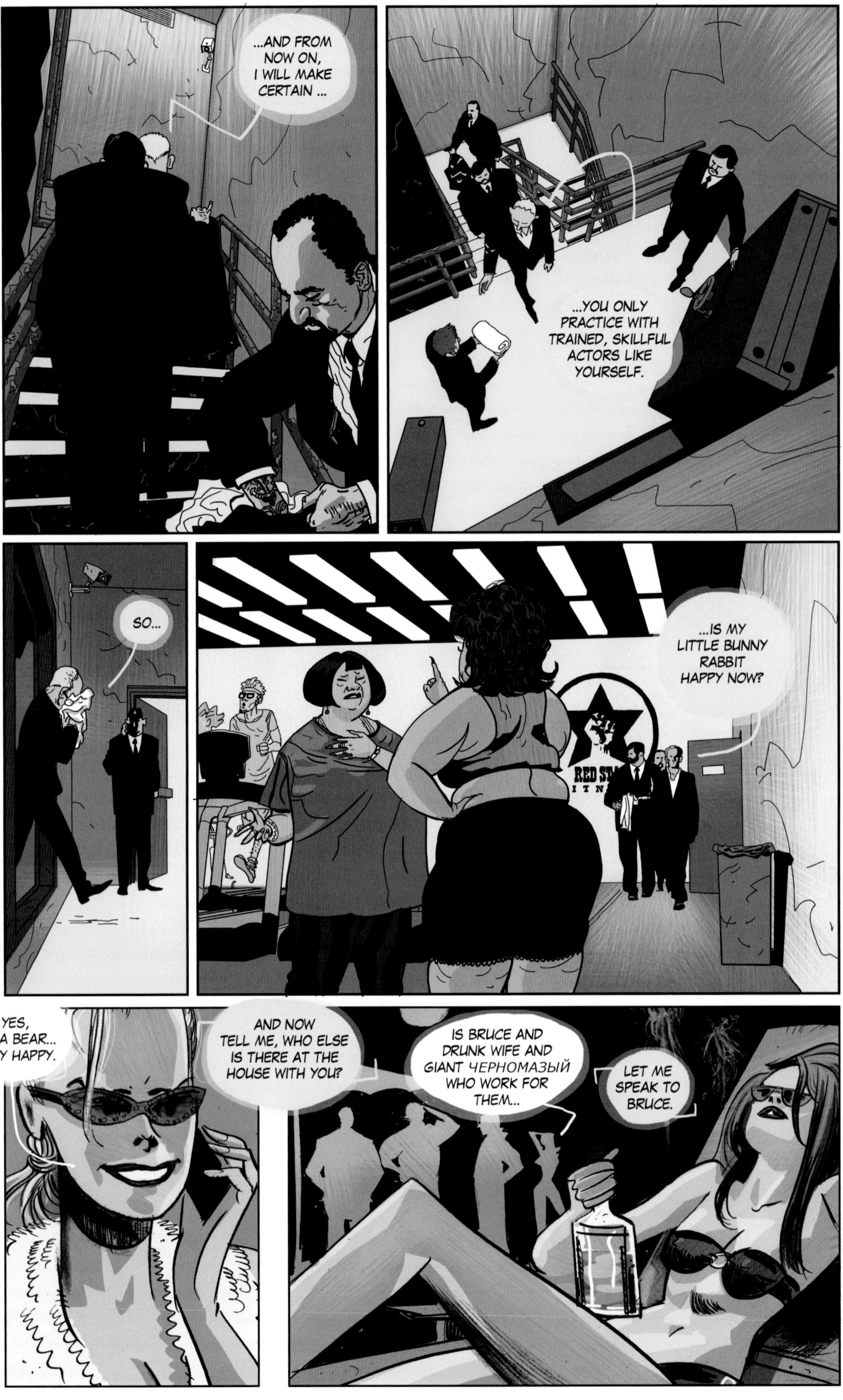
...AND FROM NOW ON, I WILL MAKE CERTAIN ...
...YOU ONLY PRACTICE WITH TRAINED, SKILLFUL ACTORS LIKE YOURSELF.
SO...
...IS MY LITTLE BUNNY RABBIT HAPPY NOW?
YES, PAPA BEAR... VERY HAPPY.
AND NOW TELL ME, WHO ELSE IS THERE AT THE HOUSE WITH YOU?
IS BRUCE AND DRUNK WIFE AND GIANT ЧЕРНОМАЗЫЙ WHO WORK FOR THEM...
LET ME SPEAK TO BRUCE.

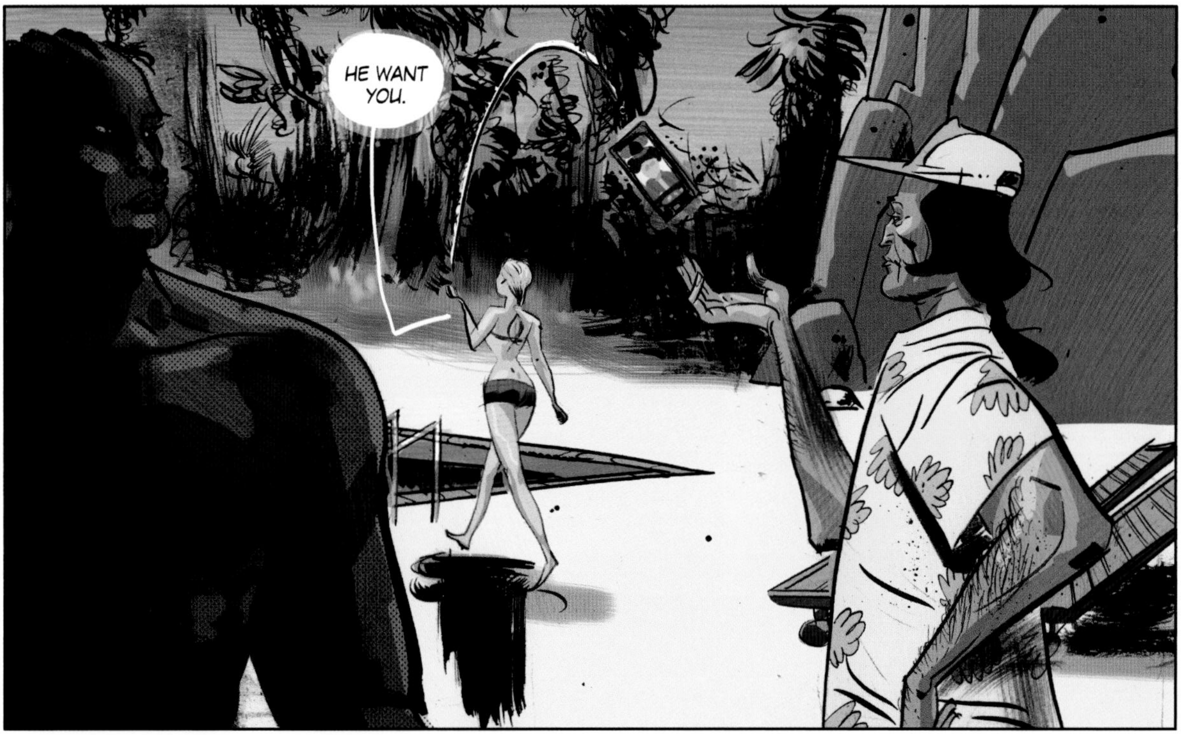
HE WANT YOU.

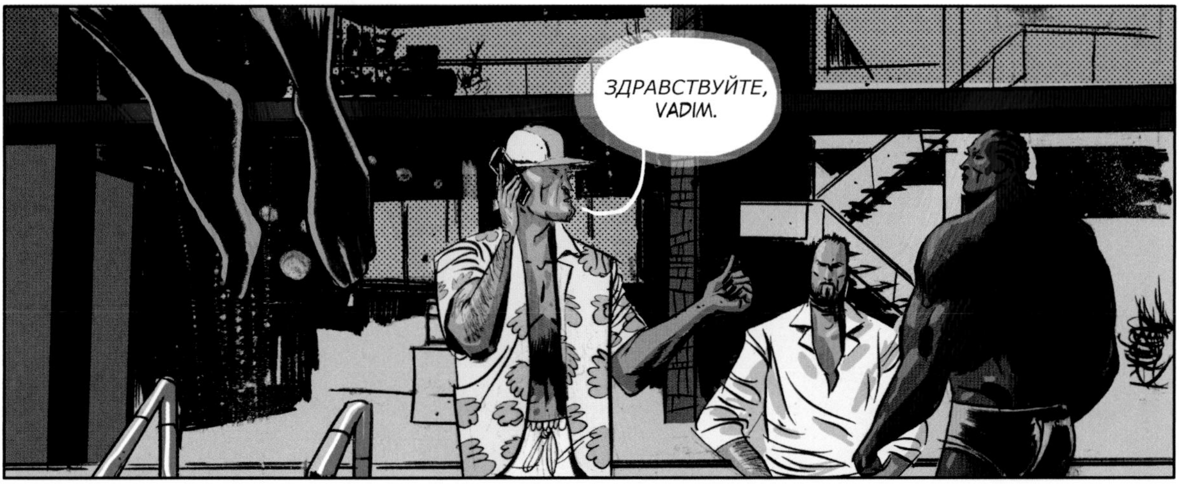
ЗДРАВСТВУЙТЕ, VADIM.

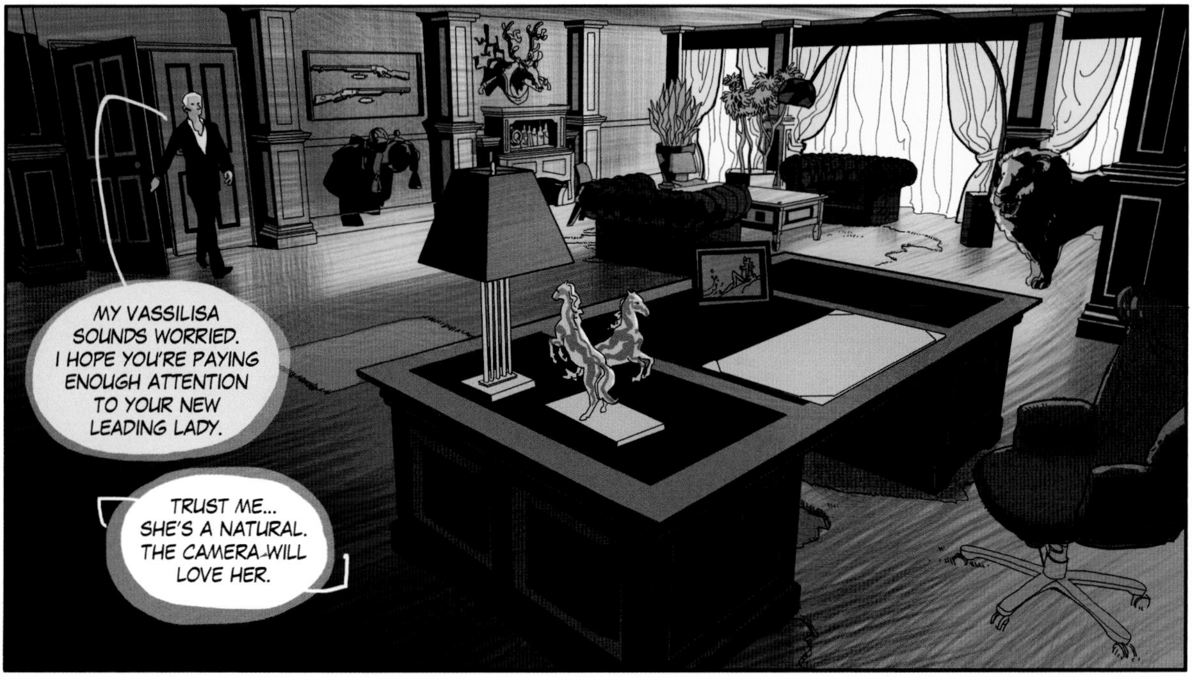
MY VASSILISA SOUNDS WORRIED. I HOPE YOU'RE PAYING ENOUGH ATTENTION TO YOUR NEW LEADING LADY.
TRUST ME... SHE'S A NATURAL. THE CAMERA WILL LOVE HER.

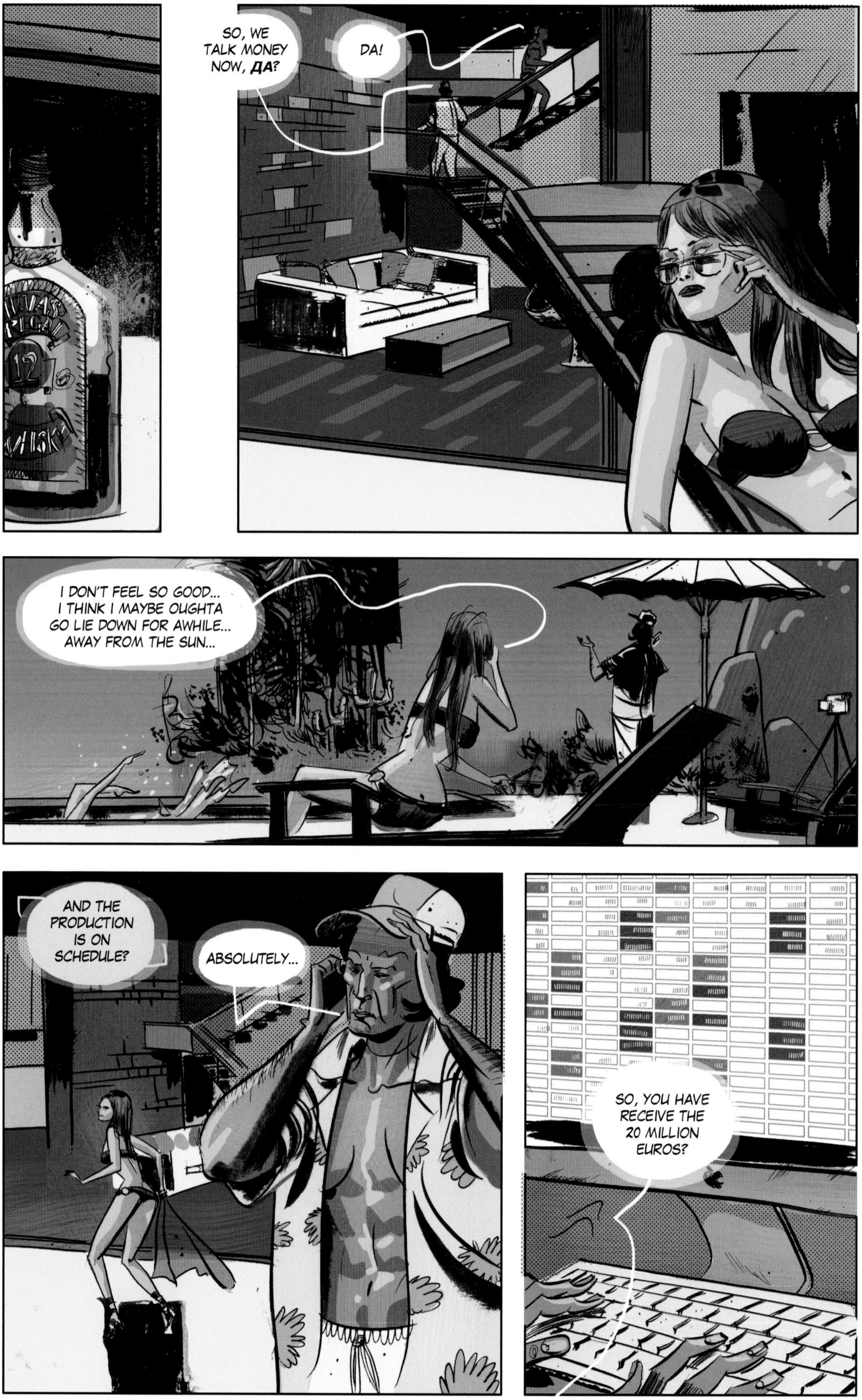
SO, WE TALK MONEY NOW, ДА?
DA!
I DON'T FEEL SO GOOD... I THINK I MAYBE OUGHTA GO LIE DOWN FOR AWHILE... AWAY FROM THE SUN...
AND THE PRODUCTION IS ON SCHEDULE?
ABSOLUTELY...
SO, YOU HAVE RECEIVE THE 20 MILLION EUROS?

OUI.

AND WHERE IS MONEY, PLEASE?

SAFE.

A SAFE? ХОРОШО.

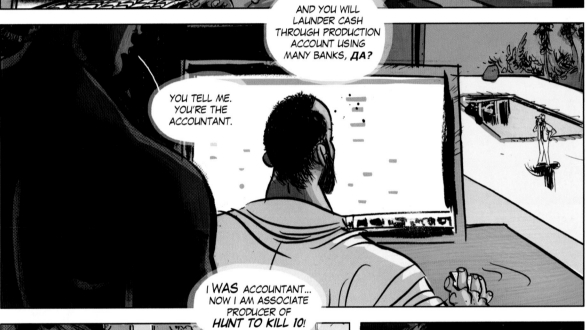

AND YOU WILL LAUNDER CASH THROUGH PRODUCTION ACCOUNT USING MANY BANKS, ДА?

YOU TELL ME. YOU'RE THE ACCOUNTANT.

I WAS ACCOUNTANT... NOW I AM ASSOCIATE PRODUCER OF HUNT TO KILL 10!

WHATEVER, G... JUST SHOW ME WHAT I'M SUPPOSED TO DO.

DETAILS IN COMPUTER... AND PLEASE TO COMPLETE ALL DEPOSITS BY FIRST OF MONTH. THIS VERY IMPORTANT.

HEY, TRUST ME... THE SOONER WE SHIFT THOSE STACKS, THE HAPPIER I'LL BE.

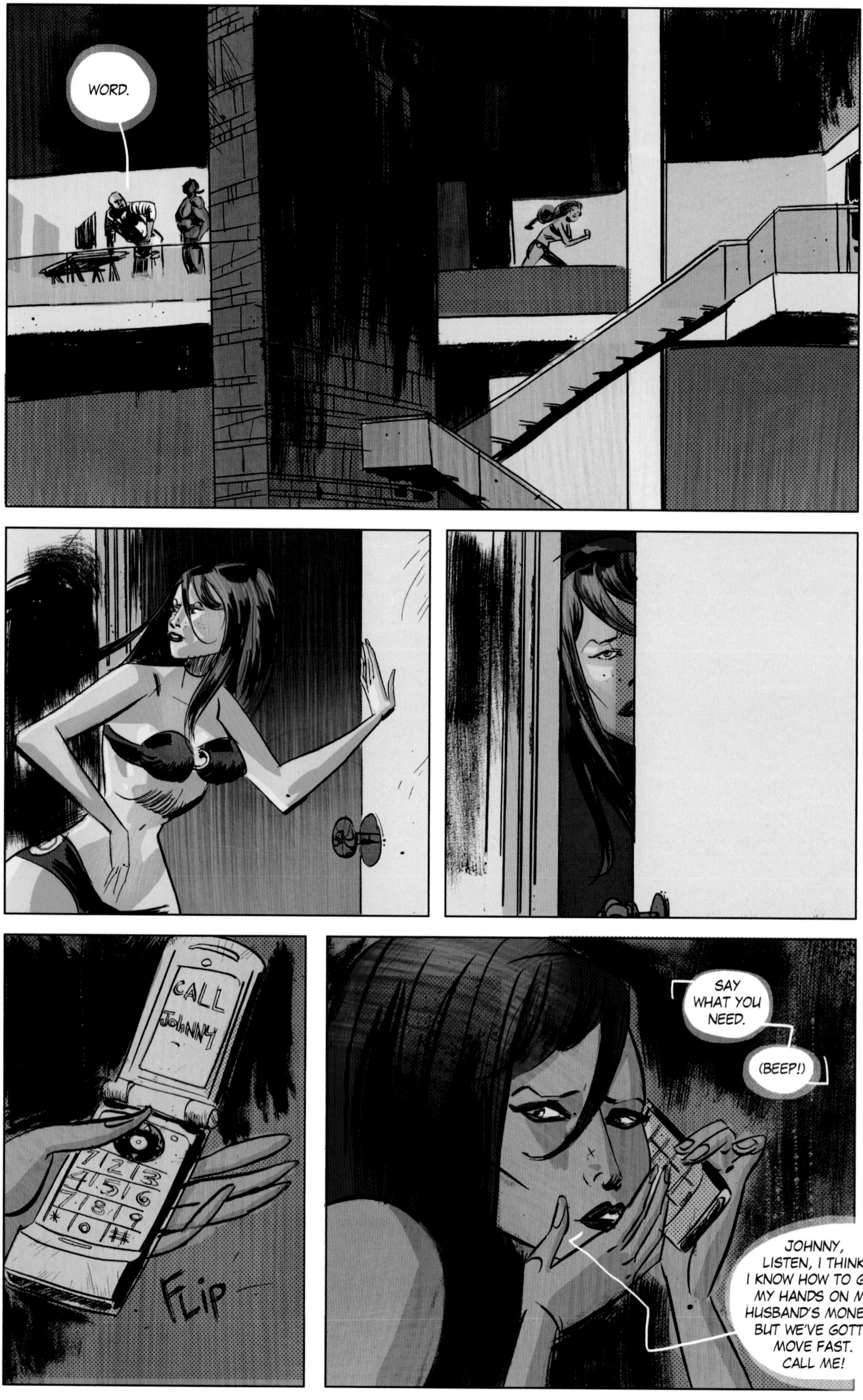
WORD.
CALL
Johnny
SAY WHAT YOU NEED.
(BEEP!)
JOHNNY, LISTEN, I THINK I KNOW HOW TO GET MY HANDS ON MY HUSBAND'S MONEY... BUT WE'VE GOTTA MOVE FAST. CALL ME!
FLIP

SO, TELL ME, OLD FRIEND... DID YOU RECEIVE THE GIFT I SENT FOR YOUR MOST BEAUTIFUL WIFE?

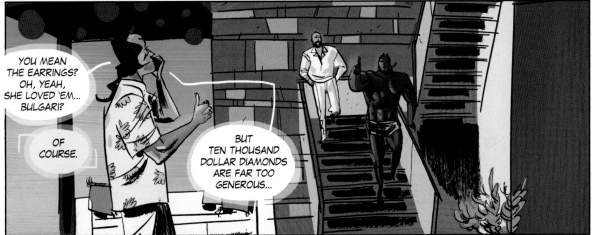

YOU MEAN THE EARRINGS? OH, YEAH, SHE LOVED 'EM... BULGARI?

OF COURSE.

BUT TEN THOUSAND DOLLAR DIAMONDS ARE FAR TOO GENEROUS...

FIFTEEN THOUSAND...

...AND IT WAS MY PLEASURE.

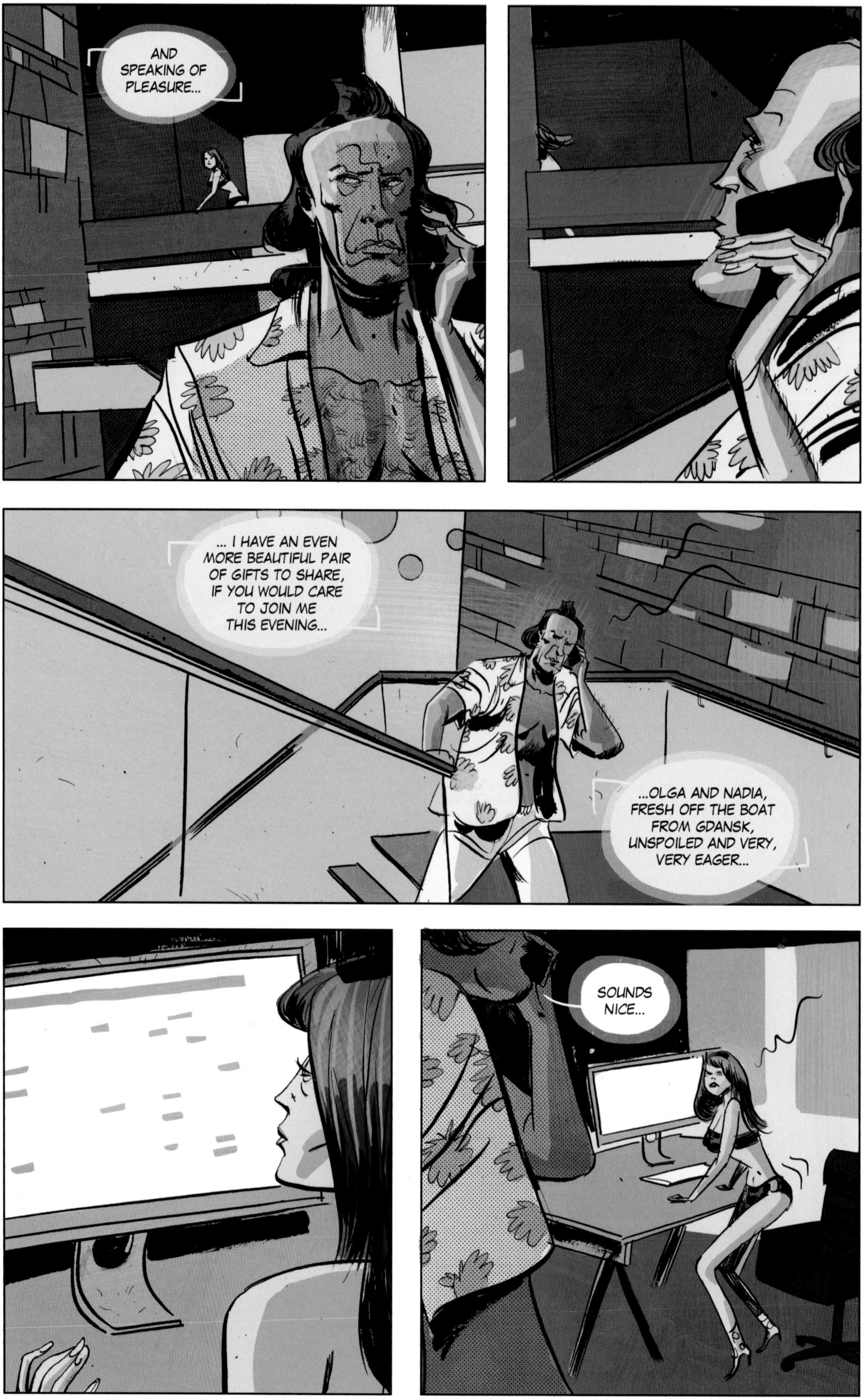
AND SPEAKING OF PLEASURE...
... I HAVE AN EVEN MORE BEAUTIFUL PAIR OF GIFTS TO SHARE, IF YOU WOULD CARE TO JOIN ME THIS EVENING...
...OLGA AND NADIA, FRESH OFF THE BOAT FROM GDANSK, UNSPOILED AND VERY, VERY EAGER...
SOUNDS NICE...

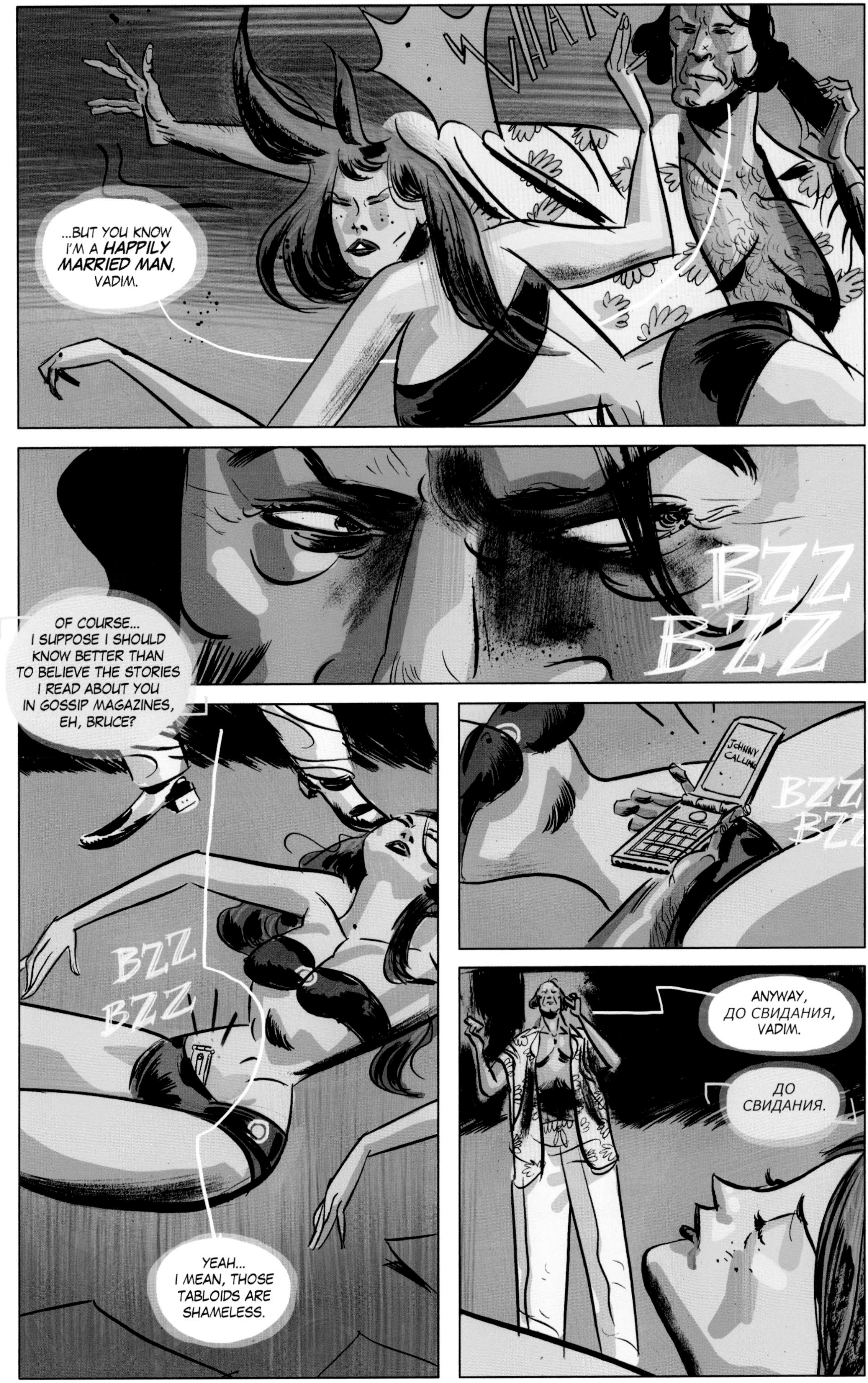
...BUT YOU KNOW I'M A HAPPILY MARRIED MAN, VADIM.
BZZ BZZ
OF COURSE... I SUPPOSE I SHOULD KNOW BETTER THAN TO BELIEVE THE STORIES I READ ABOUT YOU IN GOSSIP MAGAZINES, EH, BRUCE?
BZZ BZZ
YEAH... I MEAN, THOSE TABLOIDS ARE SHAMELESS.
JOHNNY CALLING
BZZ BZZ
ANYWAY, ДО СВИДАНИЯ, VADIM.
ДО СВИДАНИЯ.

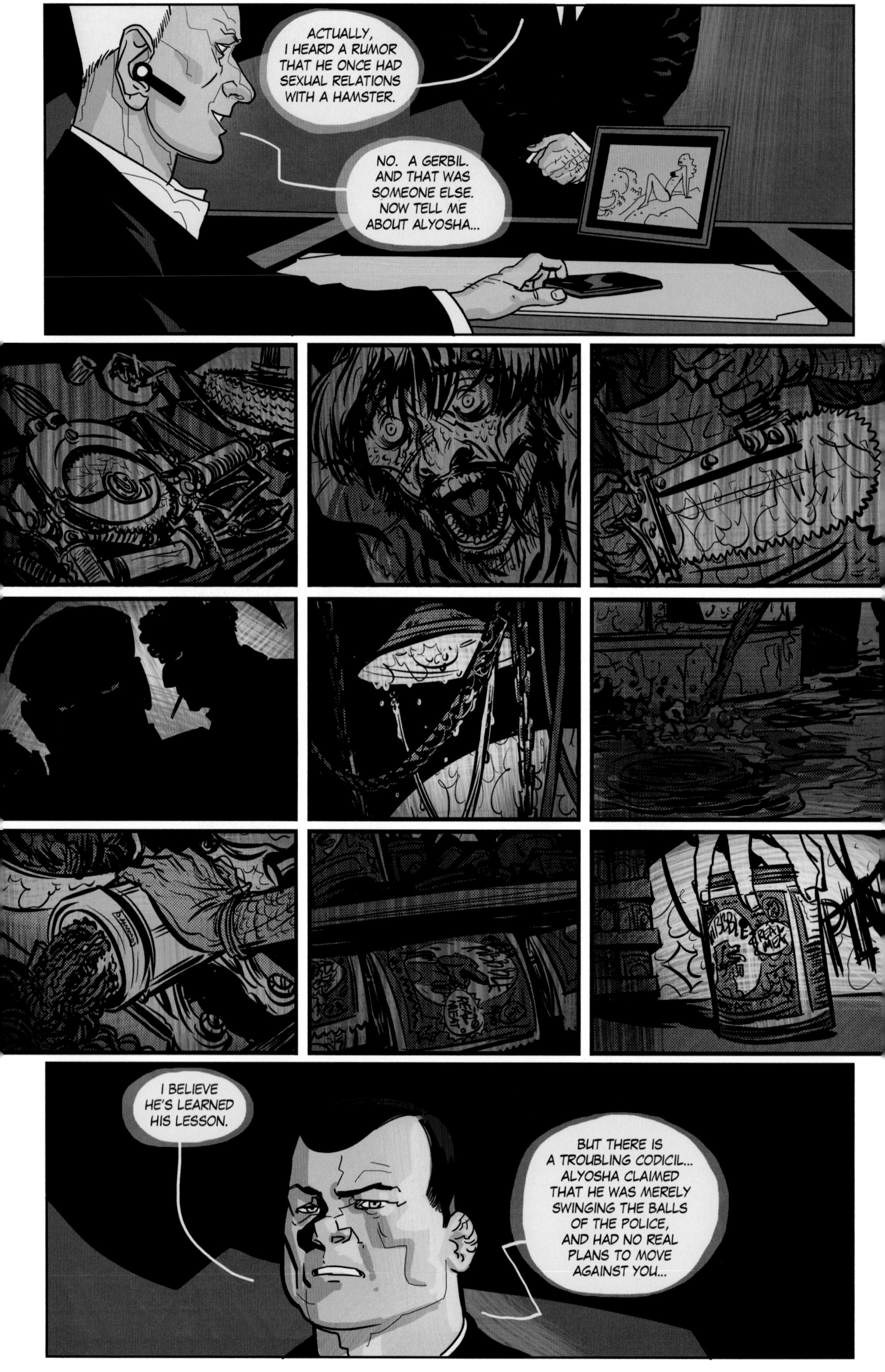
ACTUALLY, I HEARD A RUMOR THAT HE ONCE HAD SEXUAL RELATIONS WITH A HAMSTER.
NO. A GERBIL. AND THAT WAS SOMEONE ELSE. NOW TELL ME ABOUT ALYOSHA...
I BELIEVE HE'S LEARNED HIS LESSON.
BUT THERE IS A TROUBLING CODICIL... ALYOSHA CLAIMED THAT HE WAS MERELY SWINGING THE BALLS OF THE POLICE, AND HAD NO REAL PLANS TO MOVE AGAINST YOU...

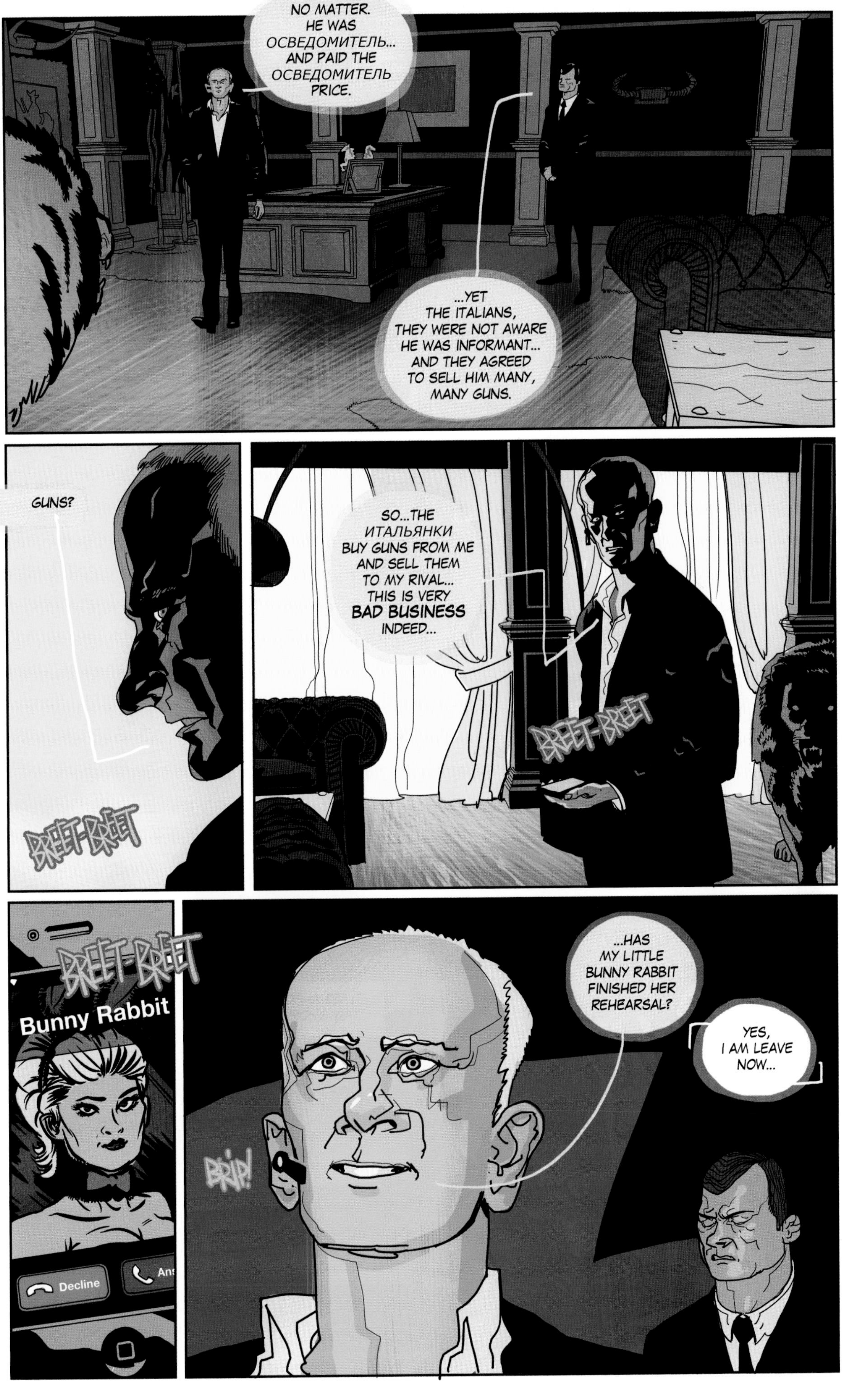
NO MATTER. HE WAS ОСВЕДОМИТЕЛЬ... AND PAID THE ОСВЕДОМИТЕЛЬ PRICE.
...YET THE ITALIANS, THEY WERE NOT AWARE HE WAS INFORMANT... AND THEY AGREED TO SELL HIM MANY, MANY GUNS.
GUNS?
BREET-BREET
SO...THE ИТАЛЬЯНКИ BUY GUNS FROM ME AND SELL THEM TO MY RIVAL... THIS IS VERY **BAD BUSINESS** INDEED...
BREET-BREET
BREET-BREET
Bunny Rabbit
Decline
BRIP!
...HAS MY LITTLE BUNNY RABBIT FINISHED HER REHEARSAL?
YES, I AM LEAVE NOW...

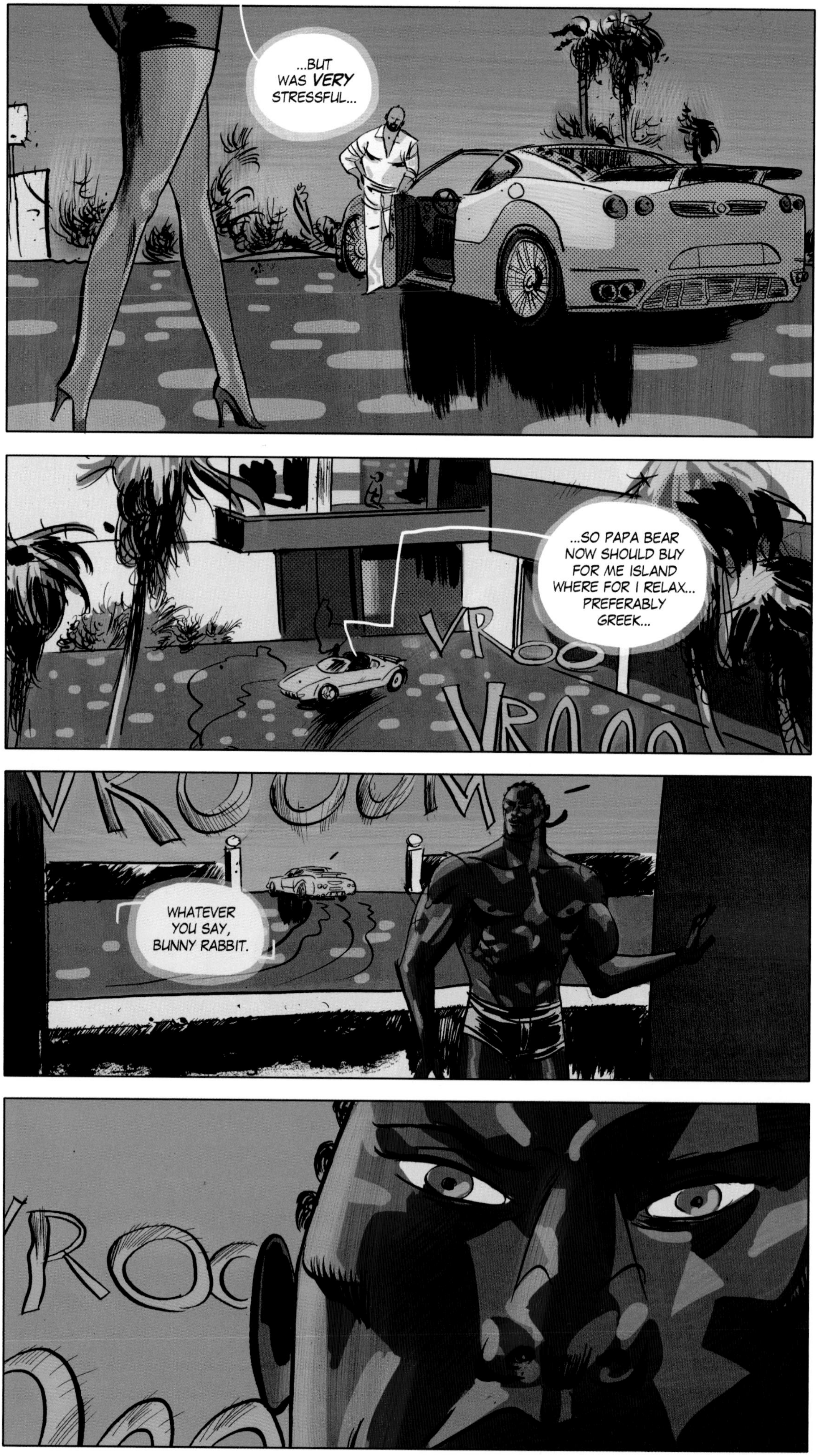
...BUT WAS VERY STRESSFUL...
...SO PAPA BEAR NOW SHOULD BUY FOR ME ISLAND WHERE FOR I RELAX... PREFERABLY GREEK...
VROOOM
WHATEVER YOU SAY, BUNNY RABBIT.

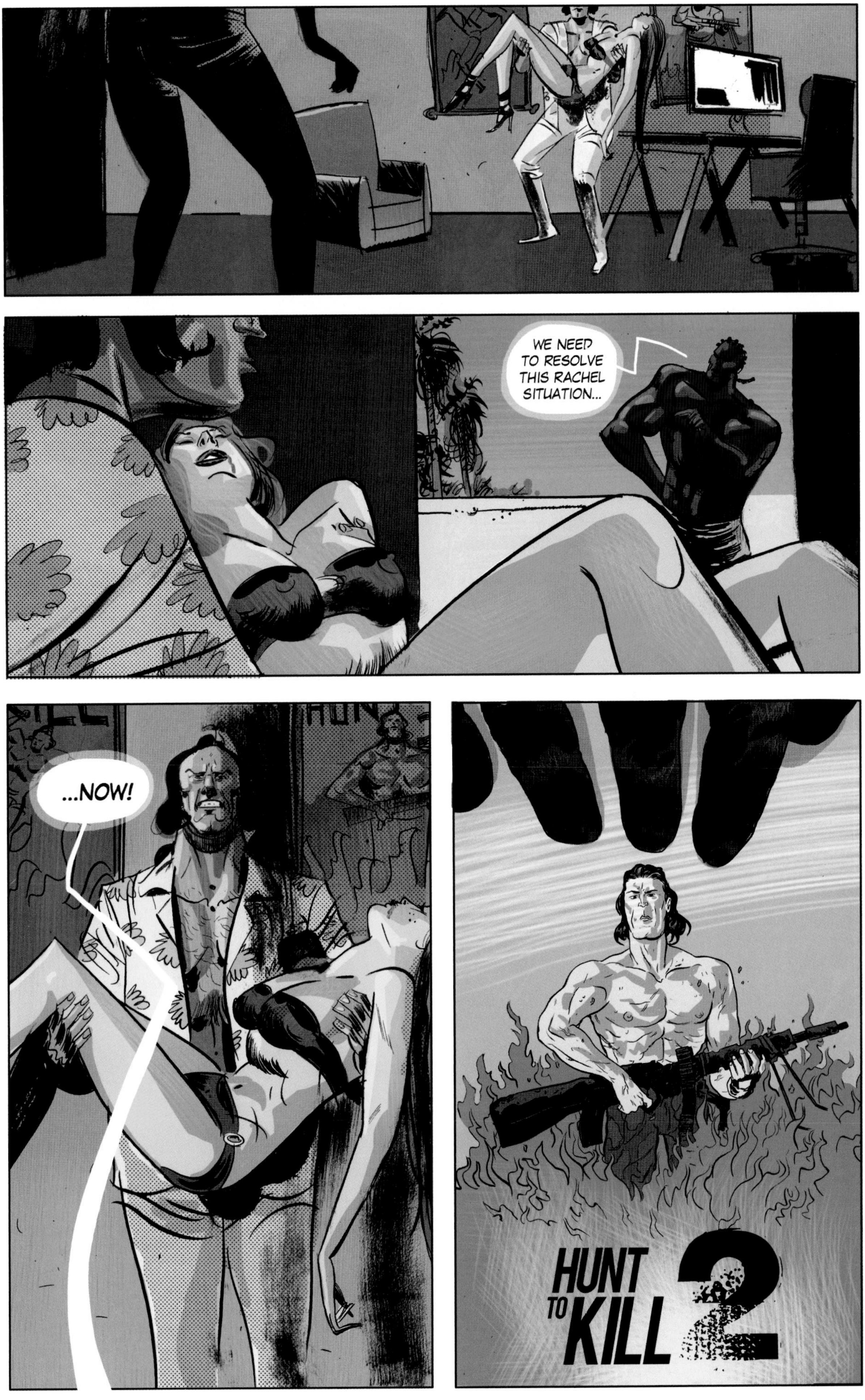
WE NEED TO RESOLVE THIS RACHEL SITUATION...
...NOW!
HUNT TO KILL 2

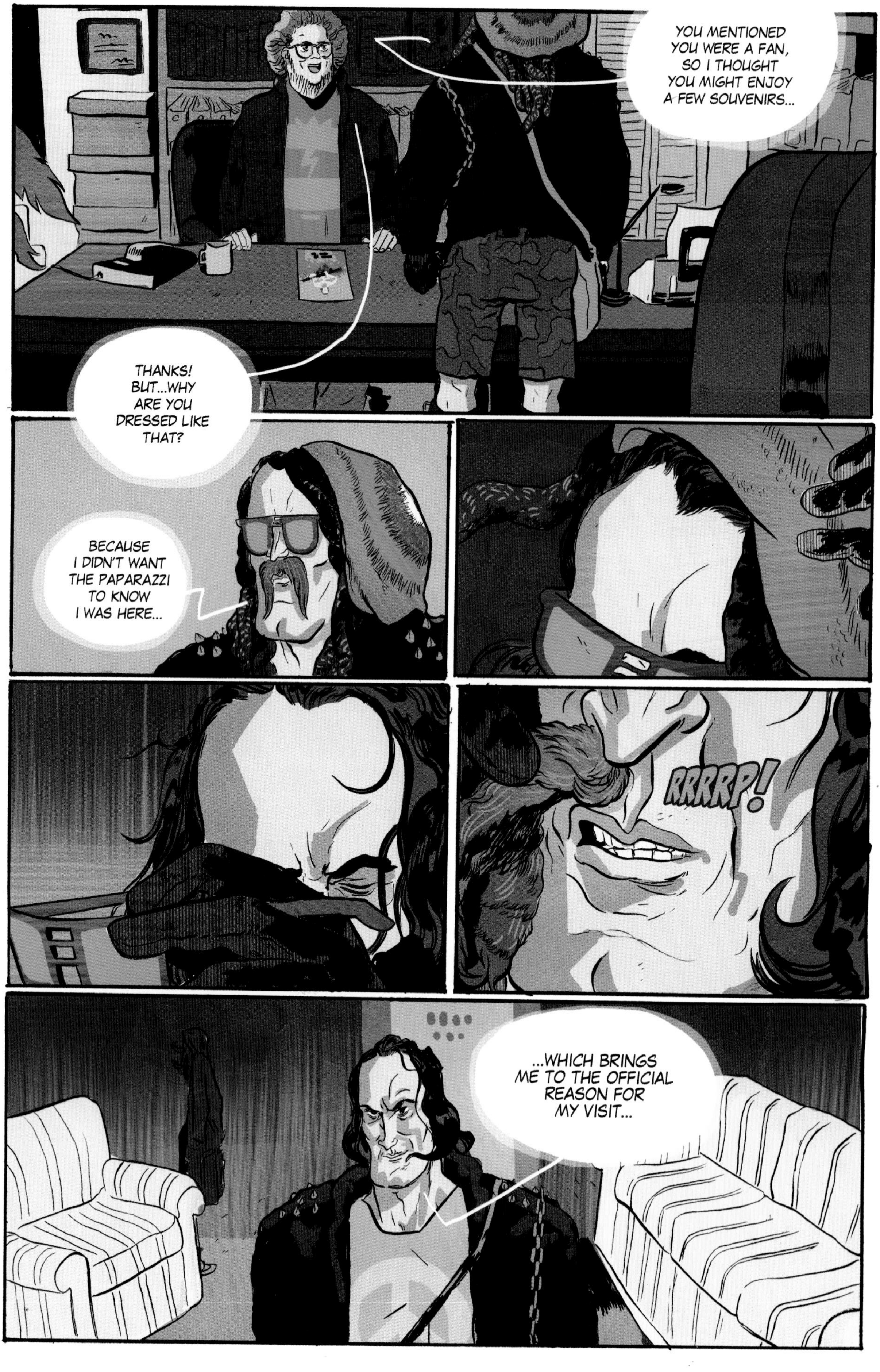
YOU MENTIONED YOU WERE A FAN, SO I THOUGHT YOU MIGHT ENJOY A FEW SOUVENIRS...
THANKS! BUT...WHY ARE YOU DRESSED LIKE THAT?
BECAUSE I DIDN'T WANT THE PAPARAZZI TO KNOW I WAS HERE...
RRRRP!
...WHICH BRINGS ME TO THE OFFICIAL REASON FOR MY VISIT...

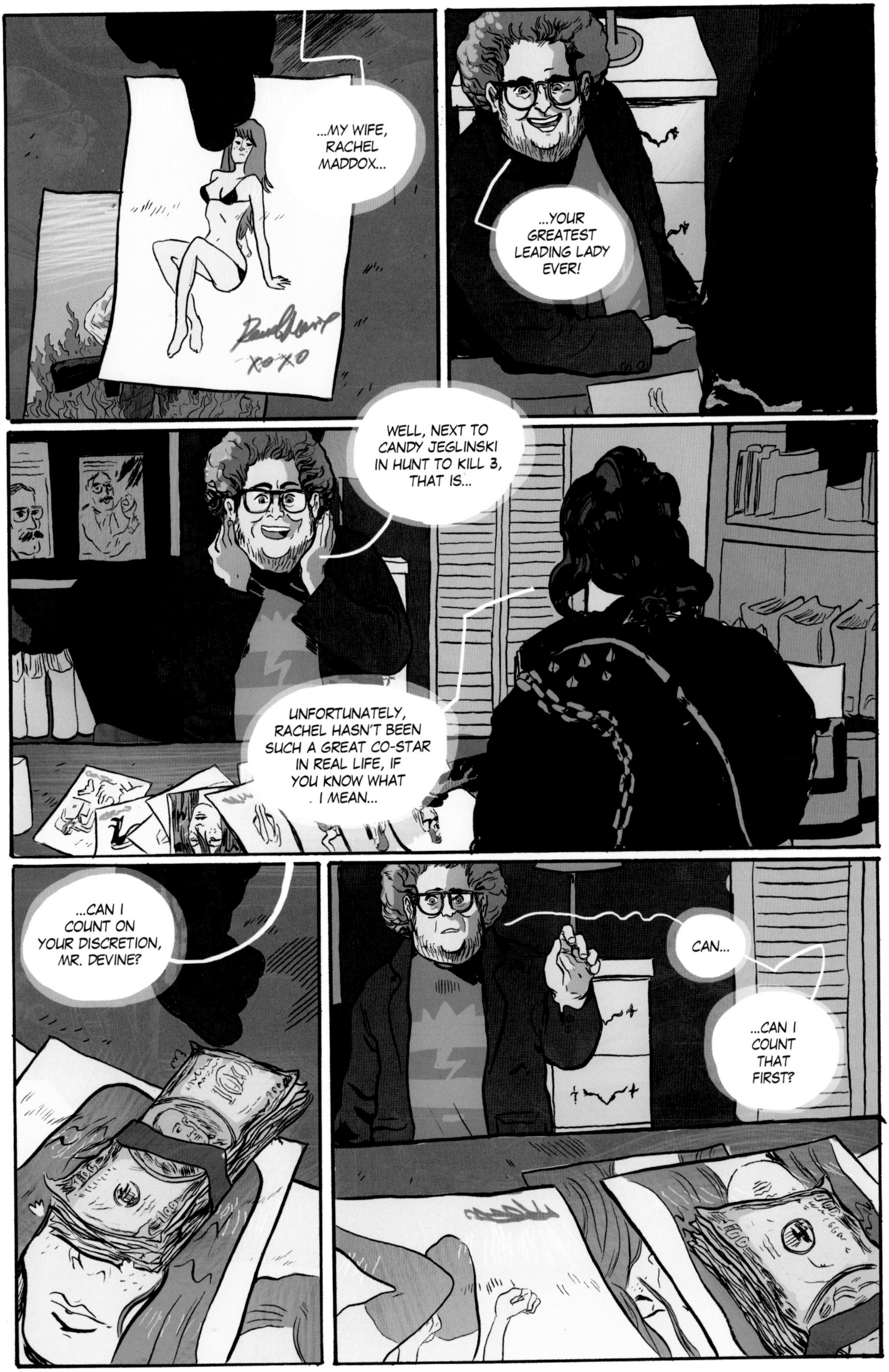
...MY WIFE, RACHEL MADDOX...
...YOUR GREATEST LEADING LADY EVER!
WELL, NEXT TO CANDY JEGLINSKI IN HUNT TO KILL 3, THAT IS...
UNFORTUNATELY, RACHEL HASN'T BEEN SUCH A GREAT CO-STAR IN REAL LIFE, IF YOU KNOW WHAT I MEAN...
...CAN I COUNT ON YOUR DISCRETION, MR. DEVINE?
CAN...
...CAN I COUNT THAT FIRST?

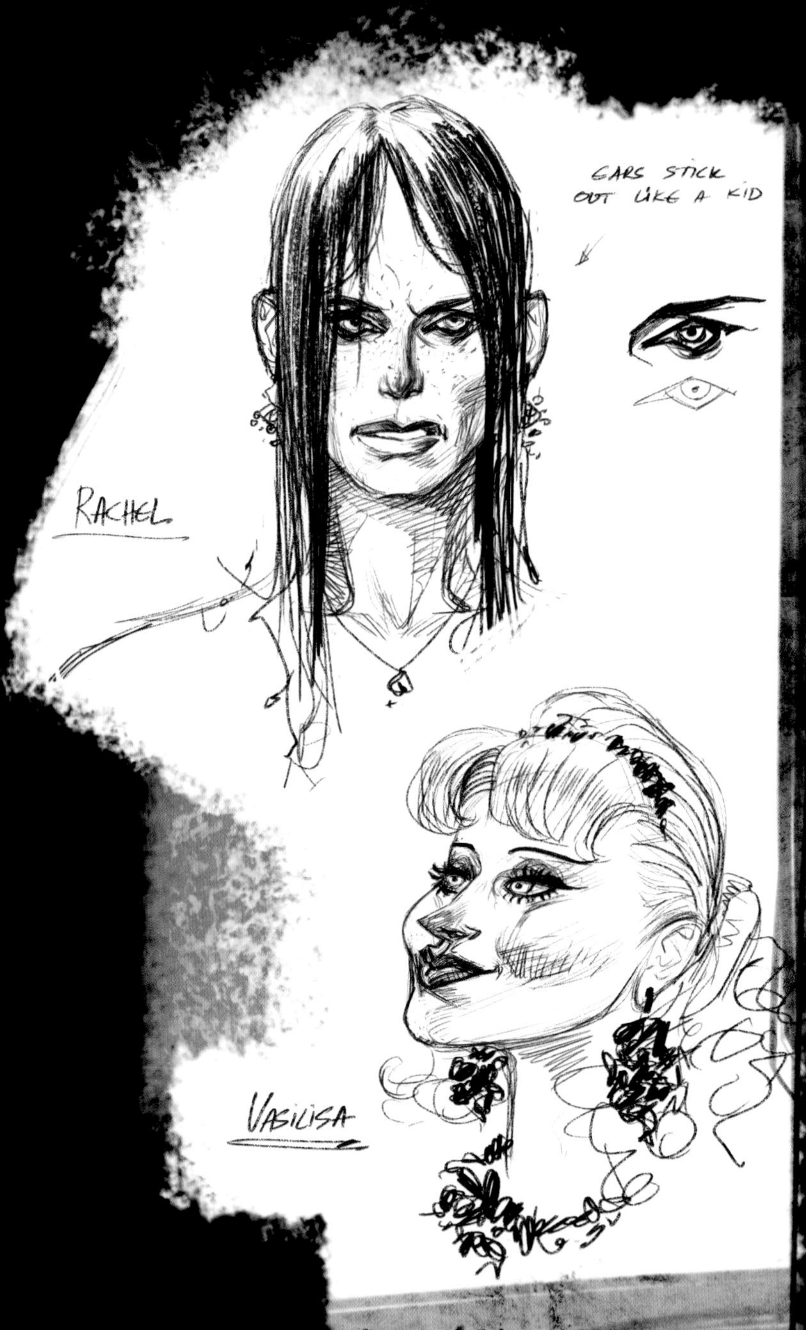
EARS STICK
OUT LIKE A KID
RACHEL
VASILISA

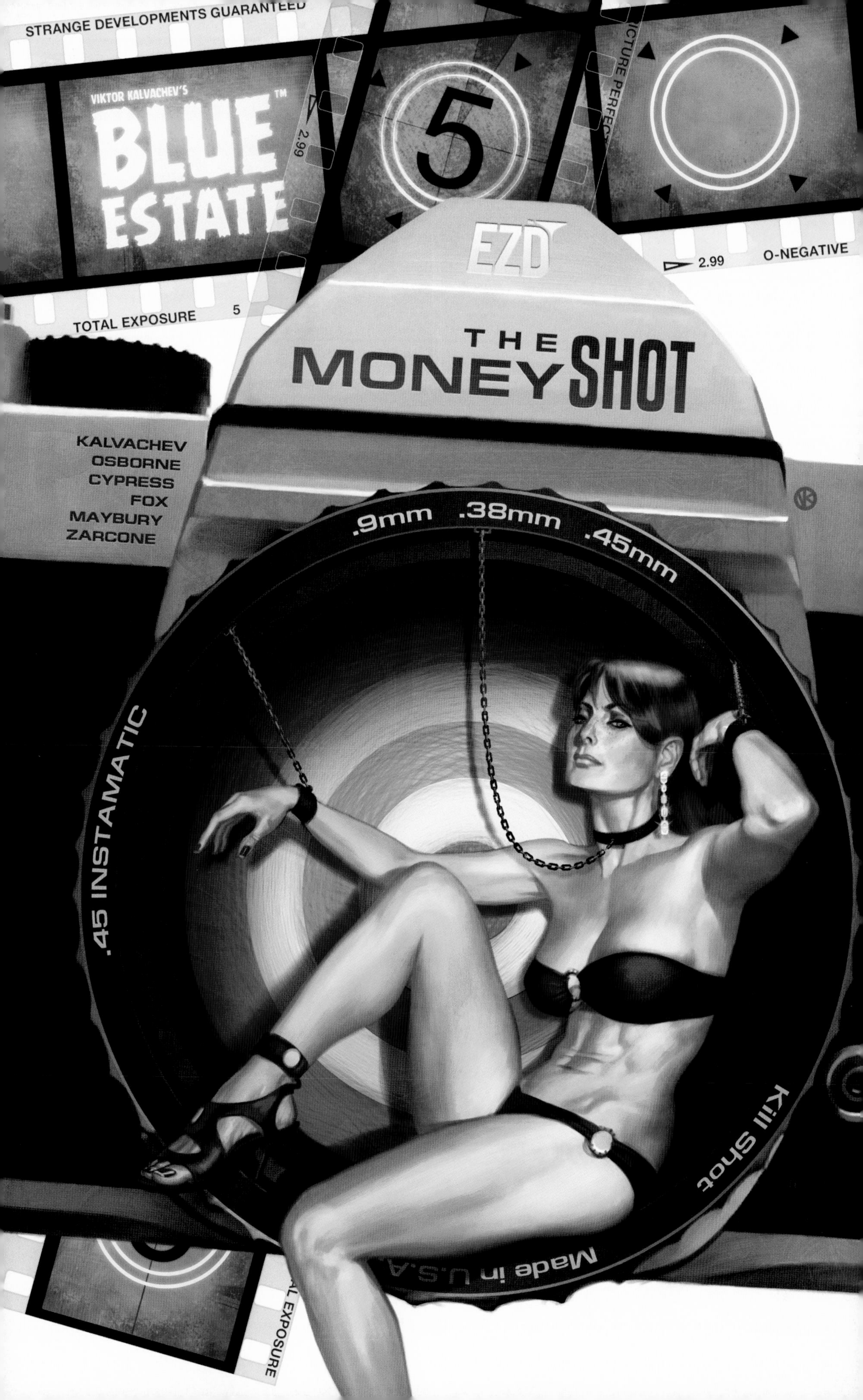
STRANGE DEVELOPMENTS GUARANTEED
VIKTOR KALVACHEV'S
BLUE ESTATE™
2.99
5
EZD
2.99
O-NEGATIVE
TOTAL EXPOSURE 5
THE MONEY SHOT
KALVACHEV
OSBORNE
CYPRESS
FOX
MAYBURY
ZARCONE
.9mm .38mm .45mm
.45 INSTAMATIC
Kill Shot
Made in U.S.A.

# BLUE™ ESTATE

### EPISODE FIVE:
## THE MONEY SHOT

ORIGINAL STORY:
### VIKTOR KALVACHEV and KOSTA YANEV

SCRIPT BY ANDREW OSBORNE

ARTISTS:
### VIKTOR KALVACHEV
### TOBY CYPRESS
### NATHAN FOX
### PAUL MAYBURY
### MARLEY ZARCONE

ART DIRECTION BY VIKTOR KALVACHEV

COVER, COLORS & DESIGN:
### VIKTOR KALVACHEV

CONTRIBUTING EDITOR:
### PHILO NORTHRUP

## WWW.BlueEstateComic.COM

EZD™
PRODUCTIONS

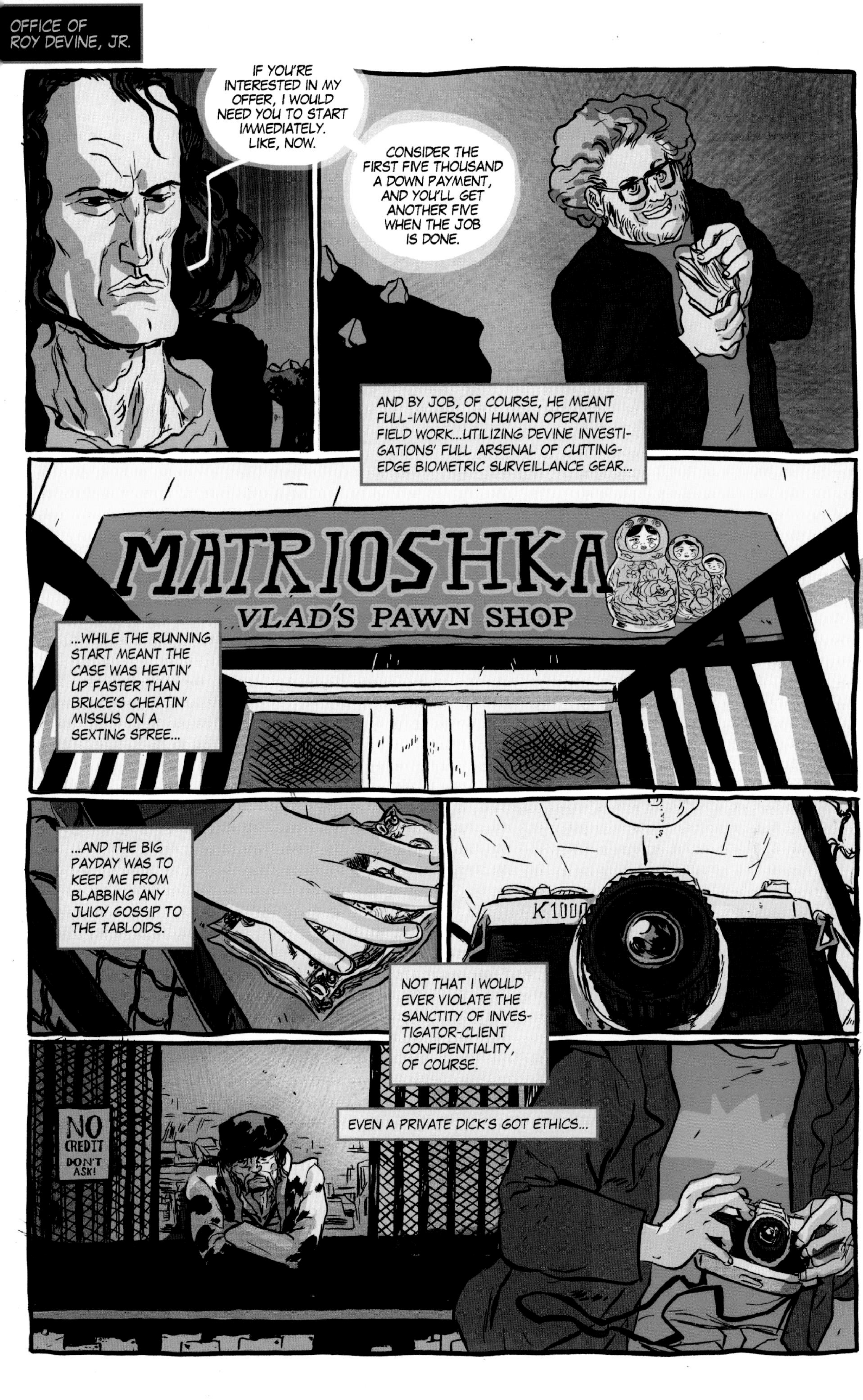
OFFICE OF ROY DEVINE, JR.
IF YOU'RE INTERESTED IN MY OFFER, I WOULD NEED YOU TO START IMMEDIATELY. LIKE, NOW.
CONSIDER THE FIRST FIVE THOUSAND A DOWN PAYMENT, AND YOU'LL GET ANOTHER FIVE WHEN THE JOB IS DONE.
AND BY JOB, OF COURSE, HE MEANT FULL-IMMERSION HUMAN OPERATIVE FIELD WORK...UTILIZING DEVINE INVESTIGATIONS' FULL ARSENAL OF CUTTING-EDGE BIOMETRIC SURVEILLANCE GEAR...
MATRIOSHKA
VLAD'S PAWN SHOP
...WHILE THE RUNNING START MEANT THE CASE WAS HEATIN' UP FASTER THAN BRUCE'S CHEATIN' MISSUS ON A SEXTING SPREE...
...AND THE BIG PAYDAY WAS TO KEEP ME FROM BLABBING ANY JUICY GOSSIP TO THE TABLOIDS.
K1000
NOT THAT I WOULD EVER VIOLATE THE SANCTITY OF INVESTIGATOR-CLIENT CONFIDENTIALITY, OF COURSE.
EVEN A PRIVATE DICK'S GOT ETHICS...
NO CREDIT
DON'T ASK!

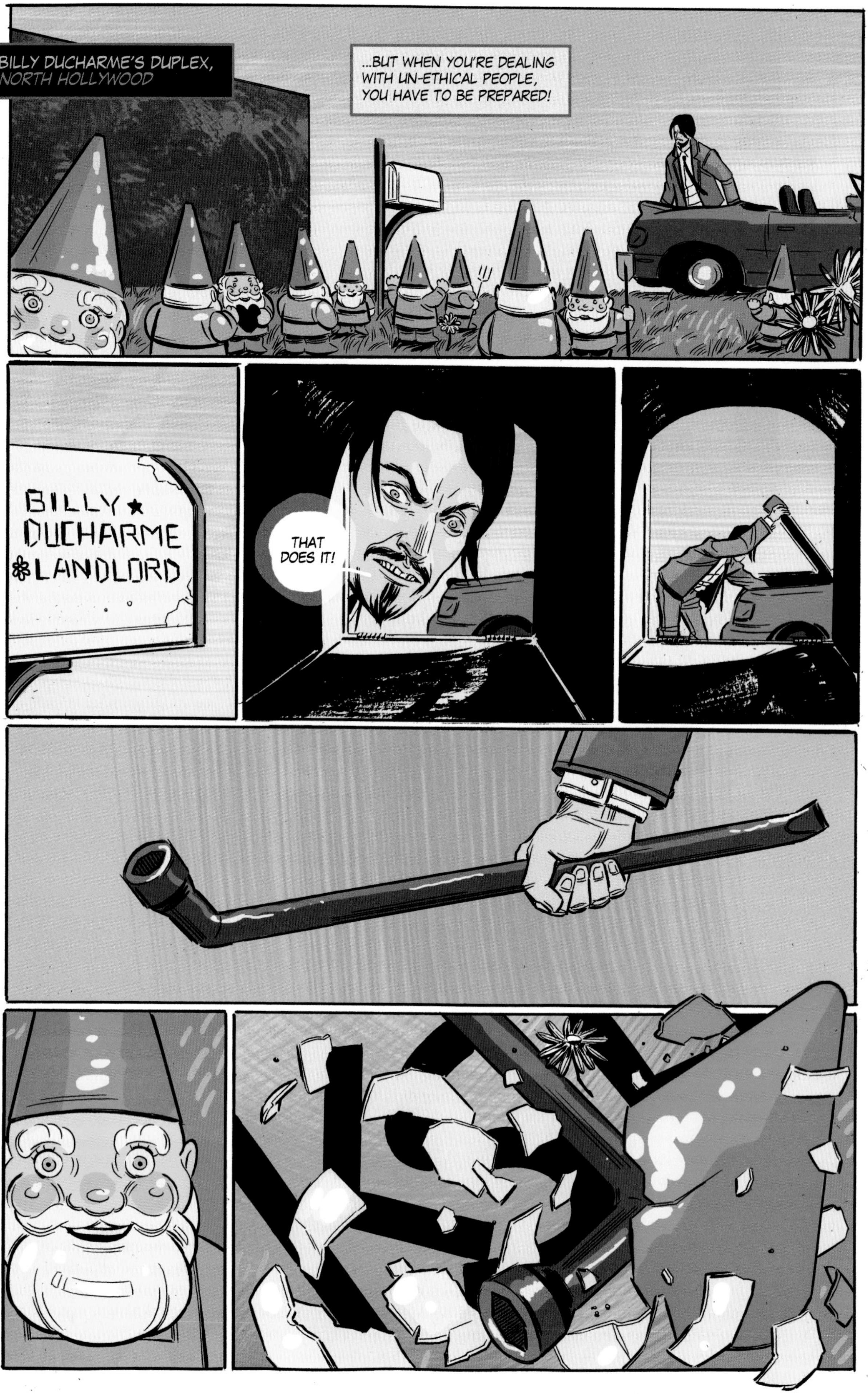
BILLY DUCHARME'S DUPLEX,
NORTH HOLLYWOOD
...BUT WHEN YOU'RE DEALING WITH UN-ETHICAL PEOPLE, YOU HAVE TO BE PREPARED!
BILLY DUCHARME LANDLORD
THAT DOES IT!

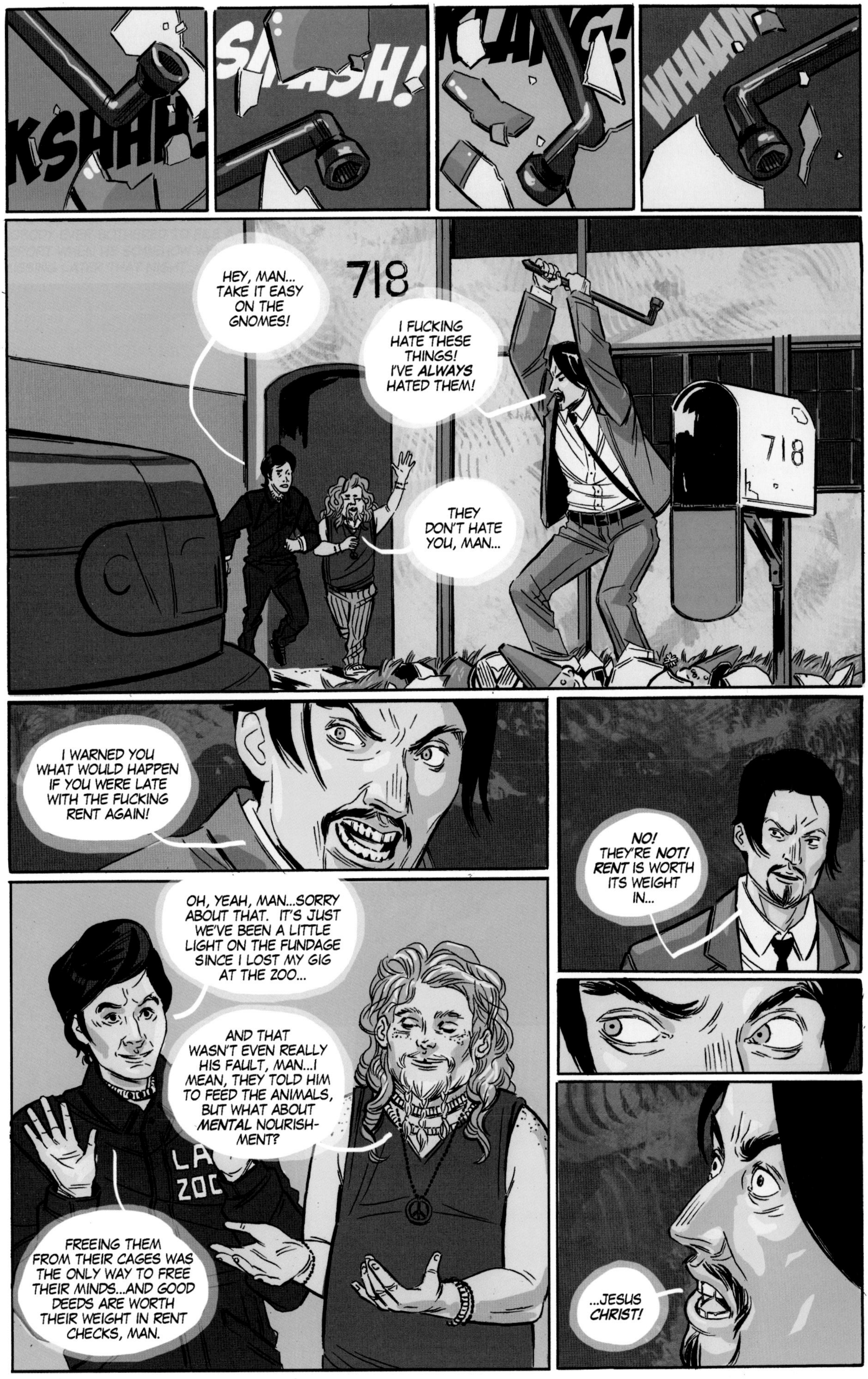
KSHHH!
SMASH!
KLANG!
WHAAM!
718
HEY, MAN... TAKE IT EASY ON THE GNOMES!
I FUCKING HATE THESE THINGS! I'VE ALWAYS HATED THEM!
718
THEY DON'T HATE YOU, MAN...
I WARNED YOU WHAT WOULD HAPPEN IF YOU WERE LATE WITH THE FUCKING RENT AGAIN!
OH, YEAH, MAN...SORRY ABOUT THAT. IT'S JUST WE'VE BEEN A LITTLE LIGHT ON THE FUNDAGE SINCE I LOST MY GIG AT THE ZOO...
AND THAT WASN'T EVEN REALLY HIS FAULT, MAN...I MEAN, THEY TOLD HIM TO FEED THE ANIMALS, BUT WHAT ABOUT MENTAL NOURISHMENT?
FREEING THEM FROM THEIR CAGES WAS THE ONLY WAY TO FREE THEIR MINDS...AND GOOD DEEDS ARE WORTH THEIR WEIGHT IN RENT CHECKS, MAN.
NO! THEY'RE NOT! RENT IS WORTH ITS WEIGHT IN...
...JESUS CHRIST!

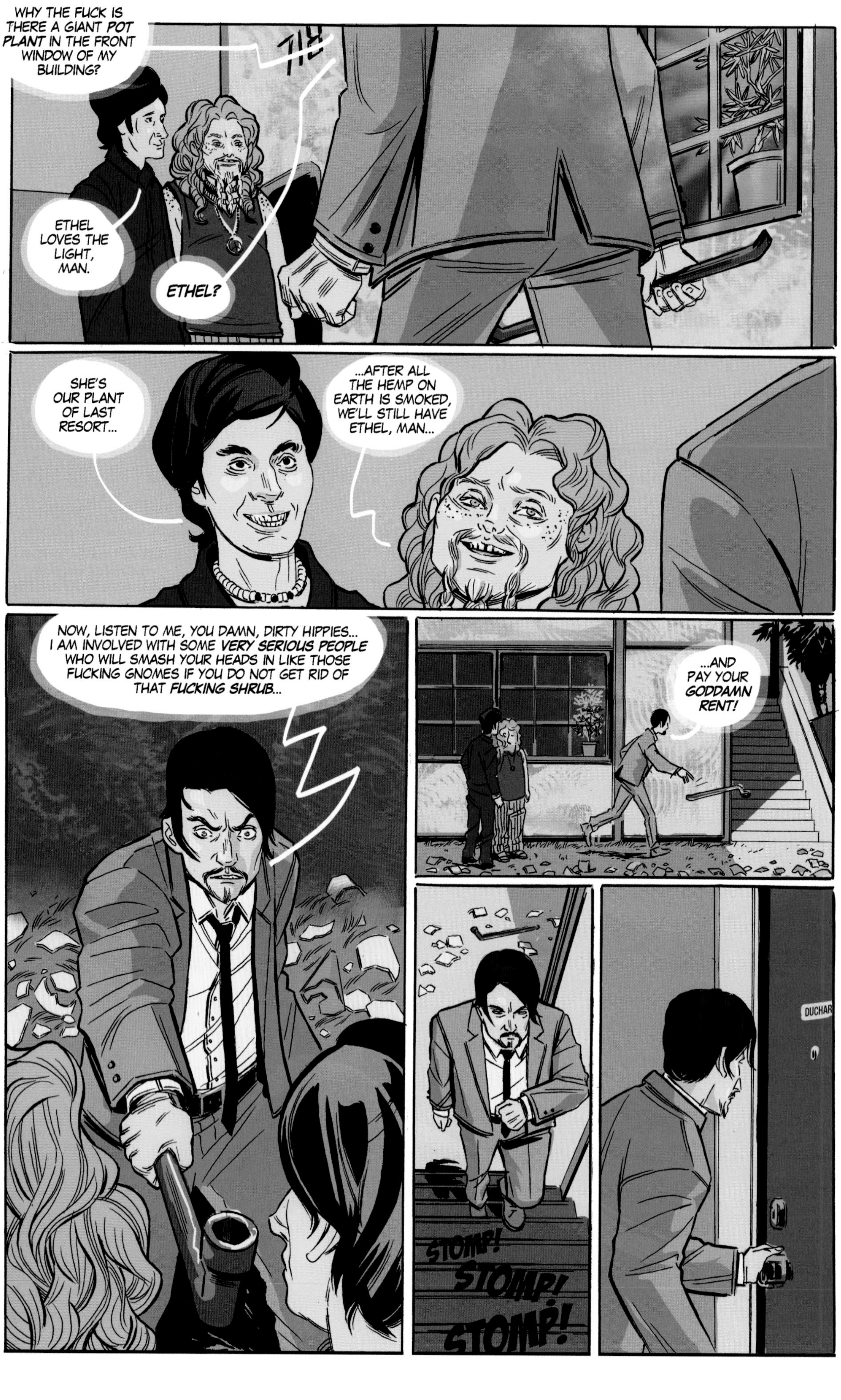
WHY THE FUCK IS THERE A GIANT POT PLANT IN THE FRONT WINDOW OF MY BUILDING?
ETHEL LOVES THE LIGHT, MAN.
ETHEL?
SHE'S OUR PLANT OF LAST RESORT...
...AFTER ALL THE HEMP ON EARTH IS SMOKED, WE'LL STILL HAVE ETHEL, MAN...
NOW, LISTEN TO ME, YOU DAMN, DIRTY HIPPIES... I AM INVOLVED WITH SOME VERY SERIOUS PEOPLE WHO WILL SMASH YOUR HEADS IN LIKE THOSE FUCKING GNOMES IF YOU DO NOT GET RID OF THAT FUCKING SHRUB...
...AND PAY YOUR GODDAMN RENT!
STOMP! STOMP! STOMP!
DUCHAR

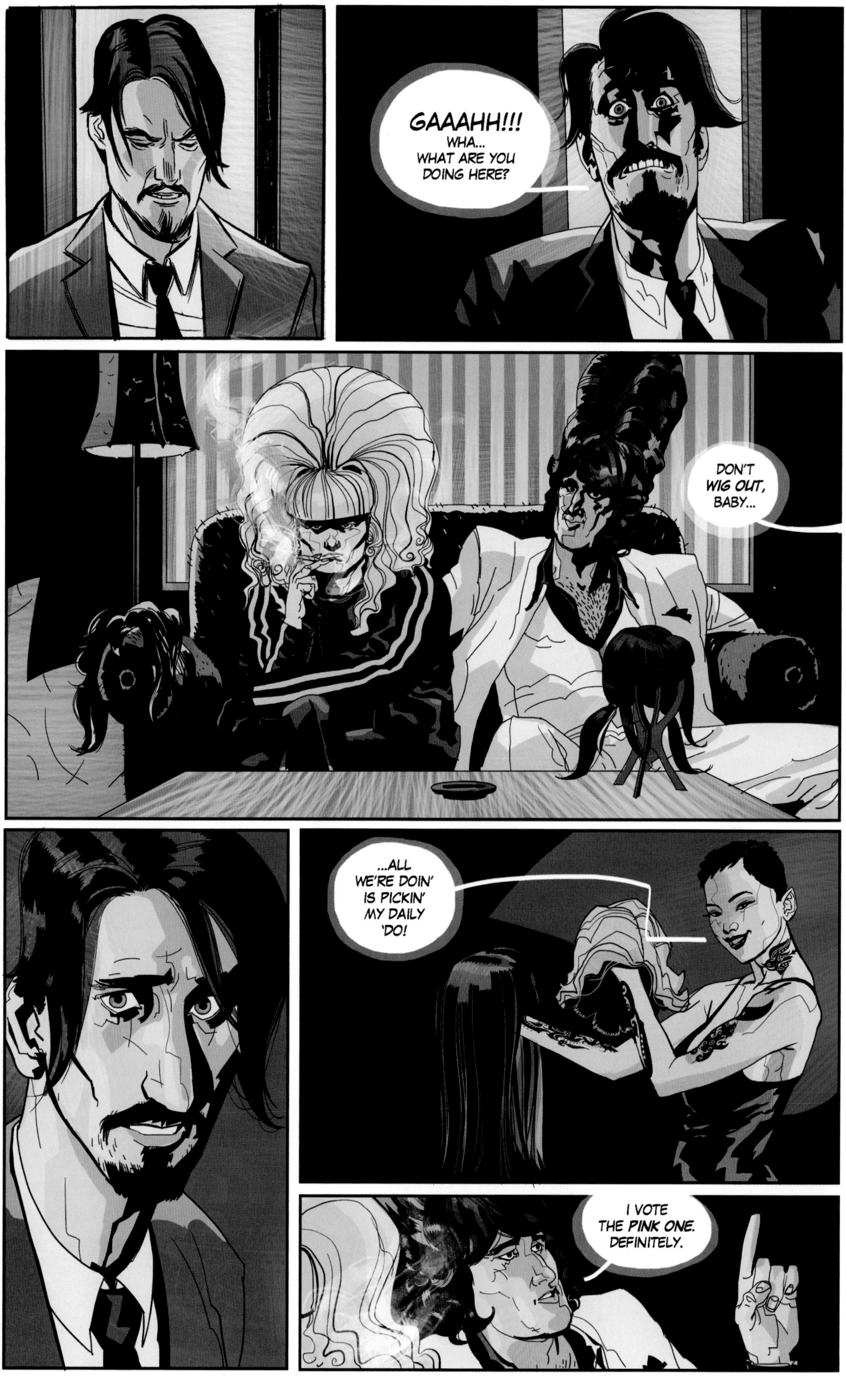
GAAAHH!!!
WHA... WHAT ARE YOU DOING HERE?
DON'T WIG OUT, BABY...
...ALL WE'RE DOIN' IS PICKIN' MY DAILY 'DO!
I VOTE THE PINK ONE. DEFINITELY.

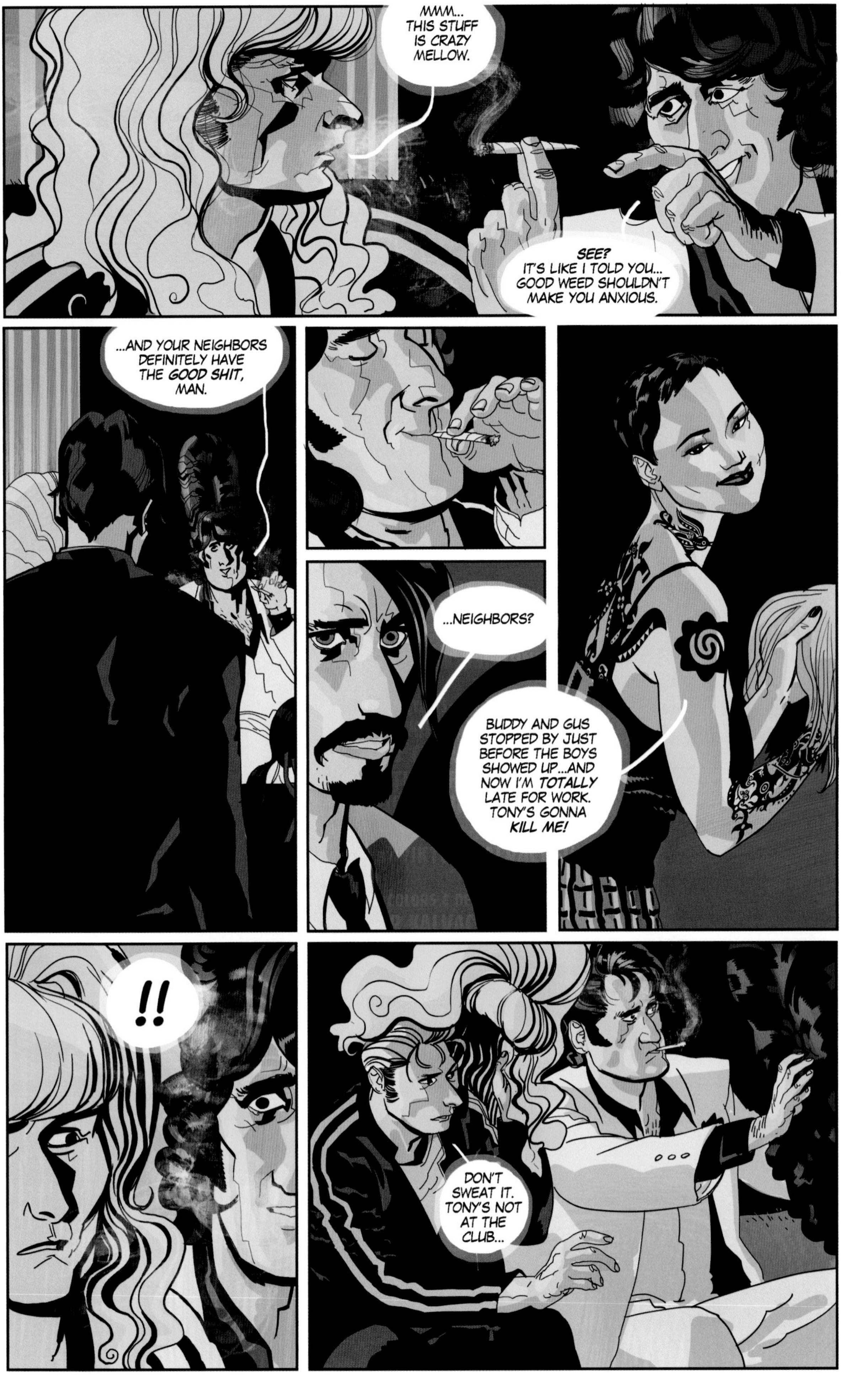
MMM... THIS STUFF IS CRAZY MELLOW.
SEE? IT'S LIKE I TOLD YOU... GOOD WEED SHOULDN'T MAKE YOU ANXIOUS.
...AND YOUR NEIGHBORS DEFINITELY HAVE THE *GOOD SHIT*, MAN.
...NEIGHBORS?
BUDDY AND GUS STOPPED BY JUST BEFORE THE BOYS SHOWED UP...AND NOW I'M *TOTALLY* LATE FOR WORK. TONY'S GONNA *KILL ME!*
!!
DON'T SWEAT IT. TONY'S NOT AT THE CLUB...

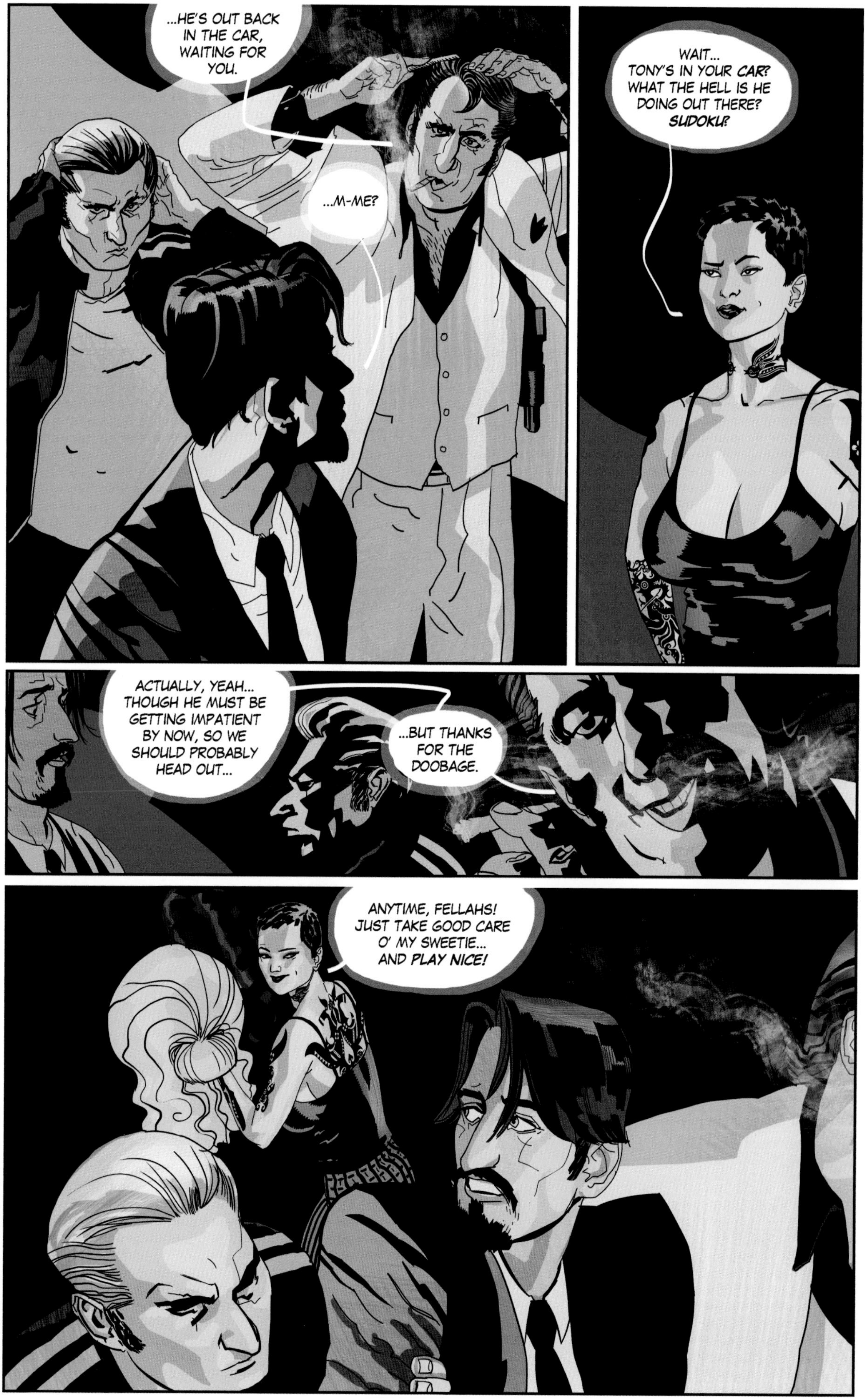
...HE'S OUT BACK IN THE CAR, WAITING FOR YOU.
...M-ME?
WAIT... TONY'S IN YOUR CAR? WHAT THE HELL IS HE DOING OUT THERE? SUDOKU?
ACTUALLY, YEAH... THOUGH HE MUST BE GETTING IMPATIENT BY NOW, SO WE SHOULD PROBABLY HEAD OUT...
...BUT THANKS FOR THE DOOBAGE.
ANYTIME, FELLAHS! JUST TAKE GOOD CARE O' MY SWEETIE... AND PLAY NICE!

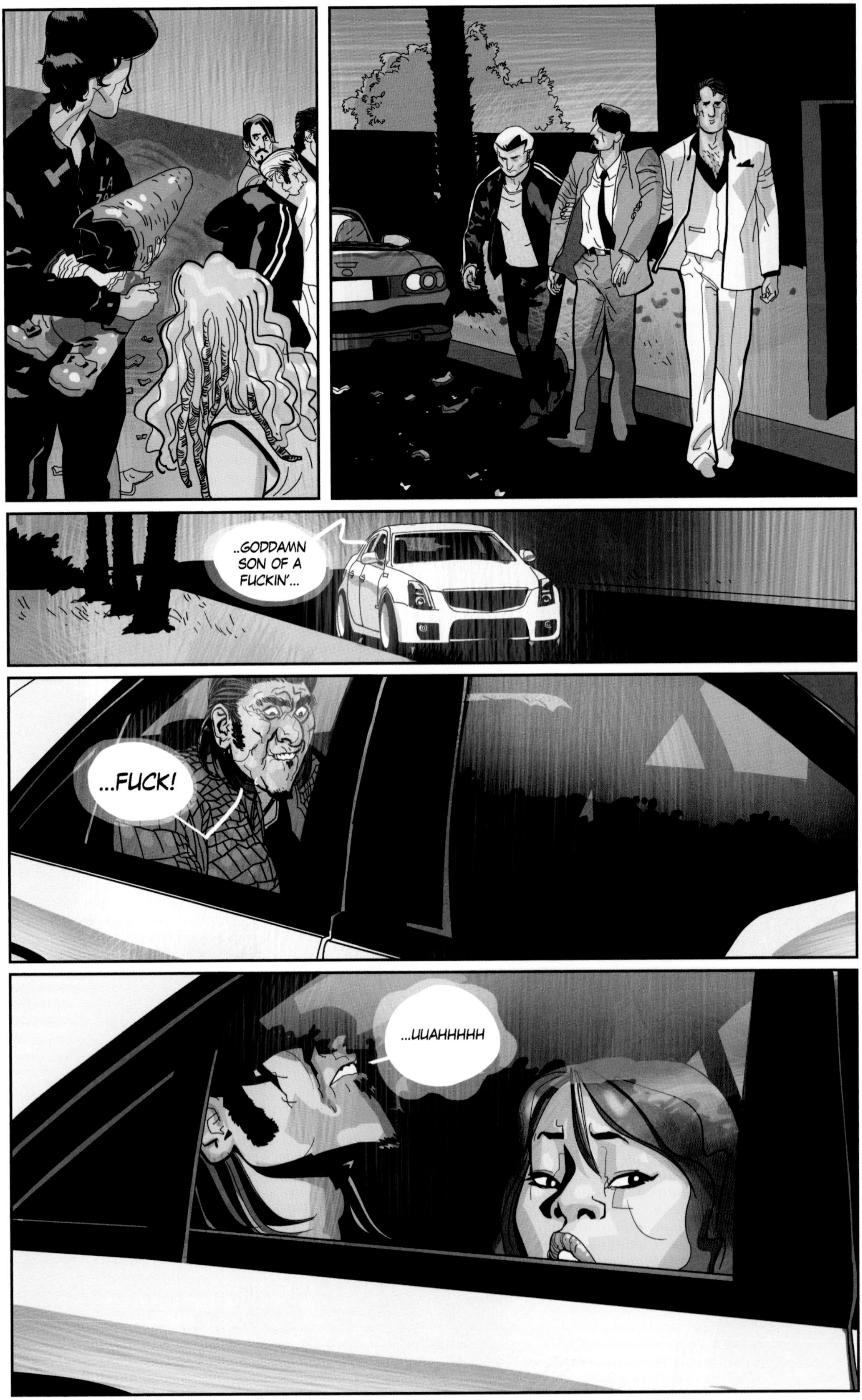

..GODDAMN SON OF A FUCKIN'...
...FUCK!
...UUAHHHHH

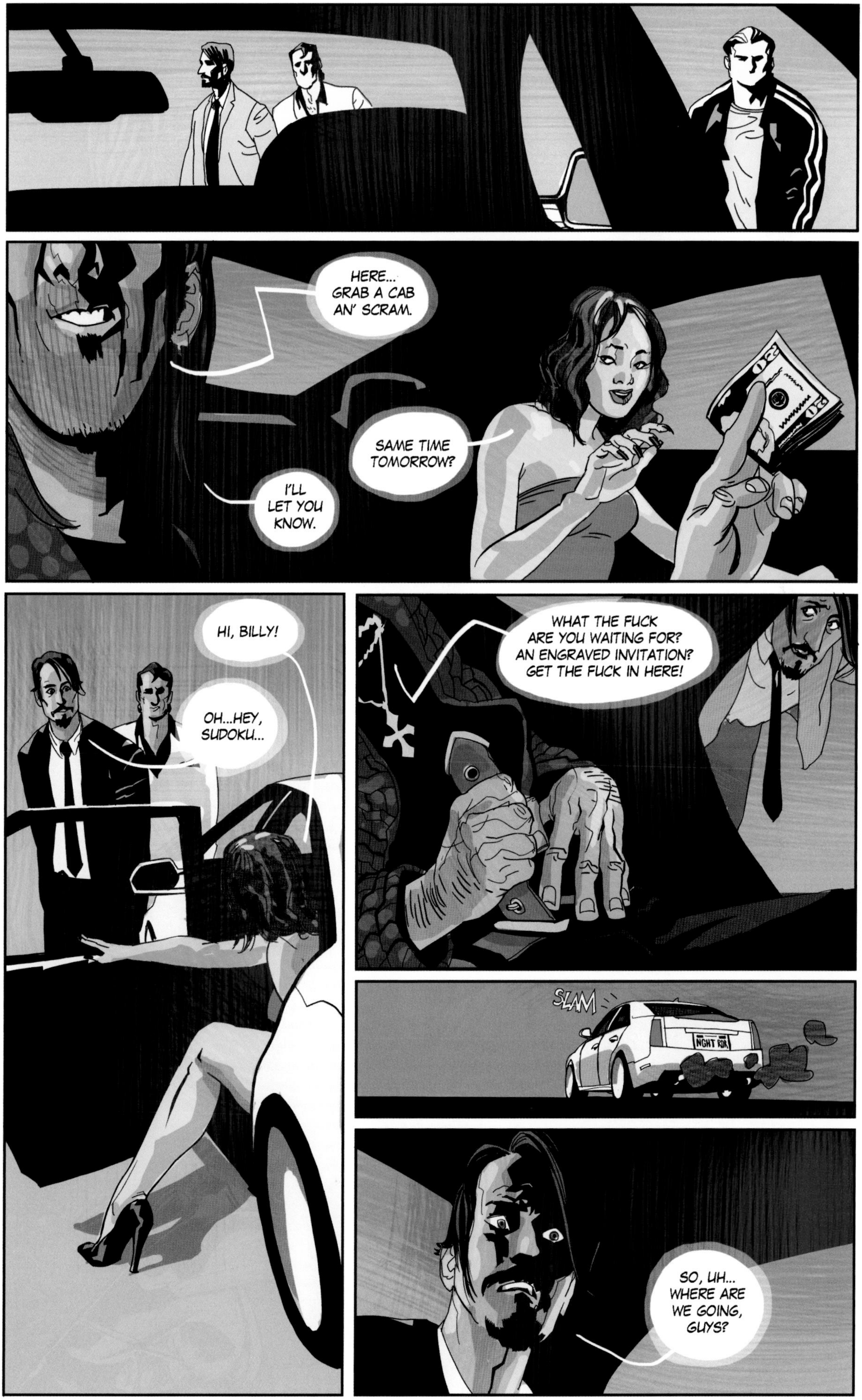
HERE... GRAB A CAB AN' SCRAM.
SAME TIME TOMORROW?
I'LL LET YOU KNOW.
HI, BILLY!
OH...HEY, SUDOKU...
WHAT THE FUCK ARE YOU WAITING FOR? AN ENGRAVED INVITATION? GET THE FUCK IN HERE!
SLAM
NGHT RDR
SO, UH... WHERE ARE WE GOING, GUYS?

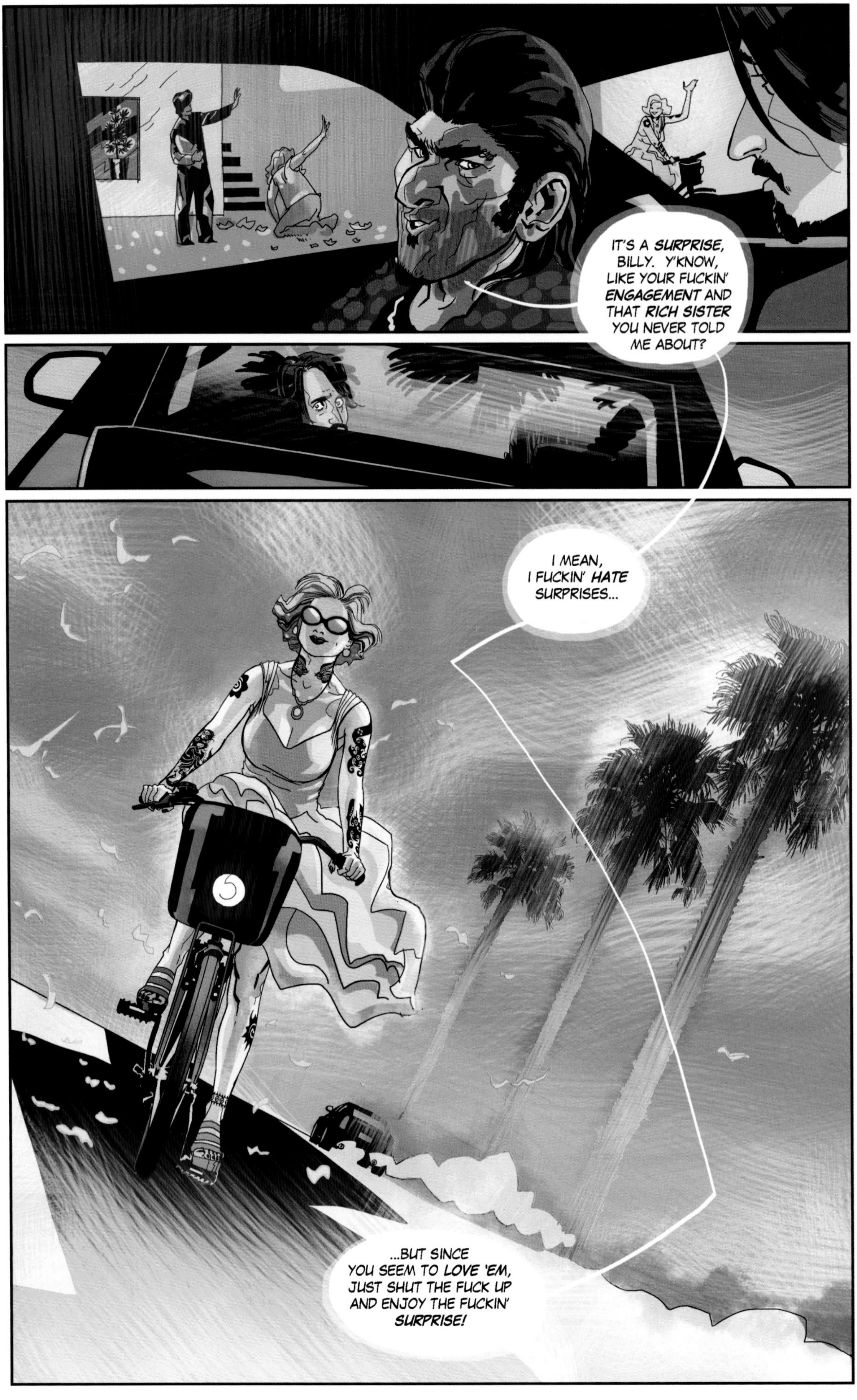
IT'S A SURPRISE, BILLY. Y'KNOW, LIKE YOUR FUCKIN' ENGAGEMENT AND THAT RICH SISTER YOU NEVER TOLD ME ABOUT?
I MEAN, I FUCKIN' HATE SURPRISES...
...BUT SINCE YOU SEEM TO LOVE 'EM, JUST SHUT THE FUCK UP AND ENJOY THE FUCKIN' SURPRISE!

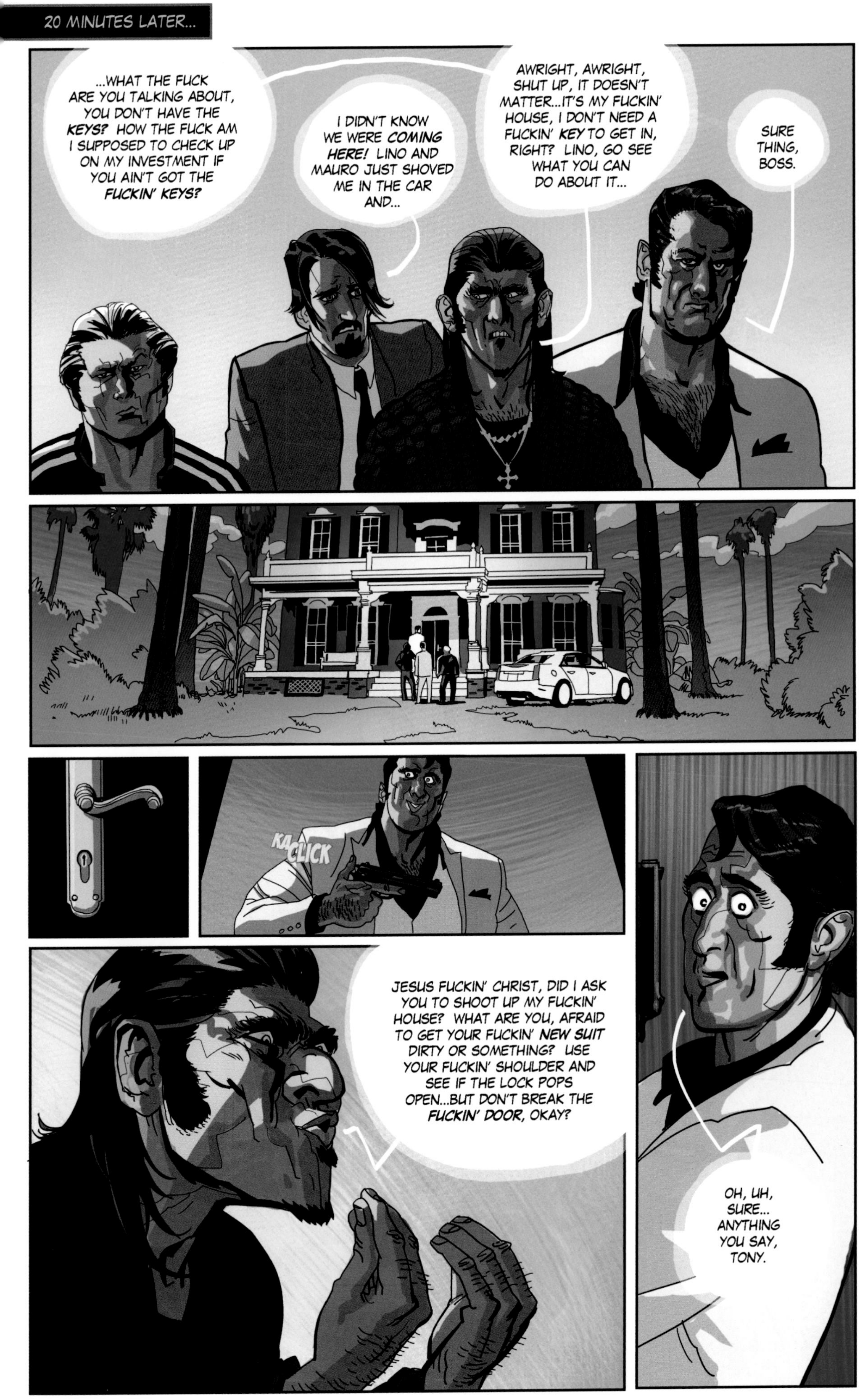
20 MINUTES LATER...
...WHAT THE FUCK ARE YOU TALKING ABOUT, YOU DON'T HAVE THE KEYS? HOW THE FUCK AM I SUPPOSED TO CHECK UP ON MY INVESTMENT IF YOU AIN'T GOT THE FUCKIN' KEYS?
I DIDN'T KNOW WE WERE COMING HERE! LINO AND MAURO JUST SHOVED ME IN THE CAR AND...
AWRIGHT, AWRIGHT, SHUT UP, IT DOESN'T MATTER...IT'S MY FUCKIN' HOUSE, I DON'T NEED A FUCKIN' KEY TO GET IN, RIGHT? LINO, GO SEE WHAT YOU CAN DO ABOUT IT...
SURE THING, BOSS.
KA CLICK
JESUS FUCKIN' CHRIST, DID I ASK YOU TO SHOOT UP MY FUCKIN' HOUSE? WHAT ARE YOU, AFRAID TO GET YOUR FUCKIN' NEW SUIT DIRTY OR SOMETHING? USE YOUR FUCKIN' SHOULDER AND SEE IF THE LOCK POPS OPEN...BUT DON'T BREAK THE FUCKIN' DOOR, OKAY?
OH, UH, SURE... ANYTHING YOU SAY, TONY.

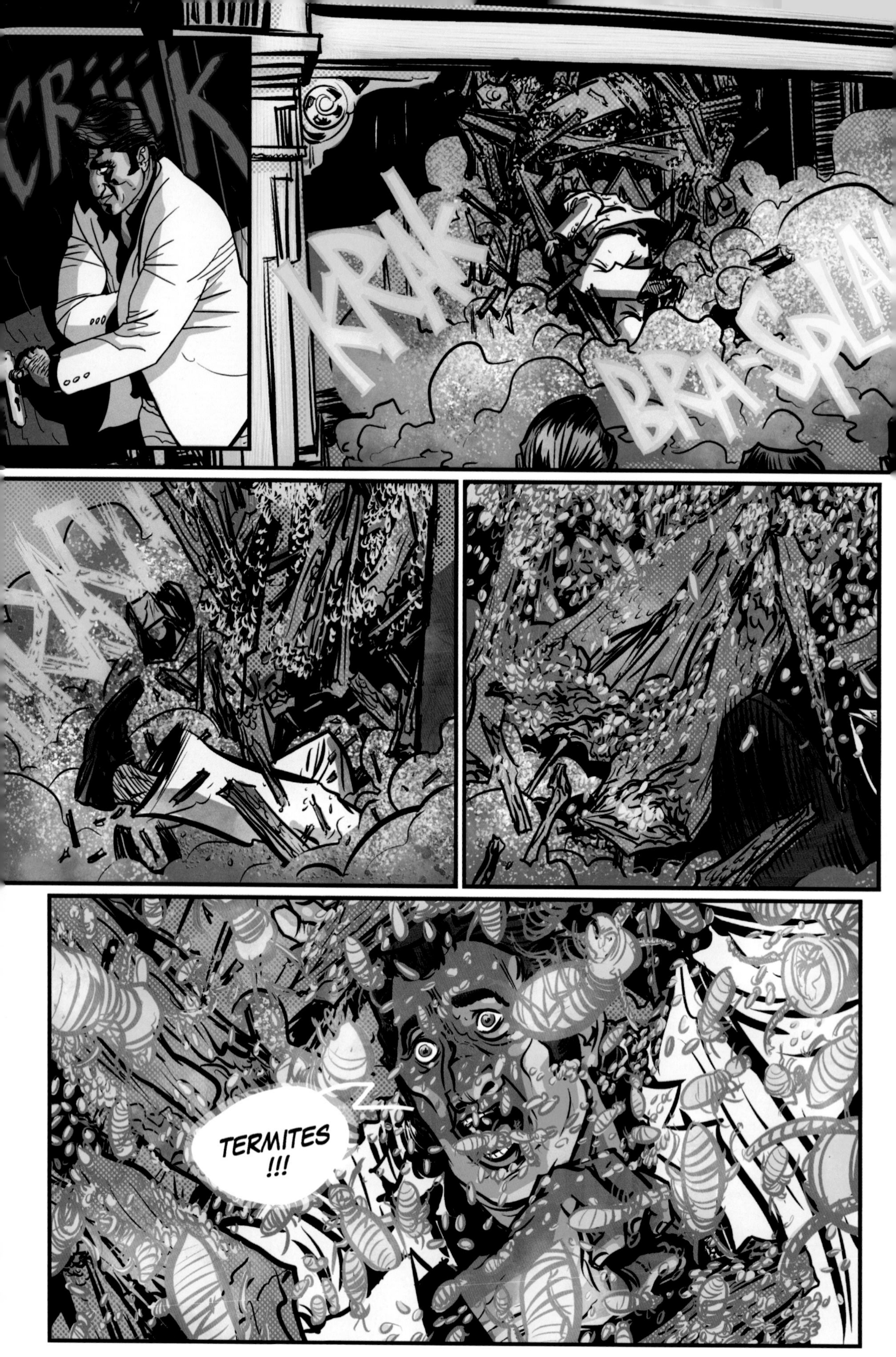
CRIIIK
KRAK
BRA-SPLA
TERMITES !!!

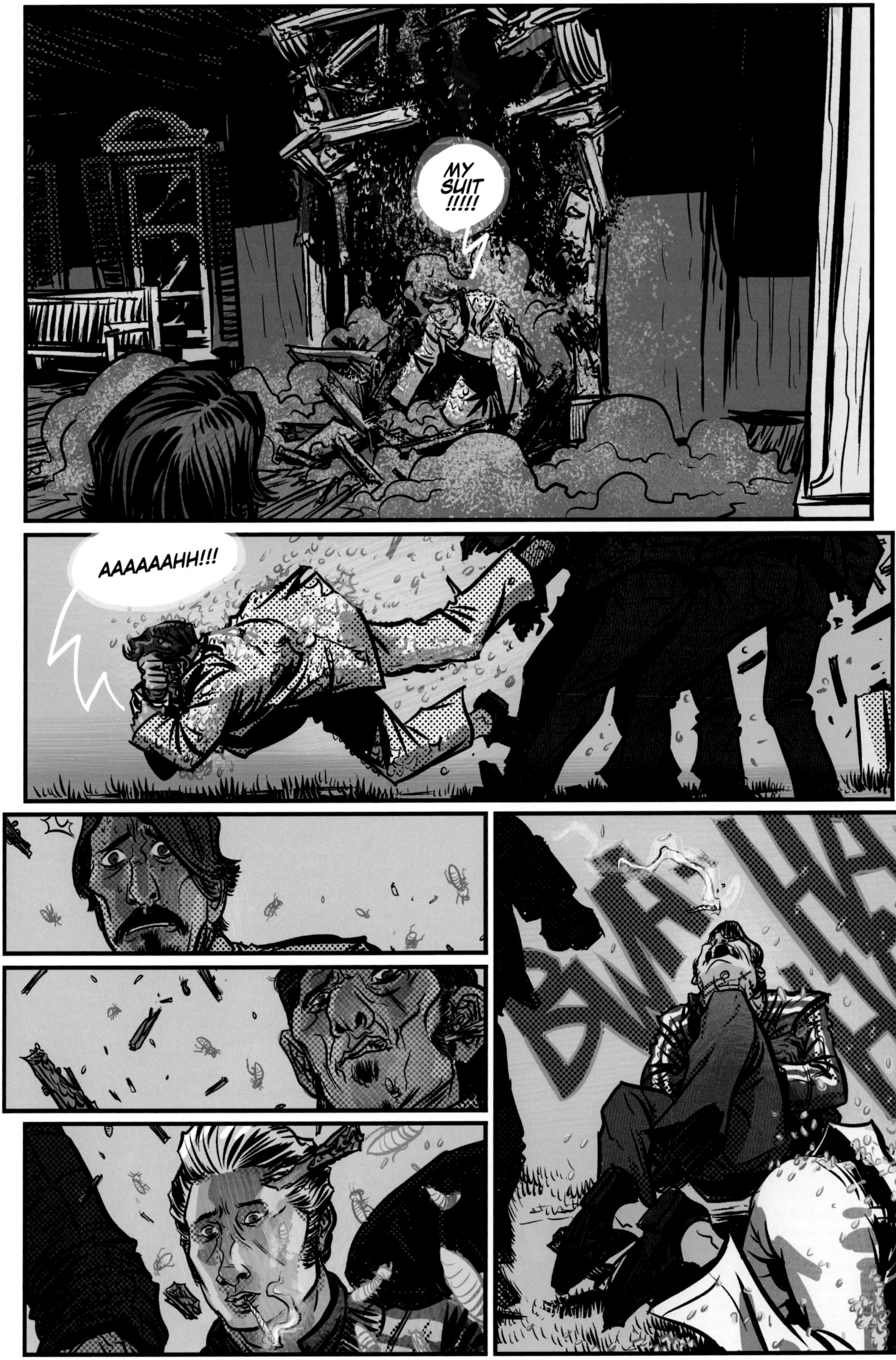
MY SUIT !!!!!
AAAAAAHH!!!

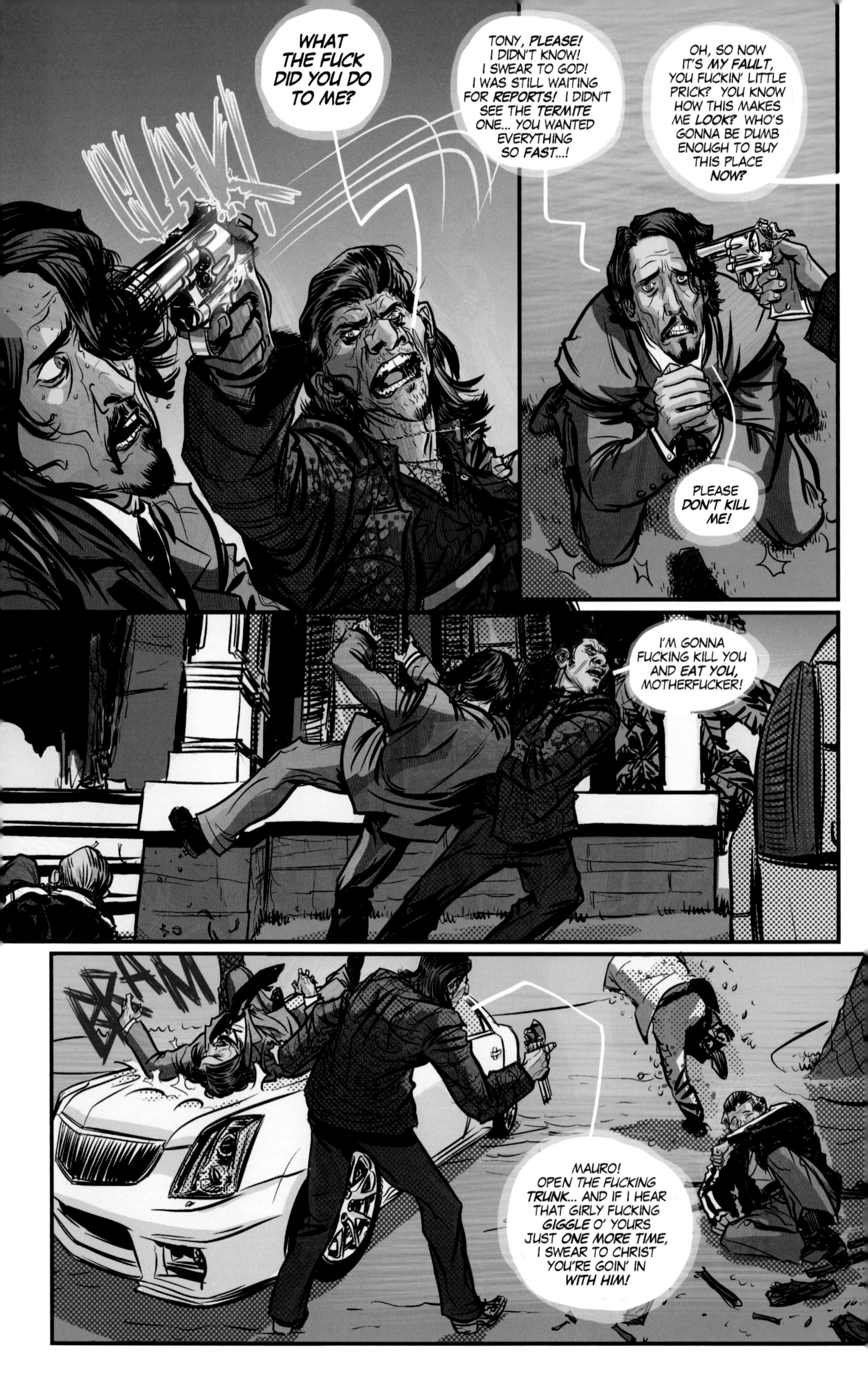
CLAK!
WHAT THE FUCK DID YOU DO TO ME?
TONY, PLEASE! I DIDN'T KNOW! I SWEAR TO GOD! I WAS STILL WAITING FOR REPORTS! I DIDN'T SEE THE TERMITE ONE... YOU WANTED EVERYTHING SO FAST...!
OH, SO NOW IT'S MY FAULT, YOU FUCKIN' LITTLE PRICK? YOU KNOW HOW THIS MAKES ME LOOK? WHO'S GONNA BE DUMB ENOUGH TO BUY THIS PLACE NOW?
PLEASE DON'T KILL ME!
I'M GONNA FUCKING KILL YOU AND EAT YOU, MOTHERFUCKER!
BAM
MAURO! OPEN THE FUCKING TRUNK... AND IF I HEAR THAT GIRLY FUCKING GIGGLE O' YOURS JUST ONE MORE TIME, I SWEAR TO CHRIST YOU'RE GOIN' IN WITH HIM!

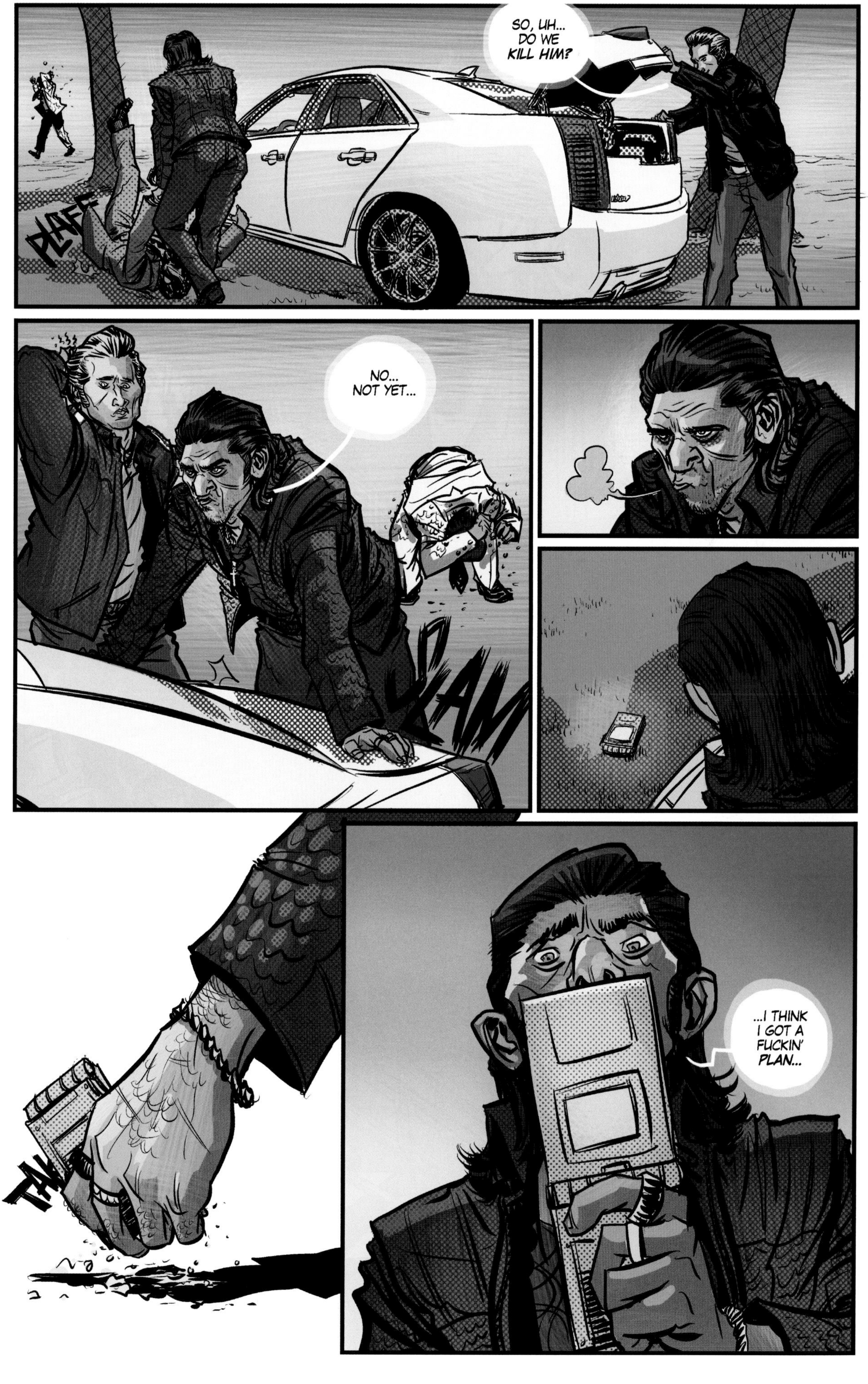
SO, UH... DO WE KILL HIM?
PLAFF
NO... NOT YET...
SLAM
TAK
...I THINK I GOT A FUCKIN' PLAN...

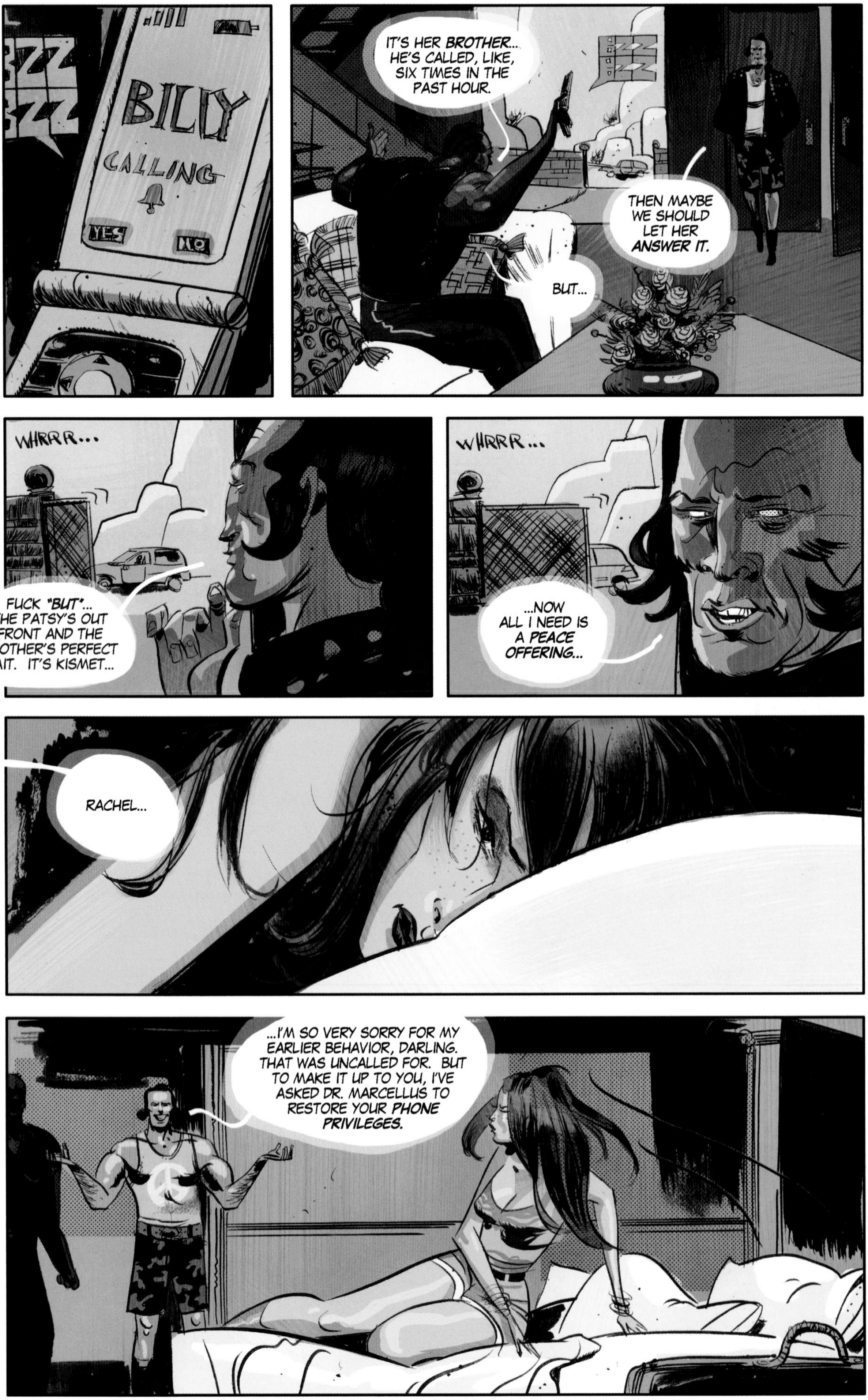
BILLY
CALLING
YES
NO
IT'S HER BROTHER... HE'S CALLED, LIKE, SIX TIMES IN THE PAST HOUR.
THEN MAYBE WE SHOULD LET HER ANSWER IT.
BUT...
WHRRR...
FUCK "BUT"... THE PATSY'S OUT FRONT AND THE BROTHER'S PERFECT BAIT. IT'S KISMET...
WHRRR...
...NOW ALL I NEED IS A PEACE OFFERING...
RACHEL...
...I'M SO VERY SORRY FOR MY EARLIER BEHAVIOR, DARLING. THAT WAS UNCALLED FOR. BUT TO MAKE IT UP TO YOU, I'VE ASKED DR. MARCELLUS TO RESTORE YOUR PHONE PRIVILEGES.

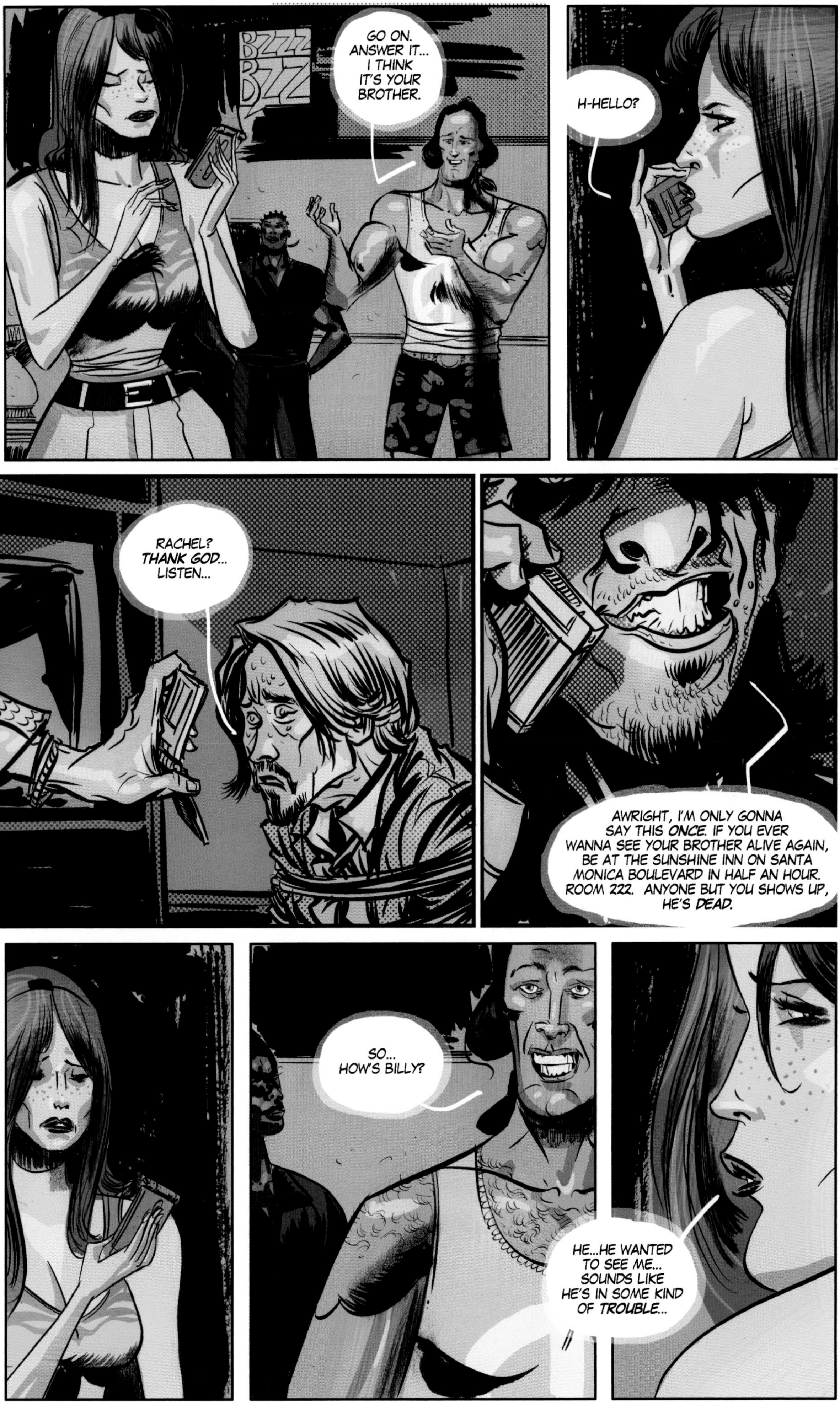
BZZZZ
BZZZ
GO ON. ANSWER IT... I THINK IT'S YOUR BROTHER.
H-HELLO?
RACHEL? THANK GOD... LISTEN...
AWRIGHT, I'M ONLY GONNA SAY THIS ONCE. IF YOU EVER WANNA SEE YOUR BROTHER ALIVE AGAIN, BE AT THE SUNSHINE INN ON SANTA MONICA BOULEVARD IN HALF AN HOUR. ROOM 222. ANYONE BUT YOU SHOWS UP, HE'S DEAD.
SO... HOW'S BILLY?
HE...HE WANTED TO SEE ME... SOUNDS LIKE HE'S IN SOME KIND OF TROUBLE...

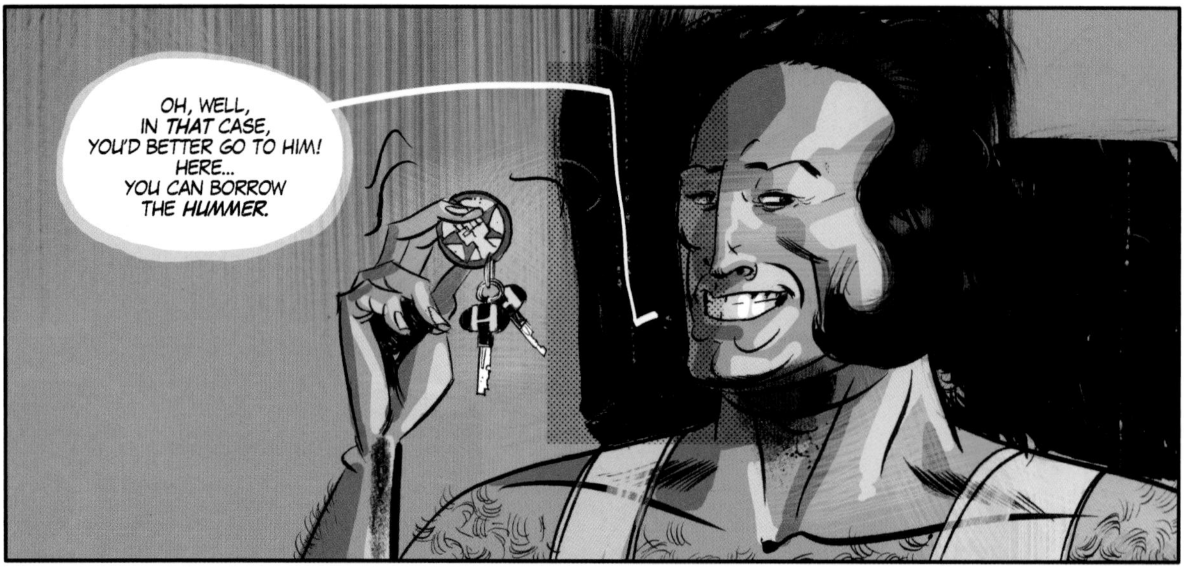
OH, WELL, IN *THAT* CASE, YOU'D BETTER GO TO HIM! HERE... YOU CAN BORROW THE *HUMMER.*

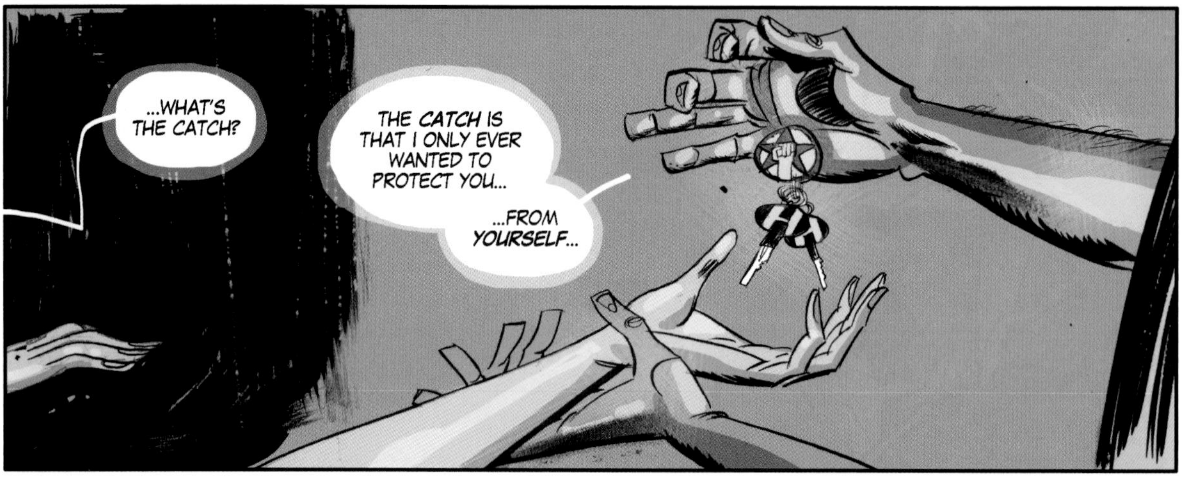
...WHAT'S THE CATCH?
THE *CATCH* IS THAT I ONLY EVER WANTED TO PROTECT YOU...
...FROM *YOURSELF*...

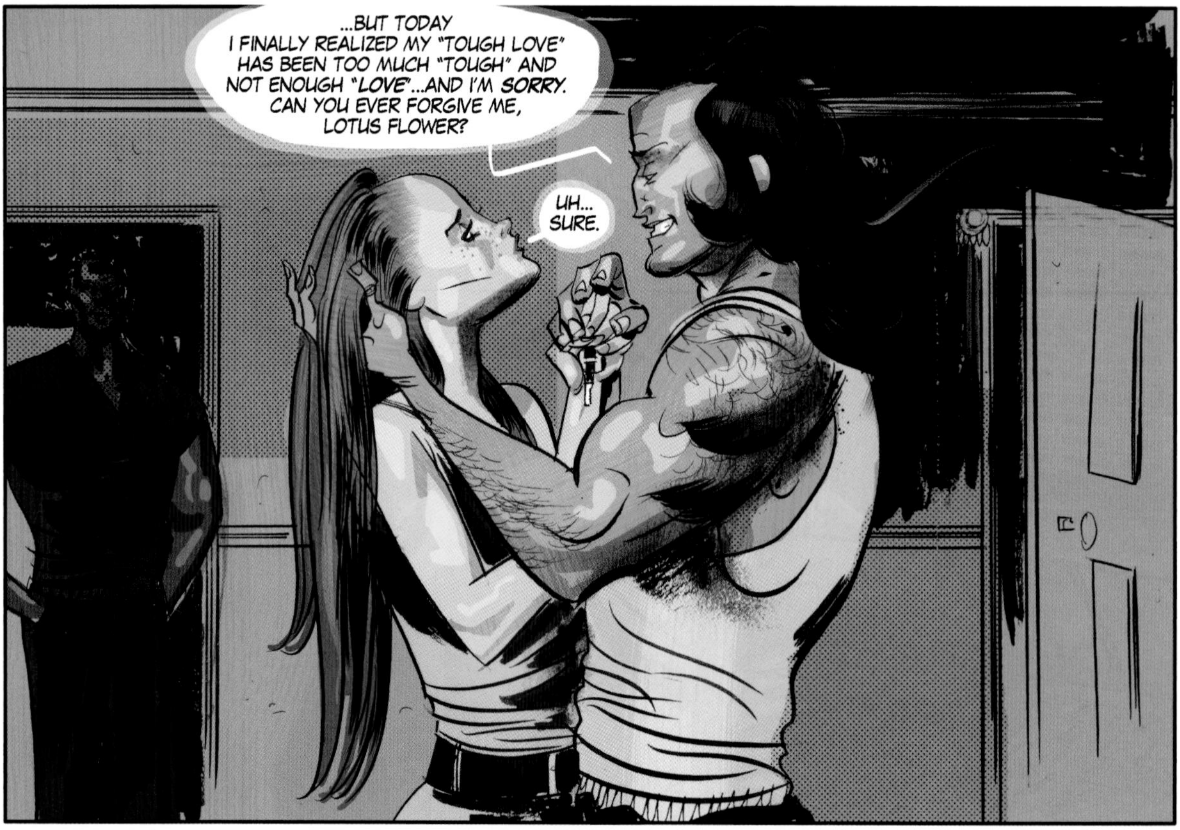
...BUT TODAY I FINALLY REALIZED MY "TOUGH LOVE" HAS BEEN TOO MUCH "TOUGH" AND NOT ENOUGH "*LOVE*"...AND I'M *SORRY.* CAN YOU EVER FORGIVE ME, LOTUS FLOWER?
UH... SURE.

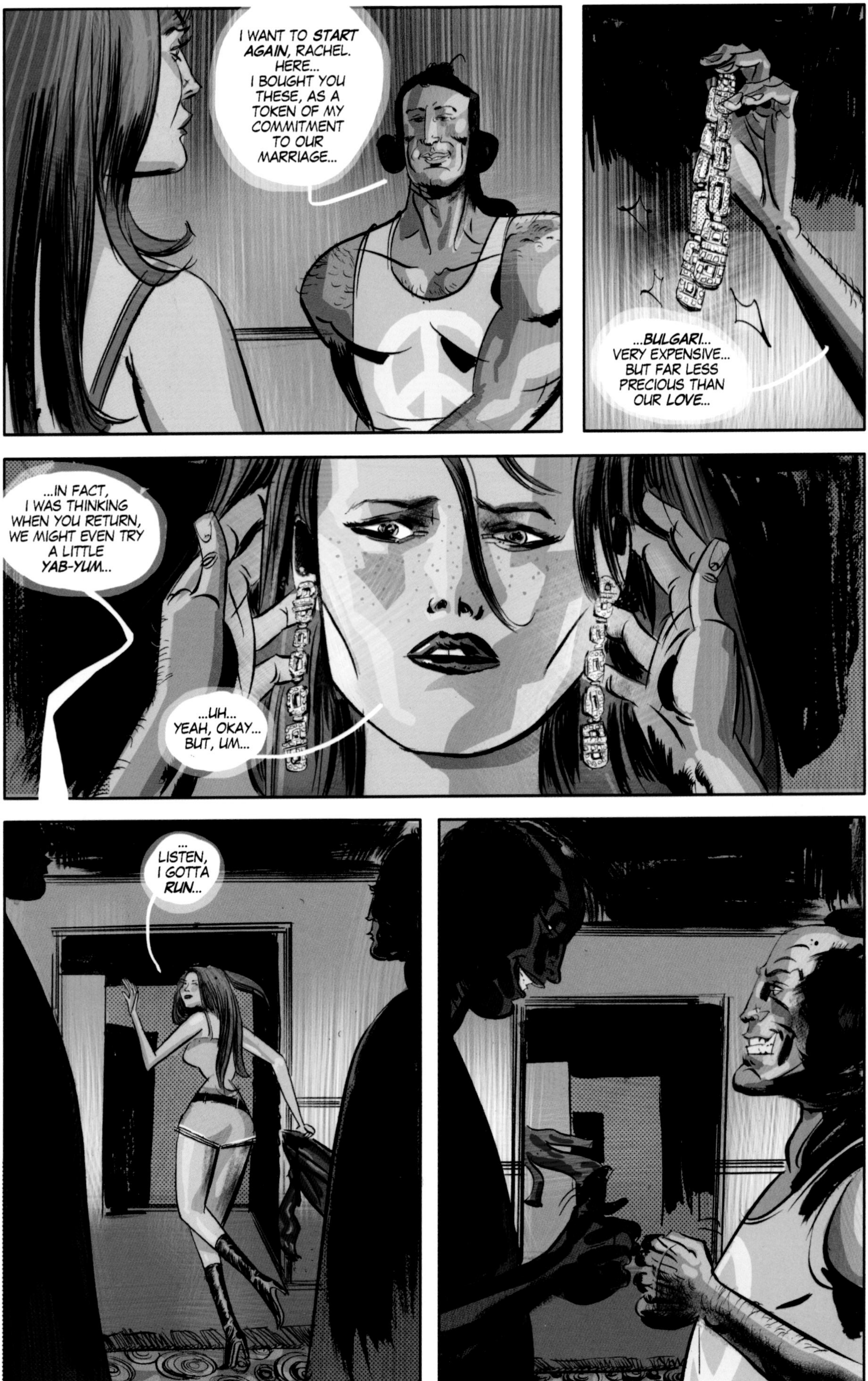
I WANT TO START AGAIN, RACHEL. HERE... I BOUGHT YOU THESE, AS A TOKEN OF MY COMMITMENT TO OUR MARRIAGE...
...BULGARI... VERY EXPENSIVE... BUT FAR LESS PRECIOUS THAN OUR LOVE...
...IN FACT, I WAS THINKING WHEN YOU RETURN, WE MIGHT EVEN TRY A LITTLE YAB-YUM...
...UH... YEAH, OKAY... BUT, UM...
... LISTEN, I GOTTA RUN...

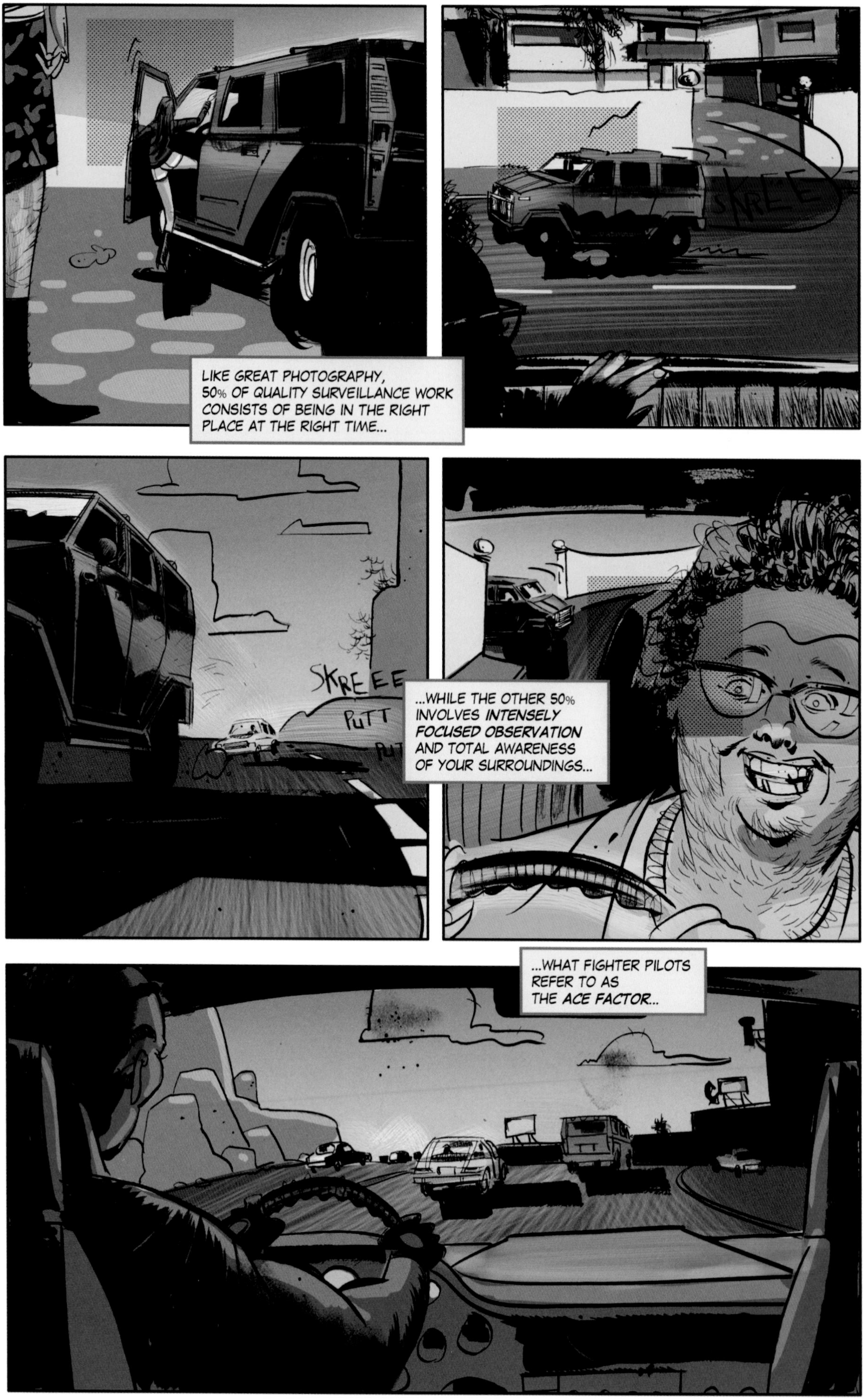
LIKE GREAT PHOTOGRAPHY, 50% OF QUALITY SURVEILLANCE WORK CONSISTS OF BEING IN THE RIGHT PLACE AT THE RIGHT TIME...
SKREEE
PUTT
...WHILE THE OTHER 50% INVOLVES INTENSELY FOCUSED OBSERVATION AND TOTAL AWARENESS OF YOUR SURROUNDINGS...
...WHAT FIGHTER PILOTS REFER TO AS THE ACE FACTOR...

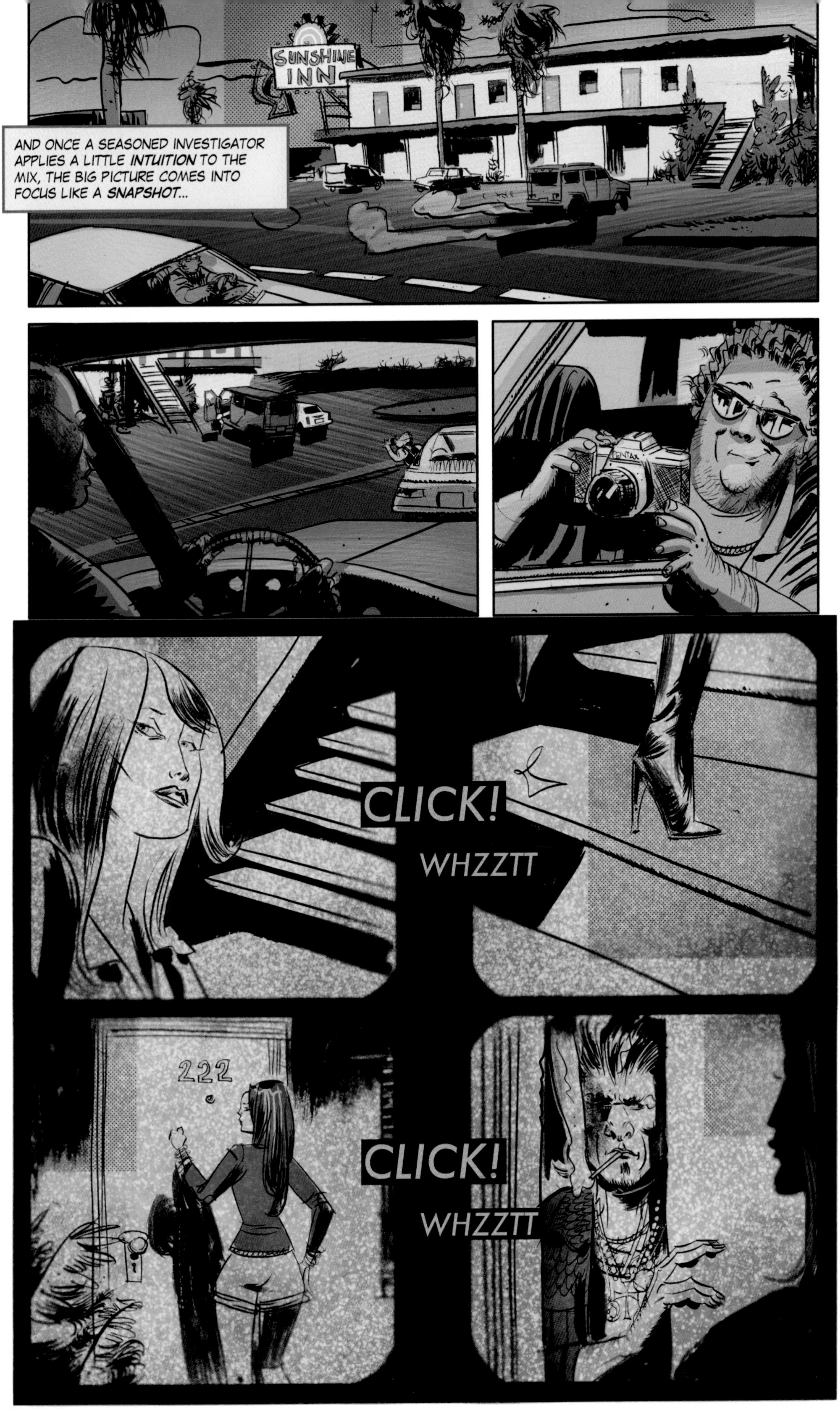
SUNSHINE INN
AND ONCE A SEASONED INVESTIGATOR APPLIES A LITTLE INTUITION TO THE MIX, THE BIG PICTURE COMES INTO FOCUS LIKE A SNAPSHOT...
CLICK!
WHZZTT
222
CLICK!
WHZZTT

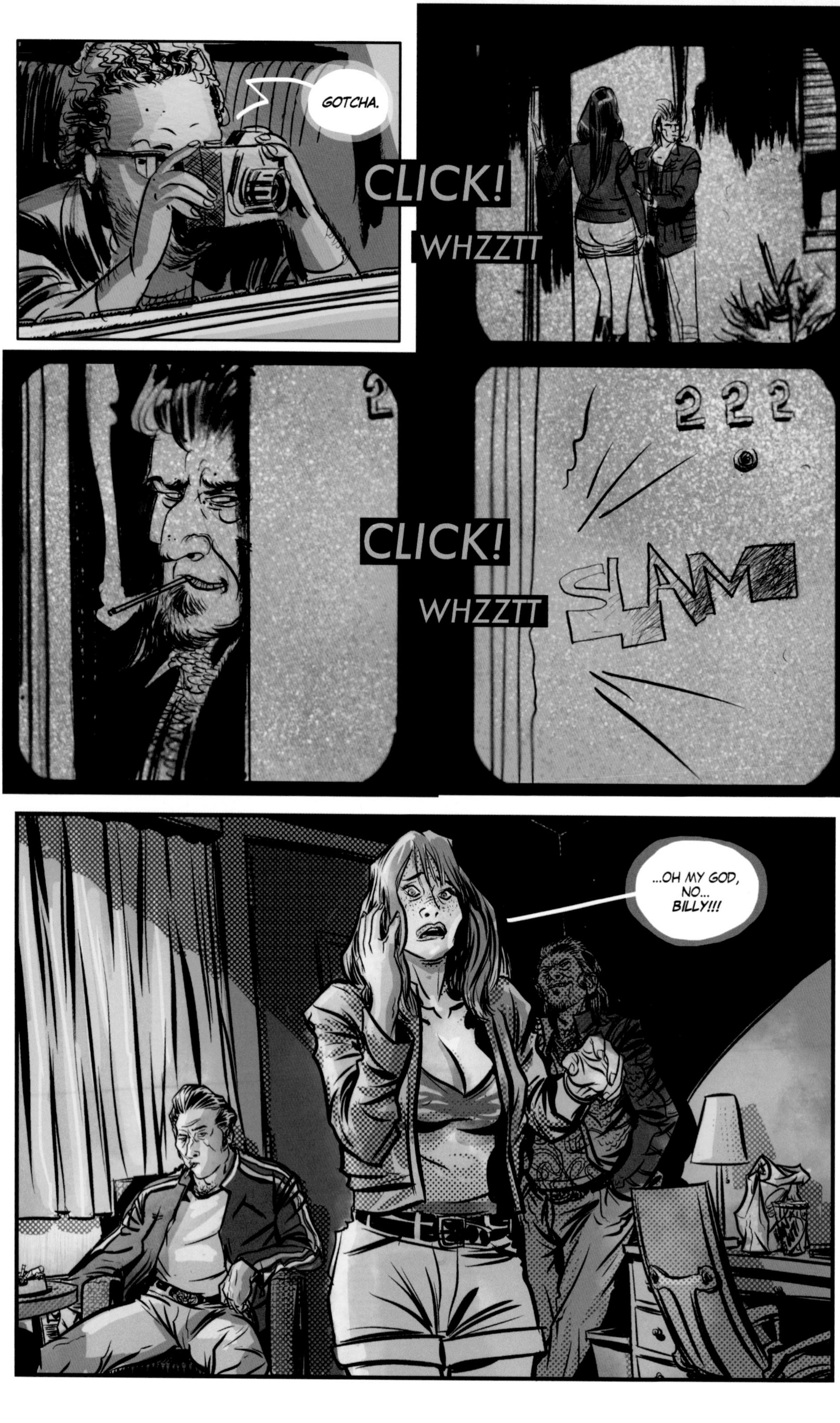
GOTCHA.
CLICK!
WHZZTT
CLICK!
WHZZTT
222
SLAM
...OH MY GOD,
NO...
BILLY!!!

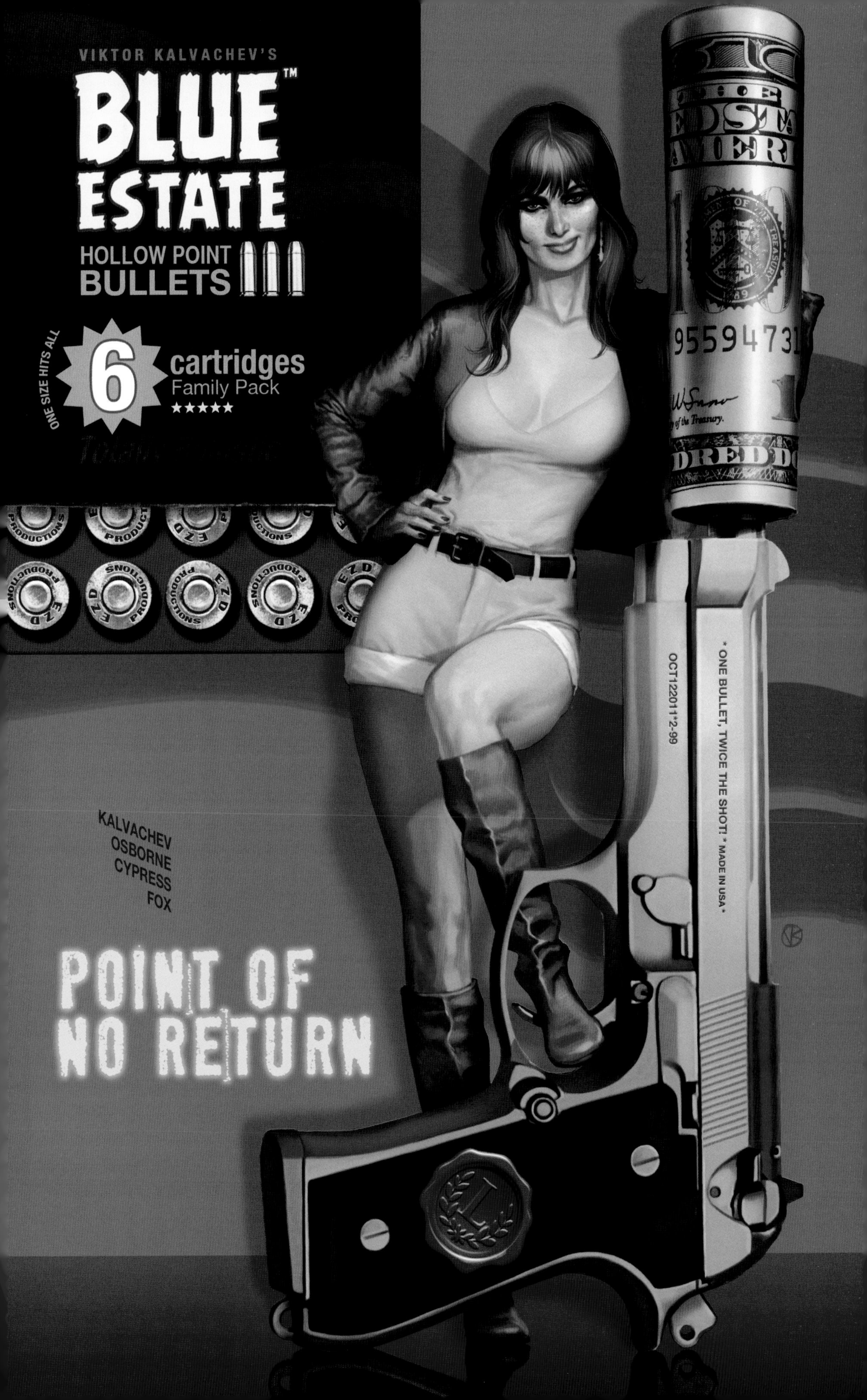
VIKTOR KALVACHEV'S
BLUE ESTATE™
HOLLOW POINT BULLETS
ONE SIZE HITS ALL
6 cartridges
Family Pack
★★★★★
EZD PRODUCTIONS
OCT112011*2.99
* ONE BULLET, TWICE THE SHOT! * MADE IN USA *
KALVACHEV
OSBORNE
CYPRESS
FOX
POINT OF NO RETURN

# BLUE ESTATE™

## EPISODE SIX:
## POINT OF NO RETURN

ORIGINAL STORY:
**VIKTOR KALVACHEV** AND **KOSTA YANEV**

SCRIPT BY **ANDREW OSBORNE**

ARTISTS:
**VIKTOR KALVACHEV**
**TOBY CYPRESS**
**NATHAN FOX**

ART DIRECTION BY **VIKTOR KALVACHEV**

COVER, COLORS & DESIGN:
**VIKTOR KALVACHEV**

CONTRIBUTING EDITOR:
**PHILO NORTHRUP**

www.BlueEstateComic.com

EZD™
PRODUCTIONS

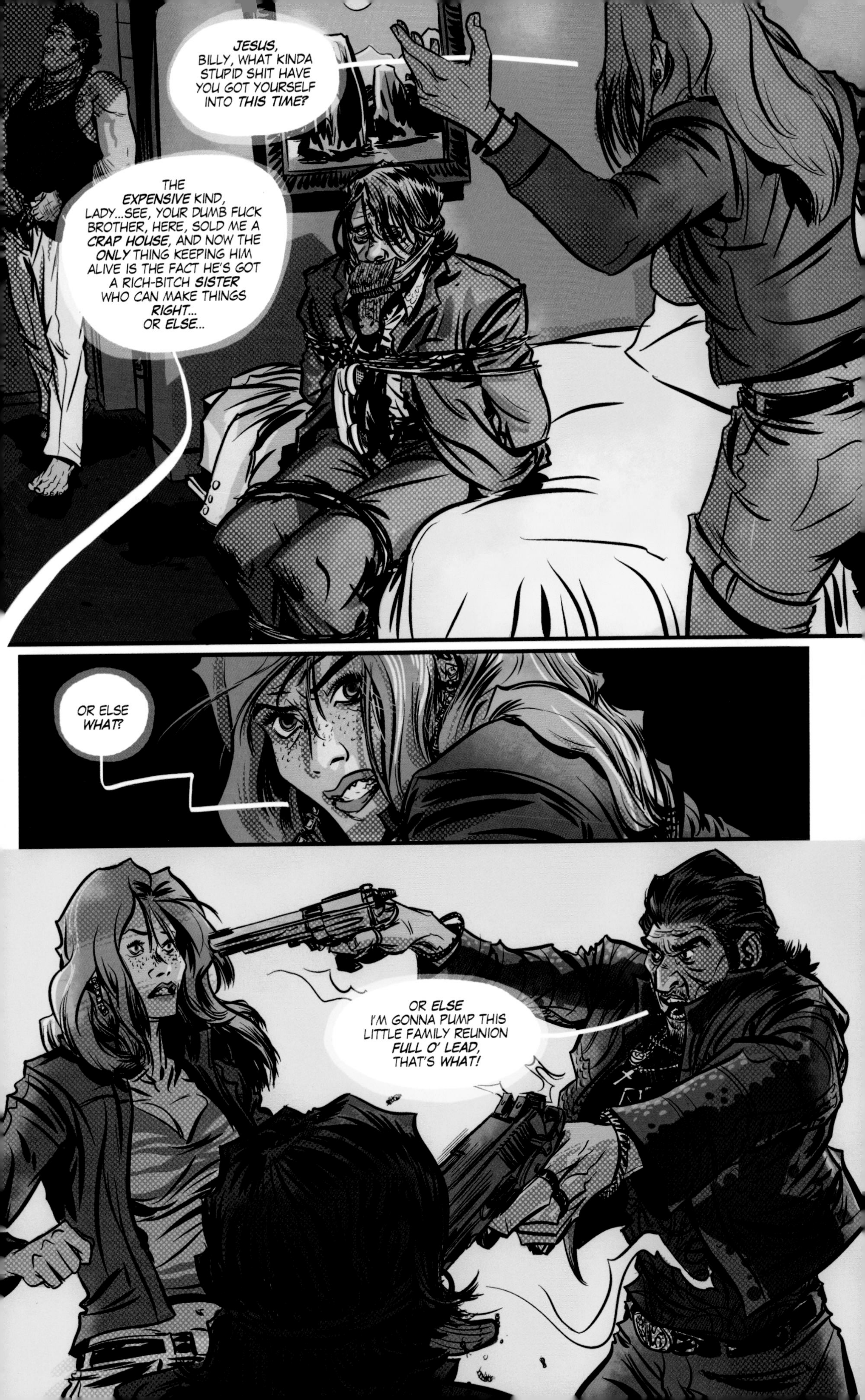
JESUS, BILLY, WHAT KINDA STUPID SHIT HAVE YOU GOT YOURSELF INTO THIS TIME?
THE EXPENSIVE KIND, LADY...SEE, YOUR DUMB FUCK BROTHER, HERE, SOLD ME A CRAP HOUSE, AND NOW THE ONLY THING KEEPING HIM ALIVE IS THE FACT HE'S GOT A RICH-BITCH SISTER WHO CAN MAKE THINGS RIGHT... OR ELSE...
OR ELSE WHAT?
OR ELSE I'M GONNA PUMP THIS LITTLE FAMILY REUNION FULL O' LEAD, THAT'S WHAT!

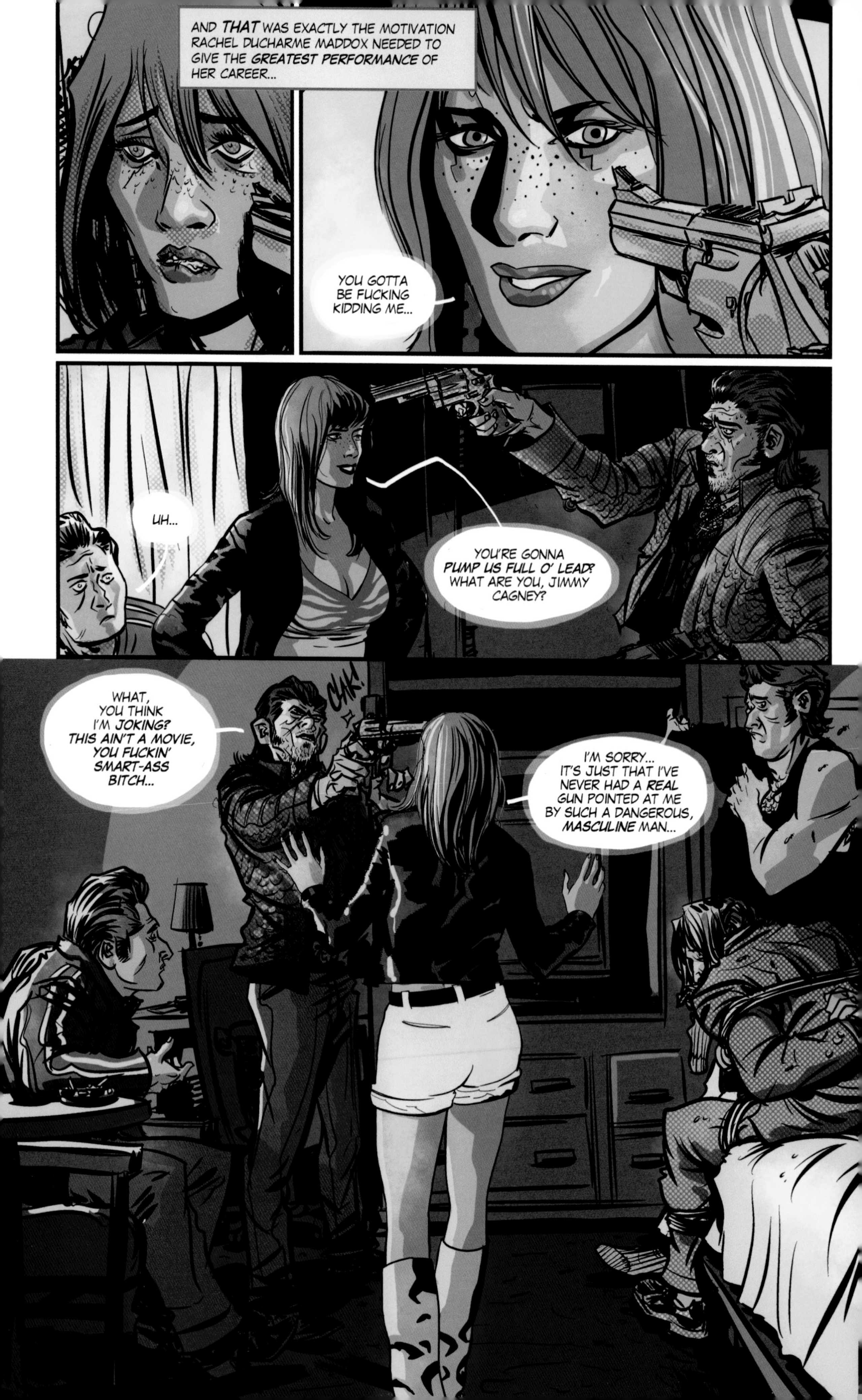
AND THAT WAS EXACTLY THE MOTIVATION RACHEL DUCHARME MADDOX NEEDED TO GIVE THE GREATEST PERFORMANCE OF HER CAREER...
YOU GOTTA BE FUCKING KIDDING ME...
UH...
YOU'RE GONNA PUMP US FULL O' LEAD? WHAT ARE YOU, JIMMY CAGNEY?
CLAK!
WHAT, YOU THINK I'M JOKING? THIS AIN'T A MOVIE, YOU FUCKIN' SMART-ASS BITCH...
I'M SORRY... IT'S JUST THAT I'VE NEVER HAD A REAL GUN POINTED AT ME BY SUCH A DANGEROUS, MASCULINE MAN...

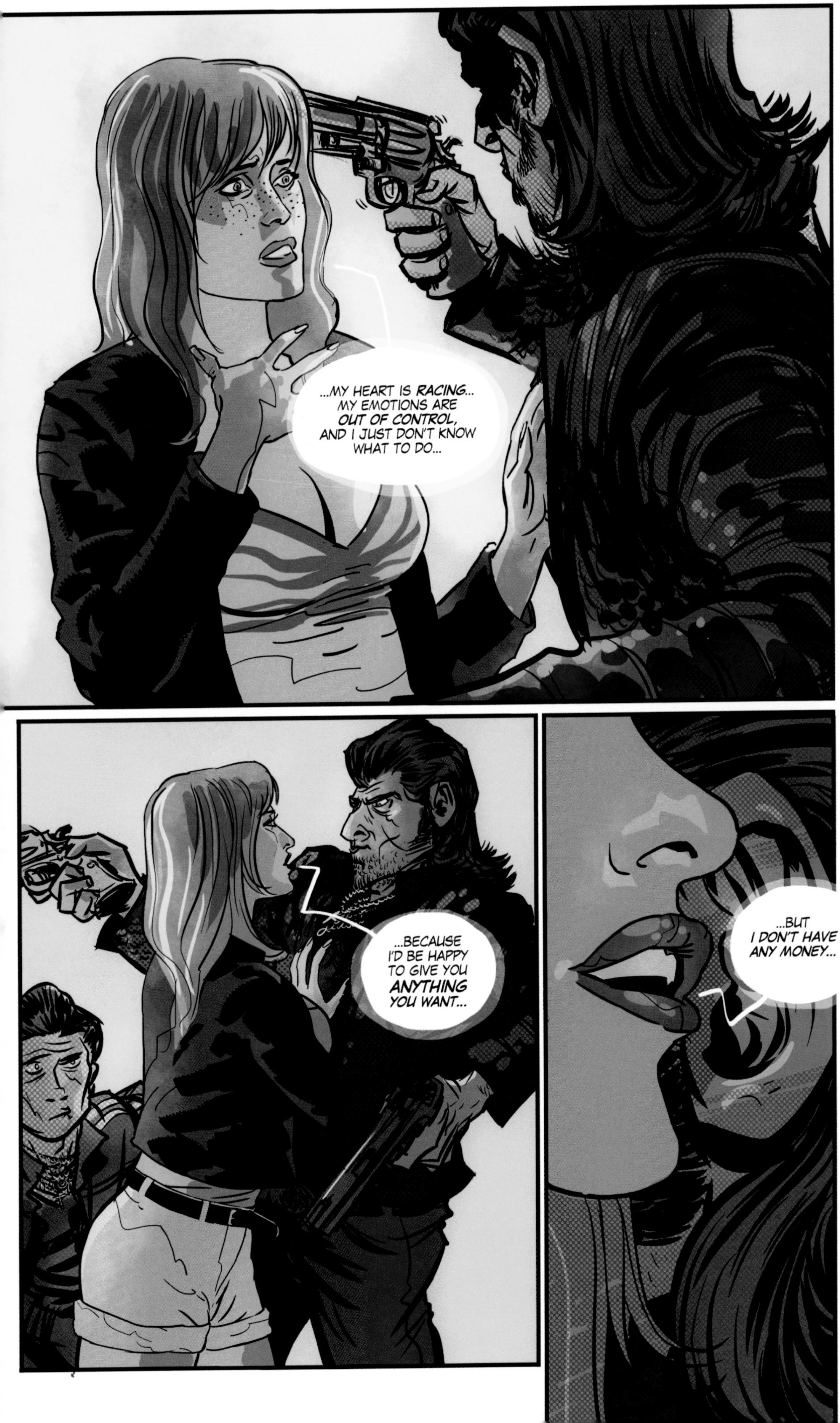
...MY HEART IS RACING... MY EMOTIONS ARE OUT OF CONTROL, AND I JUST DON'T KNOW WHAT TO DO...
...BECAUSE I'D BE HAPPY TO GIVE YOU ANYTHING YOU WANT...
...BUT I DON'T HAVE ANY MONEY...

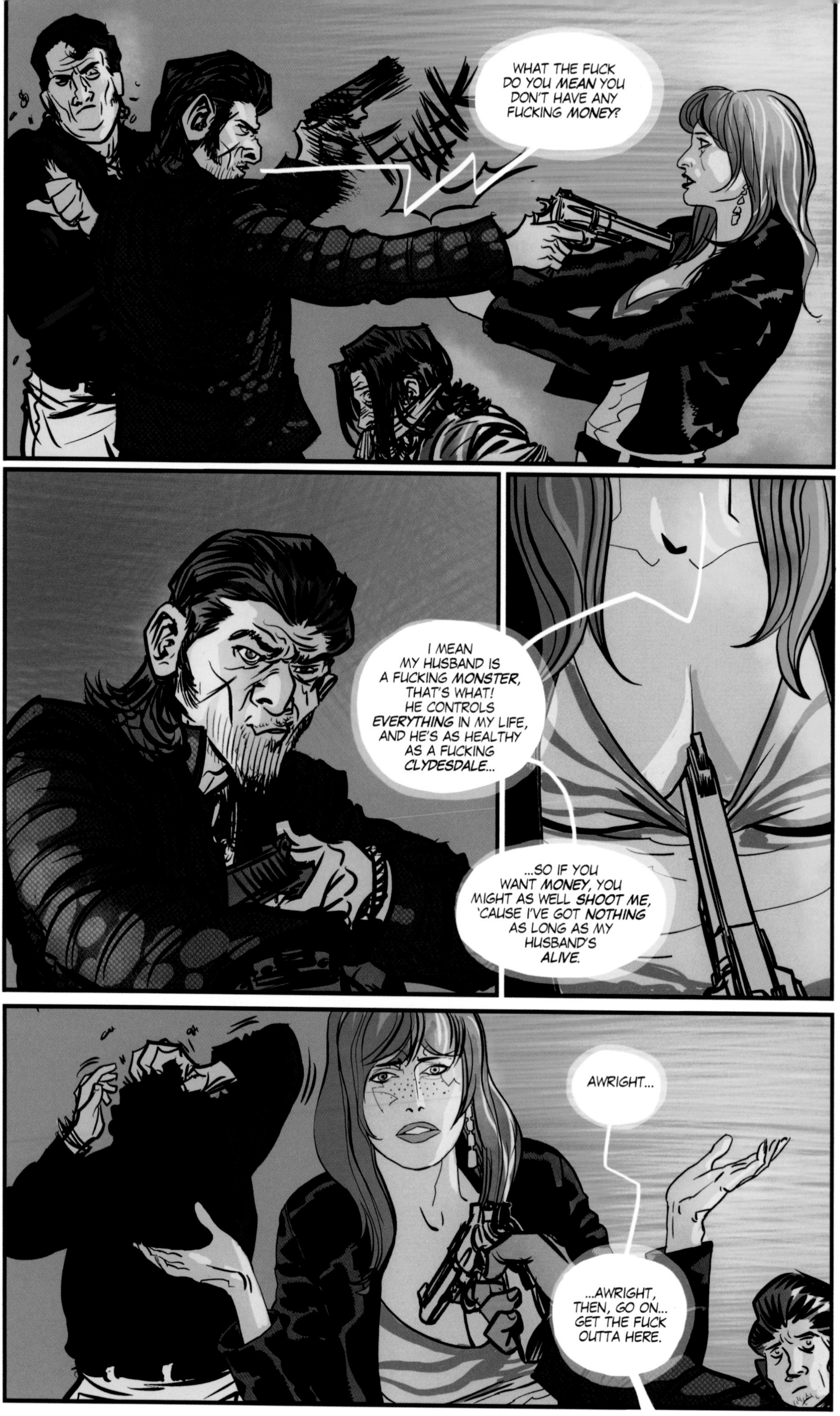
WHAT THE FUCK DO YOU MEAN YOU DON'T HAVE ANY FUCKING MONEY?
FWAK
I MEAN MY HUSBAND IS A FUCKING MONSTER, THAT'S WHAT! HE CONTROLS EVERYTHING IN MY LIFE, AND HE'S AS HEALTHY AS A FUCKING CLYDESDALE...
...SO IF YOU WANT MONEY, YOU MIGHT AS WELL SHOOT ME, 'CAUSE I'VE GOT NOTHING AS LONG AS MY HUSBAND'S ALIVE.
AWRIGHT...
...AWRIGHT, THEN, GO ON... GET THE FUCK OUTTA HERE.

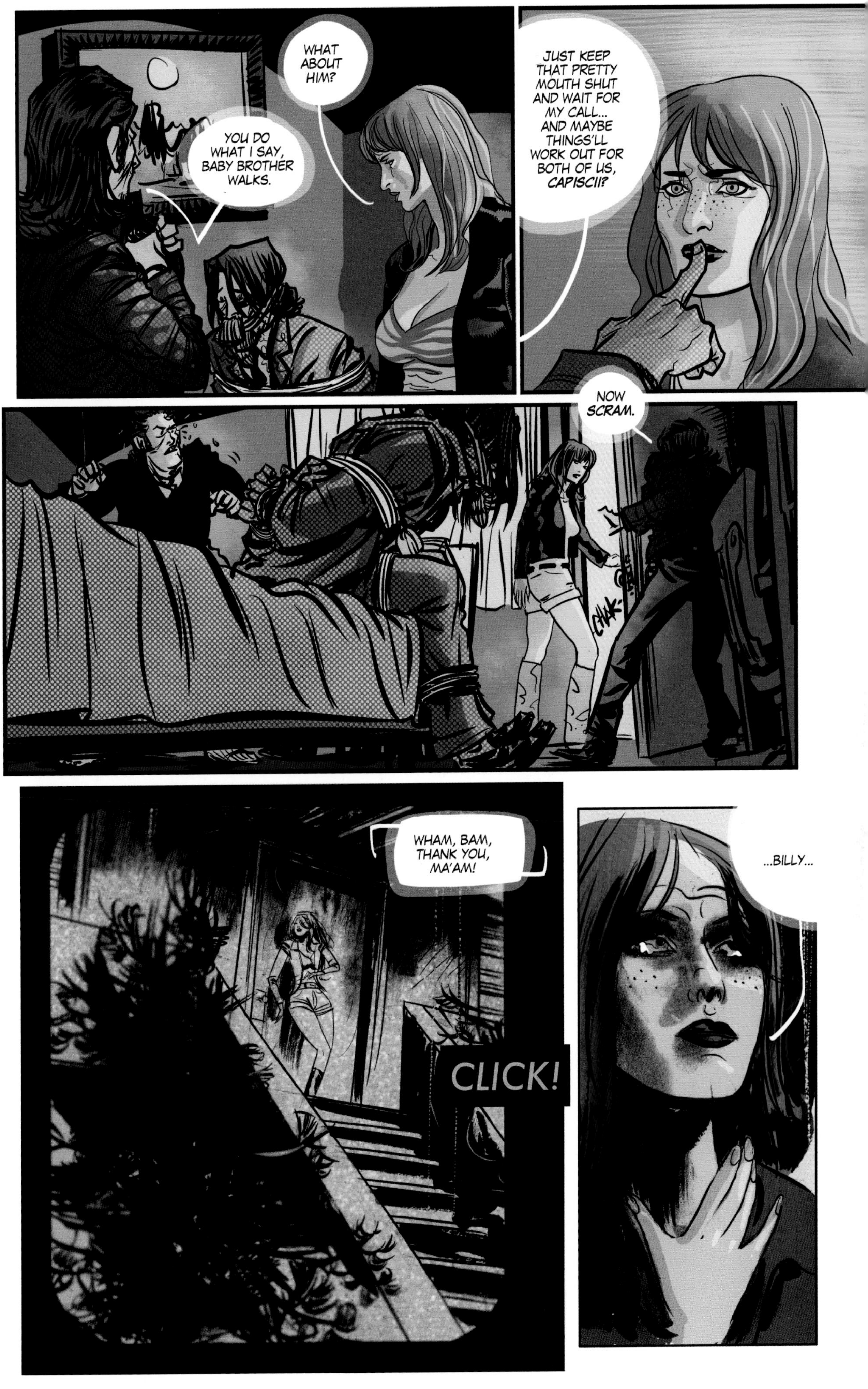
WHAT ABOUT HIM?
YOU DO WHAT I SAY, BABY BROTHER WALKS.
JUST KEEP THAT PRETTY MOUTH SHUT AND WAIT FOR MY CALL... AND MAYBE THINGS'LL WORK OUT FOR BOTH OF US, CAPISCI!?
NOW SCRAM.
CHAK
WHAM, BAM, THANK YOU, MA'AM!
CLICK!
...BILLY...

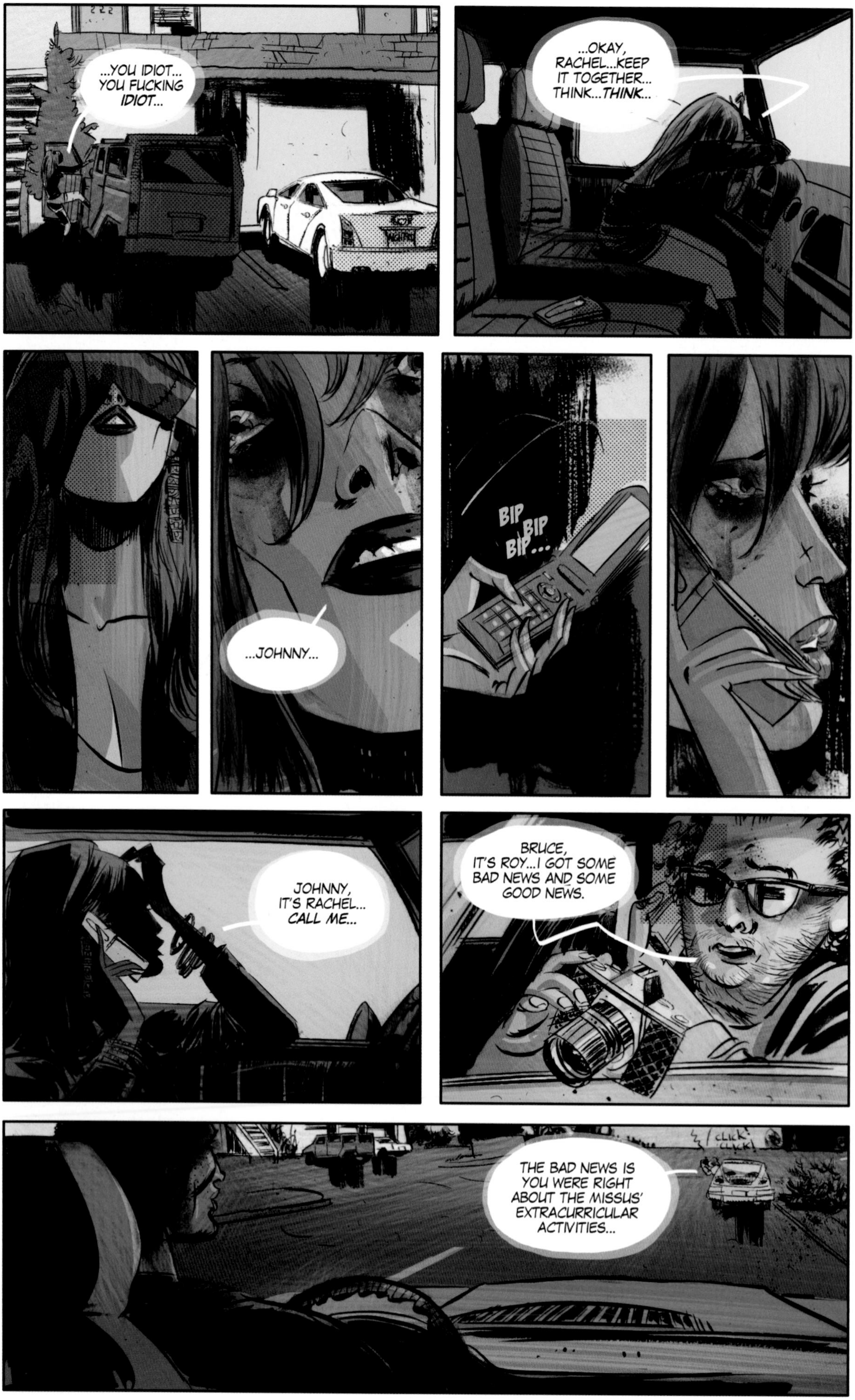

...YOU IDIOT... YOU FUCKING *IDIOT*...
...OKAY, RACHEL...KEEP IT TOGETHER... THINK...*THINK*...
...JOHNNY...
BIP BIP BIP...
JOHNNY, IT'S RACHEL... *CALL ME*...
BRUCE, IT'S ROY...I GOT SOME BAD NEWS AND SOME GOOD NEWS.
CLICK! CLICK!
THE BAD NEWS IS YOU WERE RIGHT ABOUT THE MISSUS' EXTRACURRICULAR ACTIVITIES...

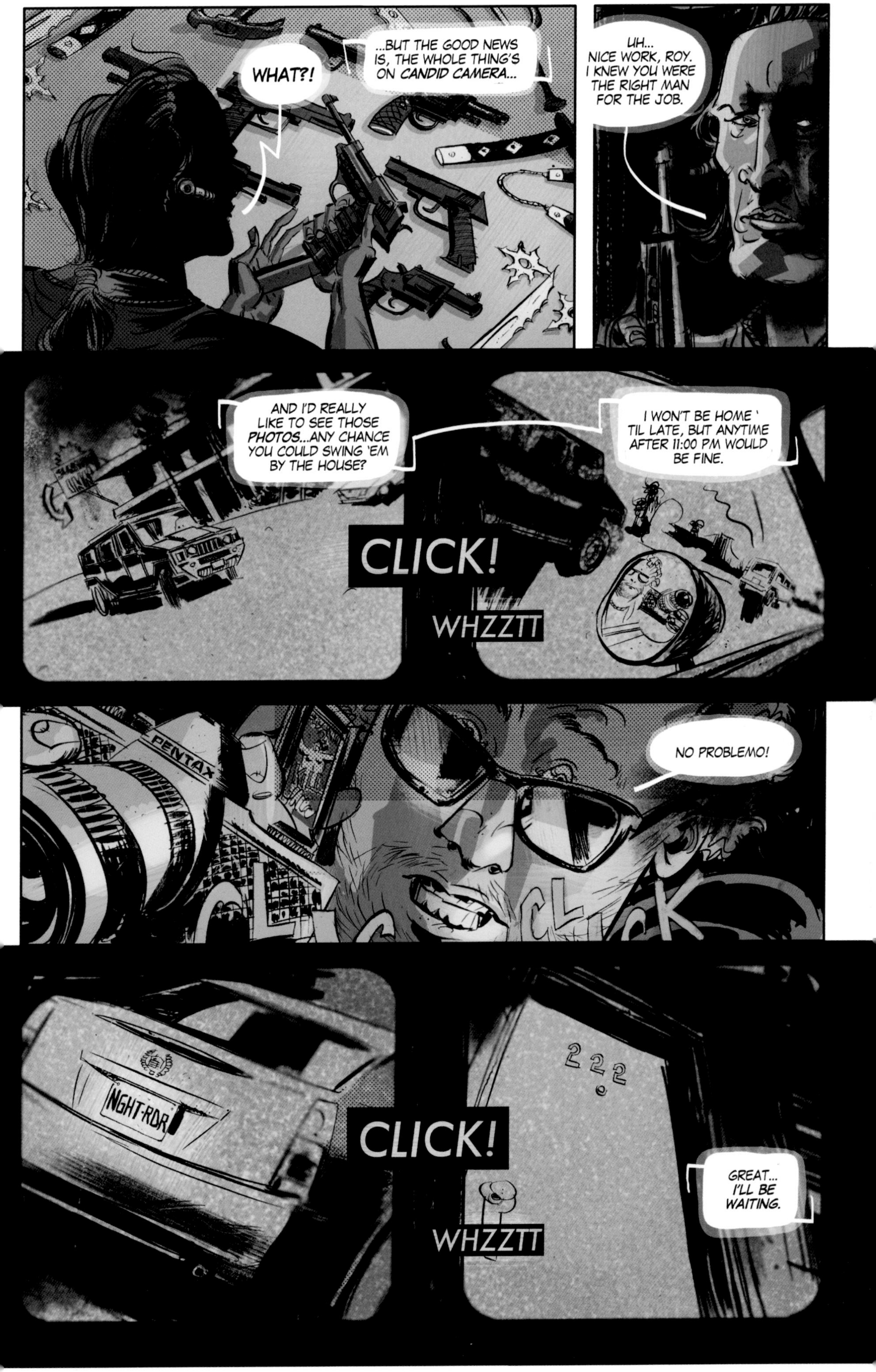
WHAT?!
...BUT THE GOOD NEWS IS, THE WHOLE THING'S ON CANDID CAMERA...
UH... NICE WORK, ROY. I KNEW YOU WERE THE RIGHT MAN FOR THE JOB.
AND I'D REALLY LIKE TO SEE THOSE PHOTOS...ANY CHANCE YOU COULD SWING 'EM BY THE HOUSE?
I WON'T BE HOME 'TIL LATE, BUT ANYTIME AFTER 11:00 PM WOULD BE FINE.
CLICK!
WHZZTT
PENTAX
NO PROBLEMO!
CLICK
NGHT-RDR
222
CLICK!
WHZZTT
GREAT... I'LL BE WAITING.

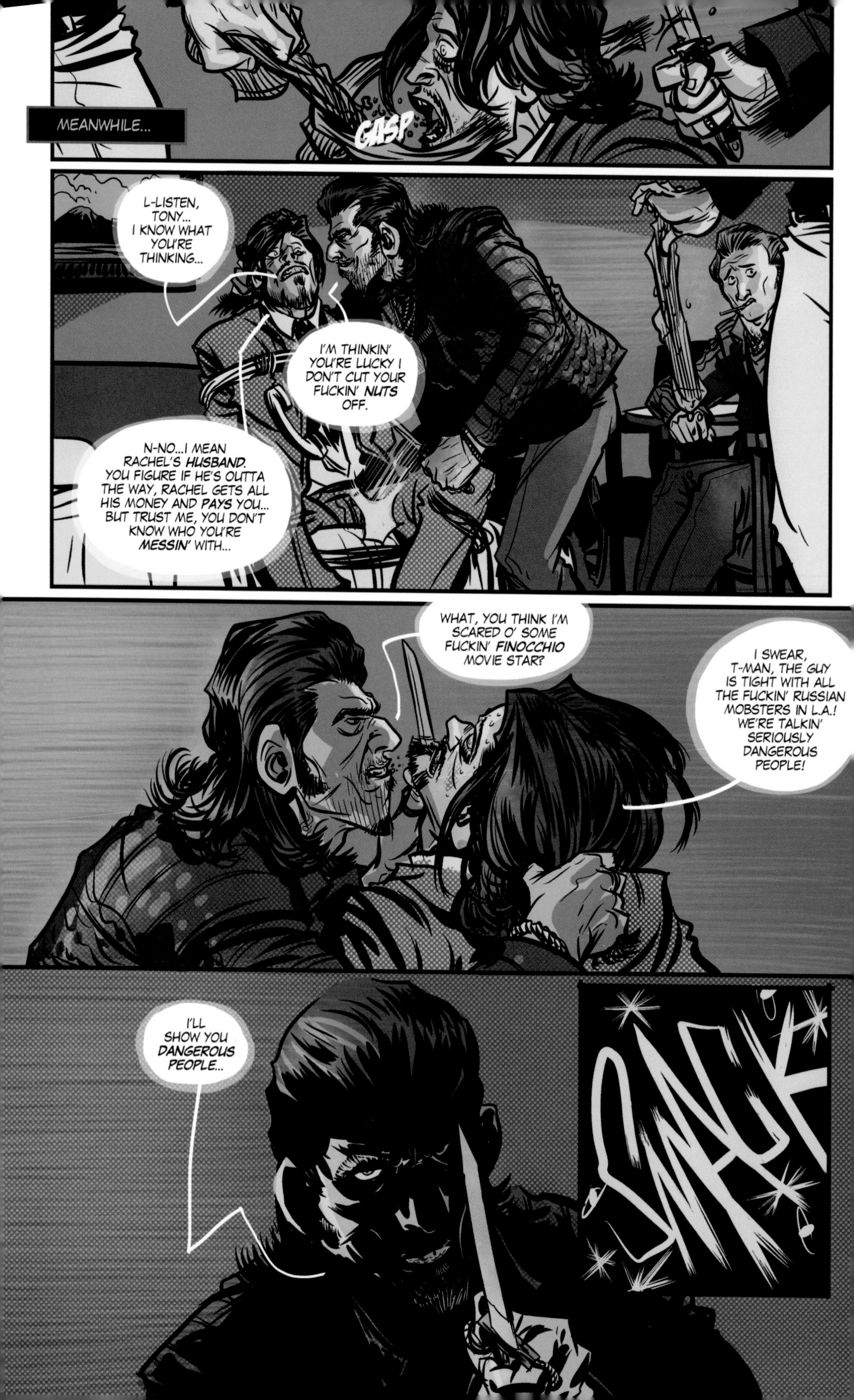
MEANWHILE...
GASP
L-LISTEN, TONY... I KNOW WHAT YOU'RE THINKING...
I'M THINKIN' YOU'RE LUCKY I DON'T CUT YOUR FUCKIN' NUTS OFF.
N-NO...I MEAN RACHEL'S HUSBAND. YOU FIGURE IF HE'S OUTTA THE WAY, RACHEL GETS ALL HIS MONEY AND PAYS YOU... BUT TRUST ME, YOU DON'T KNOW WHO YOU'RE MESSIN' WITH...
WHAT, YOU THINK I'M SCARED O' SOME FUCKIN' FINOCCHIO MOVIE STAR?
I SWEAR, T-MAN, THE GUY IS TIGHT WITH ALL THE FUCKIN' RUSSIAN MOBSTERS IN L.A.! WE'RE TALKIN' SERIOUSLY DANGEROUS PEOPLE!
I'LL SHOW YOU DANGEROUS PEOPLE...
SNICK

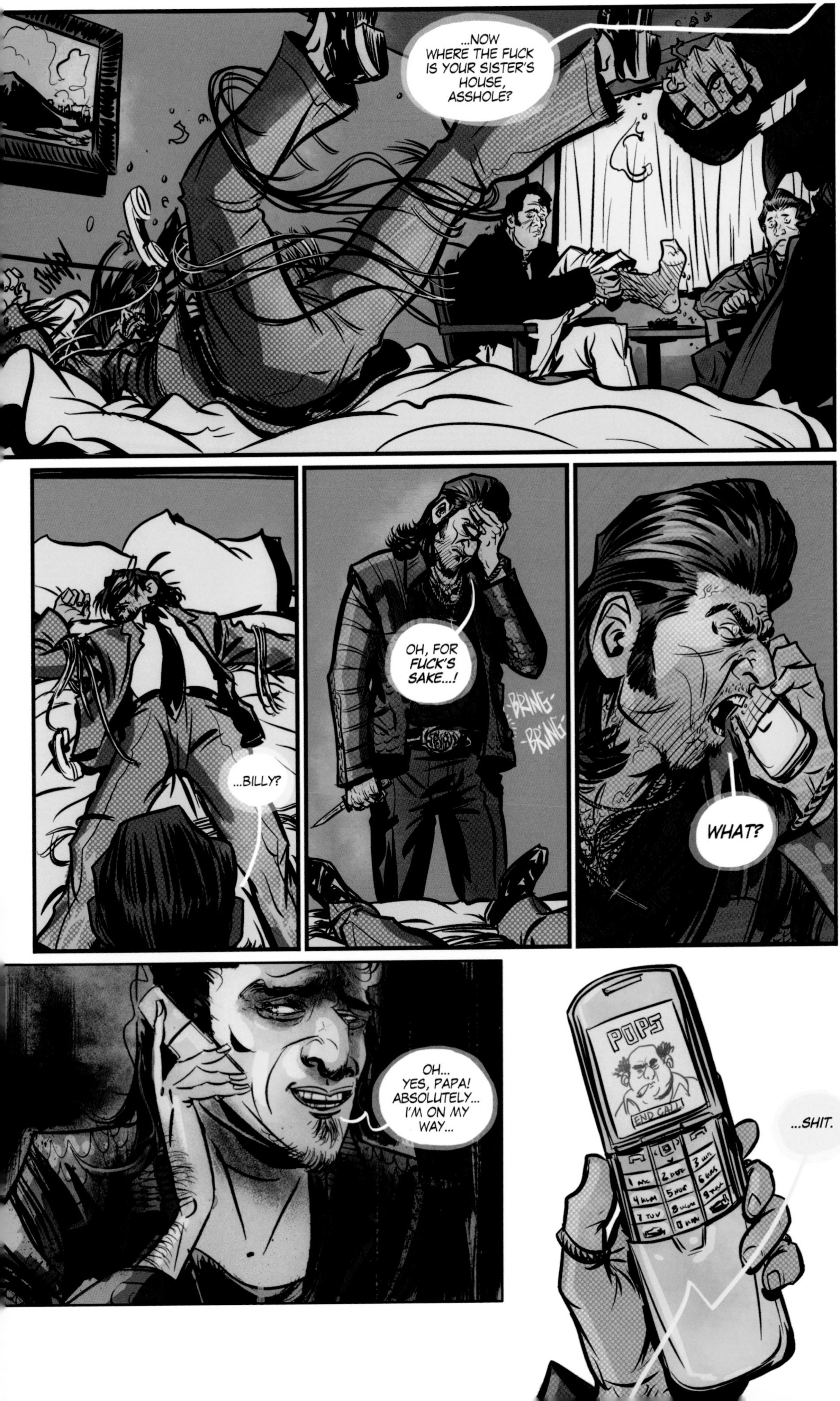
...NOW WHERE THE FUCK IS YOUR SISTER'S HOUSE, ASSHOLE?
...BILLY?
OH, FOR FUCK'S SAKE...!
BRING BRING
WHAT?
OH... YES, PAPA! ABSOLUTELY... I'M ON MY WAY...
POPS
END CALL
...SHIT.

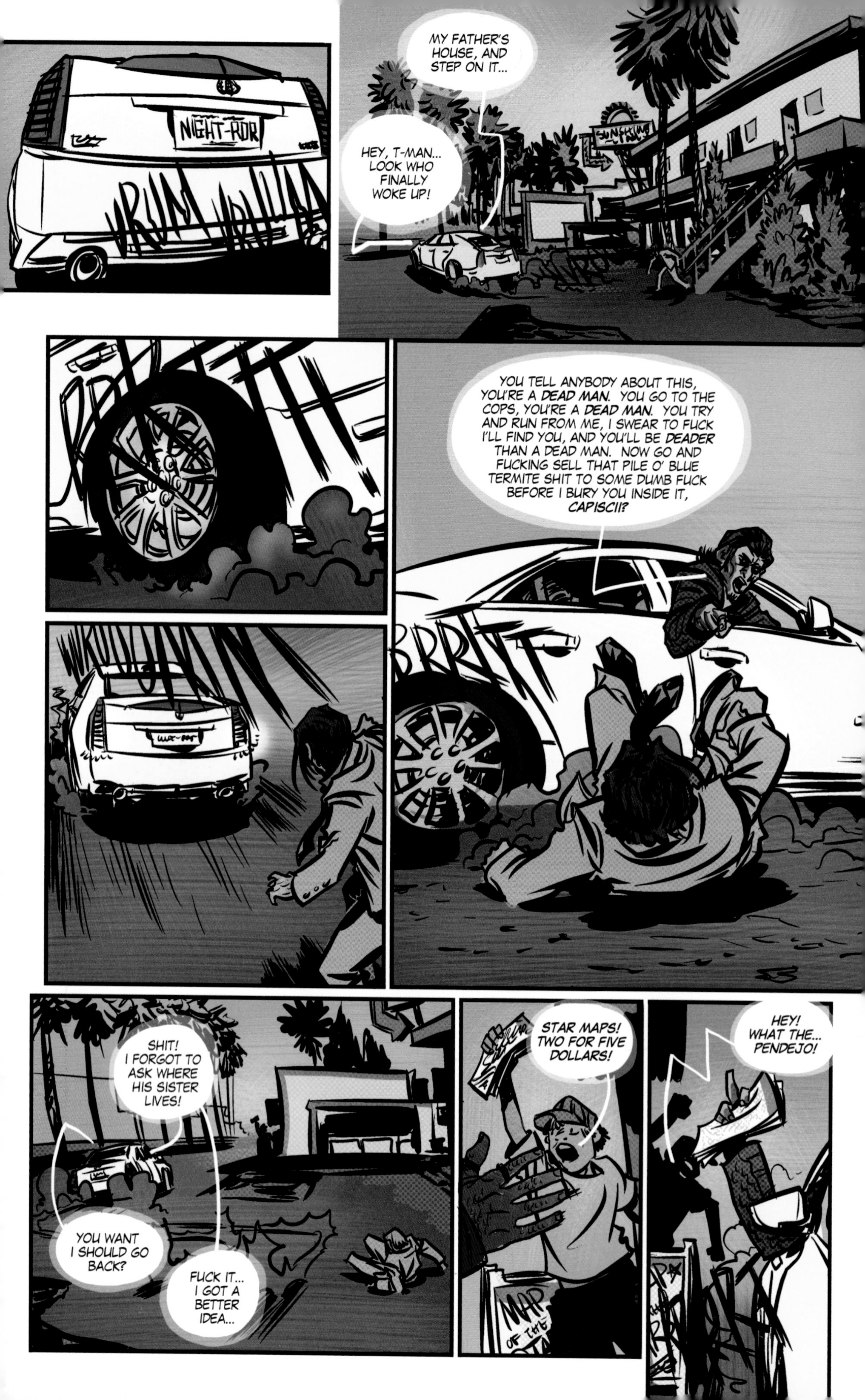
NIGHT-RDR
VRUM VRUM
MY FATHER'S HOUSE, AND STEP ON IT...
HEY, T-MAN... LOOK WHO FINALLY WOKE UP!
BRRT
YOU TELL ANYBODY ABOUT THIS, YOU'RE A DEAD MAN. YOU GO TO THE COPS, YOU'RE A DEAD MAN. YOU TRY AND RUN FROM ME, I SWEAR TO FUCK I'LL FIND YOU, AND YOU'LL BE DEADER THAN A DEAD MAN. NOW GO AND FUCKING SELL THAT PILE O' BLUE TERMITE SHIT TO SOME DUMB FUCK BEFORE I BURY YOU INSIDE IT, CAPISCI!?
BRRT
SHIT! I FORGOT TO ASK WHERE HIS SISTER LIVES!
YOU WANT I SHOULD GO BACK?
FUCK IT... I GOT A BETTER IDEA...
STAR MAPS! TWO FOR FIVE DOLLARS!
MAP OF THE
HEY! WHAT THE... PENDEJO!

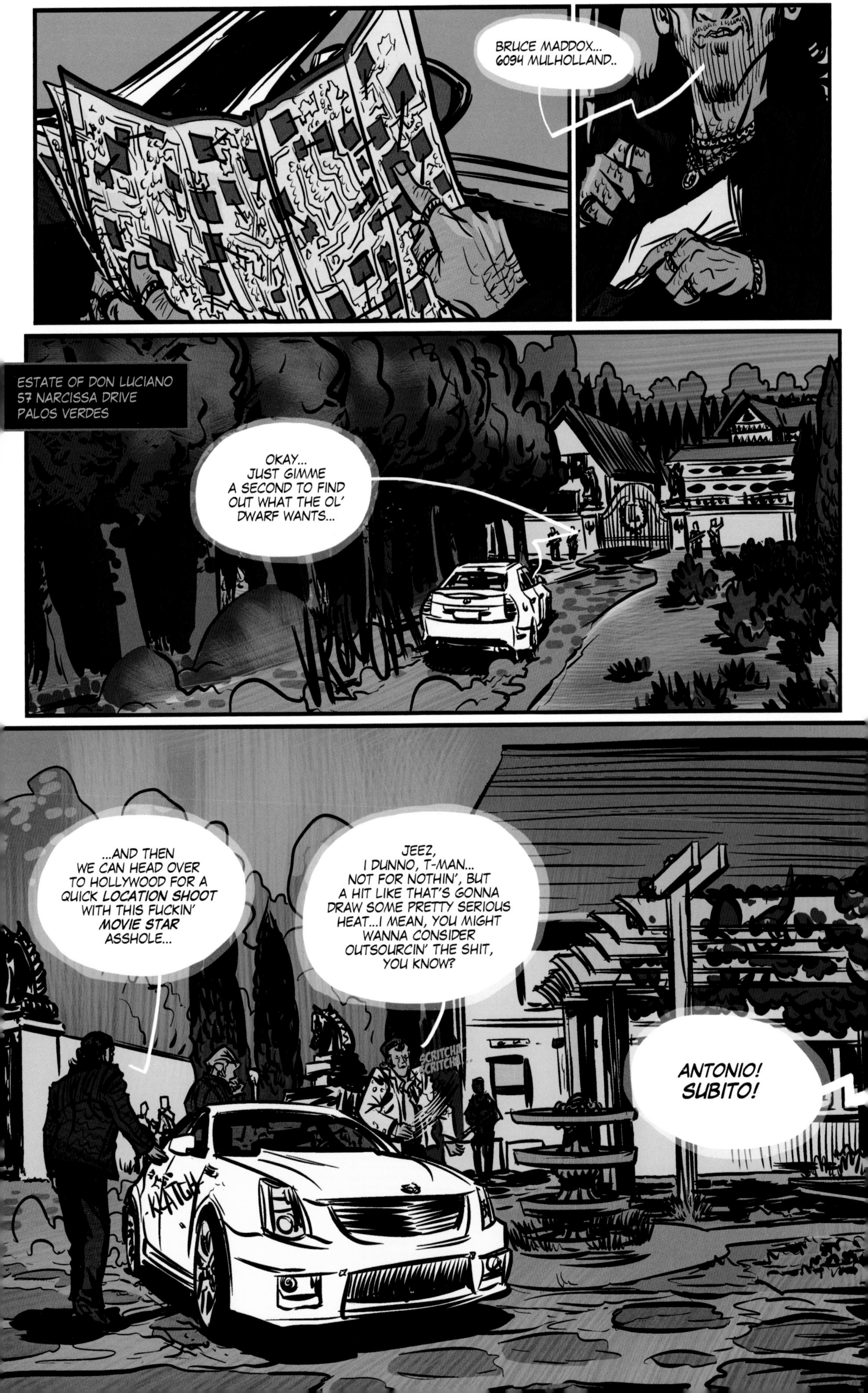
BRUCE MADDOX...
6094 MULHOLLAND..
ESTATE OF DON LUCIANO
57 NARCISSA DRIVE
PALOS VERDES
OKAY... JUST GIMME A SECOND TO FIND OUT WHAT THE OL' DWARF WANTS...
VRUUUM
...AND THEN WE CAN HEAD OVER TO HOLLYWOOD FOR A QUICK *LOCATION SHOOT* WITH THIS FUCKIN' *MOVIE STAR* ASSHOLE...
JEEZ, I DUNNO, T-MAN... NOT FOR NOTHIN', BUT A HIT LIKE THAT'S GONNA DRAW SOME PRETTY SERIOUS HEAT...I MEAN, YOU MIGHT WANNA CONSIDER OUTSOURCIN' THE SHIT, YOU KNOW?
SCRITCH SCRITCH
KATCH
*ANTONIO! SUBITO!*

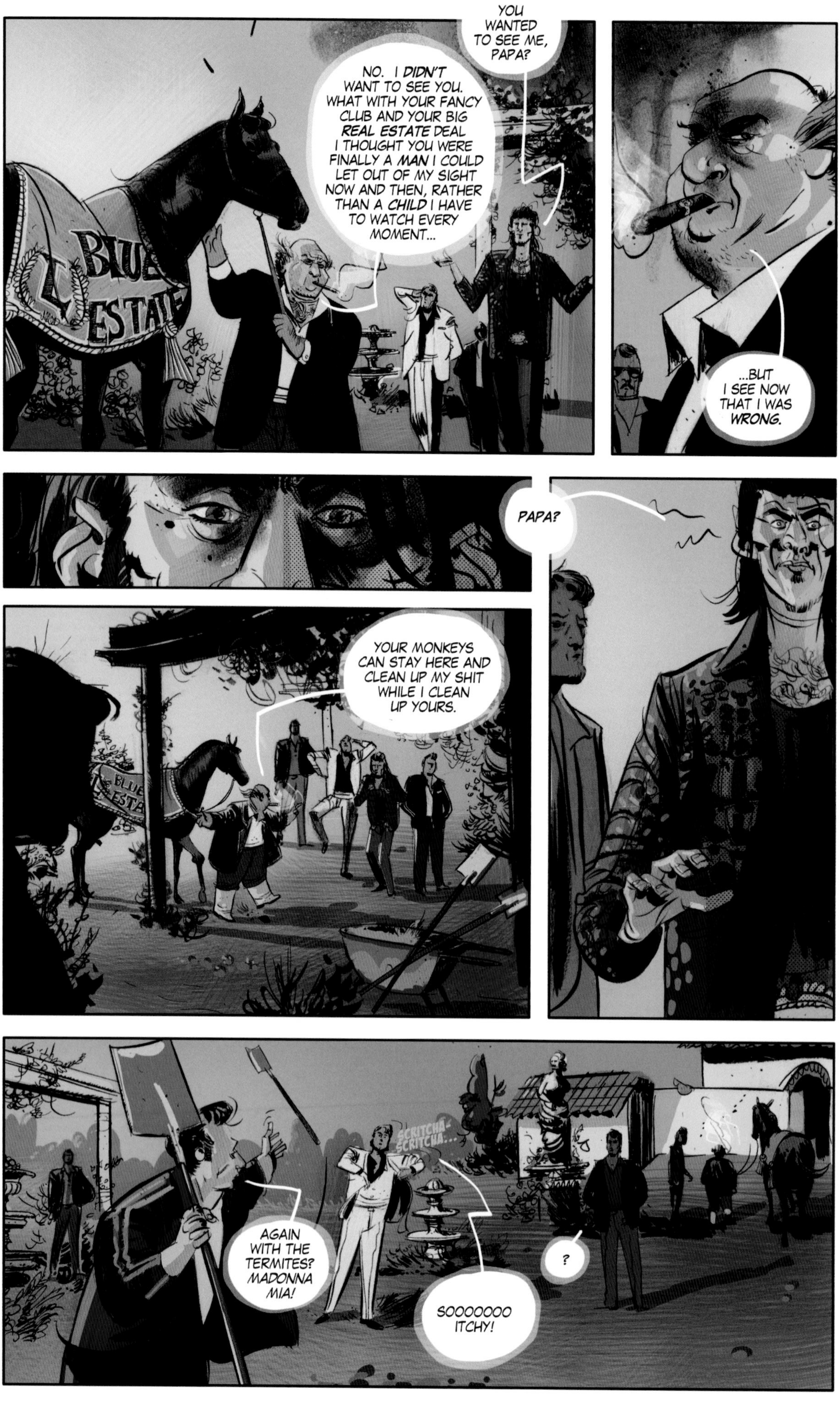
YOU WANTED TO SEE ME, PAPA?
NO. I DIDN'T WANT TO SEE YOU. WHAT WITH YOUR FANCY CLUB AND YOUR BIG REAL ESTATE DEAL I THOUGHT YOU WERE FINALLY A MAN I COULD LET OUT OF MY SIGHT NOW AND THEN, RATHER THAN A CHILD I HAVE TO WATCH EVERY MOMENT...
BLUE ESTATE
...BUT I SEE NOW THAT I WAS WRONG.
PAPA?
YOUR MONKEYS CAN STAY HERE AND CLEAN UP MY SHIT WHILE I CLEAN UP YOURS.
BLUE ESTATE
SCRITCHA-SCRITCHA...
AGAIN WITH THE TERMITES? MADONNA MIA!
SOOOOOOO ITCHY!
?

I HAD TO HEAR FROM MY SOURCE IN THE L.A.P.D. THAT MAJOR CRIMES HAS YOU *ON TAPE* MAKING AN *ARMS DEAL* WITH THIS *UZBEKI STRONZO...?*

UZBEKI... WHAT?! I DON'T KNOW WHAT YOU'RE...

-ALYOSHA KARIMOV  LAPD

BR VOO R R R R

VAFANCULO!! I'LL FUCKIN' KILL THAT RAT FUCK WITH MY BARE FUCKIN' HANDS!

NO!

YOU'VE DONE *ENOUGH!* WE CANNOT HAVE THE *CANARINO'S* DEATH CONNECTED TO THE FAMILY IN ANY WAY...

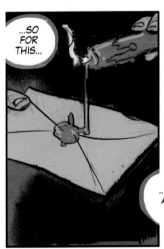

...SO FOR THIS...

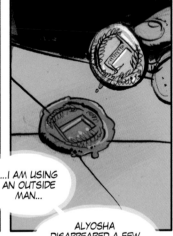

...I AM USING AN OUTSIDE MAN...

ALYOSHA DISAPPEARED A FEW DAYS AGO, SO WE NEED TO ACT FAST BEFORE THE POLICE FIND HIM.

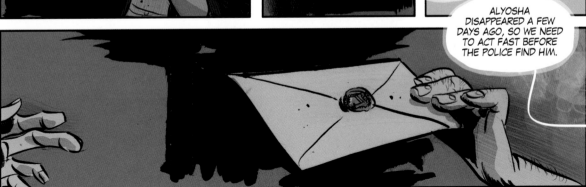

TAKE THIS. TO LOUIGI'S AND DELIVER IT TO THE MULAGNAN THERE...

AAAAAH!

...AND TRY NOT TO DISAPPOINT ME AGAIN!

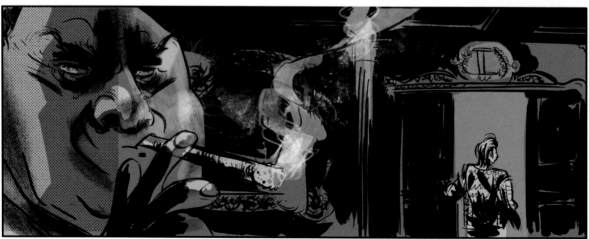

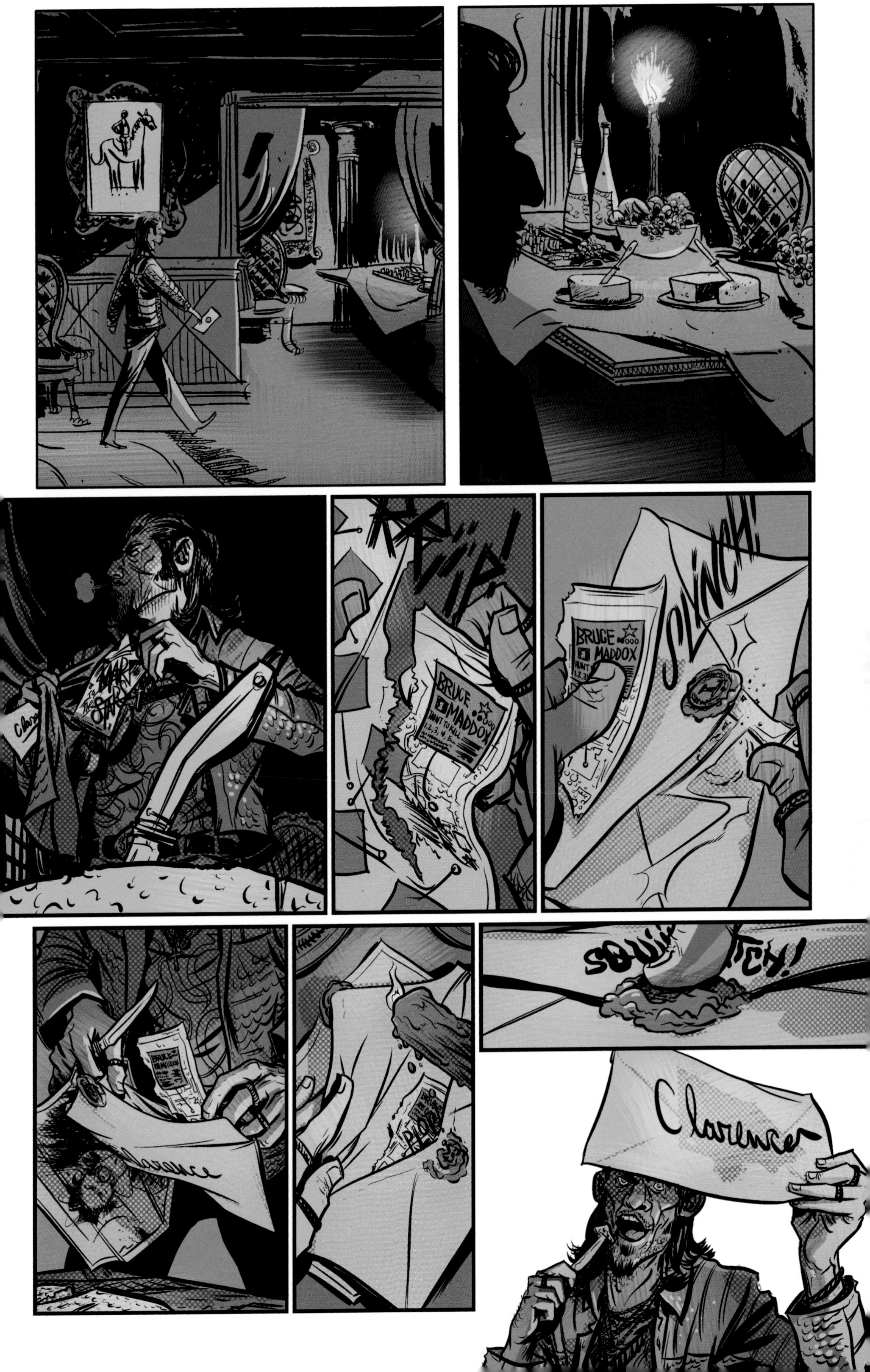

BRUCE
MADDOX
HUNT TO KILL
1,2,3,4,5...
SPLINCH!
Clarence

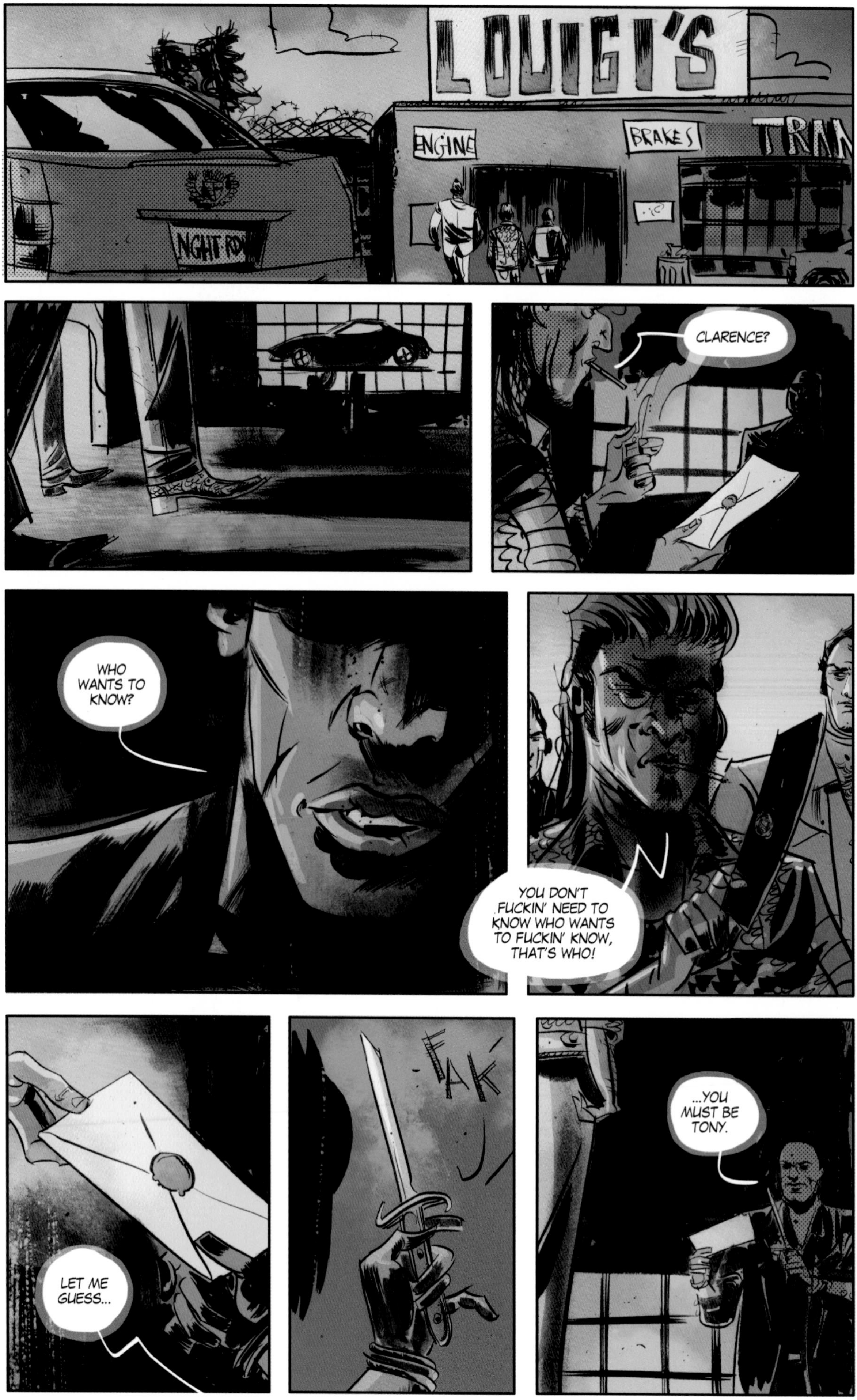
LOUIGI'S
ENGINE
BRAKES
NGHT RDR
CLARENCE?
WHO WANTS TO KNOW?
YOU DON'T FUCKIN' NEED TO KNOW WHO WANTS TO FUCKIN' KNOW, THAT'S WHO!
LET ME GUESS...
FAK
...YOU MUST BE TONY.

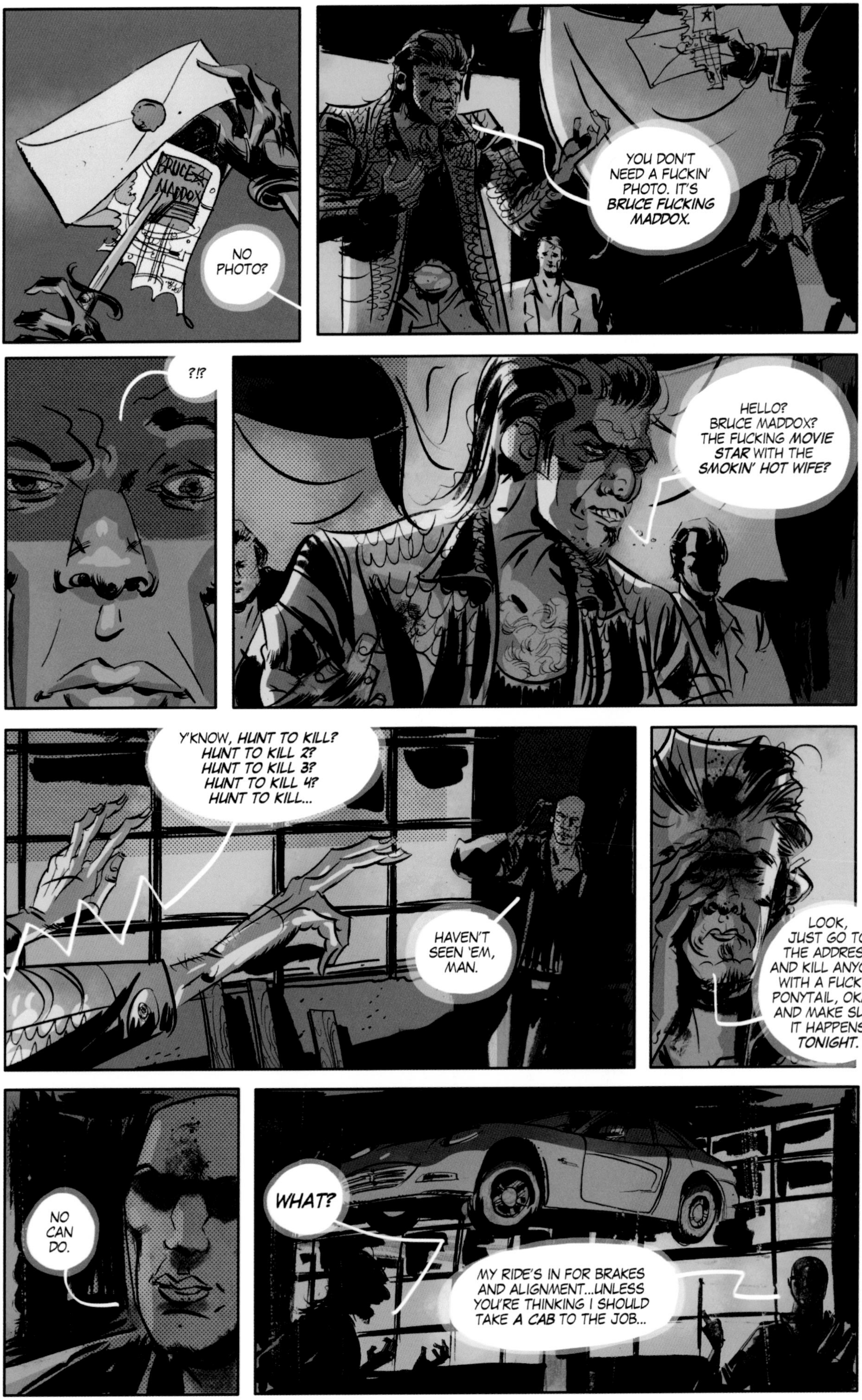
NO PHOTO?
YOU DON'T NEED A FUCKIN' PHOTO. IT'S BRUCE FUCKING MADDOX.
?!?
HELLO? BRUCE MADDOX? THE FUCKING MOVIE STAR WITH THE SMOKIN' HOT WIFE?
Y'KNOW, HUNT TO KILL? HUNT TO KILL 2? HUNT TO KILL 3? HUNT TO KILL 4? HUNT TO KILL...
HAVEN'T SEEN 'EM, MAN.
LOOK, JUST GO TO THE ADDRESS AND KILL ANYONE WITH A FUCKIN' PONYTAIL, OKAY? AND MAKE SURE IT HAPPENS TONIGHT.
NO CAN DO.
WHAT?
MY RIDE'S IN FOR BRAKES AND ALIGNMENT...UNLESS YOU'RE THINKING I SHOULD TAKE A CAB TO THE JOB...

JESUS CHRIST, I GOTTA THINK OF *EVERYTHING?*

LINO! KEYS!

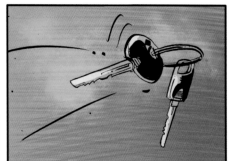

BRING IT BACK IN ONE PIECE, OKAY, SHAFT?

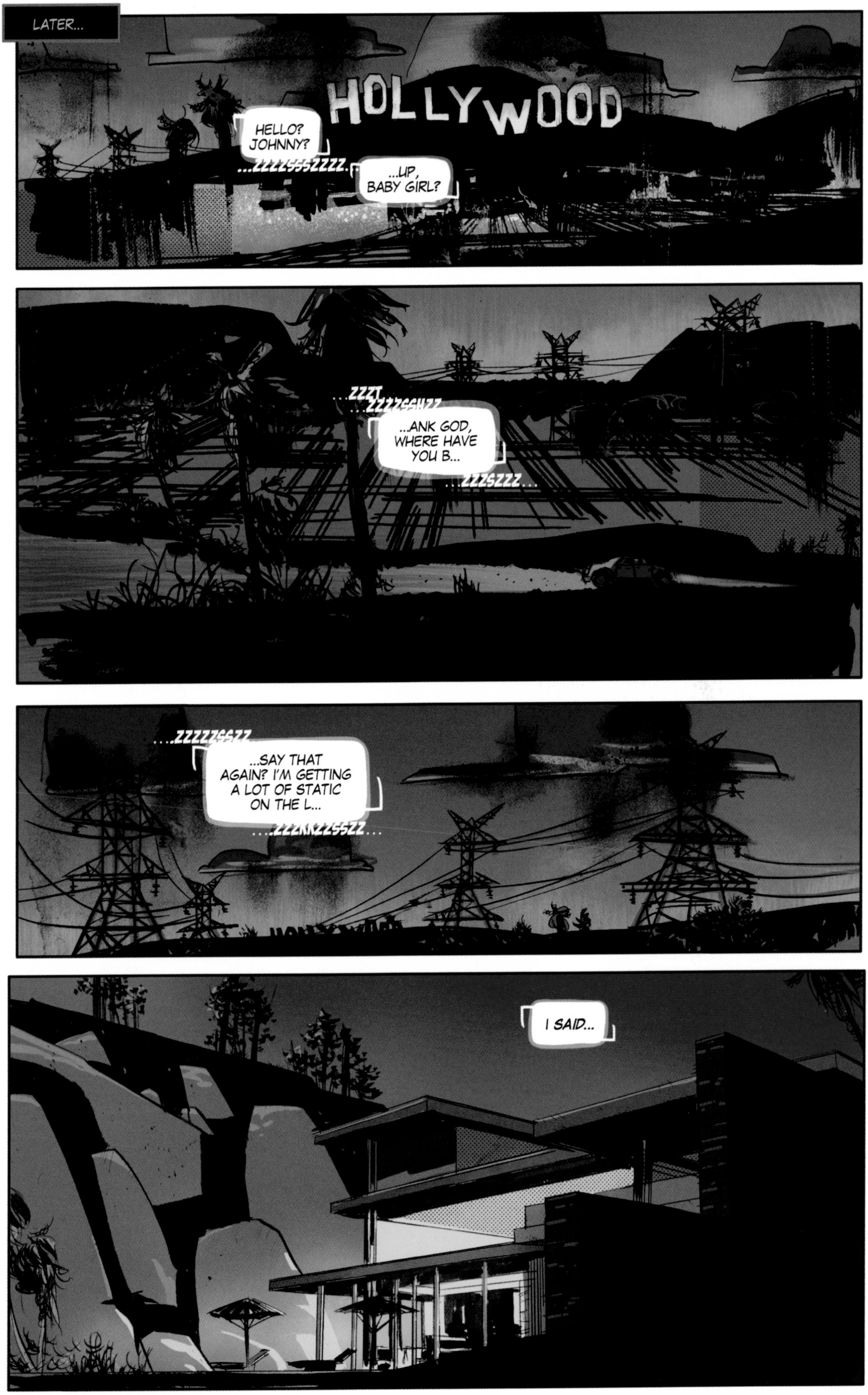
LATER...
HOLLYWOOD
HELLO? JOHNNY?
...ZZZZSSSZZZZ.
...UP, BABY GIRL?
...ZZZT ...ZZZZSSHZZ
...ANK GOD, WHERE HAVE YOU B...
...ZZZSZZZ...
...ZZZZZSSZZ
...SAY THAT AGAIN? I'M GETTING A LOT OF STATIC ON THE L...
....ZZZKKZZSSZZ...
I SAID...

...WERE YOU *SERIOUS* ABOUT WANTING A *FRESH START* IN A NEW TOWN...

...WITH *ME?*

SERIOUS AS HABAÑERO HOT SAUCE.

I'VE BEEN READY TO BLOW THIS TACO STAND FOR A WHILE NOW...

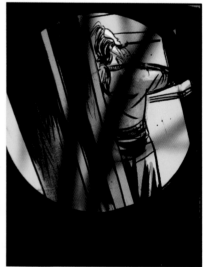

...WHY DO YOU ASK?

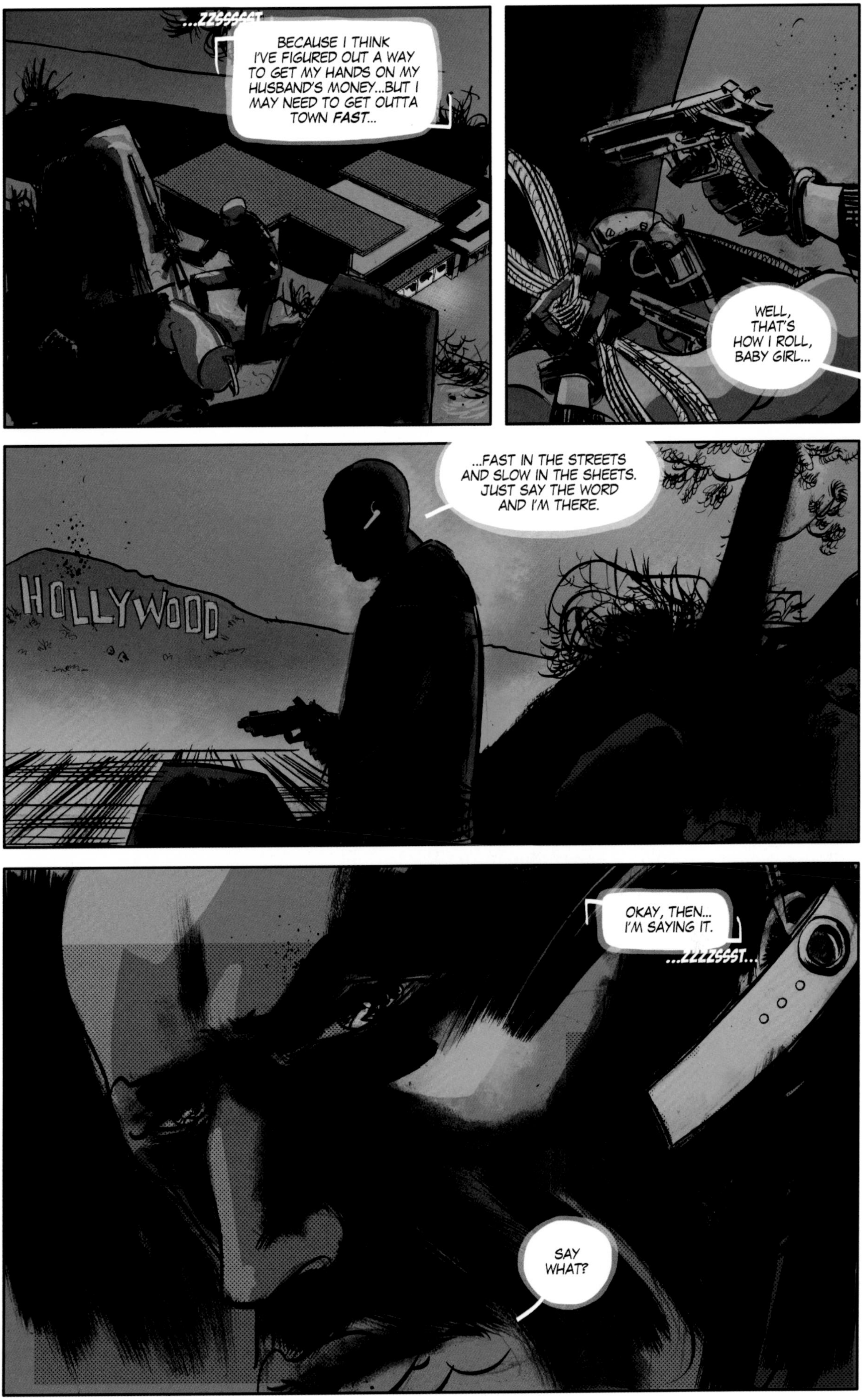
...ZZSSSST...
BECAUSE I THINK I'VE FIGURED OUT A WAY TO GET MY HANDS ON MY HUSBAND'S MONEY...BUT I MAY NEED TO GET OUTTA TOWN FAST...
WELL, THAT'S HOW I ROLL, BABY GIRL...
...FAST IN THE STREETS AND SLOW IN THE SHEETS. JUST SAY THE WORD AND I'M THERE.
HOLLYWOOD
OKAY, THEN... I'M SAYING IT.
...ZZZZSSST...
SAY WHAT?

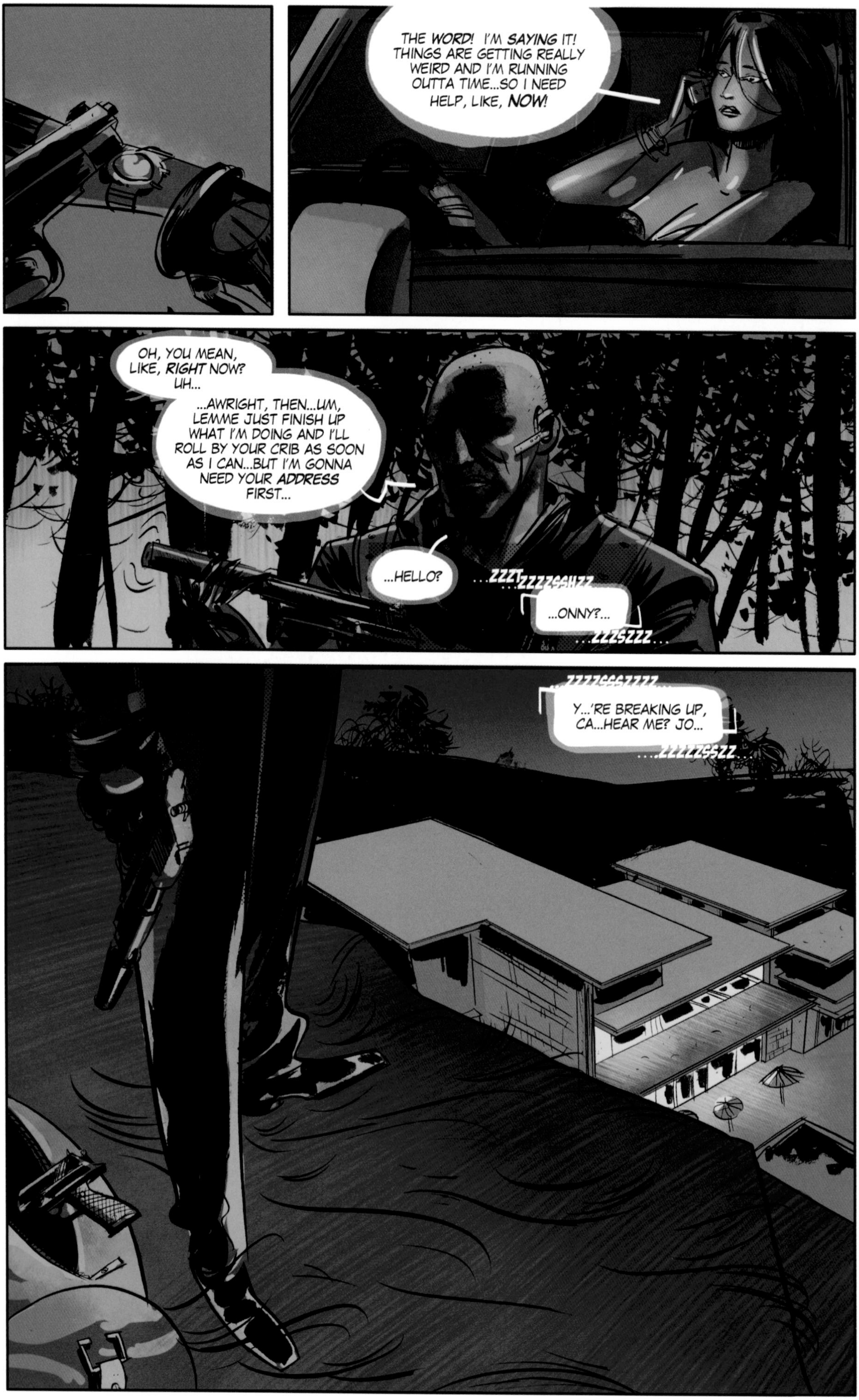
THE WORD! I'M SAYING IT! THINGS ARE GETTING REALLY WEIRD AND I'M RUNNING OUTTA TIME...SO I NEED HELP, LIKE, NOW!
OH, YOU MEAN, LIKE, RIGHT NOW? UH...
...AWRIGHT, THEN...UM, LEMME JUST FINISH UP WHAT I'M DOING AND I'LL ROLL BY YOUR CRIB AS SOON AS I CAN...BUT I'M GONNA NEED YOUR ADDRESS FIRST...
...HELLO?
...ZZZTZZZZSSHZZ...
...ONNY?...
...ZZZSZZZ...
...ZZZZSSSZZZZ...
Y...'RE BREAKING UP, CA...HEAR ME? JO...
...ZZZZZSSZZ...

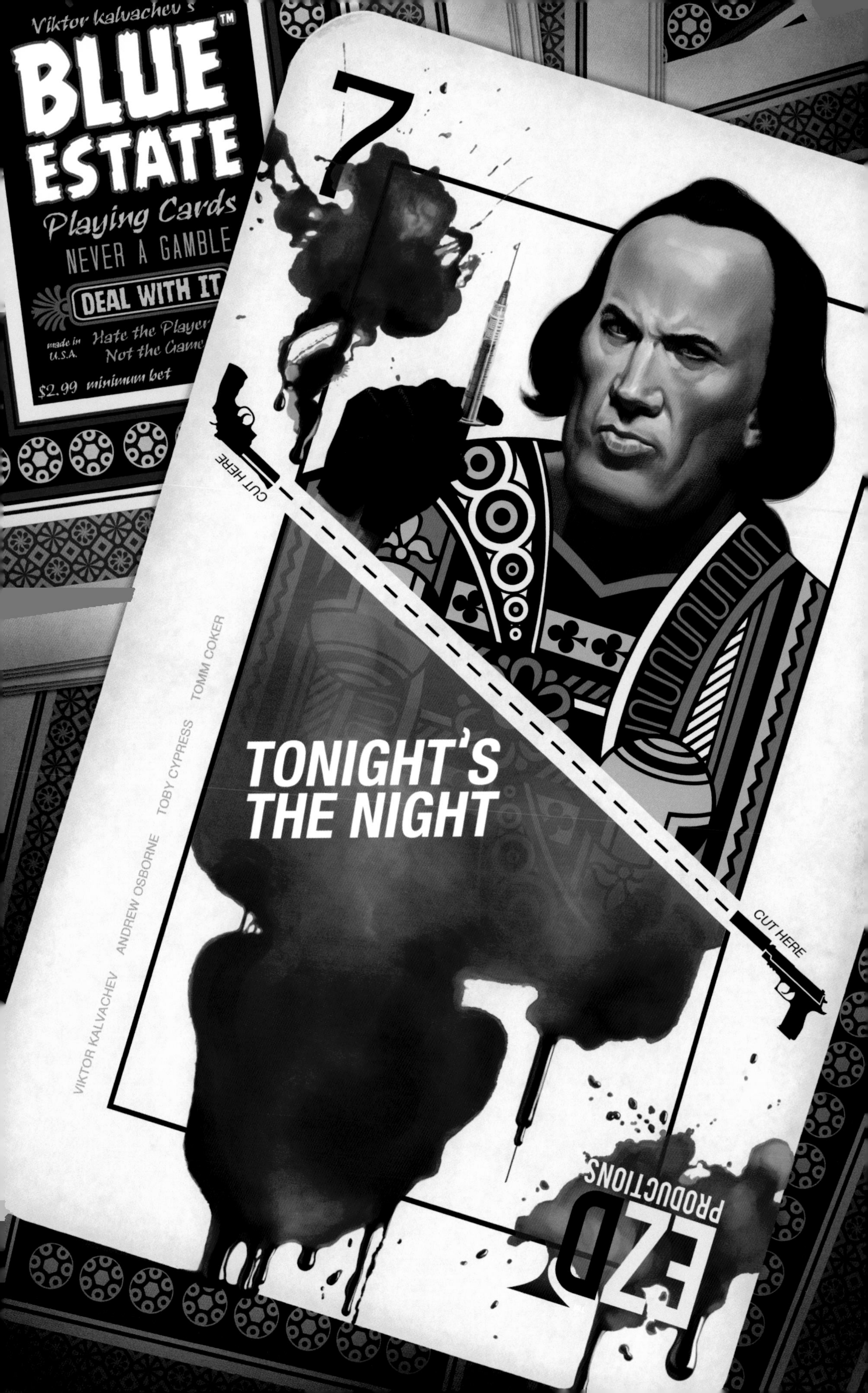
Viktor Kalvachev's
BLUE ESTATE™
Playing Cards
NEVER A GAMBLE
DEAL WITH IT
made in U.S.A.
Hate the Player Not the Game
$2.99 minimum bet
7
CUT HERE
CUT HERE
TONIGHT'S THE NIGHT
VIKTOR KALVACHEV
ANDREW OSBORNE
TOBY CYPRESS
TOMM COKER
EZD PRODUCTIONS

# BLUE™ ESTATE

EPISODE SEVEN:
## TONIGHT'S THE NIGHT

ORIGINAL STORY:
**VIKTOR KALVACHEV** AND **KOSTA YANEV**

SCRIPT BY **ANDREW OSBORNE**

ARTISTS:
**VIKTOR KALVACHEV**
**TOBY CYPRESS**
**TOMM COKER**

ART DIRECTION BY **VIKTOR KALVACHEV**

COVER, COLORS & DESIGN:
**VIKTOR KALVACHEV**

CONTRIBUTING EDITOR:
**PHILO NORTHRUP**

WWW.BlueEstateComic.com

EZD™
PRODUCTIONS

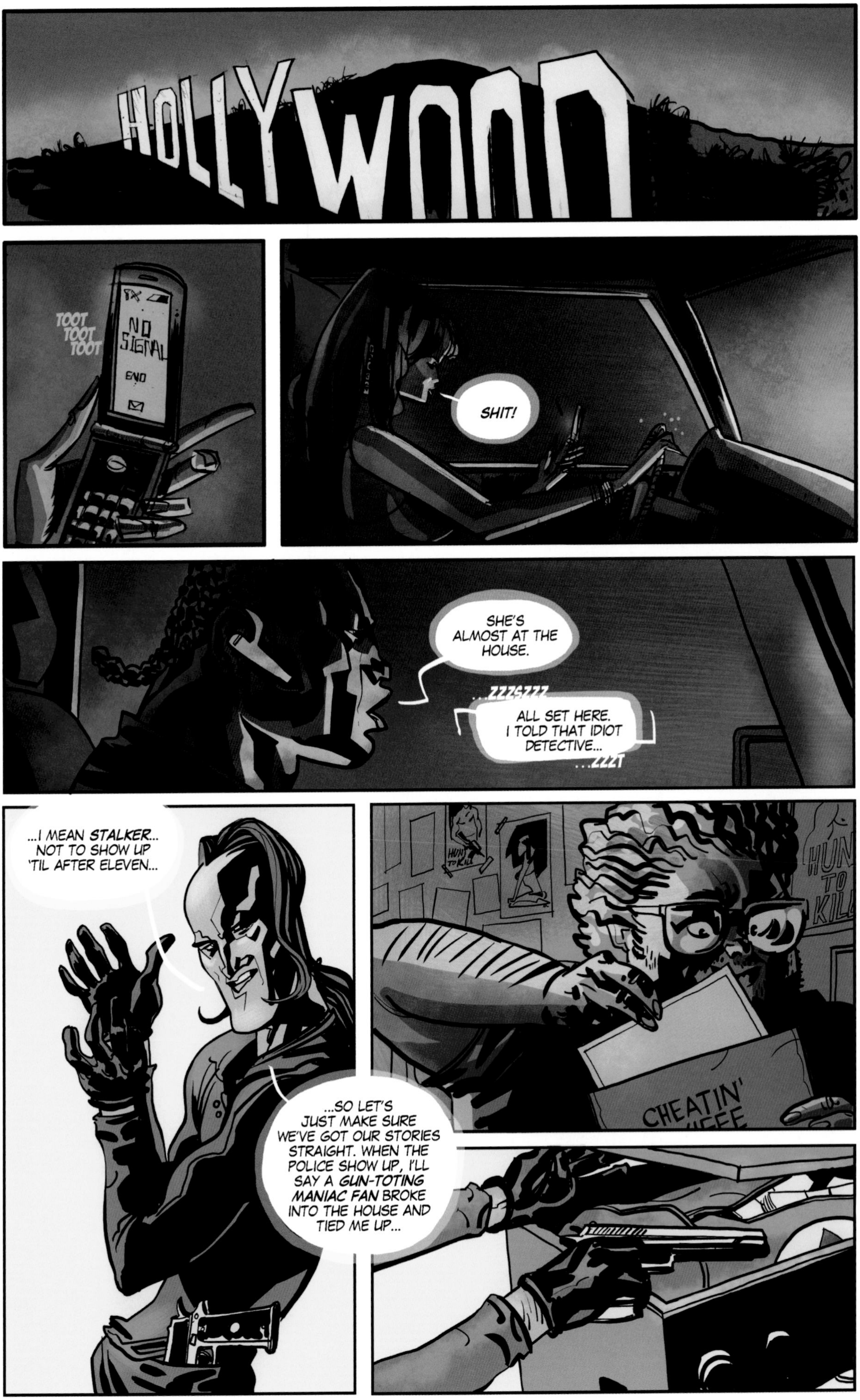
HOLLYWOOD
TOOT TOOT TOOT
NO SIGNAL
END
SHIT!
SHE'S ALMOST AT THE HOUSE.
...ZZZSZZZ
ALL SET HERE. I TOLD THAT IDIOT DETECTIVE...
...ZZZT
...I MEAN STALKER... NOT TO SHOW UP 'TIL AFTER ELEVEN...
HUNT TO KILL
...SO LET'S JUST MAKE SURE WE'VE GOT OUR STORIES STRAIGHT. WHEN THE POLICE SHOW UP, I'LL SAY A GUN-TOTING MANIAC FAN BROKE INTO THE HOUSE AND TIED ME UP...

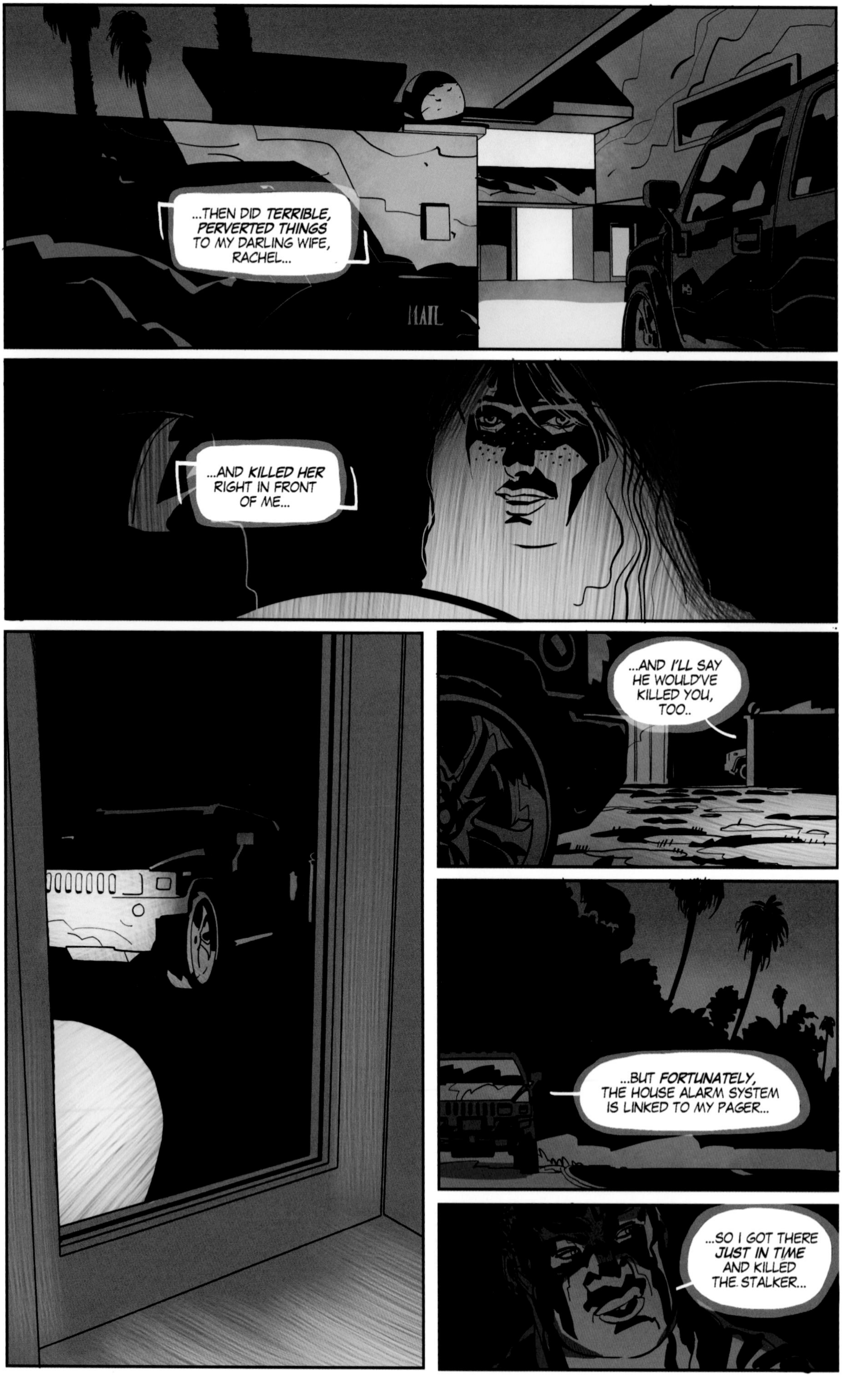
...THEN DID TERRIBLE, PERVERTED THINGS TO MY DARLING WIFE, RACHEL...
MAIL
...AND KILLED HER RIGHT IN FRONT OF ME...
...AND I'LL SAY HE WOULD'VE KILLED YOU, TOO..
...BUT FORTUNATELY, THE HOUSE ALARM SYSTEM IS LINKED TO MY PAGER...
...SO I GOT THERE JUST IN TIME AND KILLED THE STALKER...

...BUT UNFORTUNATELY, I WAS TOO LATE TO SAVE MRS. MADDOX...

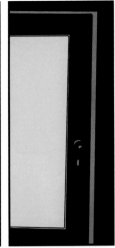

CLICK

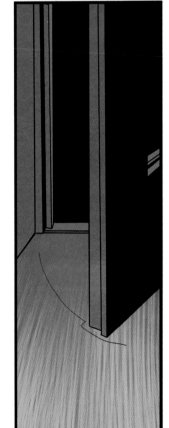

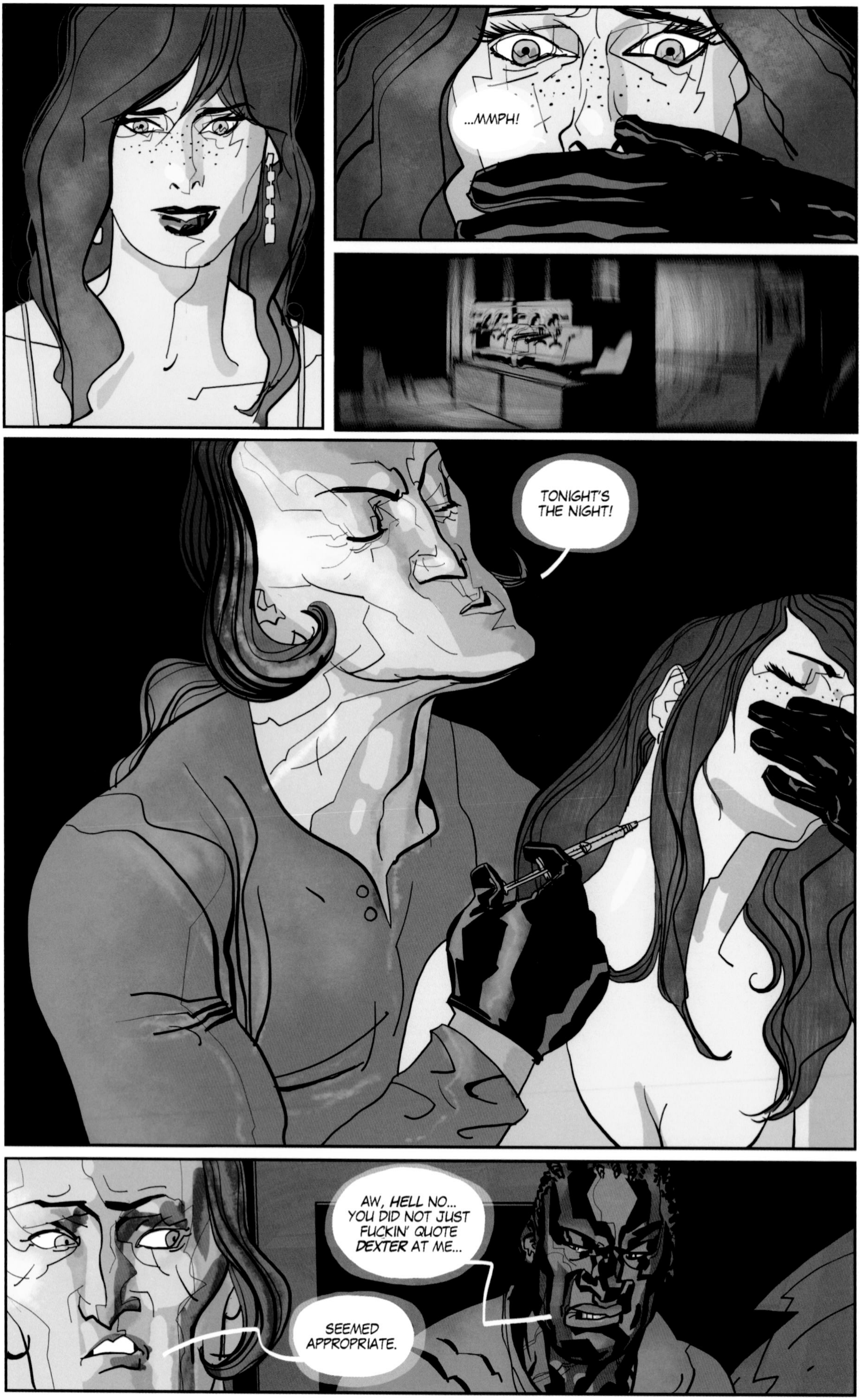
...MMPH!
TONIGHT'S THE NIGHT!
AW, HELL NO... YOU DID NOT JUST FUCKIN' QUOTE DEXTER AT ME...
SEEMED APPROPRIATE.

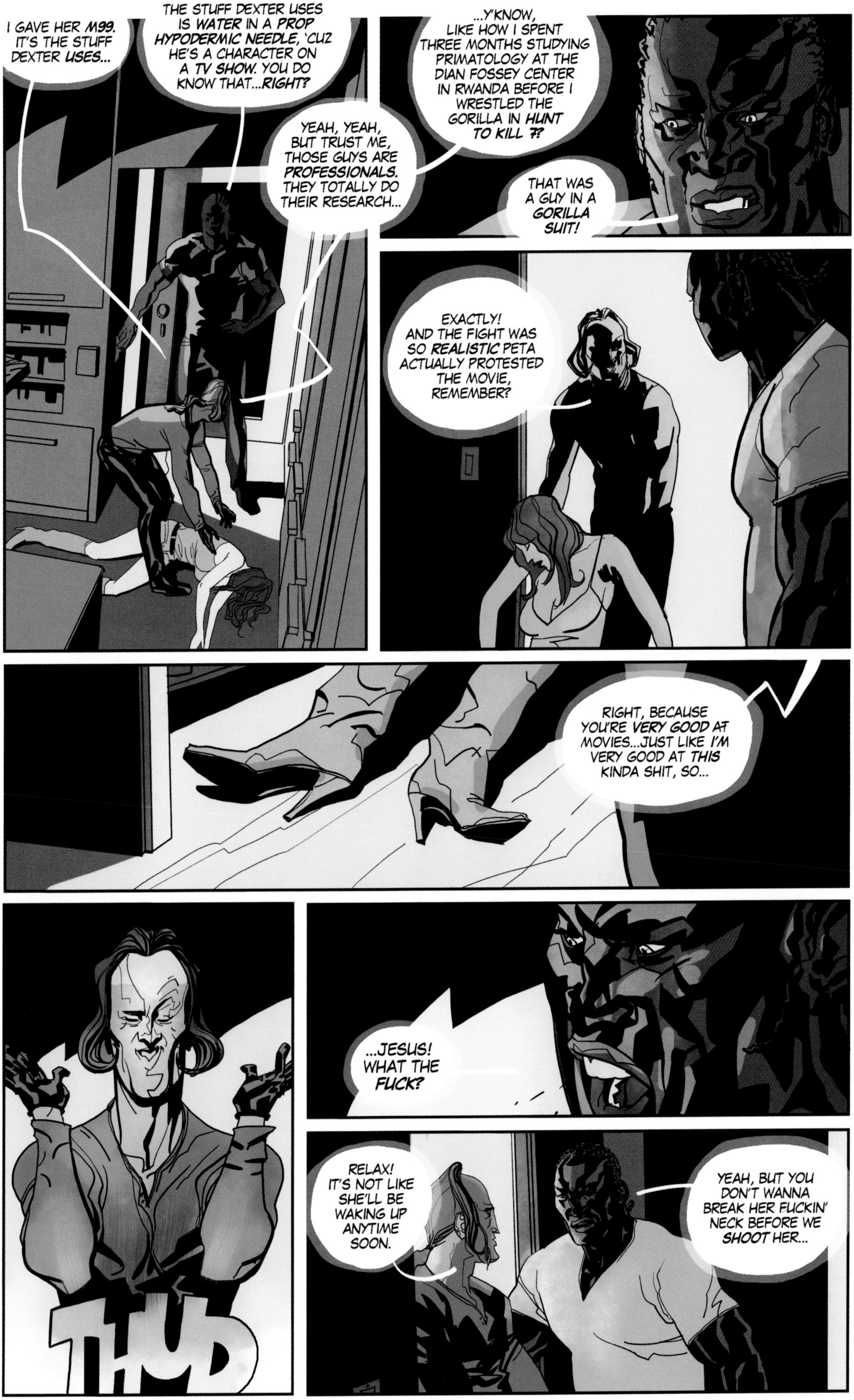
I GAVE HER M99. IT'S THE STUFF DEXTER USES...
THE STUFF DEXTER USES IS WATER IN A PROP HYPODERMIC NEEDLE, 'CUZ HE'S A CHARACTER ON A TV SHOW. YOU DO KNOW THAT...RIGHT?
YEAH, YEAH, BUT TRUST ME, THOSE GUYS ARE PROFESSIONALS. THEY TOTALLY DO THEIR RESEARCH...
...Y'KNOW, LIKE HOW I SPENT THREE MONTHS STUDYING PRIMATOLOGY AT THE DIAN FOSSEY CENTER IN RWANDA BEFORE I WRESTLED THE GORILLA IN HUNT TO KILL 7?
THAT WAS A GUY IN A GORILLA SUIT!
EXACTLY! AND THE FIGHT WAS SO REALISTIC PETA ACTUALLY PROTESTED THE MOVIE, REMEMBER?
RIGHT, BECAUSE YOU'RE VERY GOOD AT MOVIES...JUST LIKE I'M VERY GOOD AT THIS KINDA SHIT, SO...
THUD
...JESUS! WHAT THE FUCK?
RELAX! IT'S NOT LIKE SHE'LL BE WAKING UP ANYTIME SOON.
YEAH, BUT YOU DON'T WANNA BREAK HER FUCKIN' NECK BEFORE WE SHOOT HER...

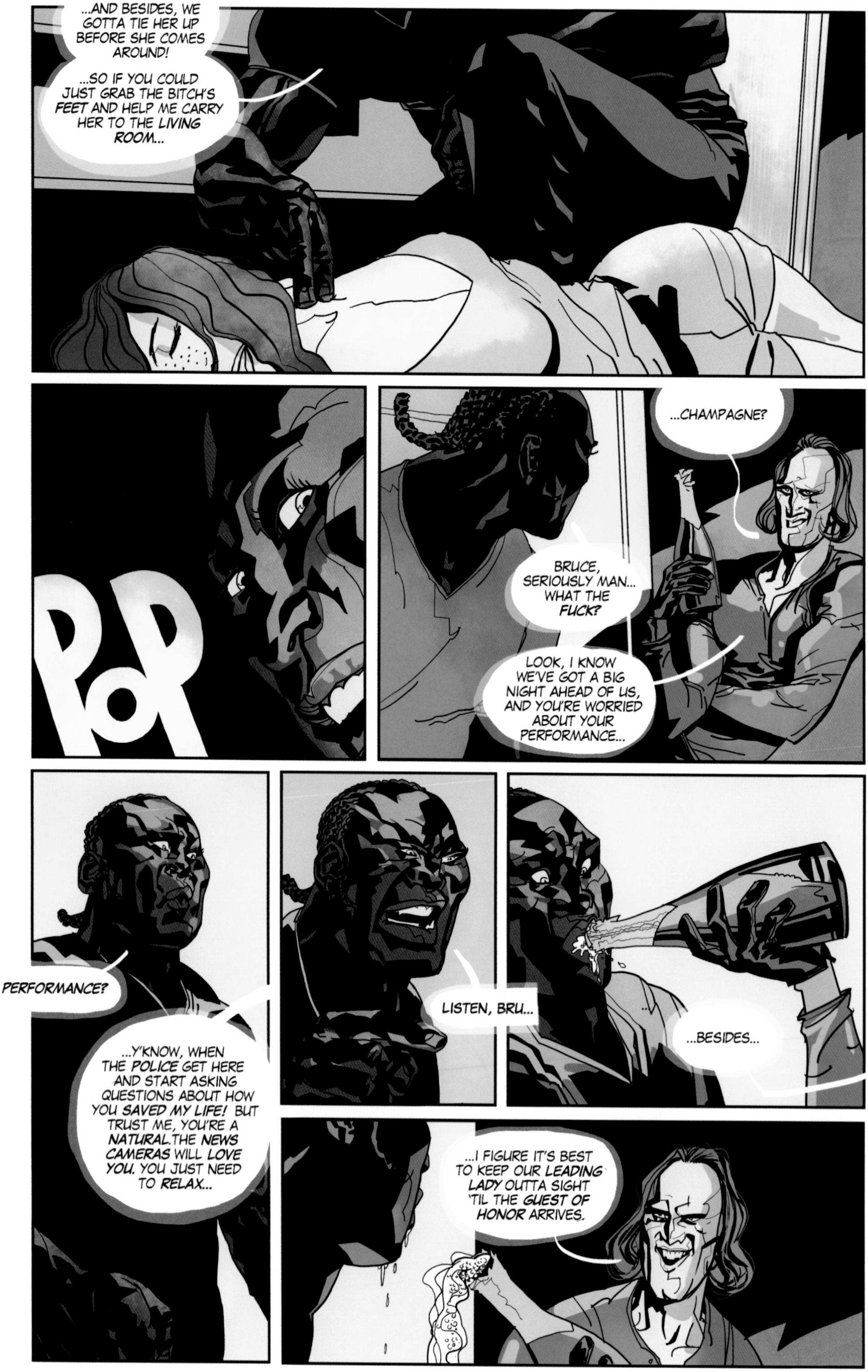
...AND BESIDES, WE GOTTA TIE HER UP BEFORE SHE COMES AROUND!
...SO IF YOU COULD JUST GRAB THE BITCH'S FEET AND HELP ME CARRY HER TO THE LIVING ROOM...
POP
...CHAMPAGNE?
BRUCE, SERIOUSLY MAN... WHAT THE FUCK?
LOOK, I KNOW WE'VE GOT A BIG NIGHT AHEAD OF US, AND YOU'RE WORRIED ABOUT YOUR PERFORMANCE...
PERFORMANCE?
...Y'KNOW, WHEN THE POLICE GET HERE AND START ASKING QUESTIONS ABOUT HOW YOU SAVED MY LIFE! BUT TRUST ME, YOU'RE A NATURAL. THE NEWS CAMERAS WILL LOVE YOU. YOU JUST NEED TO RELAX...
LISTEN, BRU...
...BESIDES...
...I FIGURE IT'S BEST TO KEEP OUR LEADING LADY OUTTA SIGHT 'TIL THE GUEST OF HONOR ARRIVES.

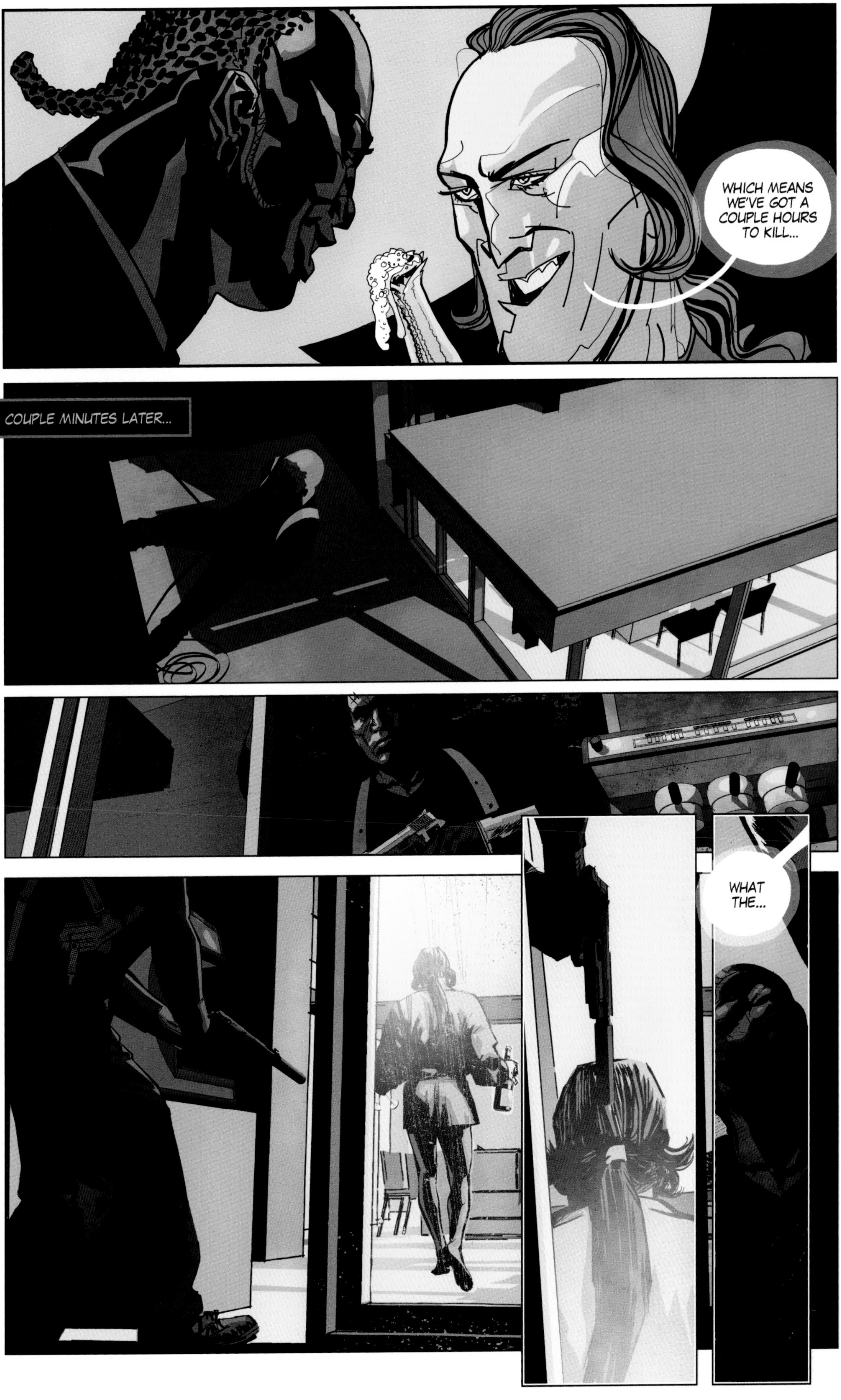
WHICH MEANS WE'VE GOT A COUPLE HOURS TO KILL...
A COUPLE MINUTES LATER...
WHAT THE...

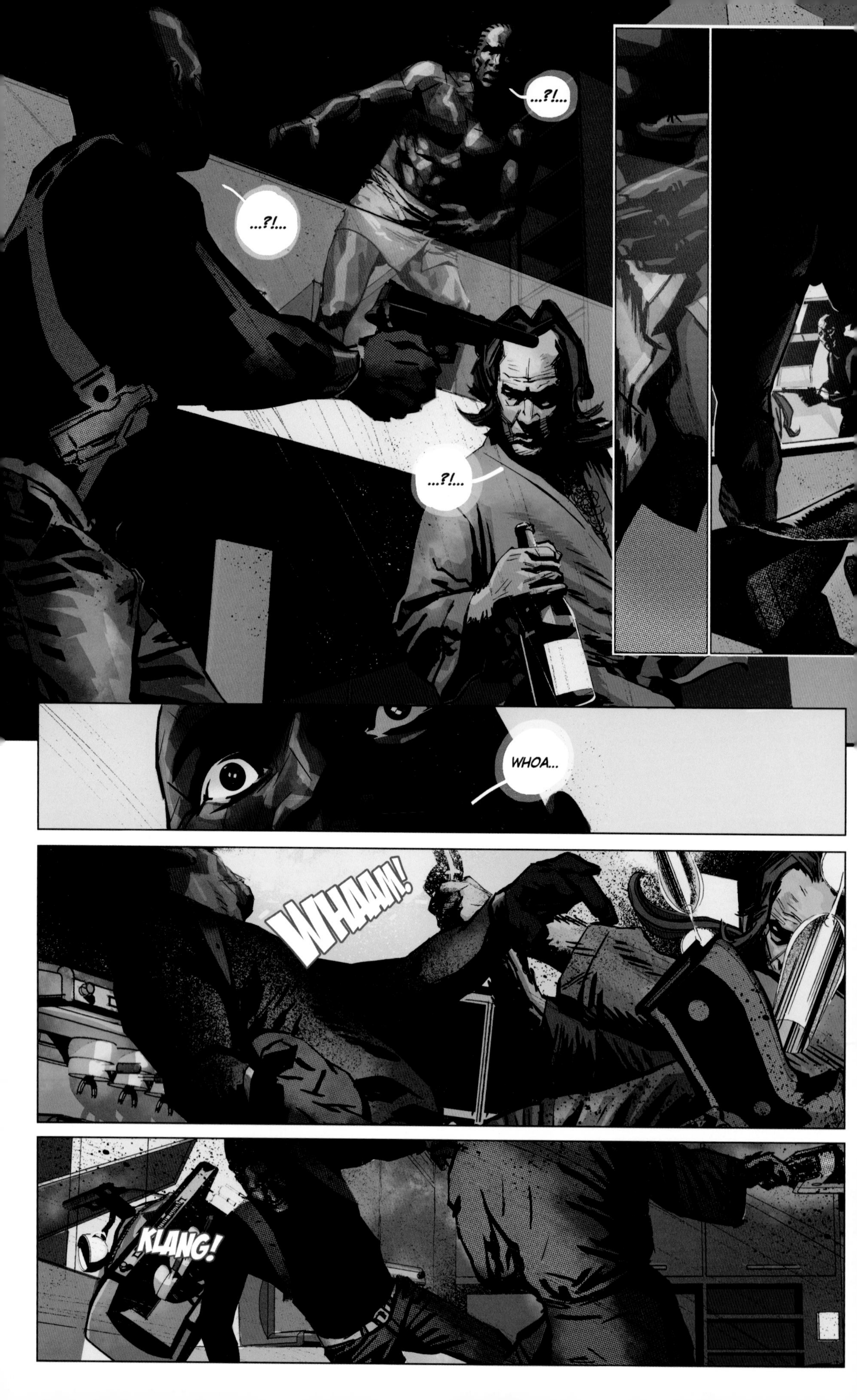
...?!...
...?!...
...?!...
WHOA...
WHAAM!
KLANG!

SKRAAAASH!

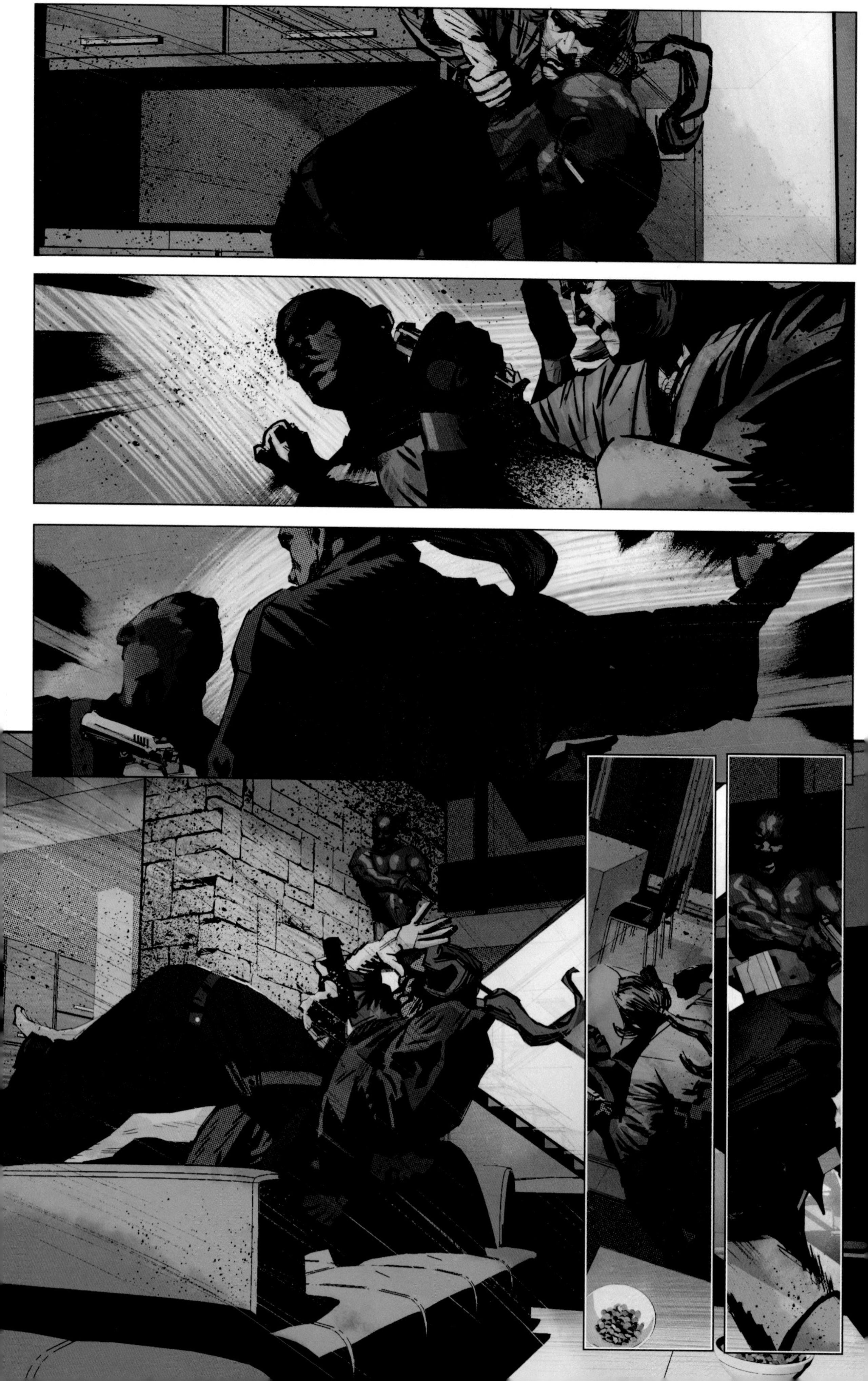

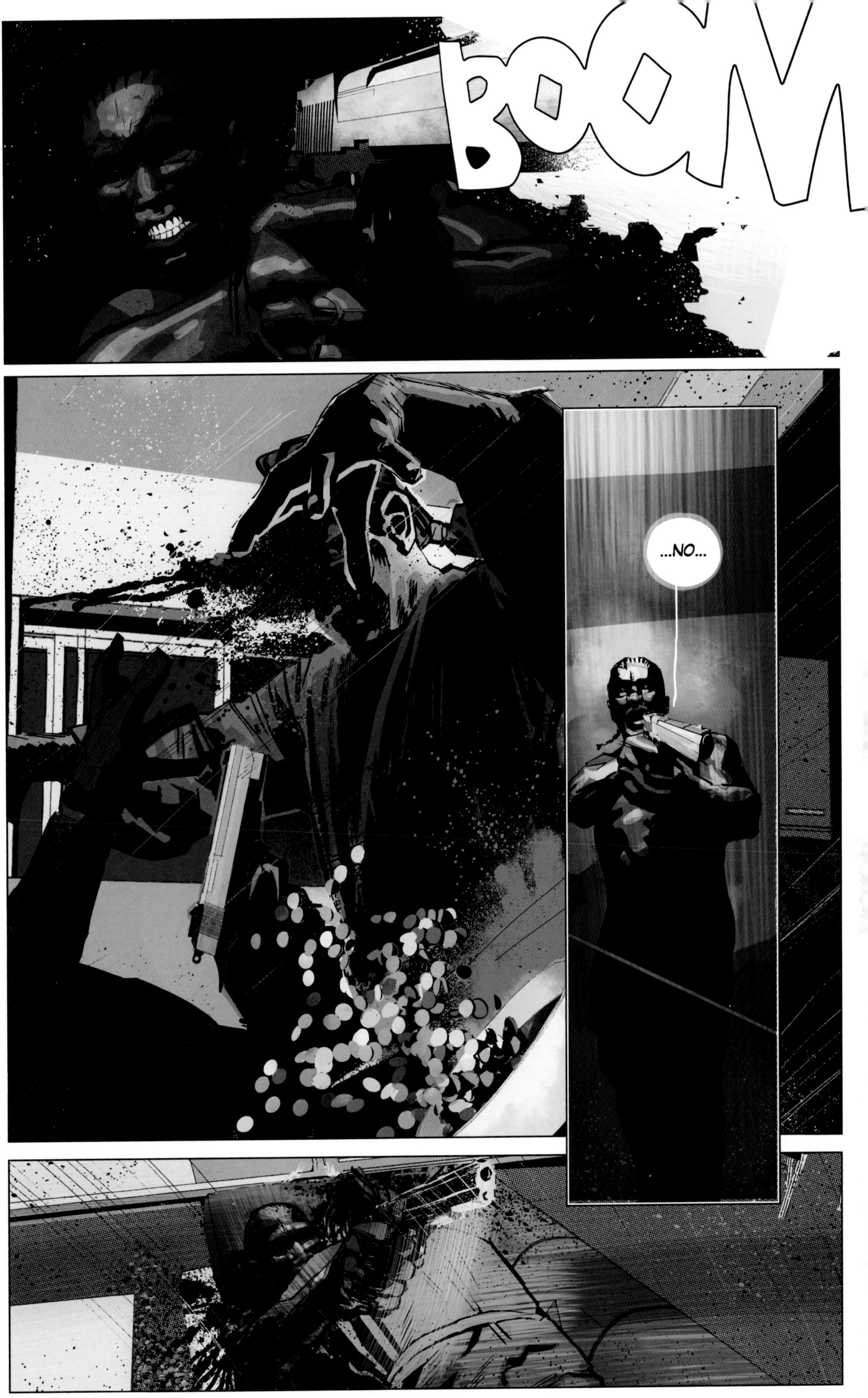
BOOM
...NO...

MMMMMUUUTTTHHHAAAFFFUUCCCKKKAAAHH!!!
BOOM
BOOM
BOOM
BOOM
BAAM
BAAM
BAAM

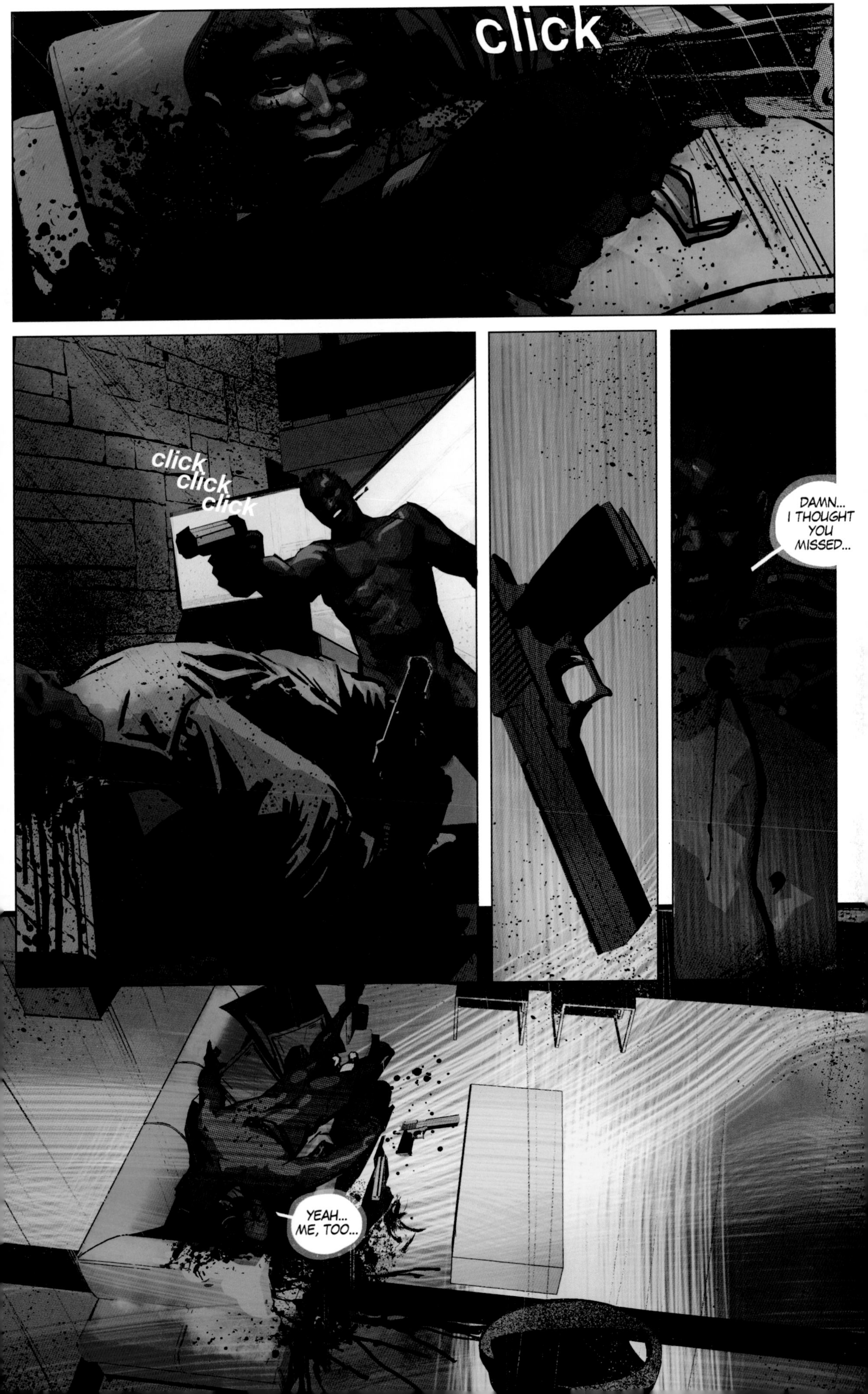
click
click
click
click
DAMN... I THOUGHT YOU MISSED...
YEAH... ME, TOO...

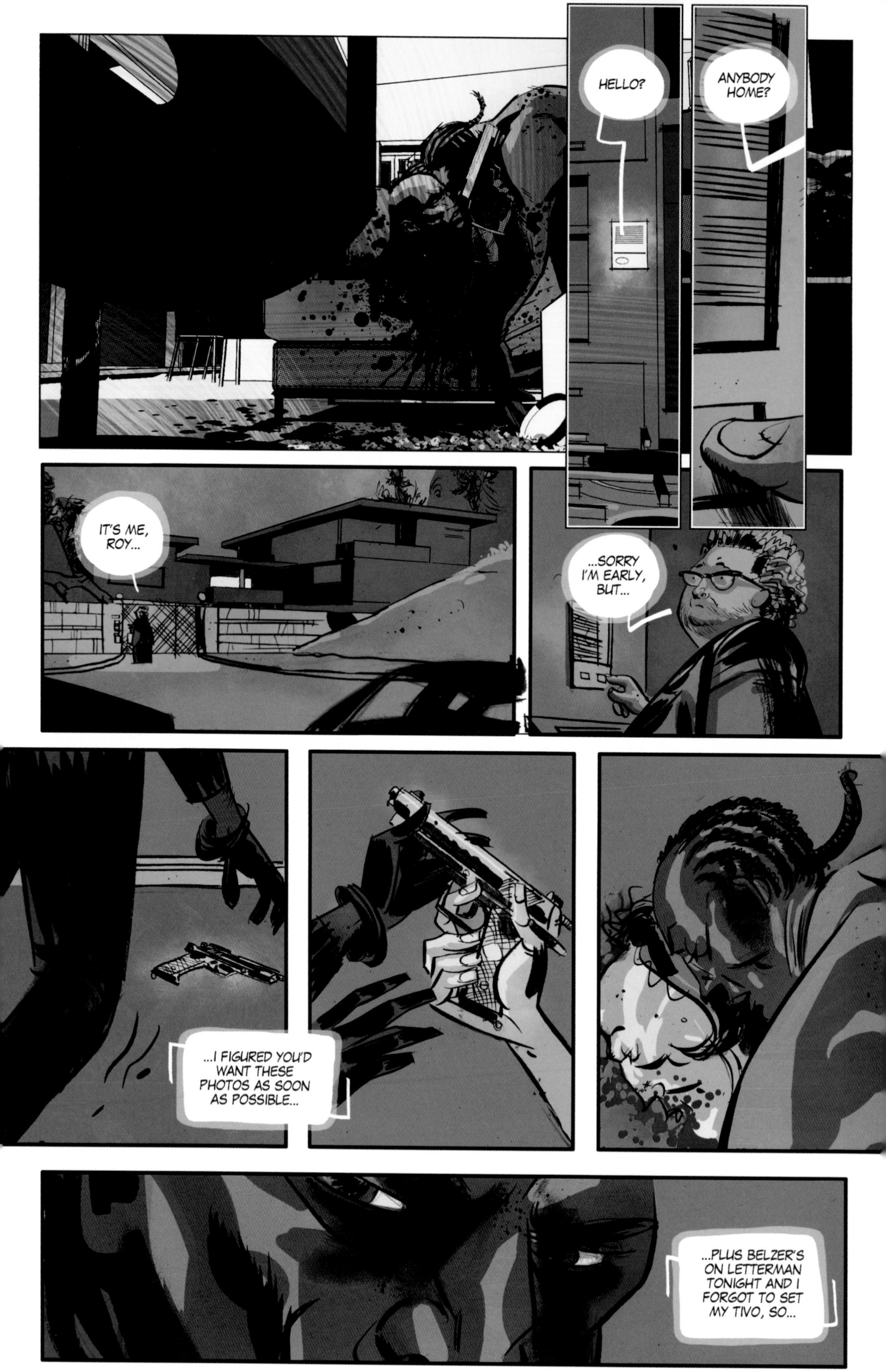
HELLO?
ANYBODY HOME?
IT'S ME, ROY...
...SORRY I'M EARLY, BUT...
...I FIGURED YOU'D WANT THESE PHOTOS AS SOON AS POSSIBLE...
...PLUS BELZER'S ON LETTERMAN TONIGHT AND I FORGOT TO SET MY TIVO, SO...

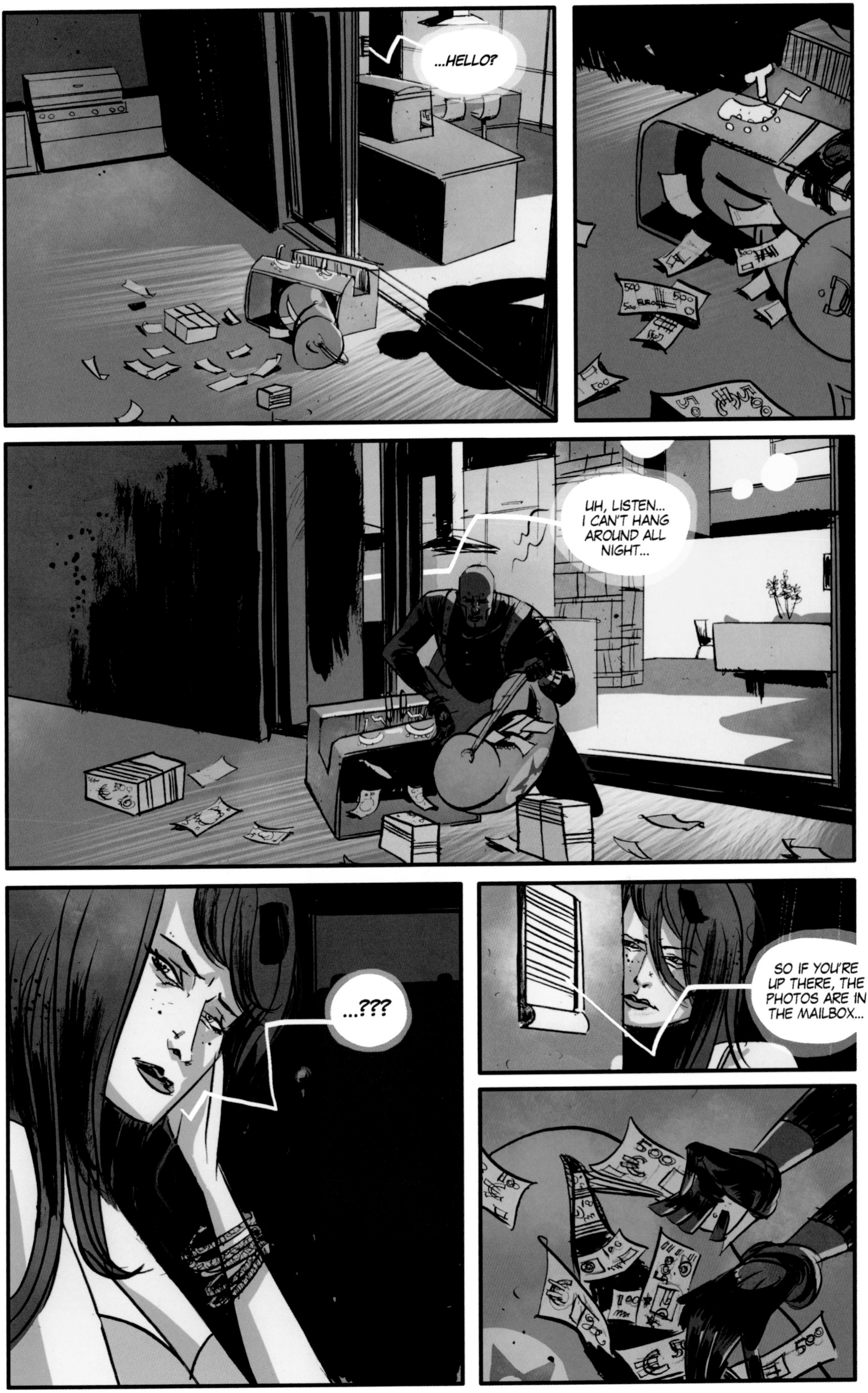
...HELLO?
UH, LISTEN... I CAN'T HANG AROUND ALL NIGHT...
...???
SO IF YOU'RE UP THERE, THE PHOTOS ARE IN THE MAILBOX...

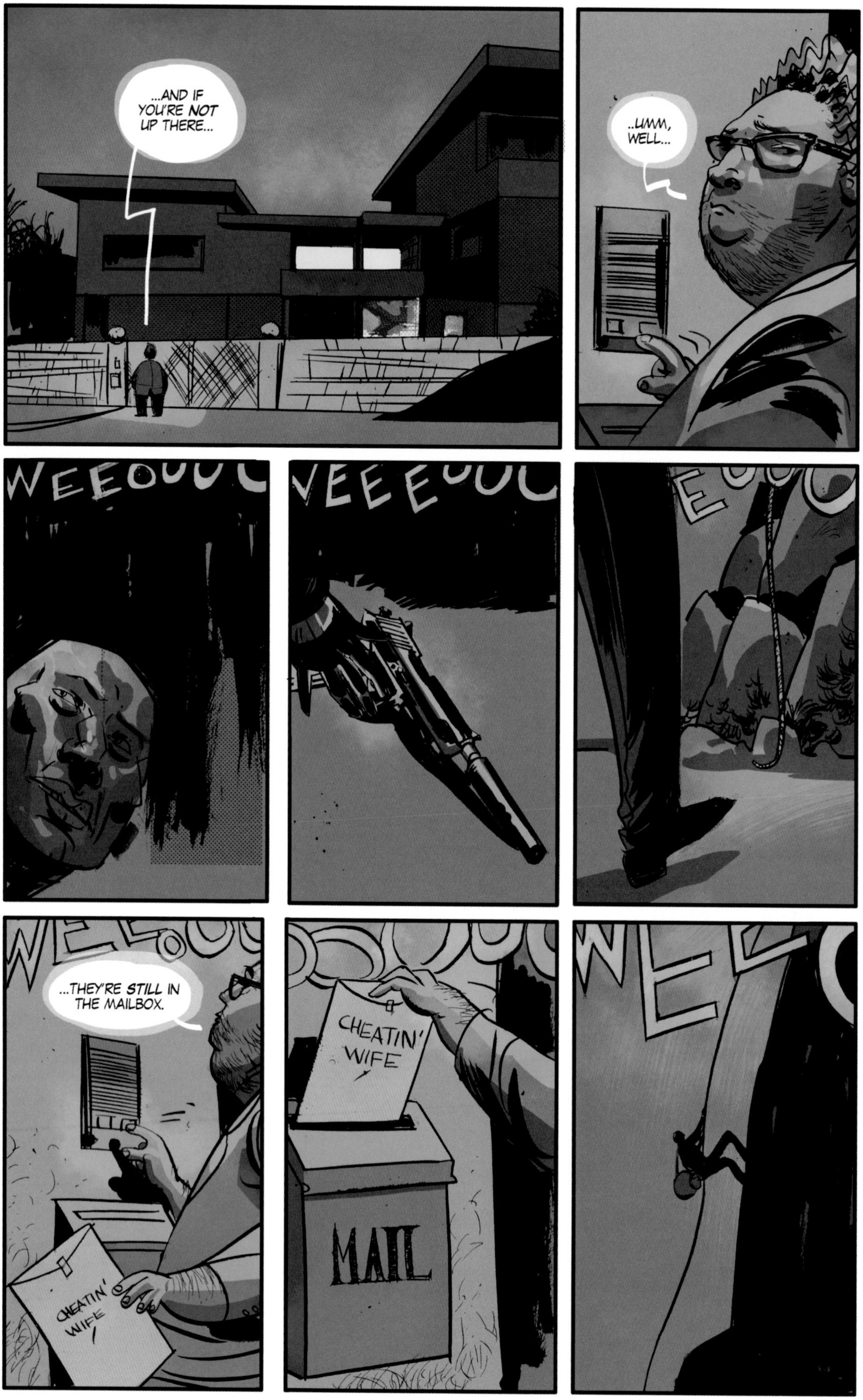
...AND IF YOU'RE NOT UP THERE...
..UMM, WELL...
WEEOOOO
WEEEEOOOO
...THEY'RE STILL IN THE MAILBOX.
CHEATIN' WIFE
CHEATIN' WIFE
MAIL

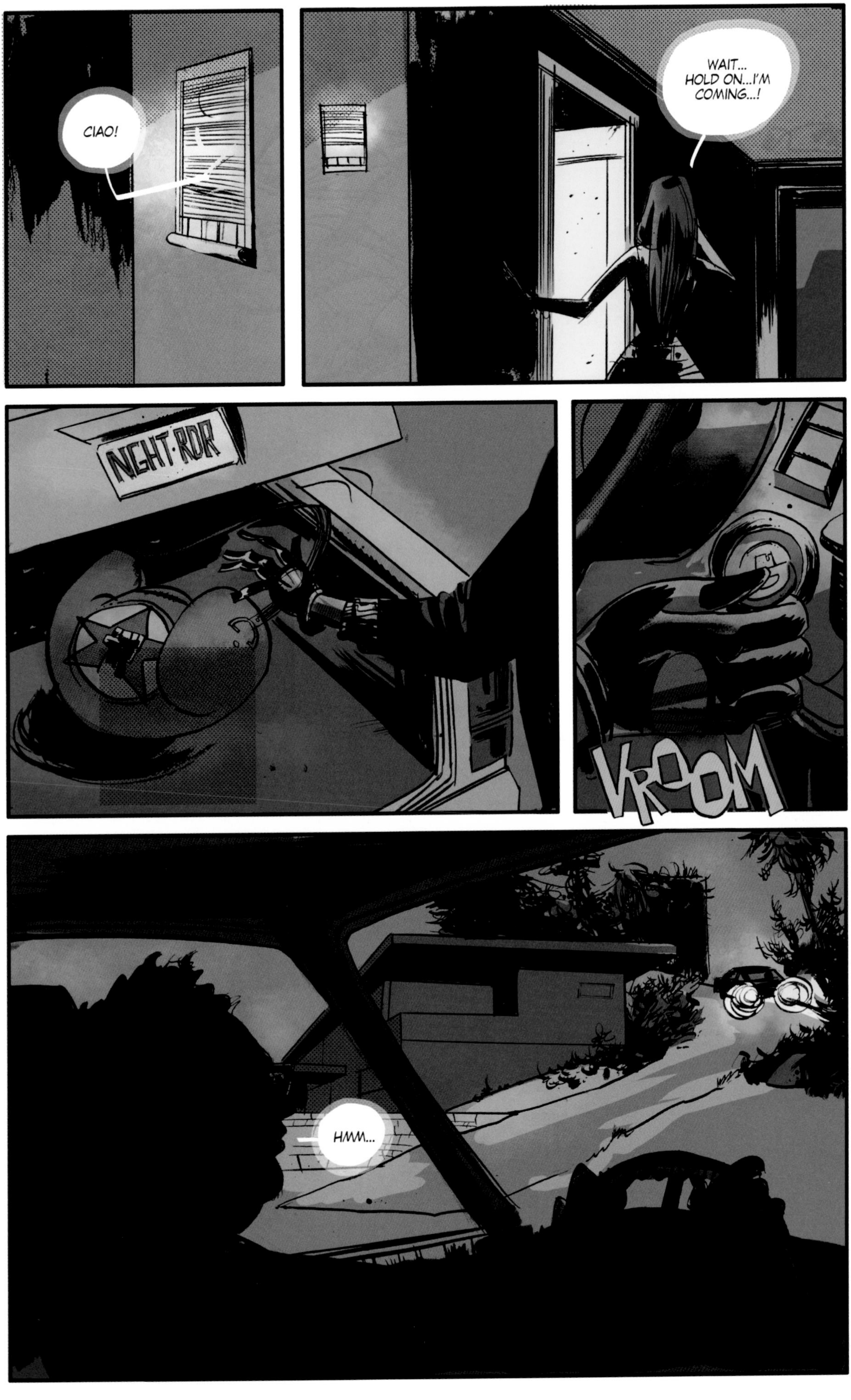
CIAO!
WAIT... HOLD ON...I'M COMING...!
NGHT·RDR
VROOM
HMM...

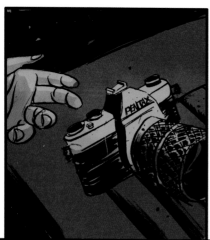

CLICK!

WHZZZZT

HELLO?

HELLO?

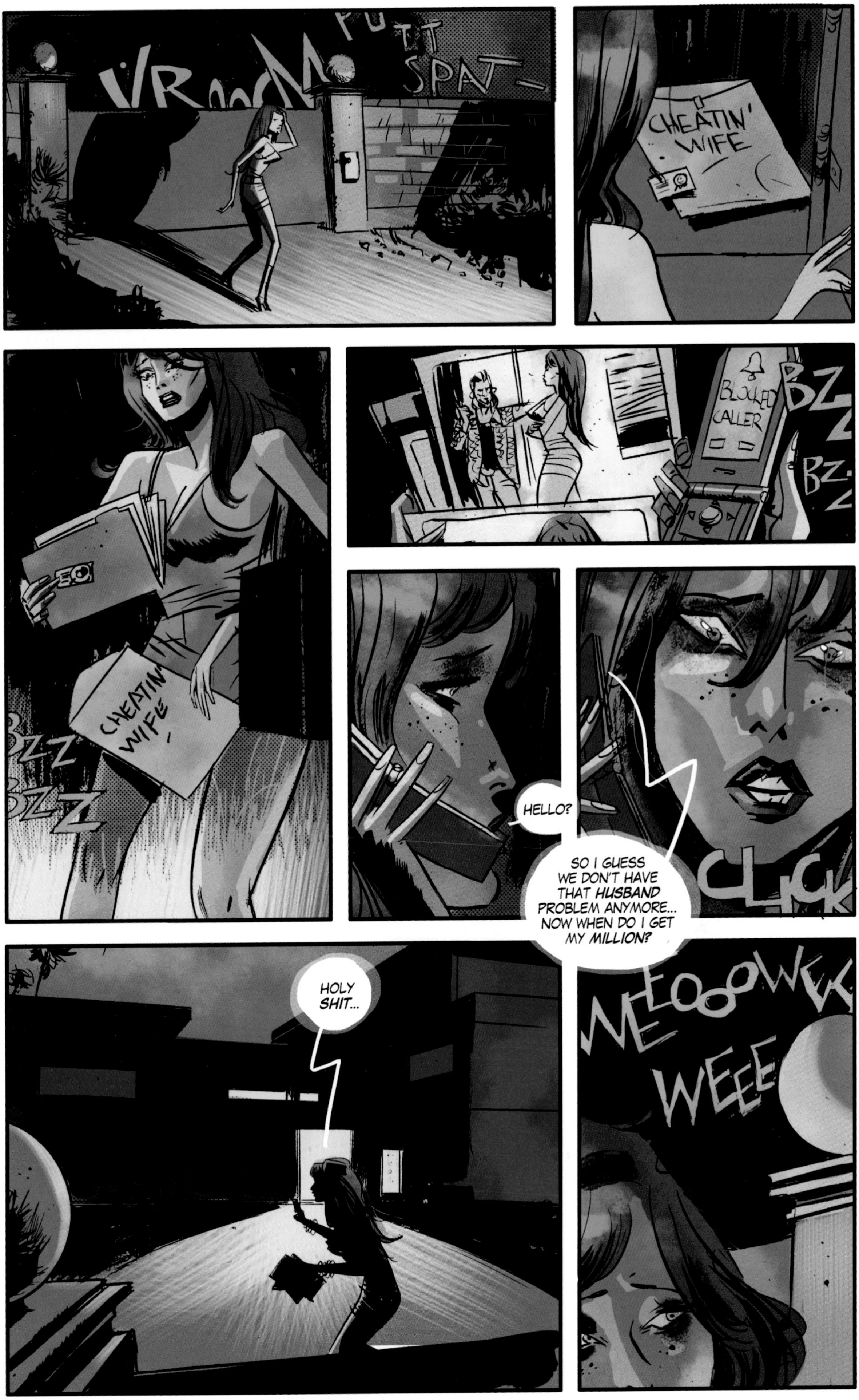
VROOM
PUTT
SPAT—
CHEATIN' WIFE
CHEATIN' WIFE
BZZ
BZZ
BLOCKED CALLER
BZZ
BZZ
HELLO?
SO I GUESS WE DON'T HAVE THAT *HUSBAND* PROBLEM ANYMORE... NOW WHEN DO I GET MY *MILLION?*
CLICK
HOLY *SHIT*...
WEEOOOWEE
WEEE

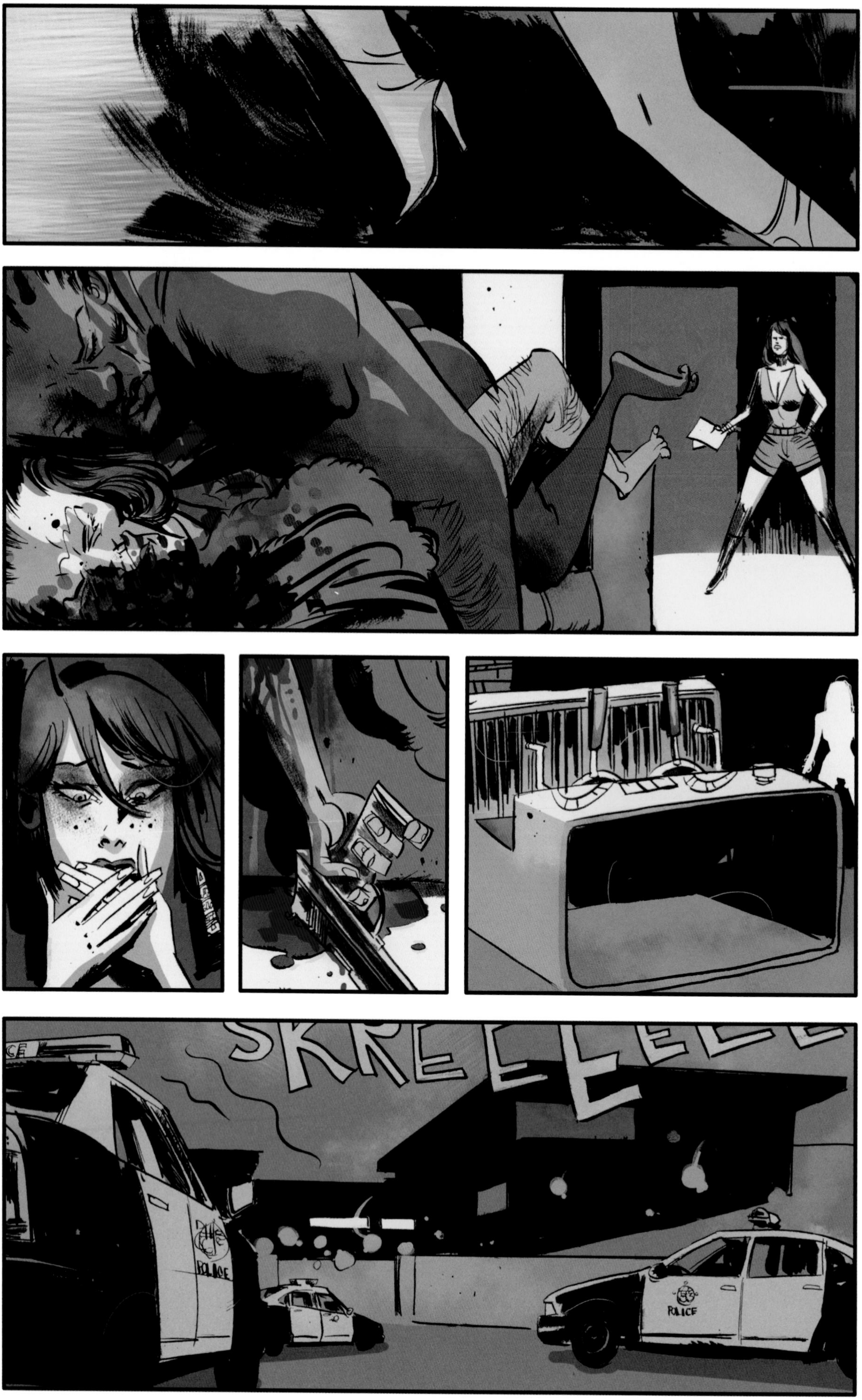
SKREEEEEEE
POLICE
POLICE

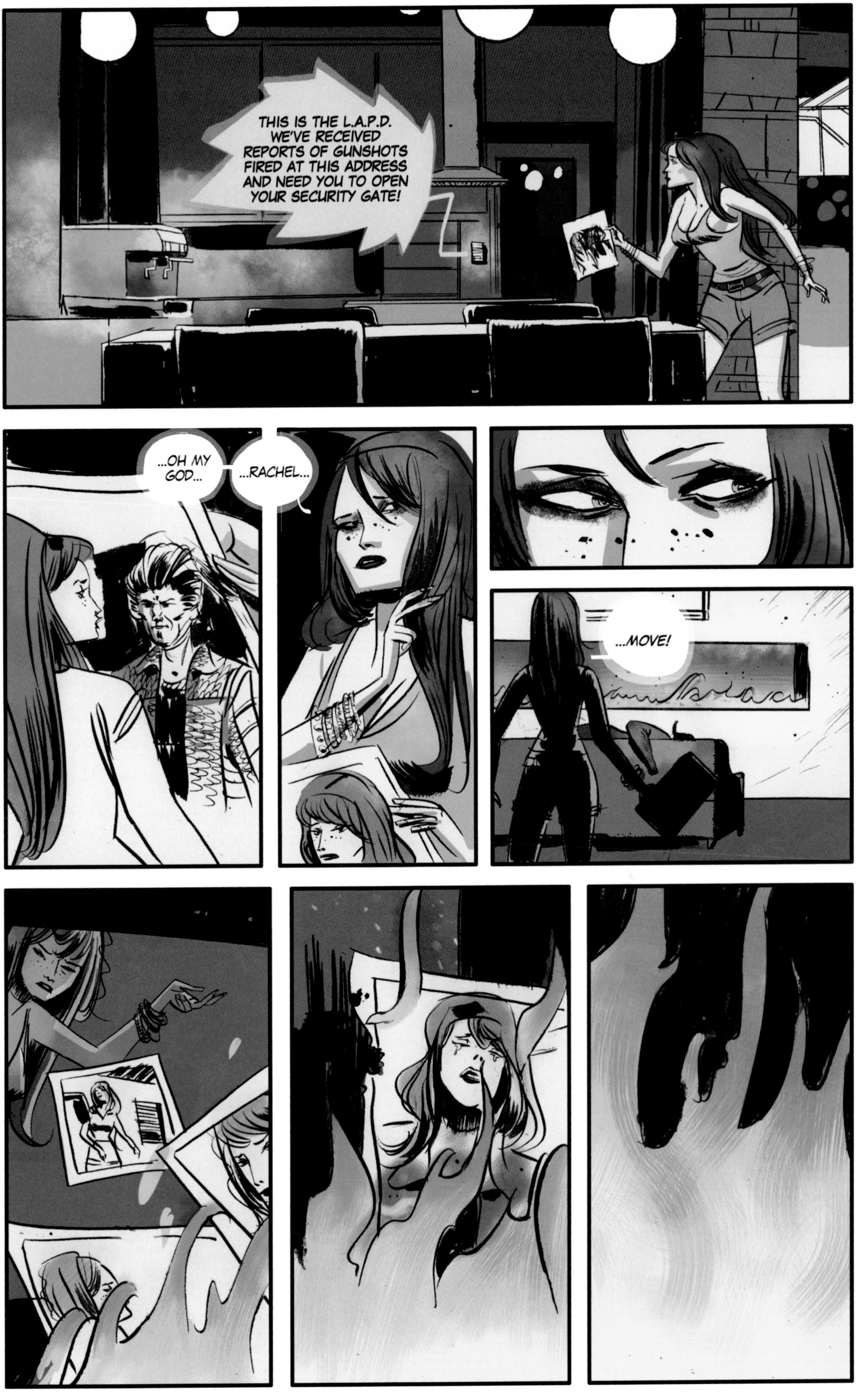
THIS IS THE L.A.P.D. WE'VE RECEIVED REPORTS OF GUNSHOTS FIRED AT THIS ADDRESS AND NEED YOU TO OPEN YOUR SECURITY GATE!
...OH MY GOD...
...RACHEL...
...MOVE!

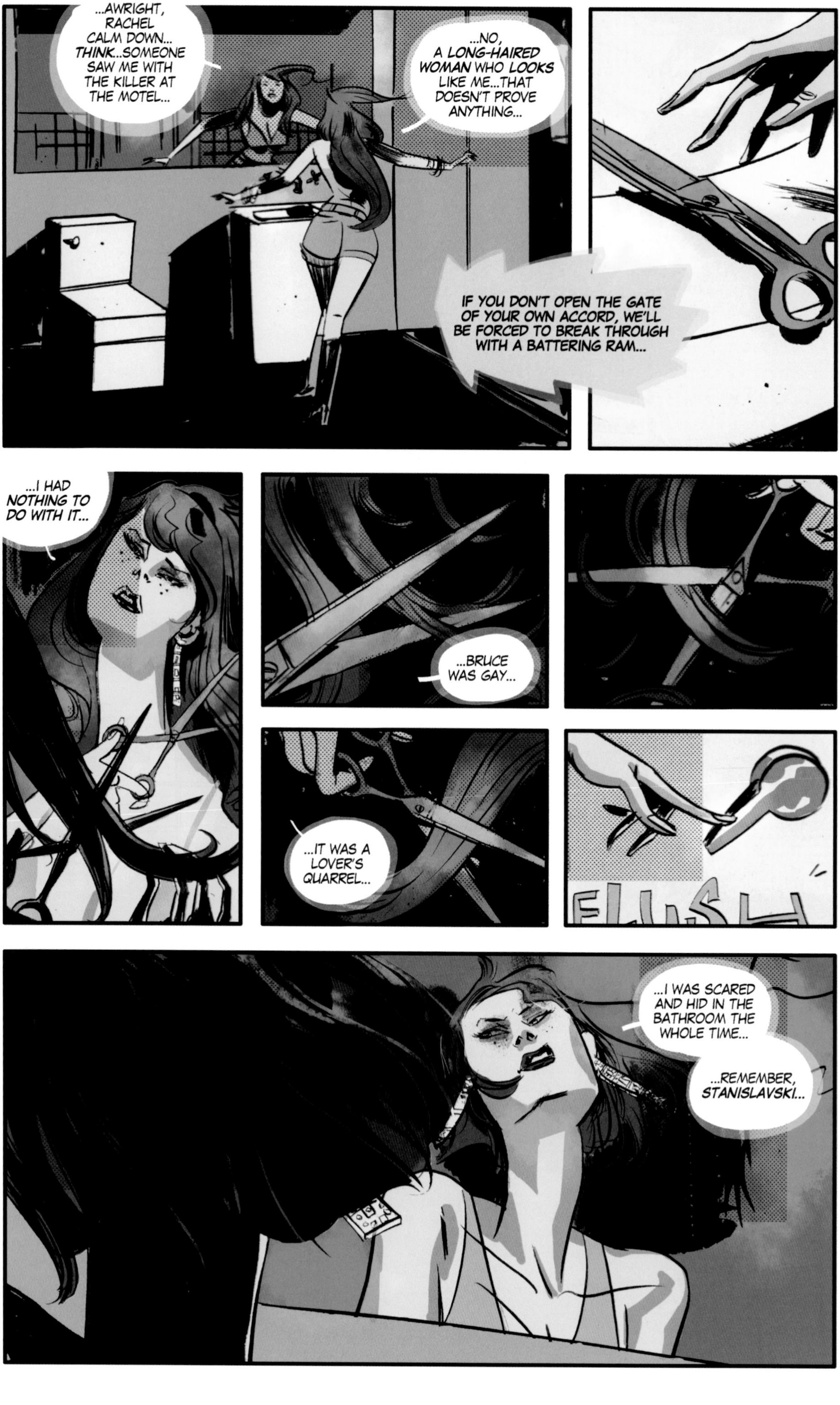
...AWRIGHT, RACHEL CALM DOWN... THINK...SOMEONE SAW ME WITH THE KILLER AT THE MOTEL...
...NO, A LONG-HAIRED WOMAN WHO LOOKS LIKE ME...THAT DOESN'T PROVE ANYTHING...
IF YOU DON'T OPEN THE GATE OF YOUR OWN ACCORD, WE'LL BE FORCED TO BREAK THROUGH WITH A BATTERING RAM...
...I HAD NOTHING TO DO WITH IT...
...BRUCE WAS GAY...
...IT WAS A LOVER'S QUARREL...
FLUSH
...I WAS SCARED AND HID IN THE BATHROOM THE WHOLE TIME...
...REMEMBER, STANISLAVSKI...

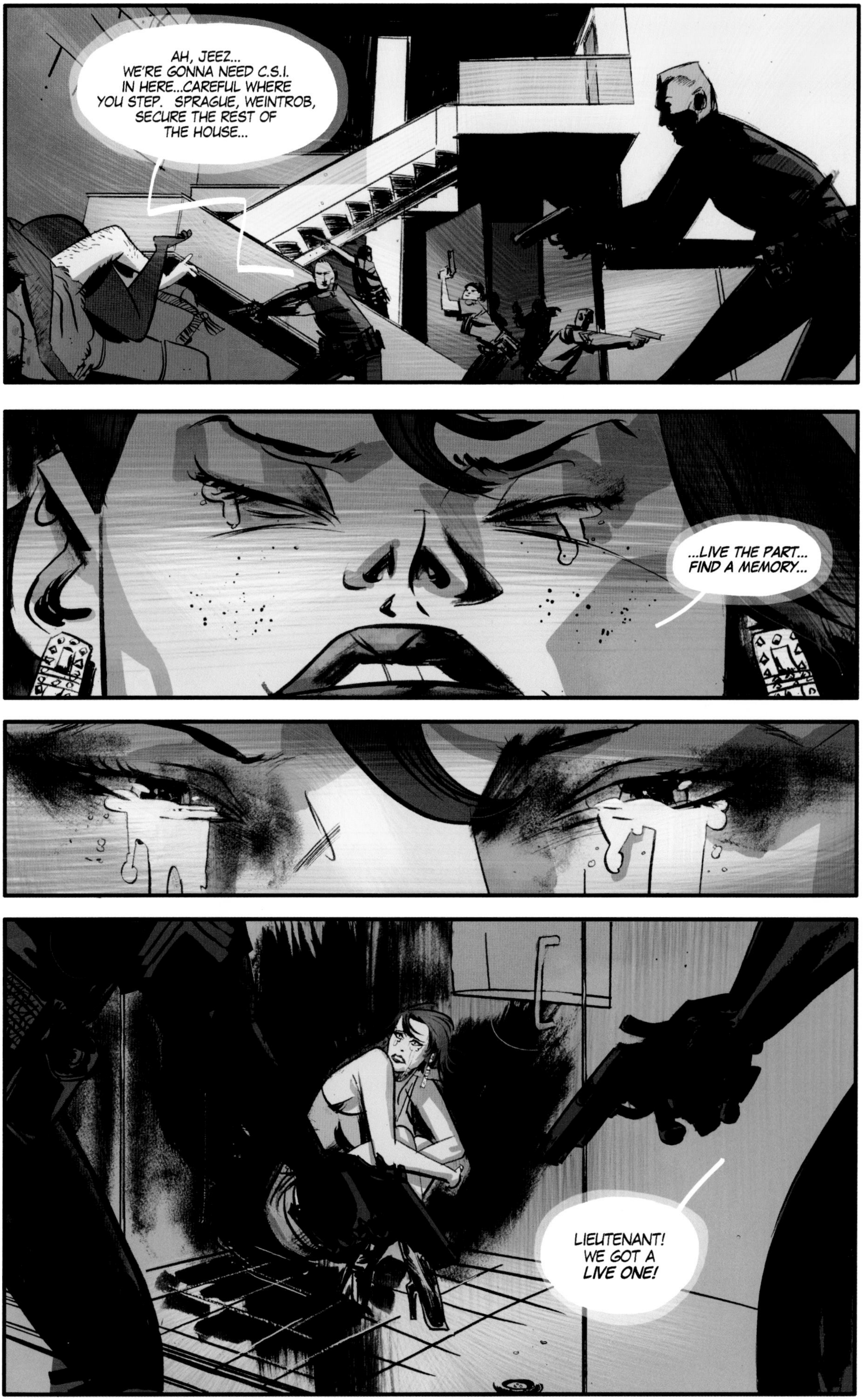
AH, JEEZ... WE'RE GONNA NEED C.S.I. IN HERE...CAREFUL WHERE YOU STEP. SPRAGUE, WEINTROB, SECURE THE REST OF THE HOUSE...
...LIVE THE PART... FIND A MEMORY...
LIEUTENANT! WE GOT A LIVE ONE!

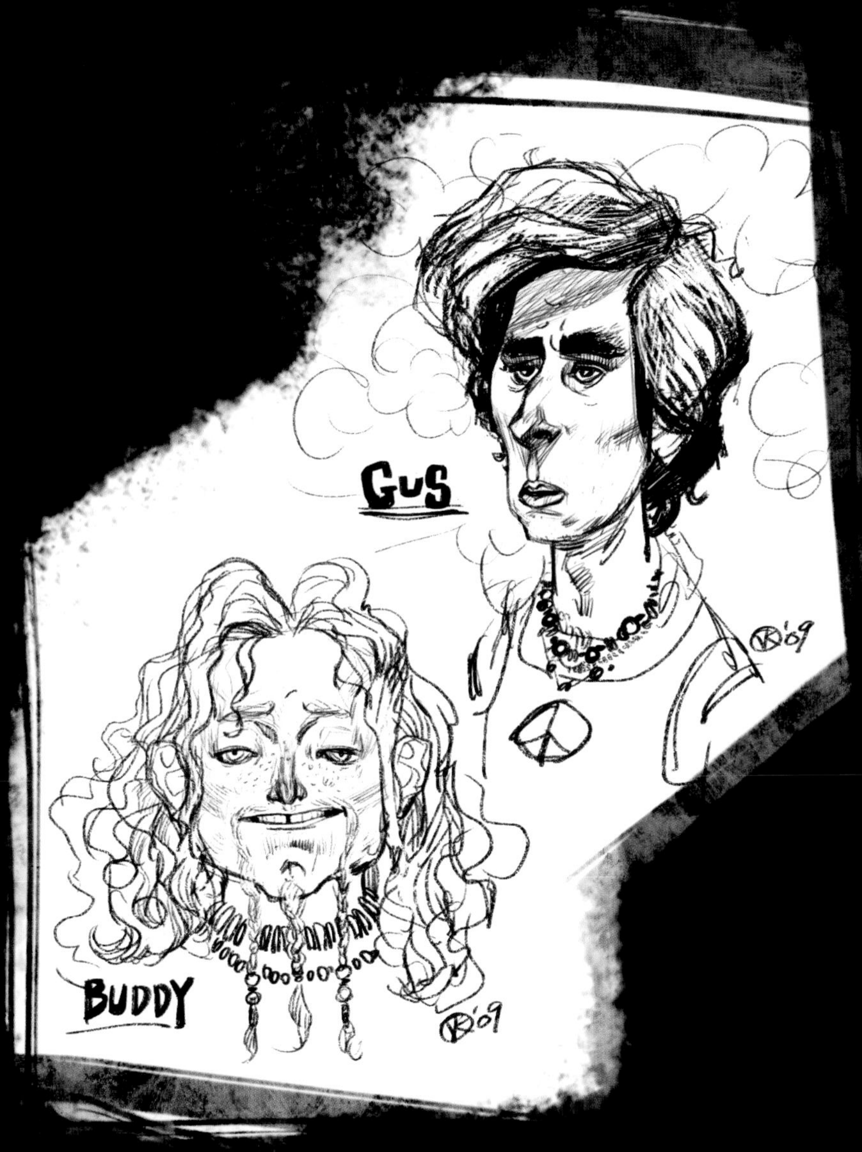
GUS
BUDDY

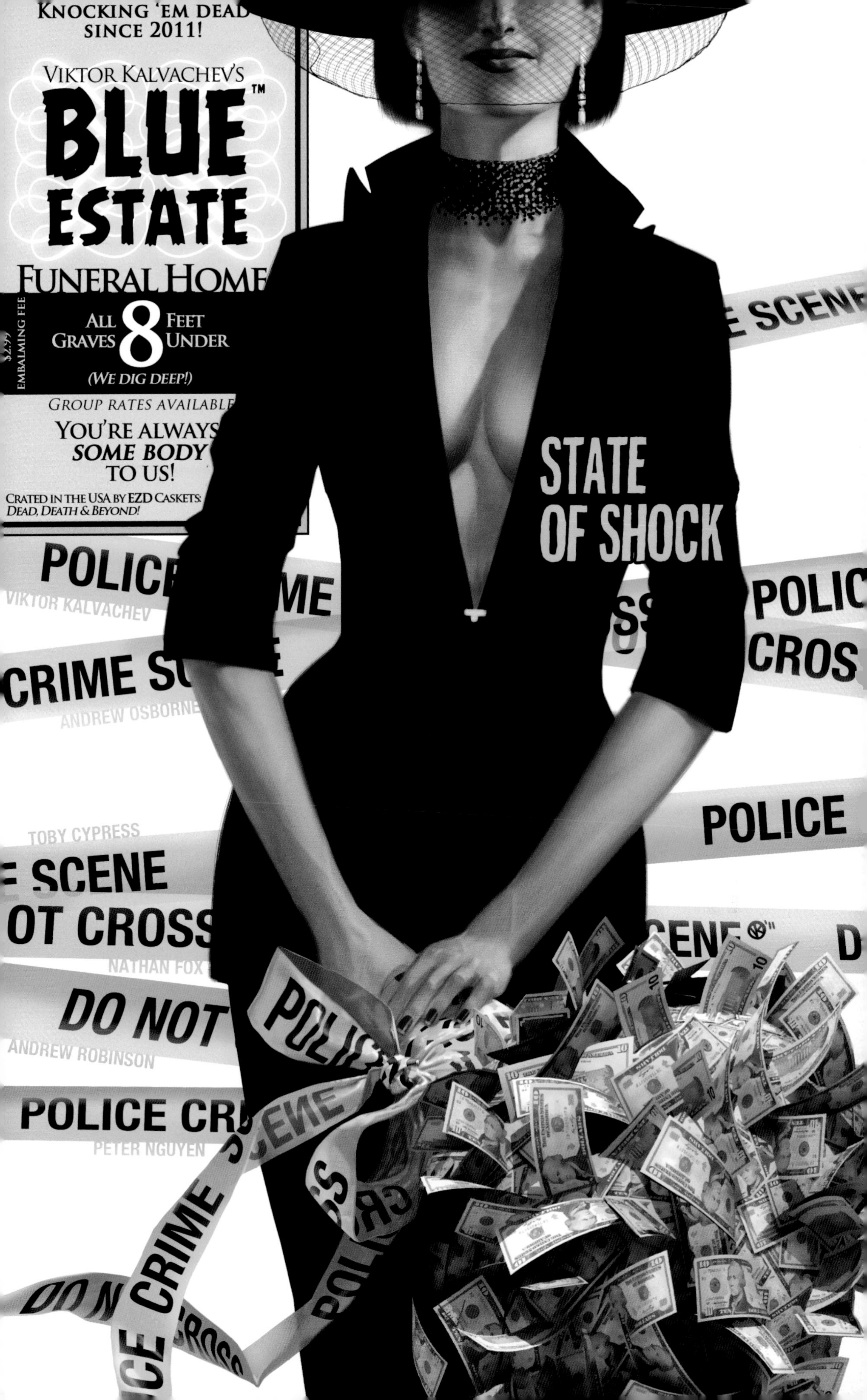
KNOCKING 'EM DEAD SINCE 2011!
VIKTOR KALVACHEV'S
BLUE ESTATE™
FUNERAL HOME
$2.99 EMBALMING FEE
ALL 8 FEET
GRAVES UNDER
(WE DIG DEEP!)
GROUP RATES AVAILABLE
YOU'RE ALWAYS SOME BODY TO US!
CRATED IN THE USA BY EZD CASKETS: DEAD, DEATH & BEYOND!
STATE OF SHOCK
VIKTOR KALVACHEV
ANDREW OSBORNE
TOBY CYPRESS
NATHAN FOX
ANDREW ROBINSON
PETER NGUYEN
POLICE

# BLUE™ ESTATE

EPISODE EIGHT:
## STATE OF SHOCK

ORIGINAL STORY:
**VIKTOR KALVACHEV** AND **KOSTA YANEV**

SCRIPT BY **ANDREW OSBORNE**

ARTISTS:
**VIKTOR KALVACHEV**
**NATHAN FOX**
**TOBY CYPRESS**
**ANDREW ROBINSON**
**PETER NGUYEN**

ART DIRECTION BY **VIKTOR KALVACHEV**

COVER, COLORS & DESIGN:
**VIKTOR KALVACHEV**

CONTRIBUTING EDITOR:
**PHILO NORTHRUP**

WWW.BlueEstateComic.com

EZD™
PRODUCTIONS

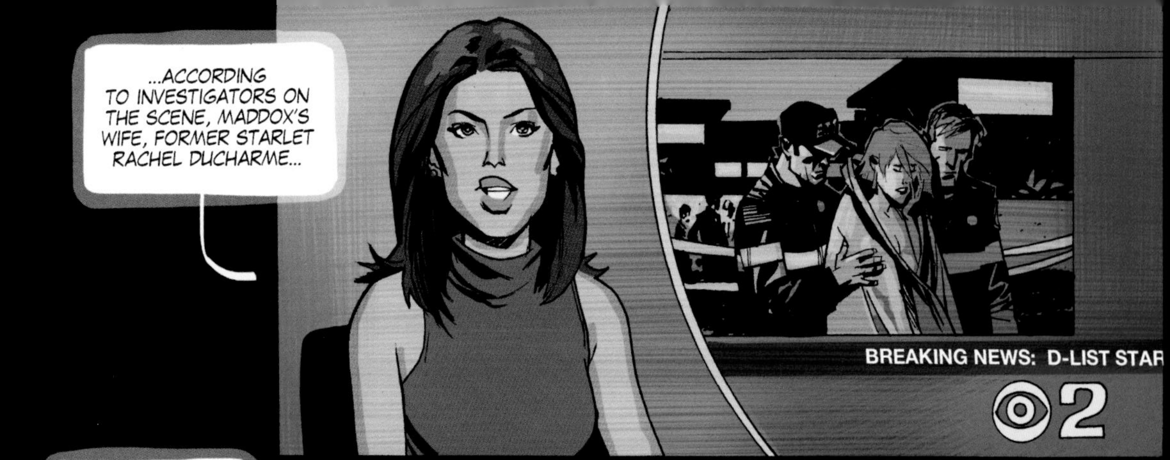
...ACCORDING TO INVESTIGATORS ON THE SCENE, MADDOX'S WIFE, FORMER STARLET RACHEL DUCHARME...
BREAKING NEWS: D-LIST STAR
2

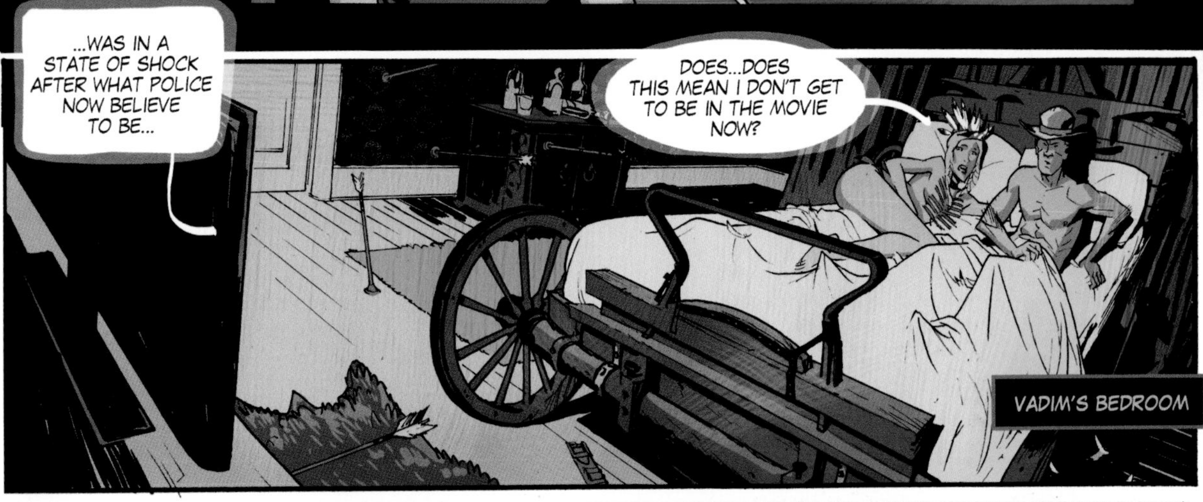
...WAS IN A STATE OF SHOCK AFTER WHAT POLICE NOW BELIEVE TO BE...
DOES...DOES THIS MEAN I DON'T GET TO BE IN THE MOVIE NOW?
VADIM'S BEDROOM

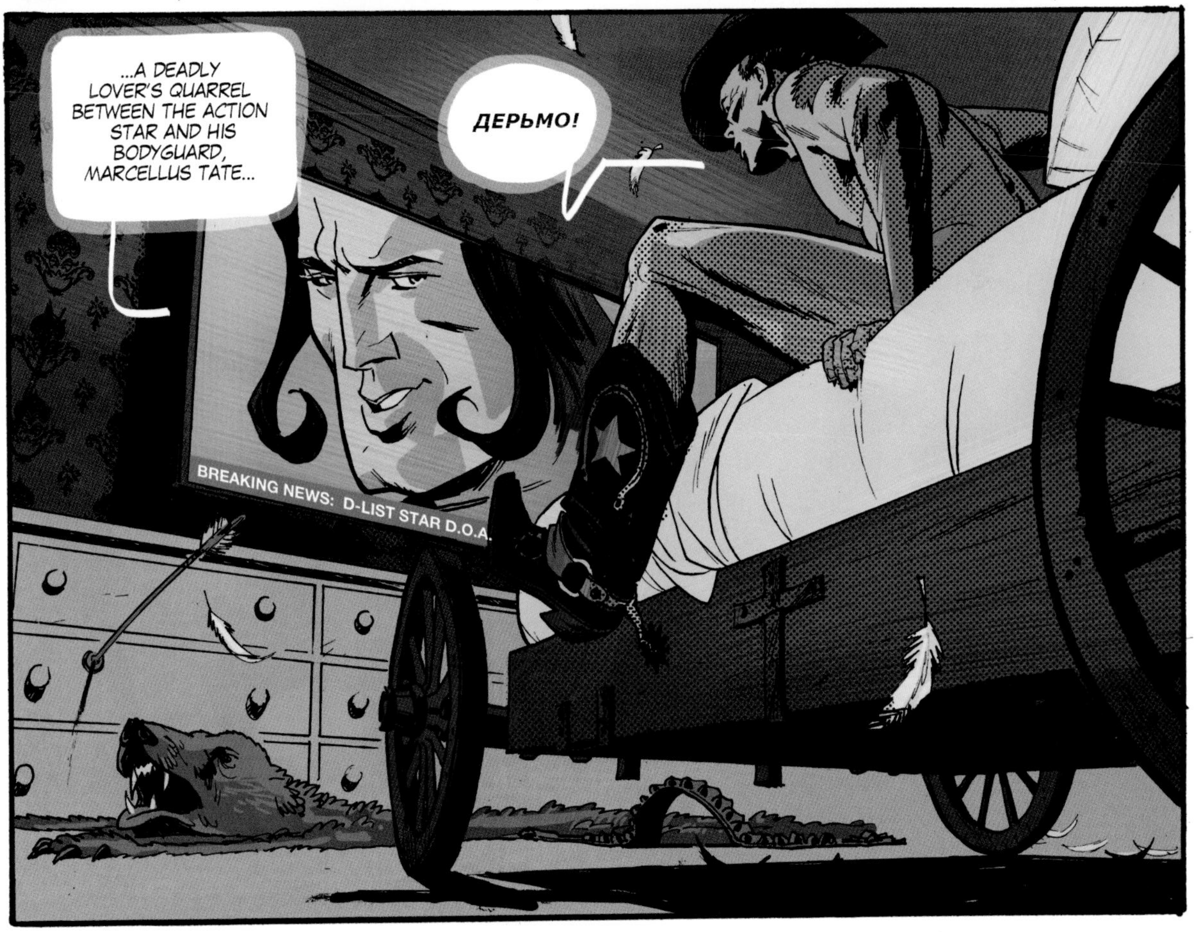
...A DEADLY LOVER'S QUARREL BETWEEN THE ACTION STAR AND HIS BODYGUARD, MARCELLUS TATE...
ДЕРЬМО!
BREAKING NEWS: D-LIST STAR D.O.A.

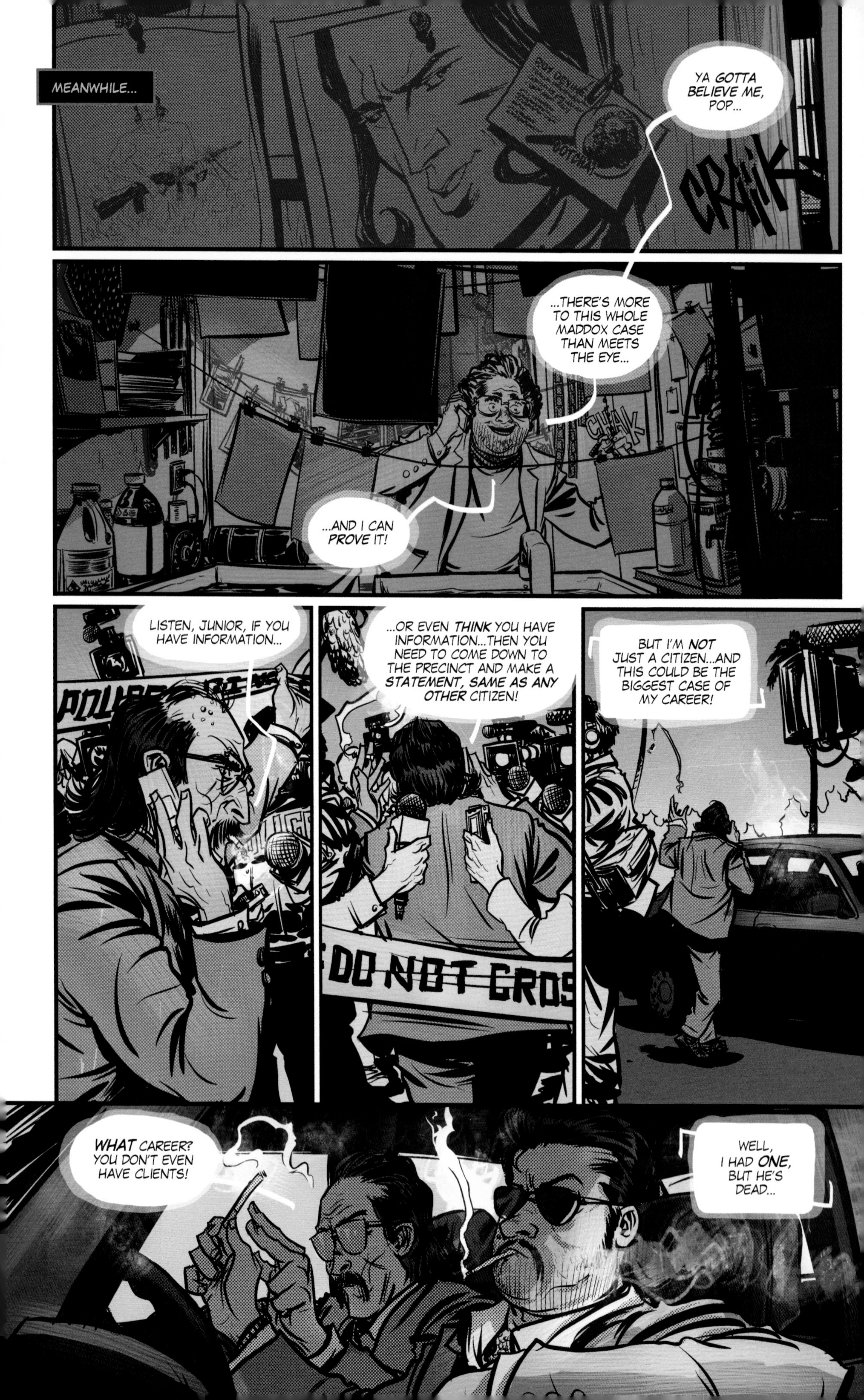
MEANWHILE...
YA GOTTA BELIEVE ME, POP...
CRAiK
...THERE'S MORE TO THIS WHOLE MADDOX CASE THAN MEETS THE EYE...
CHAK
...AND I CAN PROVE IT!
LISTEN, JUNIOR, IF YOU HAVE INFORMATION...
...OR EVEN THINK YOU HAVE INFORMATION...THEN YOU NEED TO COME DOWN TO THE PRECINCT AND MAKE A STATEMENT, SAME AS ANY OTHER CITIZEN!
DO NOT CROS
BUT I'M NOT JUST A CITIZEN...AND THIS COULD BE THE BIGGEST CASE OF MY CAREER!
WHAT CAREER? YOU DON'T EVEN HAVE CLIENTS!
WELL, I HAD ONE, BUT HE'S DEAD...

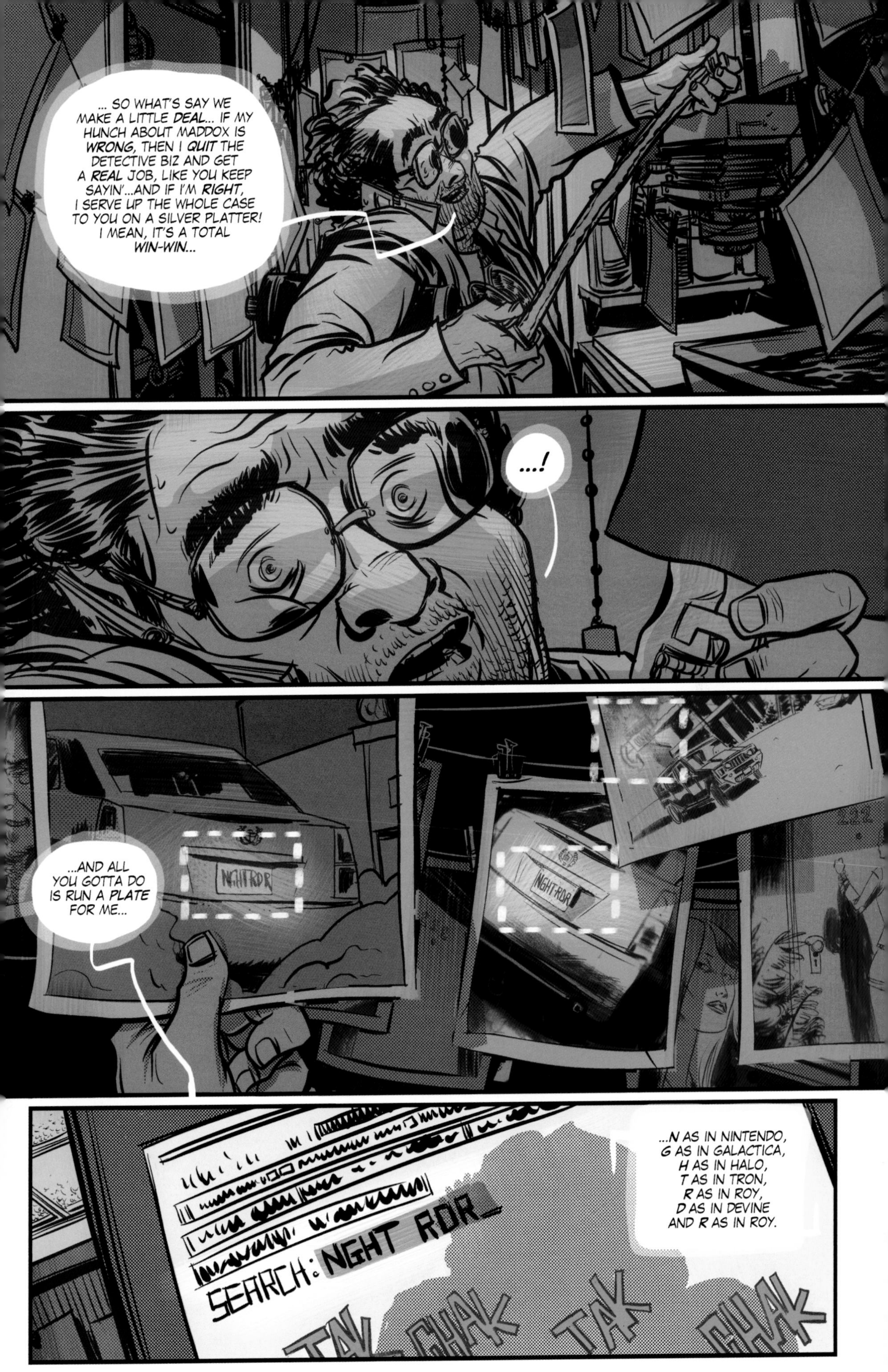
... SO WHAT'S SAY WE MAKE A LITTLE DEAL... IF MY HUNCH ABOUT MADDOX IS WRONG, THEN I QUIT THE DETECTIVE BIZ AND GET A REAL JOB, LIKE YOU KEEP SAYIN'...AND IF I'M RIGHT, I SERVE UP THE WHOLE CASE TO YOU ON A SILVER PLATTER! I MEAN, IT'S A TOTAL WIN-WIN...
...!
...AND ALL YOU GOTTA DO IS RUN A PLATE FOR ME...
SEARCH: NGHT RDR_
...N AS IN NINTENDO, G AS IN GALACTICA, H AS IN HALO, T AS IN TRON, R AS IN ROY, D AS IN DEVINE AND R AS IN ROY.
CHAK
TAK
CHAK

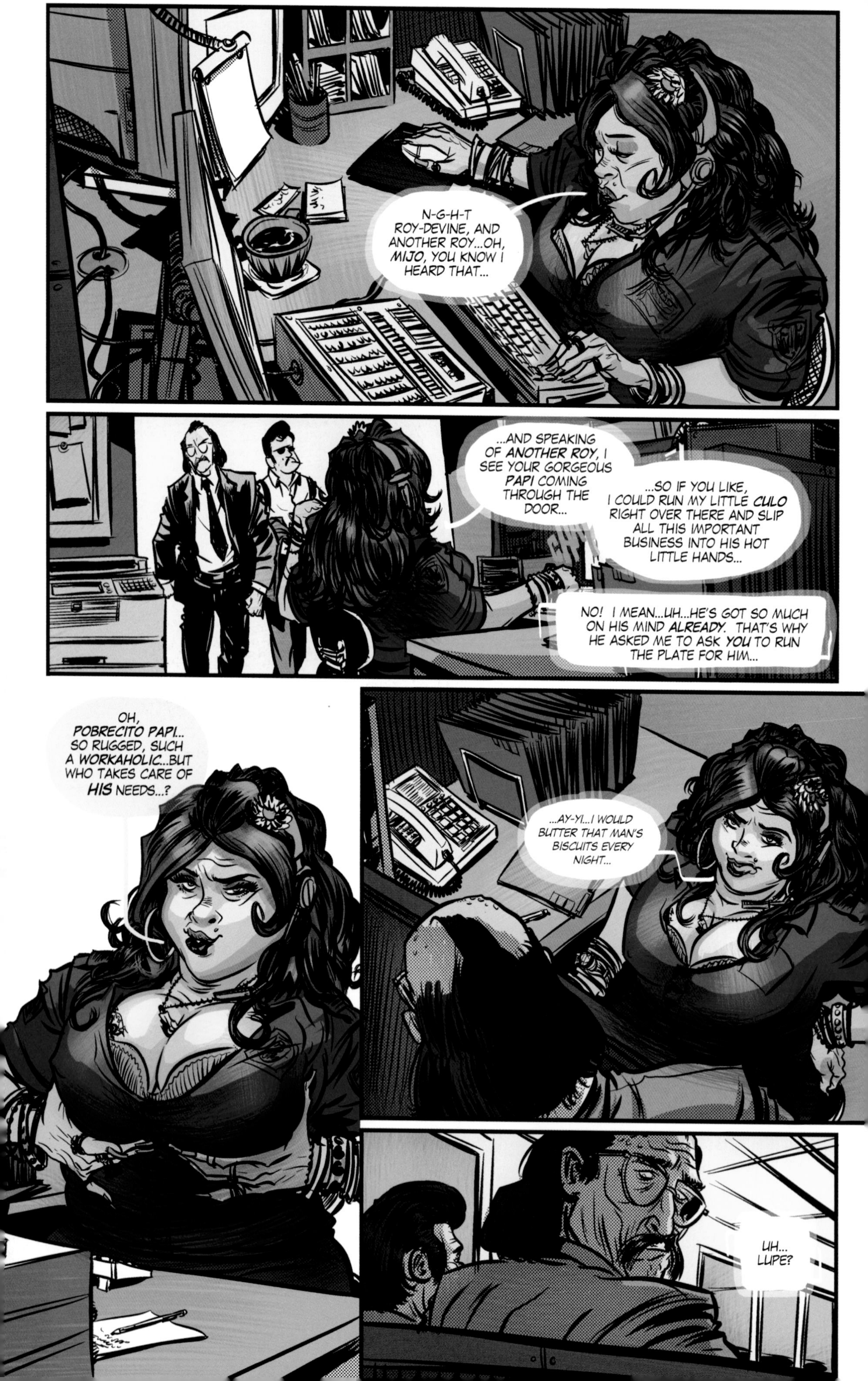
N-G-H-T ROY-DEVINE, AND ANOTHER ROY...OH, MIJO, YOU KNOW I HEARD THAT...
...AND SPEAKING OF ANOTHER ROY, I SEE YOUR GORGEOUS PAPI COMING THROUGH THE DOOR...
...SO IF YOU LIKE, I COULD RUN MY LITTLE CULO RIGHT OVER THERE AND SLIP ALL THIS IMPORTANT BUSINESS INTO HIS HOT LITTLE HANDS...
NO! I MEAN...UH...HE'S GOT SO MUCH ON HIS MIND ALREADY. THAT'S WHY HE ASKED ME TO ASK YOU TO RUN THE PLATE FOR HIM...
OH, POBRECITO PAPI... SO RUGGED, SUCH A WORKAHOLIC...BUT WHO TAKES CARE OF HIS NEEDS...?
...AY-YI...I WOULD BUTTER THAT MAN'S BISCUITS EVERY NIGHT...
UH... LUPE?

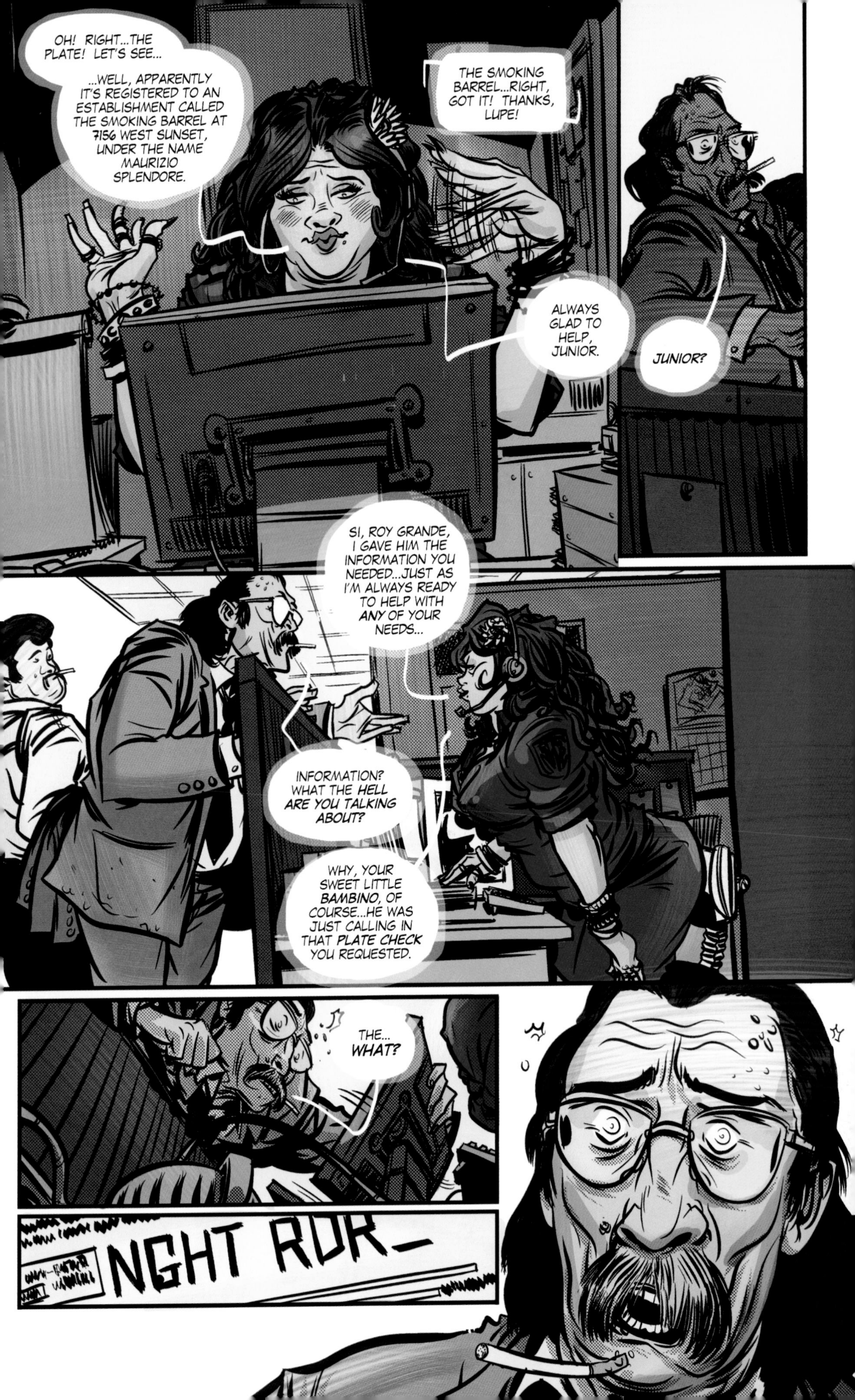
OH! RIGHT...THE PLATE! LET'S SEE...
...WELL, APPARENTLY IT'S REGISTERED TO AN ESTABLISHMENT CALLED THE SMOKING BARREL AT 7156 WEST SUNSET, UNDER THE NAME MAURIZIO SPLENDORE.
THE SMOKING BARREL...RIGHT, GOT IT! THANKS, LUPE!
ALWAYS GLAD TO HELP, JUNIOR.
JUNIOR?
SI, ROY GRANDE, I GAVE HIM THE INFORMATION YOU NEEDED...JUST AS I'M ALWAYS READY TO HELP WITH ANY OF YOUR NEEDS...
INFORMATION? WHAT THE HELL ARE YOU TALKING ABOUT?
WHY, YOUR SWEET LITTLE BAMBINO, OF COURSE...HE WAS JUST CALLING IN THAT PLATE CHECK YOU REQUESTED.
THE... WHAT?
NGHT RDR_

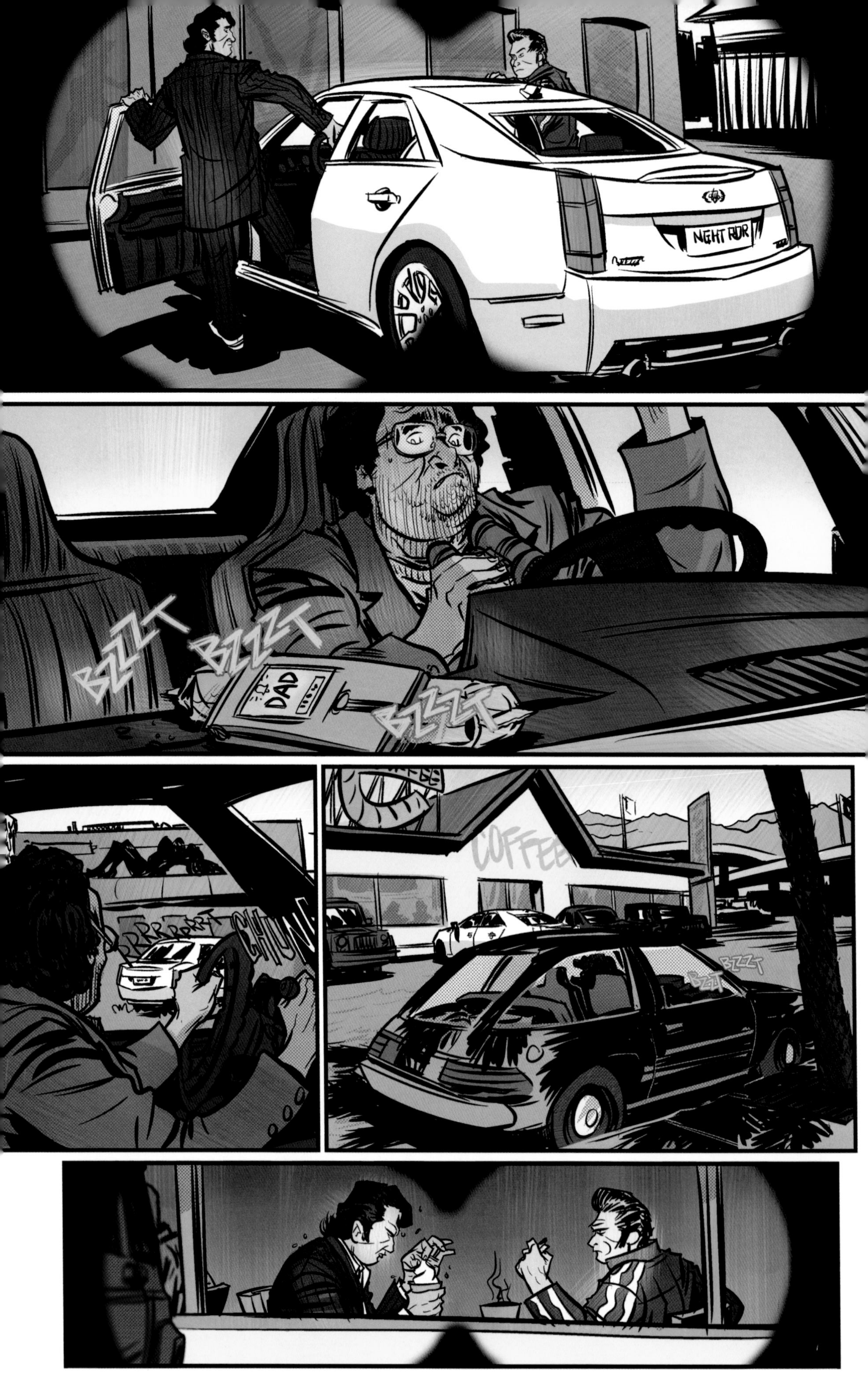
NGHT RDR
BZZZT
BZZZT
DAD
BZZZT
BRRRRRRRT
COFFEE
BZZZT
BZZZT

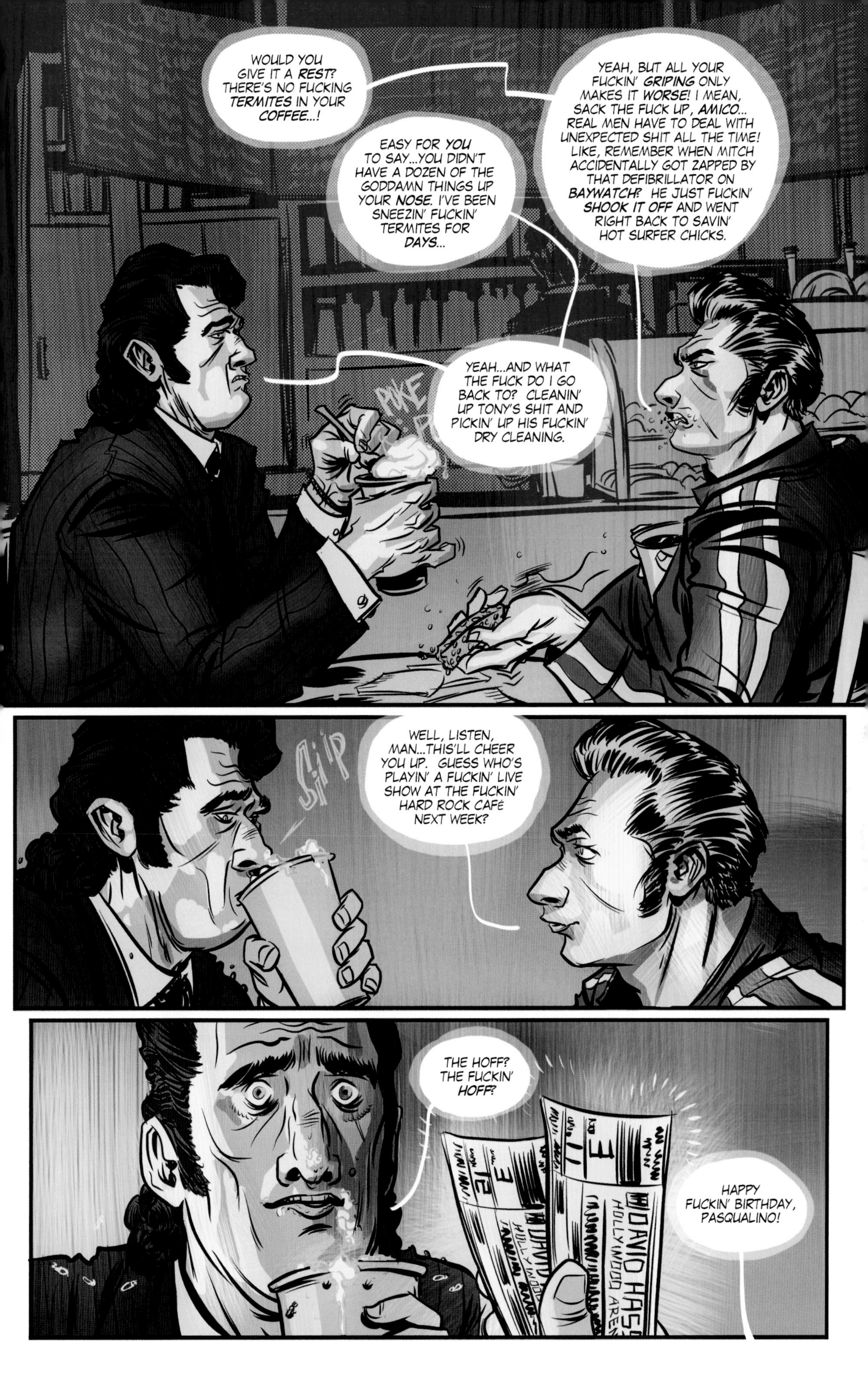

WOULD YOU GIVE IT A REST? THERE'S NO FUCKING TERMITES IN YOUR COFFEE...!
EASY FOR YOU TO SAY...YOU DIDN'T HAVE A DOZEN OF THE GODDAMN THINGS UP YOUR NOSE. I'VE BEEN SNEEZIN' FUCKIN' TERMITES FOR DAYS...
YEAH, BUT ALL YOUR FUCKIN' GRIPING ONLY MAKES IT WORSE! I MEAN, SACK THE FUCK UP, AMICO... REAL MEN HAVE TO DEAL WITH UNEXPECTED SHIT ALL THE TIME! LIKE, REMEMBER WHEN MITCH ACCIDENTALLY GOT ZAPPED BY THAT DEFIBRILLATOR ON BAYWATCH? HE JUST FUCKIN' SHOOK IT OFF AND WENT RIGHT BACK TO SAVIN' HOT SURFER CHICKS.
YEAH...AND WHAT THE FUCK DO I GO BACK TO? CLEANIN' UP TONY'S SHIT AND PICKIN' UP HIS FUCKIN' DRY CLEANING.
WELL, LISTEN, MAN...THIS'LL CHEER YOU UP. GUESS WHO'S PLAYIN' A FUCKIN' LIVE SHOW AT THE FUCKIN' HARD ROCK CAFÉ NEXT WEEK?
THE HOFF? THE FUCKIN' HOFF?
HAPPY FUCKIN' BIRTHDAY, PASQUALINO!

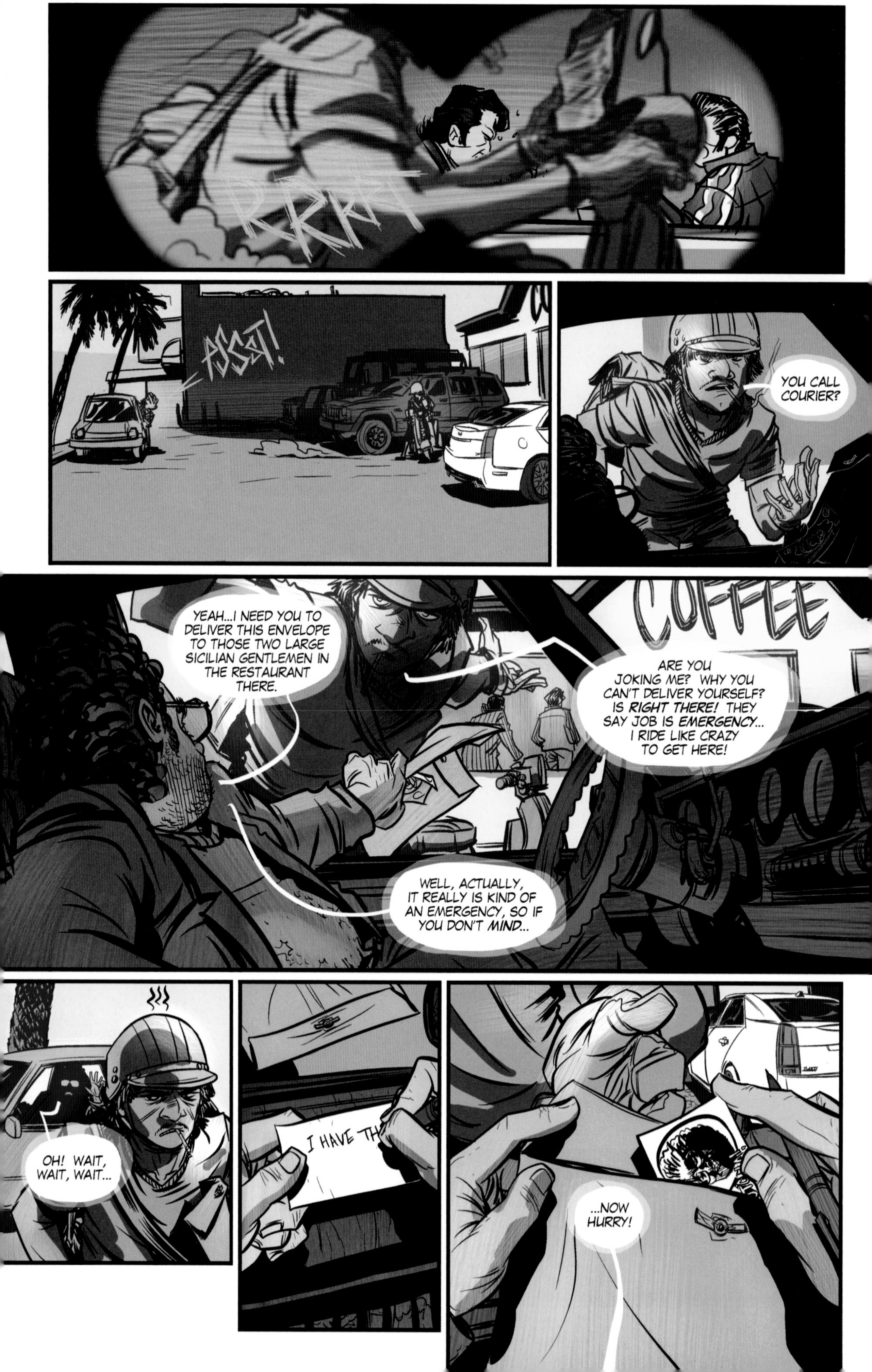
RRRRT
PSSST!
YOU CALL COURIER?
YEAH...I NEED YOU TO DELIVER THIS ENVELOPE TO THOSE TWO LARGE SICILIAN GENTLEMEN IN THE RESTAURANT THERE.
COFFEE
ARE YOU JOKING ME? WHY YOU CAN'T DELIVER YOURSELF? IS RIGHT THERE! THEY SAY JOB IS EMERGENCY... I RIDE LIKE CRAZY TO GET HERE!
WELL, ACTUALLY, IT REALLY IS KIND OF AN EMERGENCY, SO IF YOU DON'T MIND...
OH! WAIT, WAIT, WAIT...
I HAVE TH
...NOW HURRY!

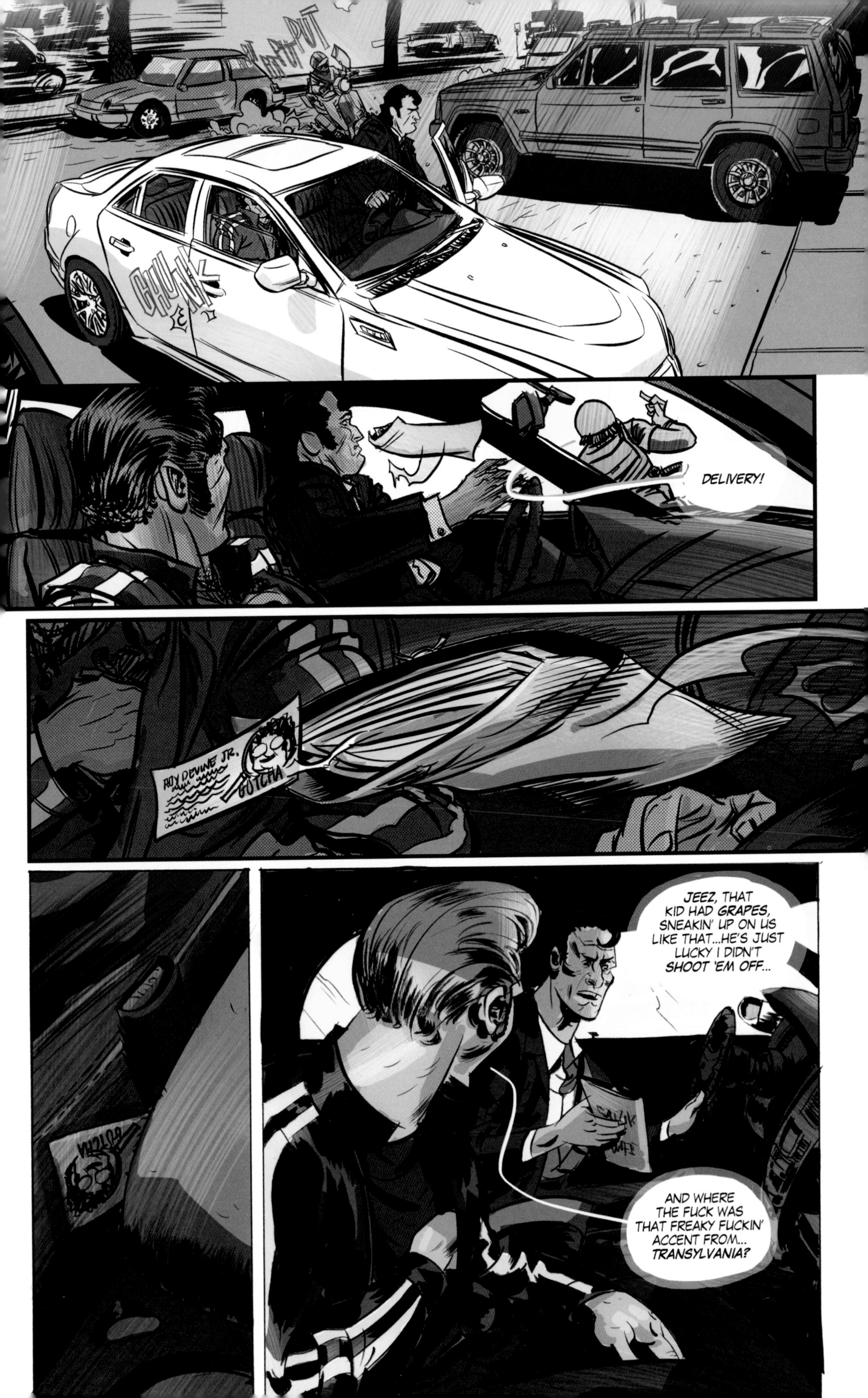
PUT PUT PUT
CHUNK
DELIVERY!
ROY DEVINE JR.
GOTCHA
JEEZ, THAT KID HAD GRAPES, SNEAKIN' UP ON US LIKE THAT...HE'S JUST LUCKY I DIDN'T SHOOT 'EM OFF...
AND WHERE THE FUCK WAS THAT FREAKY FUCKIN' ACCENT FROM... TRANSYLVANIA?

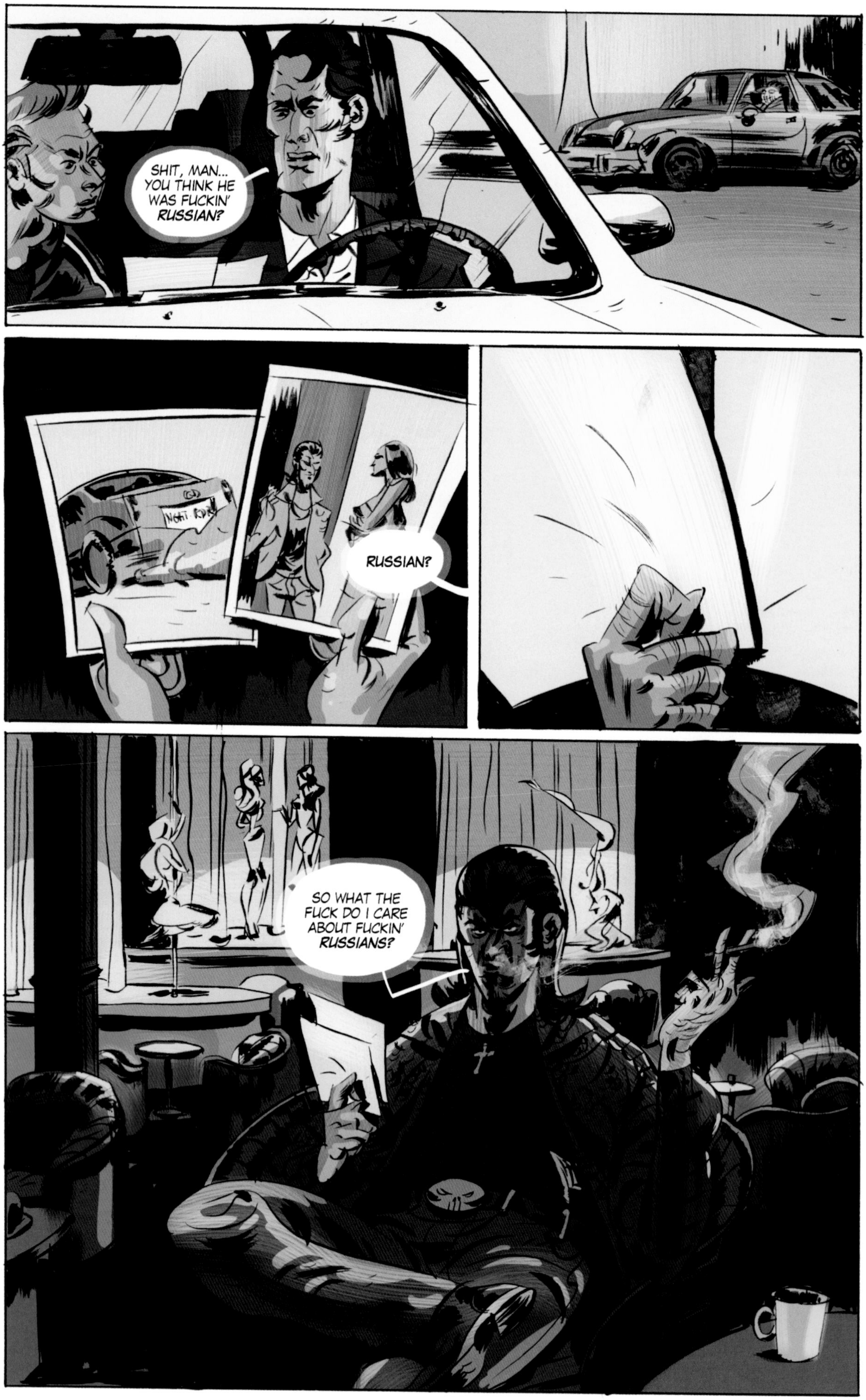
SHIT, MAN... YOU THINK HE WAS FUCKIN' *RUSSIAN?*
RUSSIAN?
SO WHAT THE FUCK DO I CARE ABOUT FUCKIN' *RUSSIANS?*

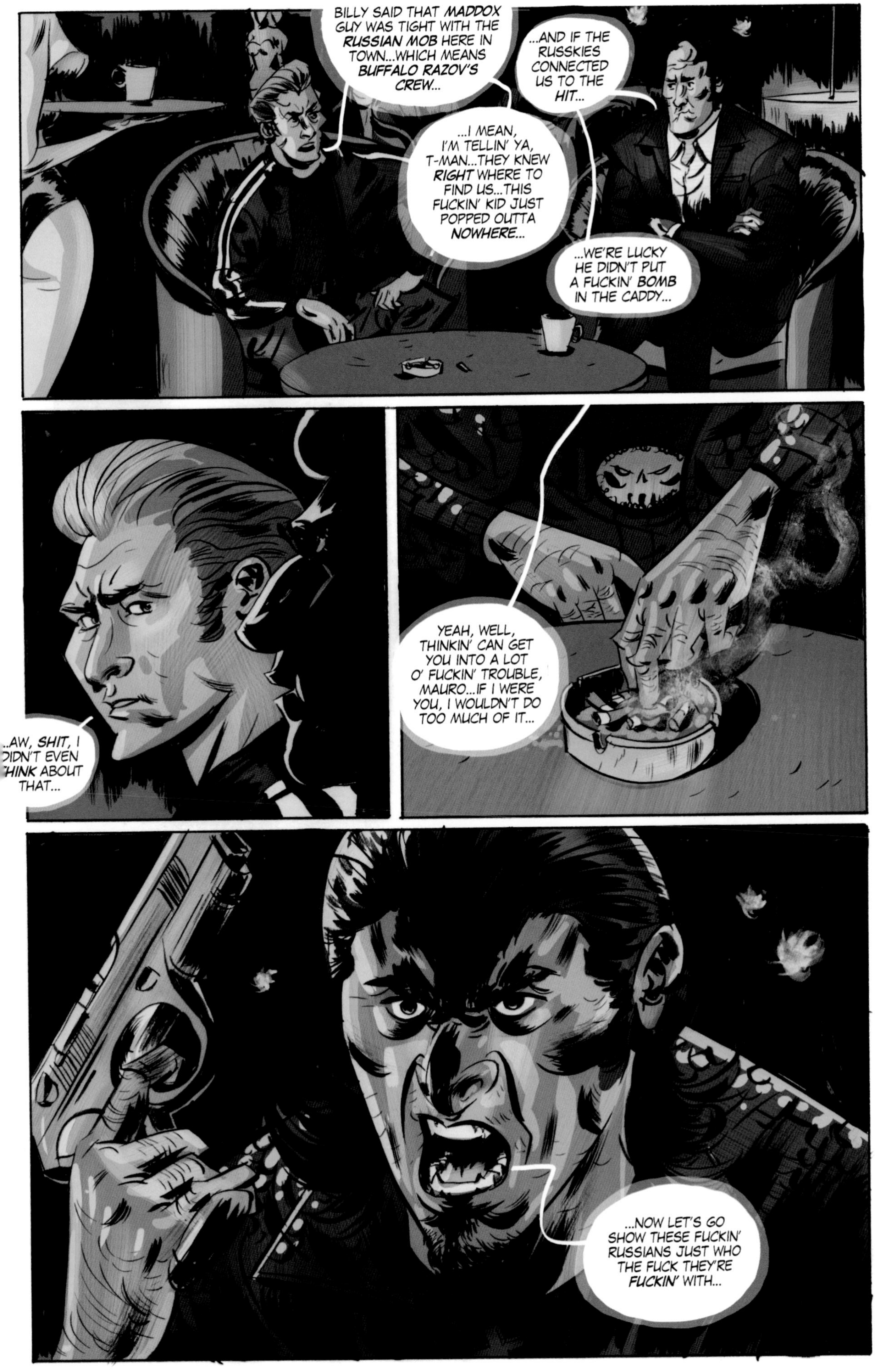
BILLY SAID THAT MADDOX GUY WAS TIGHT WITH THE RUSSIAN MOB HERE IN TOWN...WHICH MEANS BUFFALO RAZOV'S CREW...
...I MEAN, I'M TELLIN' YA, T-MAN...THEY KNEW RIGHT WHERE TO FIND US...THIS FUCKIN' KID JUST POPPED OUTTA NOWHERE...
...AND IF THE RUSSKIES CONNECTED US TO THE HIT...
...WE'RE LUCKY HE DIDN'T PUT A FUCKIN' BOMB IN THE CADDY...
...AW, SHIT, I DIDN'T EVEN THINK ABOUT THAT...
YEAH, WELL, THINKIN' CAN GET YOU INTO A LOT O' FUCKIN' TROUBLE, MAURO...IF I WERE YOU, I WOULDN'T DO TOO MUCH OF IT...
...NOW LET'S GO SHOW THESE FUCKIN' RUSSIANS JUST WHO THE FUCK THEY'RE FUCKIN' WITH...

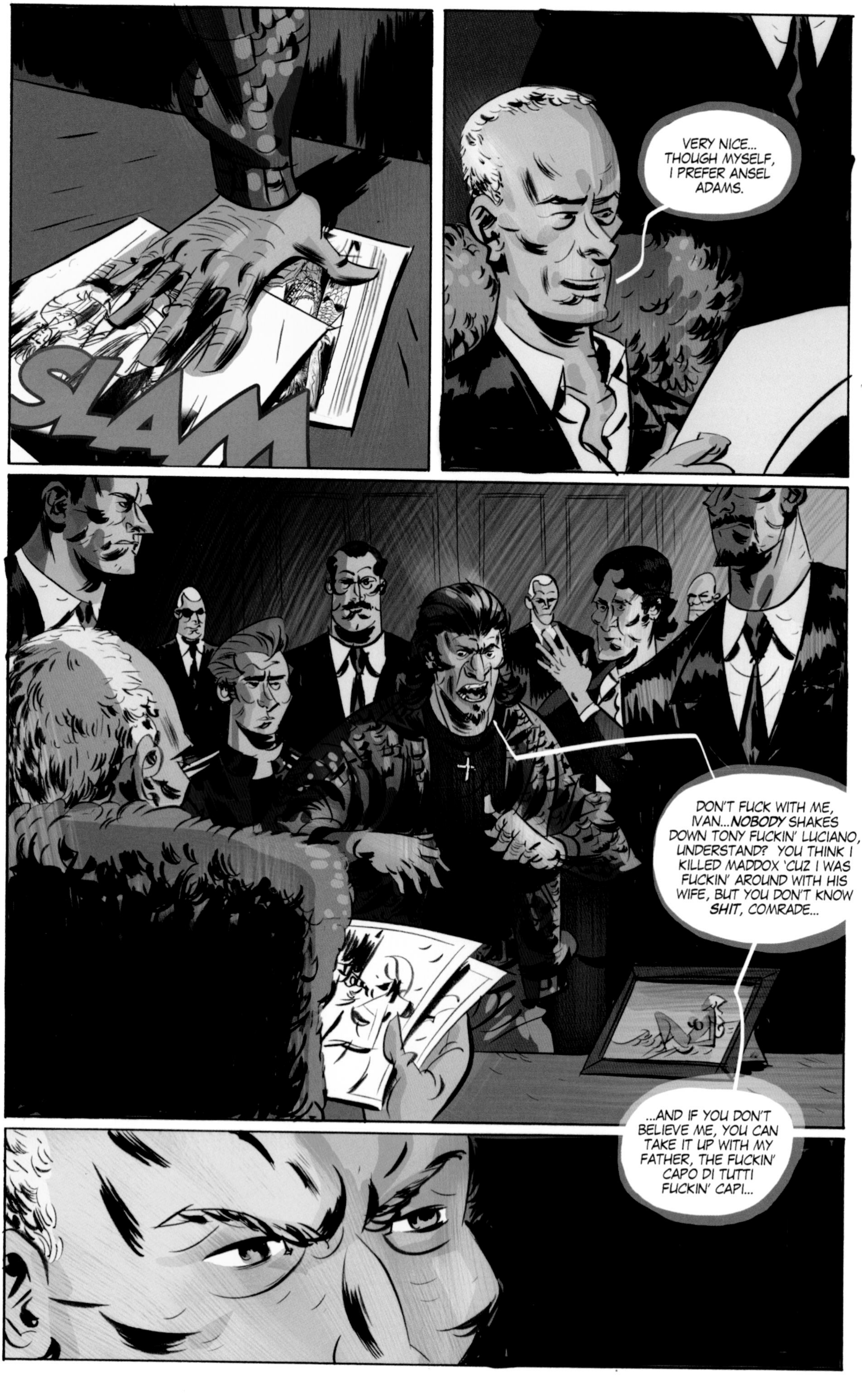
SLAM
VERY NICE... THOUGH MYSELF, I PREFER ANSEL ADAMS.
DON'T FUCK WITH ME, IVAN...**NOBODY** SHAKES DOWN TONY FUCKIN' LUCIANO, UNDERSTAND? YOU THINK I KILLED MADDOX 'CUZ I WAS FUCKIN' AROUND WITH HIS WIFE, BUT YOU DON'T KNOW **SHIT**, COMRADE...
...AND IF YOU DON'T BELIEVE ME, YOU CAN TAKE IT UP WITH MY FATHER, THE FUCKIN' CAPO DI TUTTI FUCKIN' CAPI...

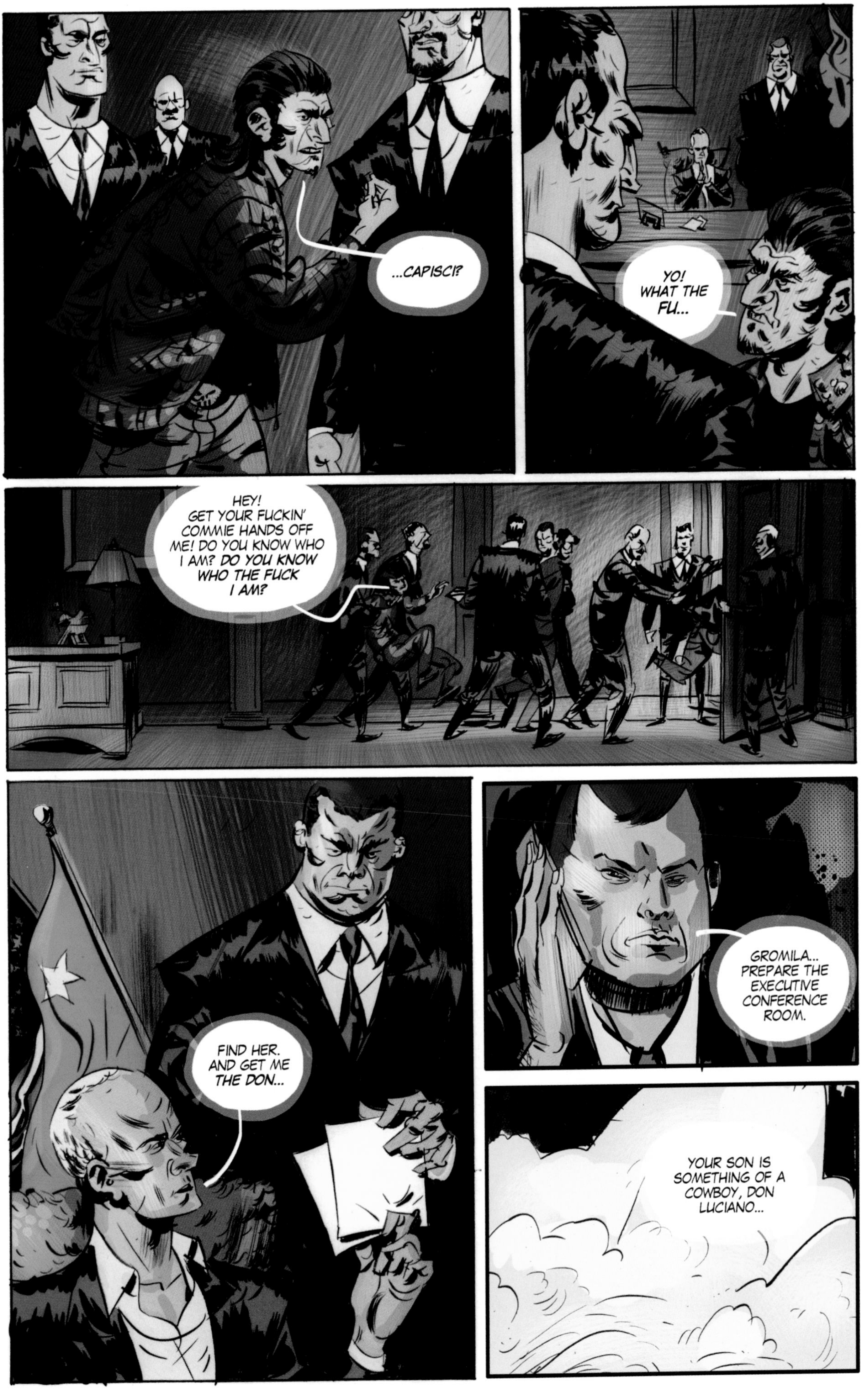
...CAPISCI?
YO! WHAT THE FU...
HEY! GET YOUR FUCKIN' COMMIE HANDS OFF ME! DO YOU KNOW WHO I AM? DO YOU KNOW WHO THE FUCK I AM?
FIND HER. AND GET ME THE DON...
GROMILA... PREPARE THE EXECUTIVE CONFERENCE ROOM.
YOUR SON IS SOMETHING OF A COWBOY, DON LUCIANO...

...AND, TO BE HONEST, I HAVE NEVER BEEN A FAN OF *SPAGHETTI WESTERNS.*

*SI...*AND *GRAZIE, AMICO MIO,* FOR BRINGING THIS UNPLEASANT SITUATION TO MY ATTENTION... I WOULD NEVER DO *ANYTHING* TO JEOPARDIZE THE PEACE BETWEEN OUR TWO ORGANIZATIONS.

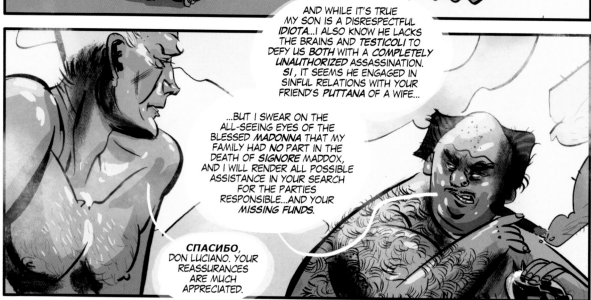

AND WHILE IT'S TRUE MY SON IS A DISRESPECTFUL *IDIOTA*...I ALSO KNOW HE LACKS THE BRAINS AND *TESTICOLI* TO DEFY US *BOTH* WITH A *COMPLETELY UNAUTHORIZED* ASSASSINATION. *SI,* IT SEEMS HE ENGAGED IN SINFUL RELATIONS WITH YOUR FRIEND'S *PUTTANA* OF A WIFE...

...BUT I SWEAR ON THE ALL-SEEING EYES OF THE BLESSED *MADONNA* THAT MY FAMILY HAD *NO* PART IN THE DEATH OF *SIGNORE* MADDOX, AND I WILL RENDER ALL POSSIBLE ASSISTANCE IN YOUR SEARCH FOR THE PARTIES RESPONSIBLE...AND YOUR *MISSING FUNDS.*

СПАСИБО, DON LUCIANO. YOUR REASSURANCES ARE MUCH APPRECIATED.

VOSTRA MADRE ANCORA SI ADDORNENTA PIANGENDO PER AVER DATO ALLA LUCE UN'IMBECILLE...*

* "YOUR MOTHER STILL CRIES HERSELF TO SLEEP FOR GIVING BIRTH TO SUCH AN IMBECILE..."

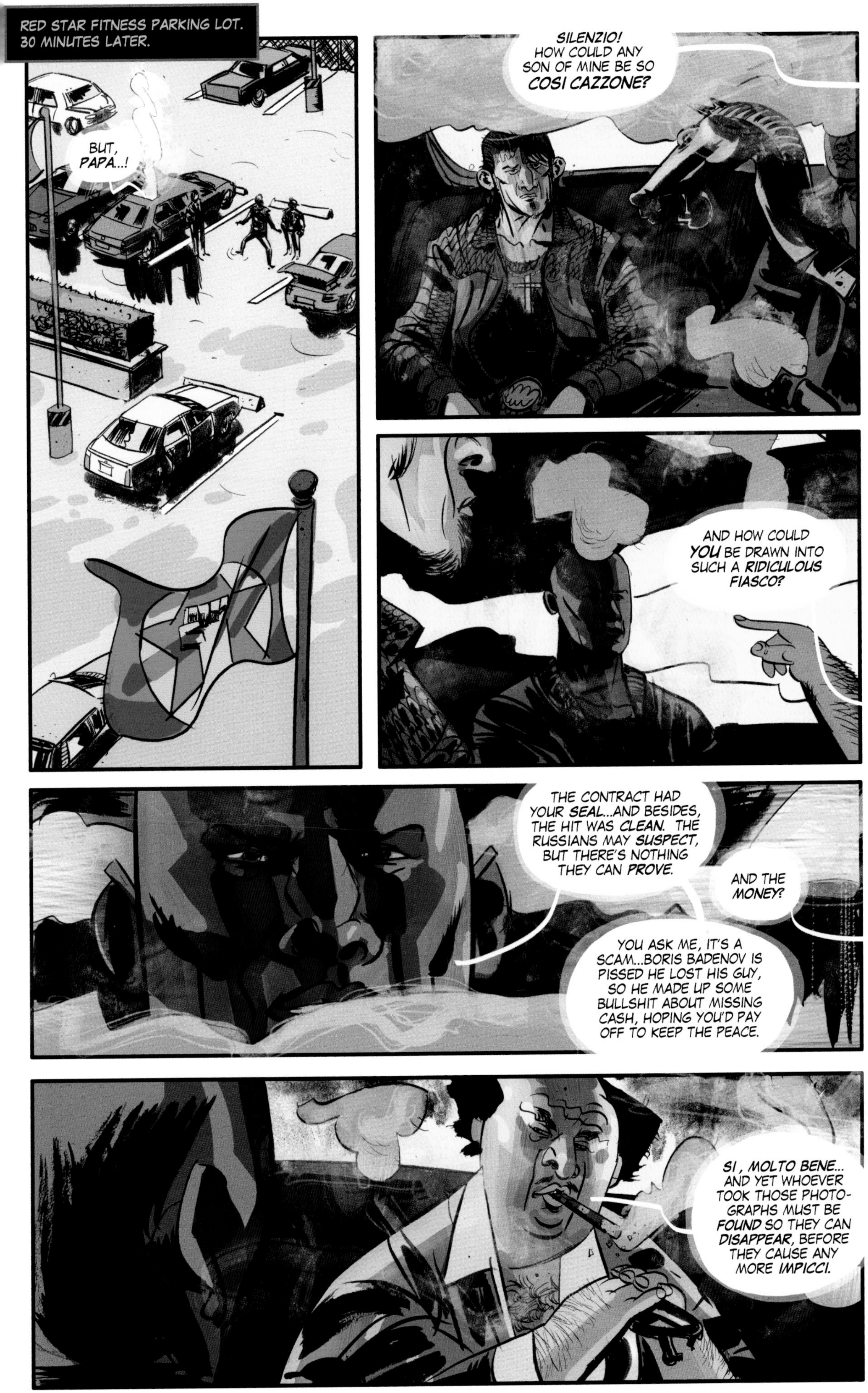
RED STAR FITNESS PARKING LOT.
30 MINUTES LATER.
BUT, PAPA...!
SILENZIO! HOW COULD ANY SON OF MINE BE SO COSI CAZZONE?
AND HOW COULD YOU BE DRAWN INTO SUCH A RIDICULOUS FIASCO?
THE CONTRACT HAD YOUR SEAL...AND BESIDES, THE HIT WAS CLEAN. THE RUSSIANS MAY SUSPECT, BUT THERE'S NOTHING THEY CAN PROVE.
AND THE MONEY?
YOU ASK ME, IT'S A SCAM...BORIS BADENOV IS PISSED HE LOST HIS GUY, SO HE MADE UP SOME BULLSHIT ABOUT MISSING CASH, HOPING YOU'D PAY OFF TO KEEP THE PEACE.
SI, MOLTO BENE... AND YET WHOEVER TOOK THOSE PHOTO-GRAPHS MUST BE FOUND SO THEY CAN DISAPPEAR, BEFORE THEY CAUSE ANY MORE IMPICCI.

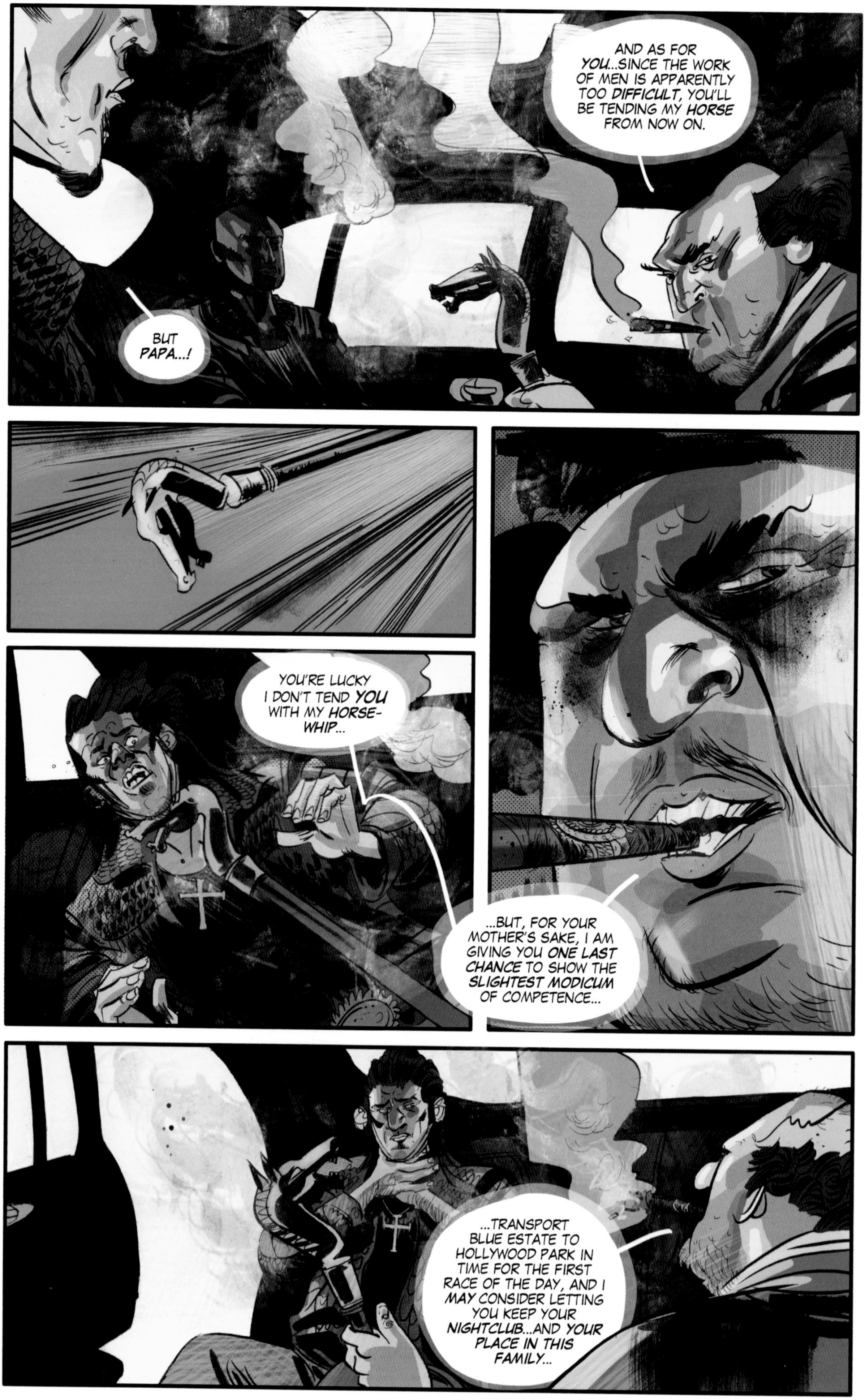
AND AS FOR YOU...SINCE THE WORK OF MEN IS APPARENTLY TOO DIFFICULT, YOU'LL BE TENDING MY HORSE FROM NOW ON.
BUT PAPA...!
YOU'RE LUCKY I DON'T TEND YOU WITH MY HORSE-WHIP...
...BUT, FOR YOUR MOTHER'S SAKE, I AM GIVING YOU ONE LAST CHANCE TO SHOW THE SLIGHTEST MODICUM OF COMPETENCE...
...TRANSPORT BLUE ESTATE TO HOLLYWOOD PARK IN TIME FOR THE FIRST RACE OF THE DAY, AND I MAY CONSIDER LETTING YOU KEEP YOUR NIGHTCLUB...AND YOUR PLACE IN THIS FAMILY...

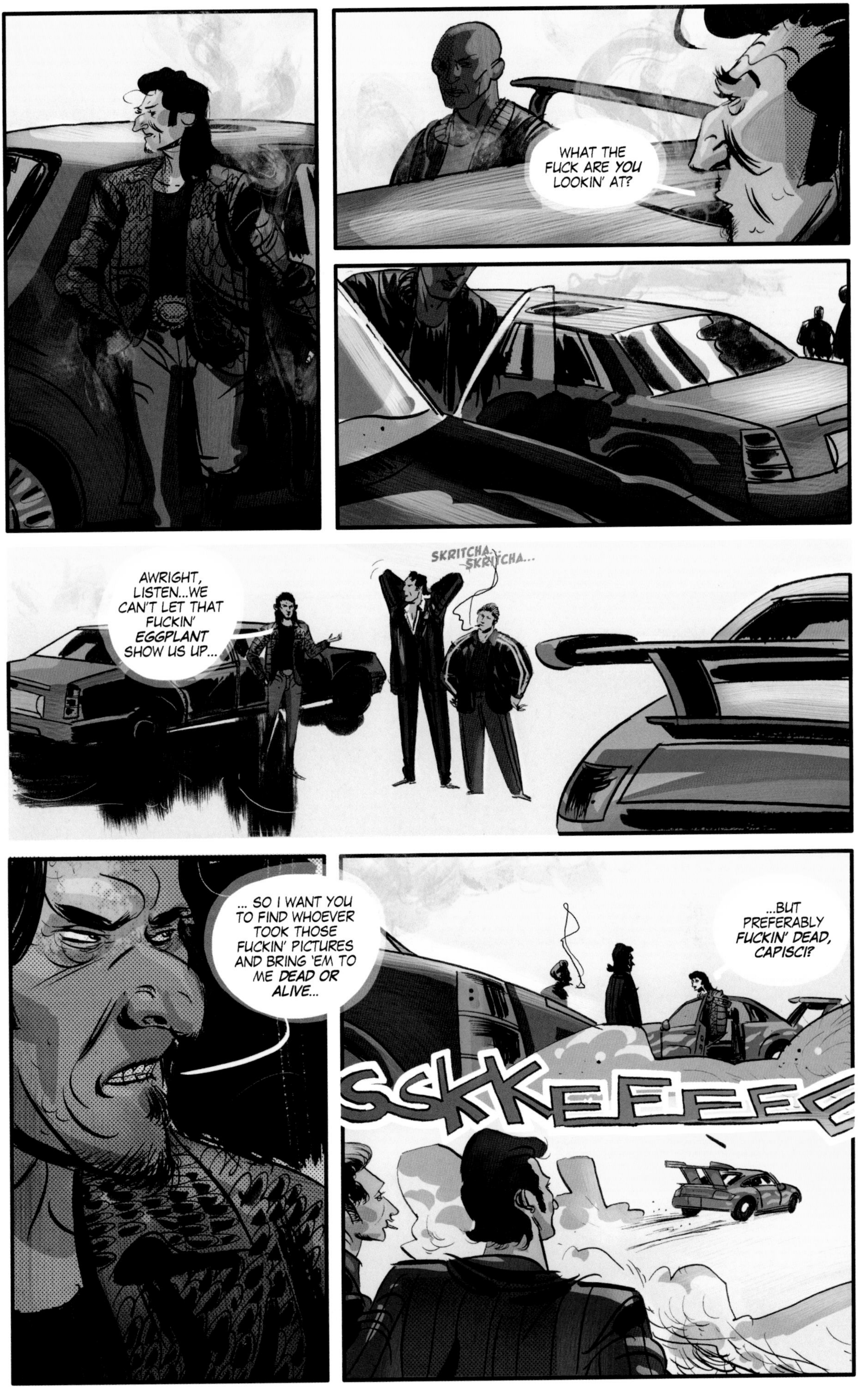
WHAT THE FUCK ARE YOU LOOKIN' AT?
SKRITCHA... SKRITCHA...
AWRIGHT, LISTEN...WE CAN'T LET THAT FUCKIN' EGGPLANT SHOW US UP...
... SO I WANT YOU TO FIND WHOEVER TOOK THOSE FUCKIN' PICTURES AND BRING 'EM TO ME DEAD OR ALIVE...
...BUT PREFERABLY FUCKIN' DEAD, CAPISCI?
SSKKEEEEE

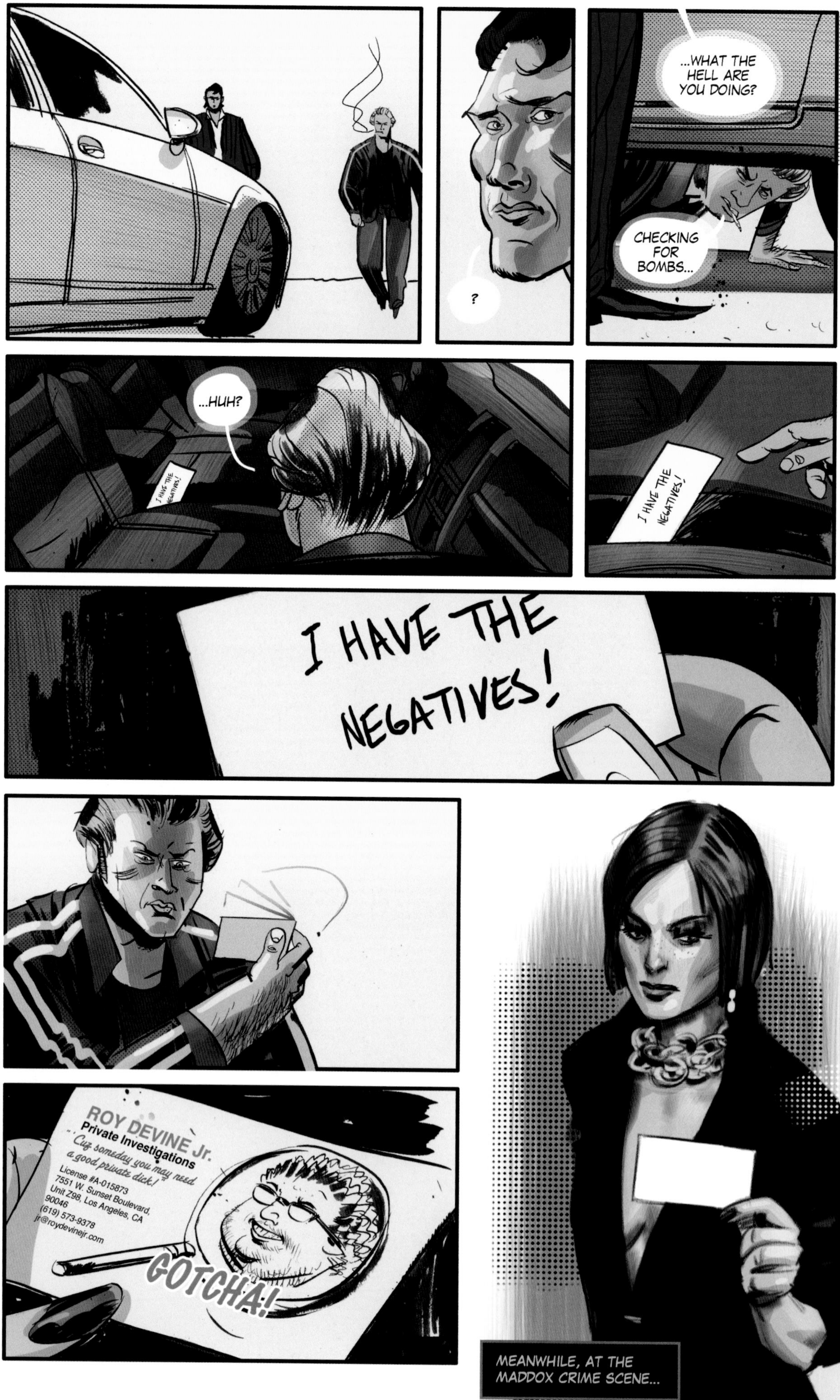
?
...WHAT THE HELL ARE YOU DOING?
CHECKING FOR BOMBS...
...HUH?
I HAVE THE NEGATIVES!
I HAVE THE NEGATIVES!
I HAVE THE NEGATIVES!
ROY DEVINE Jr.
Private Investigations
"'Cuz someday you may need a good private dick!"
License #A-015873
7551 W. Sunset Boulevard,
Unit Z98, Los Angeles, CA
90046
(619) 573-9378
jr@roydevinejr.com
GOTCHA!
MEANWHILE, AT THE MADDOX CRIME SCENE...

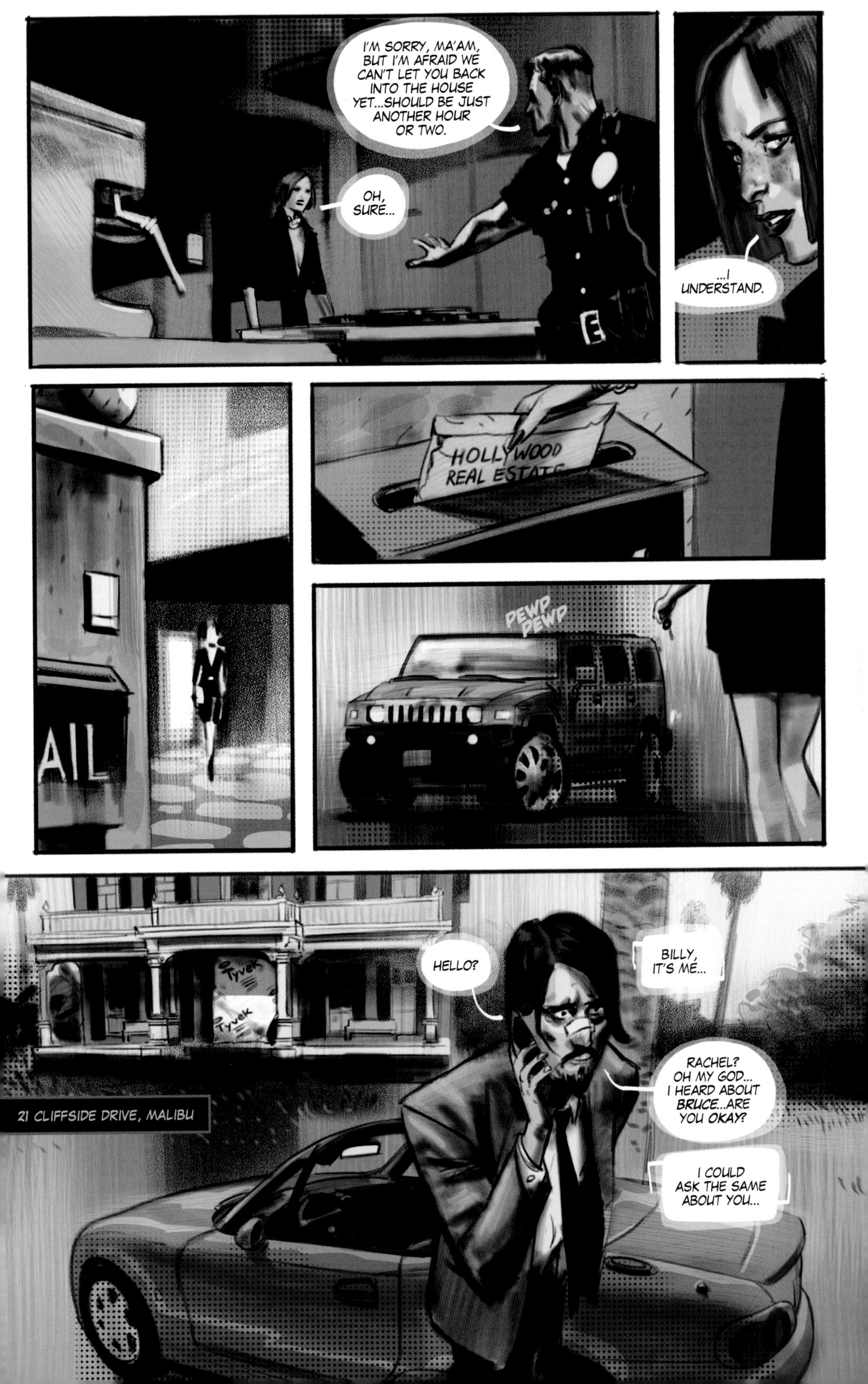
I'M SORRY, MA'AM, BUT I'M AFRAID WE CAN'T LET YOU BACK INTO THE HOUSE YET...SHOULD BE JUST ANOTHER HOUR OR TWO.
OH, SURE...
...I UNDERSTAND.
HOLLYWOOD REAL ESTATE
PEWP PEWP
21 CLIFFSIDE DRIVE, MALIBU
Tyvek
Tyvek
HELLO?
BILLY, IT'S ME...
RACHEL? OH MY GOD... I HEARD ABOUT BRUCE...ARE YOU OKAY?
I COULD ASK THE SAME ABOUT YOU...

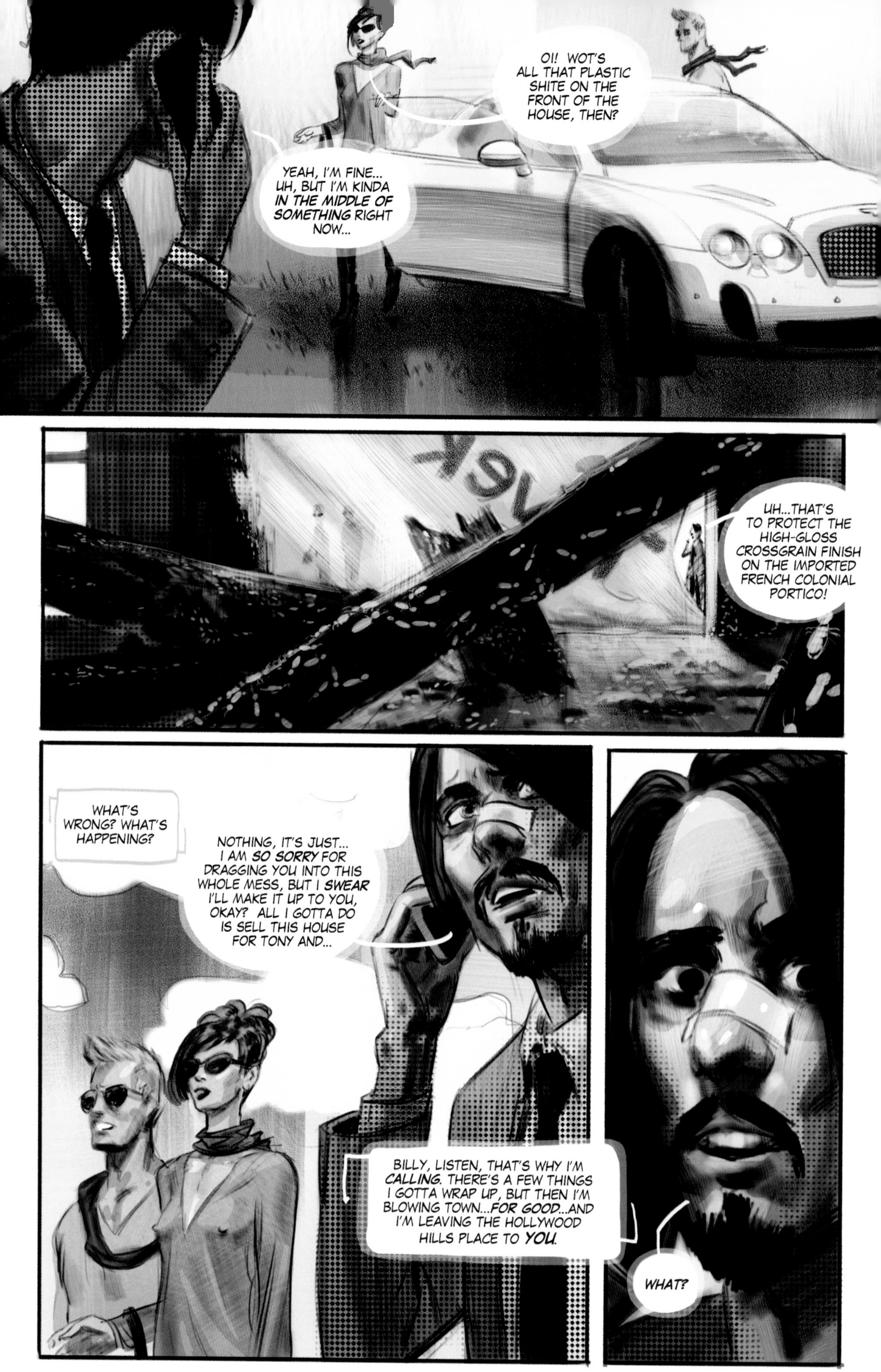
OI! WOT'S ALL THAT PLASTIC SHITE ON THE FRONT OF THE HOUSE, THEN?
YEAH, I'M FINE... UH, BUT I'M KINDA *IN THE MIDDLE OF SOMETHING* RIGHT NOW...
UH...THAT'S TO PROTECT THE HIGH-GLOSS CROSSGRAIN FINISH ON THE IMPORTED FRENCH COLONIAL PORTICO!
WHAT'S WRONG? WHAT'S HAPPENING?
NOTHING, IT'S JUST... I AM *SO SORRY* FOR DRAGGING YOU INTO THIS WHOLE MESS, BUT I *SWEAR* I'LL MAKE IT UP TO YOU, OKAY? ALL I GOTTA DO IS SELL THIS HOUSE FOR TONY AND...
BILLY, LISTEN, THAT'S WHY I'M *CALLING*. THERE'S A FEW THINGS I GOTTA WRAP UP, BUT THEN I'M BLOWING TOWN...*FOR GOOD*...AND I'M LEAVING THE HOLLYWOOD HILLS PLACE TO *YOU*.
*WHAT?*

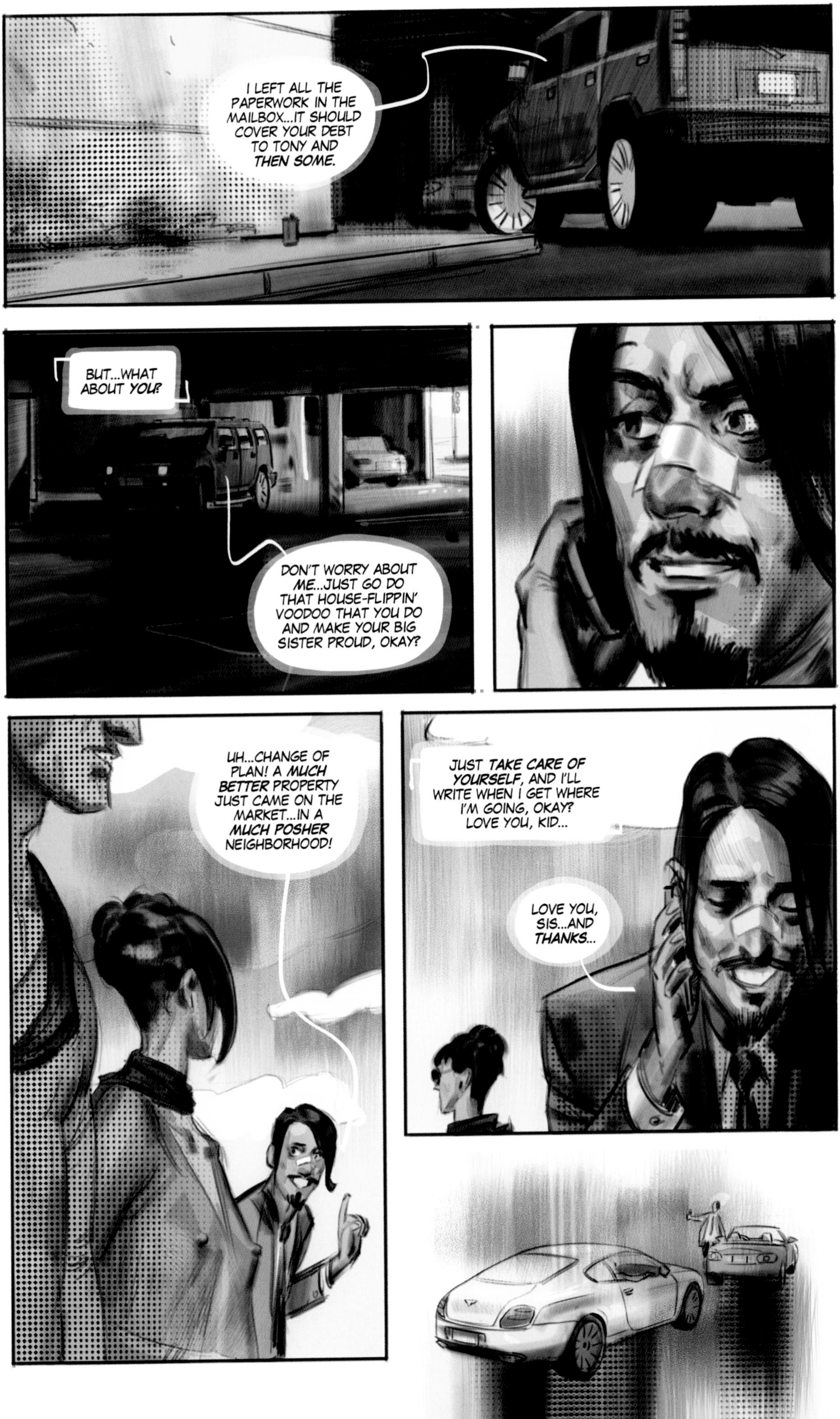
I LEFT ALL THE PAPERWORK IN THE MAILBOX...IT SHOULD COVER YOUR DEBT TO TONY AND *THEN SOME.*
BUT...WHAT ABOUT *YOU?*
DON'T WORRY ABOUT *ME*...JUST GO DO THAT HOUSE-FLIPPIN' VOODOO THAT YOU DO AND MAKE YOUR BIG SISTER PROUD, OKAY?
UH...CHANGE OF PLAN! A *MUCH BETTER* PROPERTY JUST CAME ON THE MARKET...IN A *MUCH POSHER* NEIGHBORHOOD!
JUST *TAKE CARE OF YOURSELF*, AND I'LL WRITE WHEN I GET WHERE I'M GOING, OKAY? LOVE YOU, KID...
LOVE YOU, SIS...AND *THANKS*...

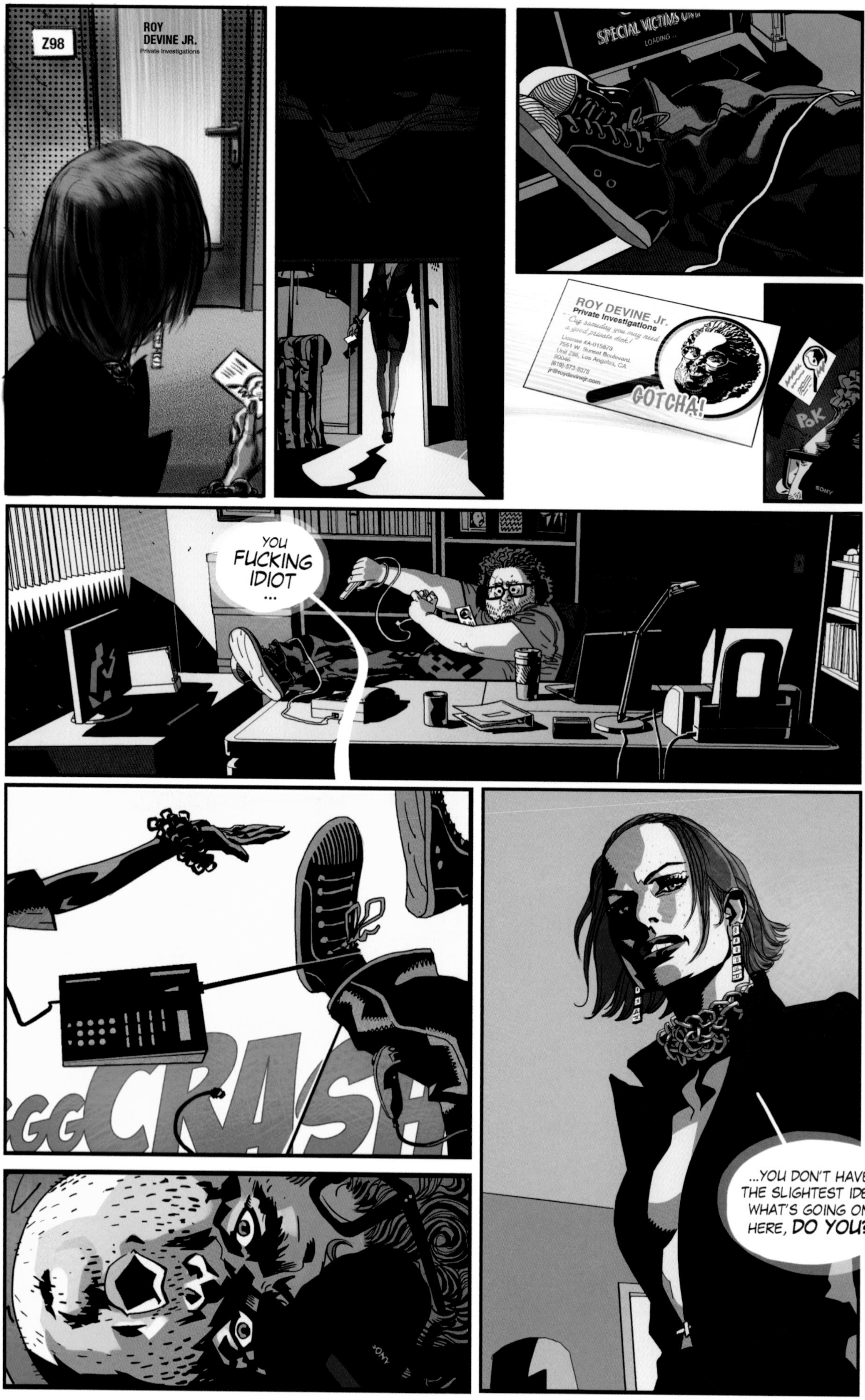
Z98
ROY DEVINE JR.
Private Investigations
LOADING...
ROY DEVINE Jr.
Private Investigations
"Cuz someday you may need a good private dick!"
License #A-015873
7551 W. Sunset Boulevard,
Unit Z98, Los Angeles, CA
90046
(619)-573-9378
jr@roydevinejr.com
GOTCHA!
POK
SONY
YOU FUCKING IDIOT ...
...YOU DON'T HAVE THE SLIGHTEST IDEA WHAT'S GOING ON HERE, DO YOU?

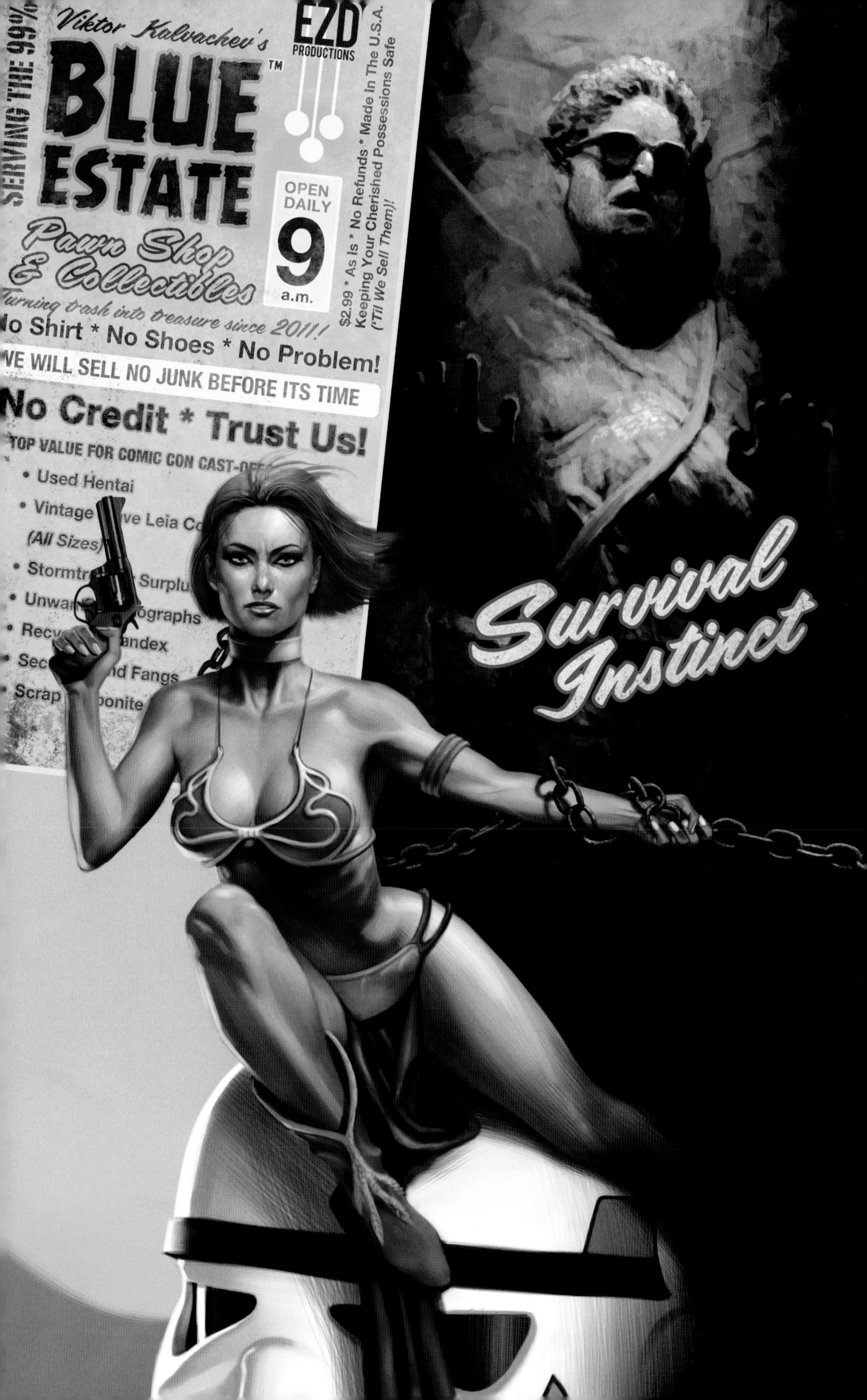

SERVING THE 99%
Viktor Kalvachev's
BLUE ESTATE™
EZD PRODUCTIONS
OPEN DAILY 9 a.m.
$2.99 * As Is * No Refunds * Made In The U.S.A.
Keeping Your Cherished Possessions Safe
('Til We Sell Them)!
Pawn Shop & Collectibles
Turning trash into treasure since 2011!
No Shirt * No Shoes * No Problem!
WE WILL SELL NO JUNK BEFORE ITS TIME
No Credit * Trust Us!
TOP VALUE FOR COMIC CON CAST-OFFS
• Used Hentai
• Vintage
(All Sizes)
• Stormtr
• Unwa
• Recy
• Sec
• Scrap
Survival Instinct

# BLUE™ ESTATE

EPISODE NINE:
## SURVIVAL INSTINCT

ORIGINAL STORY:
**VIKTOR KALVACHEV** AND **KOSTA YANEV**

SCRIPT BY **ANDREW OSBORNE**

ARTISTS:
**VIKTOR KALVACHEV**
**TOBY CYPRESS**
**ROBERT VALLEY**
**PETER NGUYEN**
**ANDY KUHN**

ART DIRECTION BY **VIKTOR KALVACHEV**

COVER, COLORS & DESIGN:
**VIKTOR KALVACHEV**

CONTRIBUTING EDITOR:
**PHILO NORTHRUP**

www.**BlueEstateComic**.com

EZD™
PRODUCTIONS

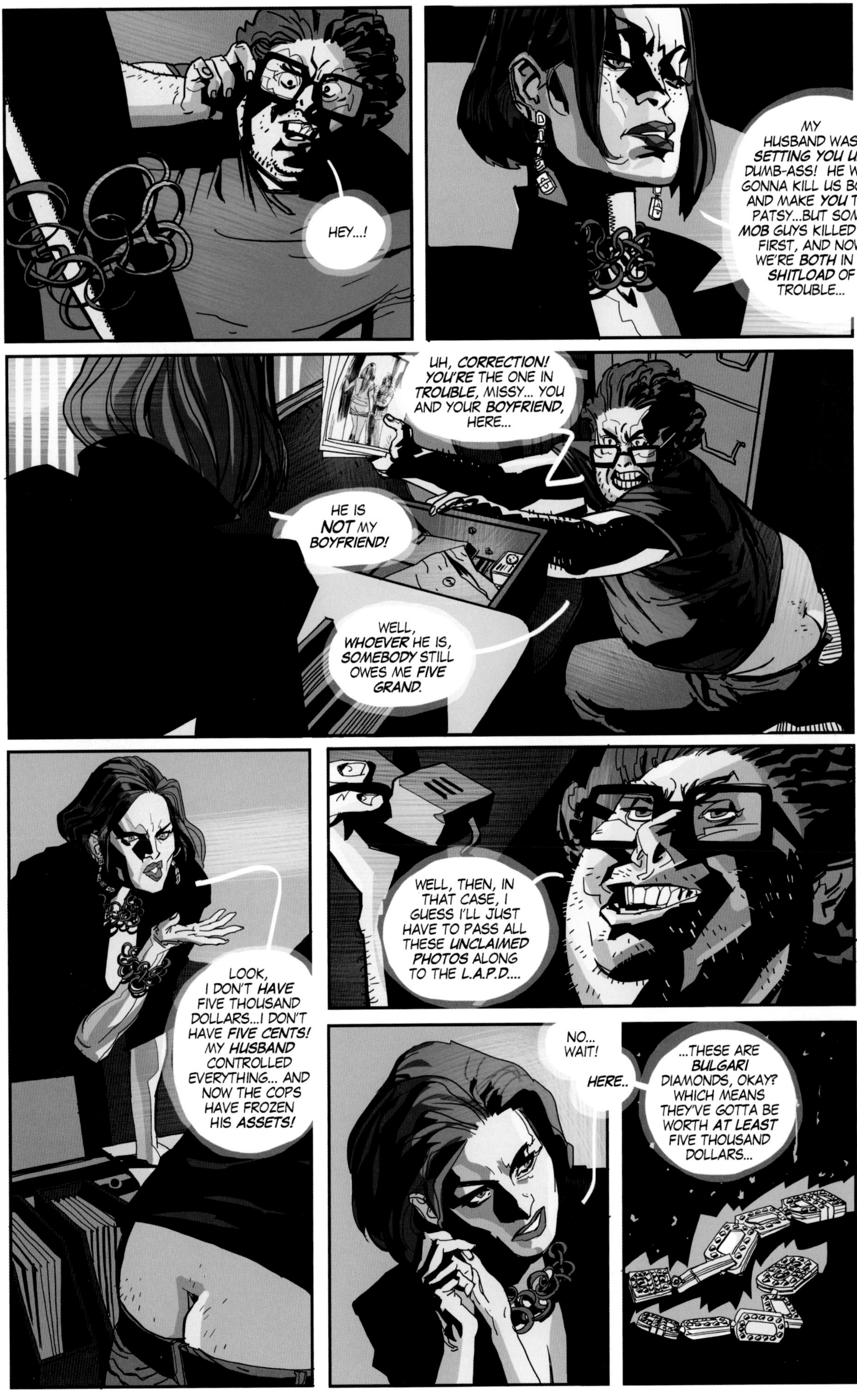
HEY...!
MY HUSBAND WAS SETTING YOU UP, DUMB-ASS! HE WAS GONNA KILL US BOTH AND MAKE YOU THE PATSY...BUT SOME MOB GUYS KILLED HIM FIRST, AND NOW WE'RE BOTH IN A SHITLOAD OF TROUBLE...
UH, CORRECTION! YOU'RE THE ONE IN TROUBLE, MISSY... YOU AND YOUR BOYFRIEND, HERE...
HE IS NOT MY BOYFRIEND!
WELL, WHOEVER HE IS, SOMEBODY STILL OWES ME FIVE GRAND.
LOOK, I DON'T HAVE FIVE THOUSAND DOLLARS...I DON'T HAVE FIVE CENTS! MY HUSBAND CONTROLLED EVERYTHING... AND NOW THE COPS HAVE FROZEN HIS ASSETS!
WELL, THEN, IN THAT CASE, I GUESS I'LL JUST HAVE TO PASS ALL THESE UNCLAIMED PHOTOS ALONG TO THE L.A.P.D....
NO... WAIT!
HERE..
...THESE ARE BULGARI DIAMONDS, OKAY? WHICH MEANS THEY'VE GOTTA BE WORTH AT LEAST FIVE THOUSAND DOLLARS...

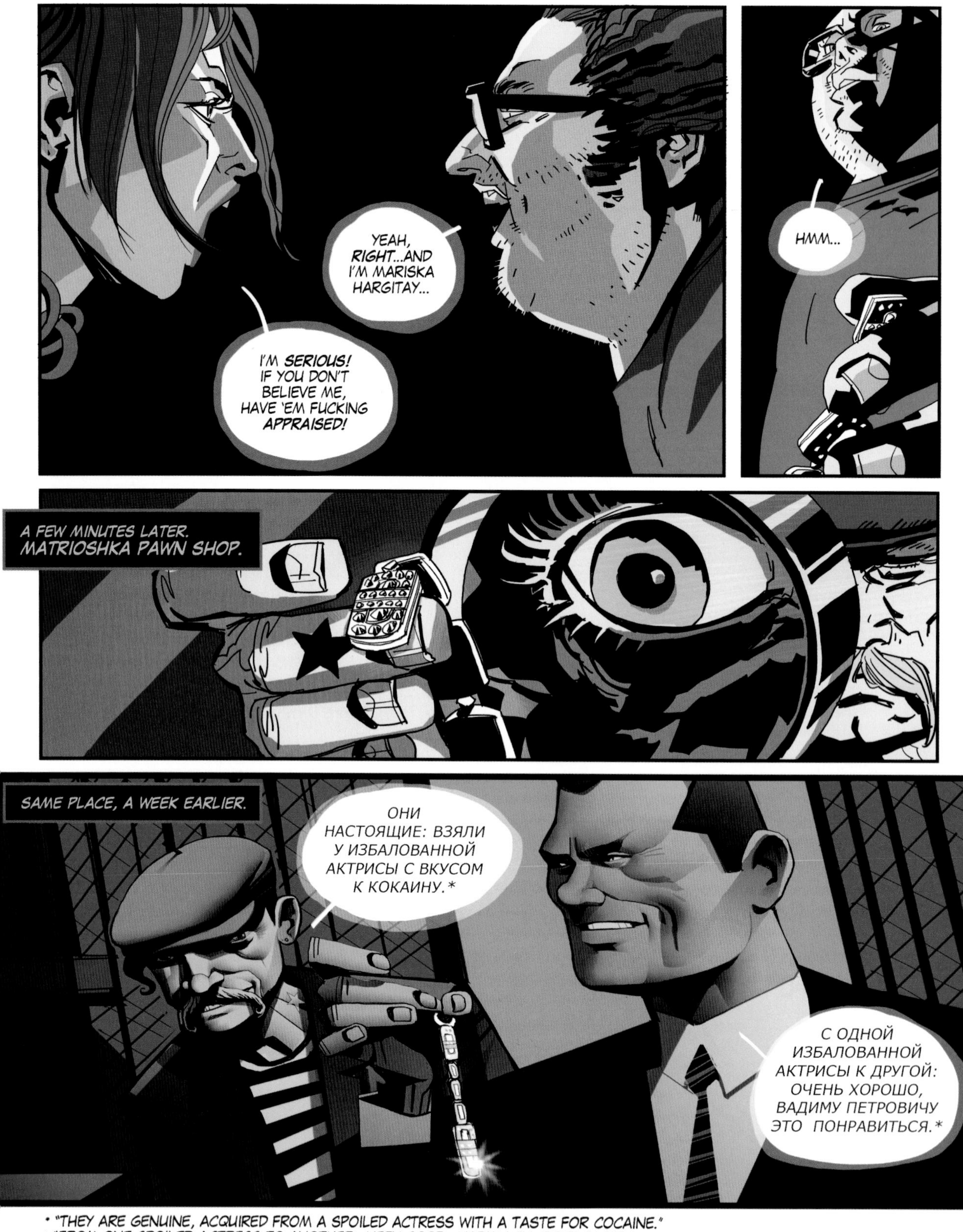
YEAH, RIGHT...AND I'M MARISKA HARGITAY...
I'M SERIOUS! IF YOU DON'T BELIEVE ME, HAVE 'EM FUCKING APPRAISED!
HMM...
A FEW MINUTES LATER. MATRIOSHKA PAWN SHOP.
SAME PLACE, A WEEK EARLIER.
ОНИ НАСТОЯЩИЕ: ВЗЯЛИ У ИЗБАЛОВАННОЙ АКТРИСЫ С ВКУСОМ К КОКАИНУ.*
С ОДНОЙ ИЗБАЛОВАННОЙ АКТРИСЫ К ДРУГОЙ: ОЧЕНЬ ХОРОШО, ВАДИМУ ПЕТРОВИЧУ ЭТО ПОНРАВИТЬСЯ.*

* "THEY ARE GENUINE, ACQUIRED FROM A SPOILED ACTRESS WITH A TASTE FOR COCAINE."
* "FROM ONE SPOILED ACTRESS TO ANOTHER. VERY GOOD. VADIM WILL BE PLEASED."

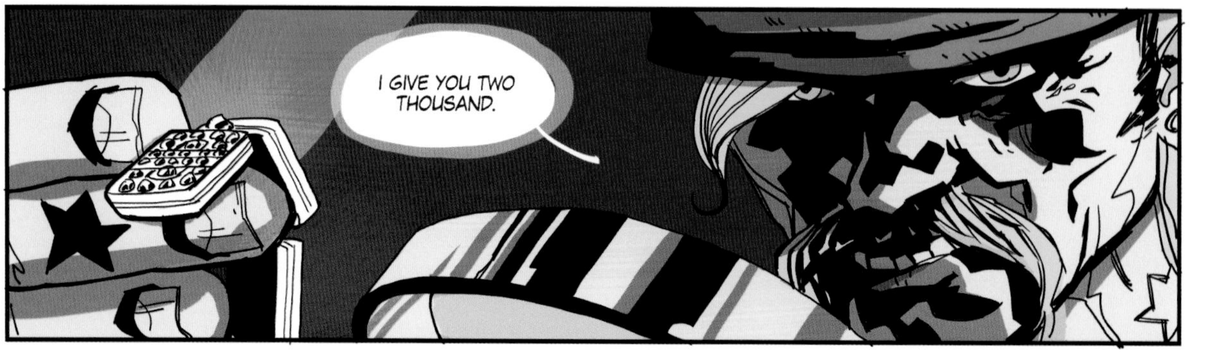
I GIVE YOU TWO THOUSAND.

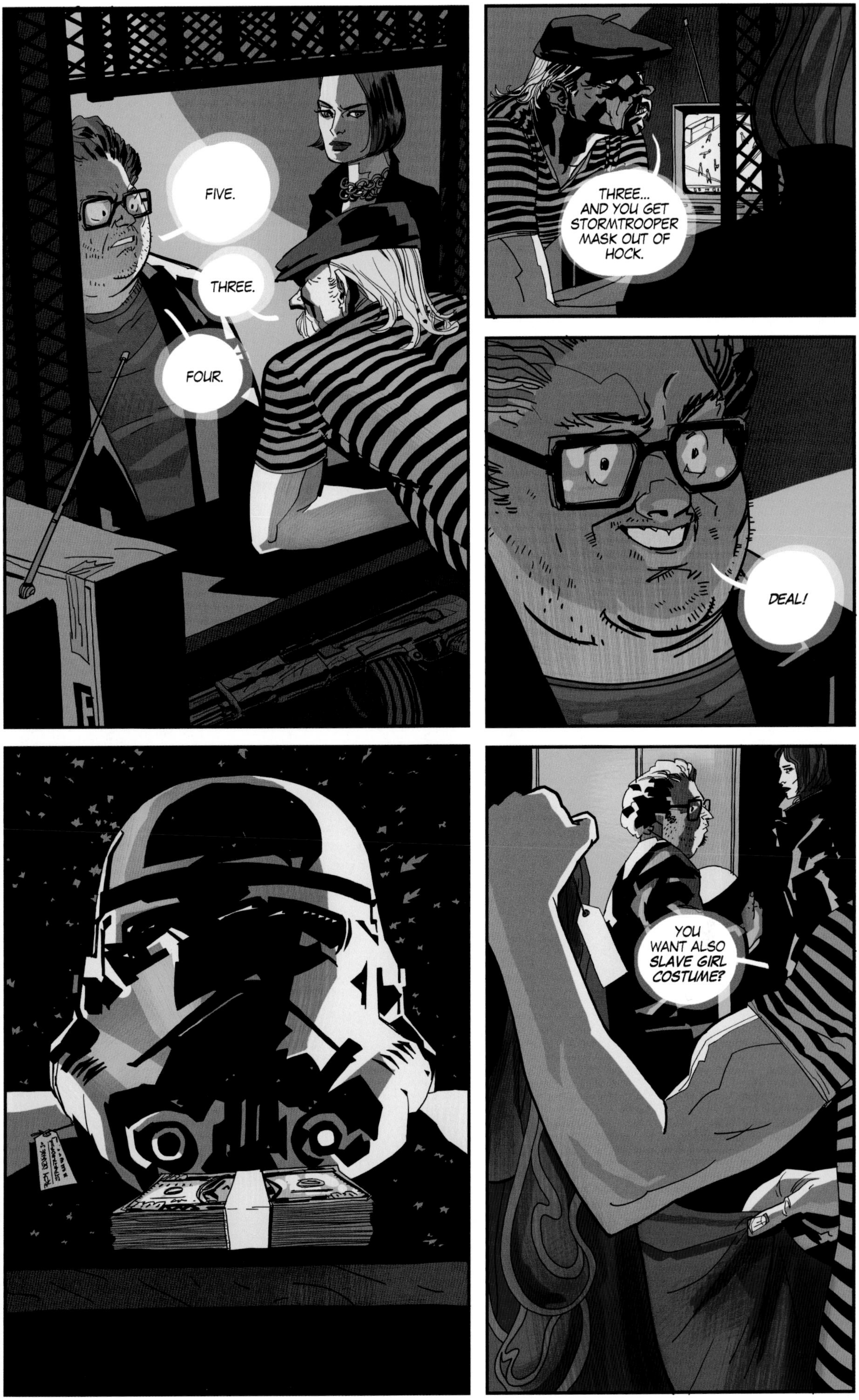
FIVE.
THREE.
FOUR.
THREE... AND YOU GET STORMTROOPER MASK OUT OF HOCK.
DEAL!
YOU WANT ALSO SLAVE GIRL COSTUME?

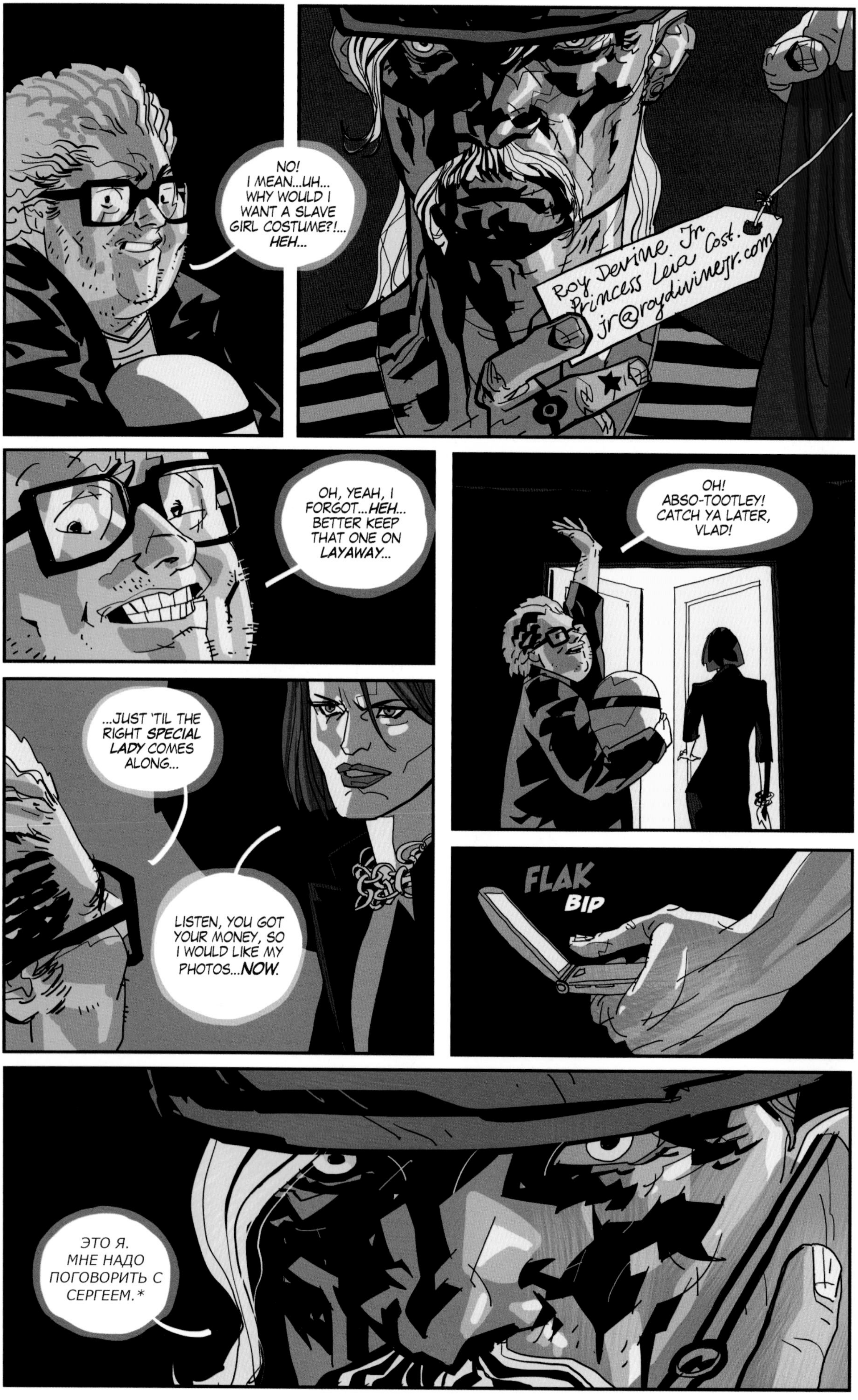
NO! I MEAN...UH... WHY WOULD I WANT A SLAVE GIRL COSTUME?!... HEH...
Roy Devine Jr
Princess Leia Cost.
jr@roydivinejr.com
OH, YEAH, I FORGOT...HEH... BETTER KEEP THAT ONE ON LAYAWAY...
...JUST 'TIL THE RIGHT SPECIAL LADY COMES ALONG...
LISTEN, YOU GOT YOUR MONEY, SO I WOULD LIKE MY PHOTOS...NOW.
OH! ABSO-TOOTLEY! CATCH YA LATER, VLAD!
FLAK
BIP
ЭТО Я. МНЕ НАДО ПОГОВОРИТЬ С СЕРГЕЕМ.*

* "IT'S ME. I MUST SPEAK WITH SERGEY."

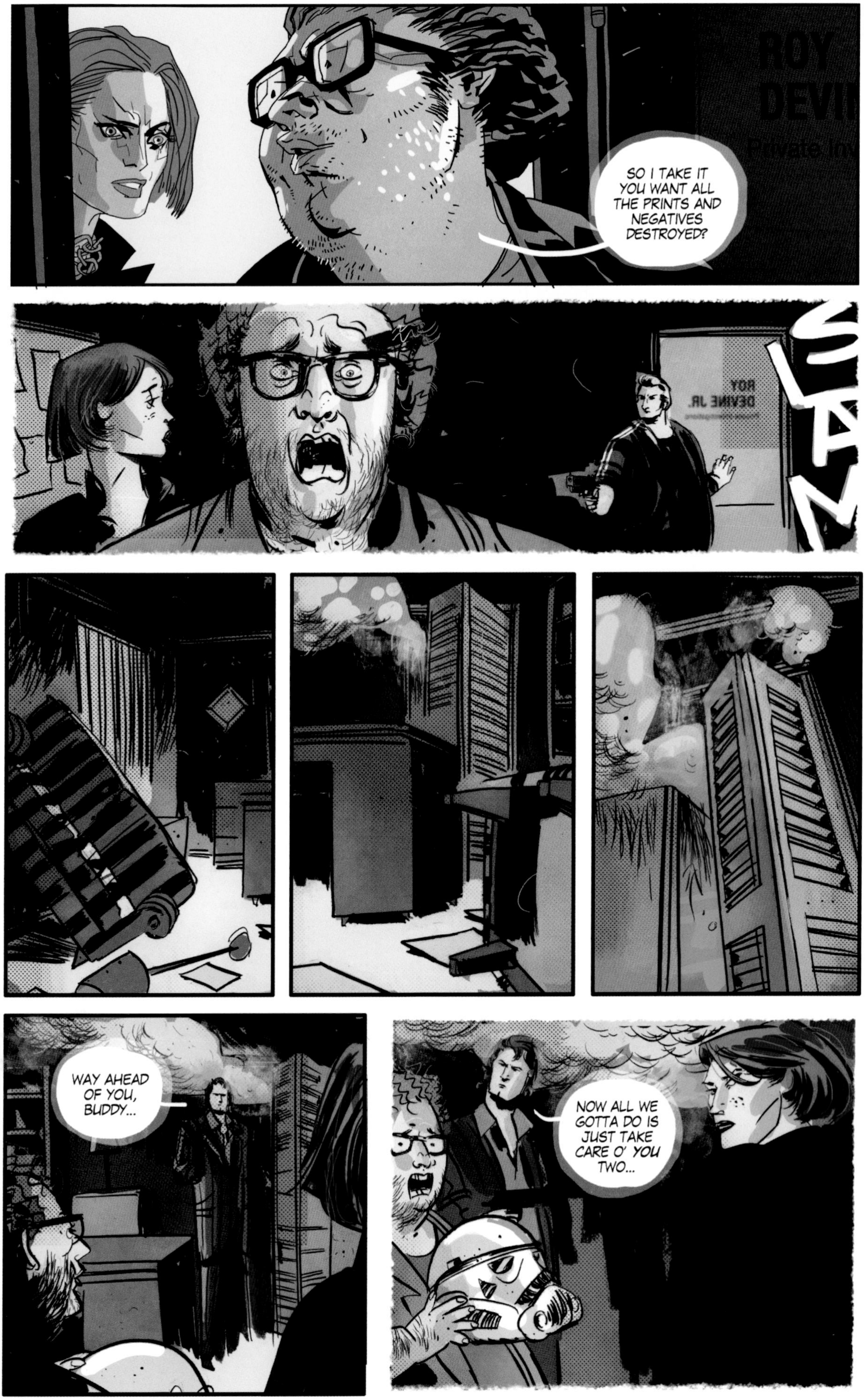
SO I TAKE IT YOU WANT ALL THE PRINTS AND NEGATIVES DESTROYED?
WAY AHEAD OF YOU, BUDDY...
NOW ALL WE GOTTA DO IS JUST TAKE CARE O' YOU TWO...

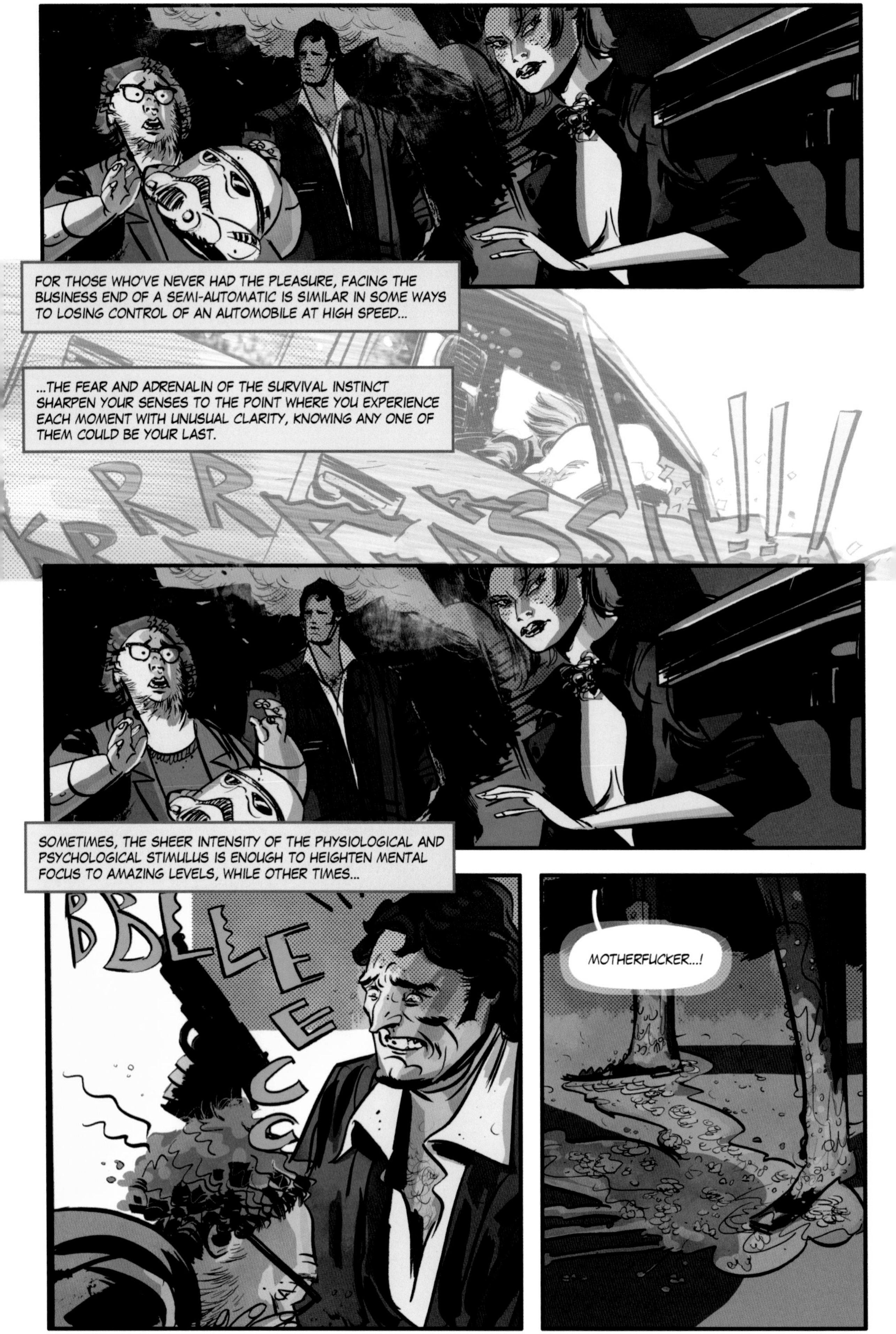

FOR THOSE WHO'VE NEVER HAD THE PLEASURE, FACING THE BUSINESS END OF A SEMI-AUTOMATIC IS SIMILAR IN SOME WAYS TO LOSING CONTROL OF AN AUTOMOBILE AT HIGH SPEED...
...THE FEAR AND ADRENALIN OF THE SURVIVAL INSTINCT SHARPEN YOUR SENSES TO THE POINT WHERE YOU EXPERIENCE EACH MOMENT WITH UNUSUAL CLARITY, KNOWING ANY ONE OF THEM COULD BE YOUR LAST.
SOMETIMES, THE SHEER INTENSITY OF THE PHYSIOLOGICAL AND PSYCHOLOGICAL STIMULUS IS ENOUGH TO HEIGHTEN MENTAL FOCUS TO AMAZING LEVELS, WHILE OTHER TIMES...
MOTHERFUCKER...!

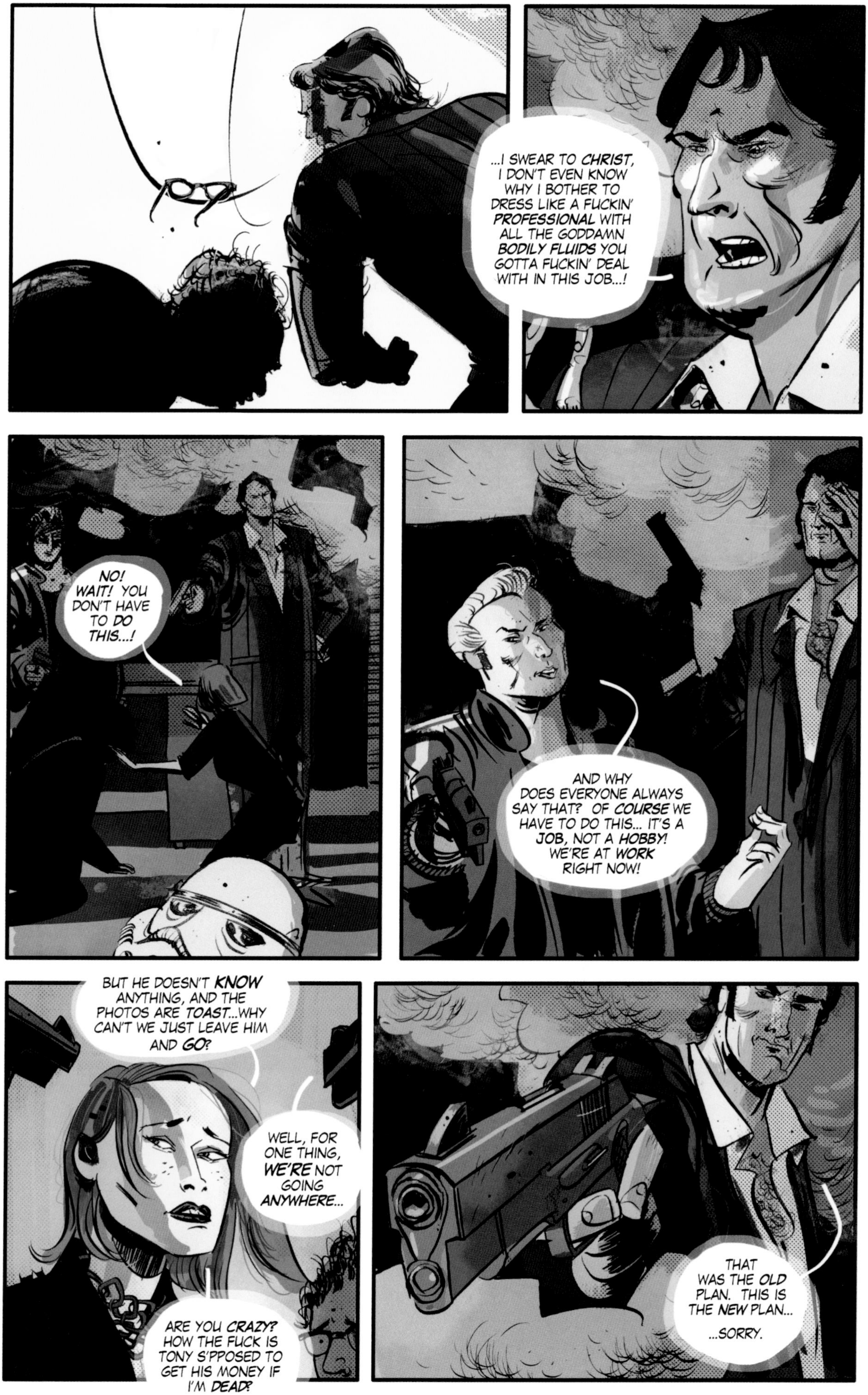
...I SWEAR TO CHRIST, I DON'T EVEN KNOW WHY I BOTHER TO DRESS LIKE A FUCKIN' PROFESSIONAL WITH ALL THE GODDAMN BODILY FLUIDS YOU GOTTA FUCKIN' DEAL WITH IN THIS JOB...!
NO! WAIT! YOU DON'T HAVE TO DO THIS...!
AND WHY DOES EVERYONE ALWAYS SAY THAT? OF COURSE WE HAVE TO DO THIS... IT'S A JOB, NOT A HOBBY! WE'RE AT WORK RIGHT NOW!
BUT HE DOESN'T KNOW ANYTHING, AND THE PHOTOS ARE TOAST...WHY CAN'T WE JUST LEAVE HIM AND GO?
WELL, FOR ONE THING, WE'RE NOT GOING ANYWHERE...
ARE YOU CRAZY? HOW THE FUCK IS TONY S'PPOSED TO GET HIS MONEY IF I'M DEAD?
THAT WAS THE OLD PLAN. THIS IS THE NEW PLAN...
...SORRY.

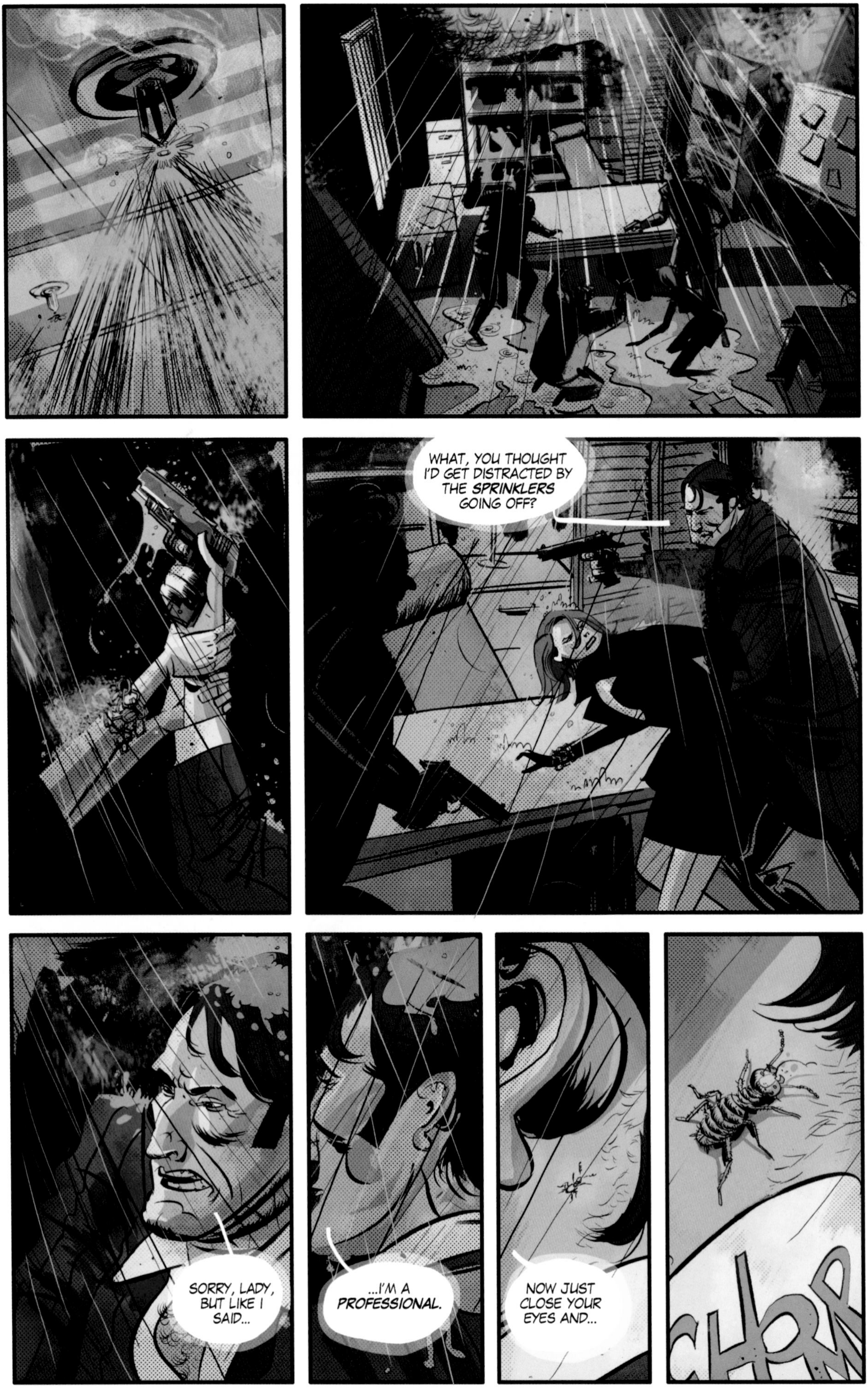
WHAT, YOU THOUGHT I'D GET DISTRACTED BY THE SPRINKLERS GOING OFF?
SORRY, LADY, BUT LIKE I SAID...
...I'M A PROFESSIONAL.
NOW JUST CLOSE YOUR EYES AND...

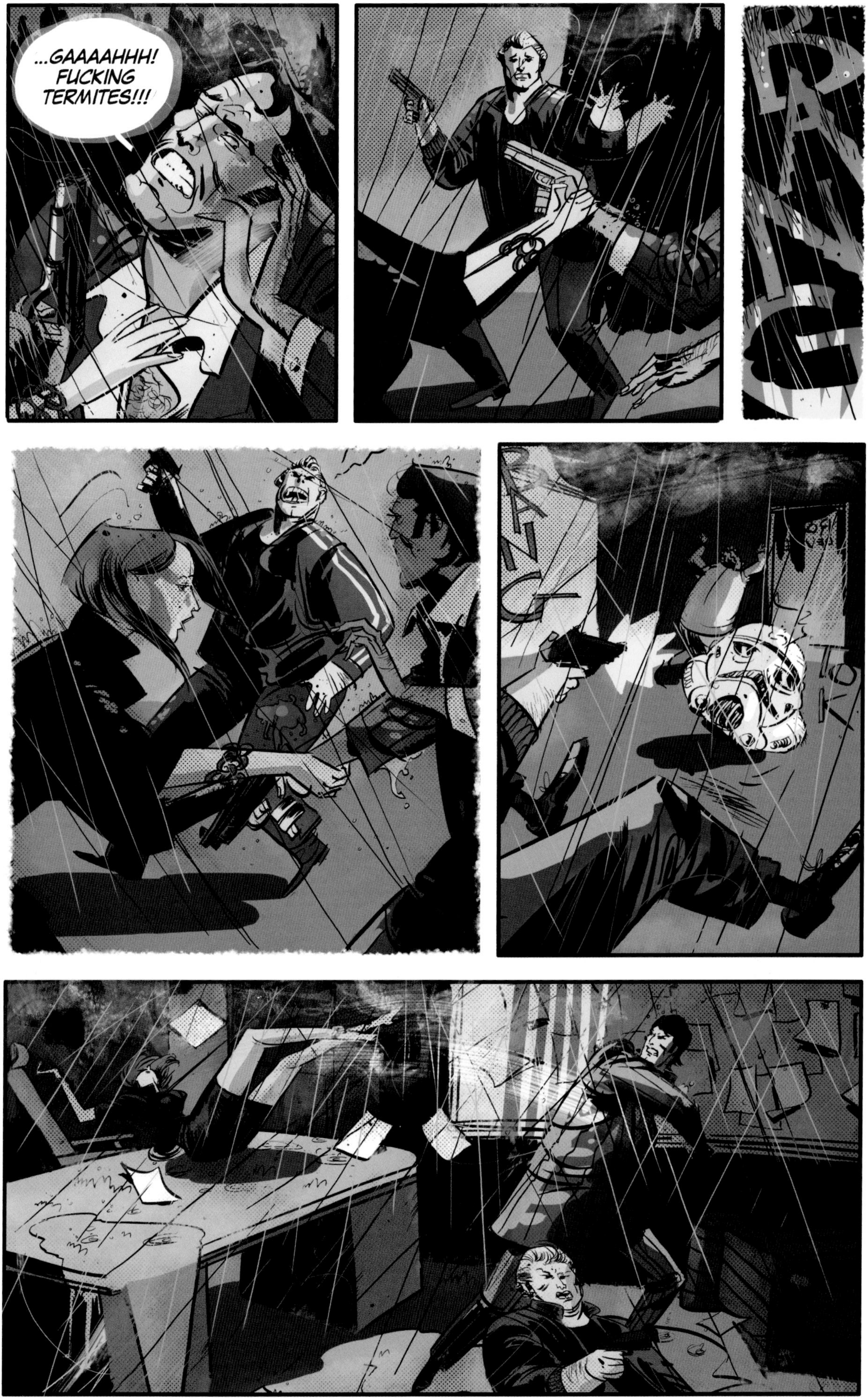
...GAAAAHHH! FUCKING TERMITES!!!

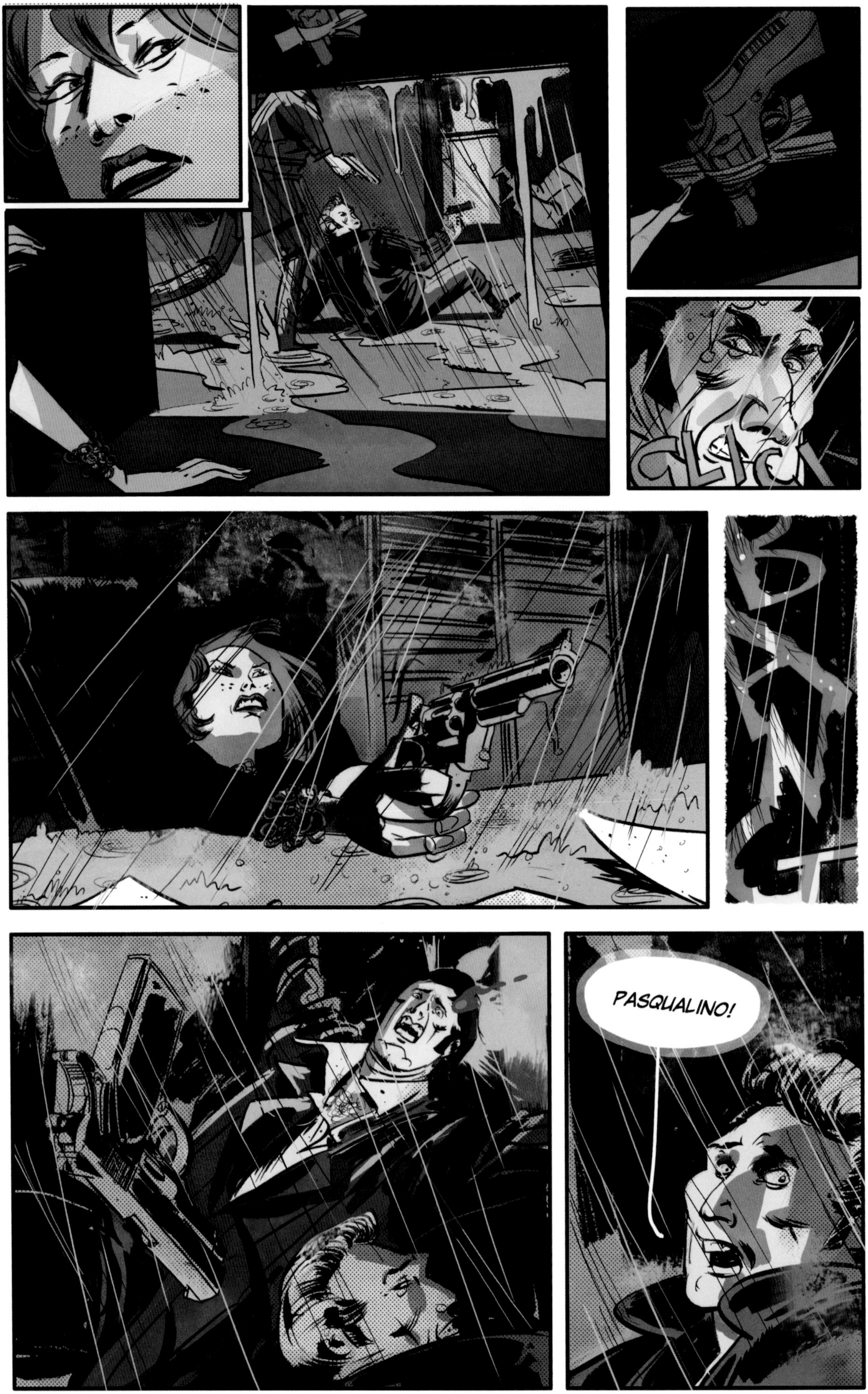
CLICK
PASQUALINO!

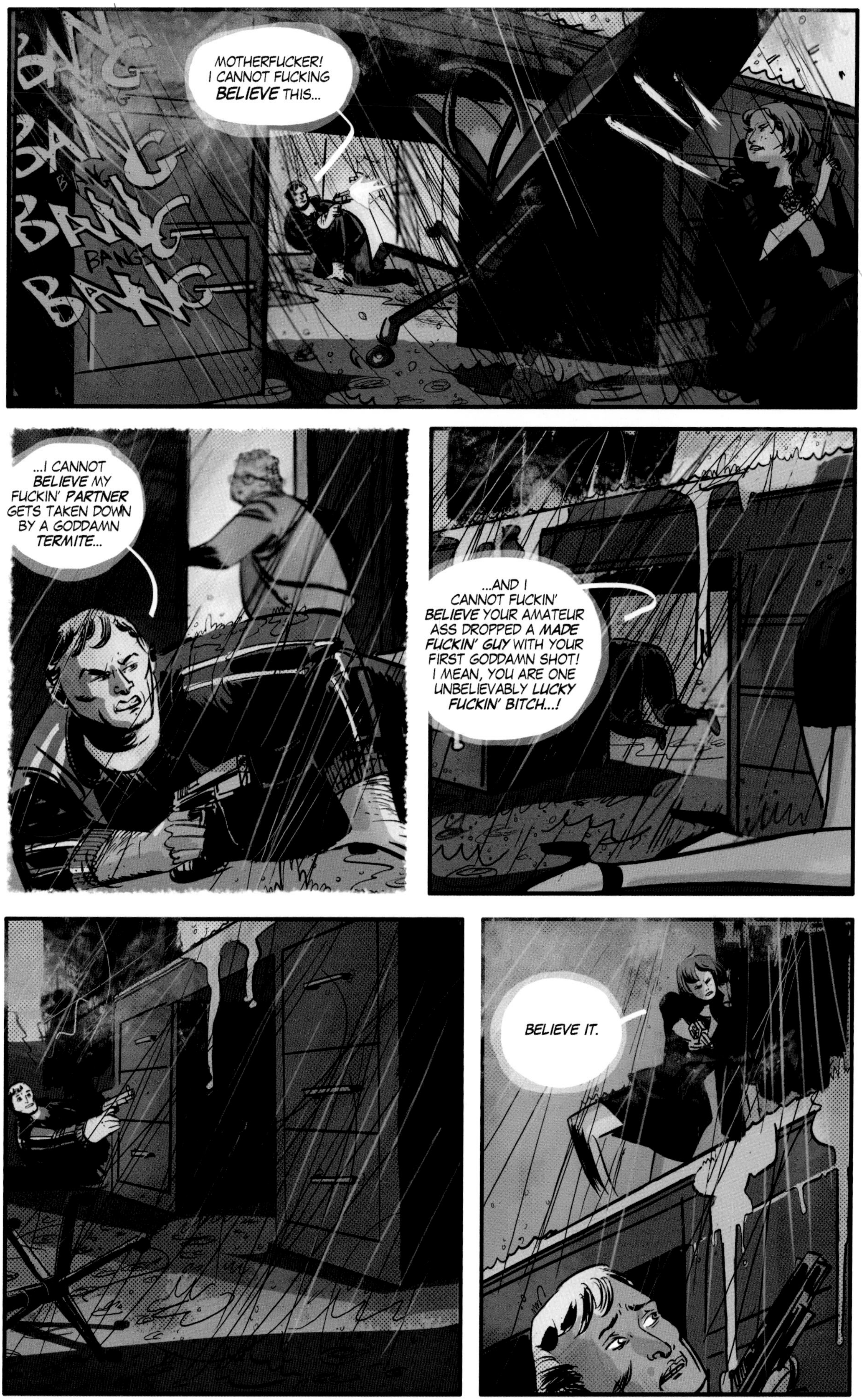
BANG BANG BANG BANG BANG BANG
MOTHERFUCKER! I CANNOT FUCKING BELIEVE THIS...
...I CANNOT BELIEVE MY FUCKIN' PARTNER GETS TAKEN DOWN BY A GODDAMN TERMITE...
...AND I CANNOT FUCKIN' BELIEVE YOUR AMATEUR ASS DROPPED A MADE FUCKIN' GUY WITH YOUR FIRST GODDAMN SHOT! I MEAN, YOU ARE ONE UNBELIEVABLY LUCKY FUCKIN' BITCH...!
BELIEVE IT.

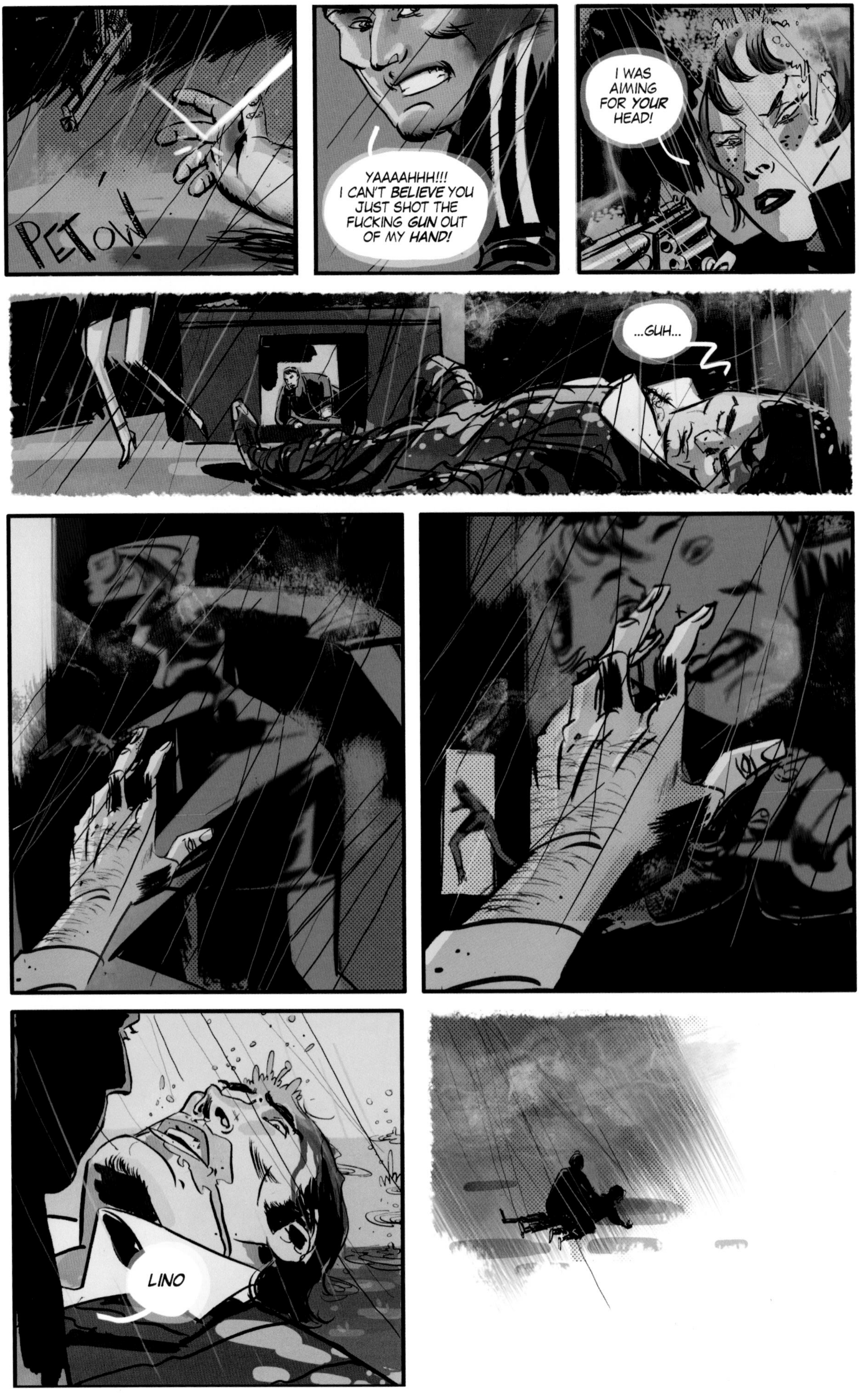
PETOW!
YAAAAHHH!!! I CAN'T BELIEVE YOU JUST SHOT THE FUCKING GUN OUT OF MY HAND!
I WAS AIMING FOR YOUR HEAD!
...GUH...
LINO

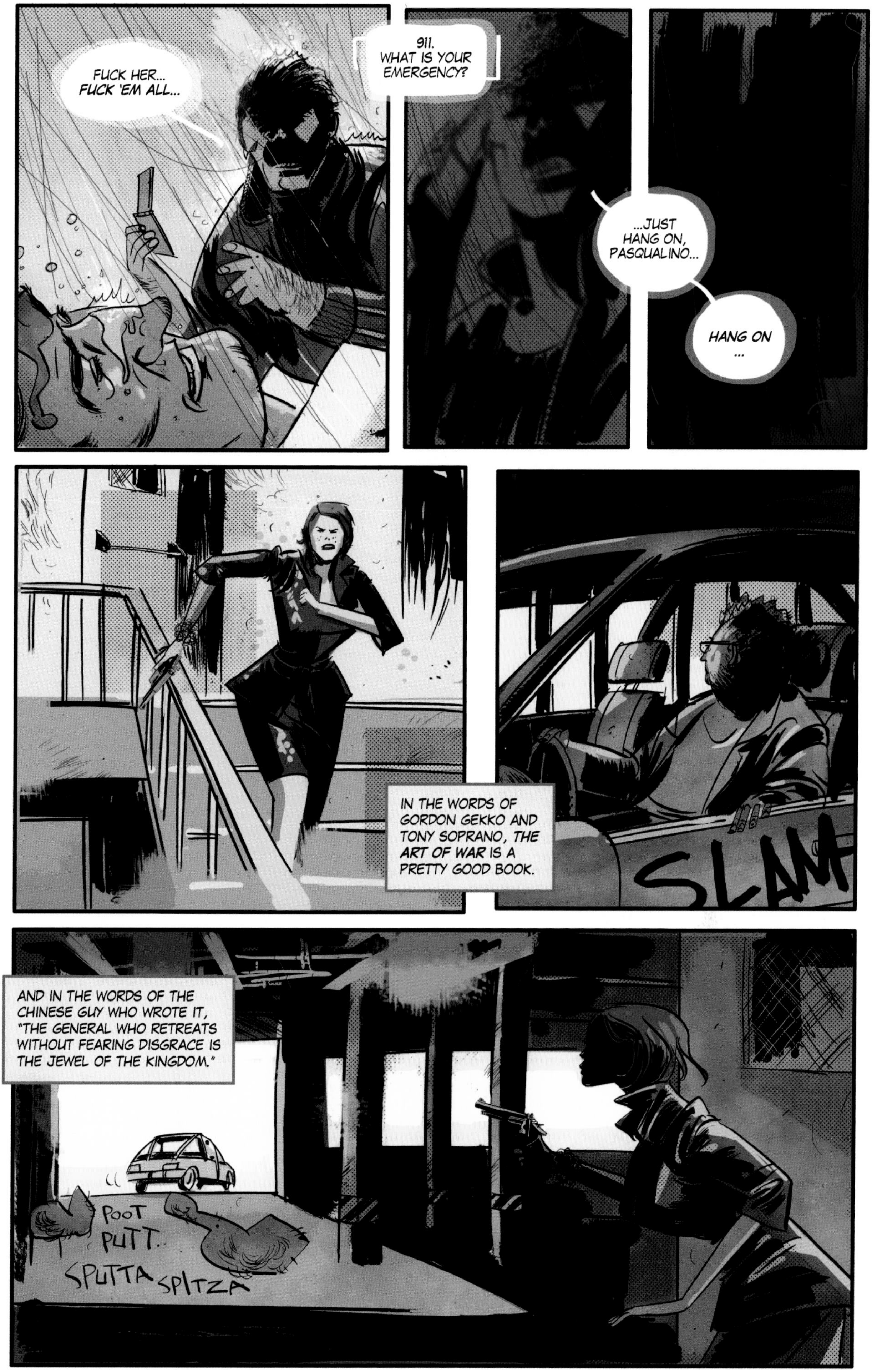
FUCK HER... FUCK 'EM ALL...
911. WHAT IS YOUR EMERGENCY?
...JUST HANG ON, PASQUALINO...
HANG ON ...
IN THE WORDS OF GORDON GEKKO AND TONY SOPRANO, THE ART OF WAR IS A PRETTY GOOD BOOK.
SLAM
AND IN THE WORDS OF THE CHINESE GUY WHO WROTE IT, "THE GENERAL WHO RETREATS WITHOUT FEARING DISGRACE IS THE JEWEL OF THE KINGDOM."
POOT
PUTT
SPUTTA SPITZA

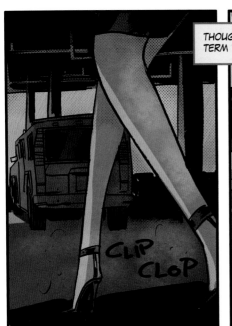

CLIP
CLOP

THOUGH PERSONALLY I PREFER THE TERM "STRATEGIC WITHDRAWAL."

HOLY SHIT...!

...OH FUCK!

SK!!!!!

WEEEOO WEEEOOOO

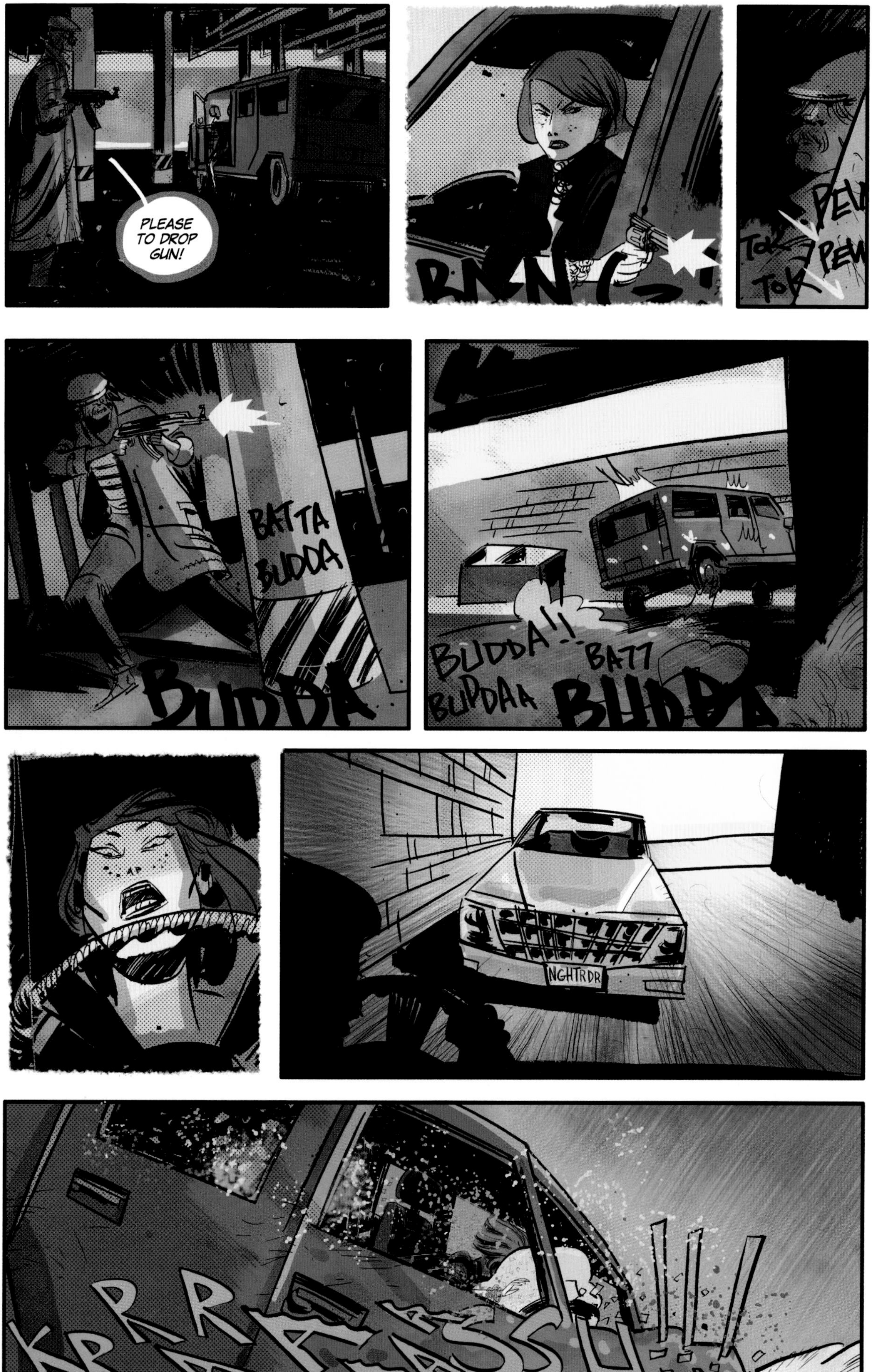
PLEASE TO DROP GUN!
TOK TOK
PEW PEW
BATTA BUDDA
BUDDA
BUDDA!!
BATT
BUDDAA
BUDDA
NGHTRDR

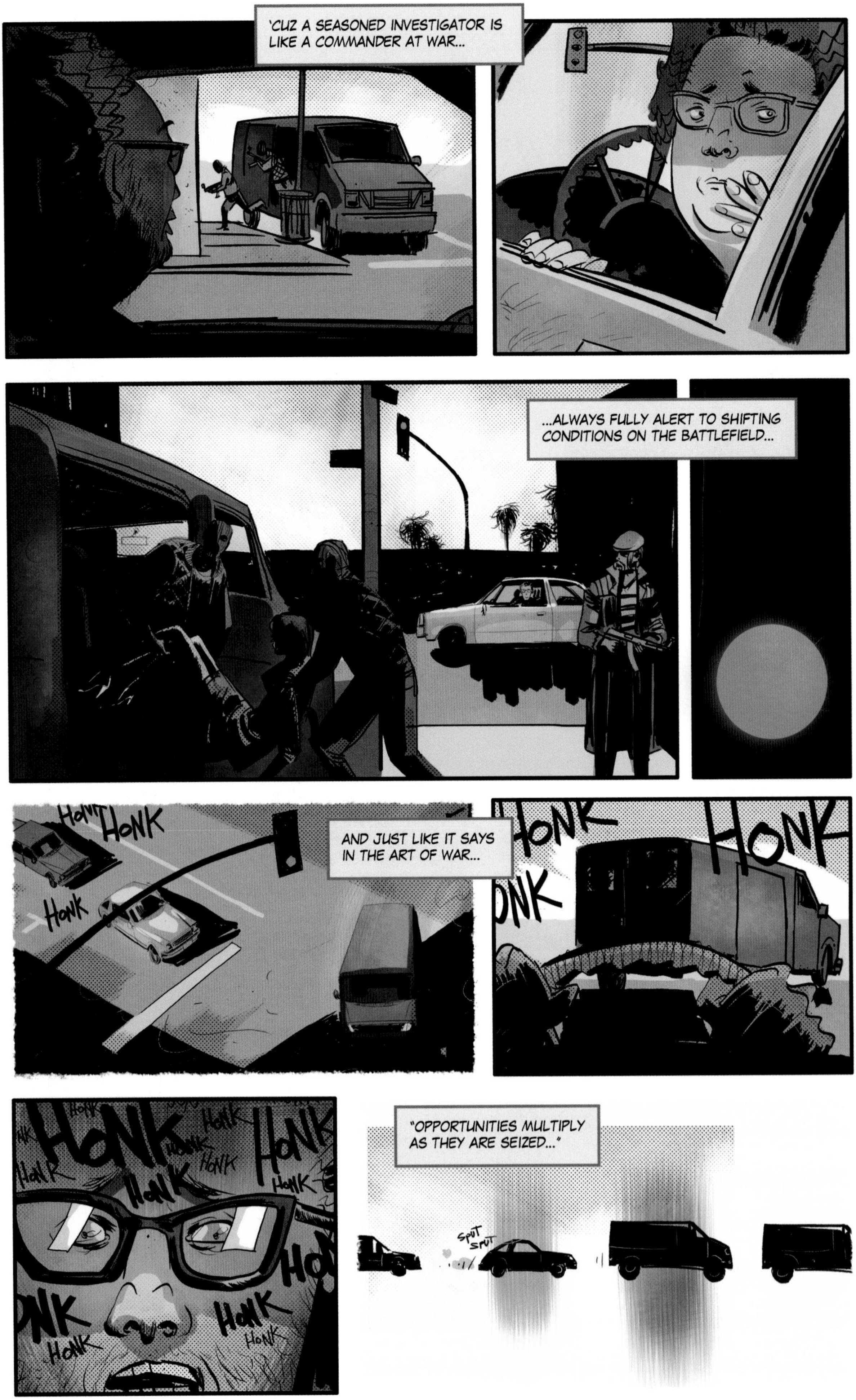
'CUZ A SEASONED INVESTIGATOR IS LIKE A COMMANDER AT WAR...
...ALWAYS FULLY ALERT TO SHIFTING CONDITIONS ON THE BATTLEFIELD...
HONK HONK
HONK
AND JUST LIKE IT SAYS IN THE ART OF WAR...
HONK
HONK
ONK
HONK
HONK
HONK
HONK
"OPPORTUNITIES MULTIPLY AS THEY ARE SEIZED..."
SPUT SPUT

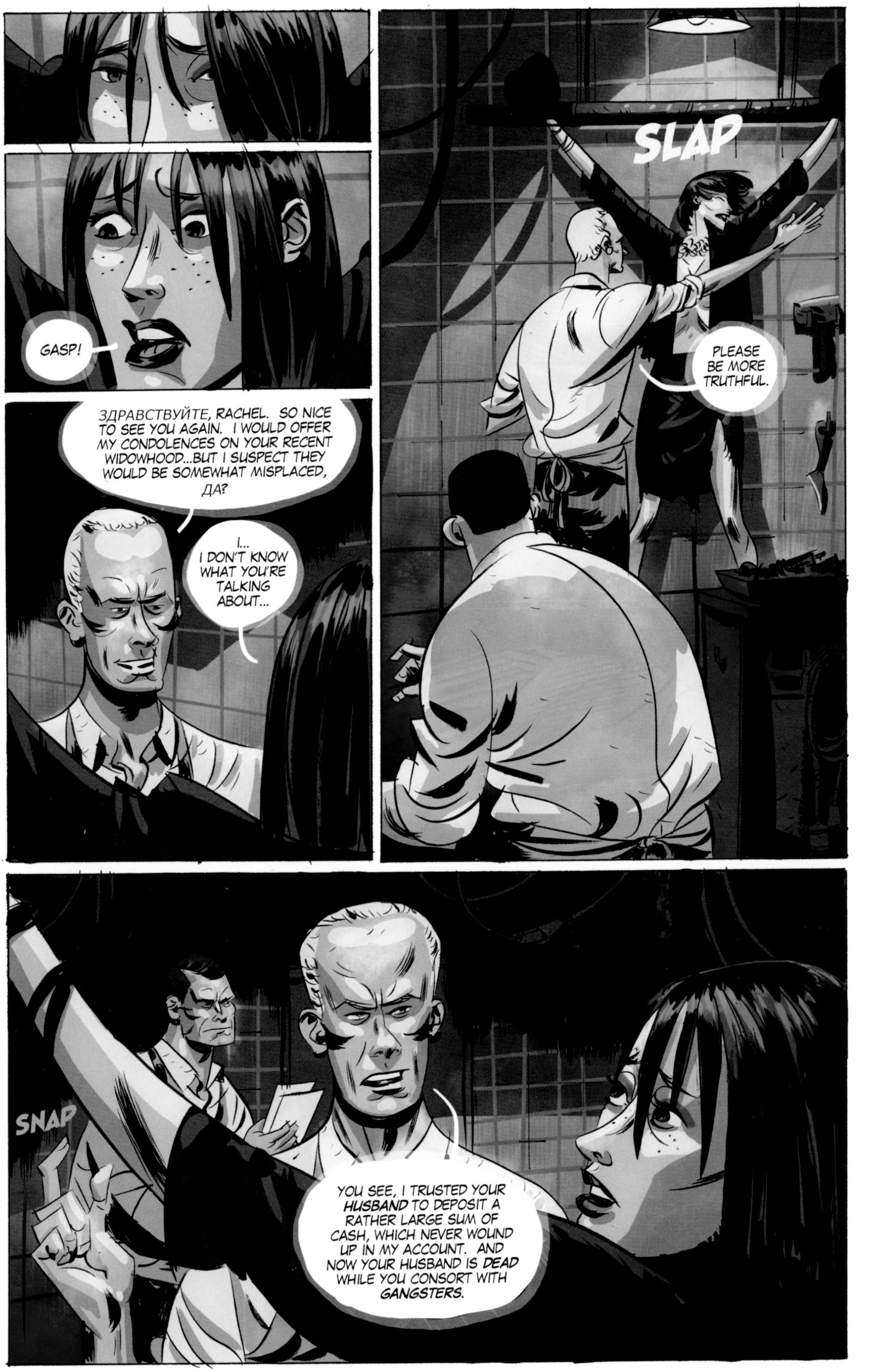
GASP!
ЗДРАВСТВУЙТЕ, RACHEL. SO NICE TO SEE YOU AGAIN. I WOULD OFFER MY CONDOLENCES ON YOUR RECENT WIDOWHOOD...BUT I SUSPECT THEY WOULD BE SOMEWHAT MISPLACED, ДА?
I... I DON'T KNOW WHAT YOU'RE TALKING ABOUT...
SLAP
PLEASE BE MORE TRUTHFUL.
SNAP
YOU SEE, I TRUSTED YOUR HUSBAND TO DEPOSIT A RATHER LARGE SUM OF CASH, WHICH NEVER WOUND UP IN MY ACCOUNT. AND NOW YOUR HUSBAND IS DEAD WHILE YOU CONSORT WITH GANGSTERS.

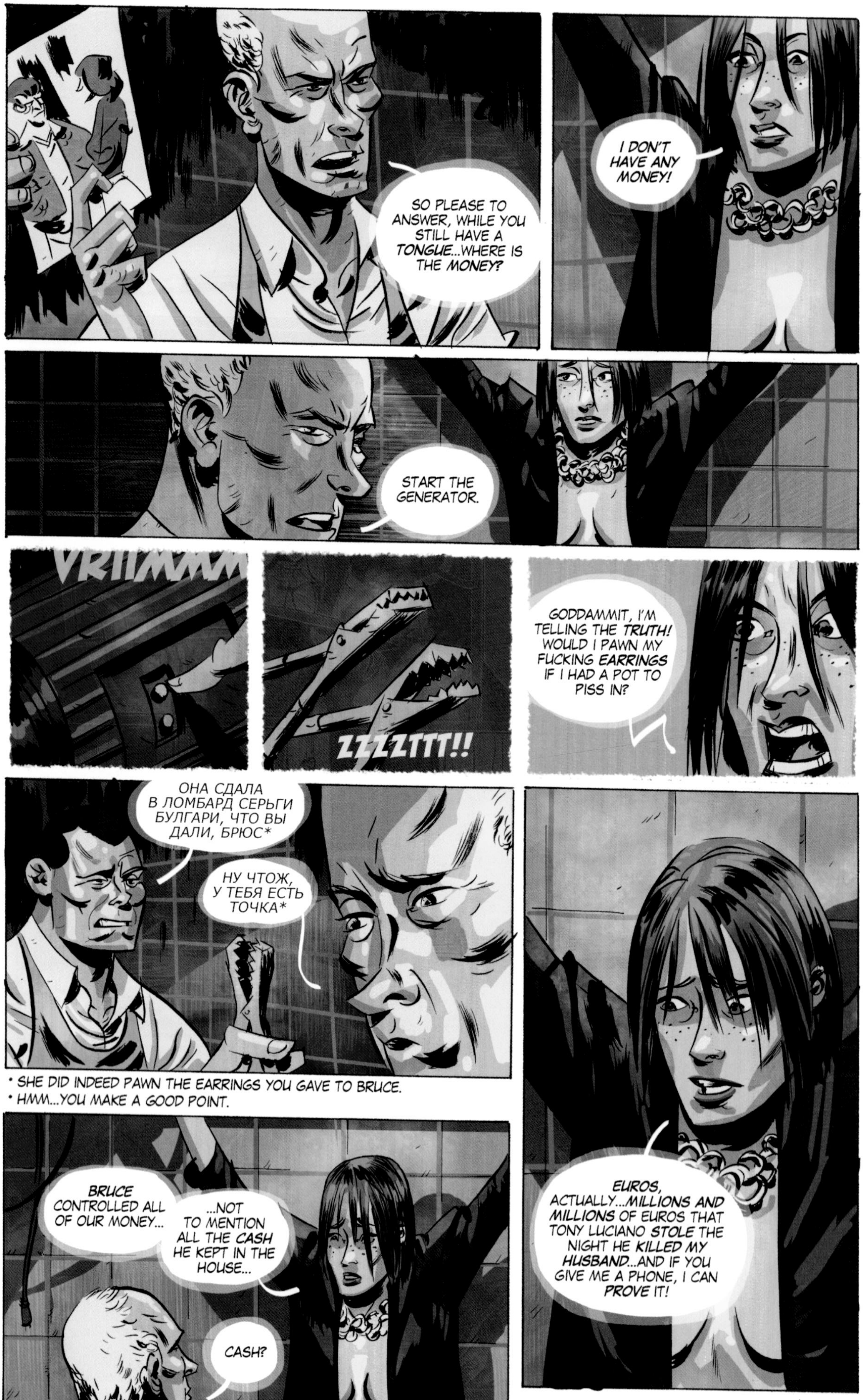
SO PLEASE TO ANSWER, WHILE YOU STILL HAVE A *TONGUE*...WHERE IS THE *MONEY?*
*I DON'T HAVE ANY MONEY!*
START THE GENERATOR.
VRIIMMM
ZZZZTTT!!
GODDAMMIT, I'M TELLING THE *TRUTH!* WOULD I PAWN MY FUCKING *EARRINGS* IF I HAD A POT TO PISS IN?
ОНА СДАЛА В ЛОМБАРД СЕРЬГИ БУЛГАРИ, ЧТО ВЫ ДАЛИ, БРЮС*
НУ ЧТОЖ, У ТЕБЯ ЕСТЬ ТОЧКА*
* SHE DID INDEED PAWN THE EARRINGS YOU GAVE TO BRUCE.
* HMM...YOU MAKE A GOOD POINT.
*EUROS,* ACTUALLY...*MILLIONS AND MILLIONS* OF EUROS THAT TONY LUCIANO *STOLE* THE NIGHT HE *KILLED MY HUSBAND*...AND IF YOU GIVE ME A PHONE, I CAN *PROVE* IT!
*BRUCE* CONTROLLED ALL OF OUR MONEY...
...NOT TO MENTION ALL THE *CASH* HE KEPT IN THE HOUSE...
CASH?

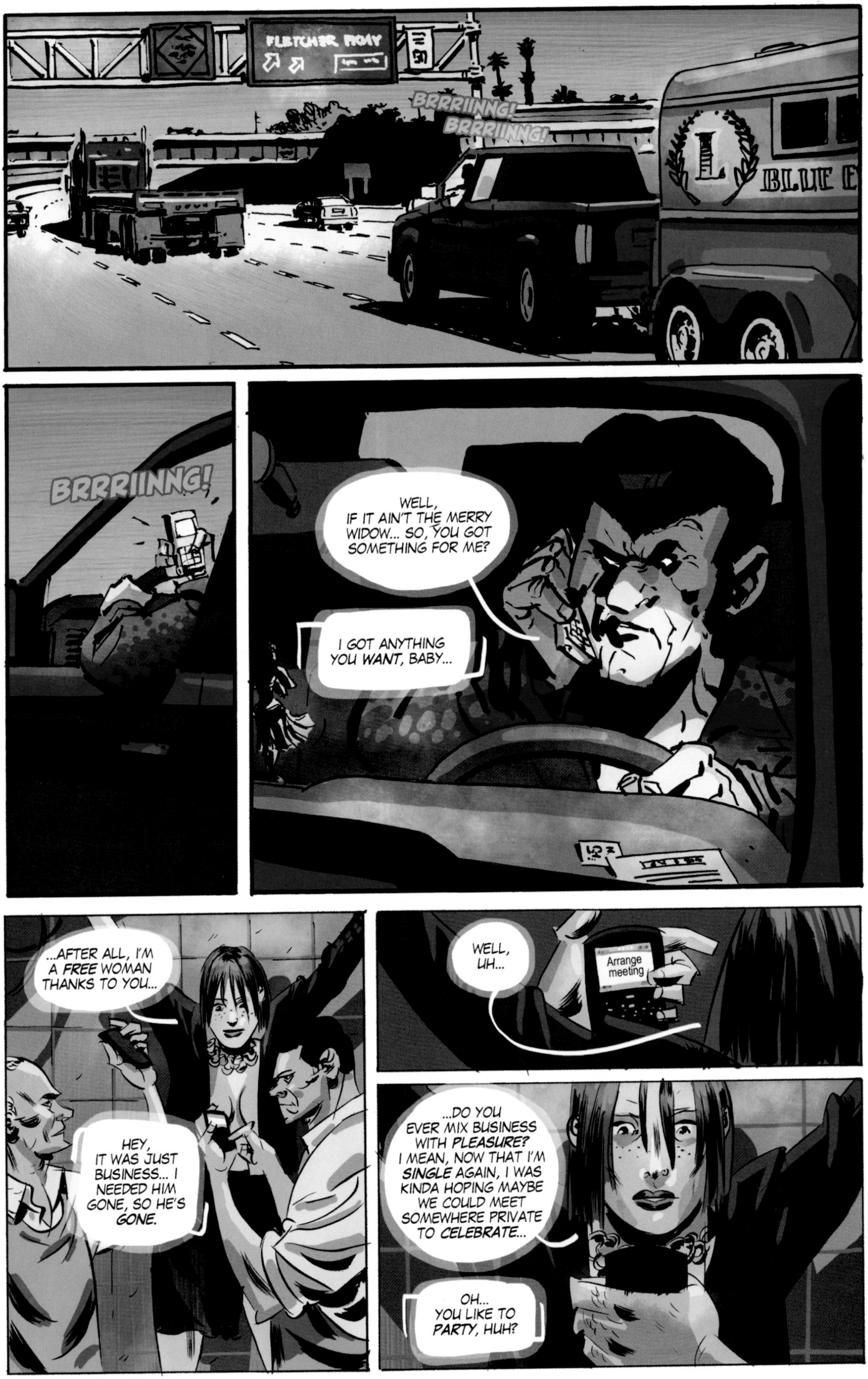
FLETCHER PKWY
BRRRIINNG!
BRRRIINNG!
BLUE
BRRRIINNG!
WELL, IF IT AIN'T THE MERRY WIDOW... SO, YOU GOT SOMETHING FOR ME?
I GOT ANYTHING YOU WANT, BABY...
...AFTER ALL, I'M A FREE WOMAN THANKS TO YOU...
HEY, IT WAS JUST BUSINESS... I NEEDED HIM GONE, SO HE'S GONE.
WELL, UH...
Arrange meeting
...DO YOU EVER MIX BUSINESS WITH PLEASURE? I MEAN, NOW THAT I'M SINGLE AGAIN, I WAS KINDA HOPING MAYBE WE COULD MEET SOMEWHERE PRIVATE TO CELEBRATE...
OH... YOU LIKE TO PARTY, HUH?

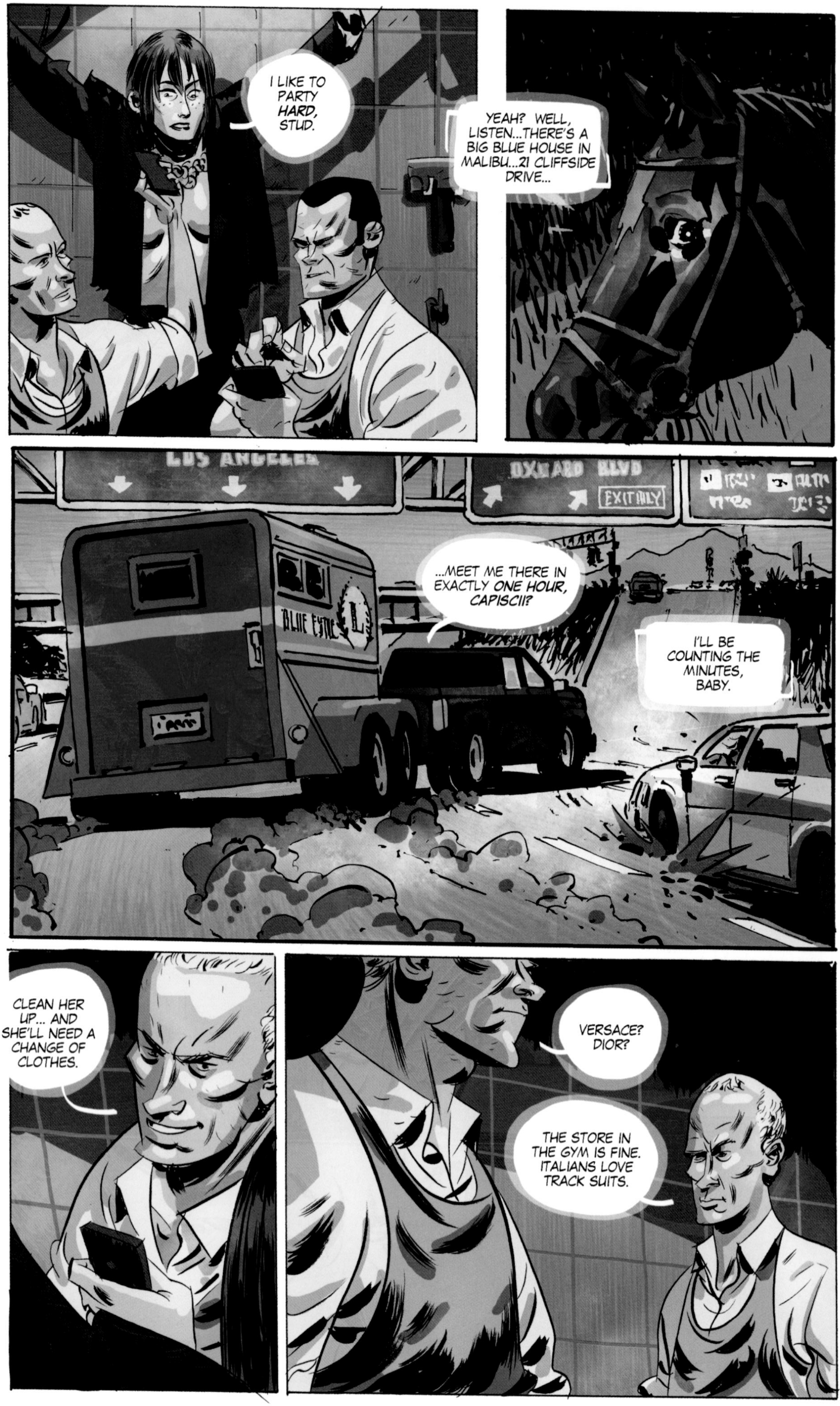
I LIKE TO PARTY HARD, STUD.
YEAH? WELL, LISTEN...THERE'S A BIG BLUE HOUSE IN MALIBU...21 CLIFFSIDE DRIVE...
LOS ANGELES
OXNARD BLVD
EXIT ONLY
...MEET ME THERE IN EXACTLY ONE HOUR, CAPISCI?
I'LL BE COUNTING THE MINUTES, BABY.
CLEAN HER UP... AND SHE'LL NEED A CHANGE OF CLOTHES.
VERSACE? DIOR?
THE STORE IN THE GYM IS FINE. ITALIANS LOVE TRACK SUITS.

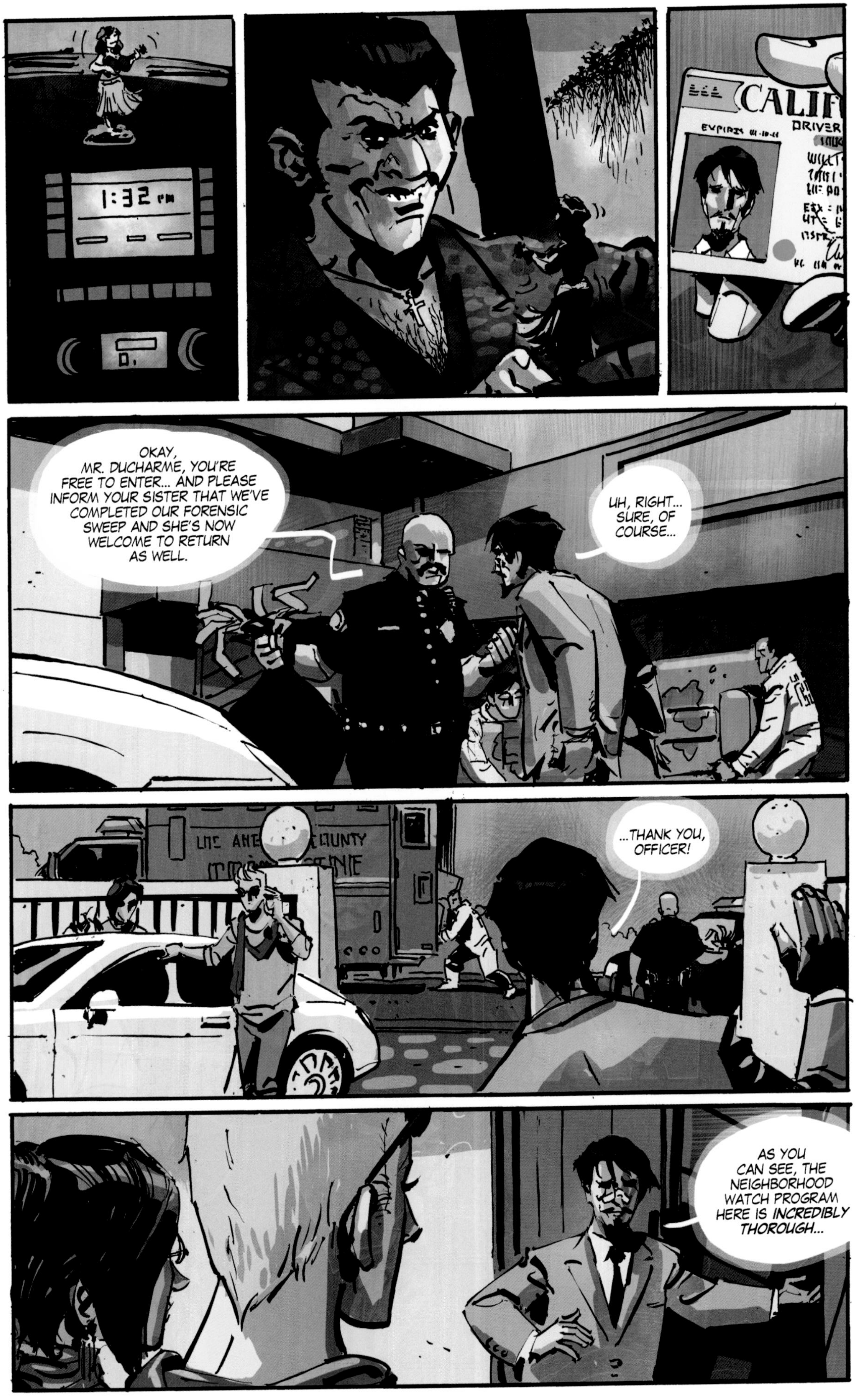
1:32 PM
CALIF
DRIVER
OKAY, MR. DUCHARME, YOU'RE FREE TO ENTER... AND PLEASE INFORM YOUR SISTER THAT WE'VE COMPLETED OUR FORENSIC SWEEP AND SHE'S NOW WELCOME TO RETURN AS WELL.
UH, RIGHT... SURE, OF COURSE...
...THANK YOU, OFFICER!
AS YOU CAN SEE, THE NEIGHBORHOOD WATCH PROGRAM HERE IS *INCREDIBLY THOROUGH*...

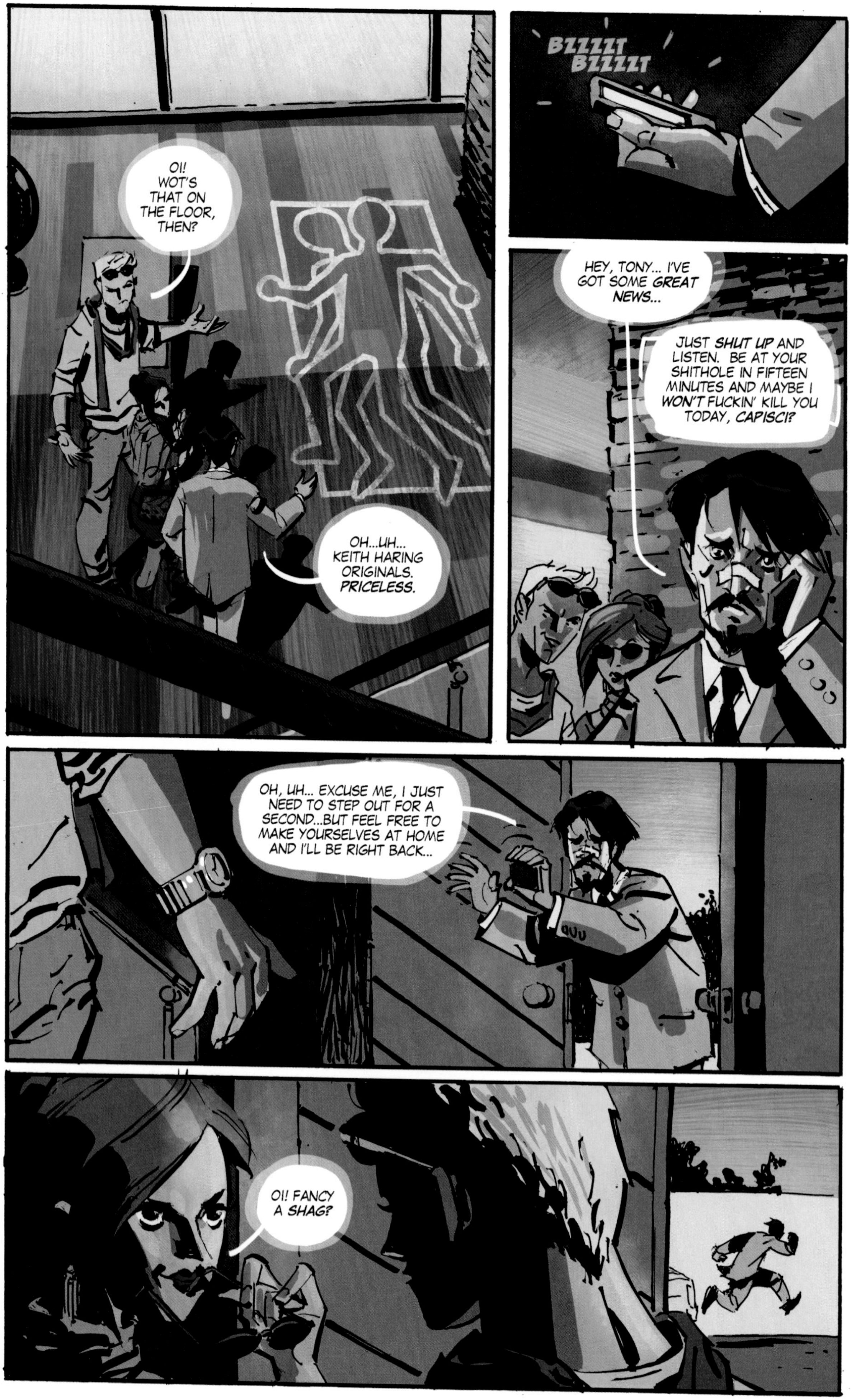
OI! WOT'S THAT ON THE FLOOR, THEN?
OH...UH... KEITH HARING ORIGINALS. PRICELESS.
BZZZZT BZZZZT
HEY, TONY... I'VE GOT SOME GREAT NEWS...
JUST SHUT UP AND LISTEN. BE AT YOUR SHITHOLE IN FIFTEEN MINUTES AND MAYBE I WON'T FUCKIN' KILL YOU TODAY, CAPISCI?
OH, UH... EXCUSE ME, I JUST NEED TO STEP OUT FOR A SECOND...BUT FEEL FREE TO MAKE YOURSELVES AT HOME AND I'LL BE RIGHT BACK...
OI! FANCY A SHAG?

EAFY GREEN

VIKTOR KALVACHEV'S

# BLUE™
## ESTATE

TRAINER:

EZD PRODUCTION
BORN & RAISED
IN THE USA

TRACK RECORD

10/10 COMICBUZZ
10/10 POPMATTERS
8.5/10 COMICBOOKNEWBIE
RANTING&RAVING
COMICSBULLETIN
CBR

10

TOTAL PURSE
WINNINGS TO DATE:
$2.99
(BY A NOSE!)

DAILY DOUBLE:
ITALIAN STALLIONS &
RUSSIAN NIGHTMARES

*White*
*Russian*

# BLUE ESTATE

## EPISODE TEN:
## WHITE RUSSIAN

ORIGINAL STORY:
**VIKTOR KALVACHEV** AND **KOSTA YANEV**

SCRIPT BY **ANDREW OSBORNE**

ARTISTS:
**VIKTOR KALVACHEV**
**TOBY CYPRESS**
**NATHAN FOX**
**REV. DAVE JOHNSON**
**PETER NGUYEN**
**KIERAN**

ART DIRECTION BY **VIKTOR KALVACHEV**

COVER, COLORS & DESIGN:
**VIKTOR KALVACHEV**

COLOR SUPPORT:
**PAUL MAYBURY**

CONTRIBUTING EDITOR:
**PHILO NORTHRUP**

www.BlueEstateComic.com

EZD
PRODUCTIONS

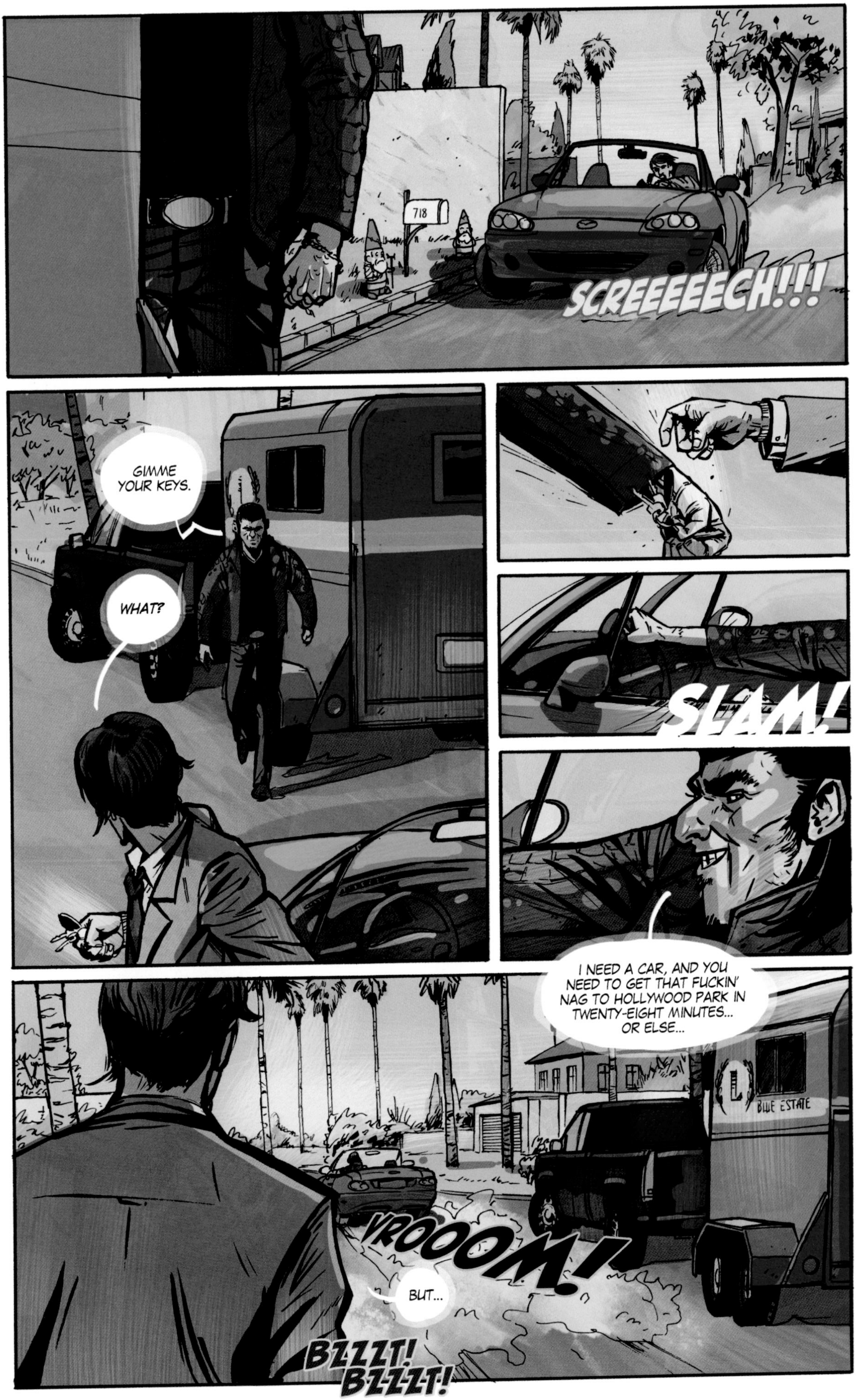
718
SCREEEEEECH!!!
GIMME YOUR KEYS.
WHAT?
SLAM!
I NEED A CAR, AND YOU NEED TO GET THAT FUCKIN' NAG TO HOLLYWOOD PARK IN TWENTY-EIGHT MINUTES... OR ELSE...
BLUE ESTATE
VROOOM!
BUT...
BZZZT! BZZZT!

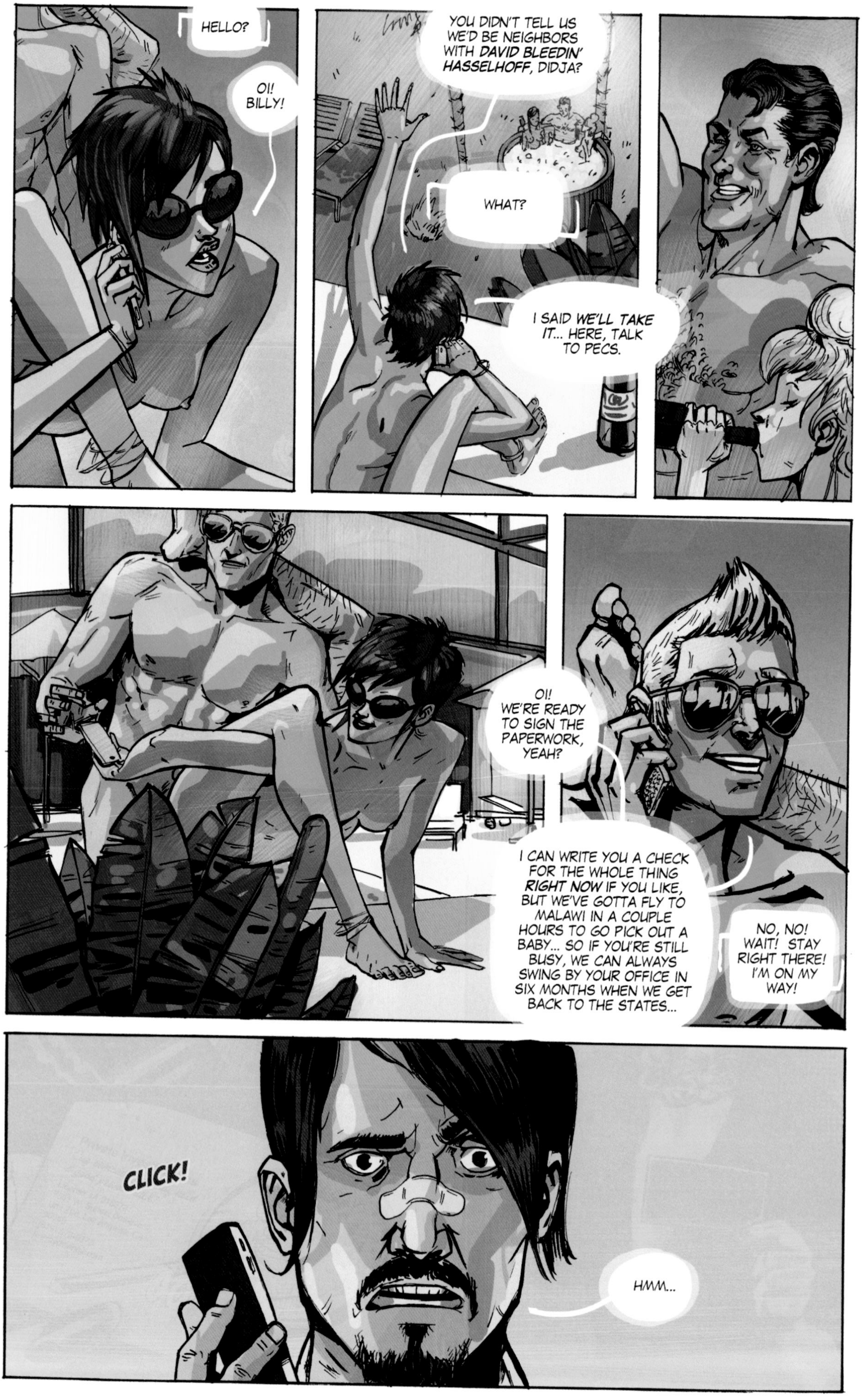
HELLO?
OI! BILLY!
YOU DIDN'T TELL US WE'D BE NEIGHBORS WITH DAVID BLEEDIN' HASSELHOFF, DIDJA?
WHAT?
I SAID WE'LL TAKE IT... HERE, TALK TO PECS.
OI! WE'RE READY TO SIGN THE PAPERWORK, YEAH?
I CAN WRITE YOU A CHECK FOR THE WHOLE THING RIGHT NOW IF YOU LIKE, BUT WE'VE GOTTA FLY TO MALAWI IN A COUPLE HOURS TO GO PICK OUT A BABY... SO IF YOU'RE STILL BUSY, WE CAN ALWAYS SWING BY YOUR OFFICE IN SIX MONTHS WHEN WE GET BACK TO THE STATES...
NO, NO! WAIT! STAY RIGHT THERE! I'M ON MY WAY!
CLICK!
HMM...

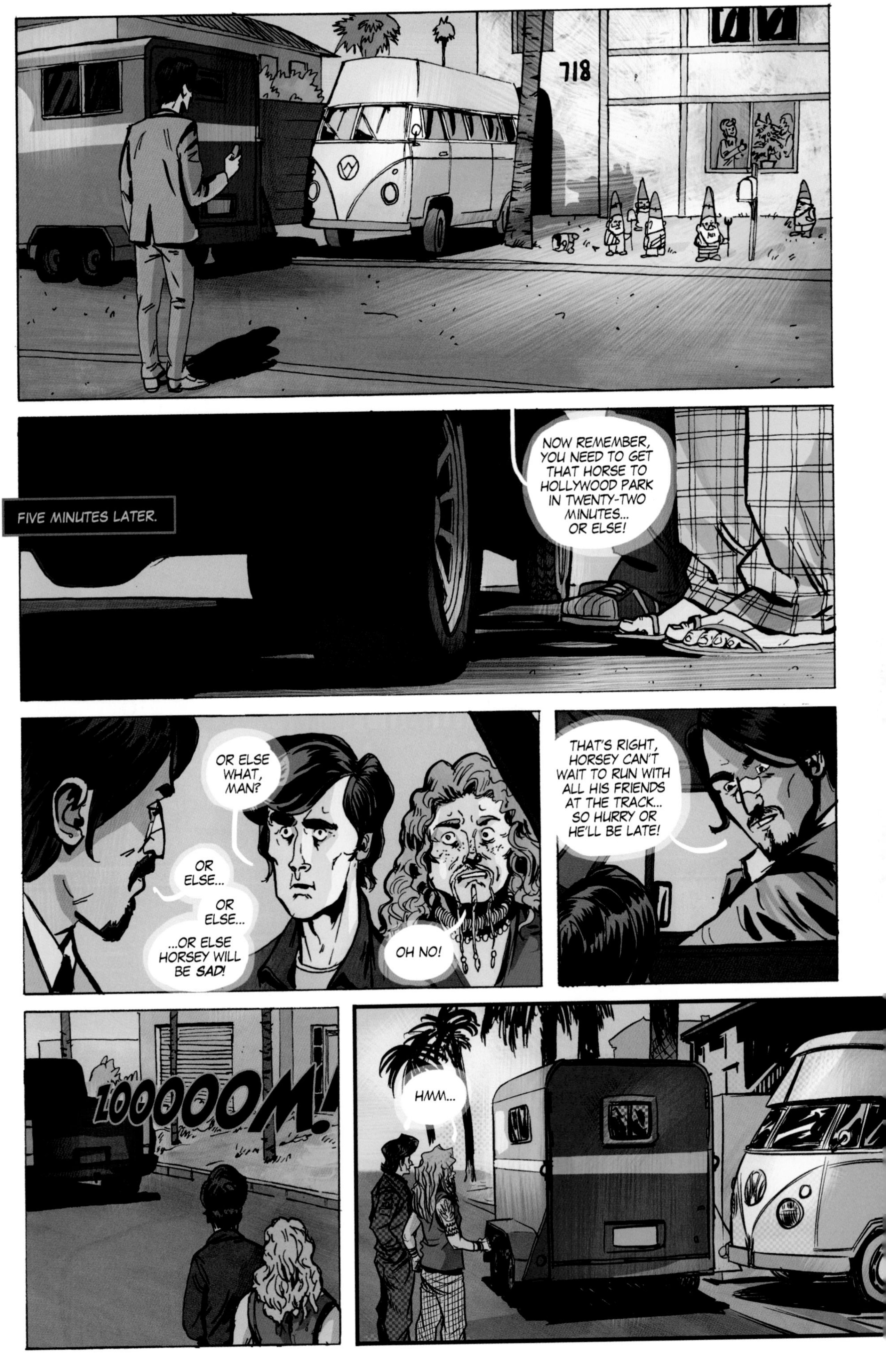
718
FIVE MINUTES LATER.
NOW REMEMBER, YOU NEED TO GET THAT HORSE TO HOLLYWOOD PARK IN TWENTY-TWO MINUTES... OR ELSE!
OR ELSE WHAT, MAN?
OR ELSE...
OR ELSE...
...OR ELSE HORSEY WILL BE SAD!
OH NO!
THAT'S RIGHT, HORSEY CAN'T WAIT TO RUN WITH ALL HIS FRIENDS AT THE TRACK... SO HURRY OR HE'LL BE LATE!
ZOOOOOM!
HMM...

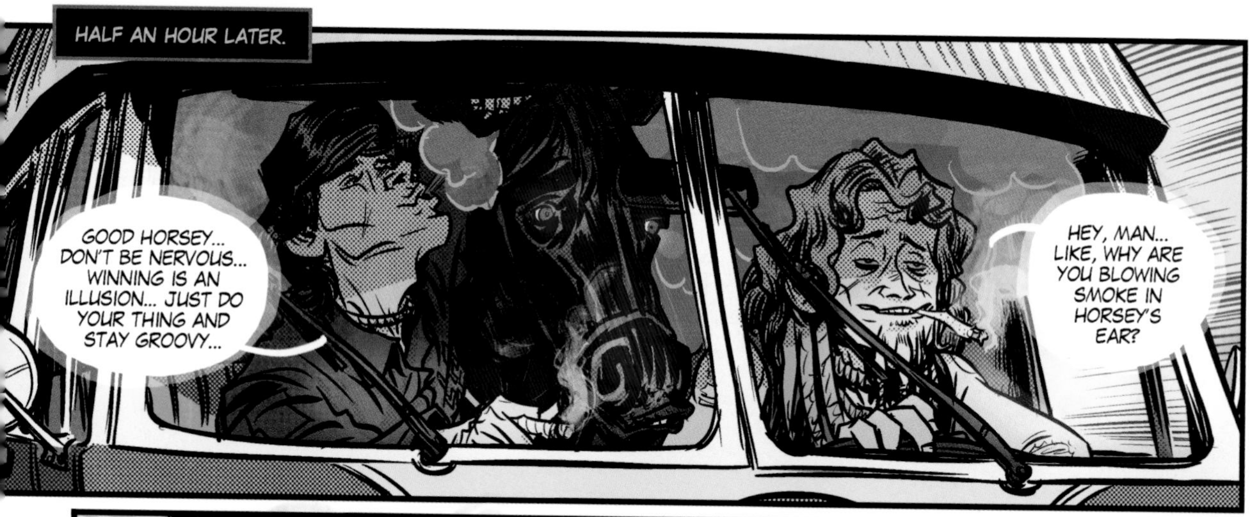
HALF AN HOUR LATER.
GOOD HORSEY... DON'T BE NERVOUS... WINNING IS AN ILLUSION... JUST DO YOUR THING AND STAY GROOVY...
HEY, MAN... LIKE, WHY ARE YOU BLOWING SMOKE IN HORSEY'S EAR?

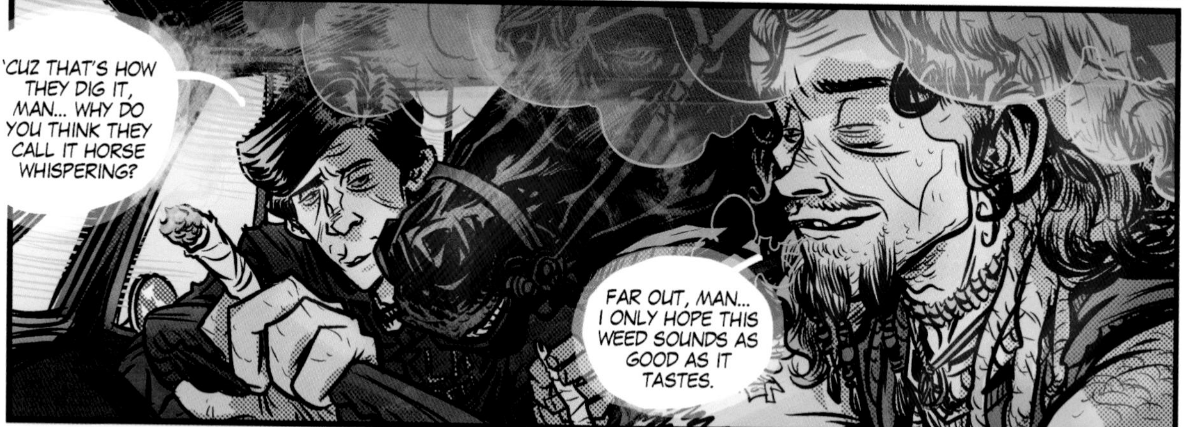
'CUZ THAT'S HOW THEY DIG IT, MAN... WHY DO YOU THINK THEY CALL IT HORSE WHISPERING?
FAR OUT, MAN... I ONLY HOPE THIS WEED SOUNDS AS GOOD AS IT TASTES.

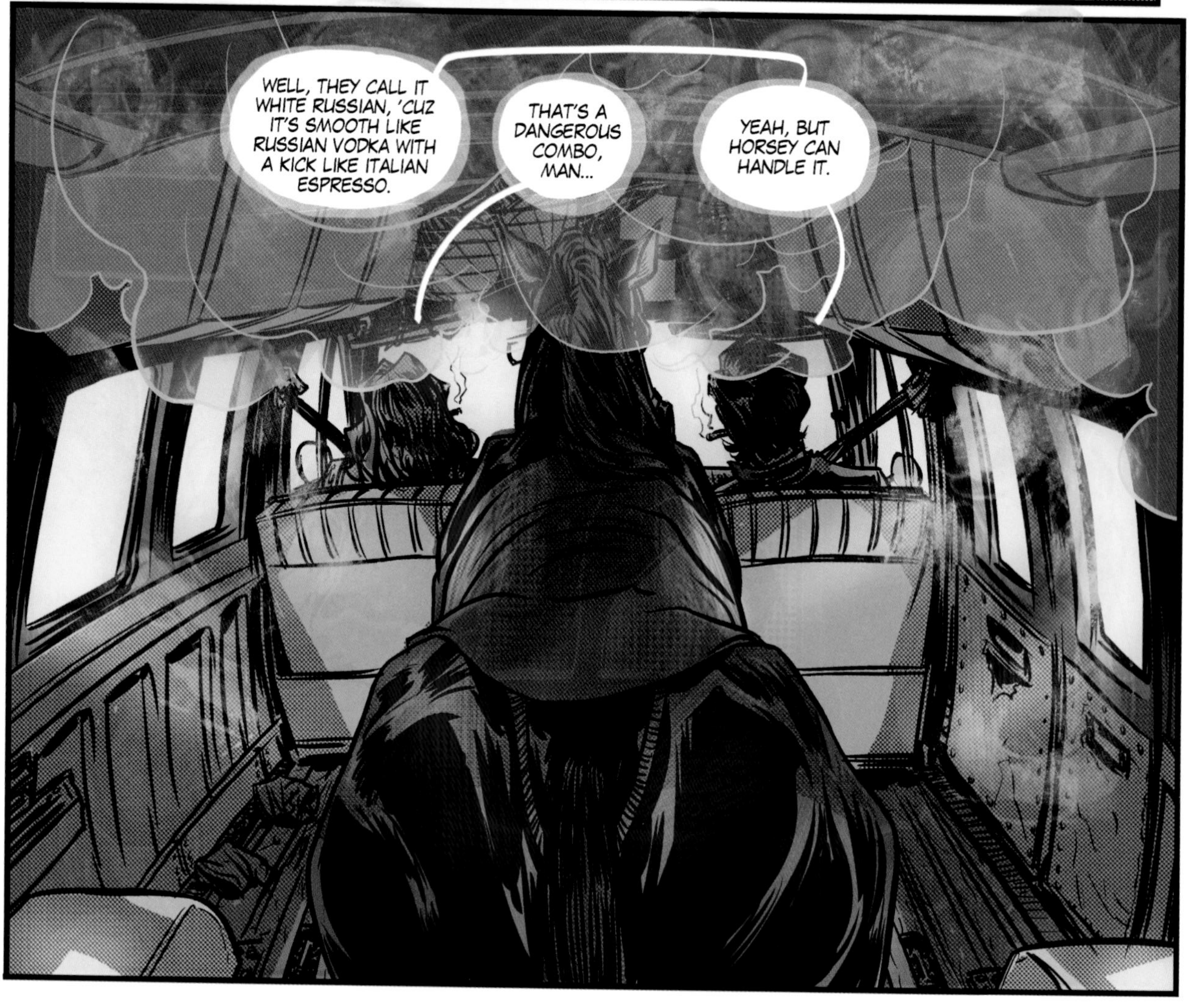
WELL, THEY CALL IT WHITE RUSSIAN, 'CUZ IT'S SMOOTH LIKE RUSSIAN VODKA WITH A KICK LIKE ITALIAN ESPRESSO.
THAT'S A DANGEROUS COMBO, MAN...
YEAH, BUT HORSEY CAN HANDLE IT.

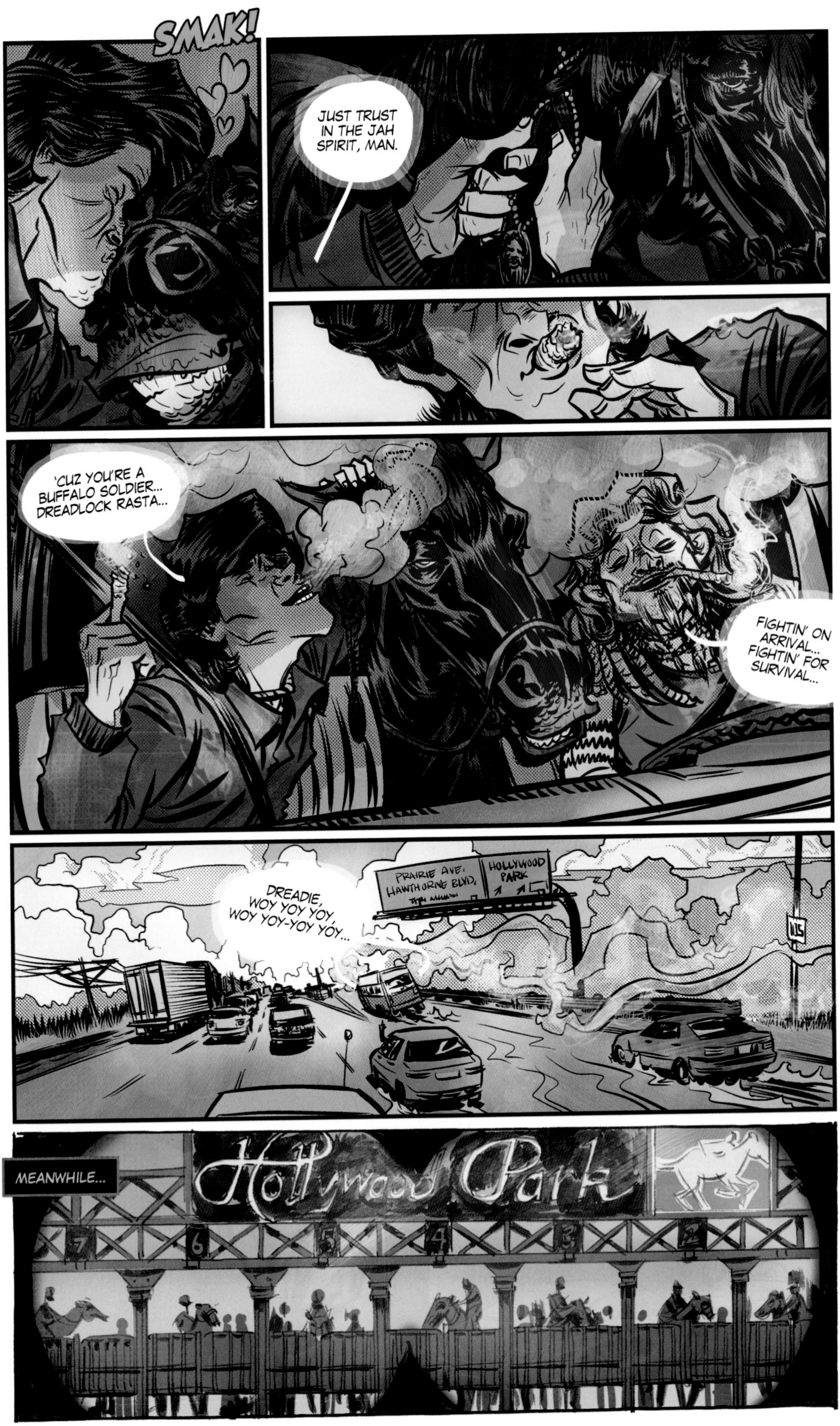
SMAK!
JUST TRUST IN THE JAH SPIRIT, MAN.
'CUZ YOU'RE A BUFFALO SOLDIER... DREADLOCK RASTA...
FIGHTIN' ON ARRIVAL... FIGHTIN' FOR SURVIVAL...
DREADIE, WOY YOY YOY, WOY YOY-YOY YOY...
PRAIRIE AVE. HAWTHORNE BLVD.
HOLLYWOOD PARK
105
MEANWHILE...
Hollywood Park

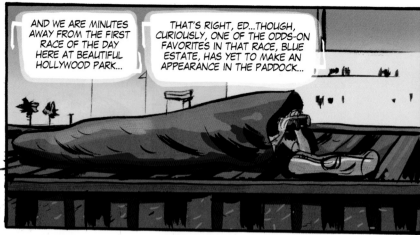

AND WE ARE MINUTES AWAY FROM THE FIRST RACE OF THE DAY HERE AT BEAUTIFUL HOLLYWOOD PARK...

THAT'S RIGHT, ED...THOUGH, CURIOUSLY, ONE OF THE ODDS-ON FAVORITES IN THAT RACE, BLUE ESTATE, HAS YET TO MAKE AN APPEARANCE IN THE PADDOCK...

ZIP

ICK

CLACK

CHICK

TACK

AERIE TO EAGLE... WHAT'S YOUR STATUS?

THE EYE OF THE EAGLE SEES ALL.

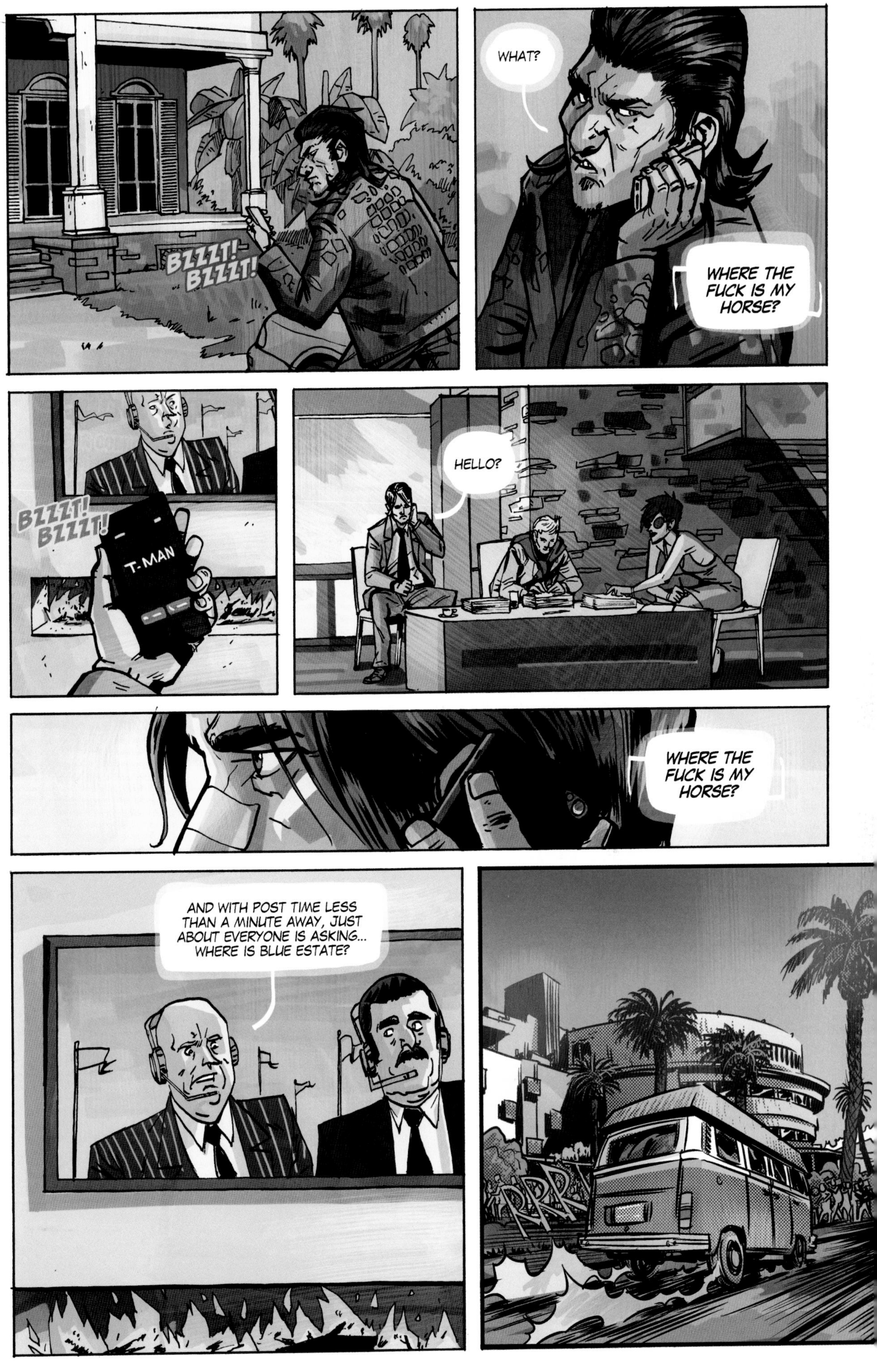
BZZZT!
BZZZT!
WHAT?
WHERE THE FUCK IS MY HORSE?
BZZZT!
BZZZT!
T-MAN
HELLO?
WHERE THE FUCK IS MY HORSE?
AND WITH POST TIME LESS THAN A MINUTE AWAY, JUST ABOUT EVERYONE IS ASKING... WHERE IS BLUE ESTATE?

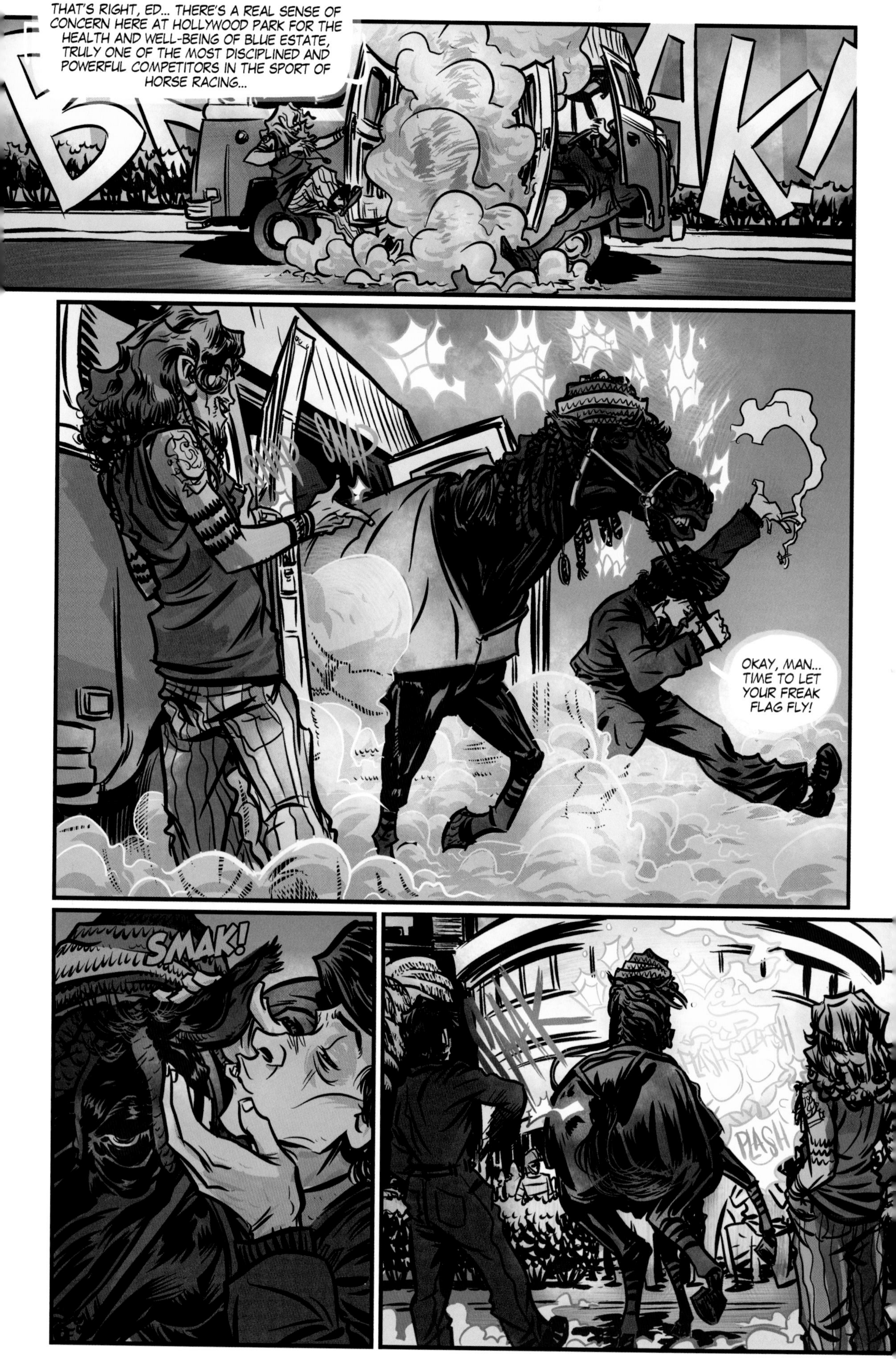
THAT'S RIGHT, ED... THERE'S A REAL SENSE OF CONCERN HERE AT HOLLYWOOD PARK FOR THE HEALTH AND WELL-BEING OF BLUE ESTATE, TRULY ONE OF THE MOST DISCIPLINED AND POWERFUL COMPETITORS IN THE SPORT OF HORSE RACING...
SNAP SNAP
OKAY, MAN... TIME TO LET YOUR FREAK FLAG FLY!
SMAK!
PLASH
PLASH

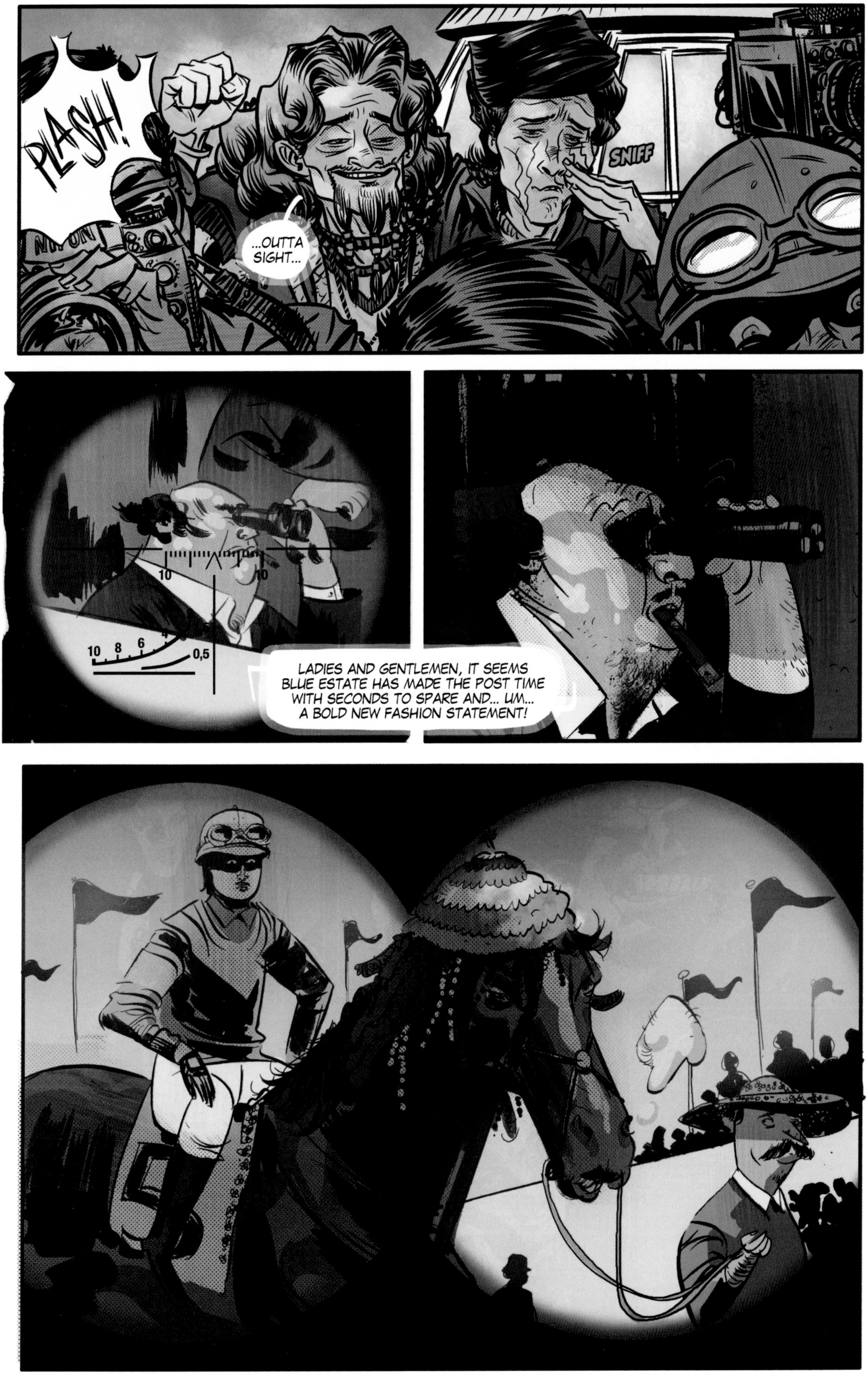
PLASH!
...OUTTA SIGHT...
SNIFF
10
10
10 8 6 4
0,5
LADIES AND GENTLEMEN, IT SEEMS BLUE ESTATE HAS MADE THE POST TIME WITH SECONDS TO SPARE AND... UM... A BOLD NEW FASHION STATEMENT!

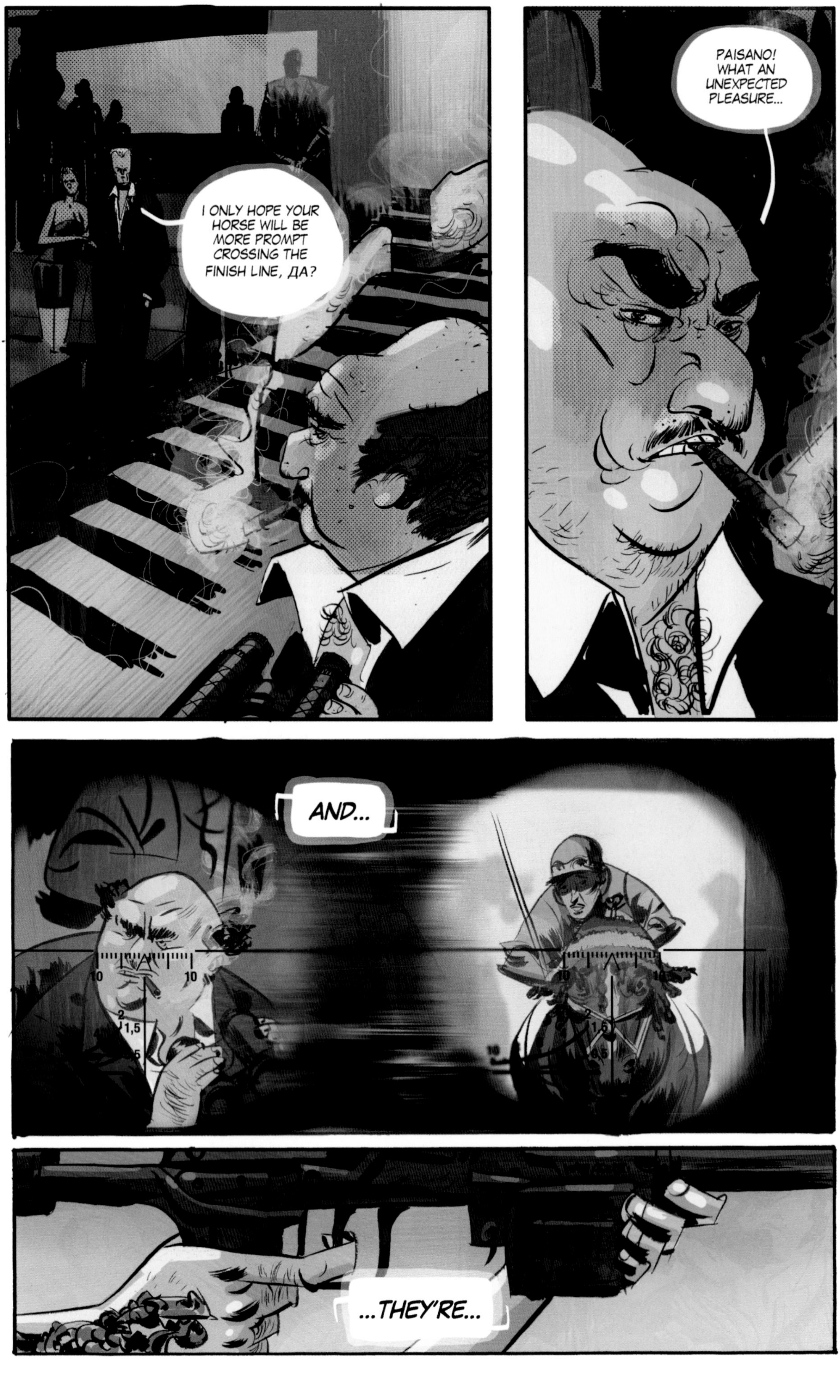
I ONLY HOPE YOUR HORSE WILL BE MORE PROMPT CROSSING THE FINISH LINE, ДА?
PAISANO! WHAT AN UNEXPECTED PLEASURE...
AND...
...THEY'RE...

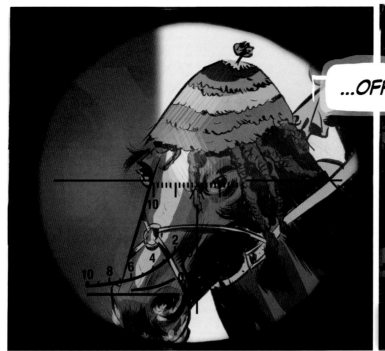

...OFF!

GIDDYAP!

NEEEEEEIIIIIGHHH!

WHAT THE...?

FUMP

OH NO! SOMETHING'S WRONG WITH BLUE ESTATE!

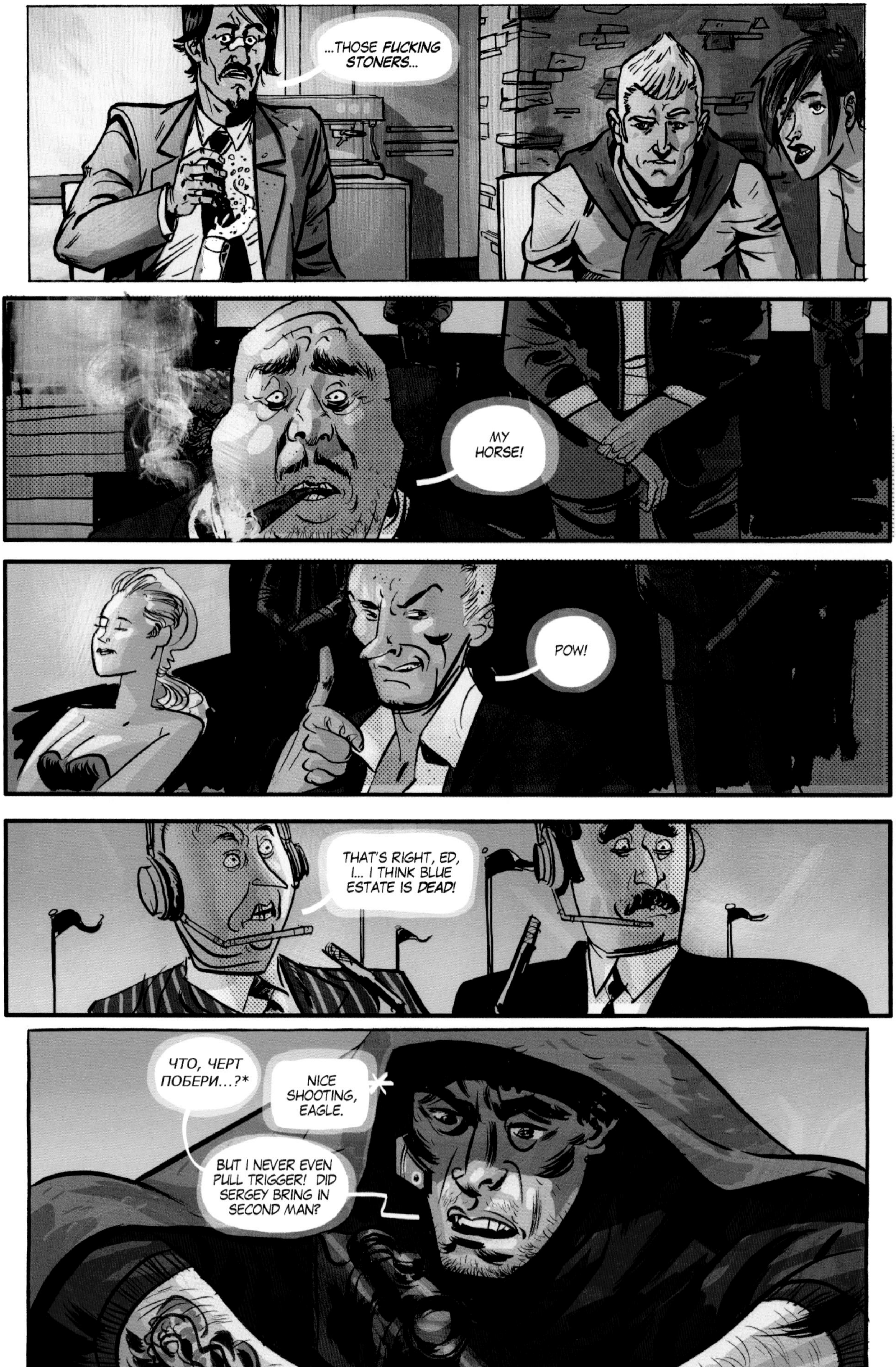
...THOSE FUCKING STONERS...
MY HORSE!
POW!
THAT'S RIGHT, ED, I... I THINK BLUE ESTATE IS DEAD!
ЧТО, ЧЕРТ ПОБЕРИ...?*
NICE SHOOTING, EAGLE.
BUT I NEVER EVEN PULL TRIGGER! DID SERGEY BRING IN SECOND MAN?

*WHAT THE HELL?

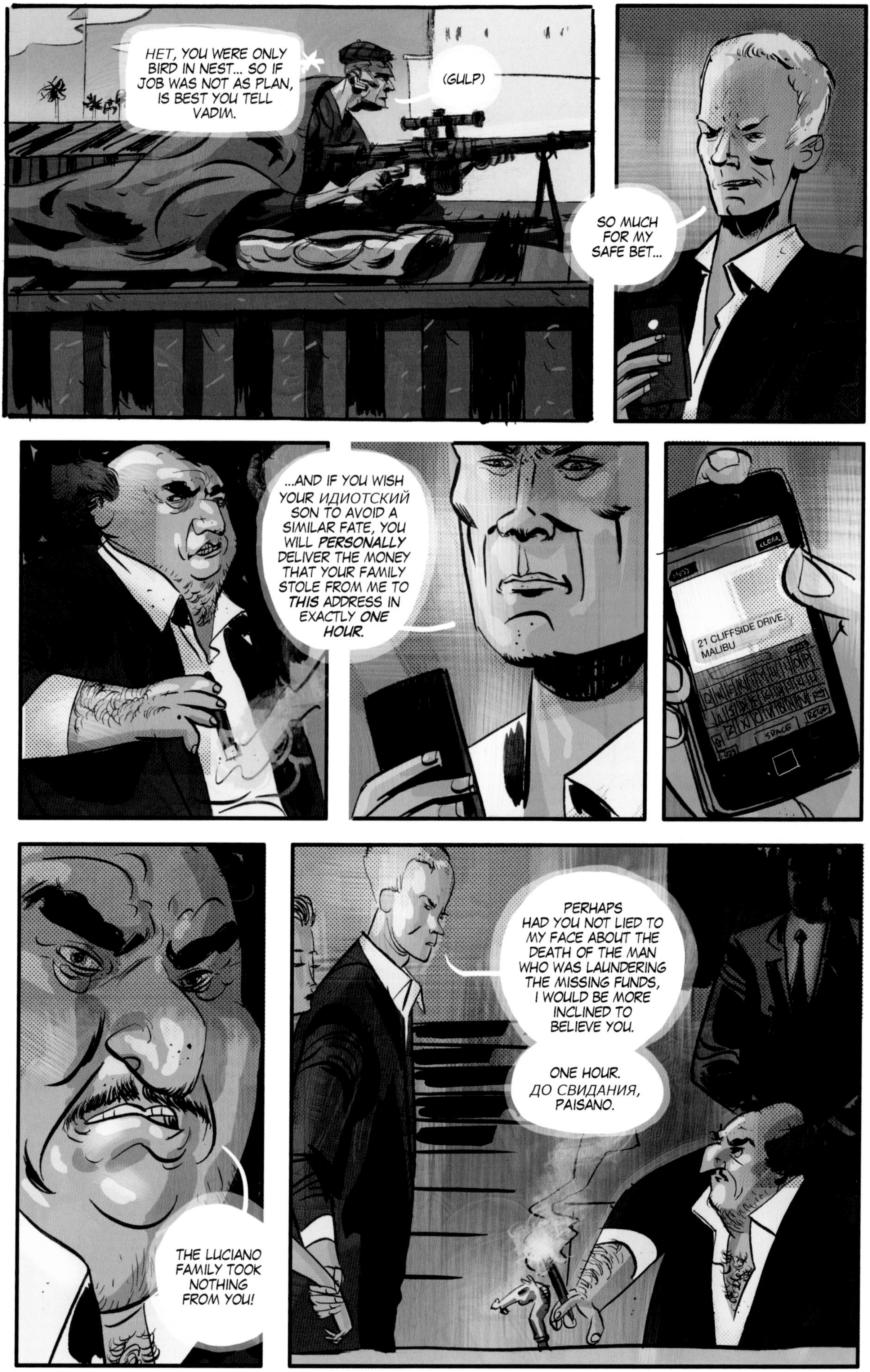
HET, YOU WERE ONLY BIRD IN NEST... SO IF JOB WAS NOT AS PLAN, IS BEST YOU TELL VADIM.
(GULP)
SO MUCH FOR MY SAFE BET...
...AND IF YOU WISH YOUR ИДИОТСКИЙ SON TO AVOID A SIMILAR FATE, YOU WILL PERSONALLY DELIVER THE MONEY THAT YOUR FAMILY STOLE FROM ME TO THIS ADDRESS IN EXACTLY ONE HOUR.
21 CLIFFSIDE DRIVE, MALIBU
SPACE
THE LUCIANO FAMILY TOOK NOTHING FROM YOU!
PERHAPS HAD YOU NOT LIED TO MY FACE ABOUT THE DEATH OF THE MAN WHO WAS LAUNDERING THE MISSING FUNDS, I WOULD BE MORE INCLINED TO BELIEVE YOU.
ONE HOUR. ДО СВИДАНИЯ, PAISANO.

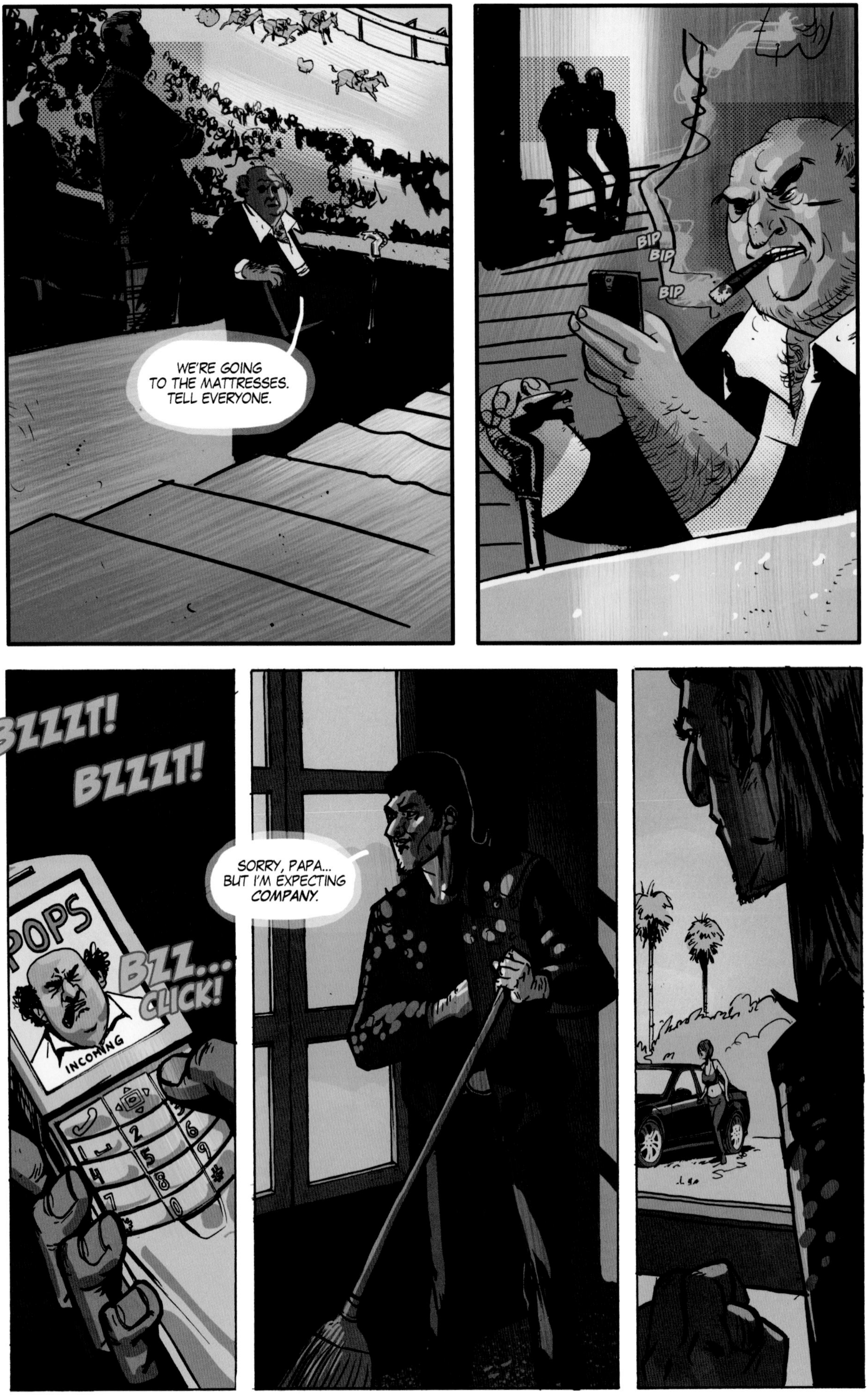
WE'RE GOING TO THE MATTRESSES. TELL EVERYONE.
BIP
BIP
BIP
BZZZT!
BZZZT!
POPS
INCOMING
BZZ... CLICK!
SORRY, PAPA... BUT I'M EXPECTING COMPANY.

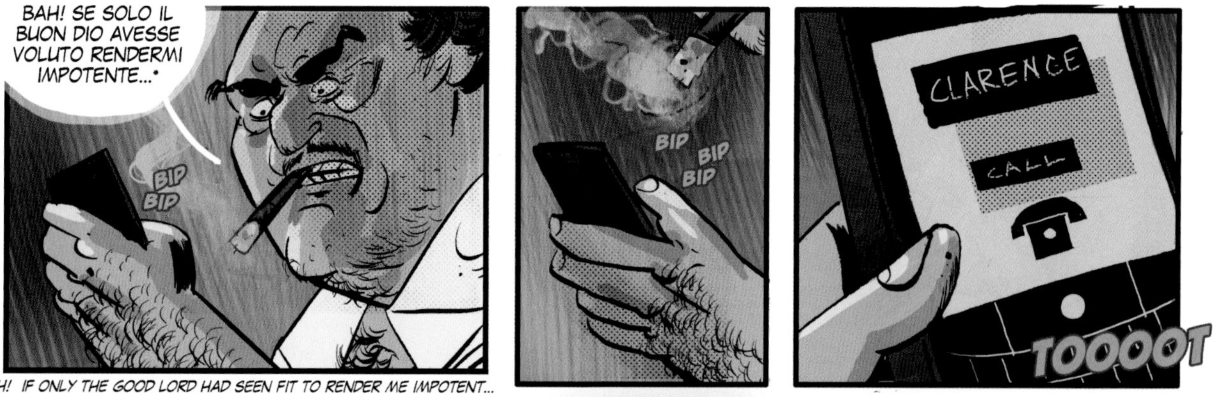
BAH! SE SOLO IL BUON DIO AVESSE VOLUTO RENDERMI IMPOTENTE...*
BIP BIP
BIP BIP BIP
CLARENCE
CALL
TOOOOT

* BAH! IF ONLY THE GOOD LORD HAD SEEN FIT TO RENDER ME IMPOTENT...

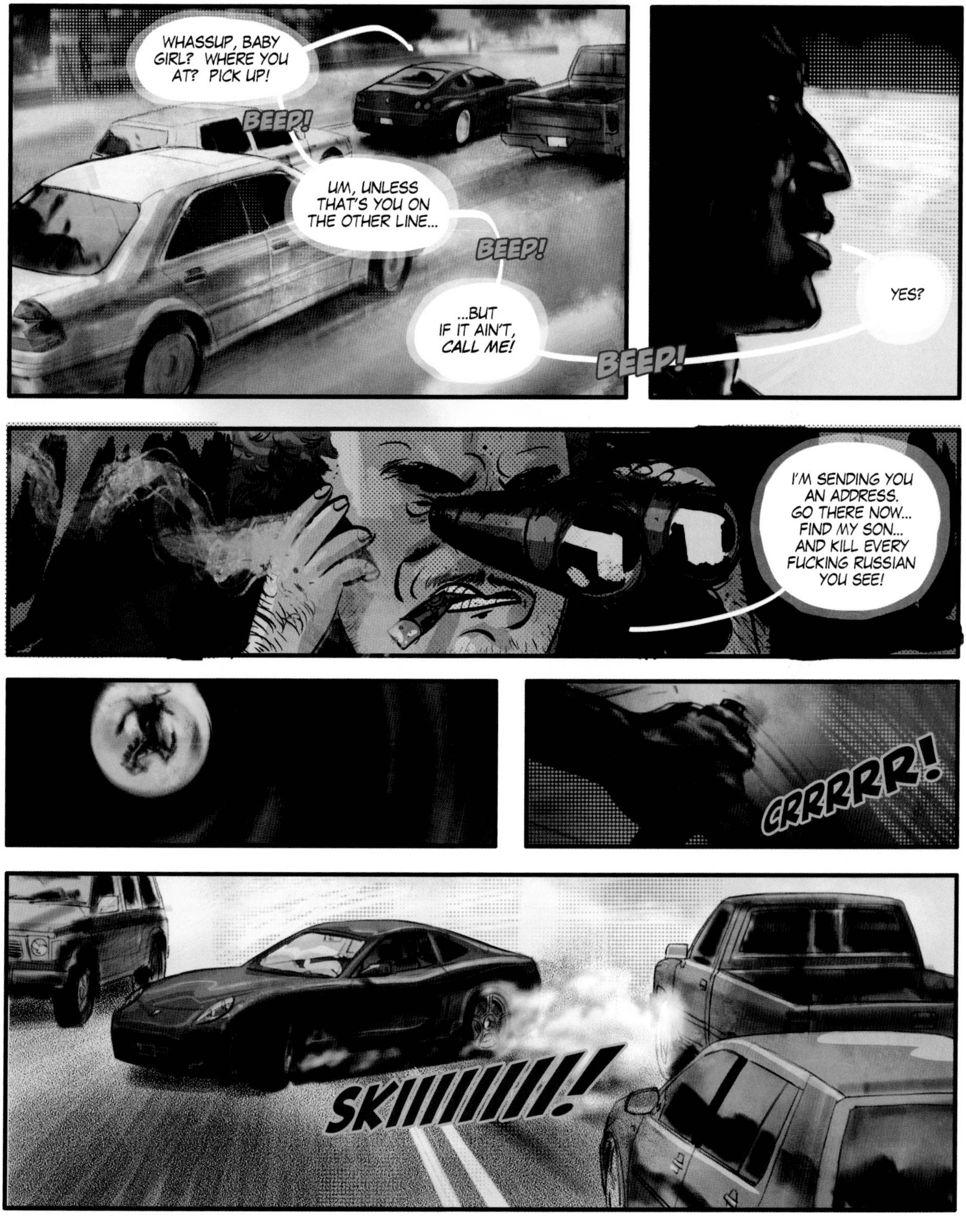
WHASSUP, BABY GIRL? WHERE YOU AT? PICK UP!
BEEP!
UM, UNLESS THAT'S YOU ON THE OTHER LINE...
BEEP!
...BUT IF IT AIN'T, CALL ME!
BEEP!
YES?
I'M SENDING YOU AN ADDRESS. GO THERE NOW... FIND MY SON... AND KILL EVERY FUCKING RUSSIAN YOU SEE!
CRRRRR!
SKIIIIIIII!

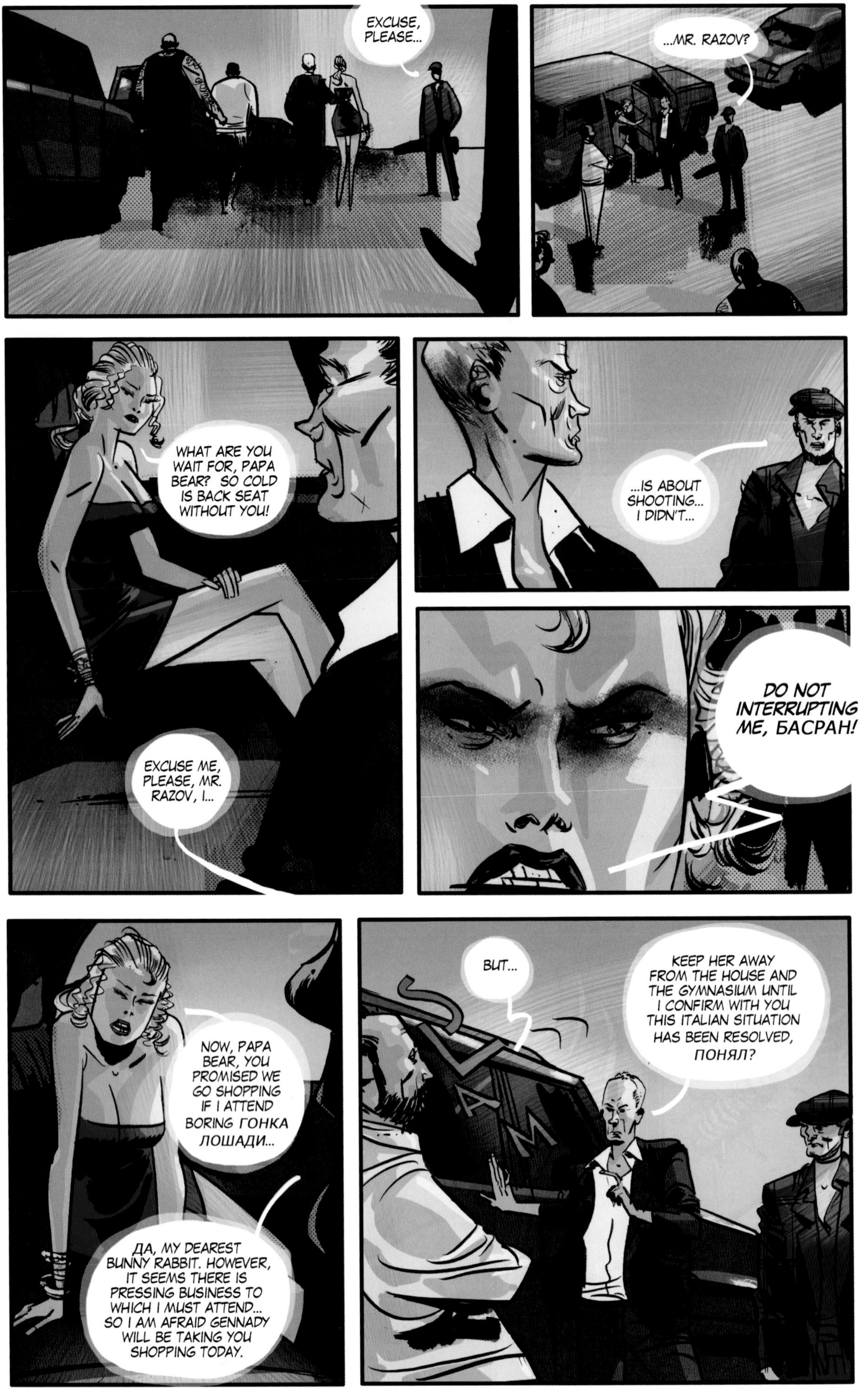
EXCUSE, PLEASE...
...MR. RAZOV?
WHAT ARE YOU WAIT FOR, PAPA BEAR? SO COLD IS BACK SEAT WITHOUT YOU!
...IS ABOUT SHOOTING... I DIDN'T...
EXCUSE ME, PLEASE, MR. RAZOV, I...
DO NOT INTERRUPTING ME, БАСРАН!
NOW, PAPA BEAR, YOU PROMISED WE GO SHOPPING IF I ATTEND BORING ГОНКА ЛОШАДИ...
ДА, MY DEAREST BUNNY RABBIT. HOWEVER, IT SEEMS THERE IS PRESSING BUSINESS TO WHICH I MUST ATTEND... SO I AM AFRAID GENNADY WILL BE TAKING YOU SHOPPING TODAY.
BUT...
KEEP HER AWAY FROM THE HOUSE AND THE GYMNASIUM UNTIL I CONFIRM WITH YOU THIS ITALIAN SITUATION HAS BEEN RESOLVED, ПОНЯЛ?

AND AS FOR *YOU*, DO NOT THINK FOR A MOMENT YOUR *DISCOURTESY* TO VASSILISA WILL BE FORGOTTEN... OR *FORGIVEN*...

MY... WHAT?

IS VADIM FOR *SERIOUS*?

*DA*... IS VERY TOUCHY WHEN COMES TO LOVE FOR VASSILISA.

*LOVE*? YOU MUST BE JOKING ME! SHE IS NOTHING BUT COMMON ШЛЮХА!

AND YET...THERE IS NOTHING COMMON IN BEDROOM WHEN SHE GIVE TO VADIM HIS NIGHTLY *BELUGA*.

*WHAT*? IS NOT *POSSIBLE*! NO WOMAN CAN DO THIS! BELUGA IS *MYTH*!

*HET*, IS *TRUE*... WITH *OWN* EYES I SEE VASSILISA GIVE *BELUGA* AT BACHELOR PARTY IN MINSK...

BUT... *HOW*? IS... IS SHE...?

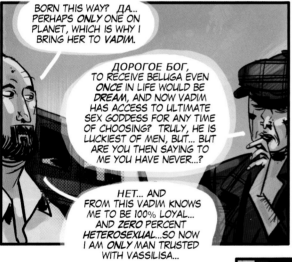

BORN THIS WAY? *DA*... PERHAPS *ONLY* ONE ON PLANET, WHICH IS WHY I BRING HER TO *VADIM*.

*ДОРОГОЕ БОГ*, TO RECEIVE BELUGA EVEN *ONCE* IN LIFE WOULD BE *DREAM*, AND NOW VADIM HAS ACCESS TO ULTIMATE SEX GODDESS FOR ANY TIME OF CHOOSING? TRULY, HE IS LUCKIEST OF MEN, BUT... BUT ARE YOU THEN SAYING TO ME YOU HAVE *NEVER*...?

*HET*... AND FROM THIS VADIM KNOWS ME TO BE 100% LOYAL... AND *ZERO* PERCENT *HETEROSEXUAL*...SO NOW I AM *ONLY* MAN TRUSTED WITH VASSILISA...

GET IN CAR AND TAKE ME TO STORE RIGHT NOW, UNLESS YOU WANT VADIM TURN YOUR ШУЛЯТА INTO *EARRINGS*!

*SIGH*... FUCKING BELUGA...

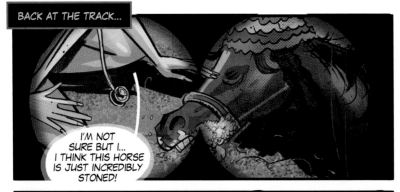

I'M NOT SURE BUT I... I THINK THIS HORSE IS JUST INCREDIBLY STONED!

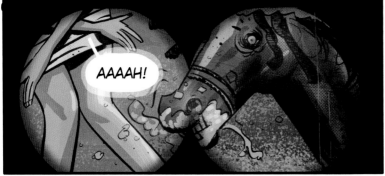

AAAAH!

AY! THAT'S-A MY BOY!

MEANWHILE, IN MALIBU...

GUESS YOU MUST'VE SENT THE MAID HOME EARLY, HUH?

HEY, YOU CAN BLAME YOUR DUMB SHIT BROTHER FOR MY FUCKED-UP *HOUSE*... BUT I DON'T KNOW *WHO* TO BLAME FOR THAT FUCKED-UP SHIT YOU'RE *WEARING.* I THOUGHT YOU RICH HOLLYWOOD SLUTS WERE AT LEAST S'POSED TO KNOW HOW TO *DRESS NICE*...

THAT'S RIGHT, *STUD*, AND WHENEVER WE'RE NOT *SHOPPING*, WE'RE AT THE *GYM*... ONLY THEY DIDN'T HAVE ANYTHING *HARD* ENOUGH THERE FOR ME TO *PUMP*, SO I CAME *HERE* INSTEAD.

YEAH? WELL, I JUST HOPE YOU BROUGHT MY FUCKIN' *MONEY* WITH YOU.

SHH, BABY... FUCKING, *THEN* MONEY...

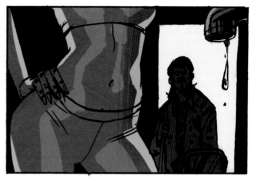

...UNLESS YOU'D RATHER KEEP PLAYING WITH YOUR LITTLE BROOM HANDLE...

GO AHEAD... WHIP IT OUT.

YOU GOT IT, BABY!

I BELIEVE SHE WAS SPEAK TO ME.

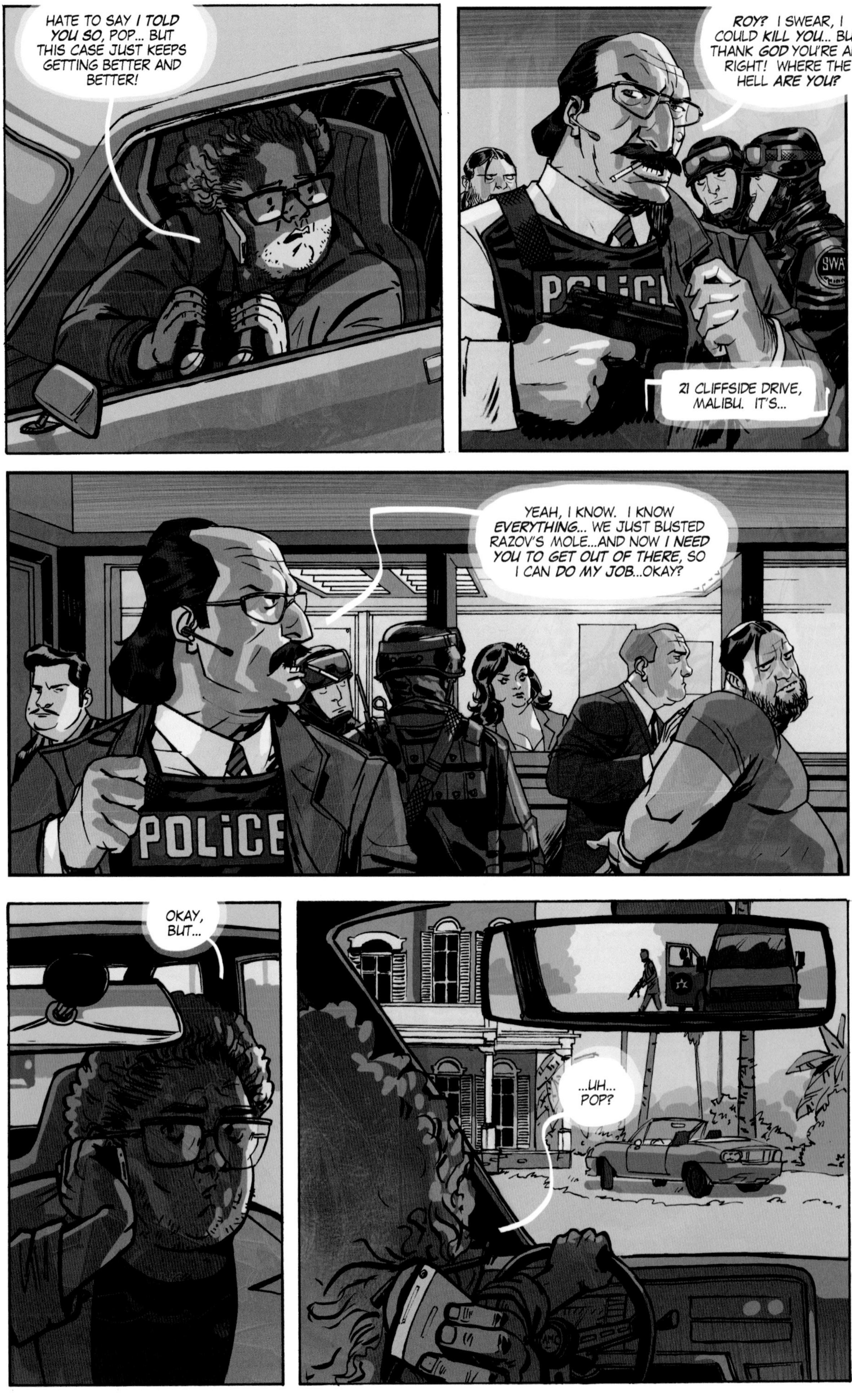
HATE TO SAY I TOLD YOU SO, POP... BUT THIS CASE JUST KEEPS GETTING BETTER AND BETTER!
ROY? I SWEAR, I COULD KILL YOU... BUT THANK GOD YOU'RE ALL RIGHT! WHERE THE HELL ARE YOU?
POLICE
SWAT
21 CLIFFSIDE DRIVE, MALIBU. IT'S...
YEAH, I KNOW. I KNOW EVERYTHING... WE JUST BUSTED RAZOV'S MOLE...AND NOW I NEED YOU TO GET OUT OF THERE, SO I CAN DO MY JOB...OKAY?
POLICE
OKAY, BUT...
...UH... POP?

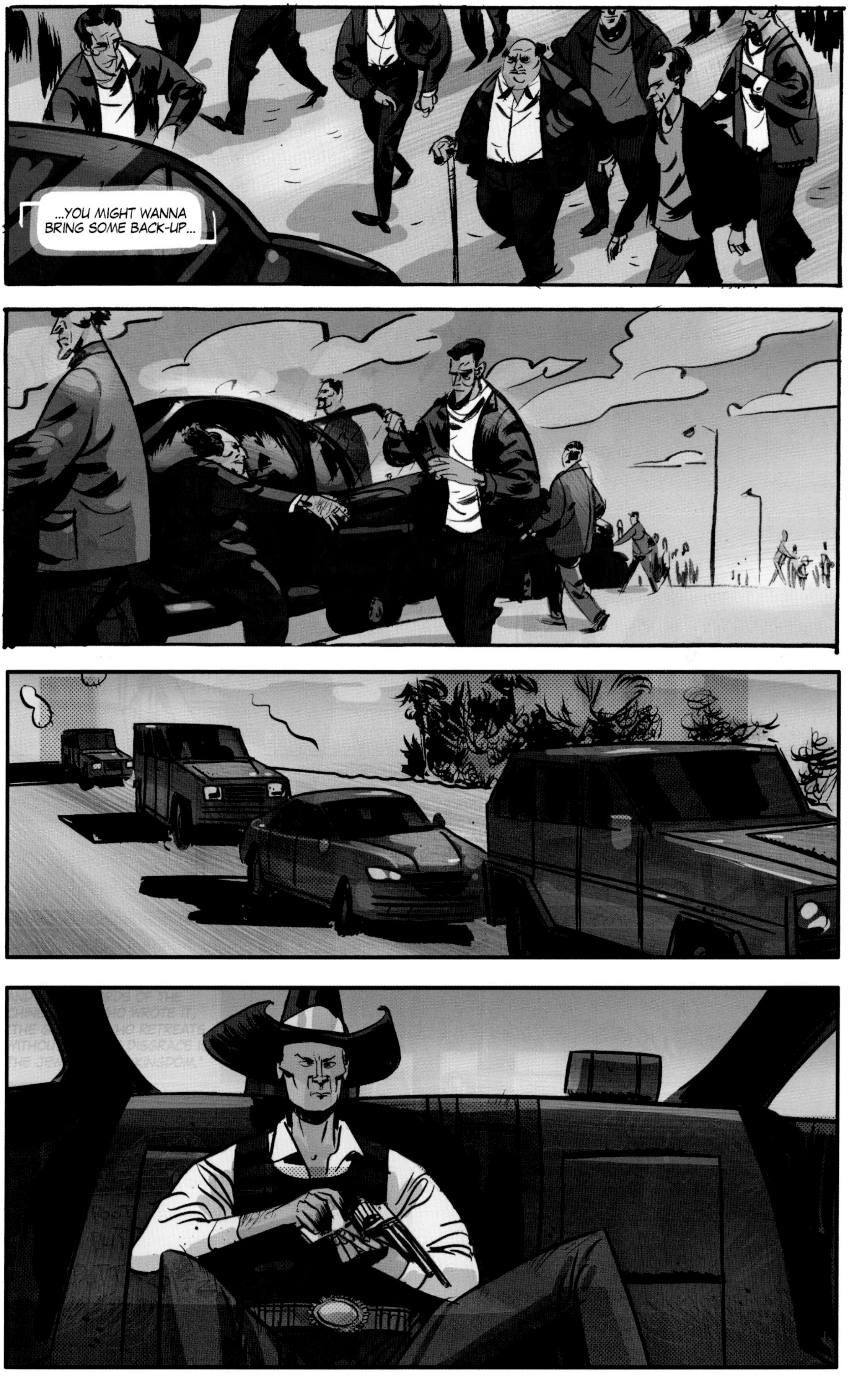
...YOU MIGHT WANNA BRING SOME BACK-UP...

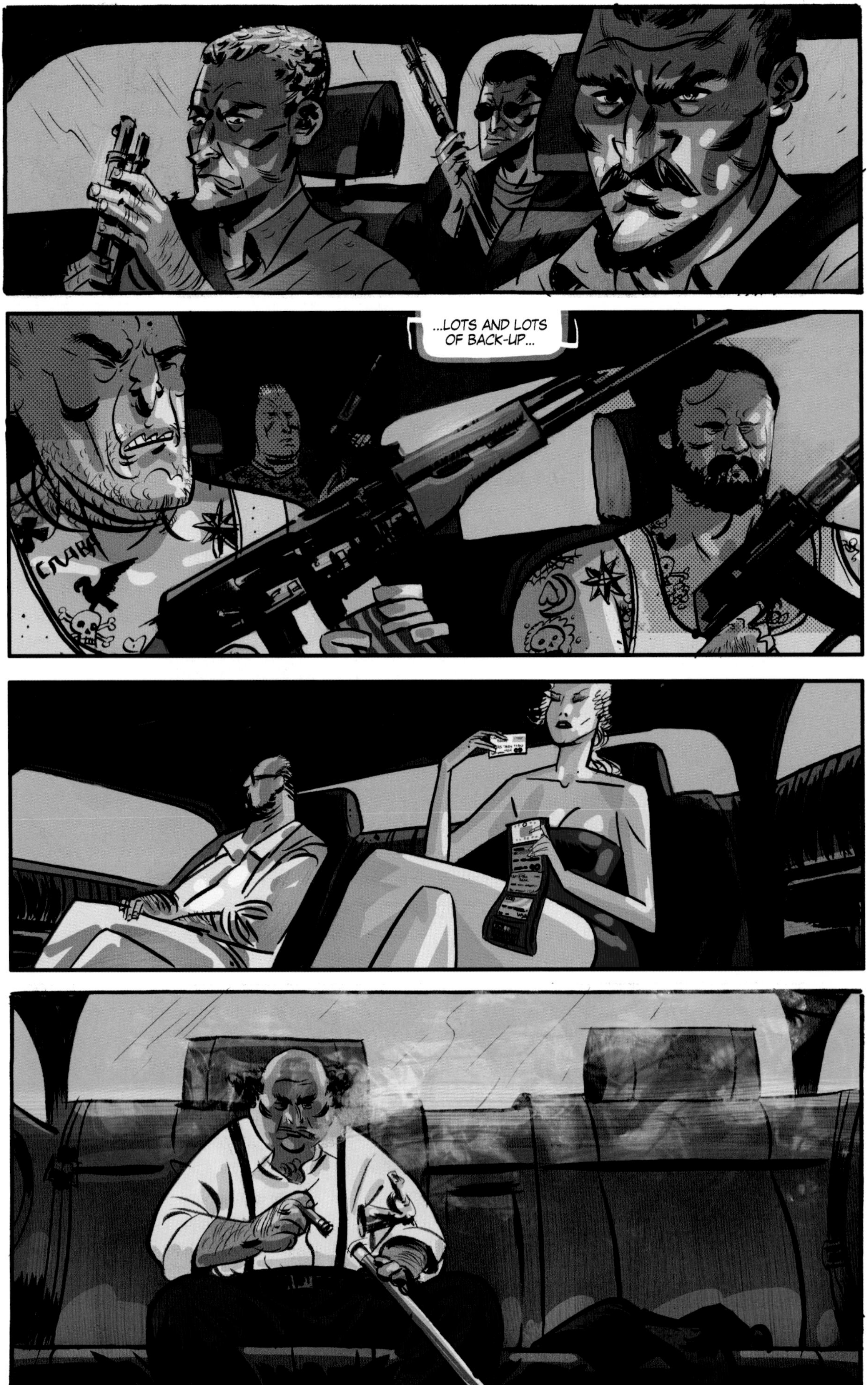
...LOTS AND LOTS OF BACK-UP...

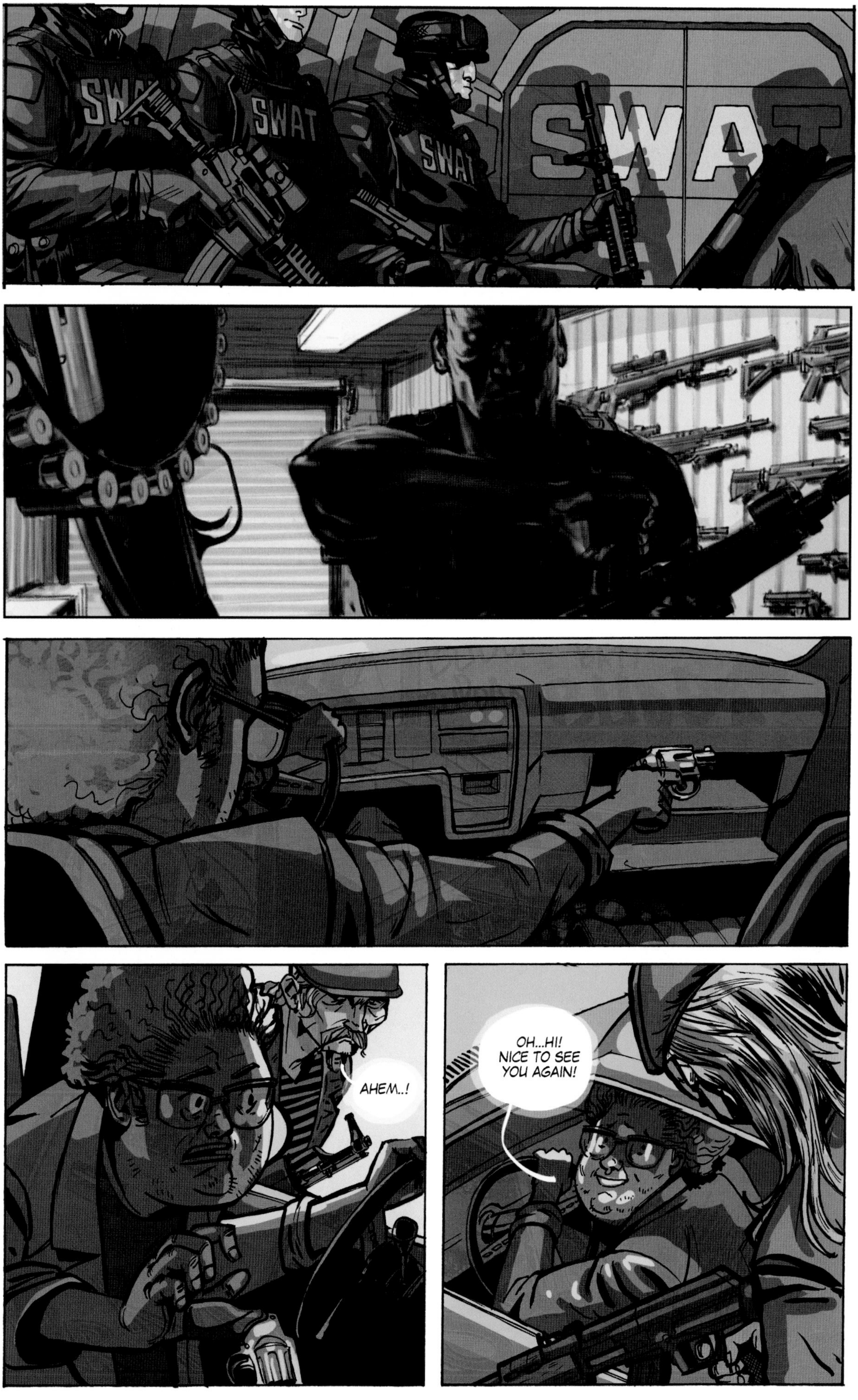
SWAT
AHEM..!
OH...HI!
NICE TO SEE
YOU AGAIN!

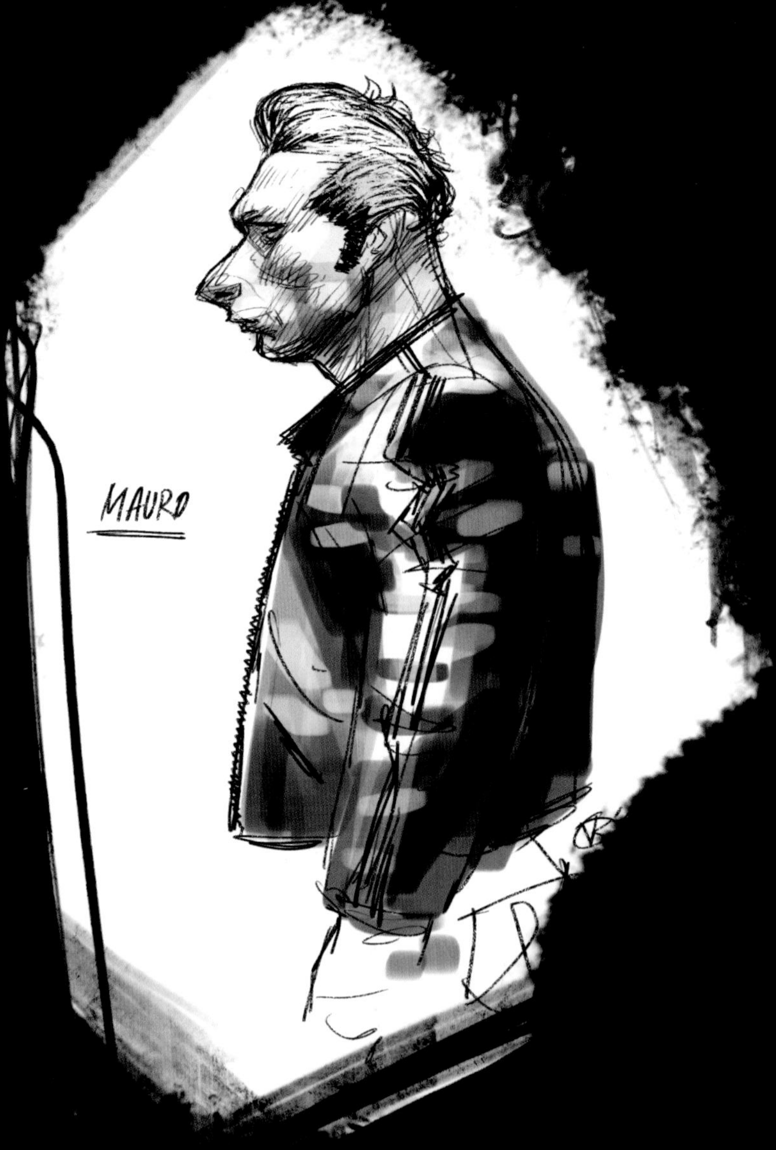
MAURO

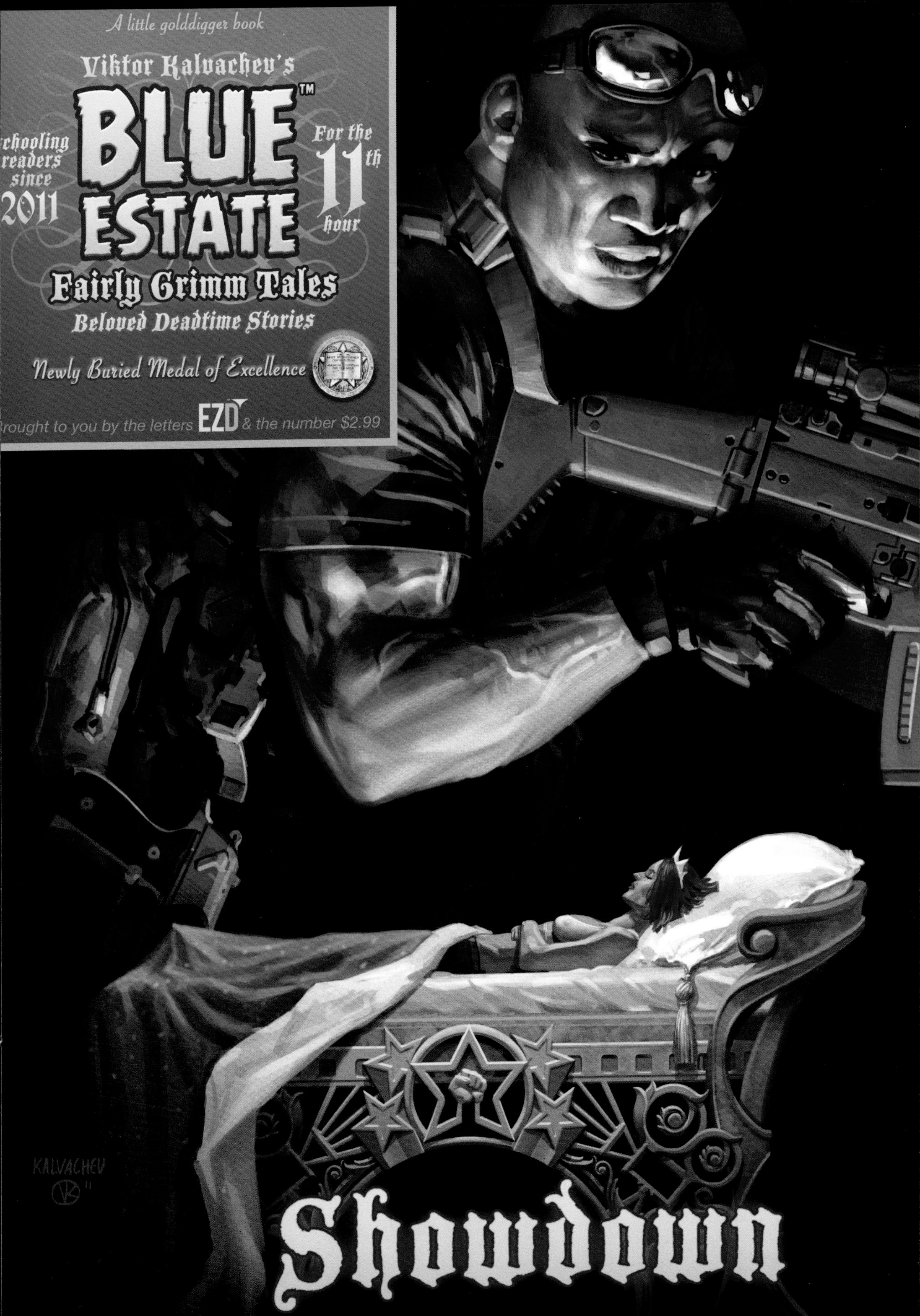
A little golddigger book
Viktor Kalvachev's
BLUE™
ESTATE
chooling readers since 2011
For the 11th hour
Fairly Grimm Tales
Beloved Deadtime Stories
Newly Buried Medal of Excellence
rought to you by the letters EZD & the number $2.99
KALVACHEV
VK '11
Showdown

# BLUE™ ESTATE

EPISODE ELEVEN:
## SHOWDOWN

ORIGINAL STORY:
**VIKTOR KALVACHEV** AND **KOSTA YANEV**

SCRIPT BY **ANDREW OSBORNE**

ARTISTS:
**TOBY CYPRESS**
**NATHAN FOX**
**ALEKSI BRICLOT**
**PETER NGUYEN**

ART DIRECTION BY **VIKTOR KALVACHEV**

COVER, COLORS & DESIGN:
**VIKTOR KALVACHEV**

CONTRIBUTING EDITOR:
**PHILO NORTHRUP**

www.**BlueEstateComic**.com

**EZD™**
PRODUCTIONS

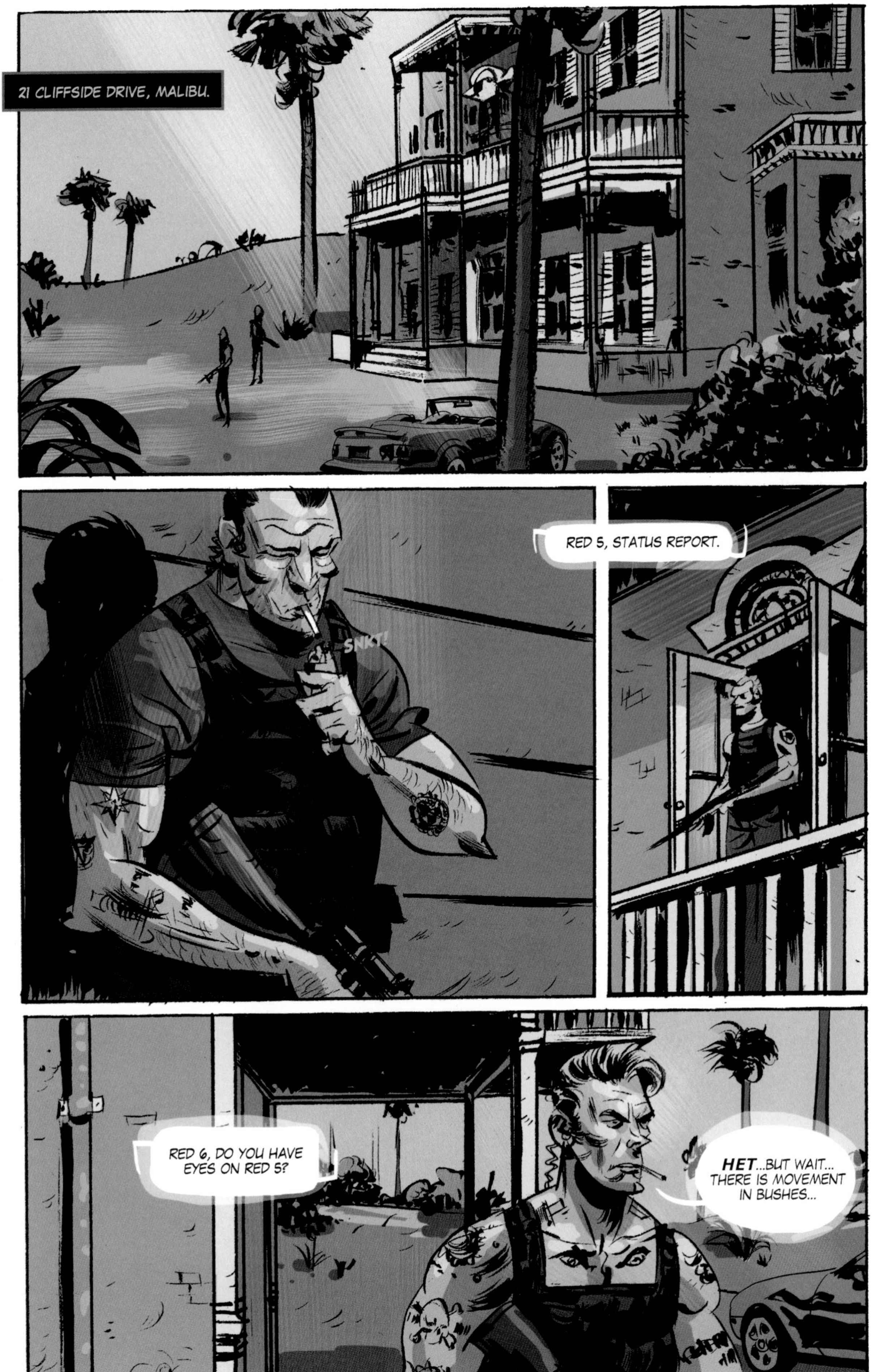
21 CLIFFSIDE DRIVE, MALIBU.
SNKT!
RED 5, STATUS REPORT.
RED 6, DO YOU HAVE EYES ON RED 5?
HET...BUT WAIT... THERE IS MOVEMENT IN BUSHES...

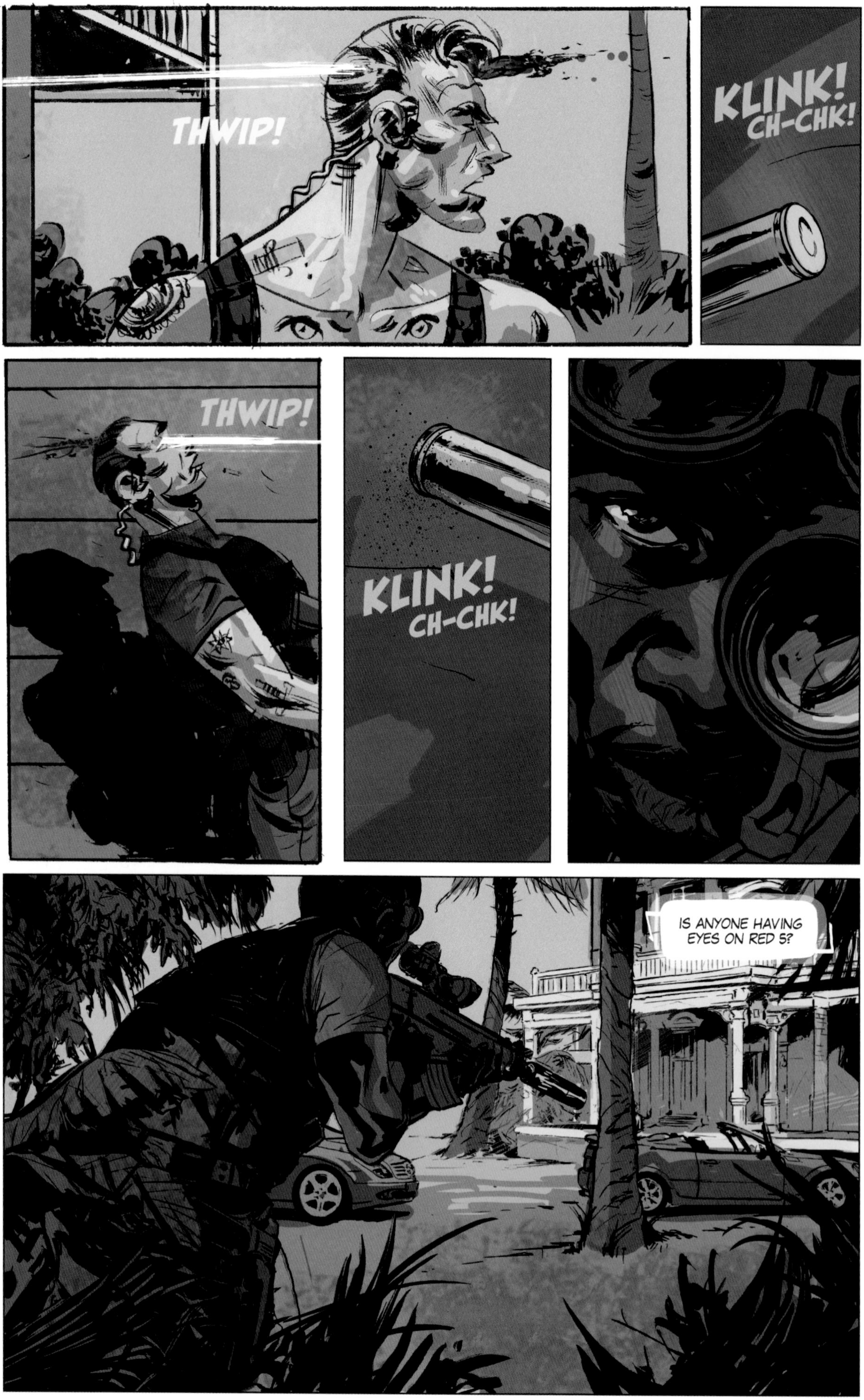
THWIP!
KLINK!
CH-CHK!
THWIP!
KLINK!
CH-CHK!
IS ANYONE HAVING
EYES ON RED 5?

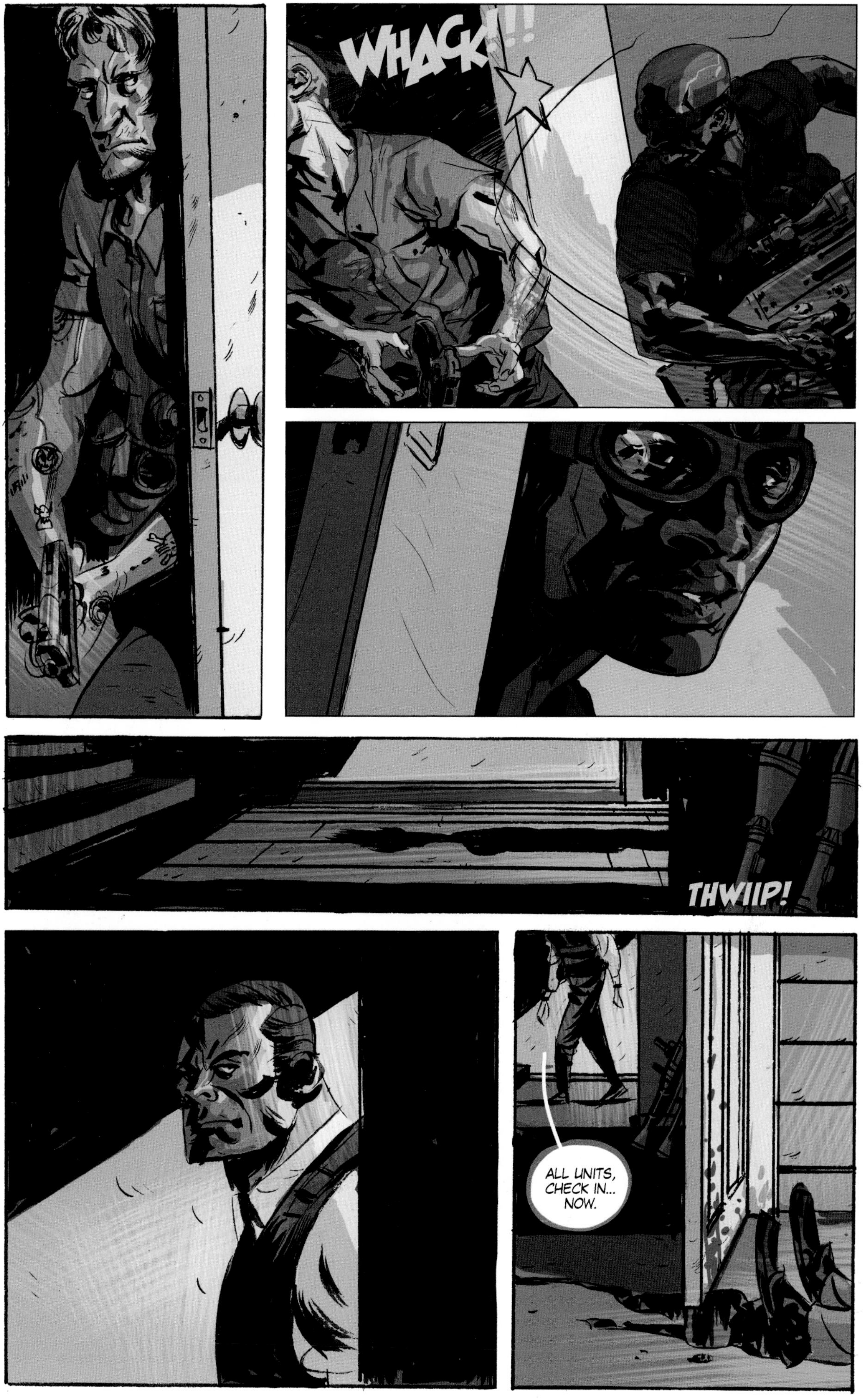
WHACK!!!
THWIIP!
ALL UNITS, CHECK IN... NOW.

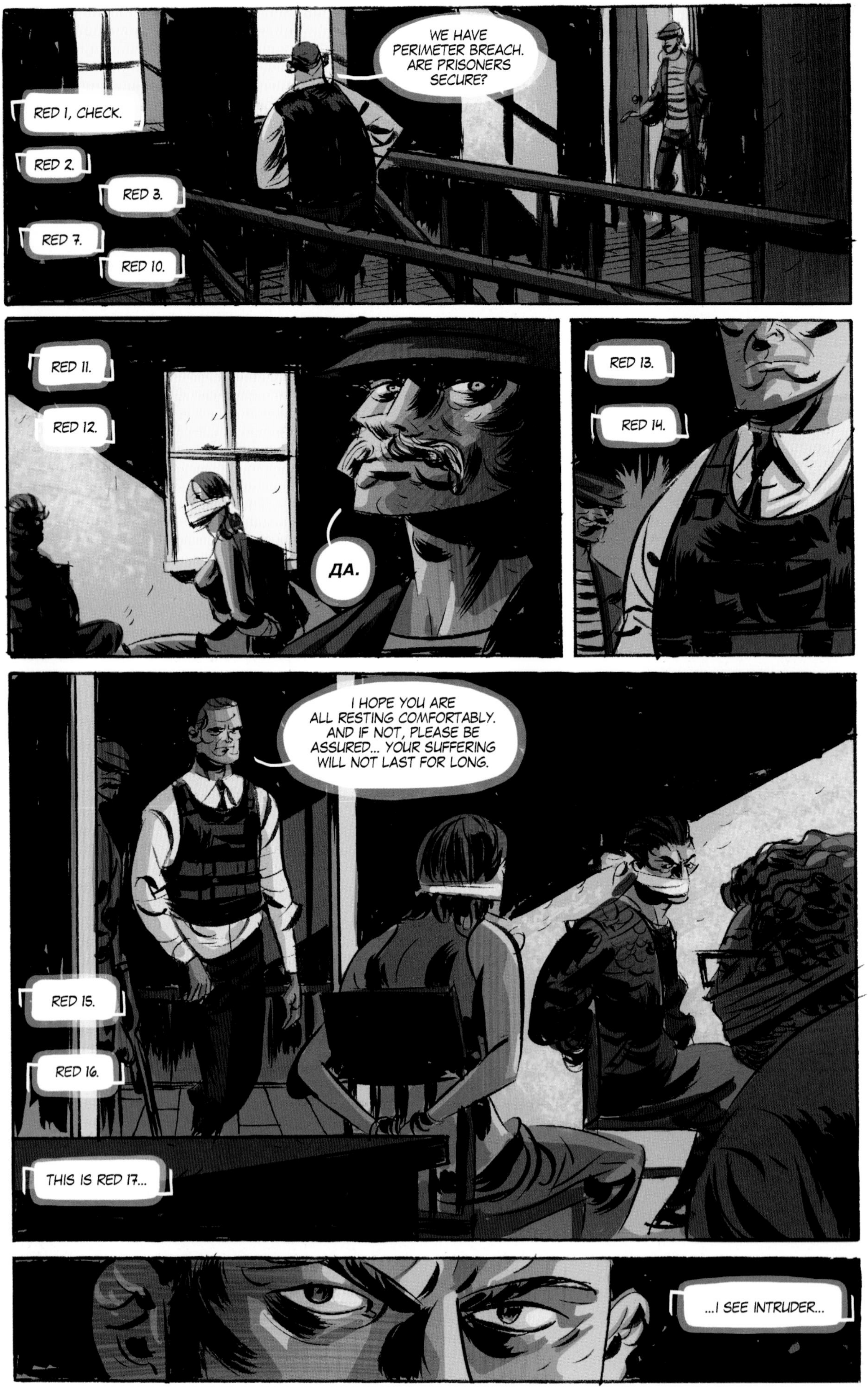
WE HAVE PERIMETER BREACH. ARE PRISONERS SECURE?
RED 1, CHECK.
RED 2.
RED 3.
RED 7.
RED 10.
RED 11.
RED 12.
ДА.
RED 13.
RED 14.
I HOPE YOU ARE ALL RESTING COMFORTABLY. AND IF NOT, PLEASE BE ASSURED... YOUR SUFFERING WILL NOT LAST FOR LONG.
RED 15.
RED 16.
THIS IS RED 17...
...I SEE INTRUDER...

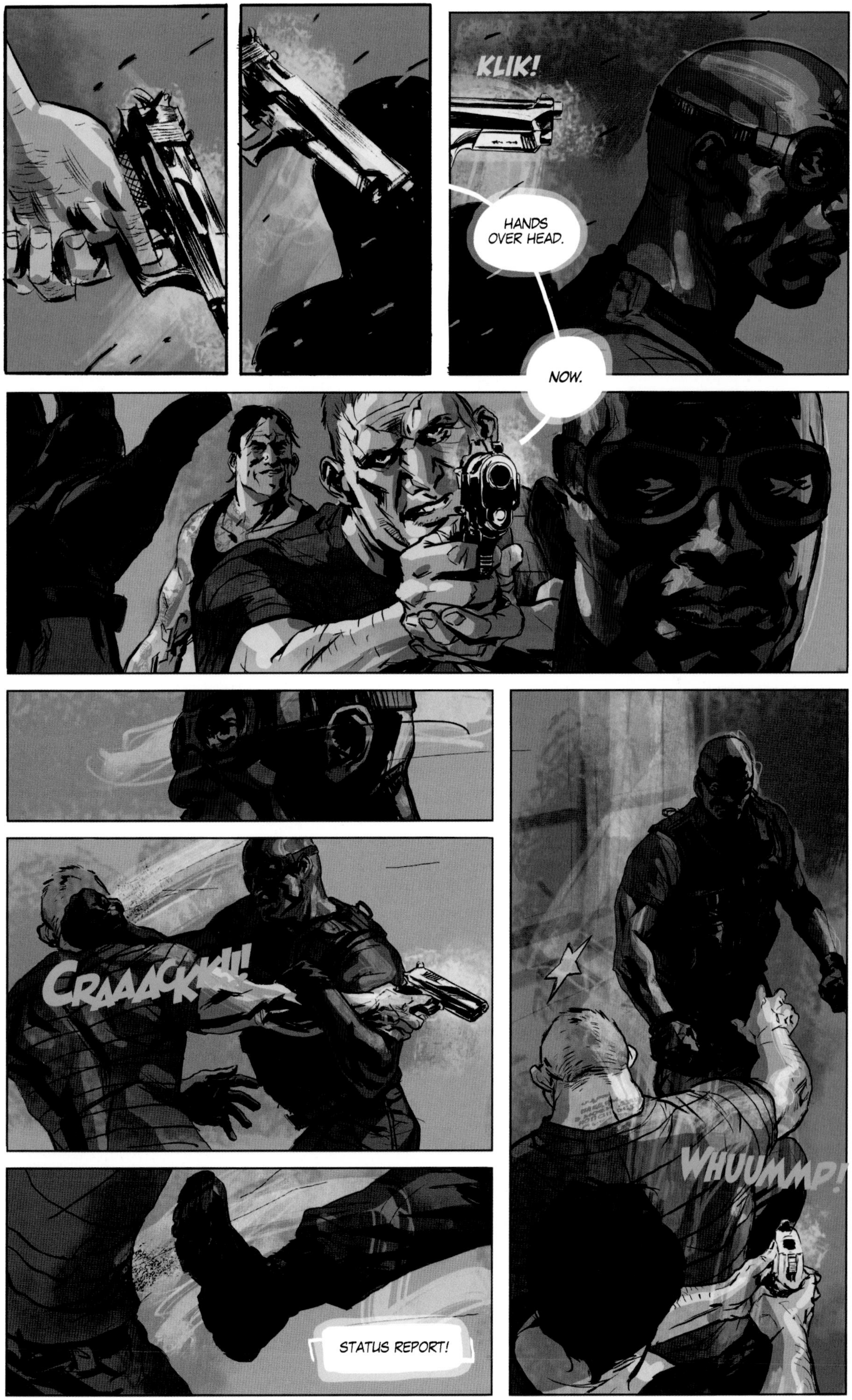
KLIK!
HANDS OVER HEAD.
NOW.
CRAAACKK!!
WHUUMMP!
STATUS REPORT!

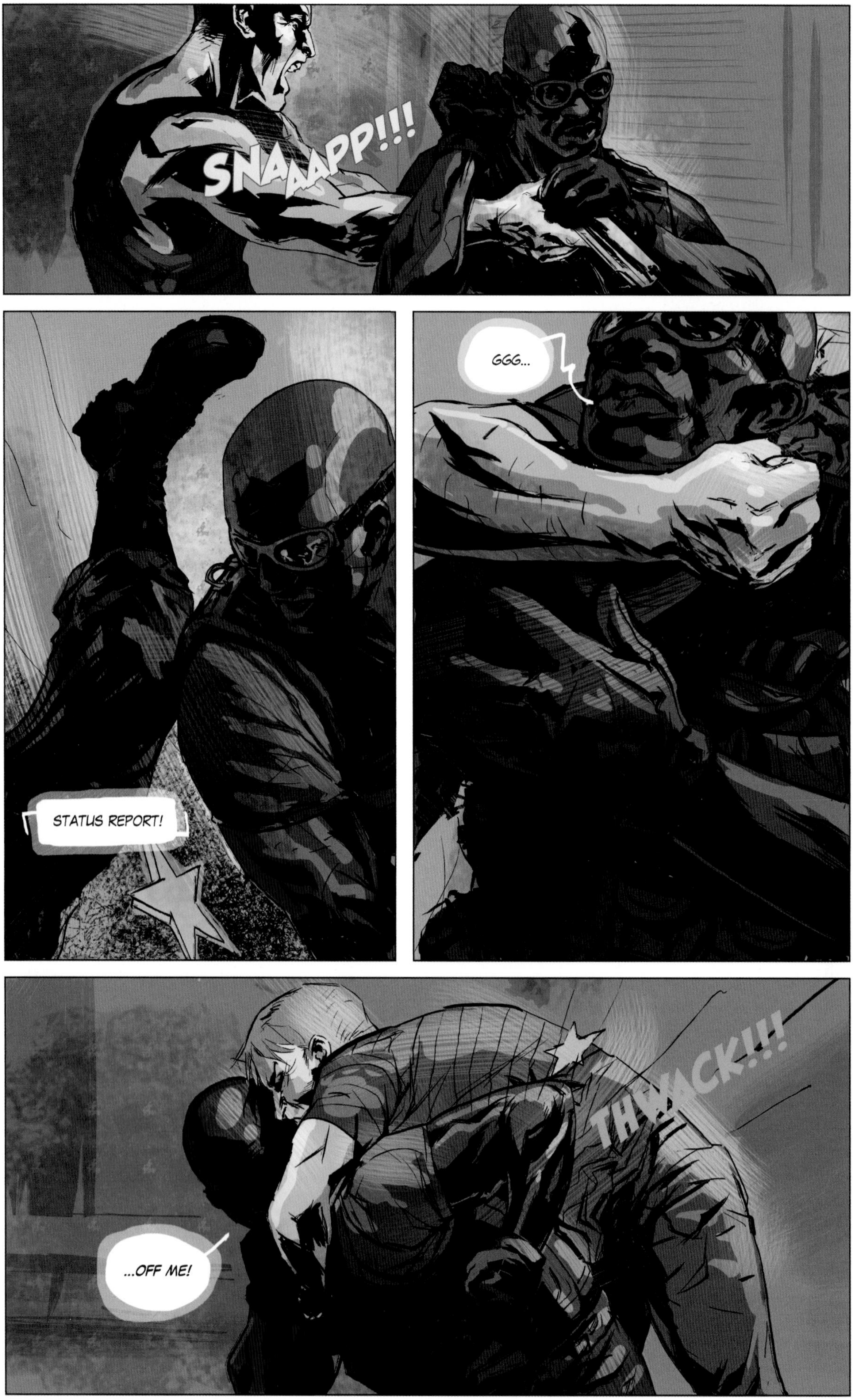
SNAAAPP!!!
STATUS REPORT!
GGG...
THWACK!!!
...OFF ME!

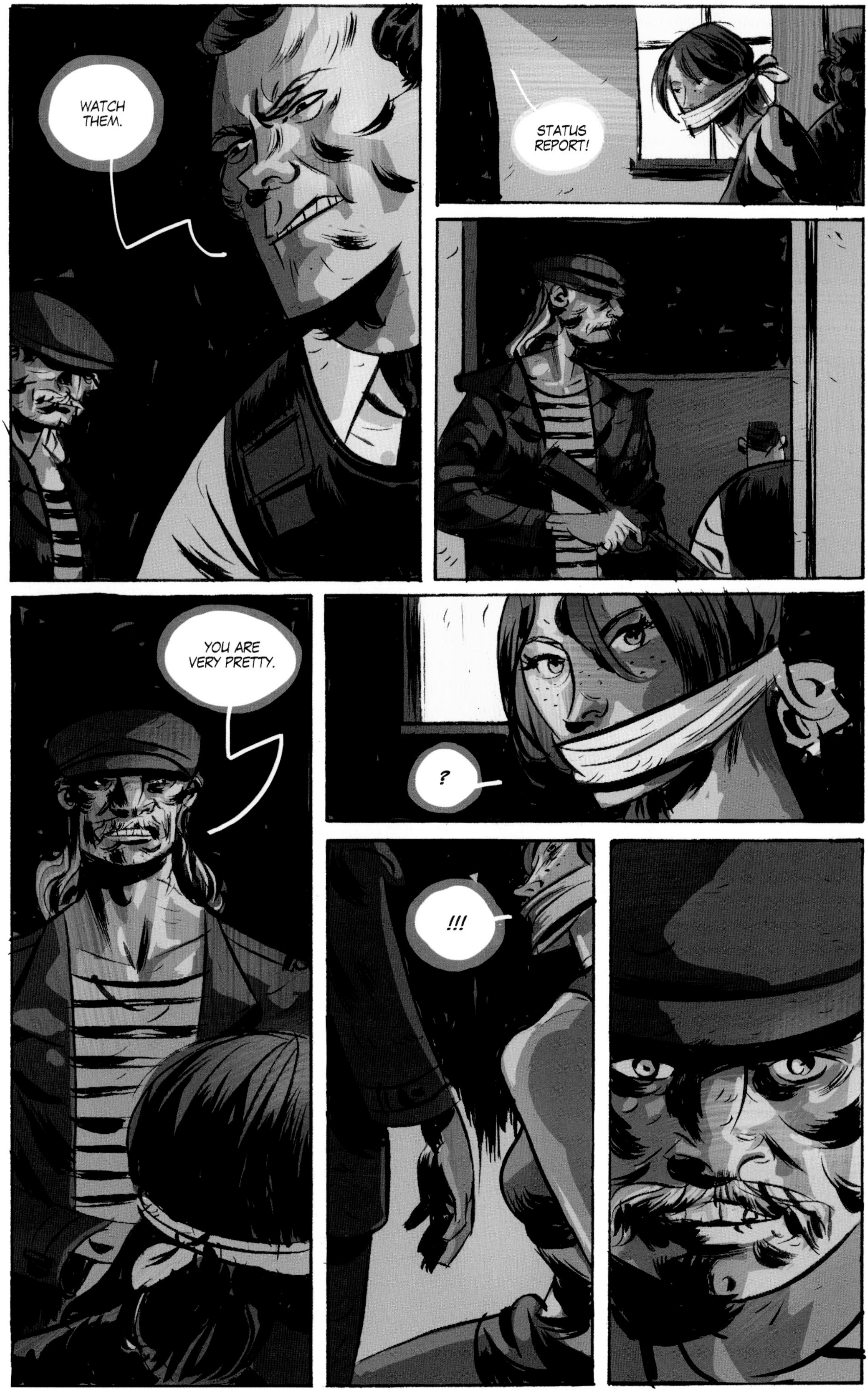
WATCH THEM.
STATUS REPORT!
YOU ARE VERY PRETTY.
?
!!!

THWIIP!

...BECKY?

TOK

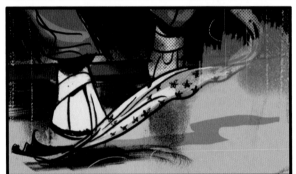

I TOLD YOU... MY REAL NAME IS *RACHEL*.

WAIT... RACHEL MADDOX? AS IN THE WIFE OF BRUCE MADDOX?

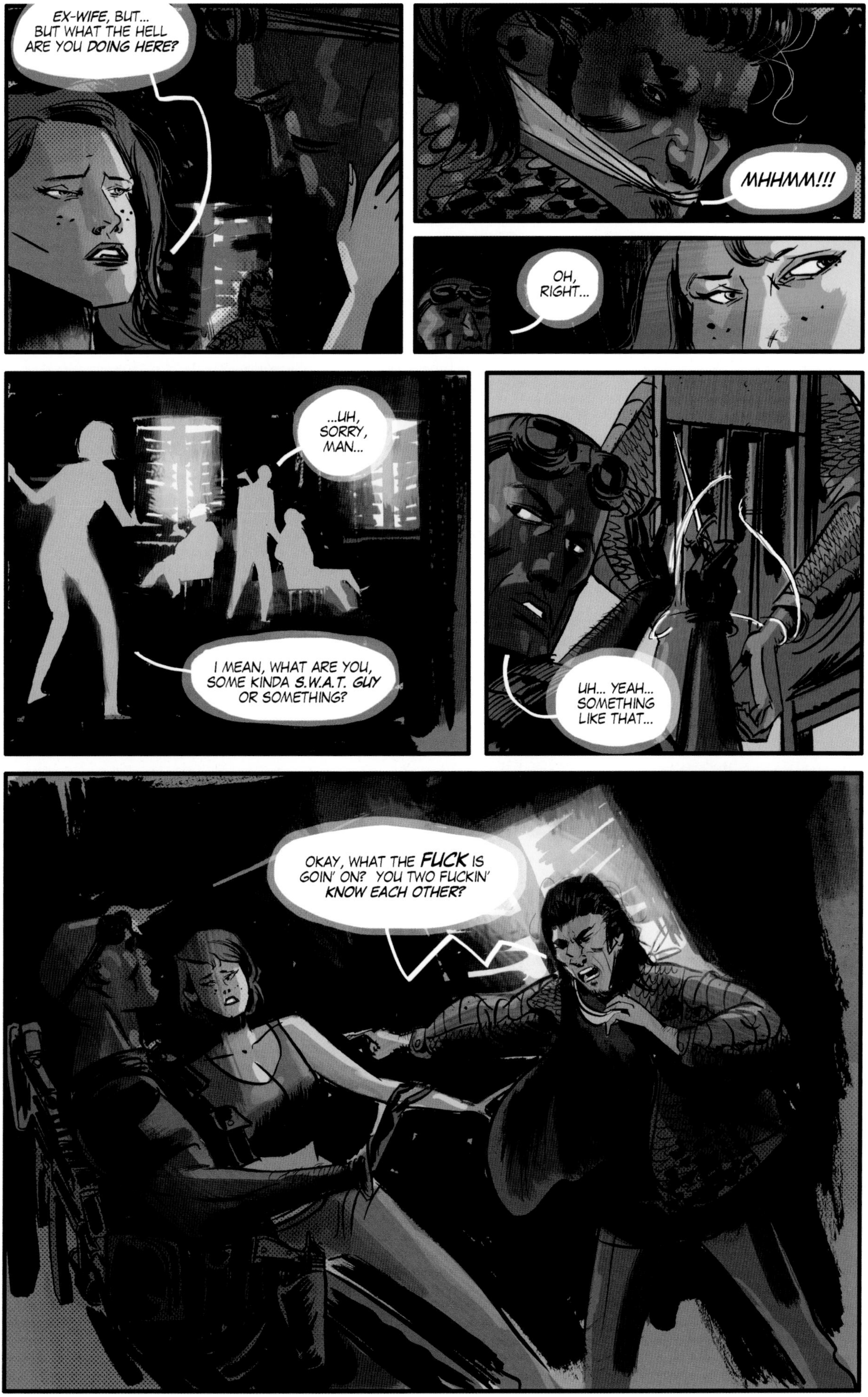
EX-WIFE, BUT... BUT WHAT THE HELL ARE YOU DOING HERE?
MHHMM!!!
OH, RIGHT...
...UH, SORRY, MAN...
I MEAN, WHAT ARE YOU, SOME KINDA S.W.A.T. GUY OR SOMETHING?
UH... YEAH... SOMETHING LIKE THAT...
OKAY, WHAT THE FUCK IS GOIN' ON? YOU TWO FUCKIN' KNOW EACH OTHER?

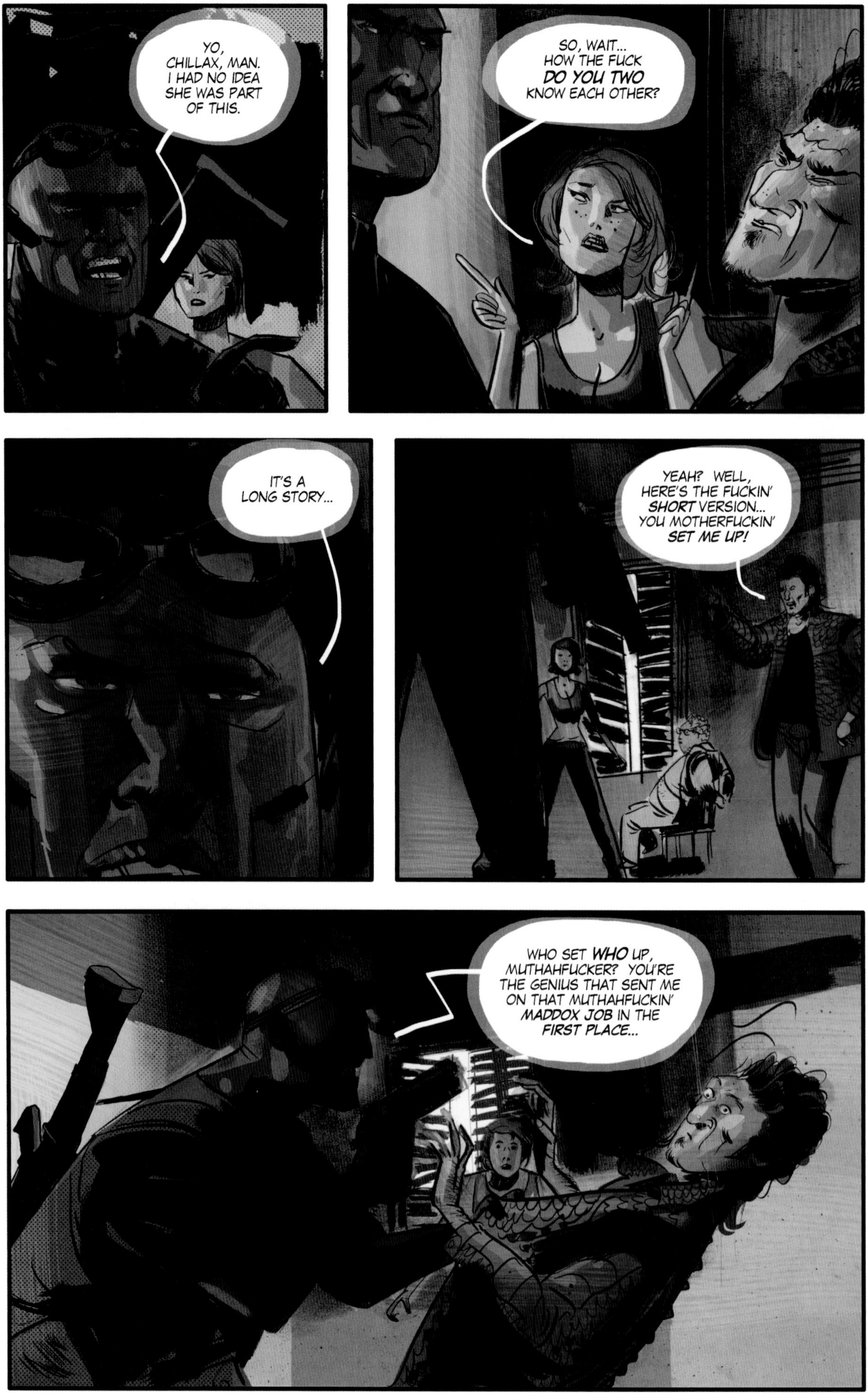
YO, CHILLAX, MAN. I HAD NO IDEA SHE WAS PART OF THIS.
SO, WAIT... HOW THE FUCK DO YOU TWO KNOW EACH OTHER?
IT'S A LONG STORY...
YEAH? WELL, HERE'S THE FUCKIN' SHORT VERSION... YOU MOTHERFUCKIN' SET ME UP!
WHO SET WHO UP, MUTHAHFUCKER? YOU'RE THE GENIUS THAT SENT ME ON THAT MUTHAHFUCKIN' MADDOX JOB IN THE FIRST PLACE...

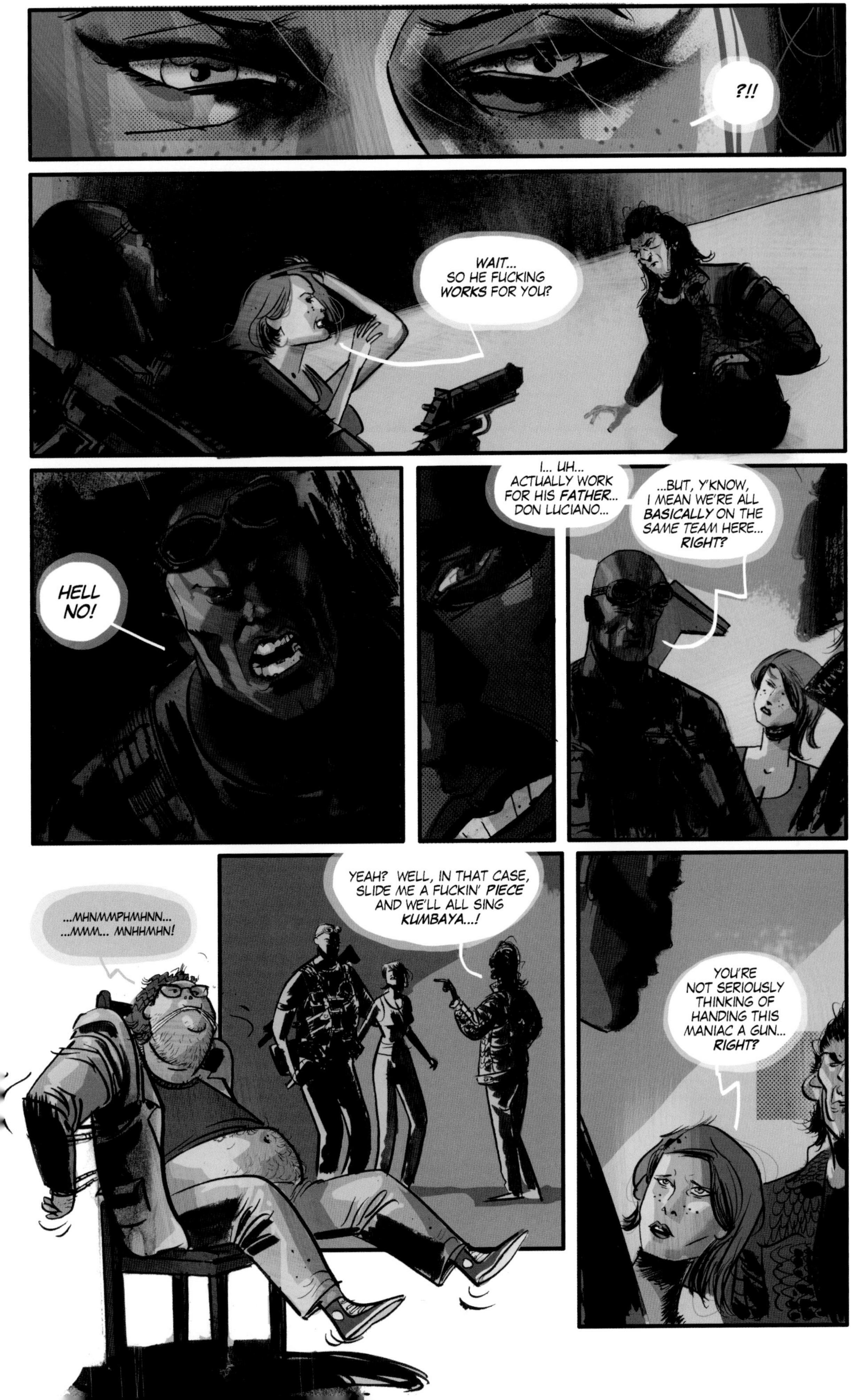
?!!
WAIT... SO HE FUCKING WORKS FOR YOU?
HELL NO!
I... UH... ACTUALLY WORK FOR HIS FATHER... DON LUCIANO...
...BUT, Y'KNOW, I MEAN WE'RE ALL BASICALLY ON THE SAME TEAM HERE... RIGHT?
...MHNMMPHMHNN... ...MMM... MNHHMHN!
YEAH? WELL, IN THAT CASE, SLIDE ME A FUCKIN' PIECE AND WE'LL ALL SING KUMBAYA...!
YOU'RE NOT SERIOUSLY THINKING OF HANDING THIS MANIAC A GUN... RIGHT?

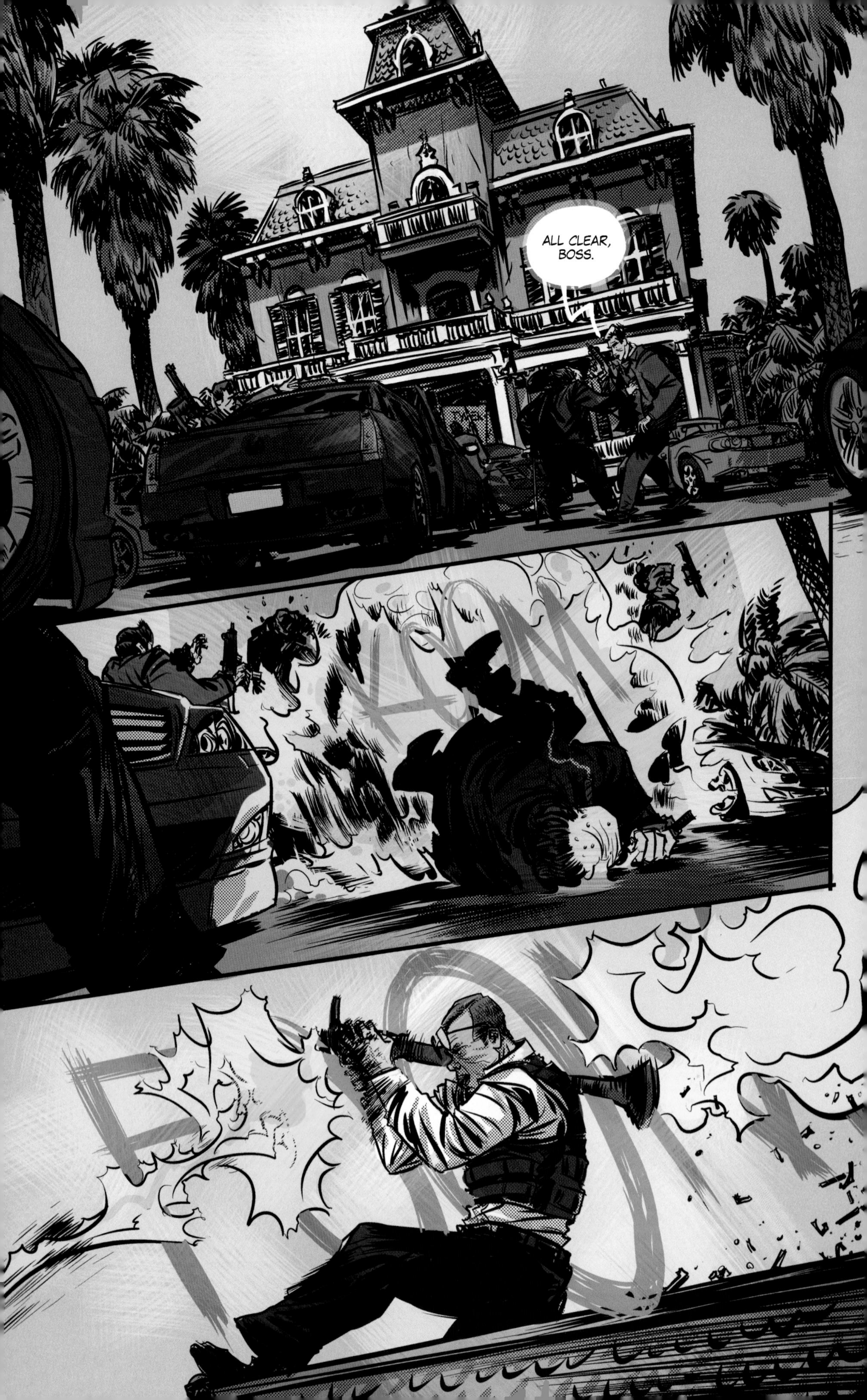
ALL CLEAR, BOSS.

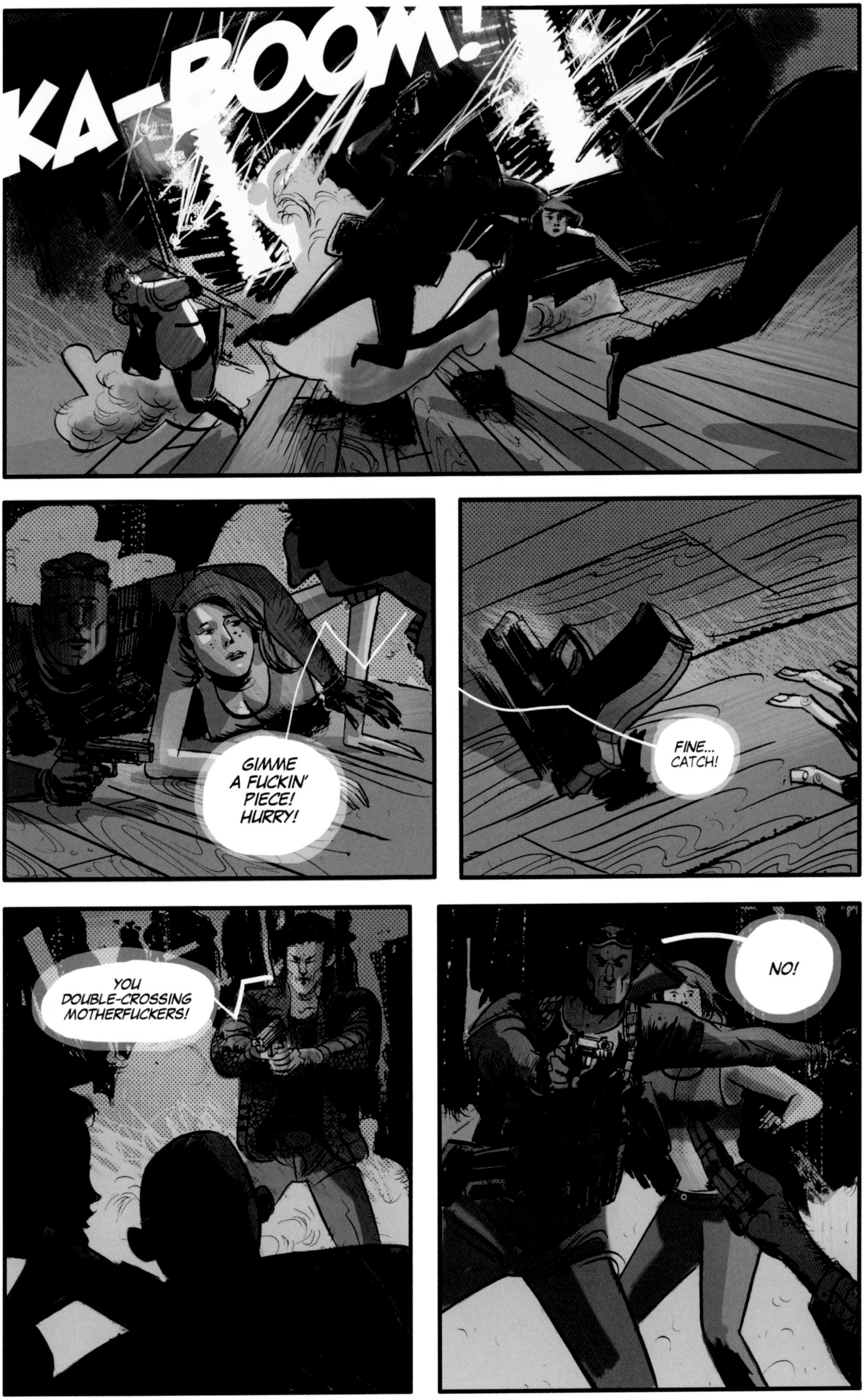
KA-BOOM!
GIMME A FUCKIN' PIECE! HURRY!
FINE... CATCH!
YOU DOUBLE-CROSSING MOTHERFUCKERS!
NO!

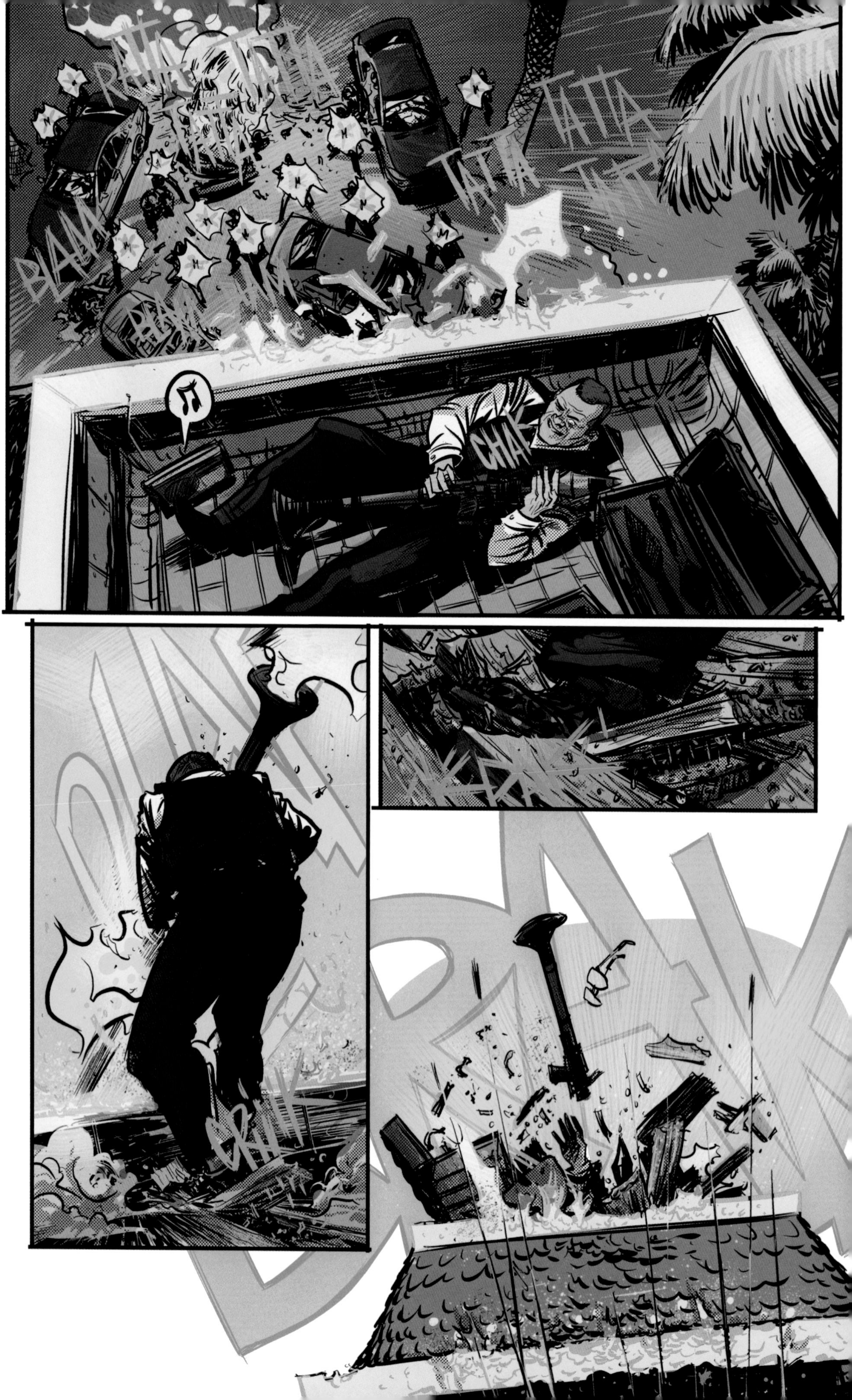
TATTA
TATTA
BLAM
CHAK

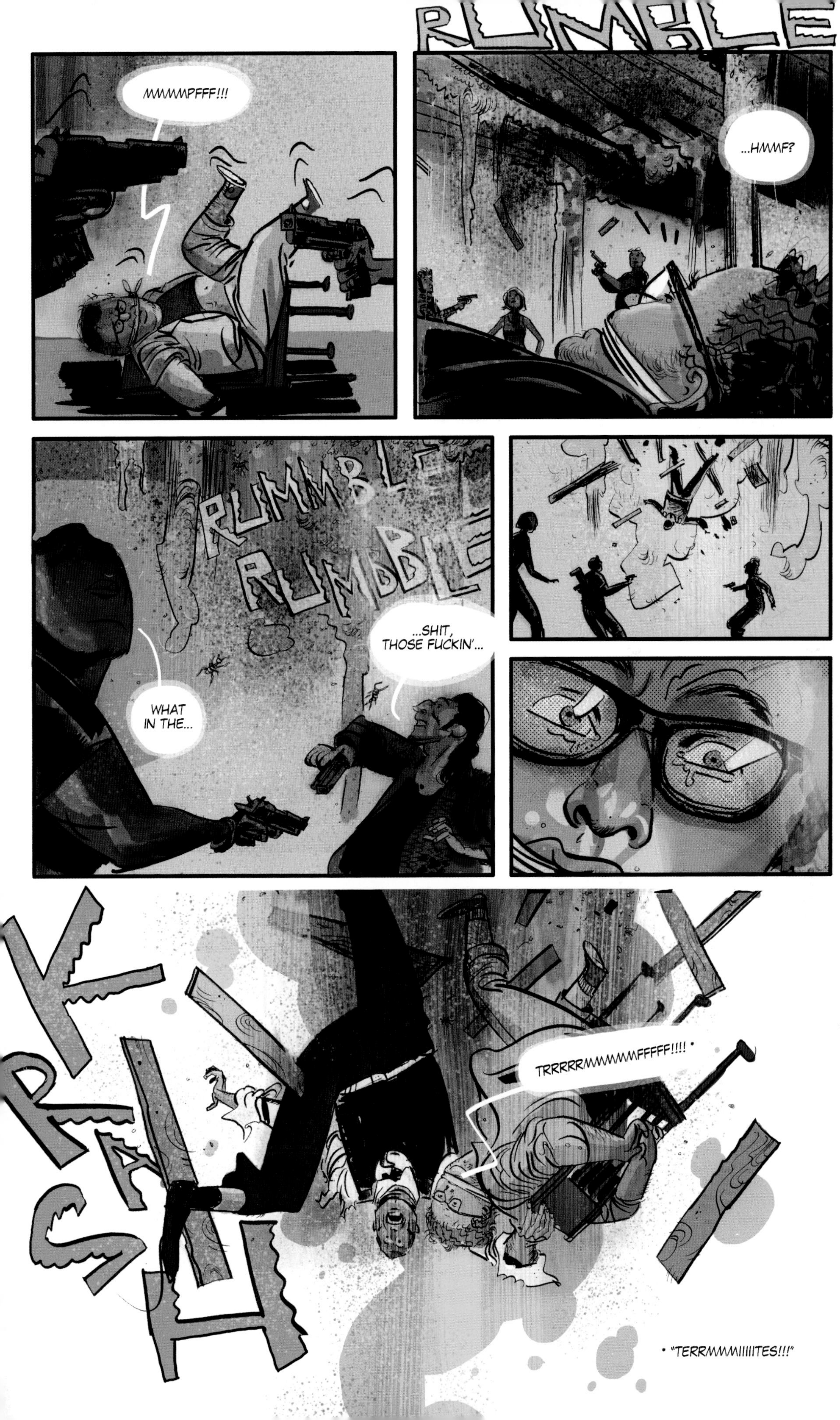
RUMBLE
MMMMPFFF!!!
...HMMF?
RUMMBLE
RUMBBLE
WHAT IN THE...
...SHIT, THOSE FUCKIN'...
KRASH
TRRRRRMMMMMFFFFF!!!! *
* "TERRMMMIIIIITES!!!"

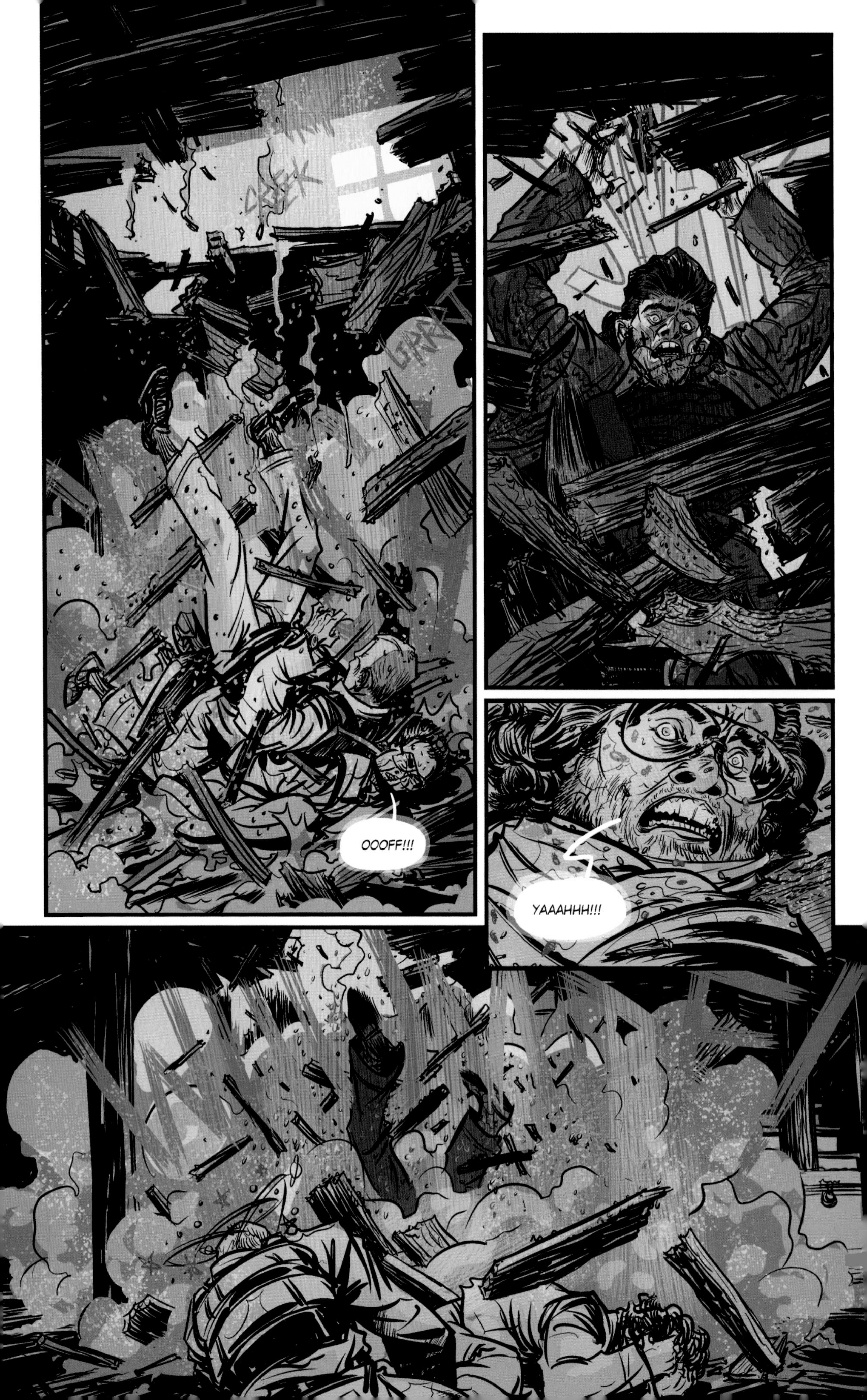
OOOFF!!!
YAAAHHH!!!

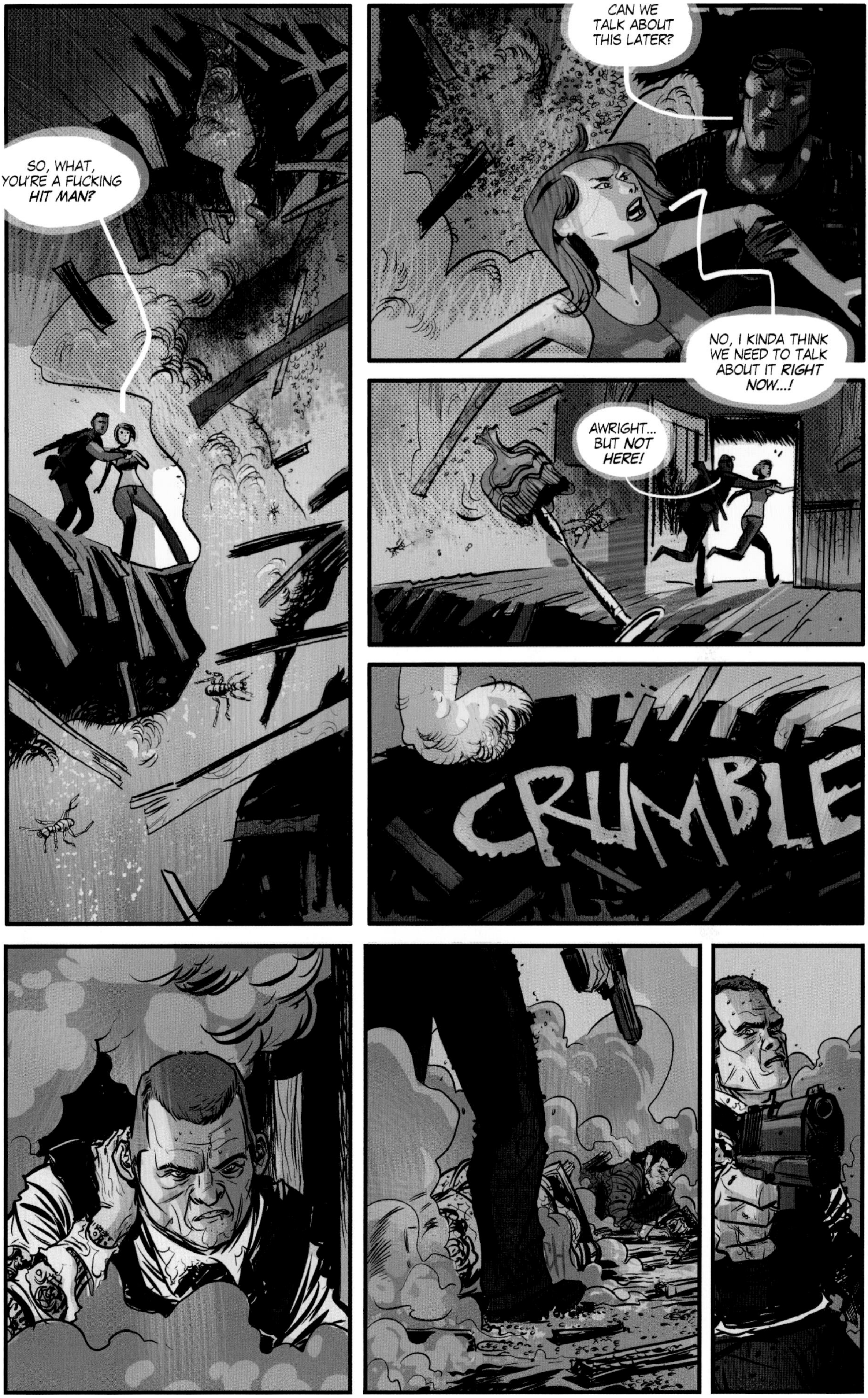
SO, WHAT, YOU'RE A FUCKING *HIT MAN?*
CAN WE TALK ABOUT THIS LATER?
NO, I KINDA THINK WE NEED TO TALK ABOUT IT *RIGHT NOW...!*
AWRIGHT... BUT *NOT HERE!*
CRUMBLE

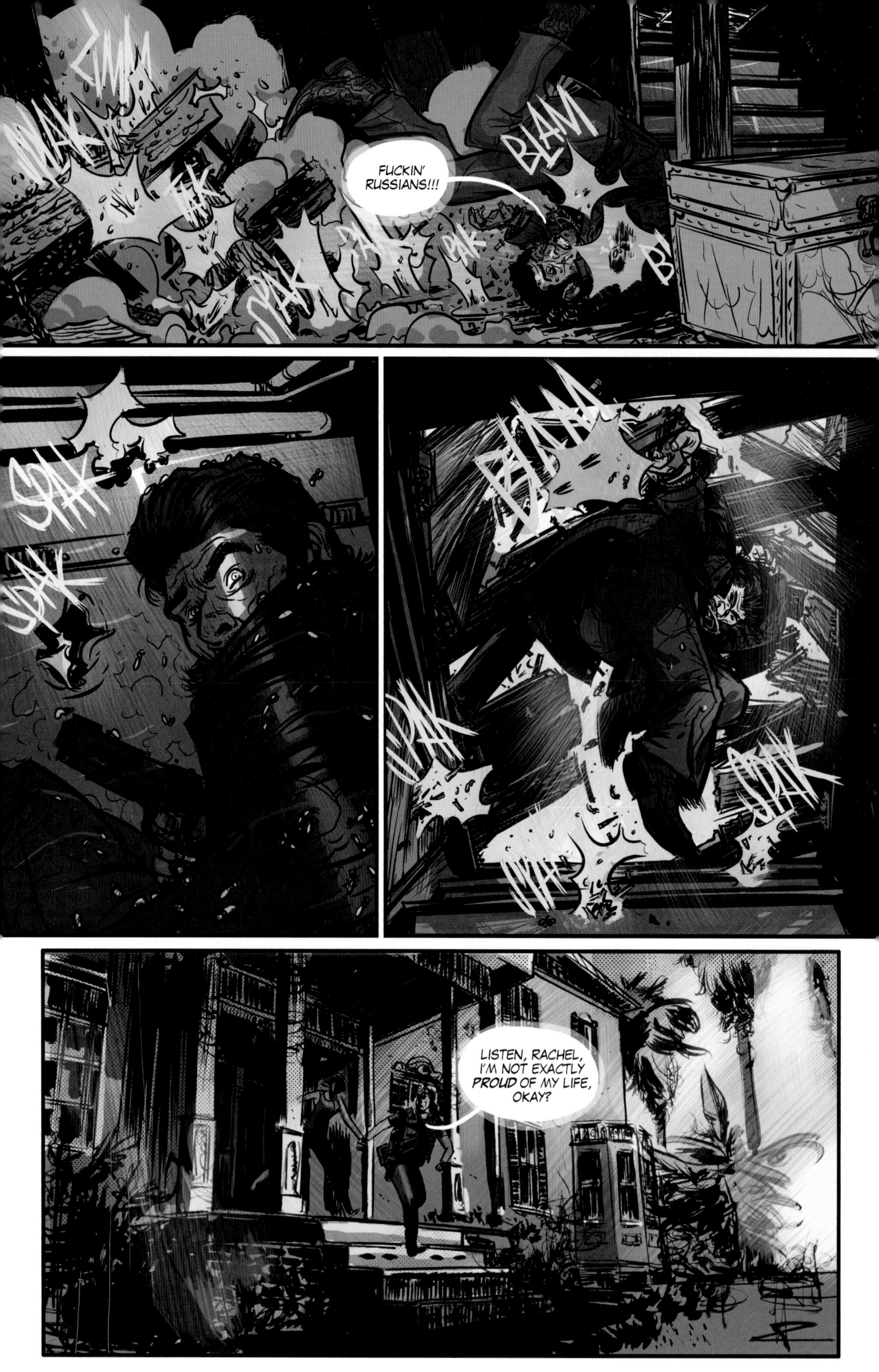

ZING
WAK
TAK
FUCKIN' RUSSIANS!!!
BLAM
SPAK
PAK
PAK
SPAK
SPAK
BLAM
SPAK
SPAK
SPAK
LISTEN, RACHEL, I'M NOT EXACTLY *PROUD* OF MY LIFE, OKAY?

RATATATA! TATATATA! POW! BLAM!
TATATA! BLAM! RATATATA!
POW! BLAM! TATAT

AND IF WE SURVIVE TO THE END OF THE DAY, I SWEAR I'M GONNA BE A BETTER MAN FROM HERE ON OUT...

JUST TELL ME ONE THING... AND I PROMISE NOT TO GET MAD, BUT I GOTTA KNOW... DID YOU KILL MY HUSBAND?

YEAH. I DID. AND I'M SORRY.

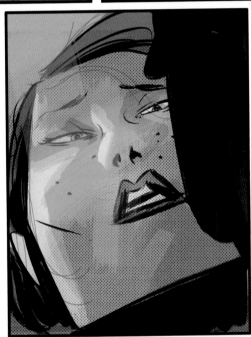

DON'T BE. YOU SAVED MY LIFE.

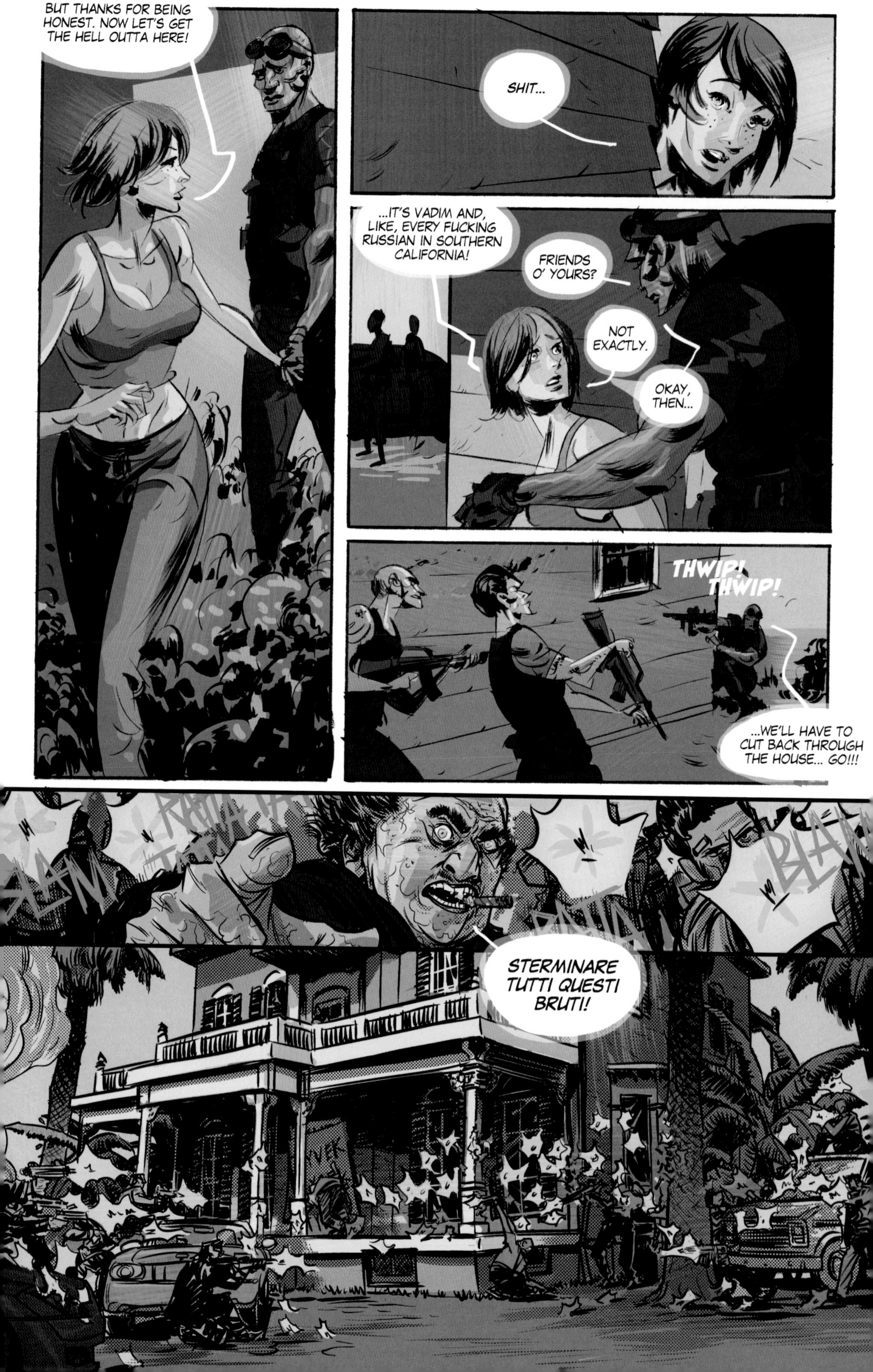
BUT THANKS FOR BEING HONEST. NOW LET'S GET THE HELL OUTTA HERE!
SHIT...
...IT'S VADIM AND, LIKE, EVERY FUCKING RUSSIAN IN SOUTHERN CALIFORNIA!
FRIENDS O' YOURS?
NOT EXACTLY.
OKAY, THEN...
THWIP! THWIP!
...WE'LL HAVE TO CUT BACK THROUGH THE HOUSE... GO!!!
STERMINARE TUTTI QUESTI BRUTI!

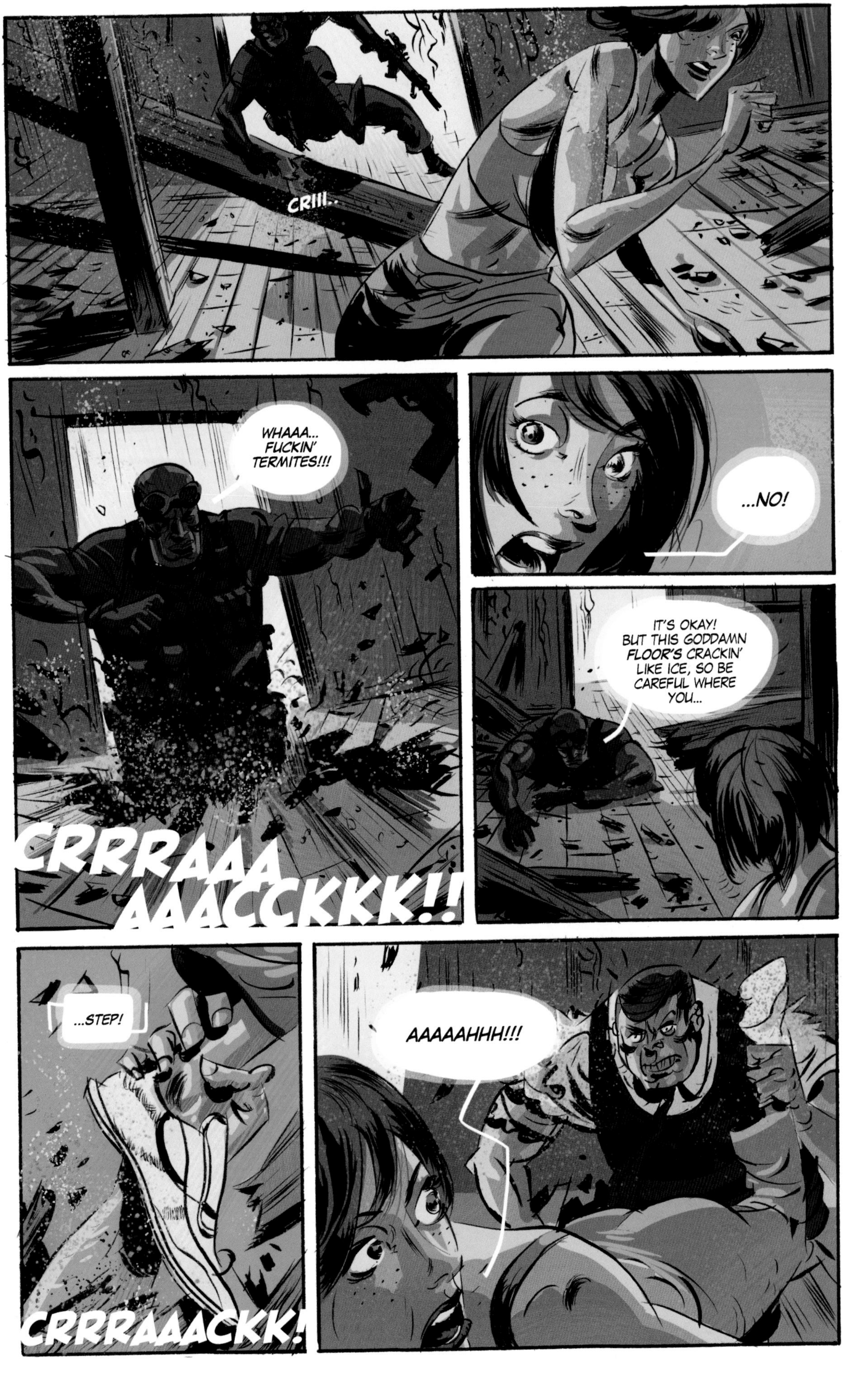
CRIII..
WHAAA... FUCKIN' TERMITES!!!
CRRRAAA AAACCKKK!!
...NO!
IT'S OKAY! BUT THIS GODDAMN FLOOR'S CRACKIN' LIKE ICE, SO BE CAREFUL WHERE YOU...
...STEP!
CRRRAAACKK!
AAAAAHHH!!!

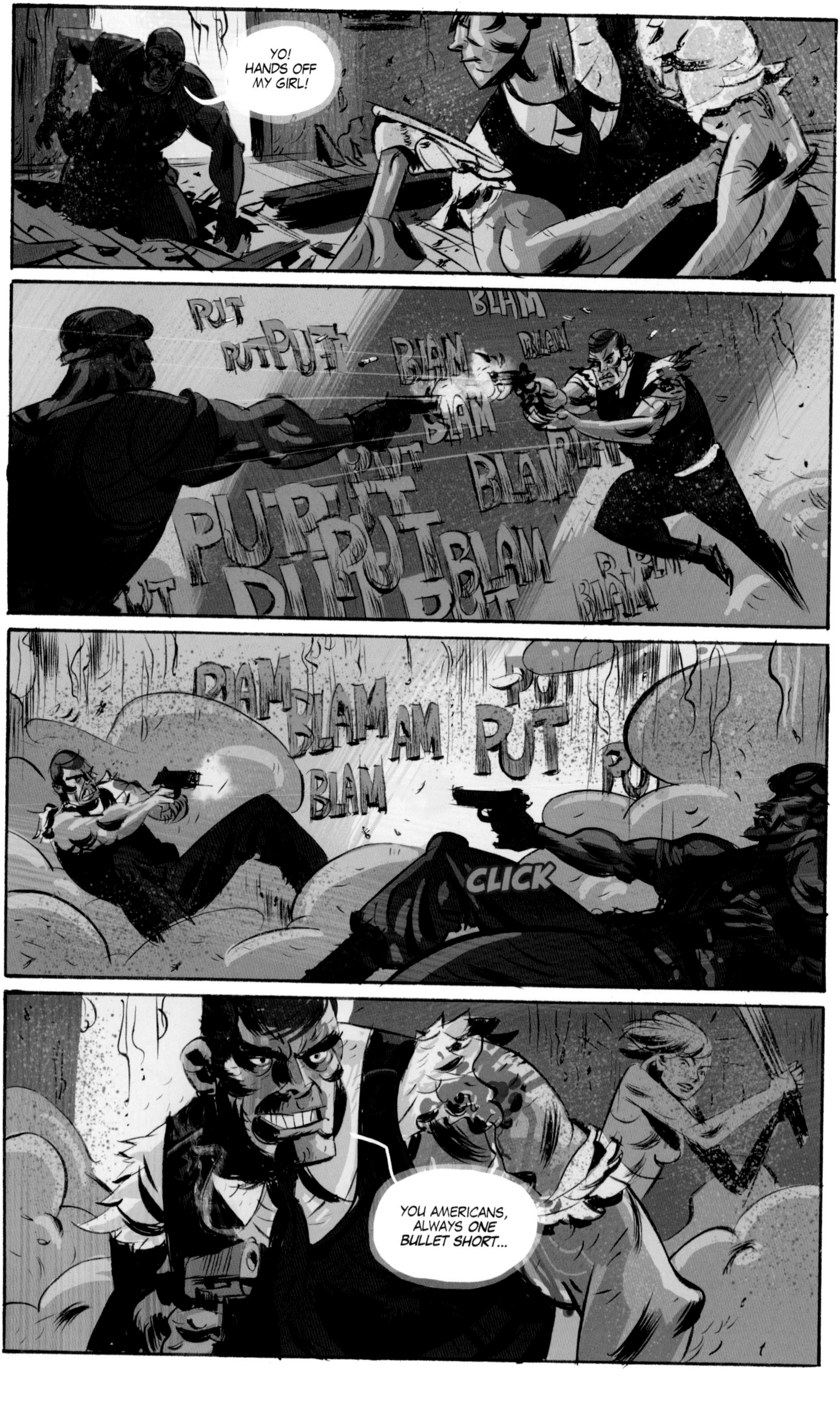
YO! HANDS OFF MY GIRL!
PUT PUT PUTT
BLAM BLAM BLAM BLAM BLAM
BLAM BLAM AM PUT BLAM
CLICK
YOU AMERICANS, ALWAYS ONE BULLET SHORT...

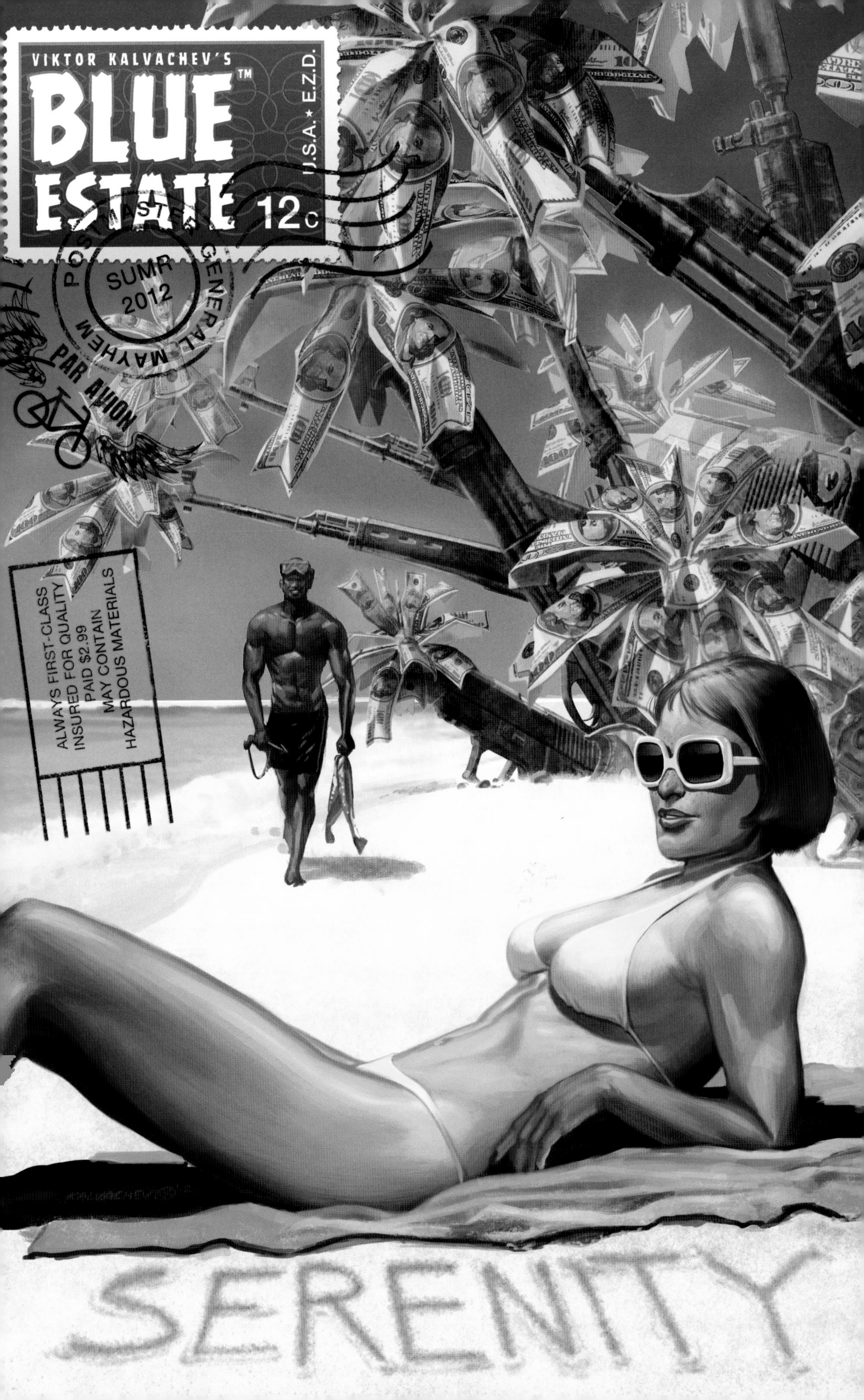

VIKTOR KALVACHEV'S
BLUE ESTATE™
U.S.A.★E.Z.D.
12c
POSTMASTER GENERAL MAYHEM
SUMR 2012
PAR AVION
ALWAYS FIRST-CLASS
INSURED FOR QUALITY
PAID $2.99
MAY CONTAIN
HAZARDOUS MATERIALS
SERENITY

# BLUE ESTATE ™

## EPISODE TWELVE:
## SERENITY

ORIGINAL STORY:
**VIKTOR KALVACHEV** AND **KOSTA YANEV**

SCRIPT BY **ANDREW OSBORNE**

ARTISTS:
**VIKTOR KALVACHEV**
**TOBY CYPRESS**
**NATHAN FOX**
**PETER NGUYEN**

ART DIRECTION BY **VIKTOR KALVACHEV**

COVER, COLORS & DESIGN:
**VIKTOR KALVACHEV**

CONTRIBUTING EDITOR:
**PHILO NORTHRUP**

www.**BlueEstateComic**.com

EZD ™
PRODUCTIONS

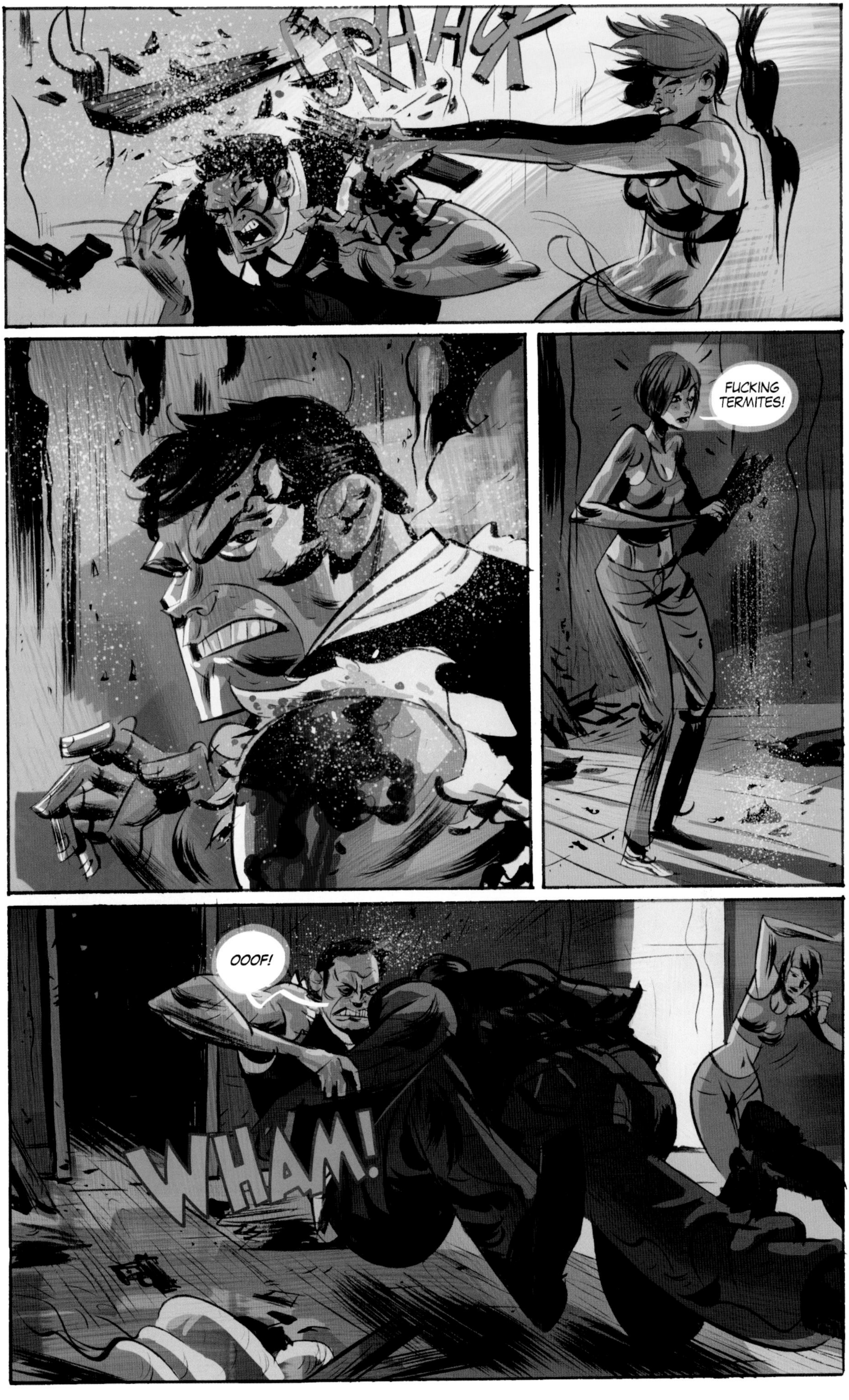
FUCKING TERMITES!
OOOF!
WHAM!

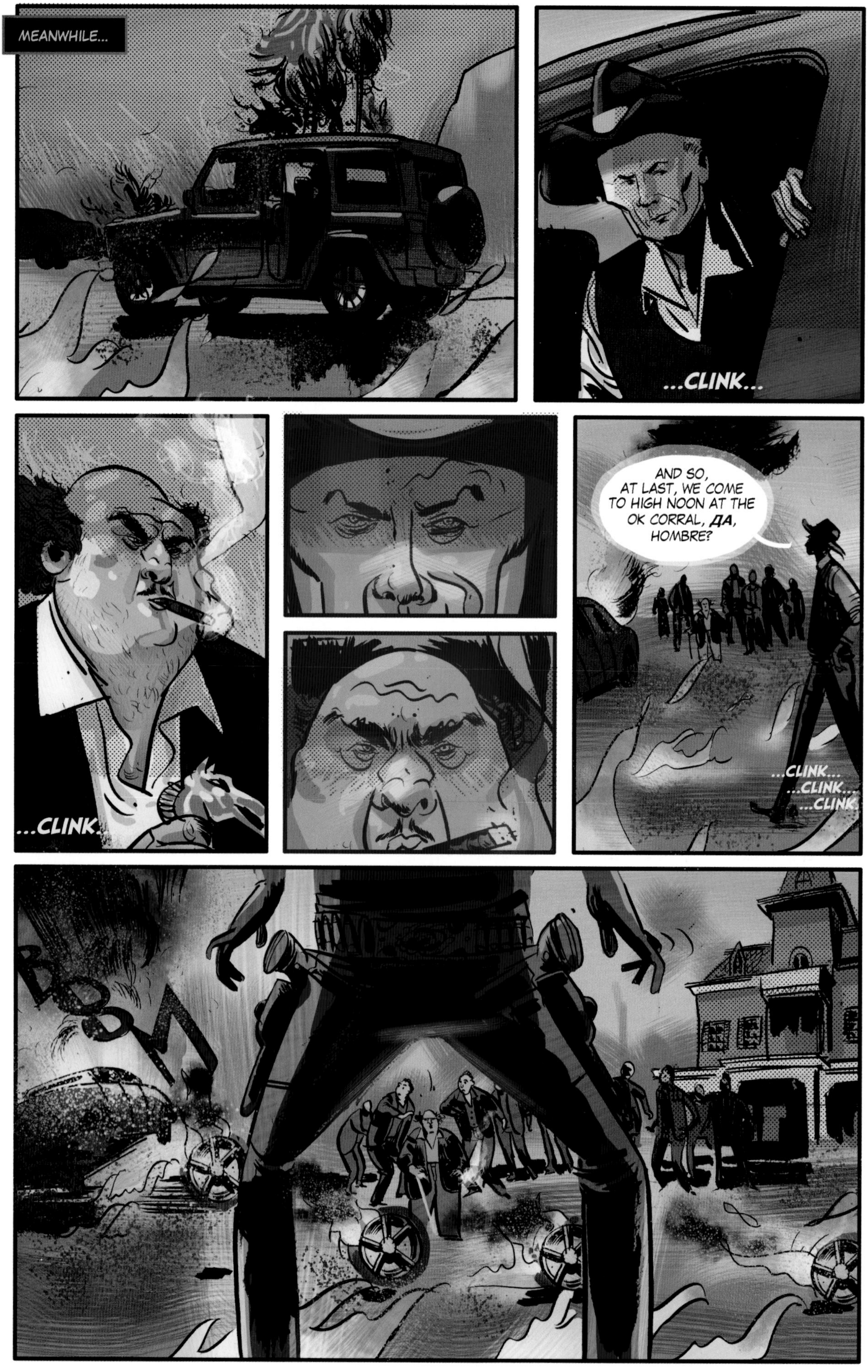
MEANWHILE...
...CLINK...
...CLINK...
AND SO, AT LAST, WE COME TO HIGH NOON AT THE OK CORRAL, ДА, HOMBRE?
...CLINK...
...CLINK...
...CLINK...
BOOM

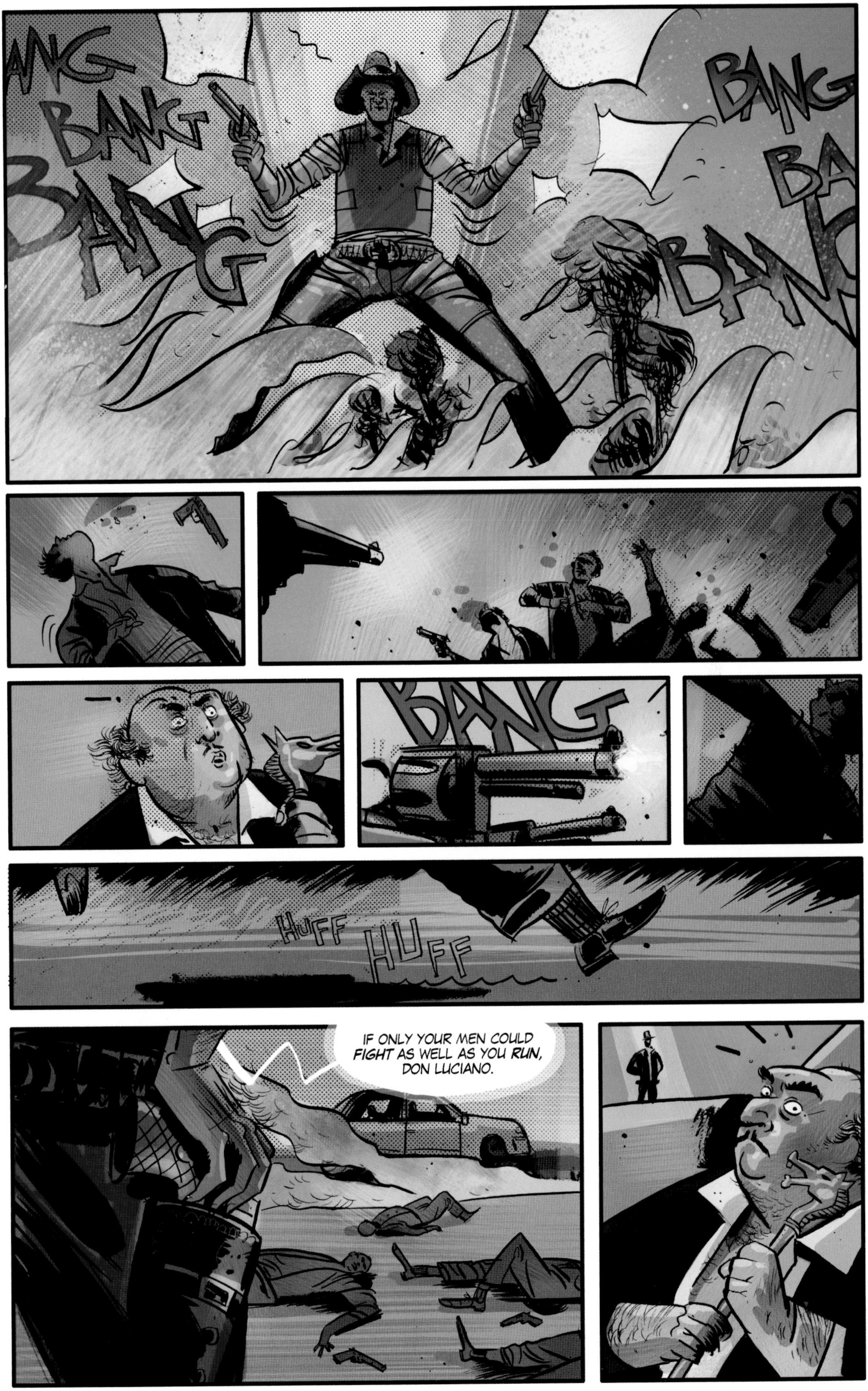
ANG
BANG
BANG
BANG
BANG
BA
BANG
BANG
HUFF
HUFF
IF ONLY YOUR MEN COULD FIGHT AS WELL AS YOU RUN, DON LUCIANO.

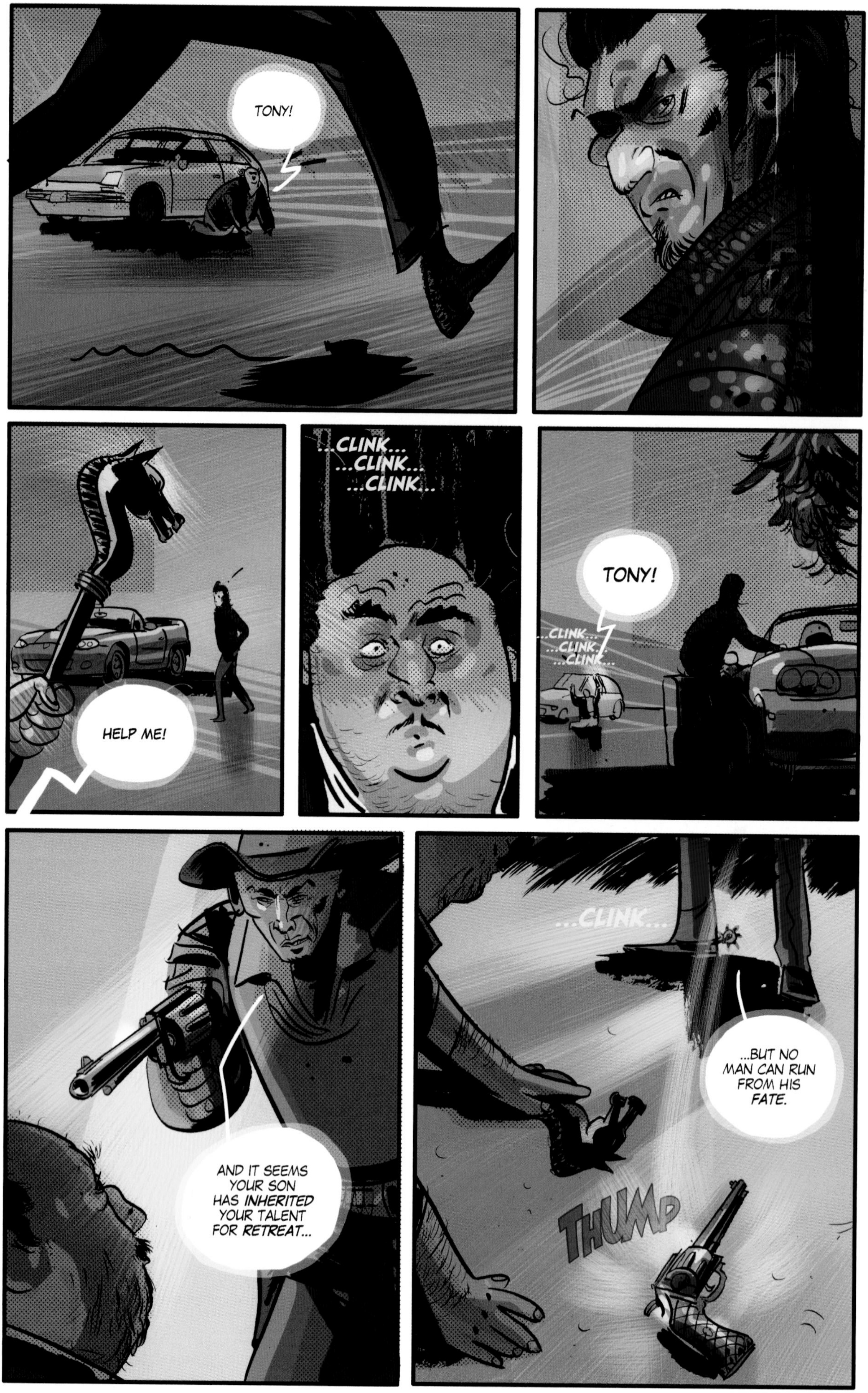
TONY!
HELP ME!
...CLINK...
...CLINK...
...CLINK...
TONY!
...CLINK...
...CLINK...
...CLINK...
AND IT SEEMS YOUR SON HAS INHERITED YOUR TALENT FOR RETREAT...
...CLINK...
...BUT NO MAN CAN RUN FROM HIS FATE.
THUMP

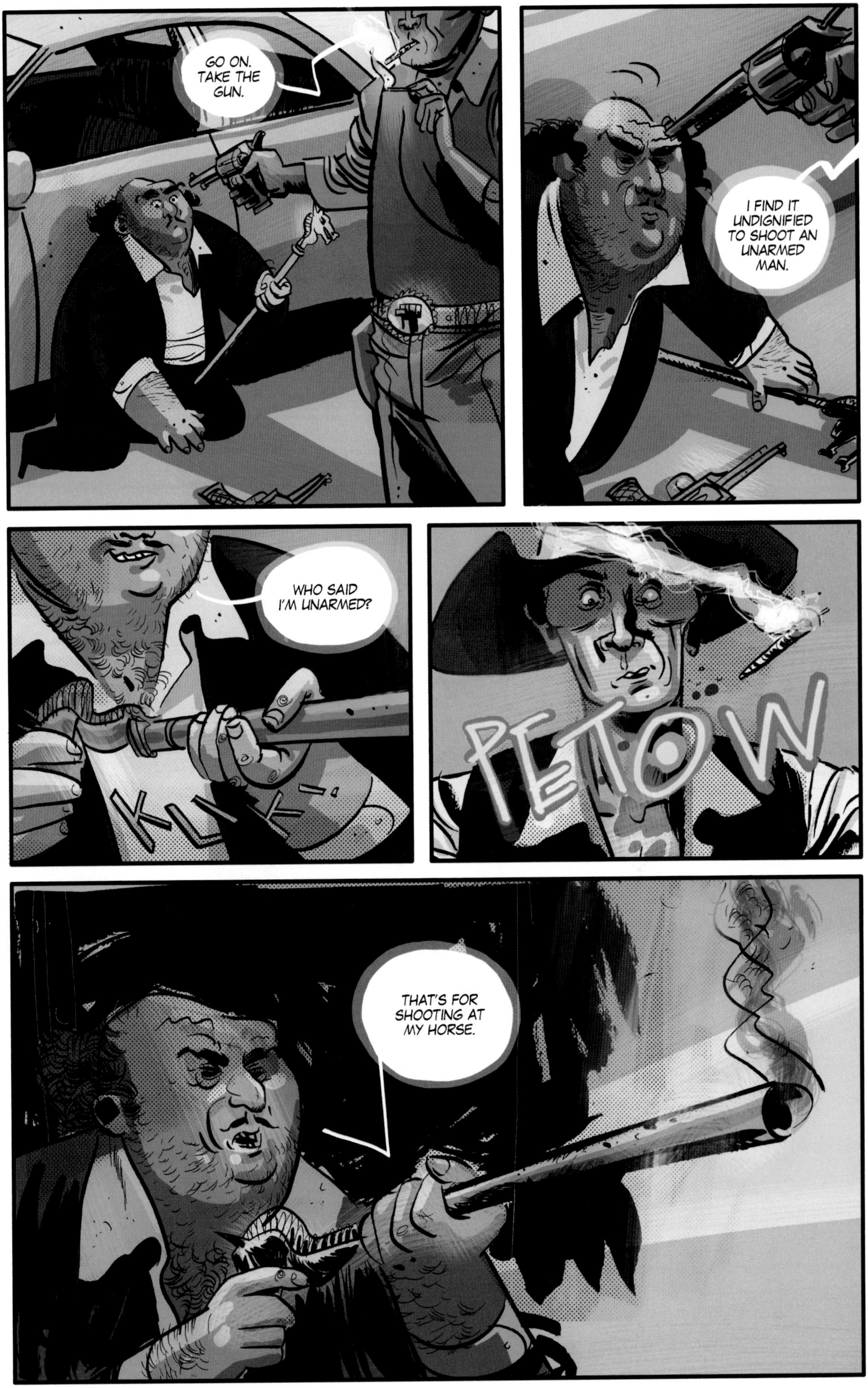
GO ON. TAKE THE GUN.
I FIND IT UNDIGNIFIED TO SHOOT AN UNARMED MAN.
WHO SAID I'M UNARMED?
PETOW
THAT'S FOR SHOOTING AT MY HORSE.

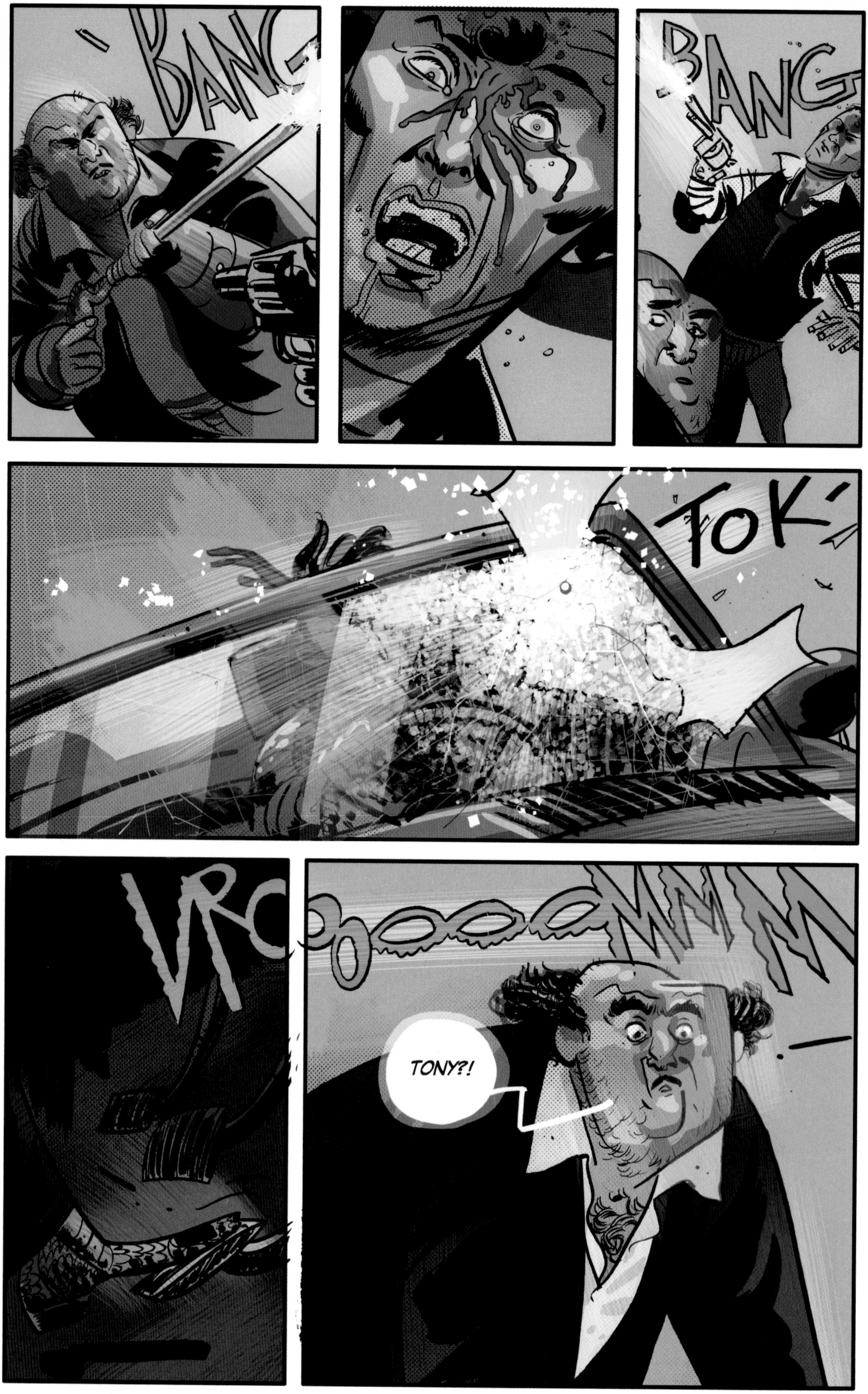
BANG
BANG
TOK
VROOOOOOMMMM
TONY?!

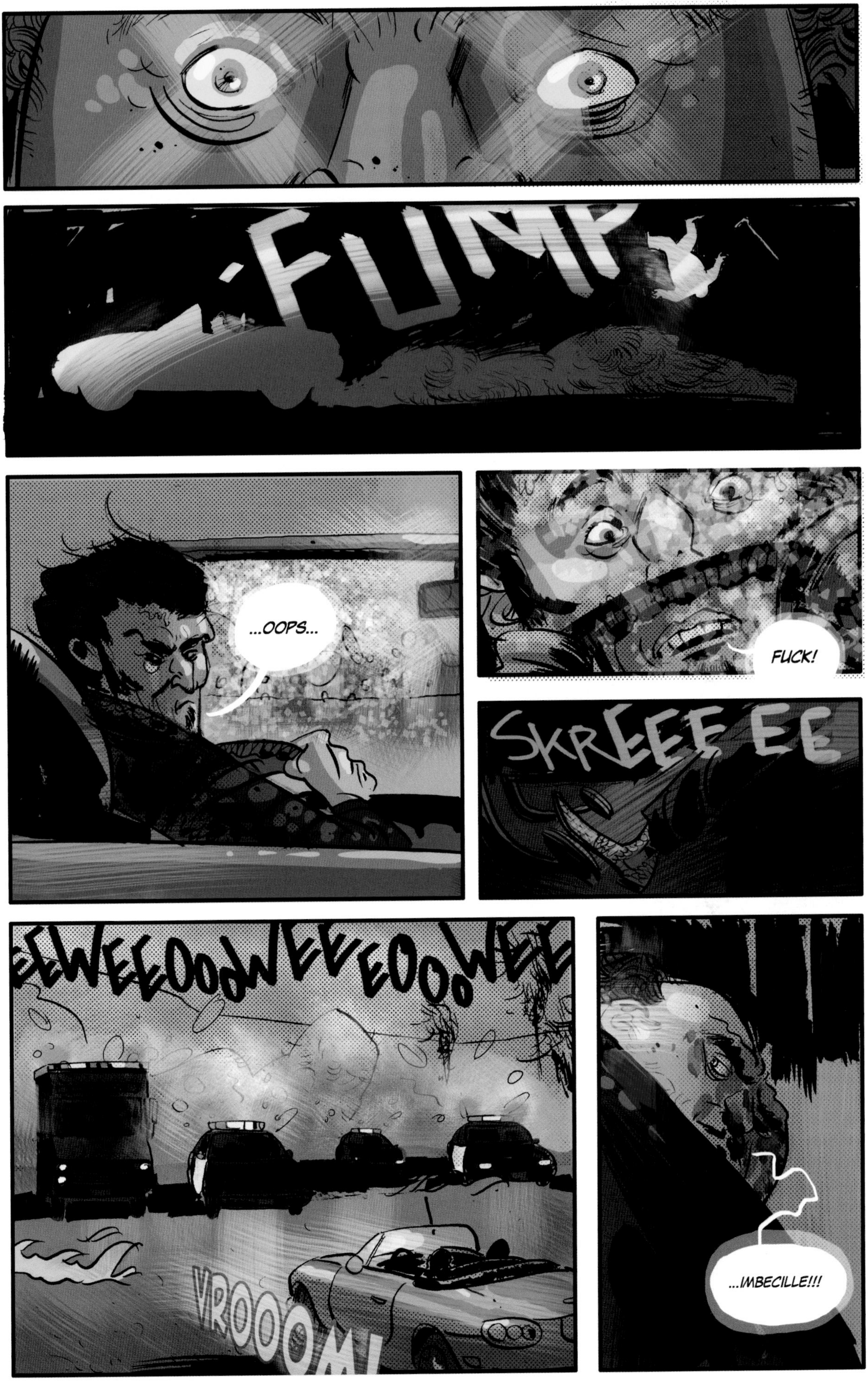
FUMP
...OOPS...
FUCK!
SKREEEEE
EEWEEOOOWEEEOOOWEE
VROOOM!
...IMBECILLE!!!

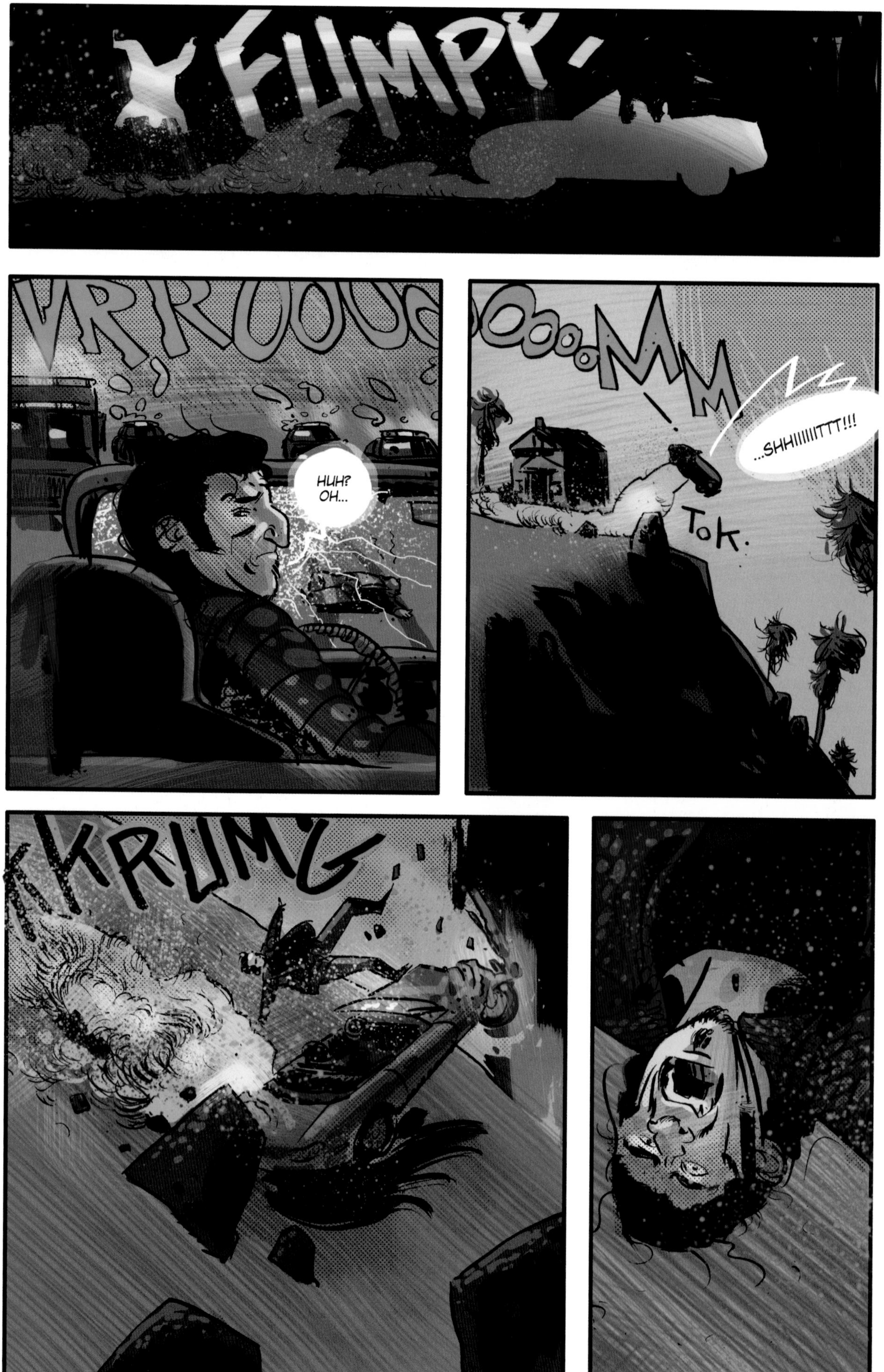

FUMPF
VRROOOOoooMM
HUH? OH...
...SHHIIIIIITTT!!!
TOK.
KRUNG

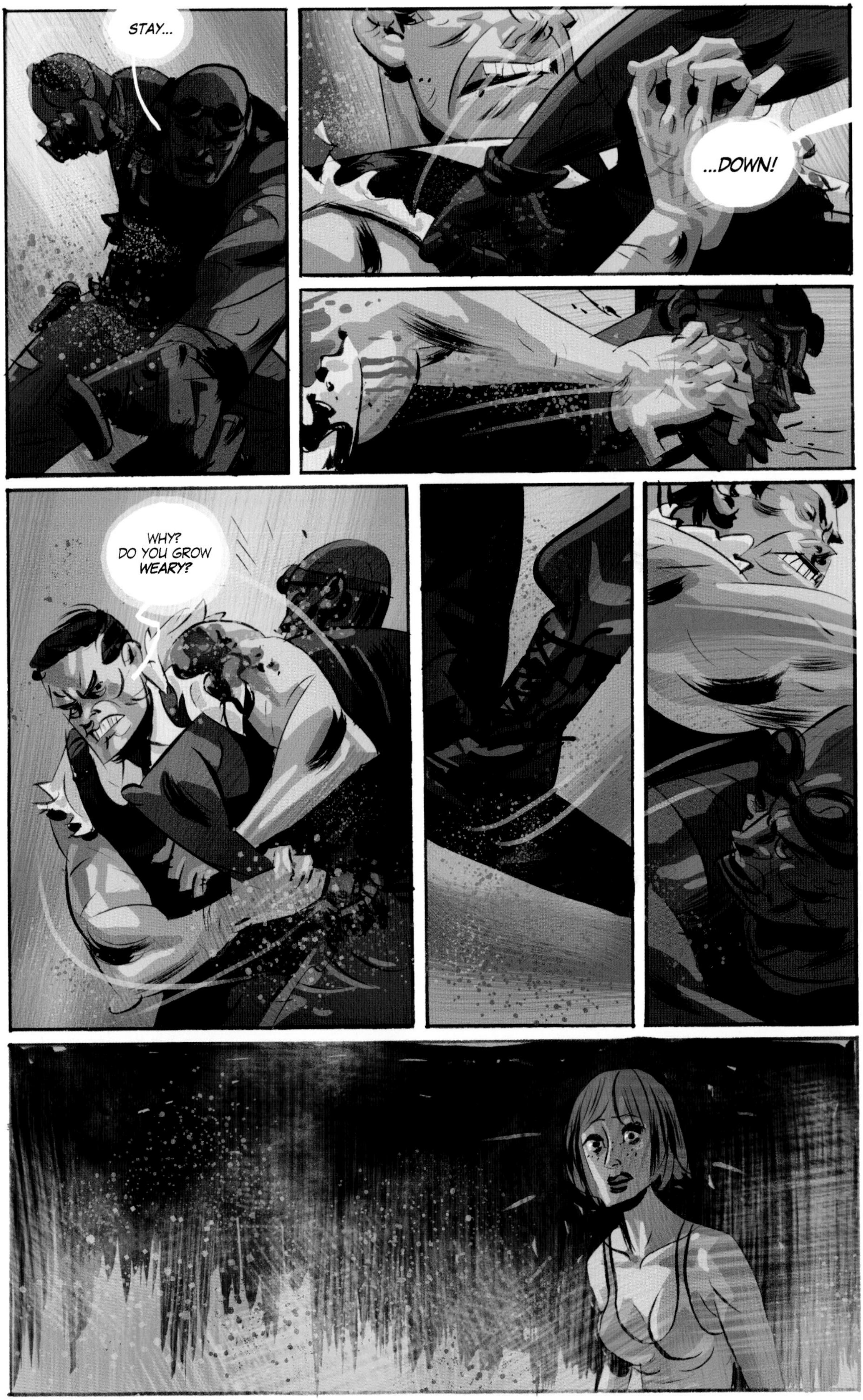
STAY...
...DOWN!
WHY? DO YOU GROW WEARY?

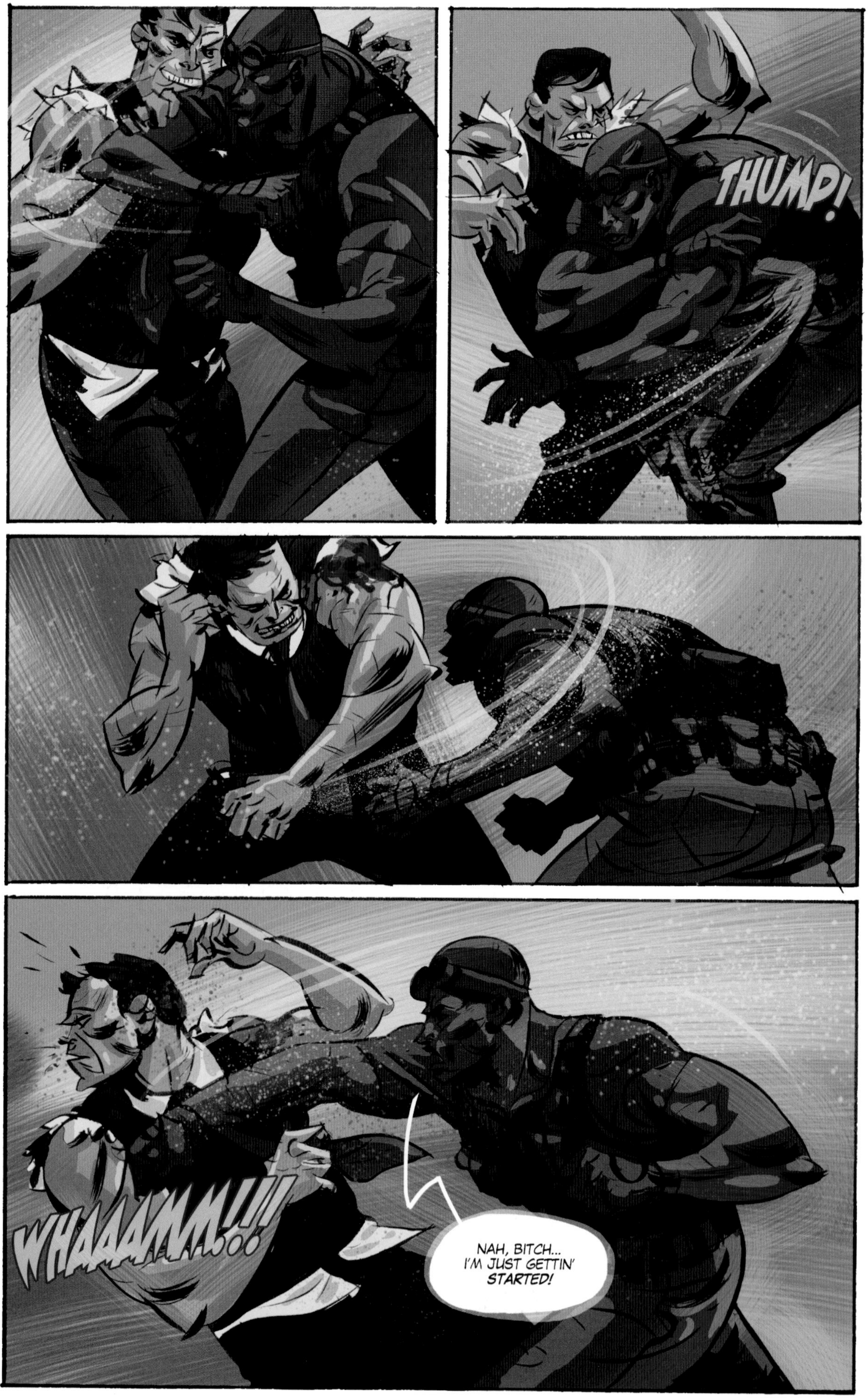
THUMP!
WHAAAMM...!!!
NAH, BITCH...
I'M JUST GETTIN'
STARTED!

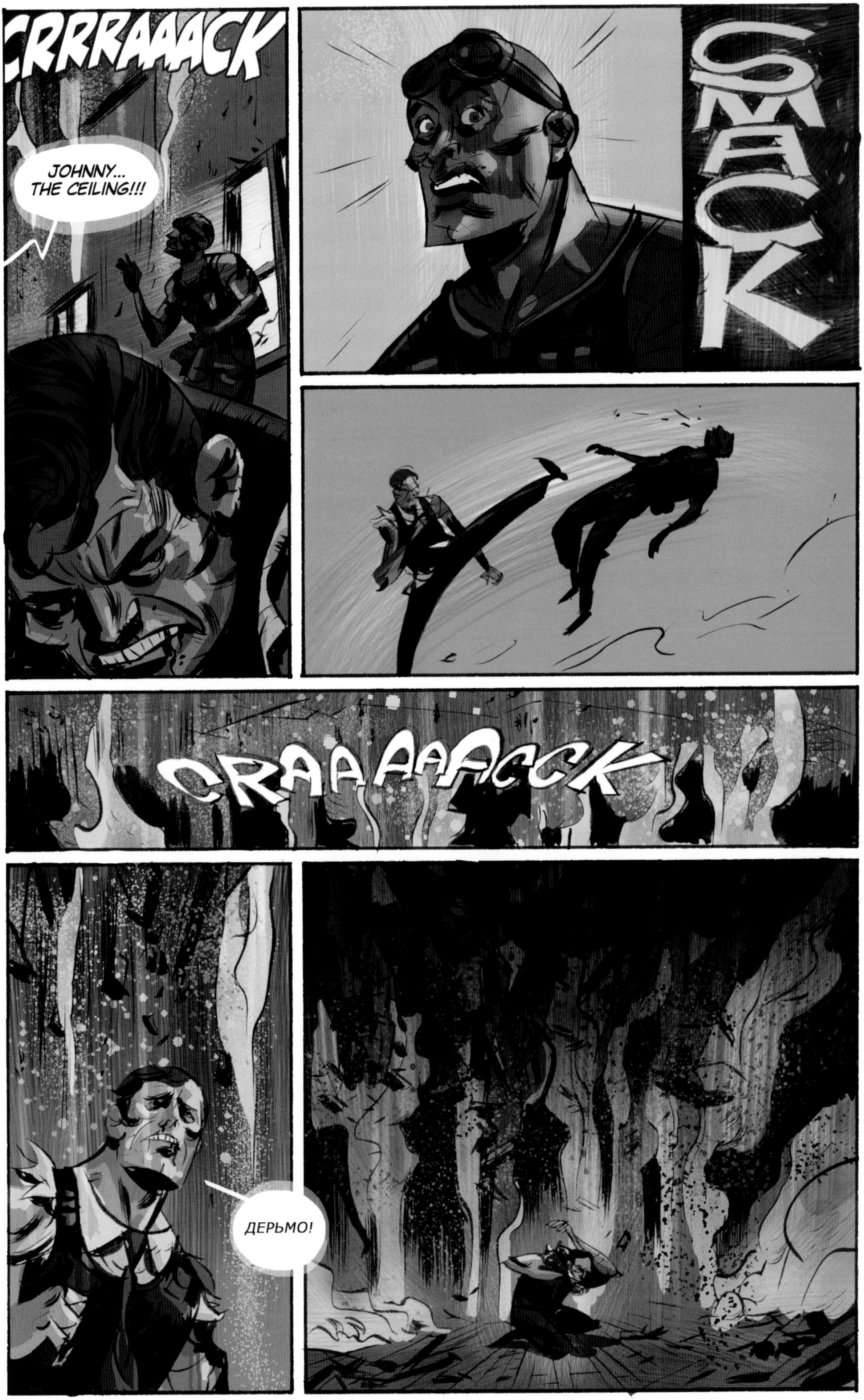
CRRRAAACK
JOHNNY... THE CEILING!!!
SMACK
CRAAAAACCK
ДЕРЬМО!

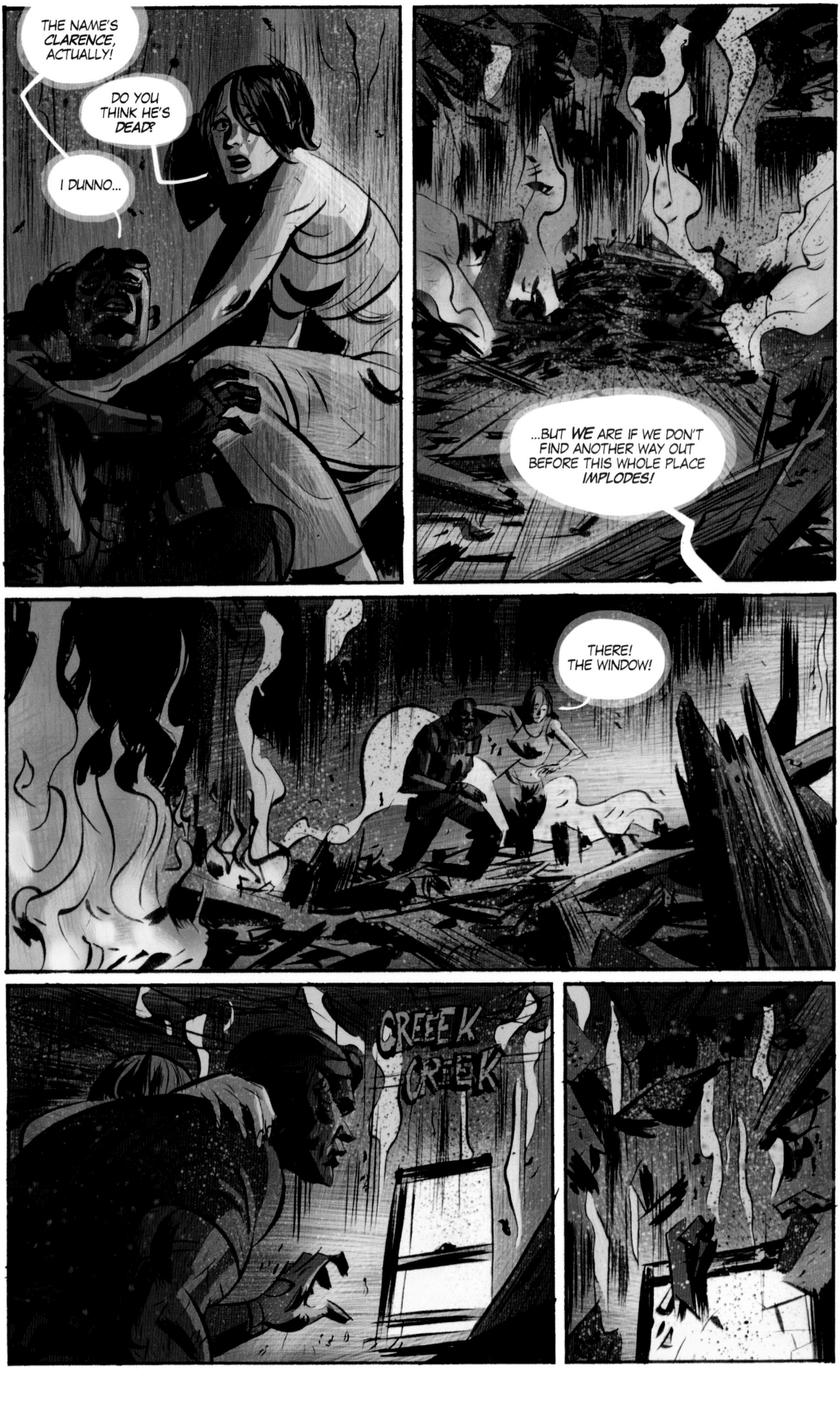
THE NAME'S CLARENCE, ACTUALLY!
DO YOU THINK HE'S DEAD?
I DUNNO...
...BUT WE ARE IF WE DON'T FIND ANOTHER WAY OUT BEFORE THIS WHOLE PLACE IMPLODES!
THERE! THE WINDOW!
CREEEK
CREEK

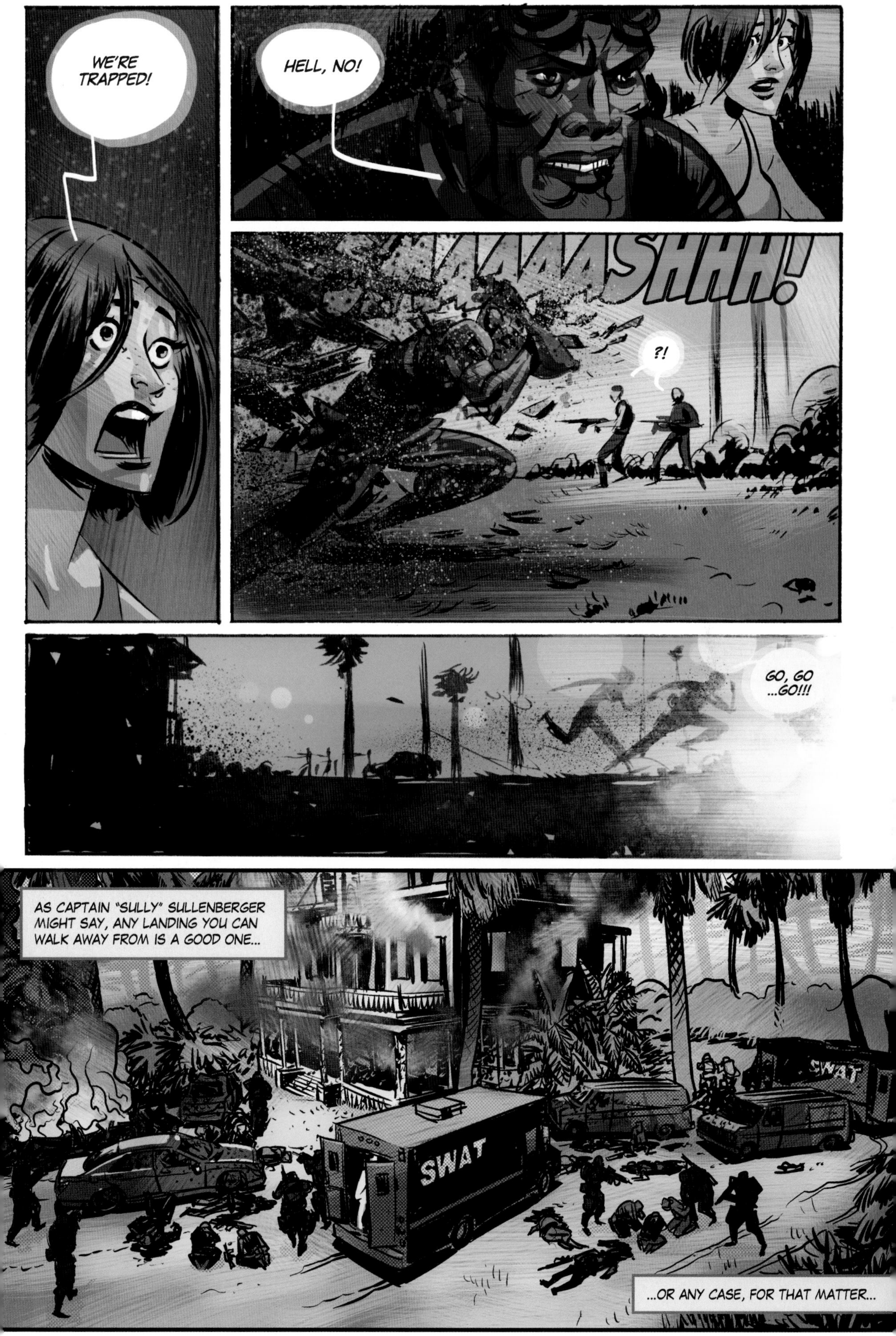
WE'RE TRAPPED!
HELL, NO!
WAAAASHHH!
?!
GO, GO ...GO!!!
AS CAPTAIN "SULLY" SULLENBERGER MIGHT SAY, ANY LANDING YOU CAN WALK AWAY FROM IS A GOOD ONE...
SWAT
SWAT
...OR ANY CASE, FOR THAT MATTER...

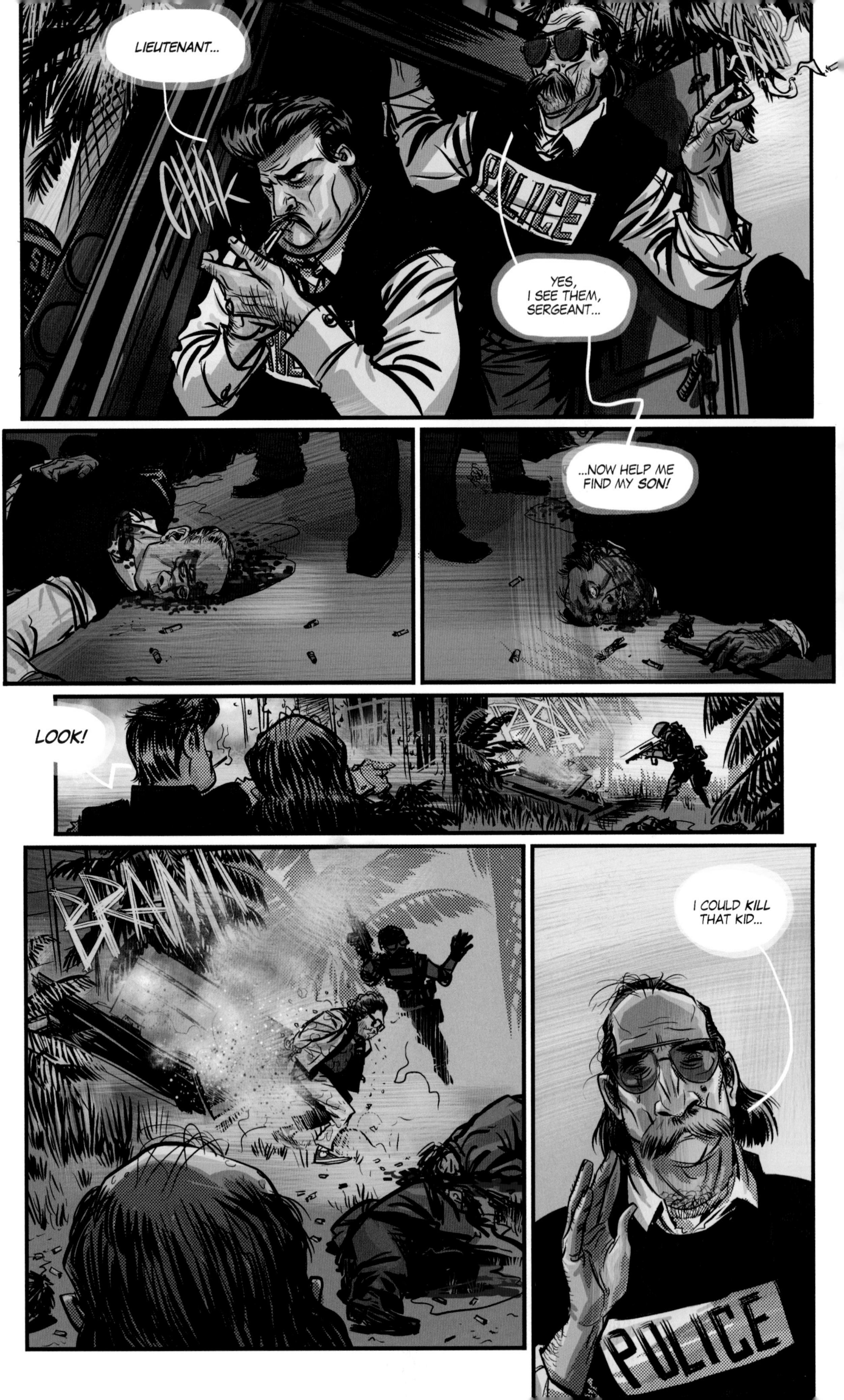
LIEUTENANT...
CHAK
YES, I SEE THEM, SERGEANT...
...NOW HELP ME FIND MY SON!
LOOK!
BRAM!
I COULD KILL THAT KID...

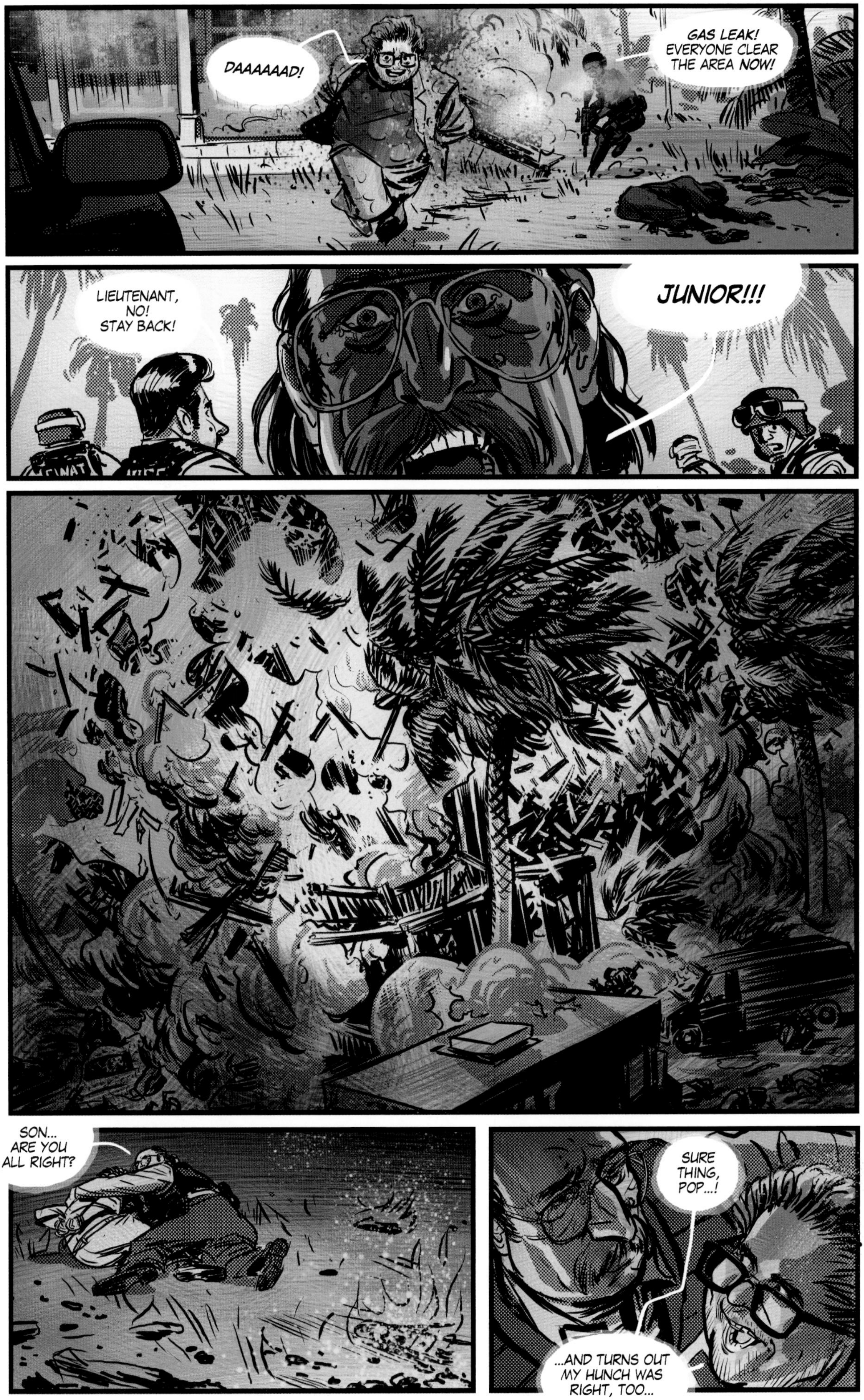
DAAAAAAD!
GAS LEAK! EVERYONE CLEAR THE AREA NOW!
LIEUTENANT, NO! STAY BACK!
JUNIOR!!!
SON... ARE YOU ALL RIGHT?
SURE THING, POP...!
...AND TURNS OUT MY HUNCH WAS RIGHT, TOO...

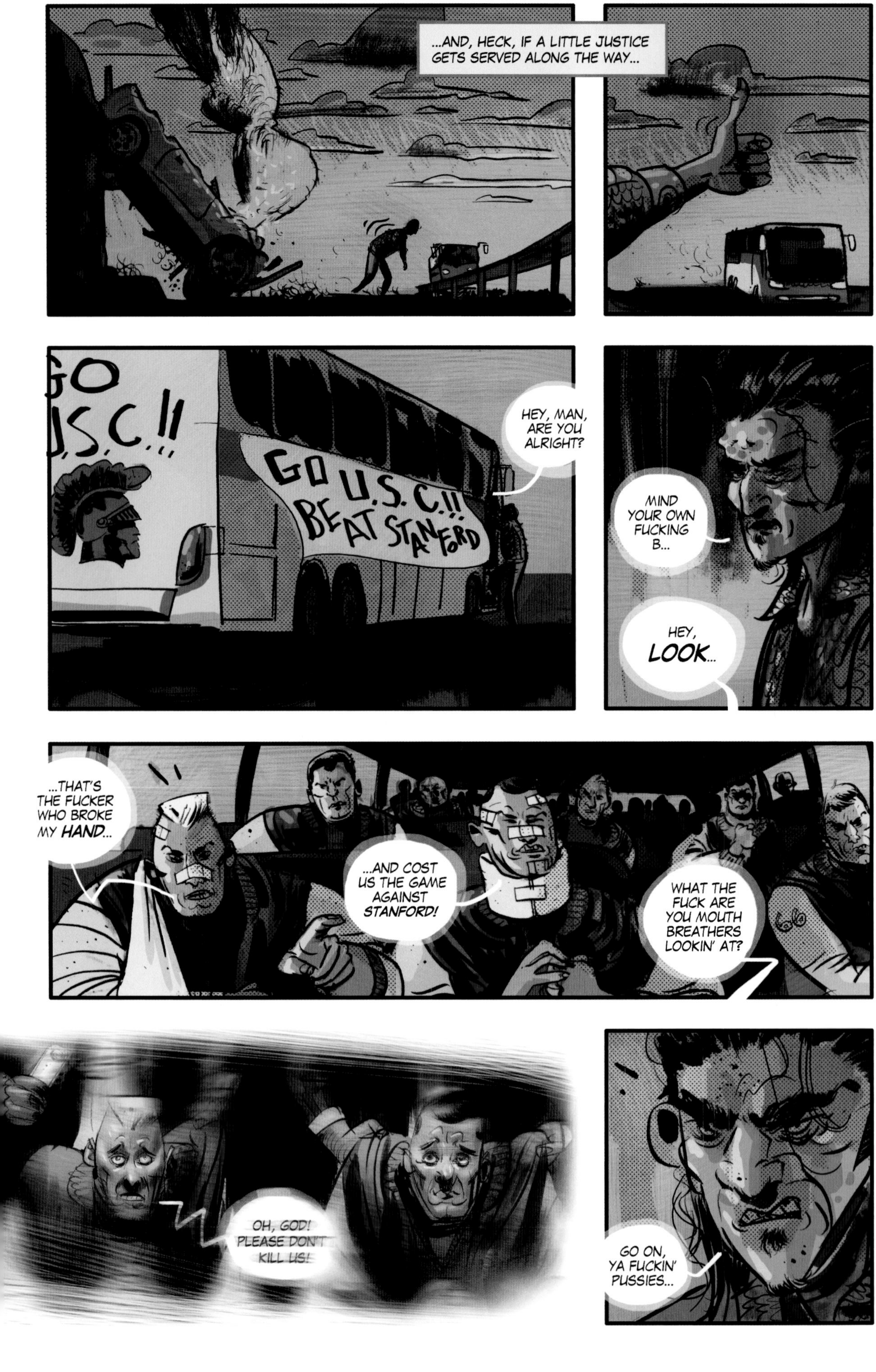
...AND, HECK, IF A LITTLE JUSTICE GETS SERVED ALONG THE WAY...
GO U.S.C.!!
GO U.S.C.!! BEAT STANFORD
HEY, MAN, ARE YOU ALRIGHT?
MIND YOUR OWN FUCKING B...
HEY, LOOK...
...THAT'S THE FUCKER WHO BROKE MY HAND...
...AND COST US THE GAME AGAINST STANFORD!
WHAT THE FUCK ARE YOU MOUTH BREATHERS LOOKIN' AT?
OH, GOD! PLEASE DON'T KILL US!
GO ON, YA FUCKIN' PUSSIES...

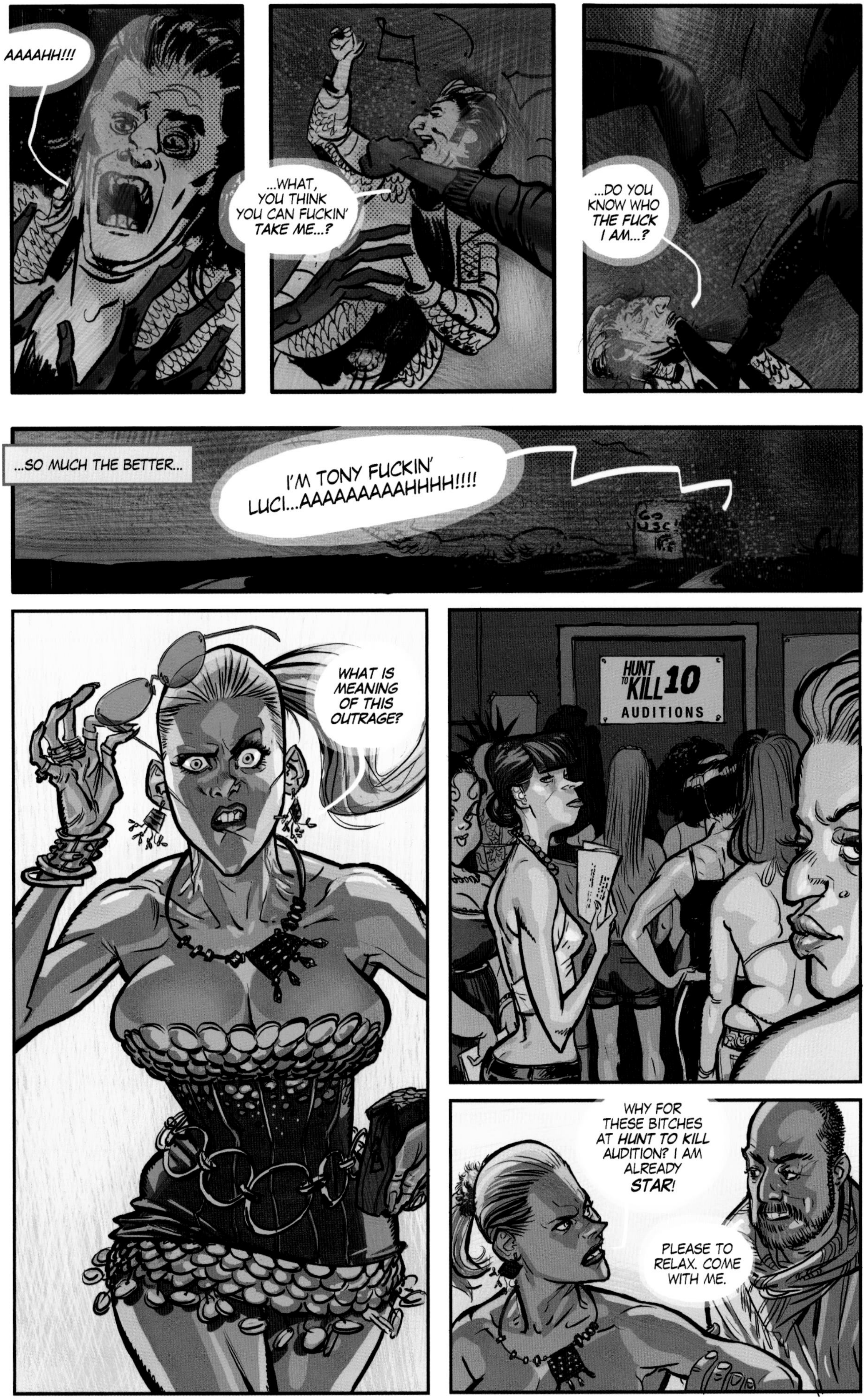
AAAAHH!!!
...WHAT, YOU THINK YOU CAN FUCKIN' TAKE ME...?
...DO YOU KNOW WHO THE FUCK I AM...?
...SO MUCH THE BETTER...
I'M TONY FUCKIN' LUCI...AAAAAAAAAHHHH!!!!
WHAT IS MEANING OF THIS OUTRAGE?
HUNT TO KILL 10 AUDITIONS
WHY FOR THESE BITCHES AT HUNT TO KILL AUDITION? I AM ALREADY STAR!
PLEASE TO RELAX. COME WITH ME.

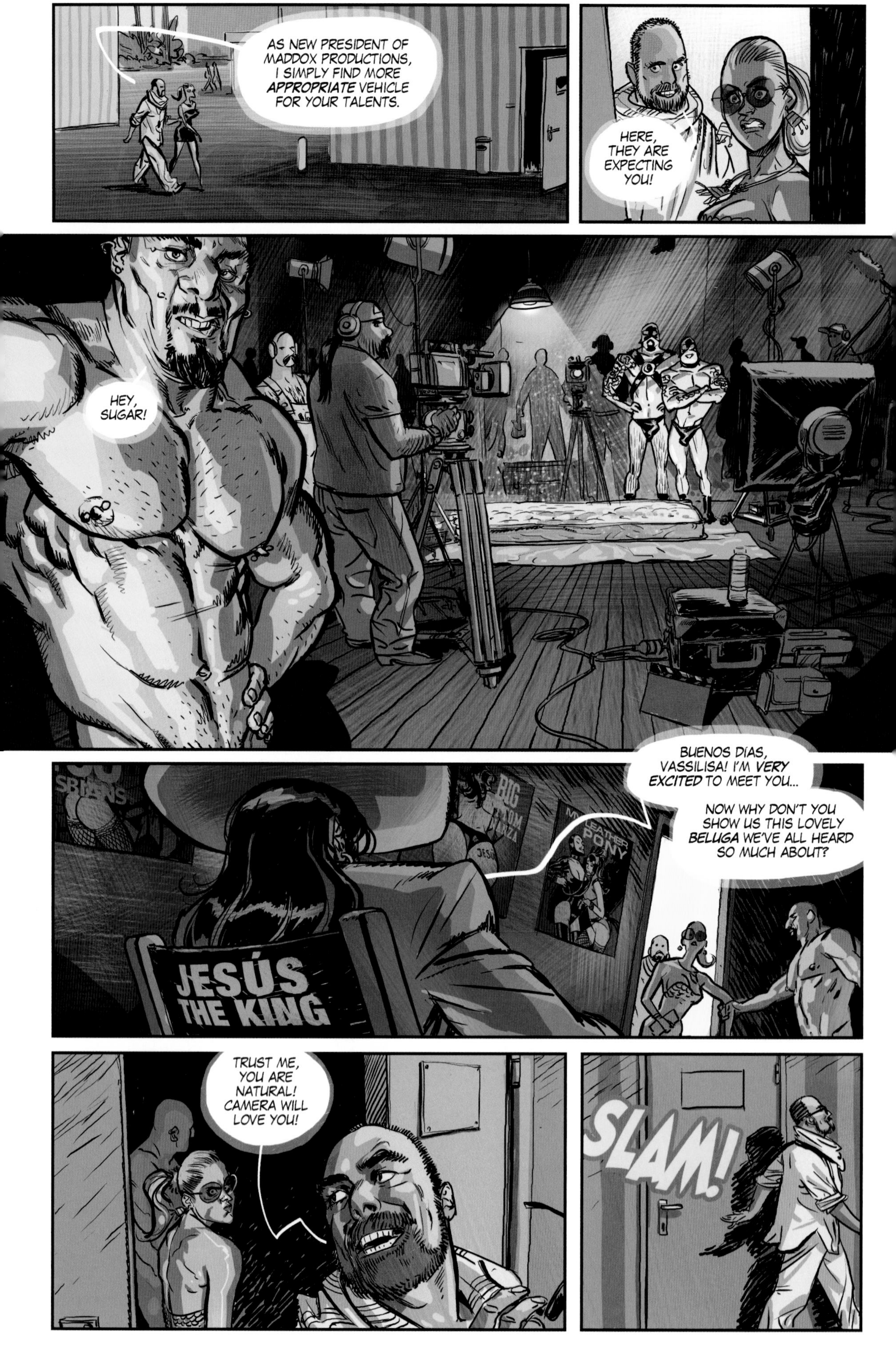
AS NEW PRESIDENT OF MADDOX PRODUCTIONS, I SIMPLY FIND MORE *APPROPRIATE* VEHICLE FOR YOUR TALENTS.
HERE, THEY ARE EXPECTING YOU!
HEY, SUGAR!
BUENOS DIAS, VASSILISA! I'M *VERY EXCITED* TO MEET YOU...
NOW WHY DON'T YOU SHOW US THIS LOVELY *BELUGA* WE'VE ALL HEARD SO MUCH ABOUT?
JESÚS THE KING
MY LEATHER PONY
TRUST ME, YOU ARE NATURAL! CAMERA WILL LOVE YOU!
SLAM!

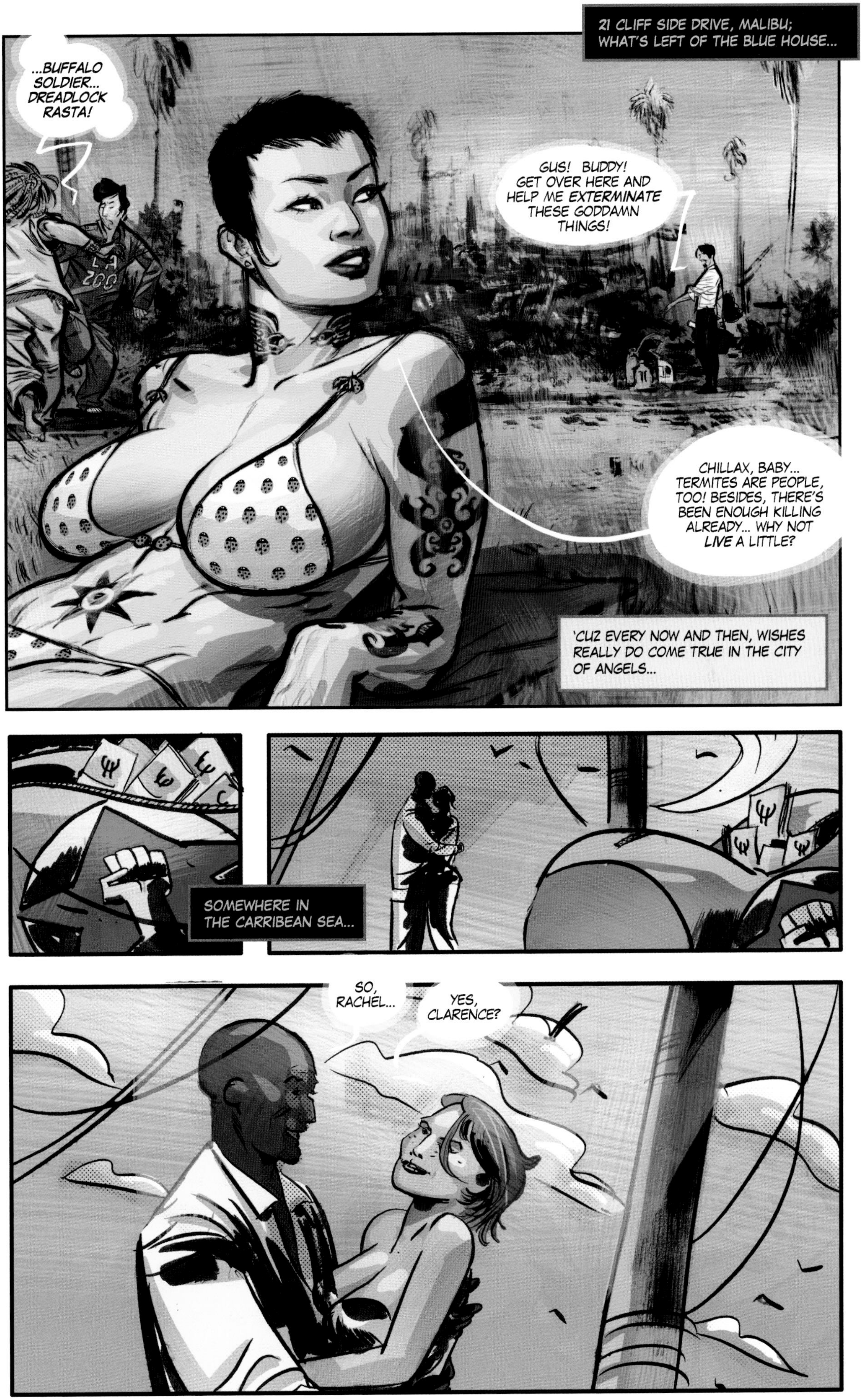
21 CLIFF SIDE DRIVE, MALIBU; WHAT'S LEFT OF THE BLUE HOUSE...
...BUFFALO SOLDIER... DREADLOCK RASTA!
GUS! BUDDY! GET OVER HERE AND HELP ME EXTERMINATE THESE GODDAMN THINGS!
CHILLAX, BABY... TERMITES ARE PEOPLE, TOO! BESIDES, THERE'S BEEN ENOUGH KILLING ALREADY... WHY NOT LIVE A LITTLE?
'CUZ EVERY NOW AND THEN, WISHES REALLY DO COME TRUE IN THE CITY OF ANGELS...
SOMEWHERE IN THE CARRIBEAN SEA...
SO, RACHEL...
YES, CLARENCE?

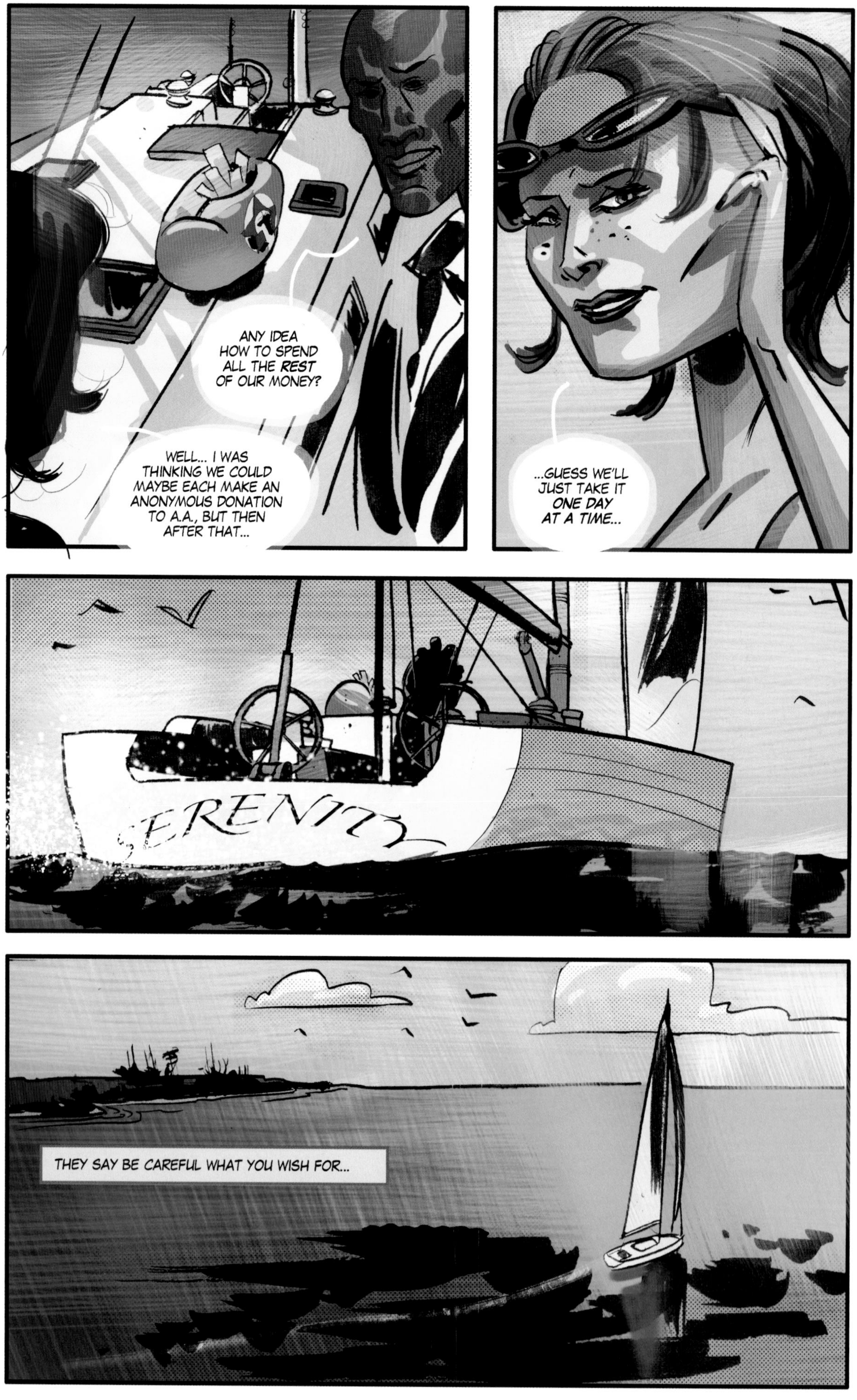
ANY IDEA HOW TO SPEND ALL THE REST OF OUR MONEY?
WELL... I WAS THINKING WE COULD MAYBE EACH MAKE AN ANONYMOUS DONATION TO A.A., BUT THEN AFTER THAT...
...GUESS WE'LL JUST TAKE IT ONE DAY AT A TIME...
SERENITY
THEY SAY BE CAREFUL WHAT YOU WISH FOR...

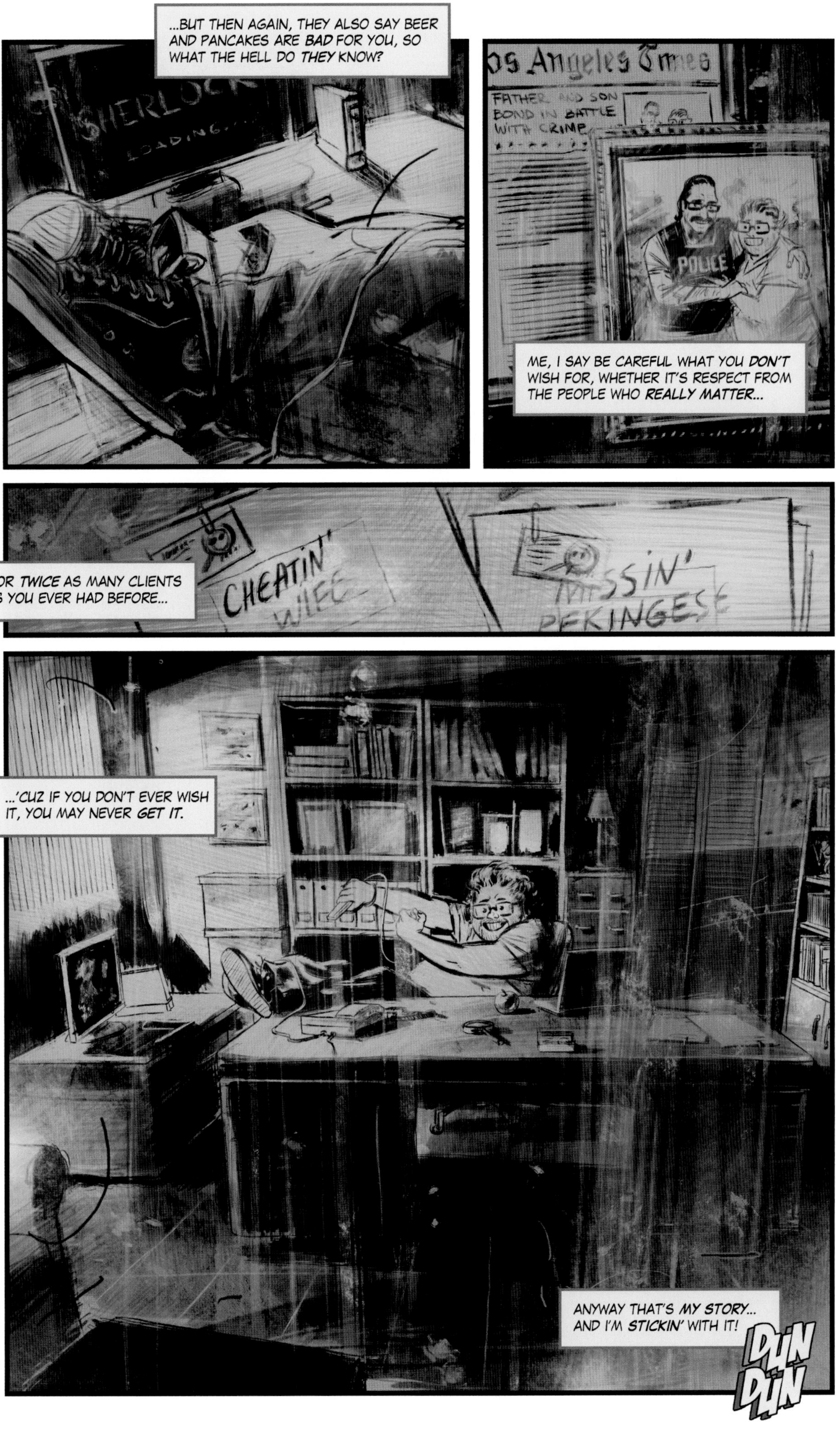
...BUT THEN AGAIN, THEY ALSO SAY BEER AND PANCAKES ARE *BAD* FOR YOU, SO WHAT THE HELL DO *THEY* KNOW?
SHERLOCK
LOADING...
os Angeles Times
FATHER AND SON BOND IN BATTLE WITH CRIME
POLICE
ME, I SAY BE CAREFUL WHAT YOU *DON'T* WISH FOR, WHETHER IT'S RESPECT FROM THE PEOPLE WHO ***REALLY MATTER***...
...OR *TWICE* AS MANY CLIENTS AS YOU EVER HAD BEFORE...
CHEATIN'
PEKINGESE
...'CUZ IF YOU DON'T EVER WISH IT, YOU MAY NEVER *GET IT.*
ANYWAY THAT'S *MY STORY*... AND I'M ***STICKIN'*** WITH IT!
DUN DUN

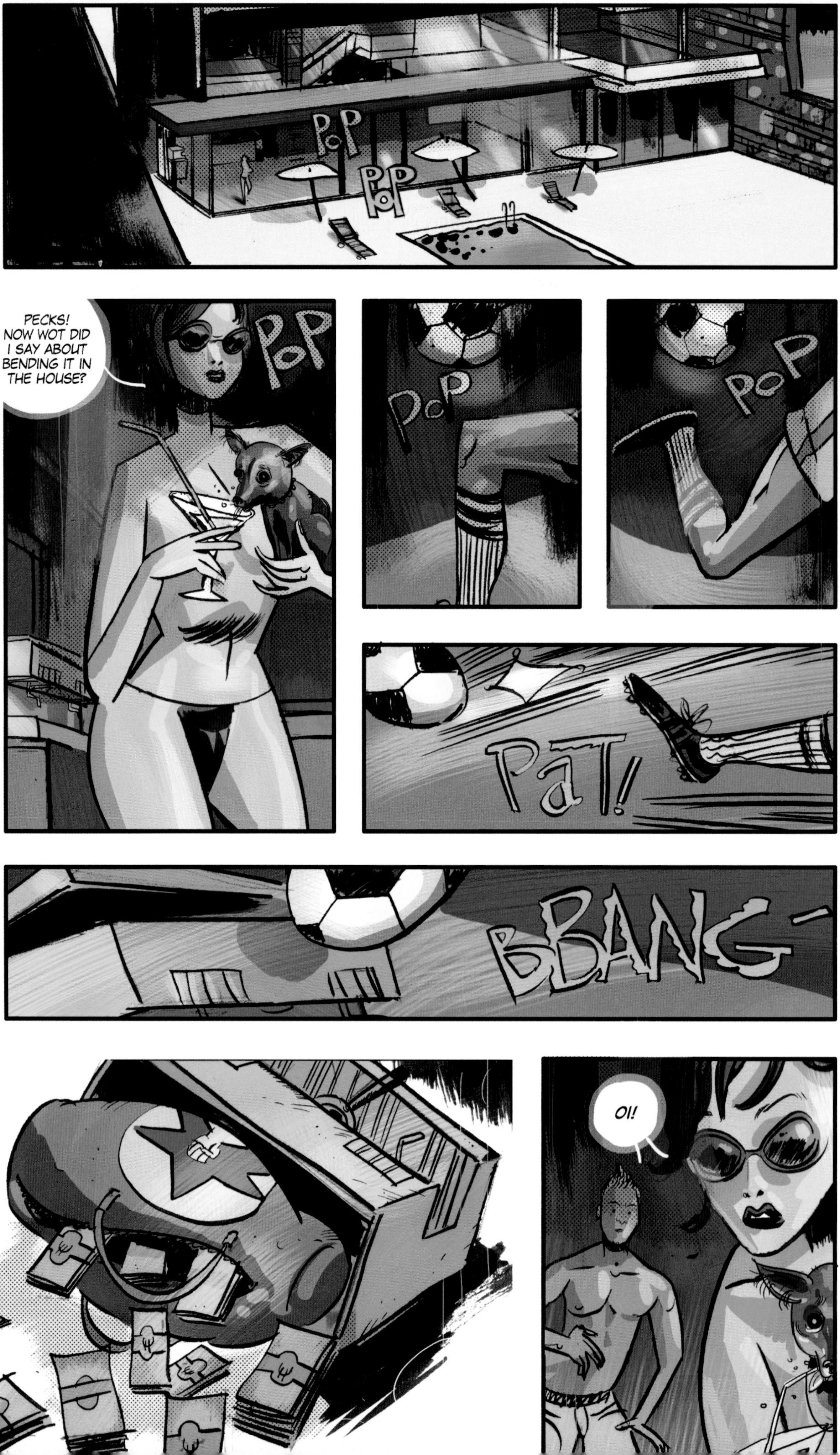
POP
POP
PECKS! NOW WOT DID I SAY ABOUT BENDING IT IN THE HOUSE?
POP
POP
POP
PAT!
BBANG
OI!

THE END?

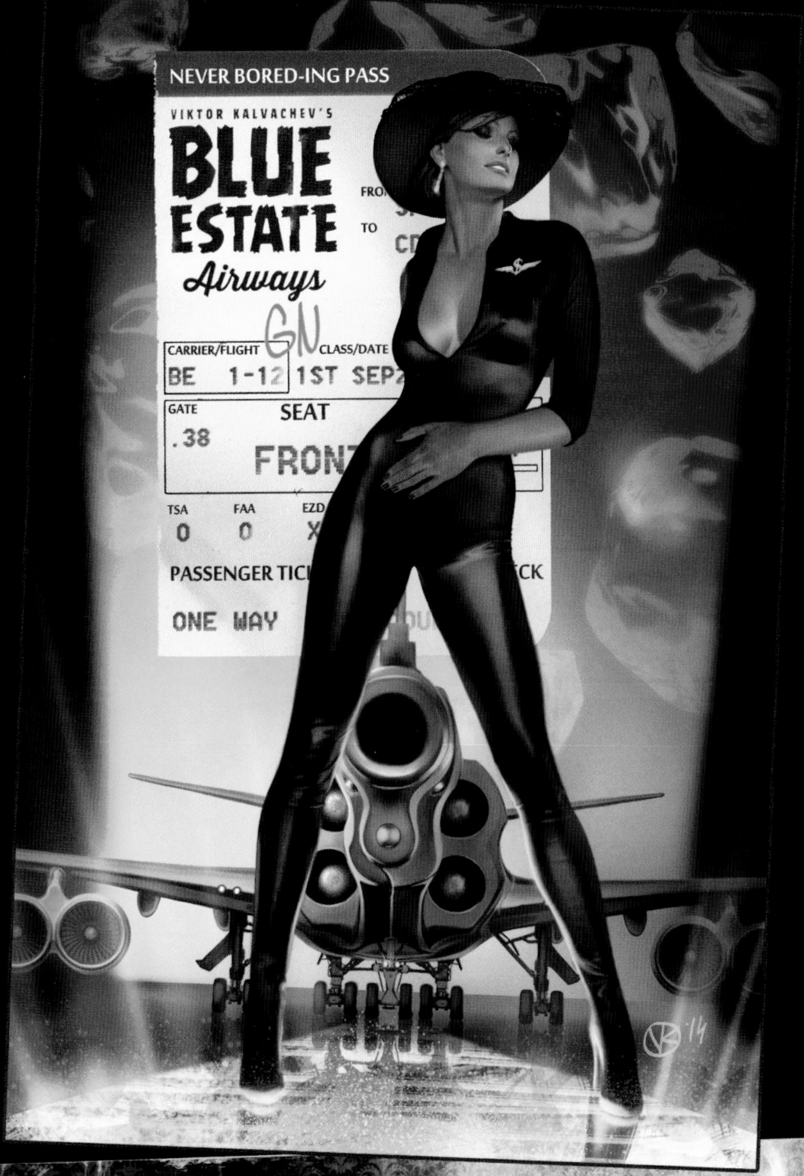
NEVER BORED-ING PASS
VIKTOR KALVACHEV'S
BLUE ESTATE
Airways
GN
CARRIER/FLIGHT
CLASS/DATE
BE 1-12
GATE
SEAT
.38
TSA
FAA
EZD
0
0
ONE WAY

# THE MAKING OF BLUE ESTATE

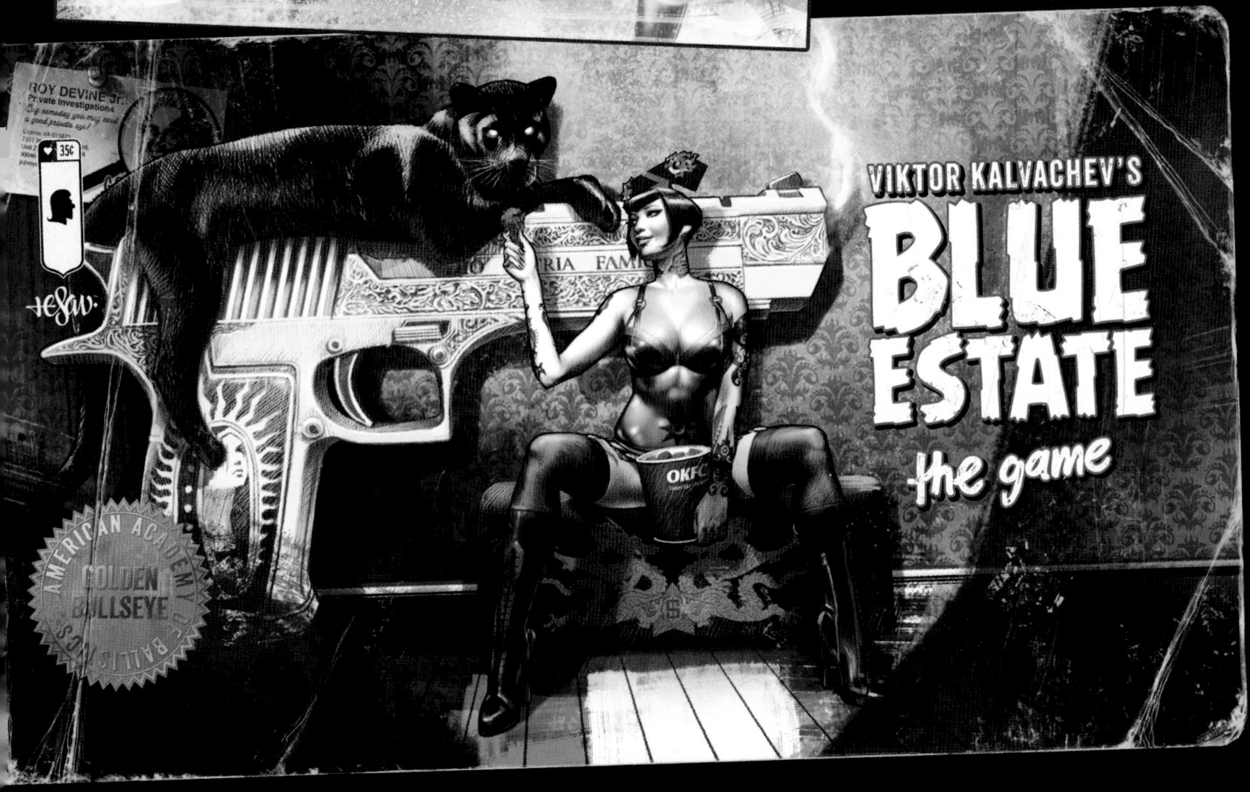
ROY DEVINE JR.
Private Investigations
35¢
VIKTOR KALVACHEV'S
BLUE ESTATE
the game
GOLDEN BULLSEYE
OKFC

Creating a big story with so many incredible artists all jamming together is a lot of fun, but if you are not well organized it can easily become a disaster. The entire script was done and split into 12 episodes before we even started. There was a diagram for each episode showing where the styles should shift, who would draw them and how. Every artist had their color code which made it very easy to quickly see who is doing what and where it fits into the larger story.

Some episodes were very straight-forward and easy to divide...

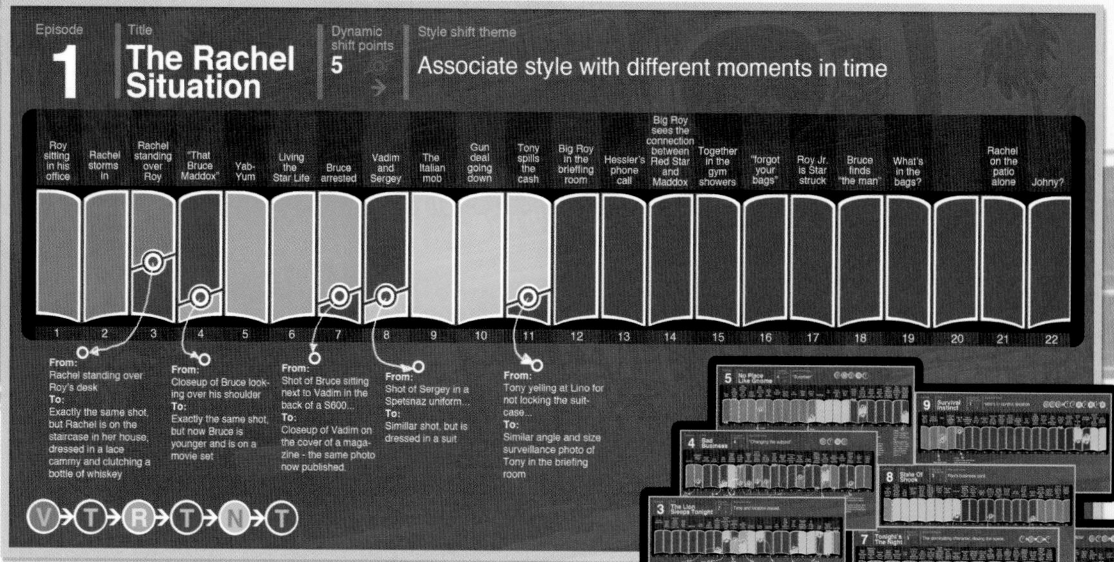

Episode
1
Title
The Rachel Situation
Dynamic shift points
5
Style shift theme
Associate style with different moments in time
Roy sitting in his office
Rachel storms in
Rachel standing over Roy
"That Bruce Maddox"
Yab-Yum
Living the Star Life
Bruce arrested
Vadim and Sergey
The Italian mob
Gun deal going down
Tony spills the cash
Big Roy in the briefing room
Hessler's phone call
Big Roy sees the connection between Red Star and Maddox
Together in the gym showers
"forgot your bags"
Roy Jr. is Star struck
Bruce finds "the man"
What's in the bags?
Rachel on the patio alone
Johny?
From:
Rachel standing over Roy's desk
To:
Exactly the same shot, but Rachel is on the staircase in her house, dressed in a lace cammy and clutching a bottle of whiskey
From:
Closeup of Bruce looking over his shoulder
To:
Exactly the same shot, but now Bruce is younger and is on a movie set
From:
Shot of Bruce sitting next to Vadim in the back of a S600...
To:
Closeup of Vadim on the cover of a magazine - the same photo now published.
From:
Shot of Sergey in a Spetsnaz uniform...
To:
Similar shot, but is dressed in a suit
From:
Tony yelling at Lino for not locking the suitcase...
To:
Similar angle and size surveillance photo of Tony in the briefing room
V T R T N T


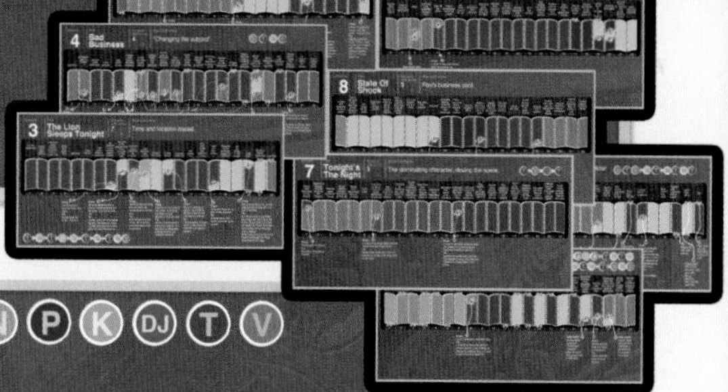

5 No Place Like Gnome
9 Survival Instinct
4 Bad Business
8 State Of Shock
3 The Lion Sleeps Tonight
7 Tonight's The Night


...but others were quite complicated.

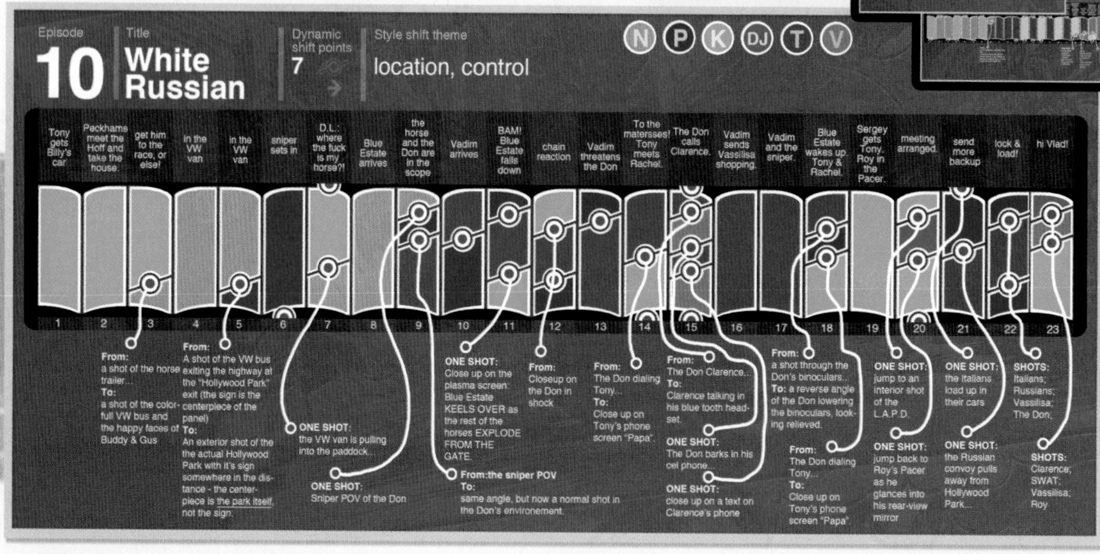

Episode
10
Title
White Russian
Dynamic shift points
7
Style shift theme
location, control
N P K DJ T V
Tony gets Billy's car
Peckhams meet the Hoff and take the house
get him to the race, or else!
in the VW van
in the VW van
sniper sets in
D.L.: where the fuck is my horse?!
Blue Estate arrives
the horse and the Don are in the scope
Vadim arrives
BAM! Blue Estate falls down
chain reaction
Vadim threatens the Don
To the matersses! Tony meets Rachel.
The Don calls Clarence.
Vadim sends Vassilisa shopping.
Vadim and the sniper.
Blue Estate wakes up Tony & Rachel.
Sergey gets Tony, Roy in the Pacer.
meeting arranged.
send more backup
lock & load!
hi Vlad!
From:
a shot of the horse trailer...
To:
a shot of the colorfull VW bus and the happy faces of Buddy & Gus
From:
A shot of the VW bus exiting the highway at the "Hollywood Park" exit (the sign is the centerpiece of the panel)
To:
An exterior shot of the the actual Hollywood Park with it's sign somewhere in the distance - the centerpiece is the park itself, not the sign.
ONE SHOT:
the VW van is pulling into the paddock...
ONE SHOT:
Sniper POV of the Don
ONE SHOT:
Close up on the plasma screen: Blue Estate KEELS OVER as the rest of the horses EXPLODE FROM THE GATE.
From:the sniper POV
To:
same angle, but now a normal shot in the Don's environement.
From:
Closeup on the Don in shock
From:
The Don dialing Tony...
To:
Close up on Tony's phone screen "Papa".
From:
The Don Clarence...
To:
Clarence talking in his blue tooth headset.
ONE SHOT:
The Don barks in his cel phone...
ONE SHOT:
close up on a text on Clarence's phone
From:
a shot through the Don's binoculars...
To: a reverse angle of the Don lowering the binoculars, looking relieved.
From:
The Don dialing Tony...
To:
Close up on Tony's phone screen "Papa".
ONE SHOT:
jump to an interior shot of the L.A.P.D.
ONE SHOT:
jump back to Roy's Pacer as he glances into his rear-view mirror
ONE SHOT:
the Italians load up in their cars
ONE SHOT:
the Russian convoy pulls away from Hollywood Park...
SHOTS:
Italians;
Russians;
Vassilisa;
The Don;
SHOTS:
Clarence;
SWAT;
Vassilisa;
Roy


In episode 6 for example, we took the style shifting to a new level when I started drawing Rachel in Nathan's panels. Just as she was manipulating Tony, we were manipulating the readers with a slight change of styles.

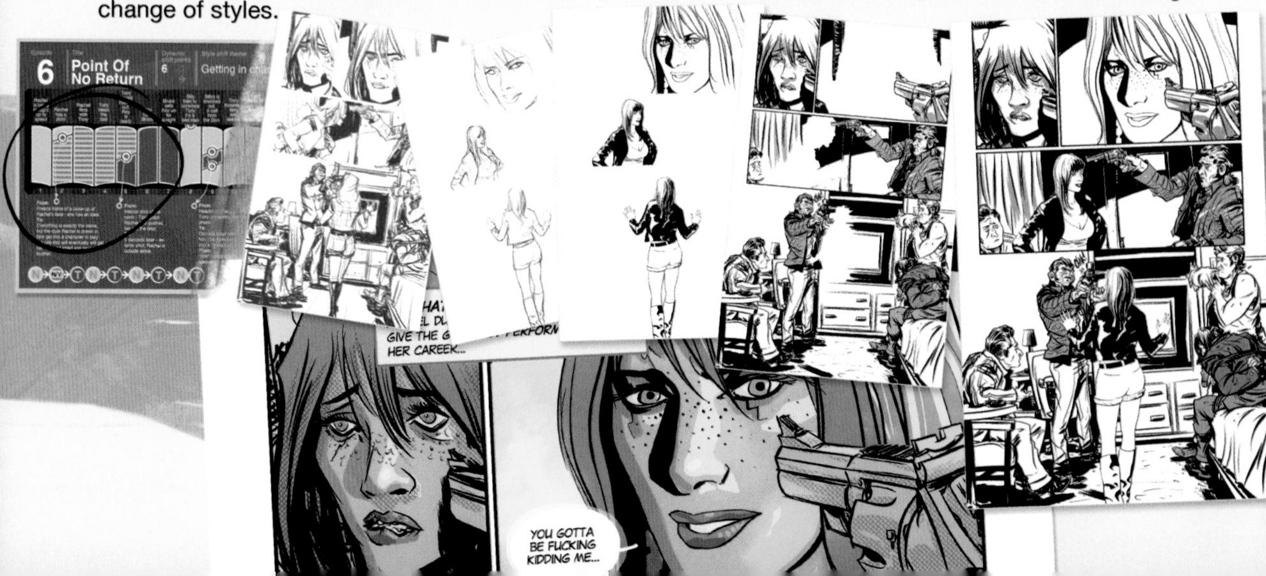

6
Point Of No Return
GIVE THE G
HER CAREER...
YOU GOTTA BE FUCKING KIDDING ME...

To make sure the story flow was consistent I did almost all of the storytelling on thumbnails leaving enough room for the artists to be creative and leave their own mark.

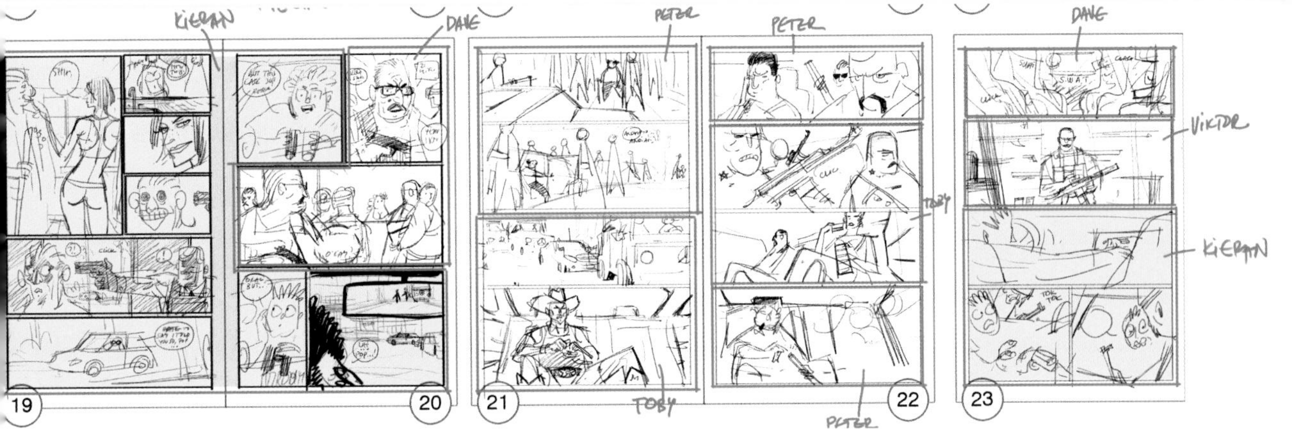
KIERAN
DAVE
PETER
PETER
DAVE
VIKTOR
TOBY
KIERAN
19
20
21
TOBY
PETER
22
23

In the end, my approach to coloring was simple and absolutely the same no matter what the inking style was. That helped unite all the different looks and give the book a cohesive voice.

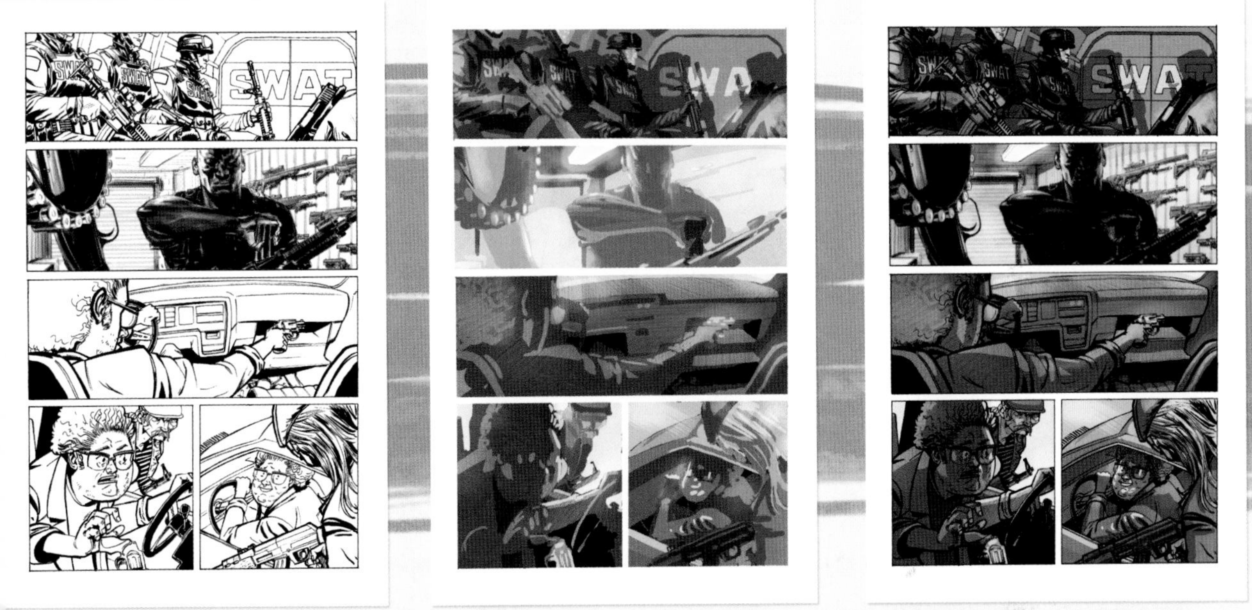
SWAT

I invited all these wonderful artists for their styles and imagination and didn't want to give them character sheets drawn by me, because I was afraid in order to stay on character they might follow my lines too closely and lose some of their uniqueness. So I decided to make miniature head sculptures of the main 12 characters that they could use as reference and re-interpret in their own styles.

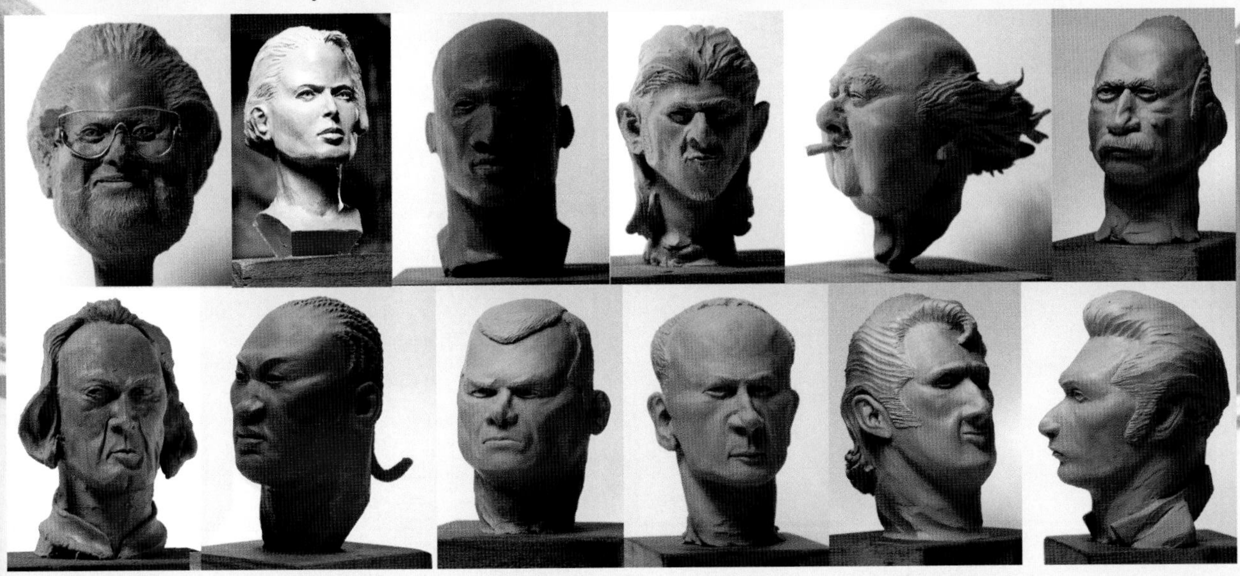

There were a few locations in the story we would be using a lot and it was important they always be consistent. I used Sketchup to design the environments and make them work for the story. It was also very helpful when planning the shots and setting up the "cameras" for the storytelling. I even used them as basis for storyboarding some of the complicated scenes in order to communicate to the artists what was going on and where a character is at a certain time, so when they draw their panels, they all stay consistent and characters and objects don't move around when a style shifts.

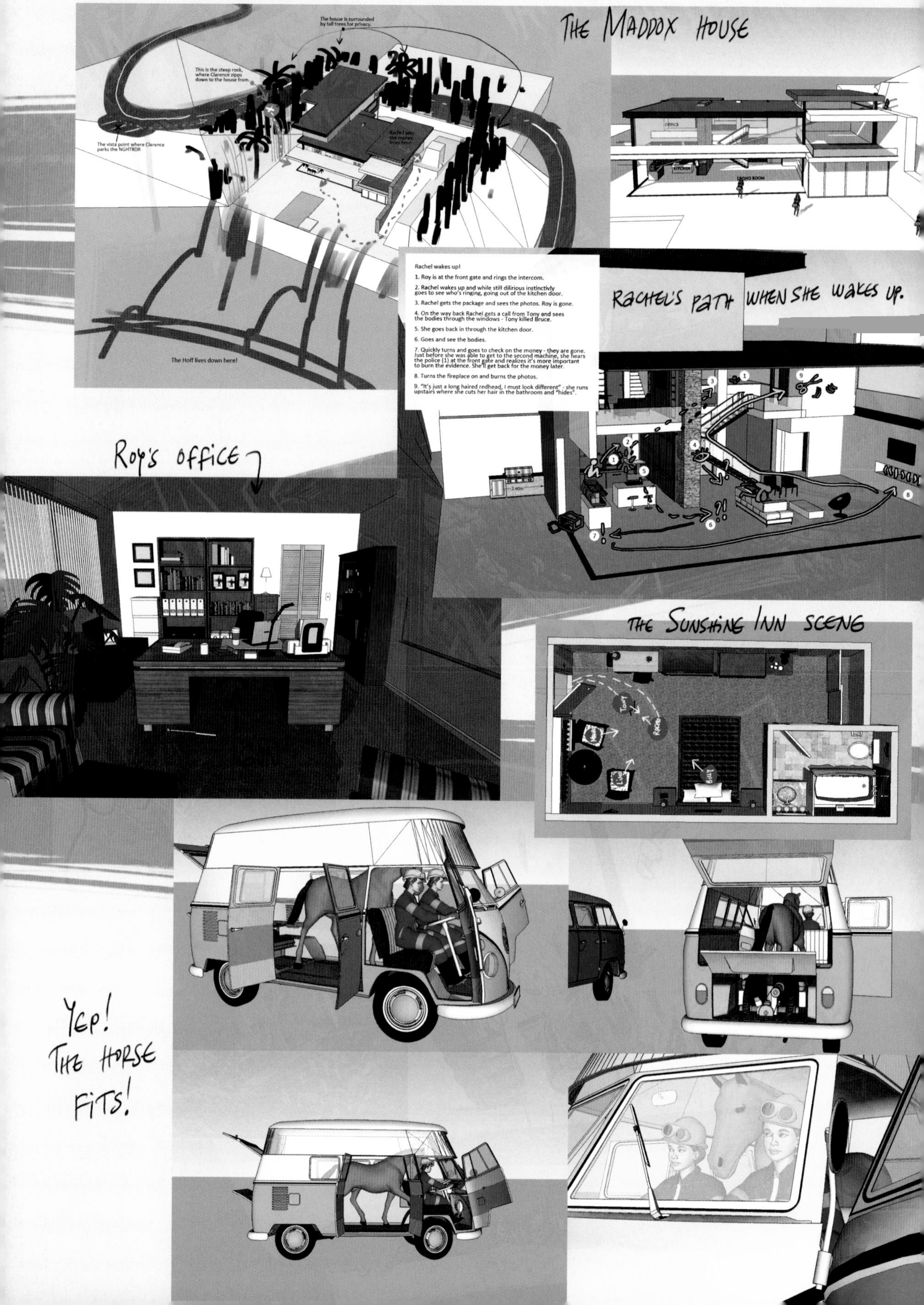

THE MADDOX HOUSE
The house is surrounded by tall trees for privacy.
This is the steep rock, where Clarence zipps down to the house from.
The vista point where Clarence parks the NGHTRDR
Rachel sees the money from here
The Hoff lives down here!
OFFICE
KITCHEN
LIVING ROOM
RACHEL'S PATH WHEN SHE WAKES UP.
Rachel wakes up!
1. Roy is at the front gate and rings the intercom.
2. Rachel wakes up and while still dilirious instinctivly goes to see who's ringing, going out of the kitchen door.
3. Rachel gets the package and sees the photos. Roy is gone.
4. On the way back Rachel gets a call from Tony and sees the bodies through the windows - Tony killed Bruce.
5. She goes back in through the kitchen door.
6. Goes and see the bodies.
7. Quickly turns and goes to check on the money - they are gone. Just before she was able to get to the second machine, she hears the police (1) at the front gate and realizes it's more important to burn the evidence. She'll get back for the money later.
8. Turns the fireplace on and burns the photos.
9. "It's just a long haired redhead, I must look different" - she runs upstairs where she cuts her hair in the bathroom and "hides".
ROY'S OFFICE
THE SUNSHINE INN SCENE
Tony
Rachel
YEP! THE HORSE FITS!

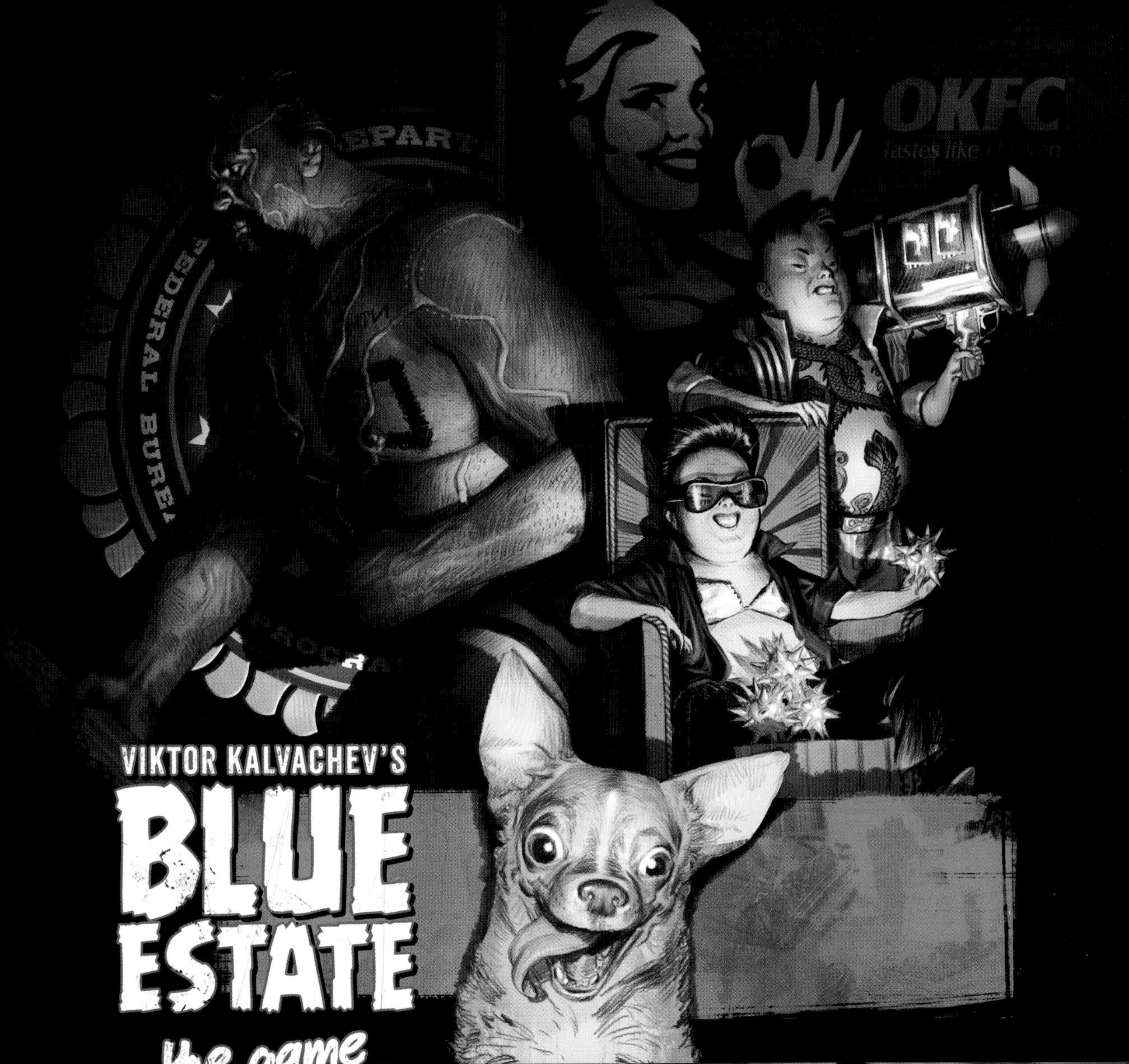
OKFC

VIKTOR KALVACHEV'S

# BLUE ESTATE

## the game

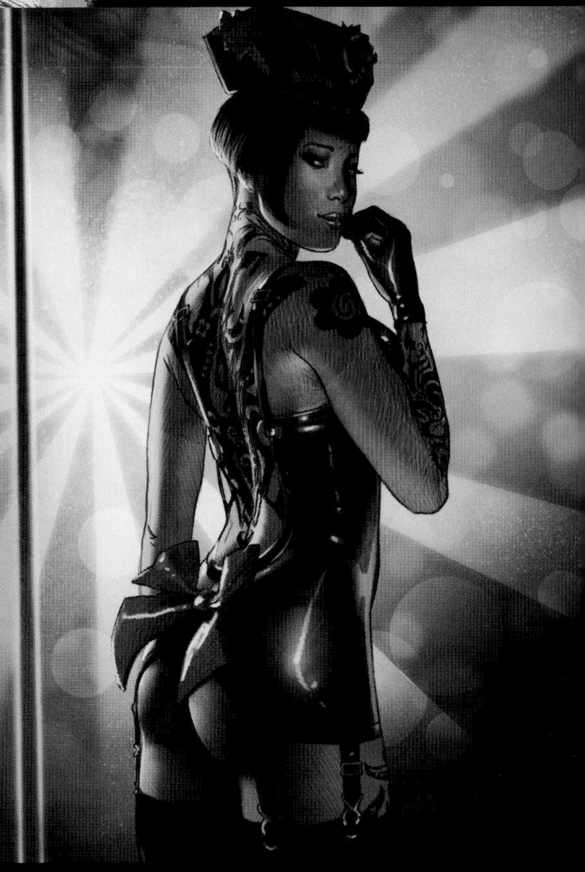

Before the comic was even finished we decided it was a great world for gameplay and started working with a small French team on what was to become Blue Estate the Game. We chose to do an old school rail shooter as we loved that genre and it also provided us with the best possible control over time and camera angles in order to try and have jokes. The theme was simple – ridicule the typical male perception of the gangster world and everything in it, bringing it completely over the top and not taking ourselves seriously. The result is hopefully scandalous and entertaining. For the PS4 version we used the gyroscopic features of the dual shock controller, turning it into a light gun with a simple L1/UP re-center at any time.

The story once again is told by Roy Devine Jr., who this time is hired by Cherry Popz to find the love of her life, Vincent, who went missing. Roy quickly pulls us into Cherry's world introduces us to Tony Luciano. In the game you play as Tony in 4 levels and Clarence, in the other 3 (with critical intel by provided by Lino and Mauro).

For info and videos on the game, go to:

**www.BlueEstateTheGame.com**

I was exploring a visual style for the two big cinematic sequences at the beginning and end of the game and my first version of Cherry was very stylized, but in the end I went with a much more realistic look and chose to color it in a rough pencil/pastel look.

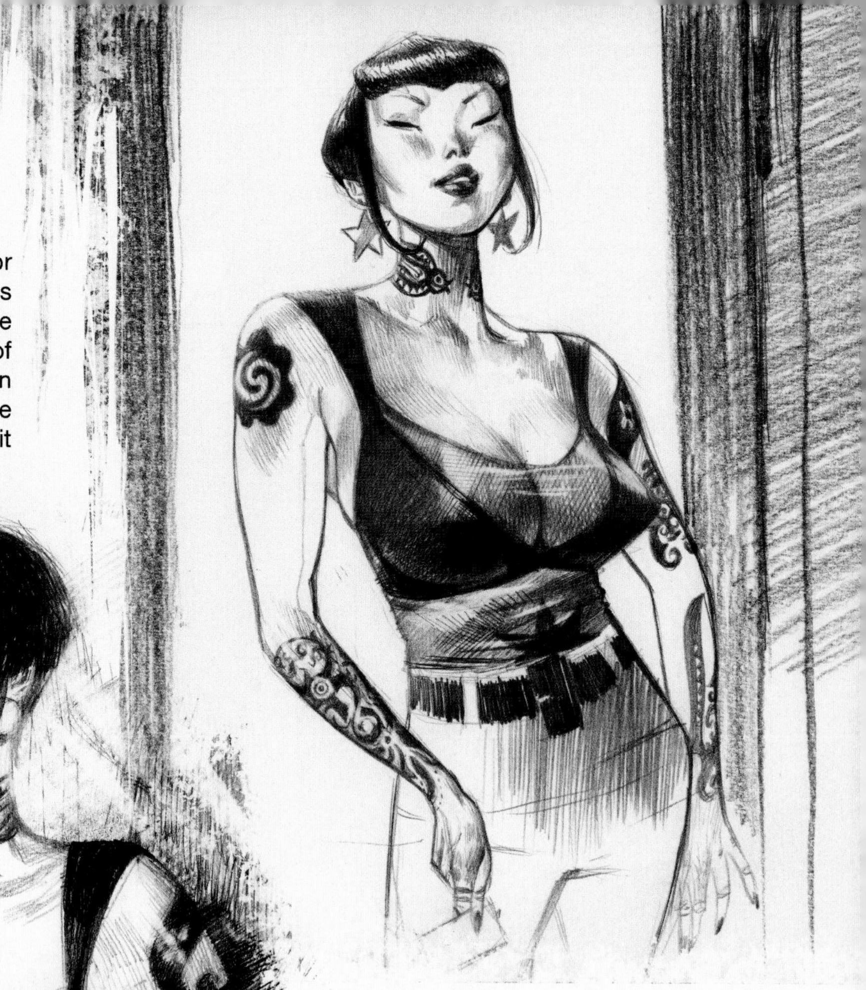

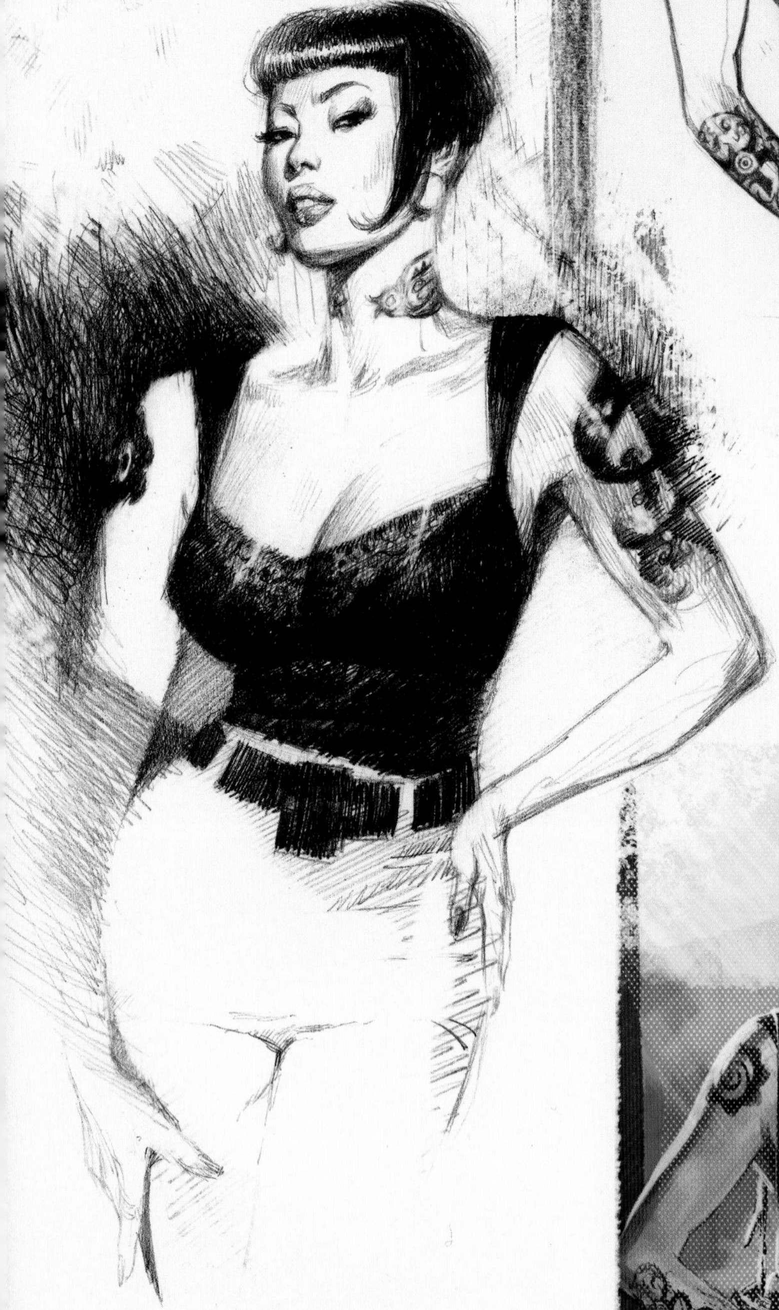

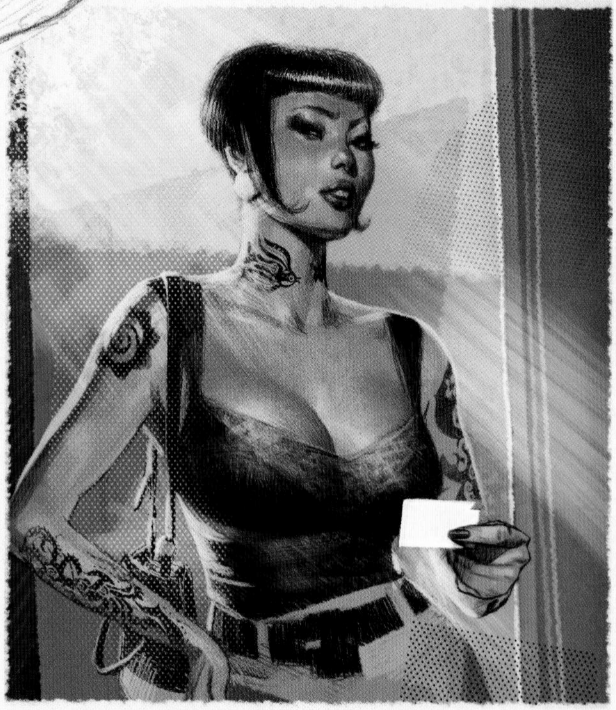

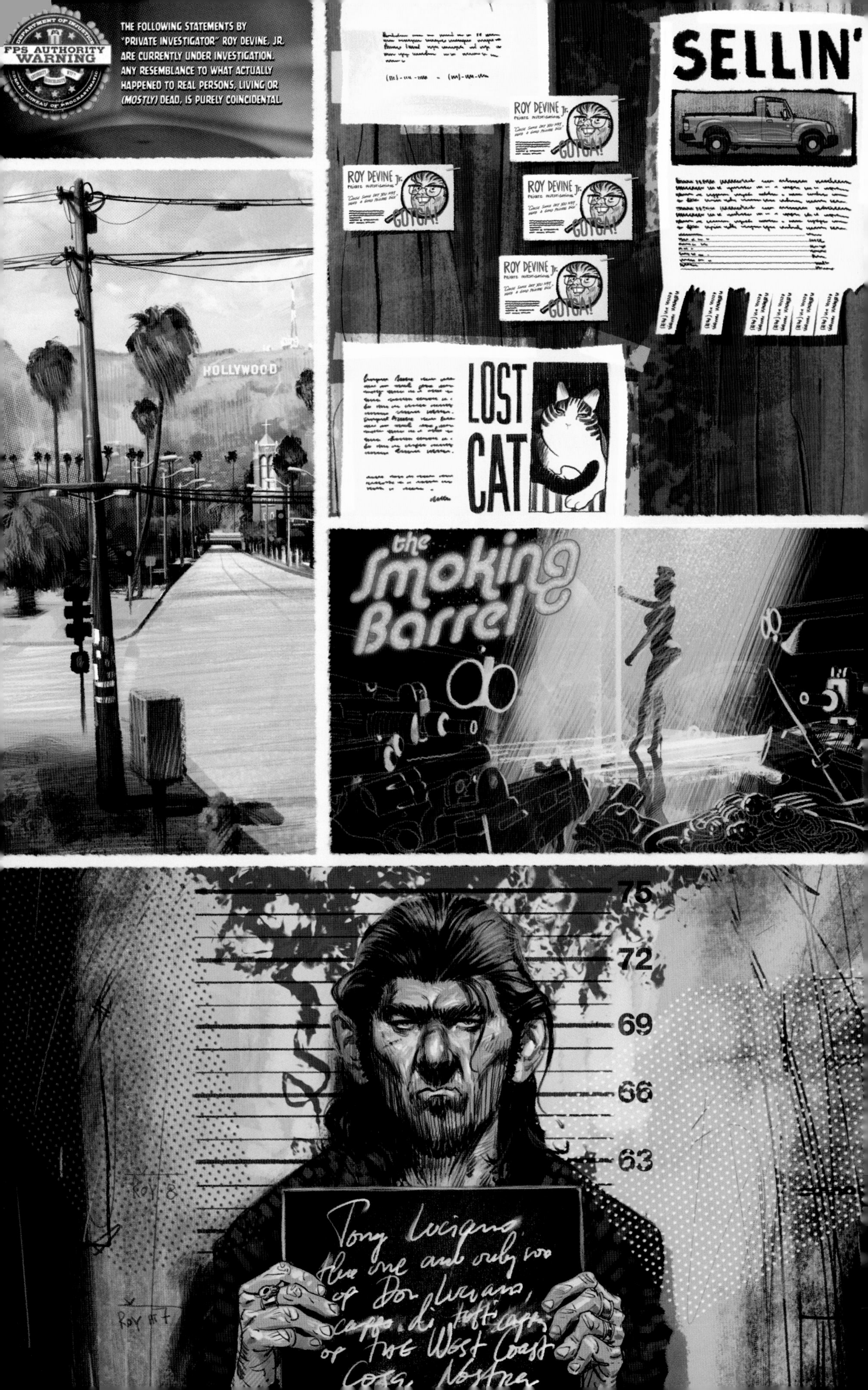
DEPARTMENT OF INJUSTICE
FPS AUTHORITY WARNING
THE FOLLOWING STATEMENTS BY "PRIVATE INVESTIGATOR" ROY DEVINE, JR. ARE CURRENTLY UNDER INVESTIGATION. ANY RESEMBLANCE TO WHAT ACTUALLY HAPPENED TO REAL PERSONS, LIVING OR (MOSTLY) DEAD, IS PURELY COINCIDENTAL.
HOLLYWOOD
ROY DEVINE Jr.
PRIVATE INVESTIGATIONS
GOTCHA!
SELLIN'
LOST CAT
the Smoking Barrel
75
72
69
66
63
Tony Luciano,
of Don Luciano,
of the West Coast
Cosa Nostra

There was no way we could shift the art style of a video game in the middle of gameplay, but I wanted to somehow bring back the iconic elements of Blue Estate. Luckily I found a way through the short level intro cinematics, where Roy Jr. updates us on the progress of his case through Polaroid shots. The team of artists was inspiring and I was really happy with the results.

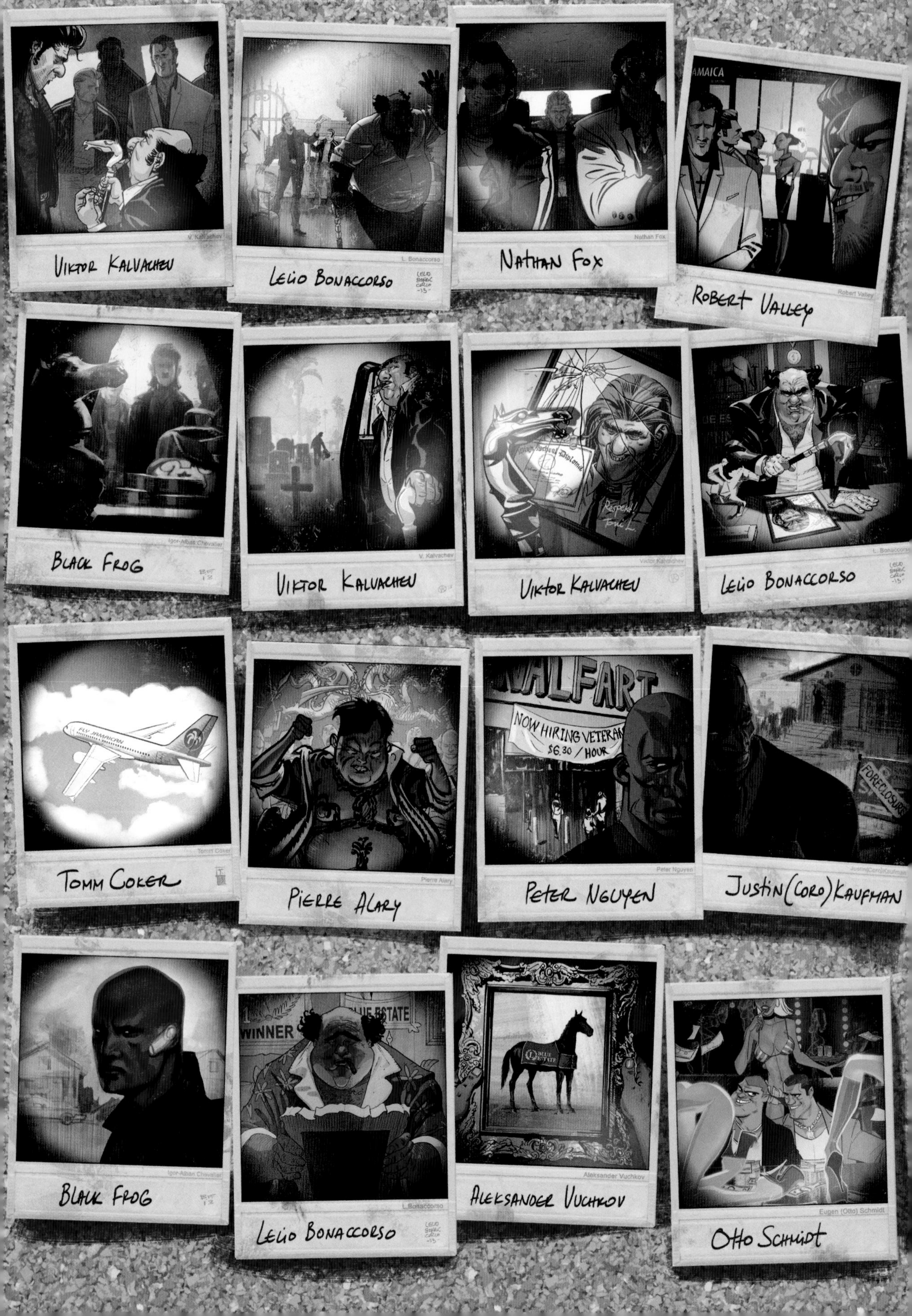
VIKTOR KALVACHEV
LELIO BONACCORSO
NATHAN FOX
ROBERT VALLEY
BLACK FROG
VIKTOR KALVACHEV
VIKTOR KALVACHEV
LELIO BONACCORSO
TOMM COKER
PIERRE ALARY
PETER NGUYEN
JUSTIN (CORO) KAUFMAN
BLACK FROG
LELIO BONACCORSO
ALEKSANDER VUCHKOV
OTTO SCHMIDT

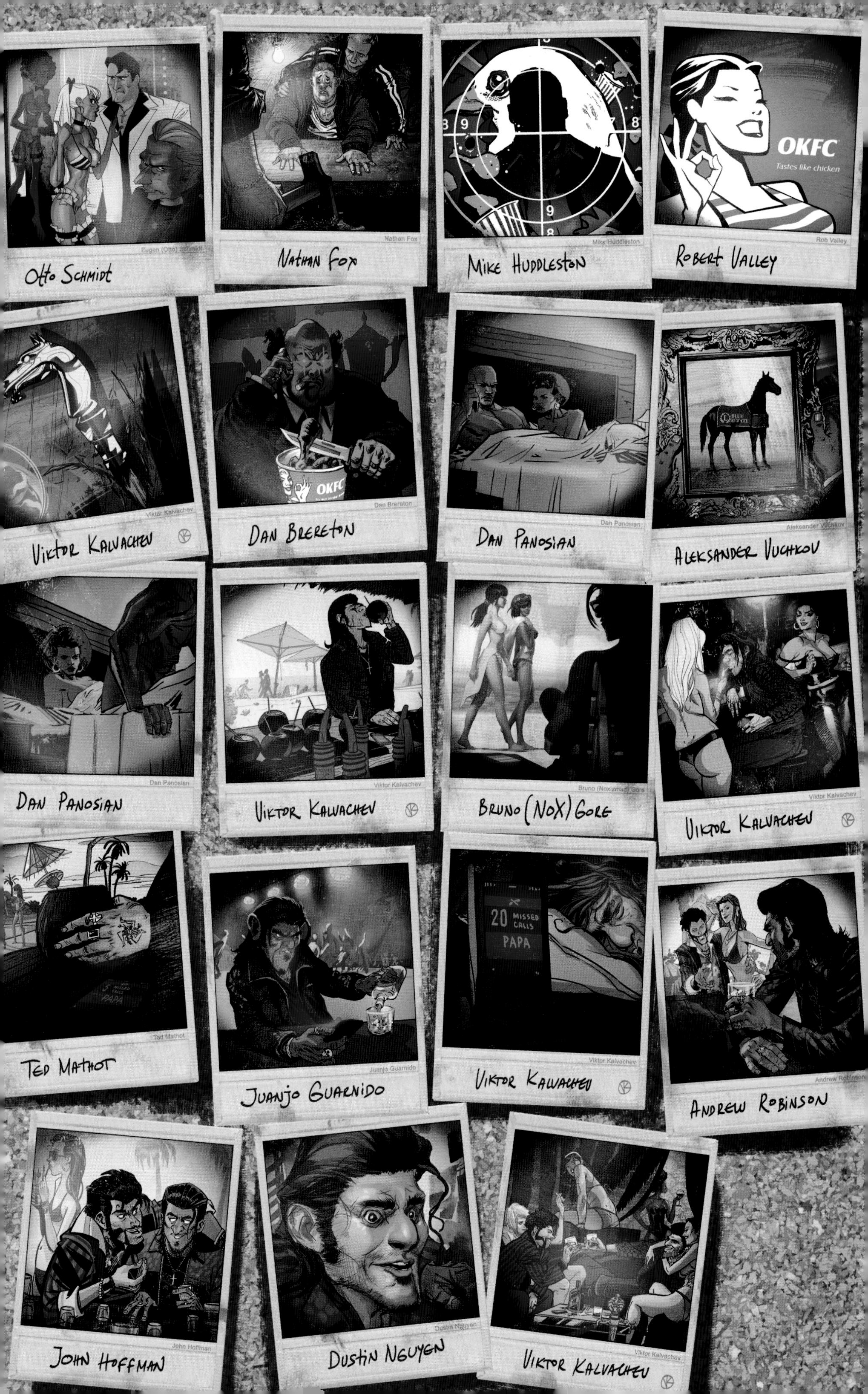

Eugen (Otto) Schmidt
Otto Schmidt
Nathan Fox
Nathan Fox
OKFC
Tastes like chicken
Mike Huddleston
Mike Huddleston
Rob Valley
Robert Valley
Viktor Kalvachev
Viktor Kalvachev
OKFC
Dan Brereton
Dan Brereton
Dan Panosian
Dan Panosian
Aleksander Vuchkov
Aleksander Vuchkov
Dan Panosian
Dan Panosian
Viktor Kalvachev
Viktor Kalvachev
Bruno (Noxizmad) Gore
Bruno (NoX) Gore
Viktor Kalvachev
Viktor Kalvachev
Ted Mathot
Ted Mathot
Juanjo Guarnido
Juanjo Guarnido
20 MISSED CALLS
PAPA
Viktor Kalvachev
Viktor Kalvachev
Andrew Robinson
Andrew Robinson
John Hoffman
John Hoffman
Dustin Nguyen
Dustin Nguyen
Viktor Kalvachev
Viktor Kalvachev

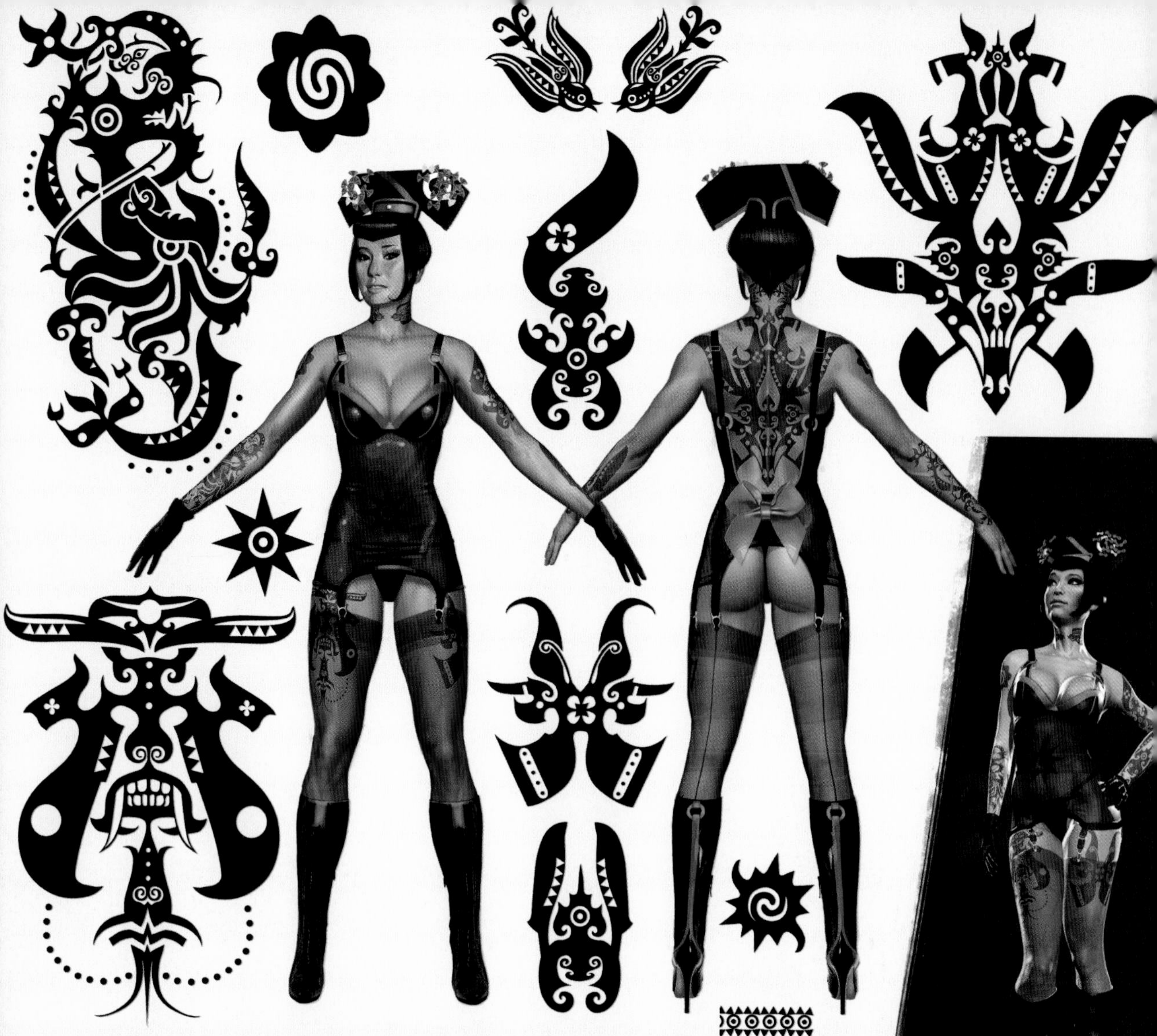

**Cherry** is the story's "Helen of Troy" and is at its Heart. We had to make sure we stay true to her character and show her at her best. The pole dancing motion capture turned out so well, we decided to have her animated in the main menu all the time.

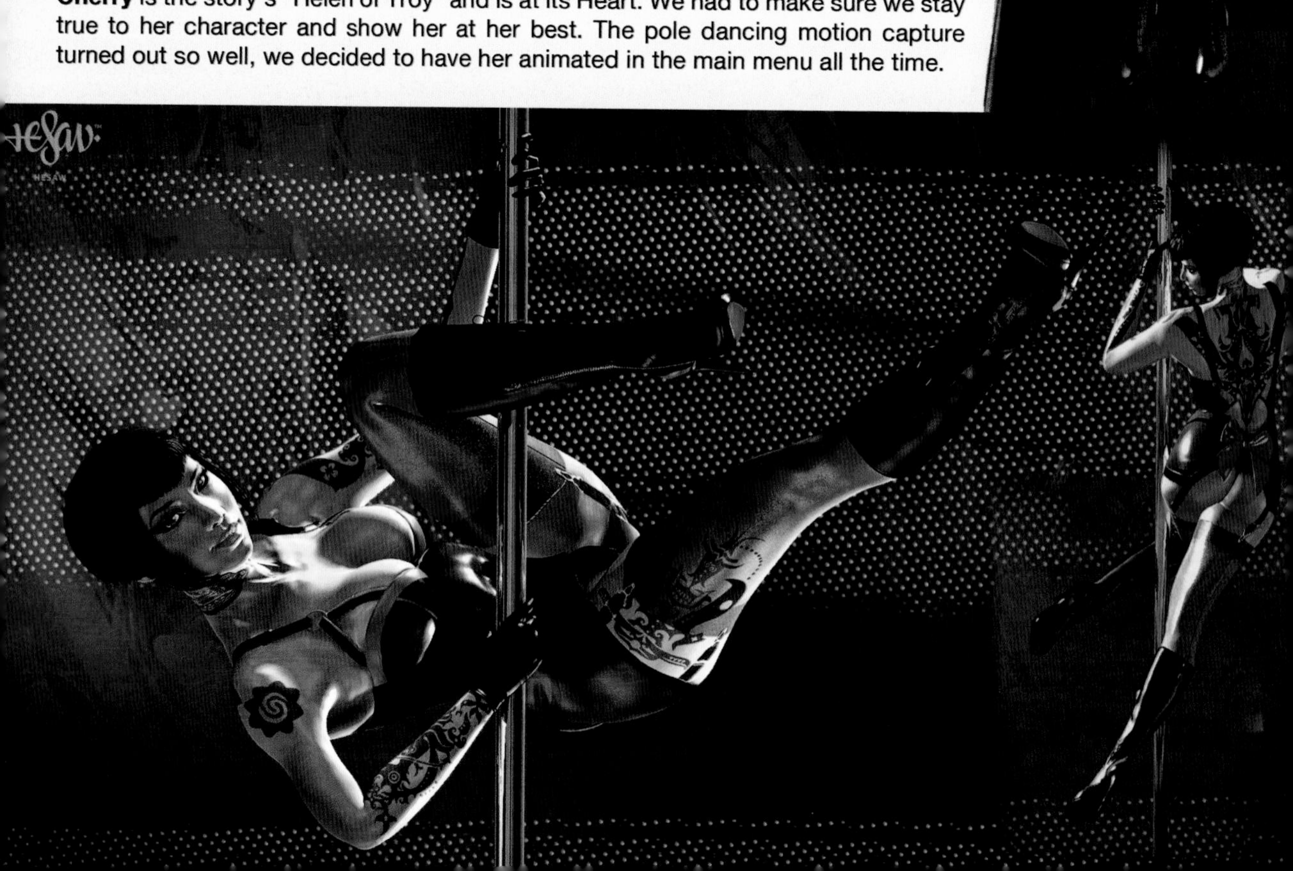

**Kim Bong Sik** and **Jin Bong Sik** are evil twins, who own the luxurious club THE TWIN DRAGON and are bosses of one of the strongest criminal organizations in LA – the Sik Bros Gang. They kidnapped Cherry to work in their club and when Tony goes to get her back, everything goes sideways…as usual. Kim has a designer white bra fetish and an extensive collection in his walking closet; and Jin has a golden rocket launcher which always misfires. Kim Sik fights Tony in the first boss level, while Jin tries in the fourth, but fails miserably.

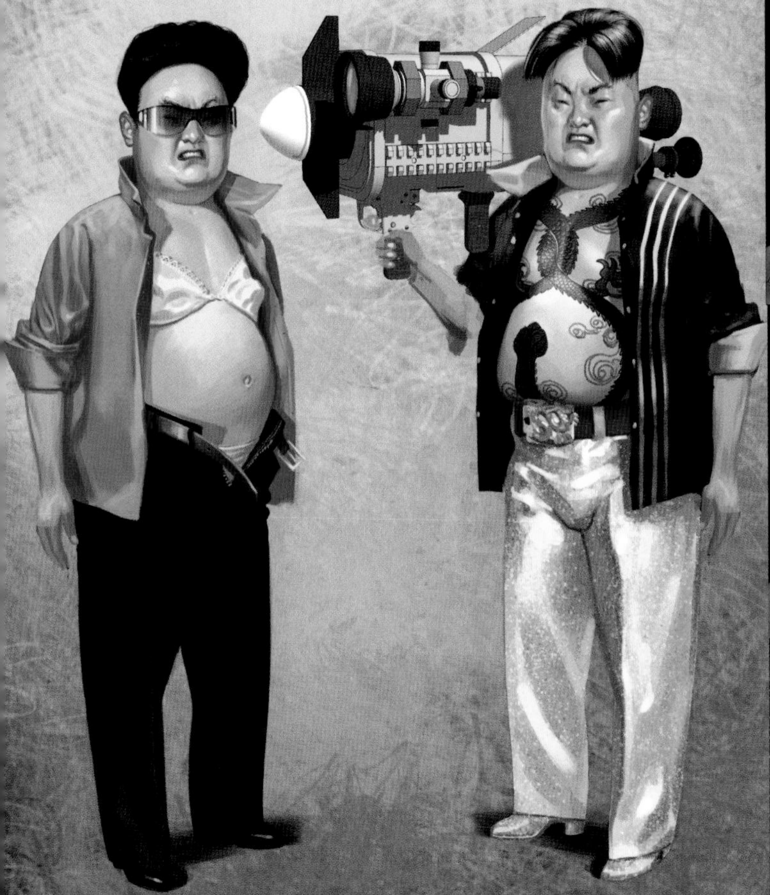

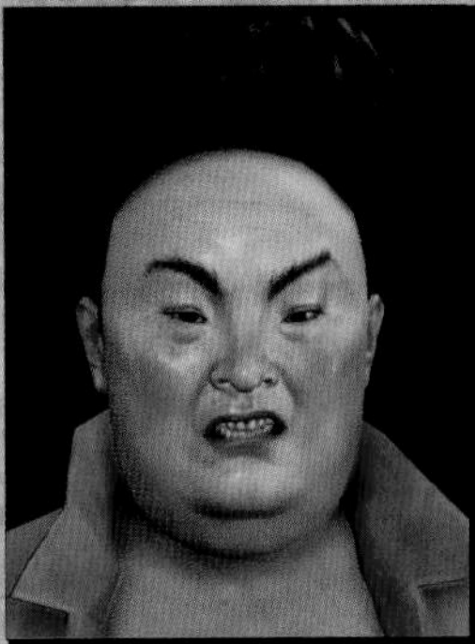

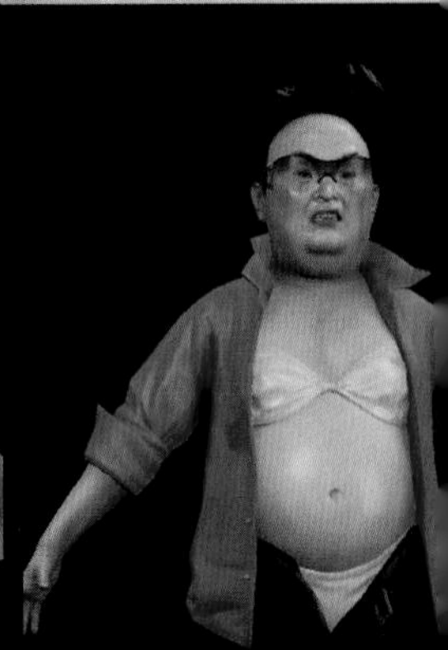

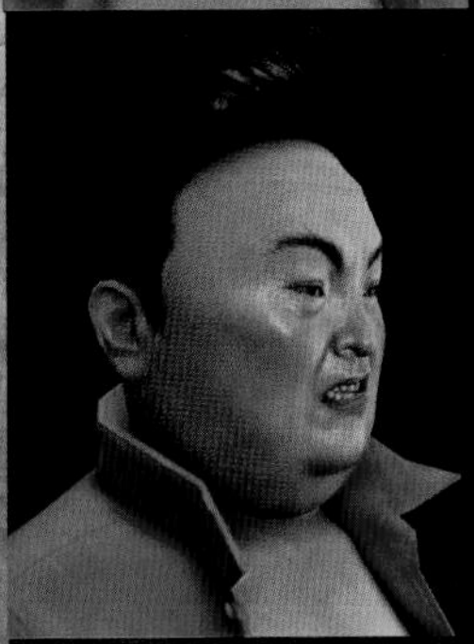

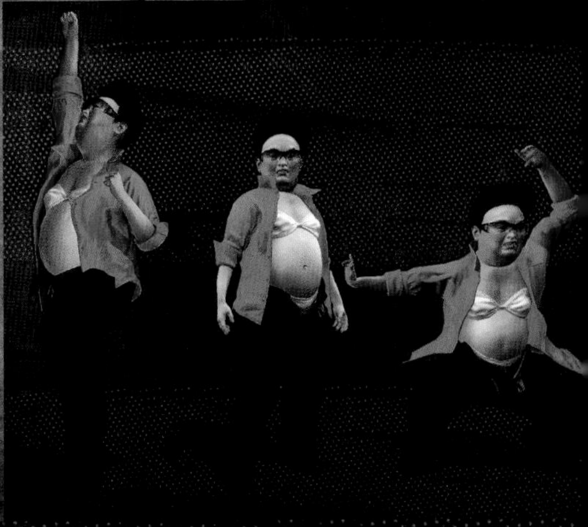

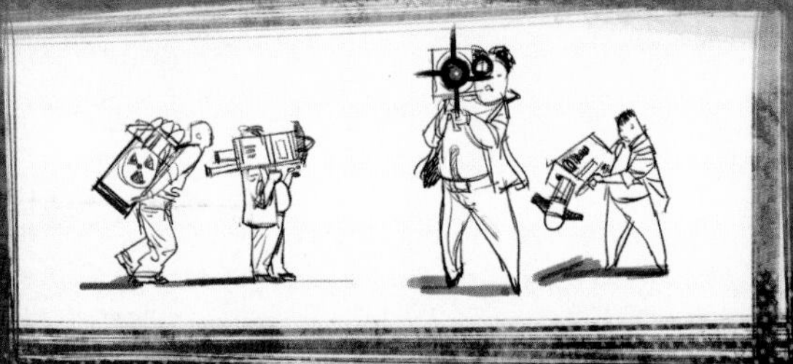

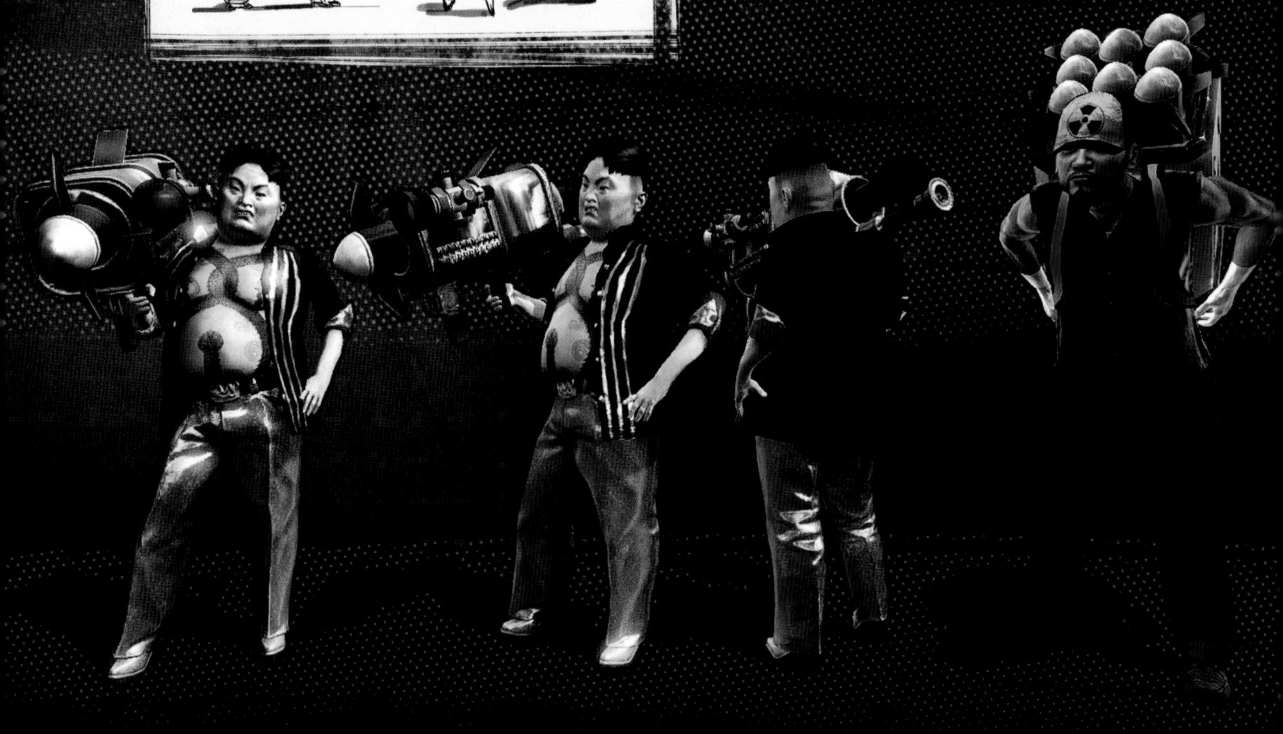

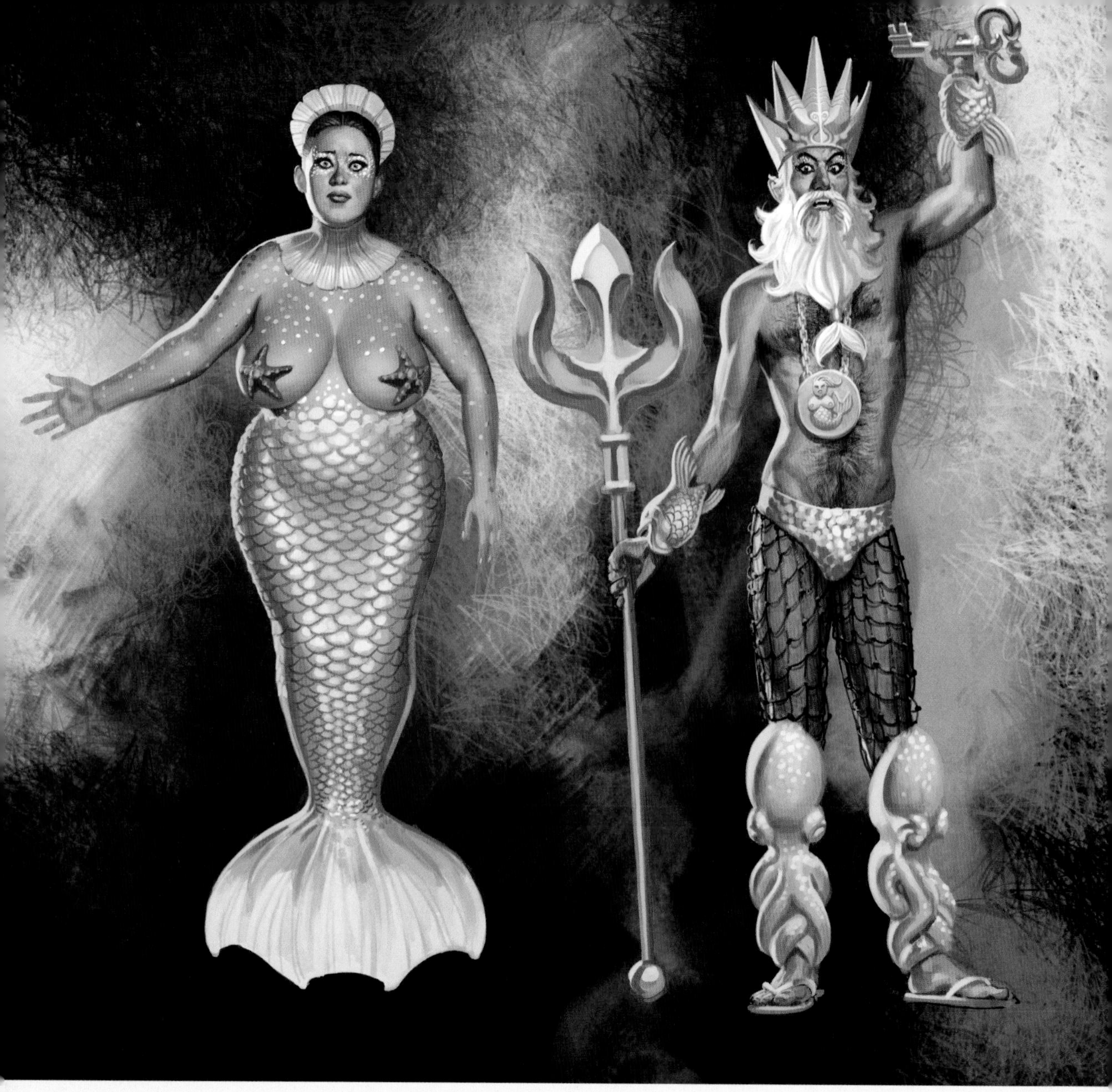

The original idea was to have a burlesque number by these two characters, but due to time and budget we had to "fire" Poseidon. He was supposed to present the Amazing Goldfish as one that can hold her breath for 5 minutes, while locked in a fish tank with no access to air. Just as he finishes the presentation and the mermaid dives in, he locks the fish tank with a giant lock and a golden key and starts counting. Unfortunately, the shooting starts and Poseidon falls dead on the ground, leaving the mermaid with no chance of survival. The sexy stunt becomes deadly and it's up to Tony to break the fish tank and save her before the time runs out. It was fun, but too expensive to do, so we decided to turn the Amazing Goldfish into "Bertha Kowalski, formerly employed by the State Senate, not good at swimming" and have her gasping for air in the middle of the battle, trying to get out. At the end, Tony does free her and she flaps away afraid but unharmed.

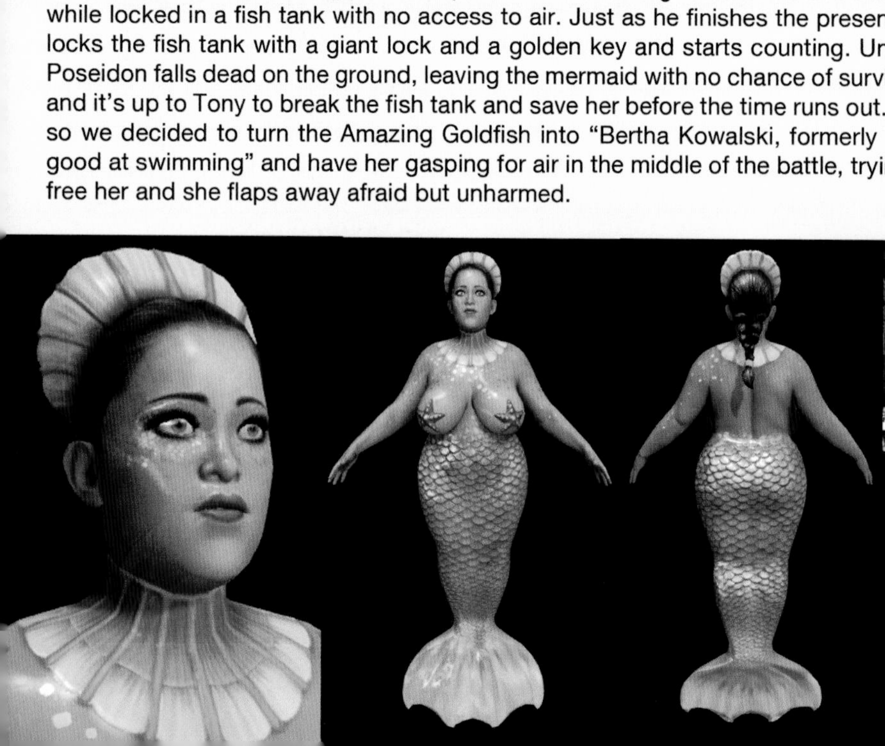

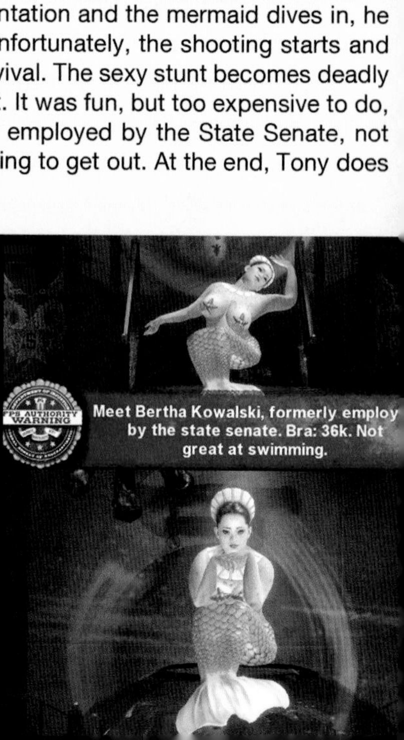
FPS AUTHORITY
WARNING
Meet Bertha Kowalski, formerly employ
by the state senate. Bra: 36k. Not
great at swimming.

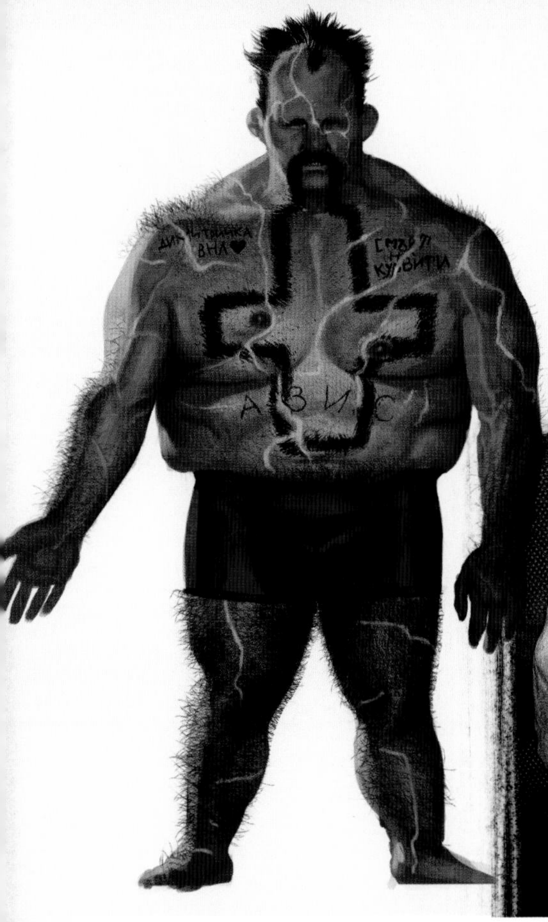

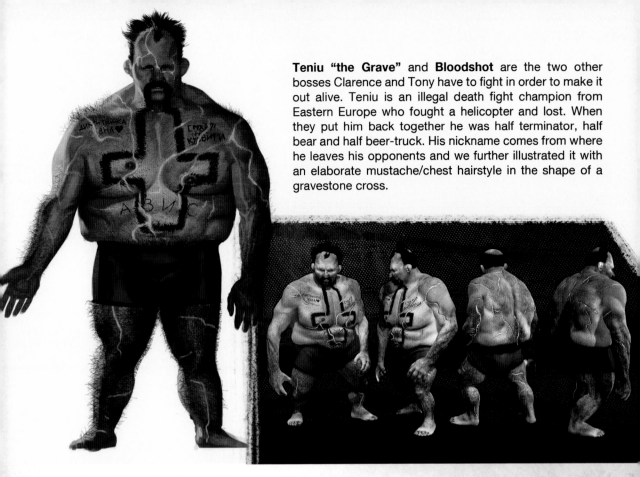

**Teniu "the Grave"** and **Bloodshot** are the two other bosses Clarence and Tony have to fight in order to make it out alive. Teniu is an illegal death fight champion from Eastern Europe who fought a helicopter and lost. When they put him back together he was half terminator, half bear and half beer-truck. His nickname comes from where he leaves his opponents and we further illustrated it with an elaborate mustache/chest hairstyle in the shape of a gravestone cross.

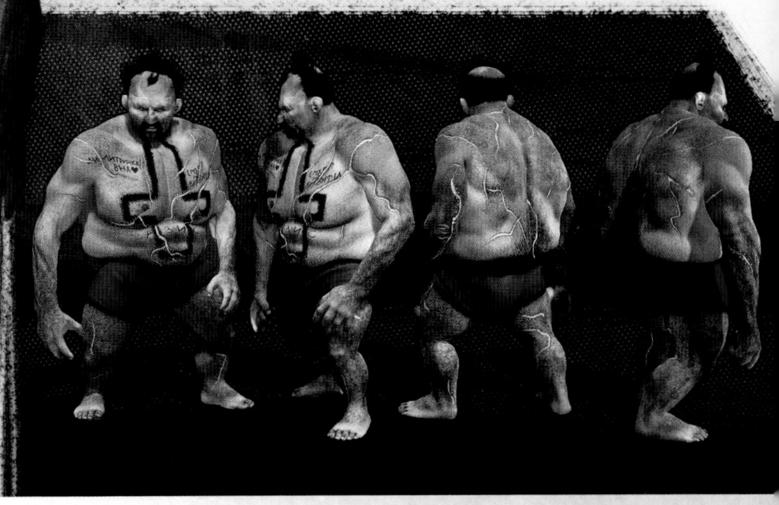

**Bloodshot** is a vicious Jamaican mob boss (and the toughest final boss in the game), whose unfortunate nickname makes everyone think he's high, his retinas are red because of albinism. Tony steals the world's most valuable "medicinal" plant from Bloodshot's personal reserve and gets himself chased by the Bloodshot gang. It wasn't entirely his fault however as his new partner, Alyosha the Lion, led him to believe they were on a field trip to gather seeds from an unique bio-fuel plant that will make them both legally rich.

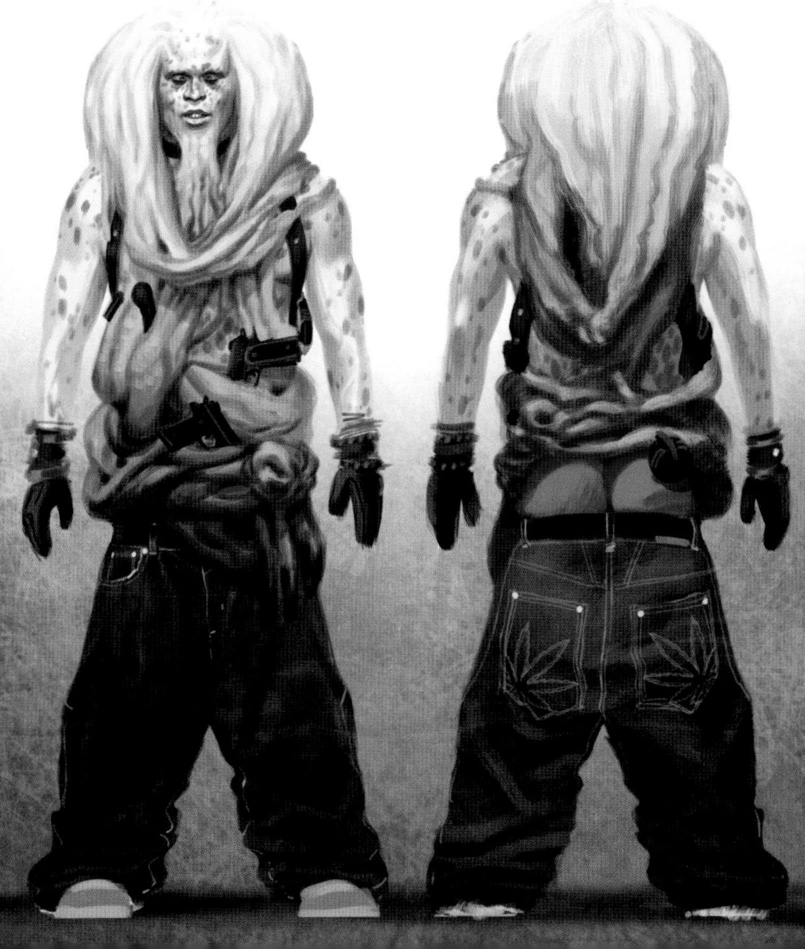

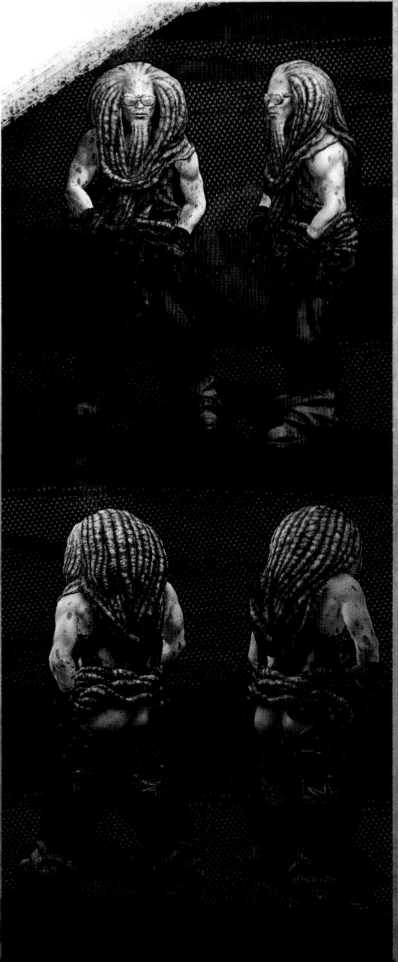

You just saw the end of **Alyosha** the lion in the book, but in the game, his relationship with Tony is just beginning.

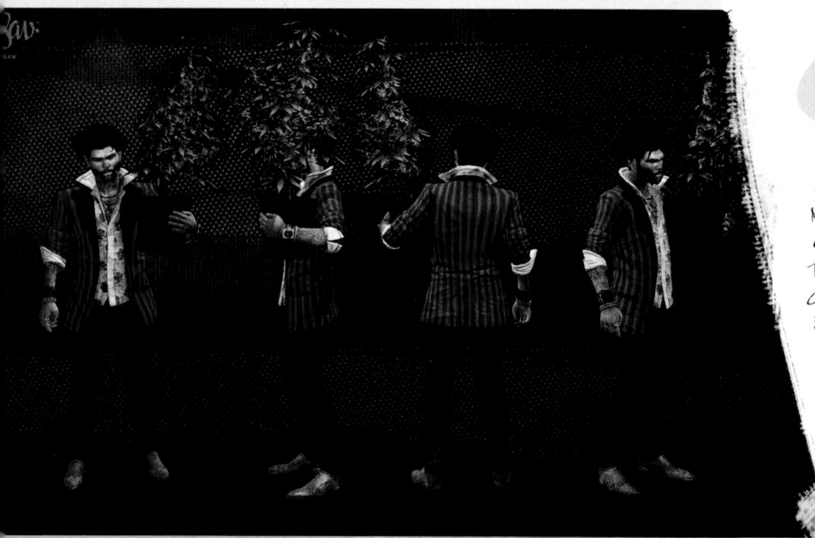

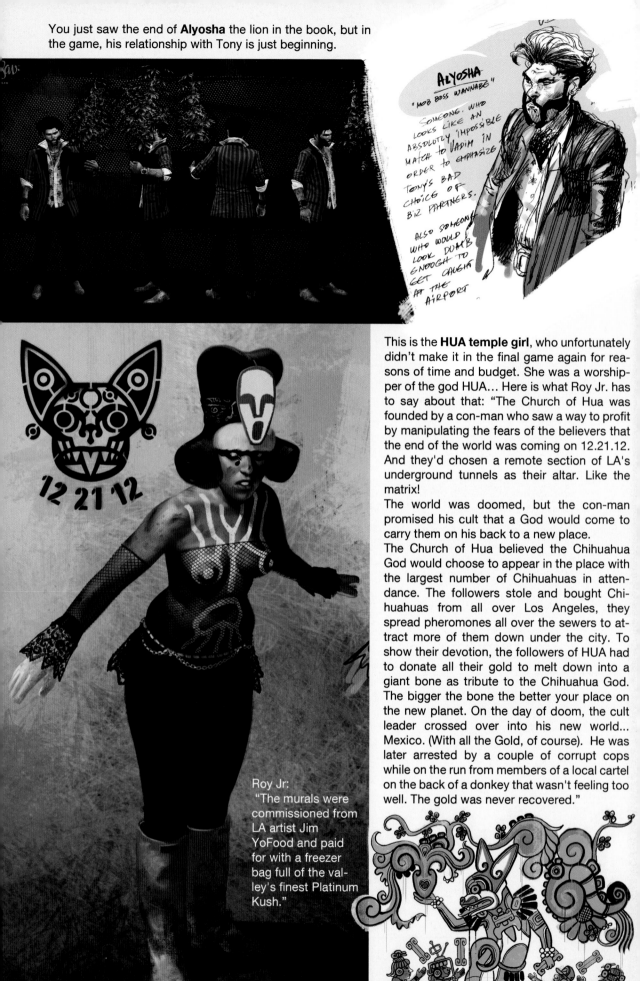

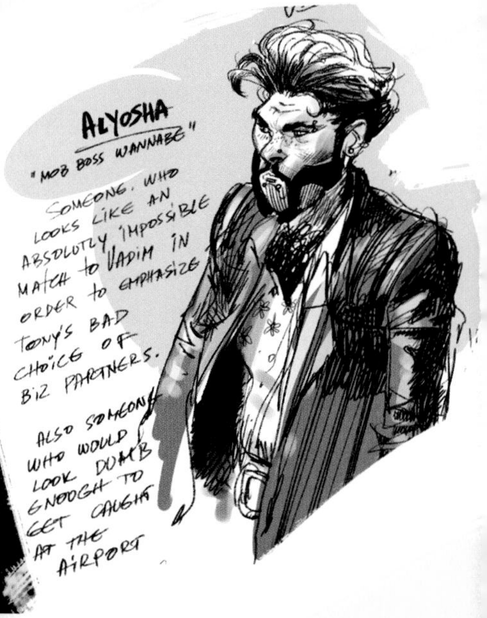
ALYOSHA
"MOB BOSS WANNABE"
SOMEONE. WHO
LOOKS LIKE AN
ABSOLUTLY 'IMPOSSIBLE
MATCH to VADIM IN
ORDER to EMPHASIZE
TONY'S BAD
CHOICE OF
BIZ PARTNERS.
ALSO SOMEONE
WHO WOULD
LOOK DUMB
ENOUGH TO
GET CAUGHT
AT THE
AIRPORT

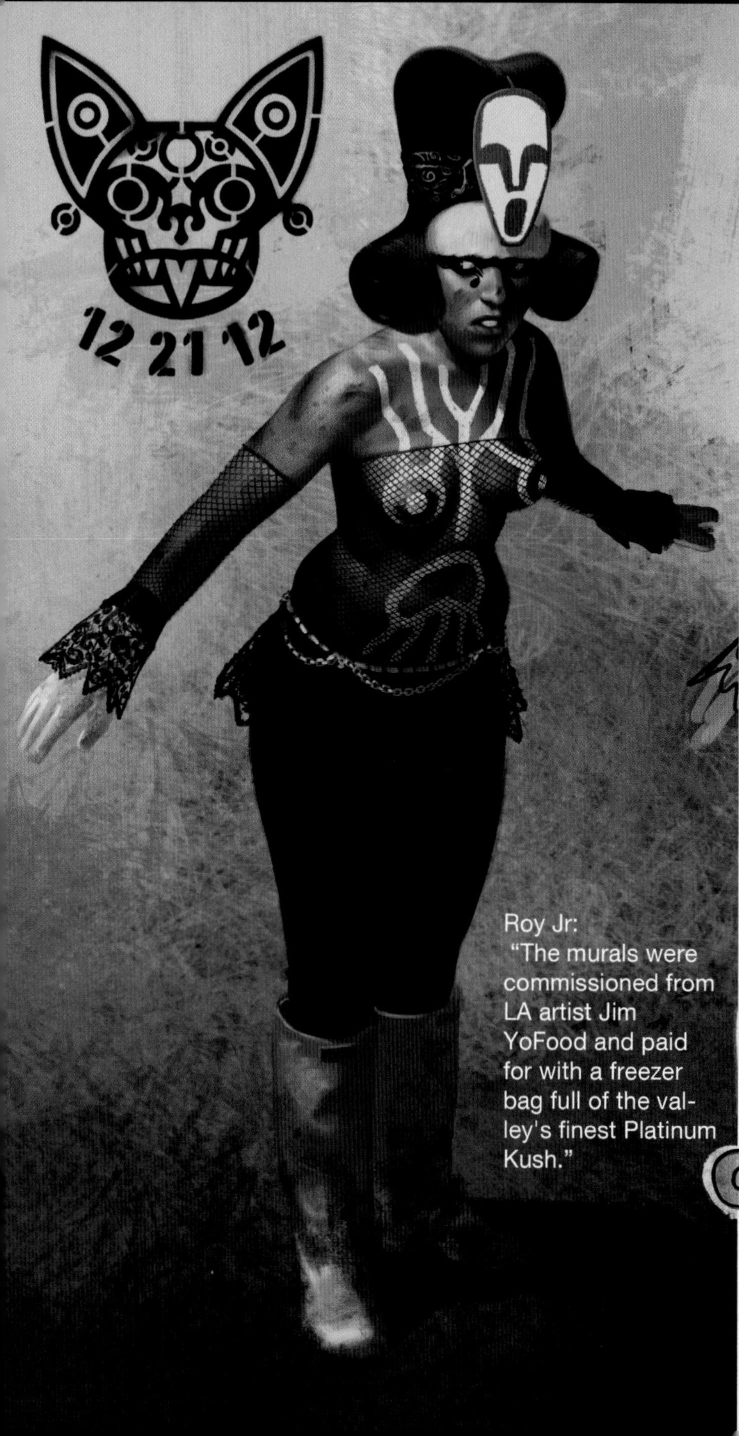
12 21 12

Roy Jr:
"The murals were commissioned from LA artist Jim YoFood and paid for with a freezer bag full of the valley's finest Platinum Kush."

This is the **HUA temple girl**, who unfortunately didn't make it in the final game again for reasons of time and budget. She was a worshipper of the god HUA… Here is what Roy Jr. has to say about that: "The Church of Hua was founded by a con-man who saw a way to profit by manipulating the fears of the believers that the end of the world was coming on 12.21.12. And they'd chosen a remote section of LA's underground tunnels as their altar. Like the matrix!

The world was doomed, but the con-man promised his cult that a God would come to carry them on his back to a new place.

The Church of Hua believed the Chihuahua God would choose to appear in the place with the largest number of Chihuahuas in attendance. The followers stole and bought Chihuahuas from all over Los Angeles, they spread pheromones all over the sewers to attract more of them down under the city. To show their devotion, the followers of HUA had to donate all their gold to melt down into a giant bone as tribute to the Chihuahua God. The bigger the bone the better your place on the new planet. On the day of doom, the cult leader crossed over into his new world... Mexico. (With all the Gold, of course). He was later arrested by a couple of corrupt cops while on the run from members of a local cartel on the back of a donkey that wasn't feeling too well. The gold was never recovered."

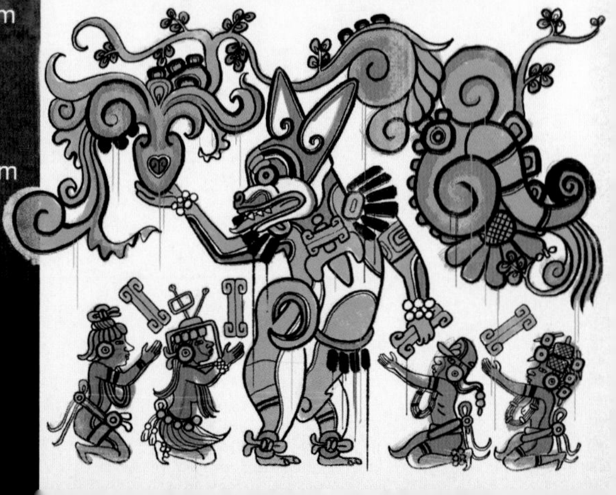

On the next few pages you will see the in-game Level cover art; concepts and final in-game screenshots from each of the 7 levels of Blue Estate the Game.

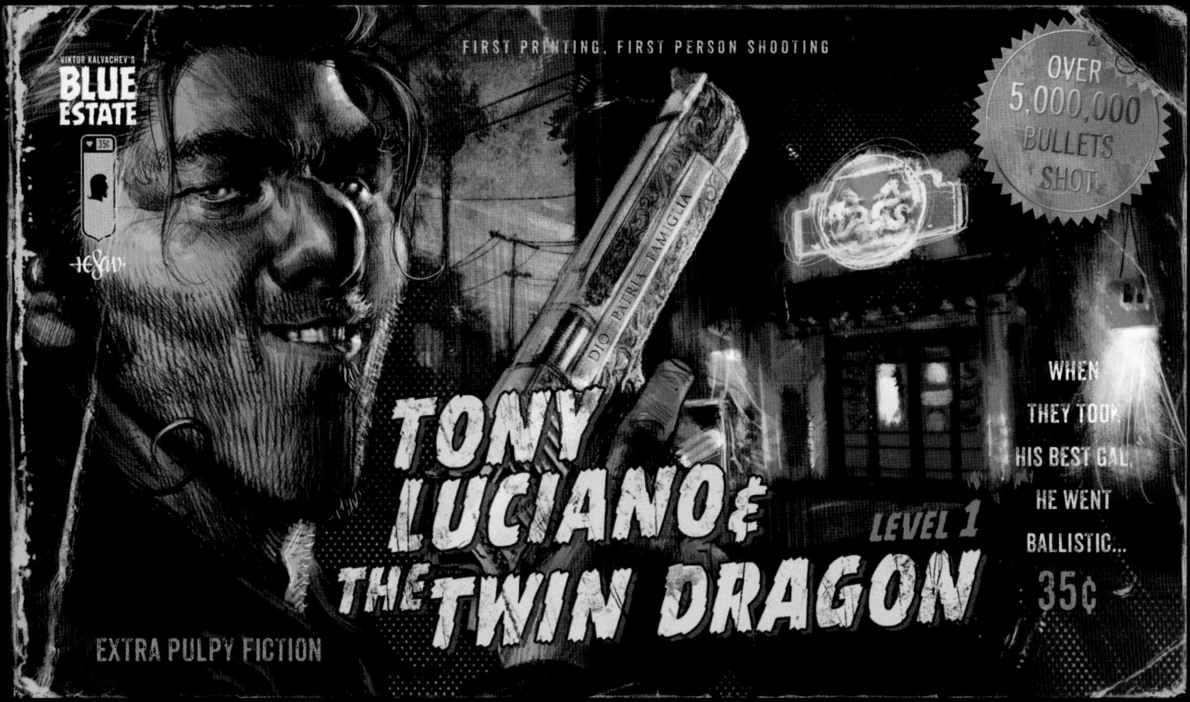
FIRST PRINTING, FIRST PERSON SHOOTING
VIKTOR KALVACHEV'S
BLUE ESTATE
35¢
OVER 5,000,000 BULLETS SHOT
DIO PATRIA FAMIGLIA
TONY LUCIANO & THE TWIN DRAGON
LEVEL 1
WHEN THEY TOOK HIS BEST GAL, HE WENT BALLISTIC...
35¢
EXTRA PULPY FICTION

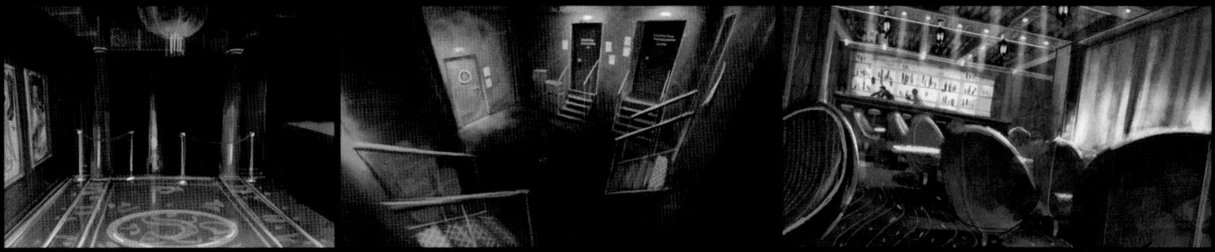

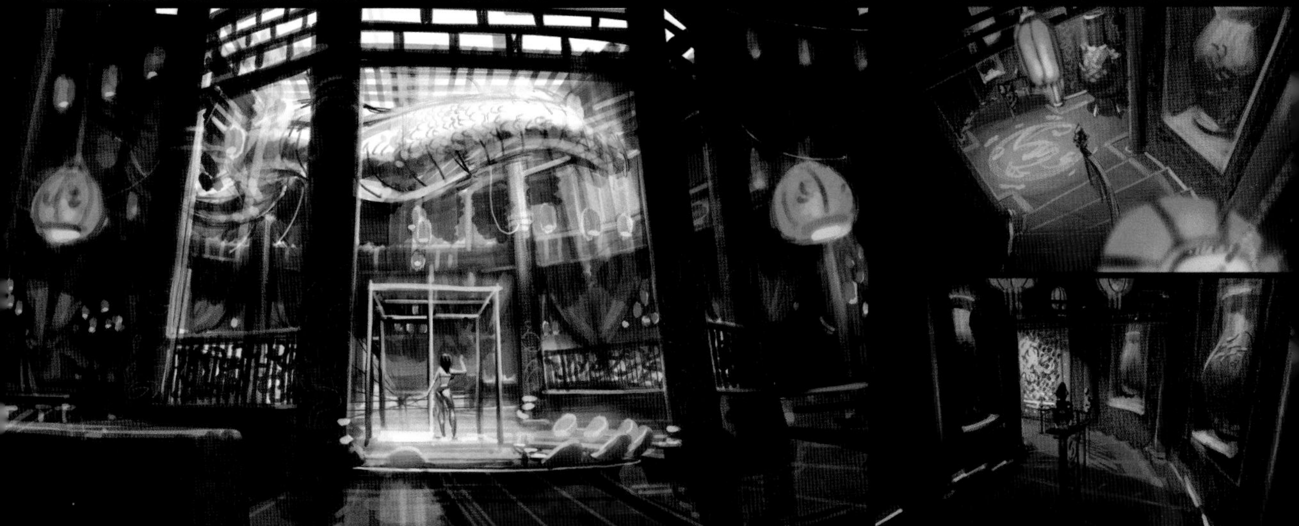

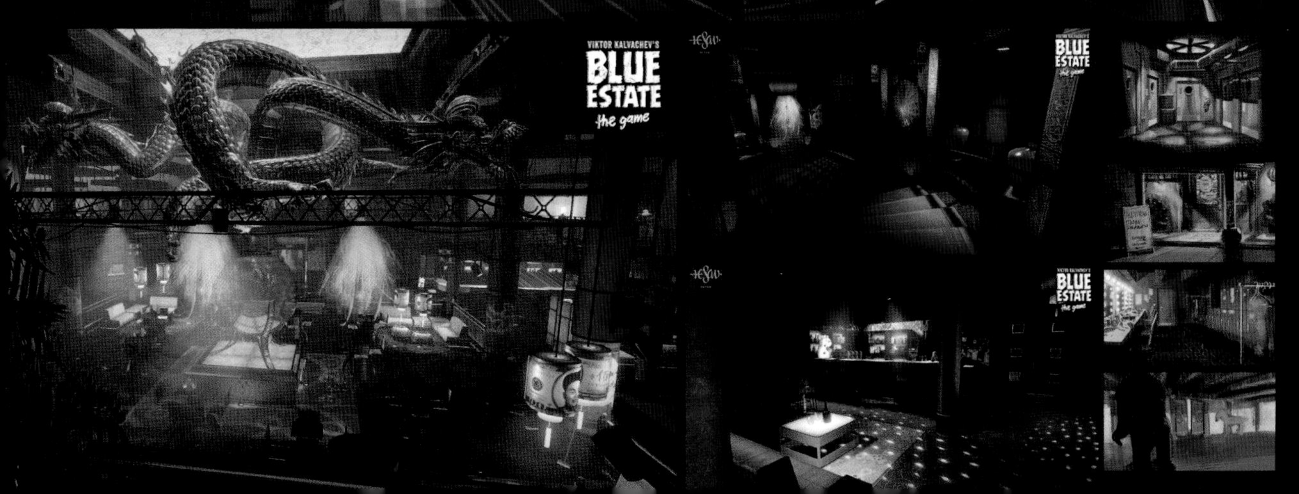
VIKTOR KALVACHEV'S
BLUE ESTATE
the game

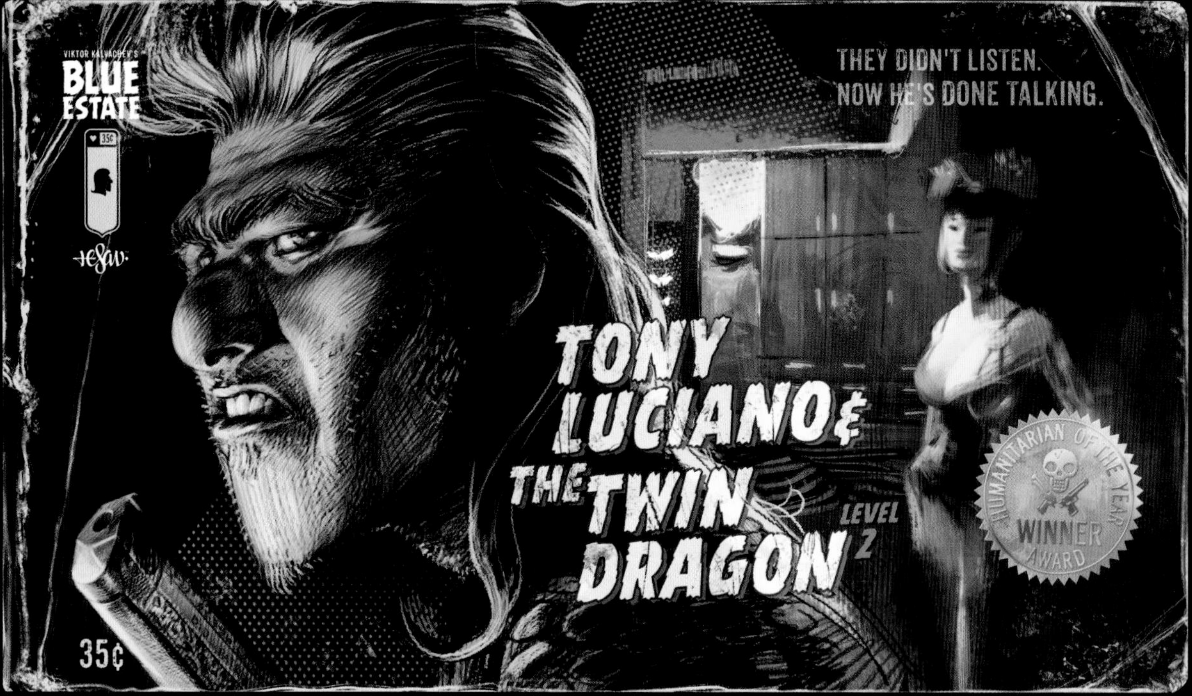
VIKTOR KALVACHEV'S
BLUE ESTATE
35¢
THEY DIDN'T LISTEN.
NOW HE'S DONE TALKING.
TONY LUCIANO & THE TWIN DRAGON
LEVEL 2
HUMANITARIAN OF THE YEAR
WINNER
AWARD
35¢

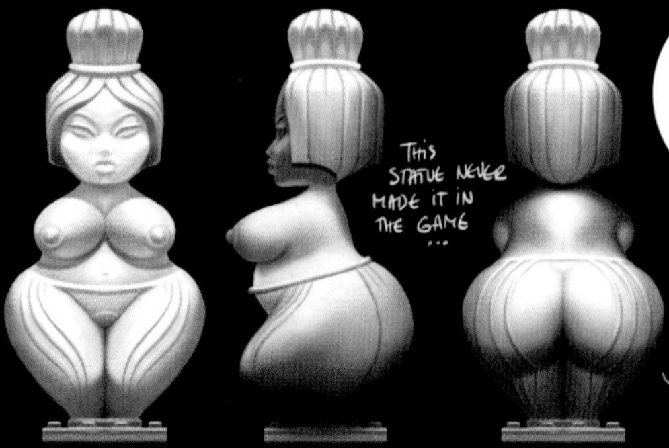
This statue never made it in the game...

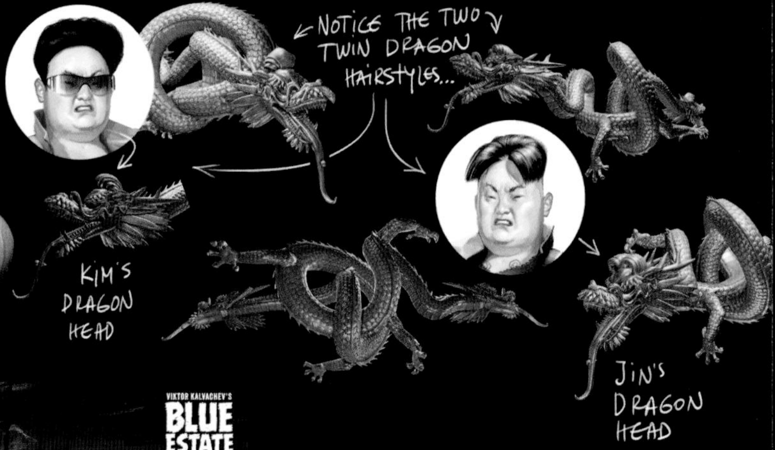
← NOTICE THE TWO TWIN DRAGON HAIRSTYLES...
KIM'S DRAGON HEAD
JIN'S DRAGON HEAD

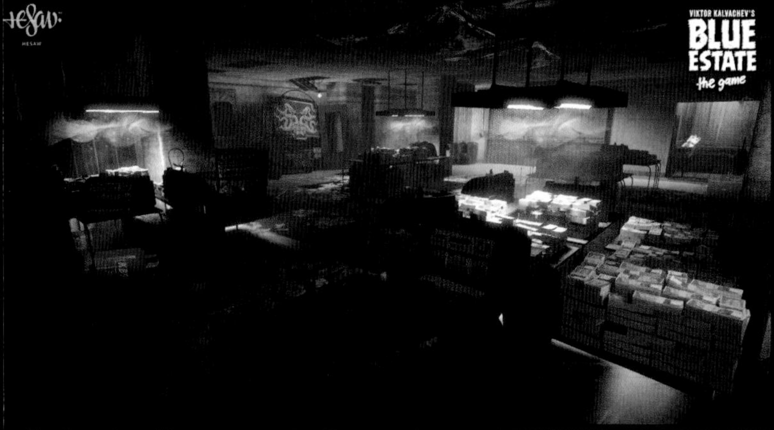
VIKTOR KALVACHEV'S
BLUE ESTATE
the game

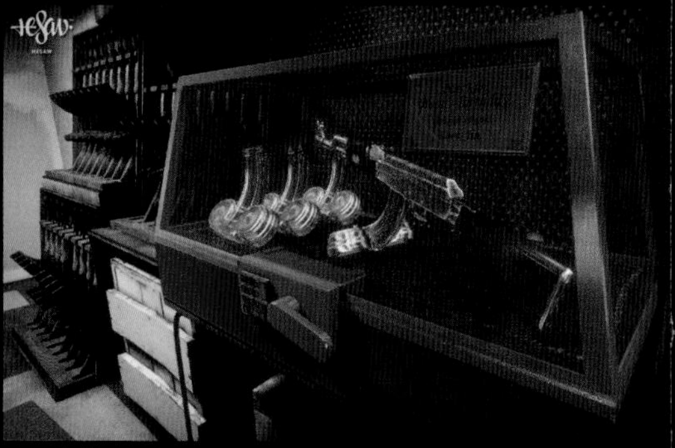

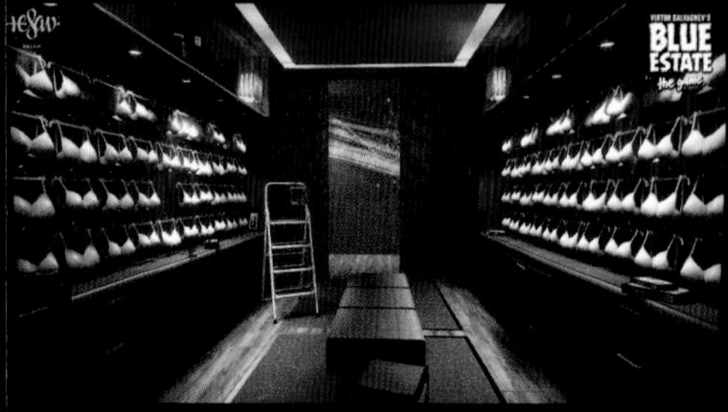
BLUE ESTATE

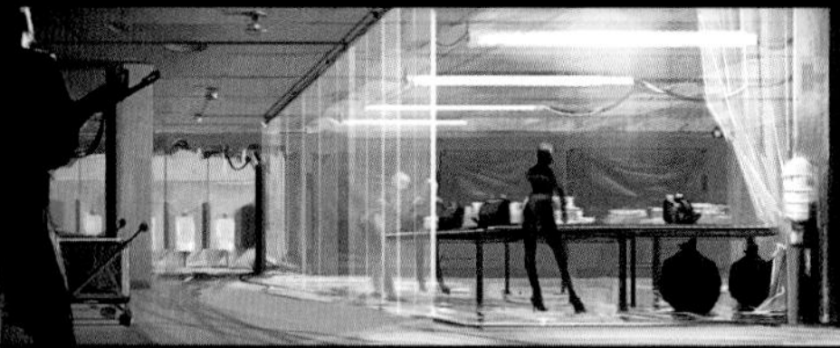

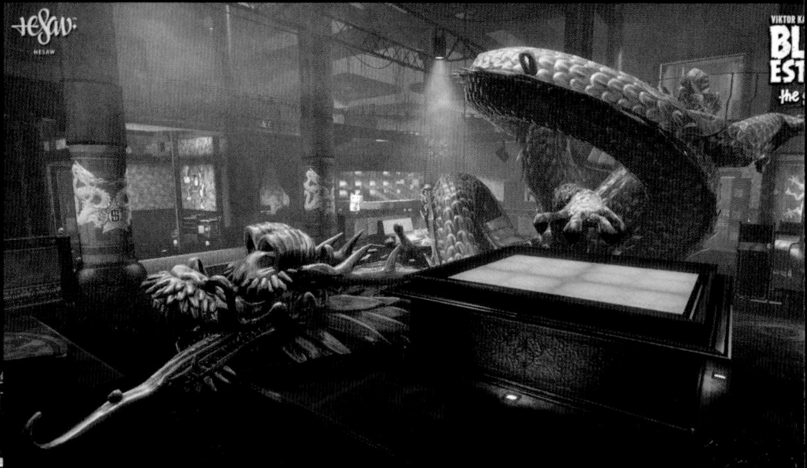

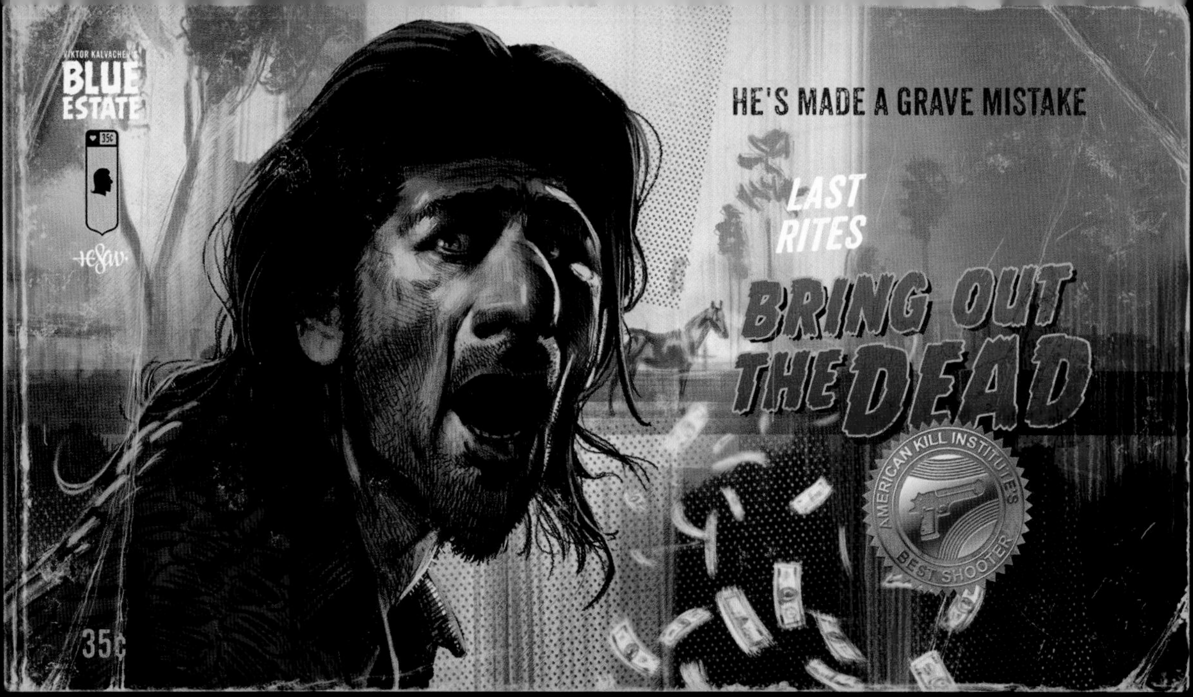
VIKTOR KALVACHEV'S
BLUE ESTATE
35¢
HE'S MADE A GRAVE MISTAKE
LAST RITES
BRING OUT THE DEAD
AMERICAN KILL INSTITUTE'S
BEST SHOOTER
35¢

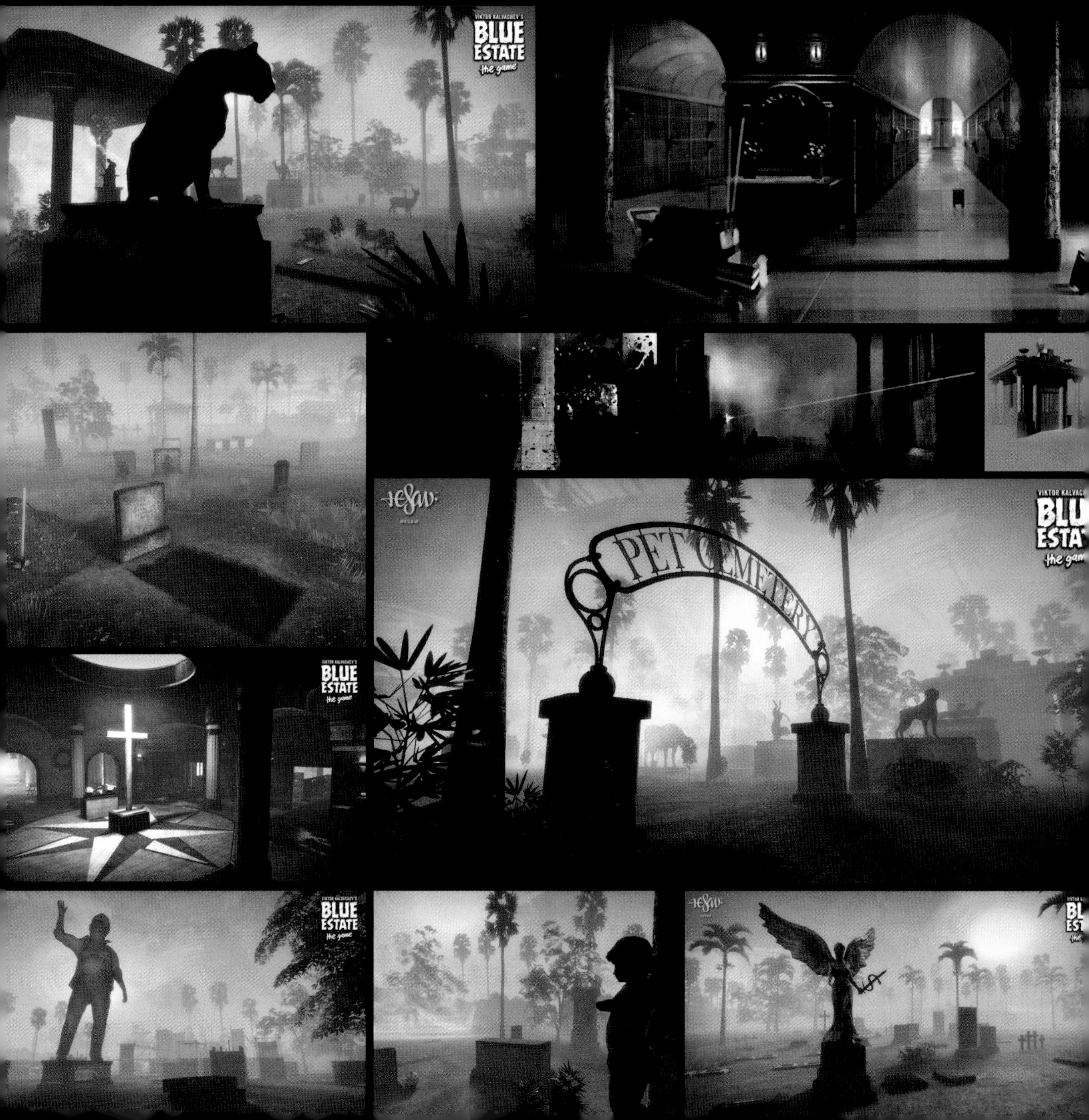
VIKTOR KALVACHEV'S
BLUE ESTATE
the game
PET CEMETERY

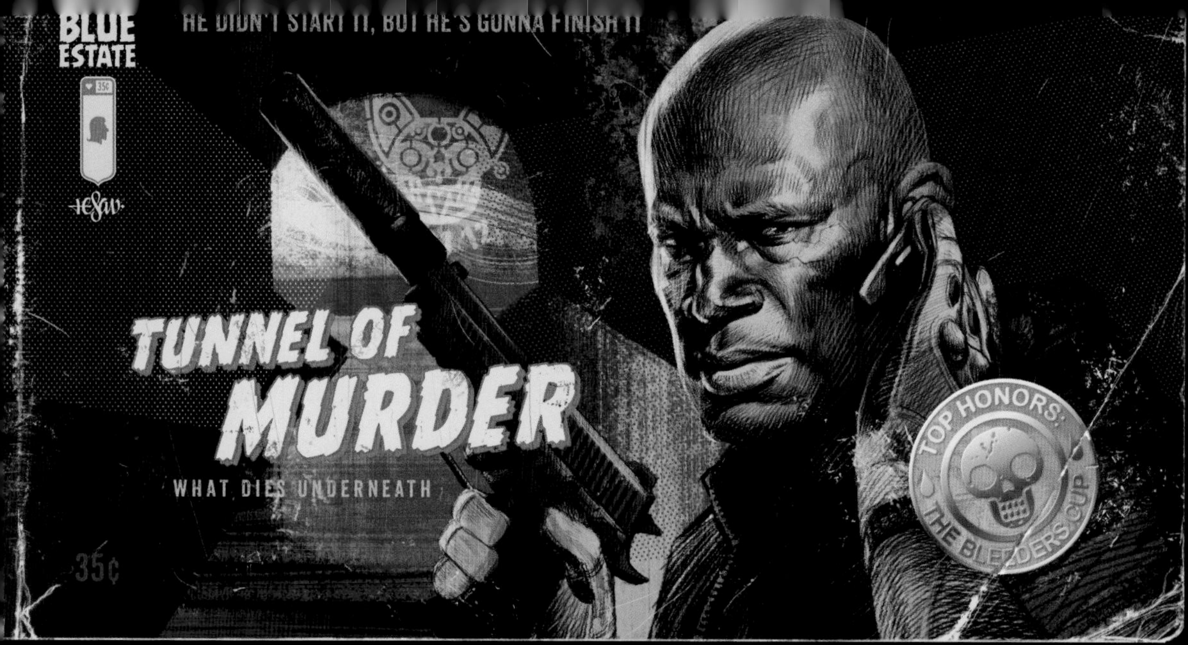
BLUE ESTATE
HE DIDN'T START IT, BUT HE'S GONNA FINISH IT
TUNNEL OF MURDER
WHAT DIES UNDERNEATH
35¢
TOP HONORS: THE BLEEDERS CUP

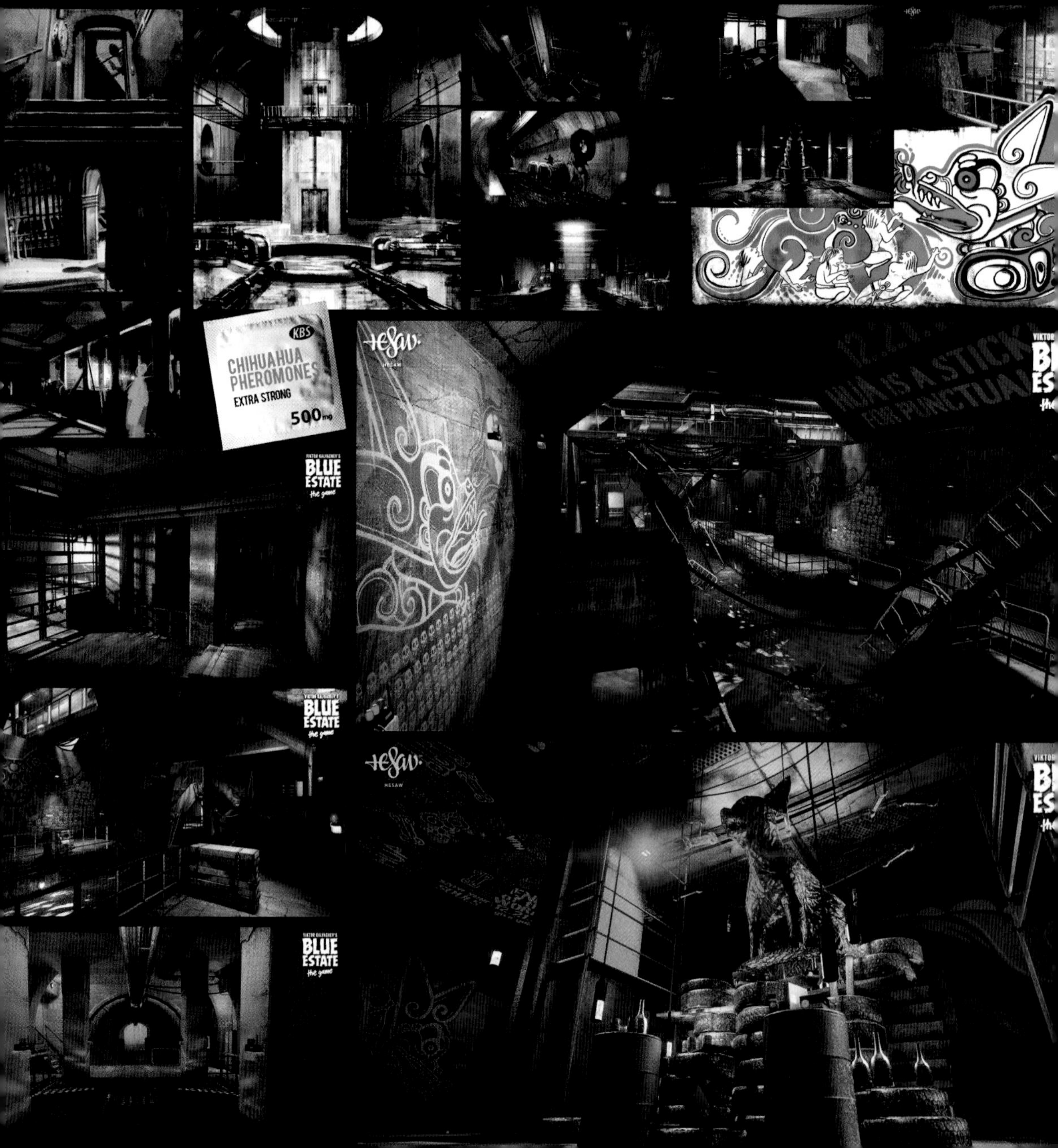
KBS
CHIHUAHUA PHEROMONES
EXTRA STRONG
500mg
BLUE ESTATE the game
HESAW

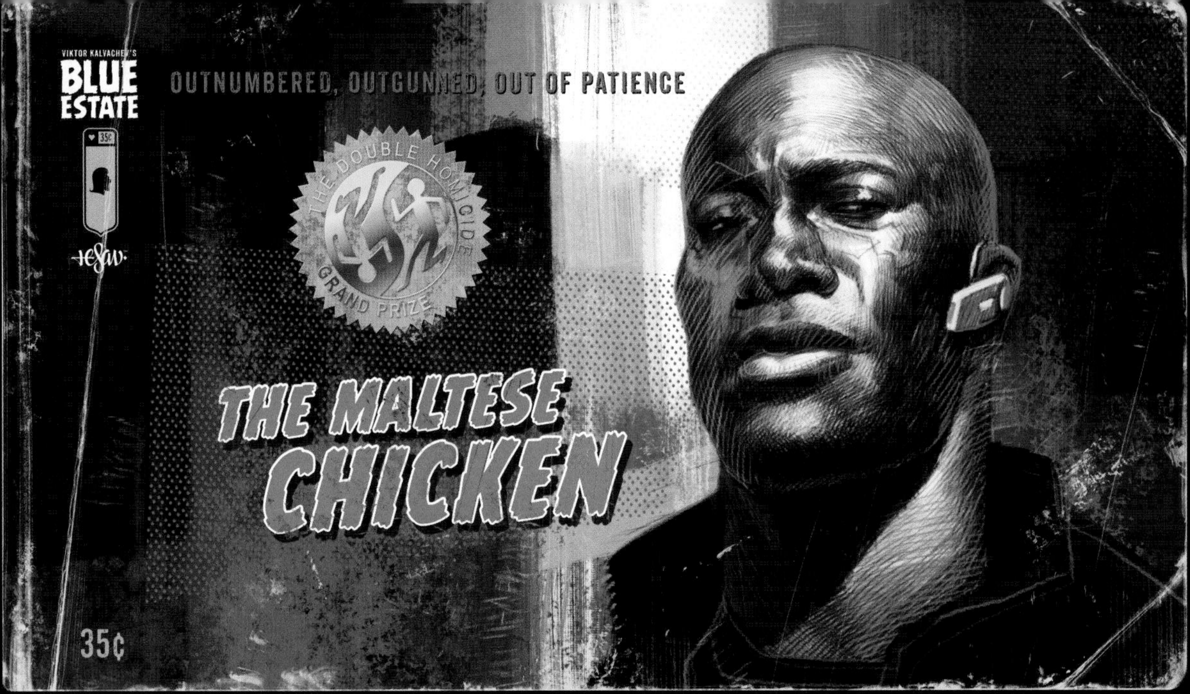
VIKTOR KALVACHEV'S
BLUE ESTATE
OUTNUMBERED, OUTGUNNED, OUT OF PATIENCE
THE DOUBLE HOMICIDE GRAND PRIZE
THE MALTESE CHICKEN
35¢

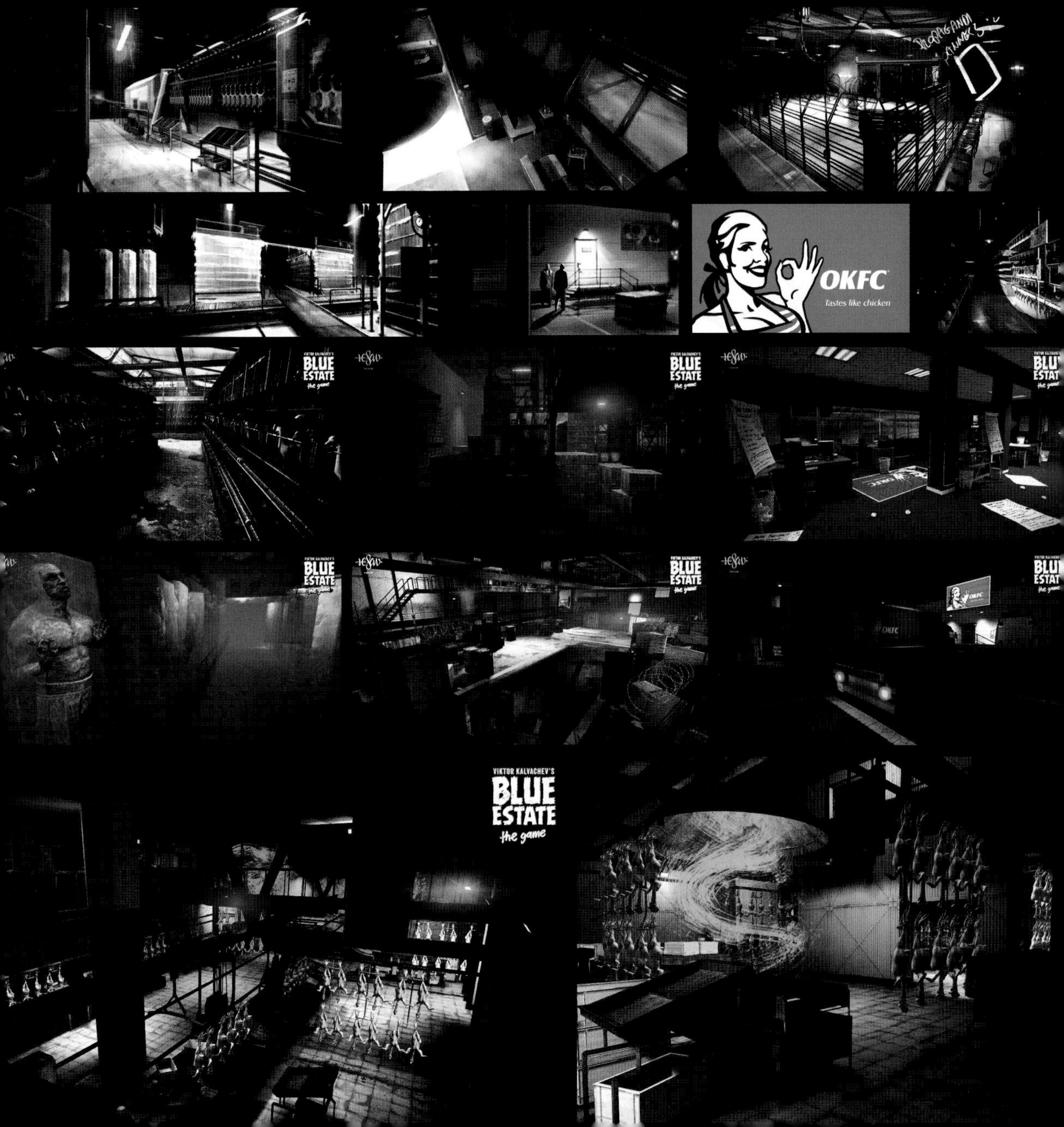
OKFC
Tastes like chicken
VIKTOR KALVACHEV'S
BLUE ESTATE
the game

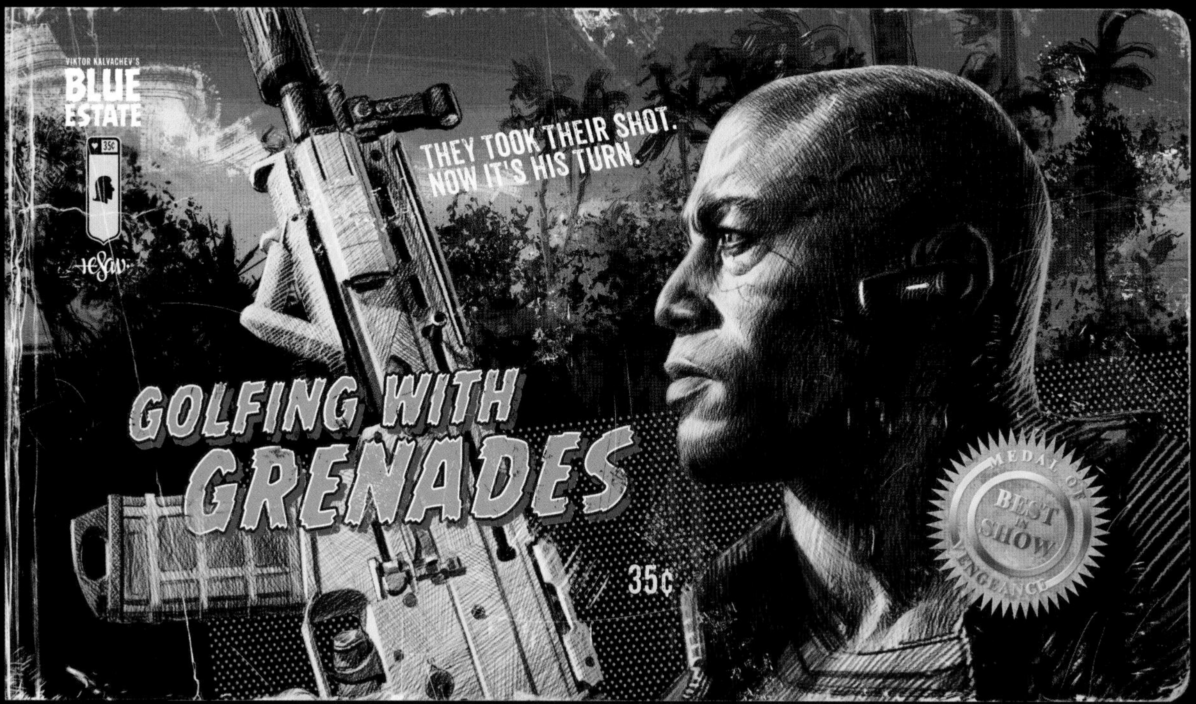

VIKTOR KALVACHEV'S
BLUE ESTATE
35¢
THEY TOOK THEIR SHOT.
NOW IT'S HIS TURN.
GOLFING WITH GRENADES
35¢
MEDAL OF VENGEANCE
BEST IN SHOW


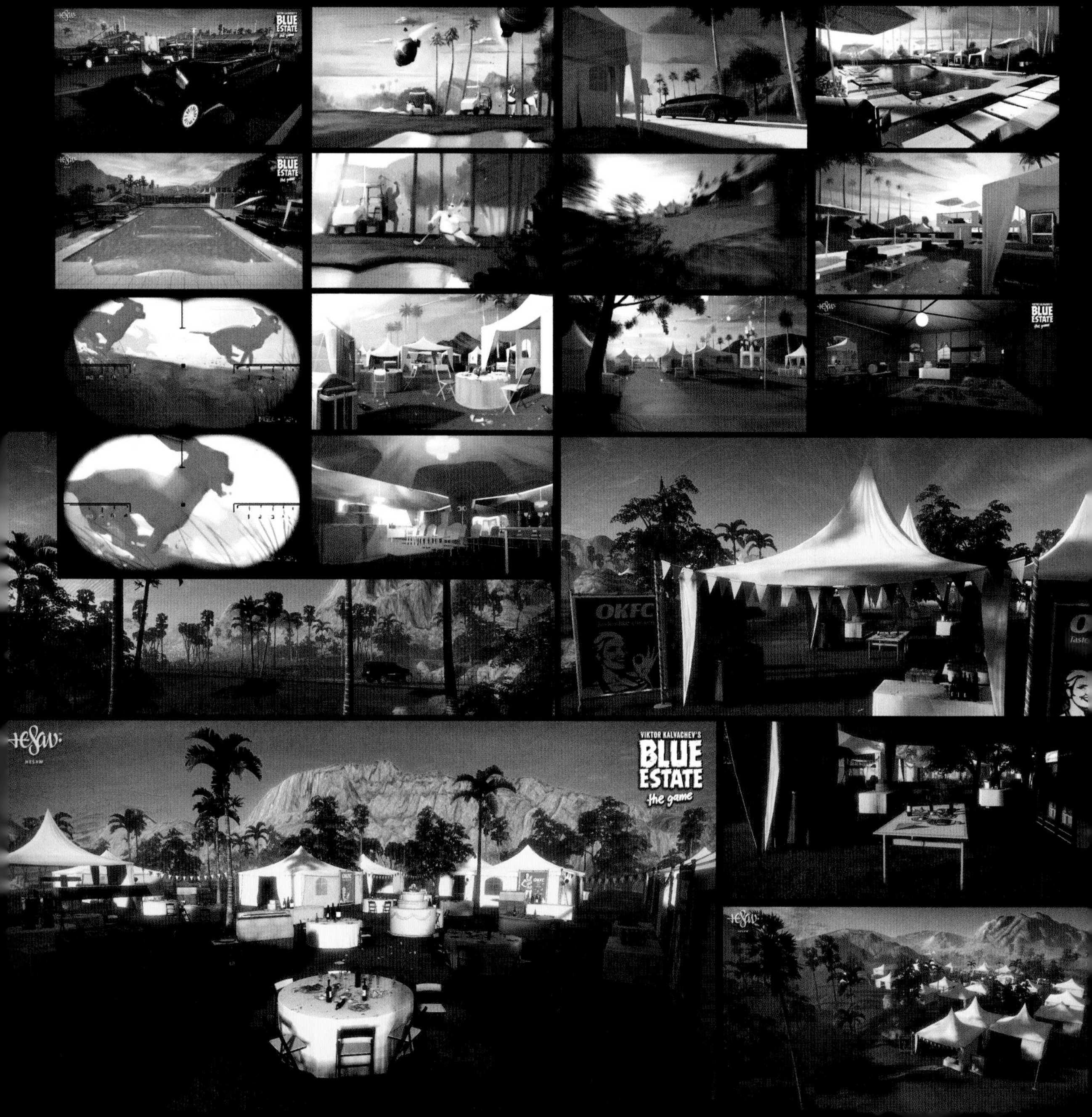

OKFC
HESAW
VIKTOR KALVACHEV'S
BLUE ESTATE
the game

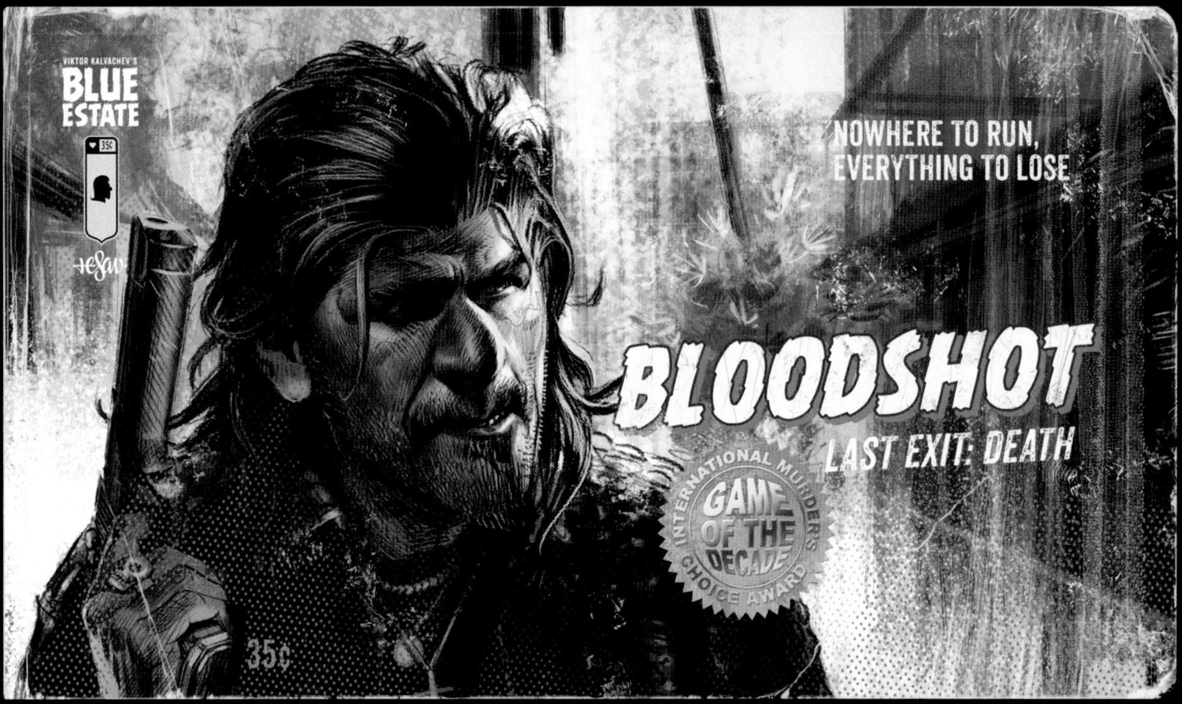
VIKTOR KALVACHEV'S
BLUE ESTATE
35¢
NOWHERE TO RUN,
EVERYTHING TO LOSE
BLOODSHOT
LAST EXIT: DEATH
INTERNATIONAL MURDERERS CHOICE AWARD
GAME OF THE DECADE
35¢

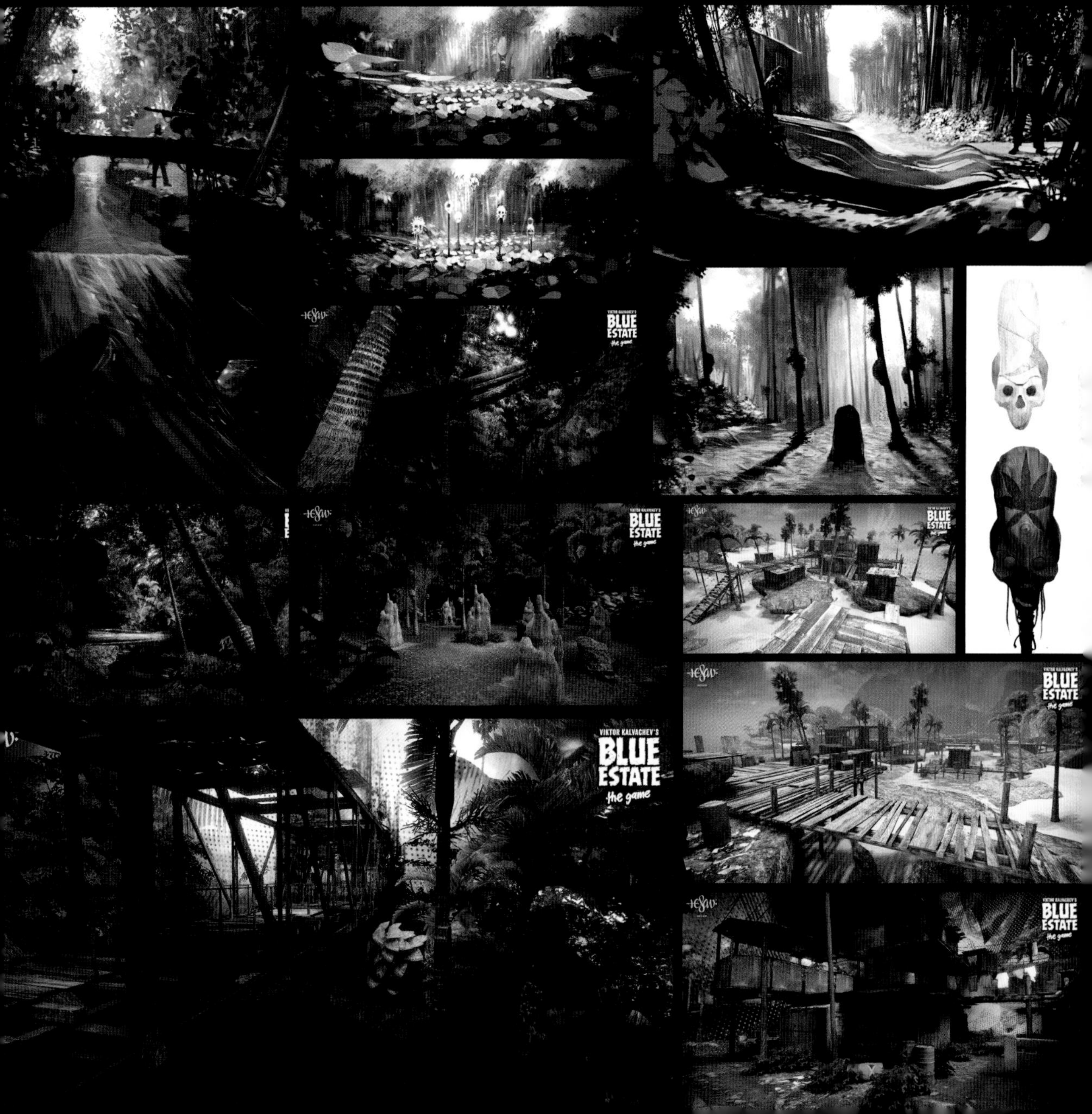
VIKTOR KALVACHEV'S
BLUE ESTATE
the game

We came up with a great system for randomizing the enemy characters allowing us to have over 70 unique looking bad guys per level. This plays a huge role in how the game feels as in a rail shooter level you are usually attacked by over 100 enemies and if unaddressed the enemies can get really repetitive. We split the models into 8 slots and created many different assets and ways to manipulate them. Here are just a few of the in-game results.

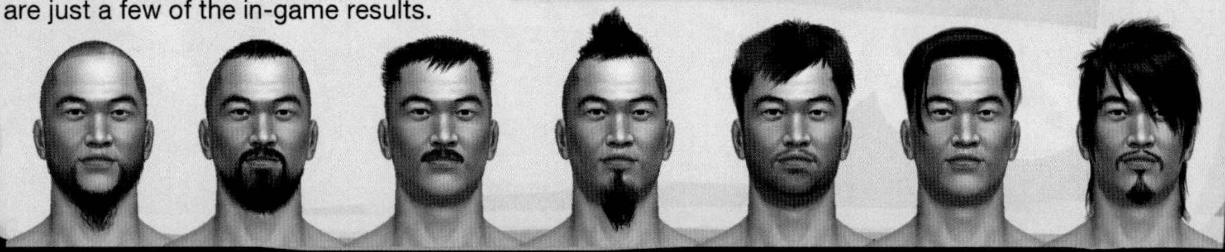

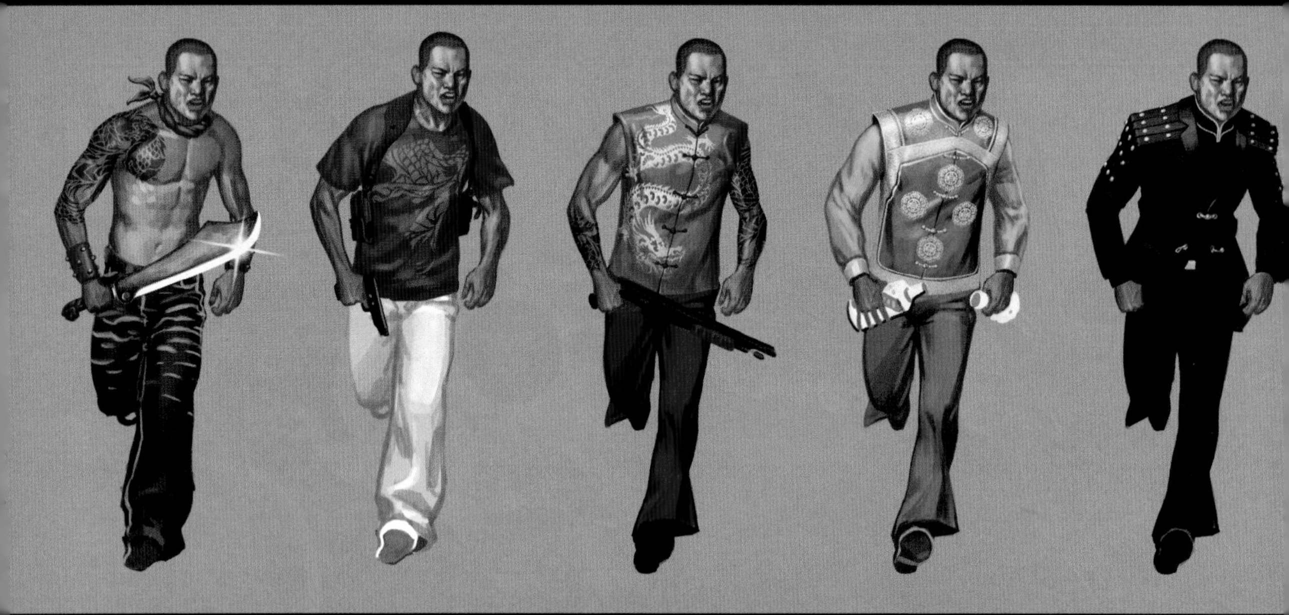

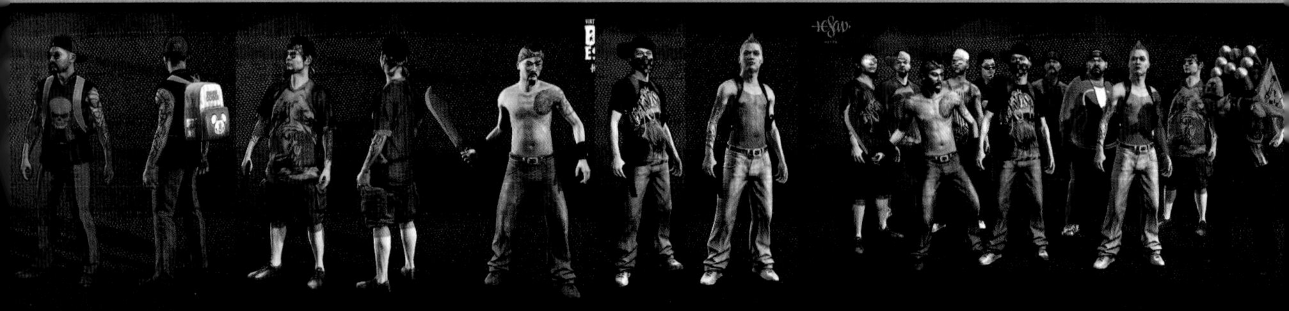

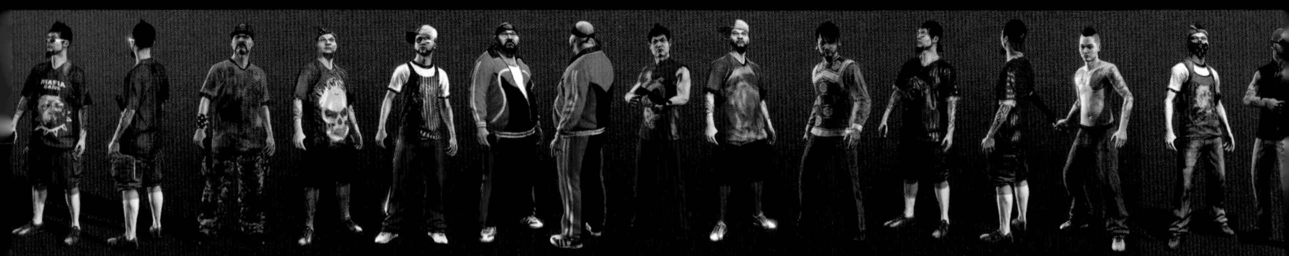

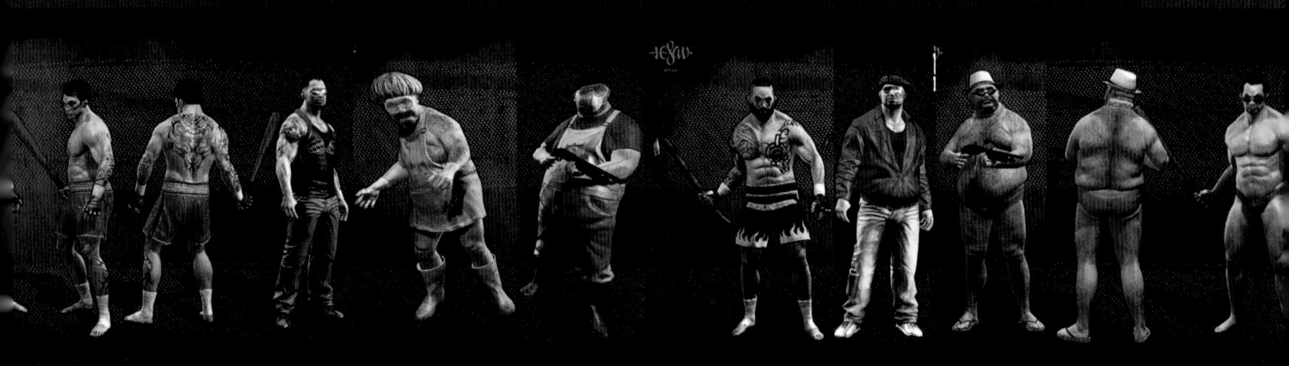

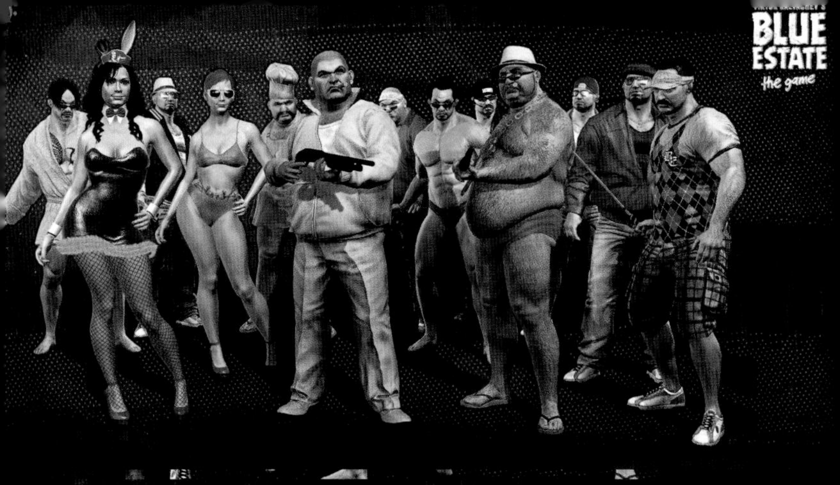
BLUE
ESTATE
the game

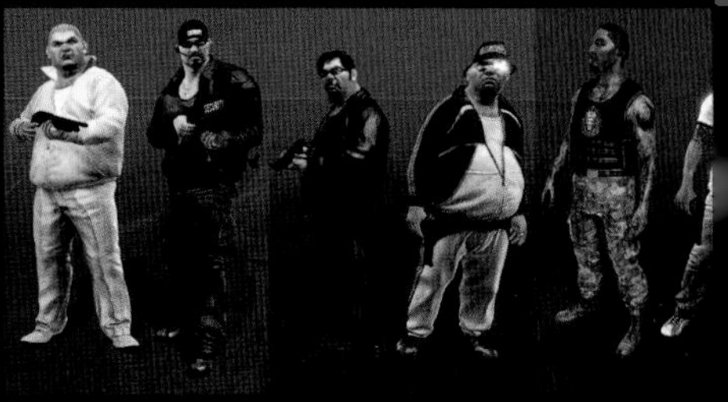

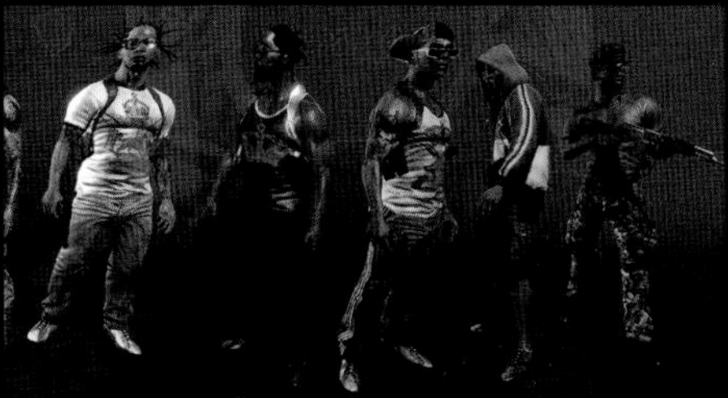

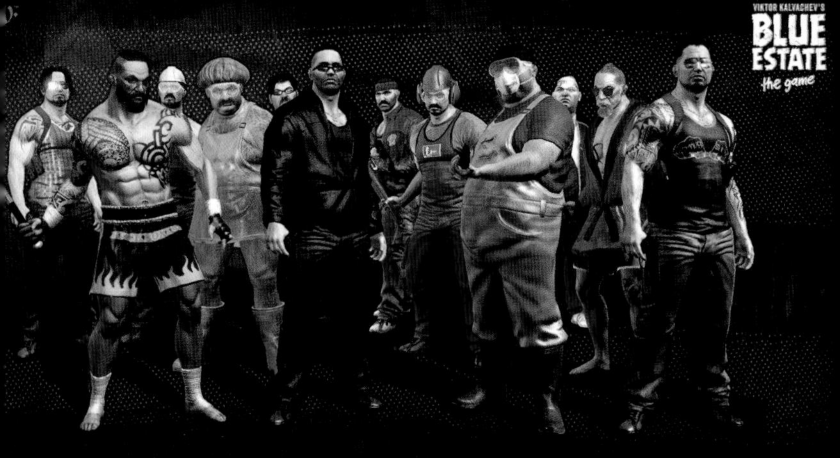
VIKTOR KALVACHEV'S
BLUE
ESTATE
the game

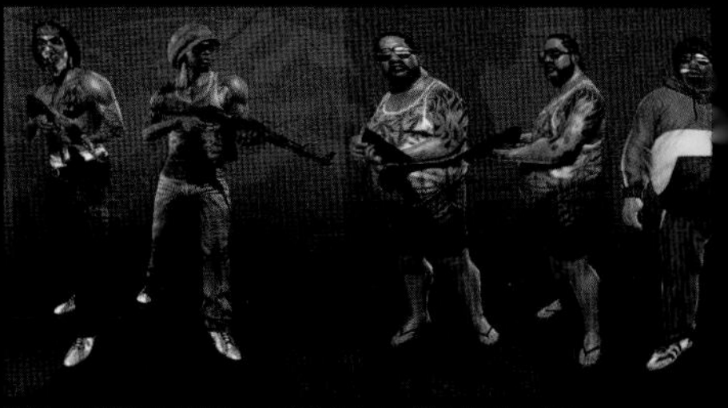

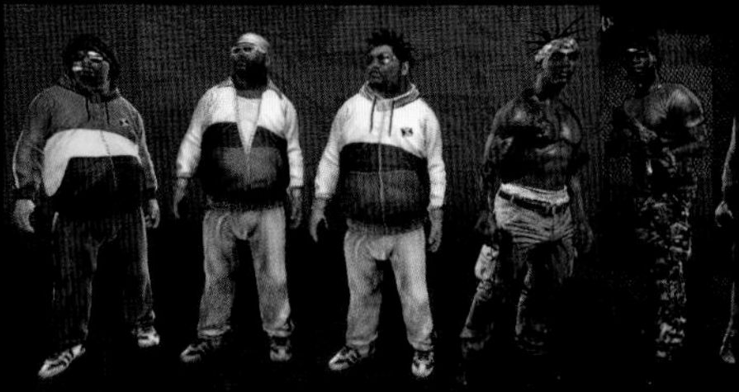

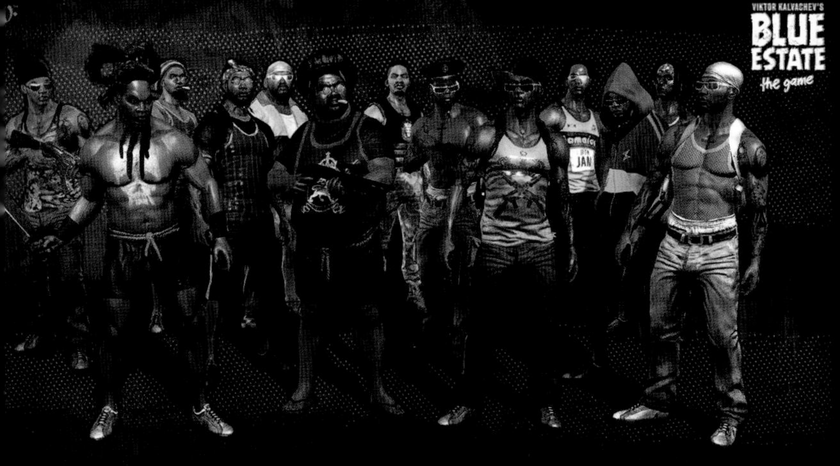
VIKTOR KALVACHEV'S
BLUE
ESTATE
the game

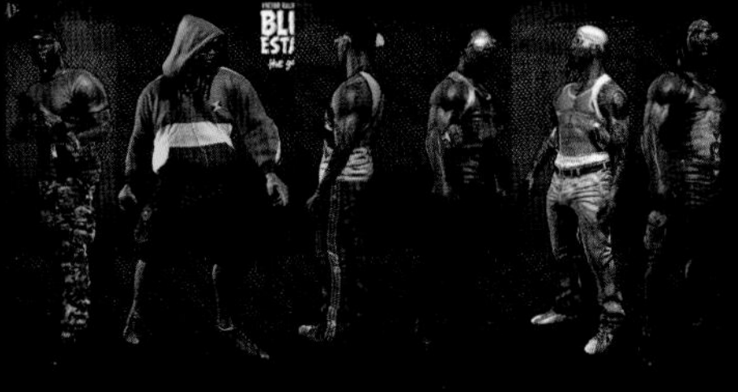

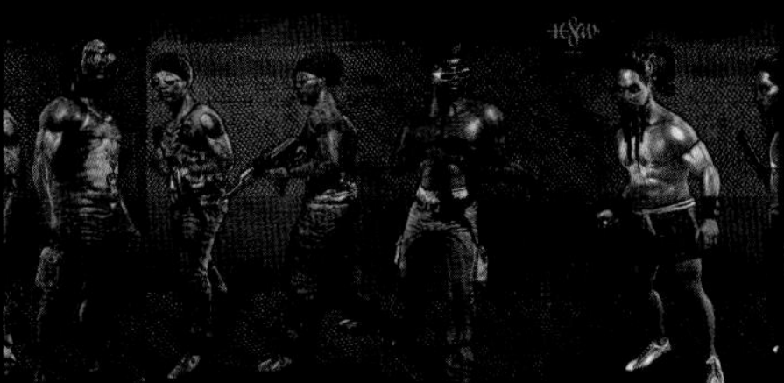

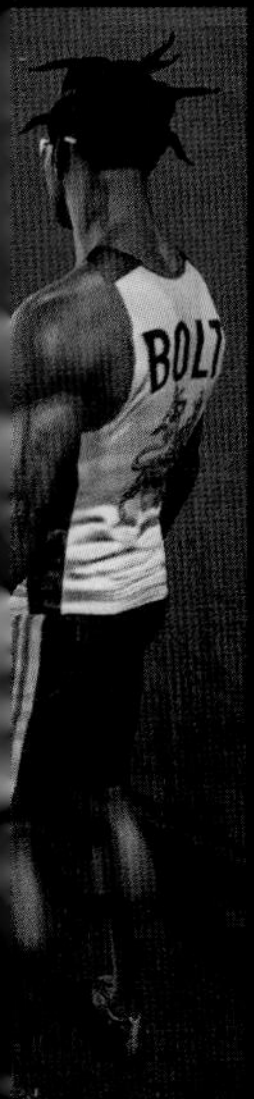
BOLT

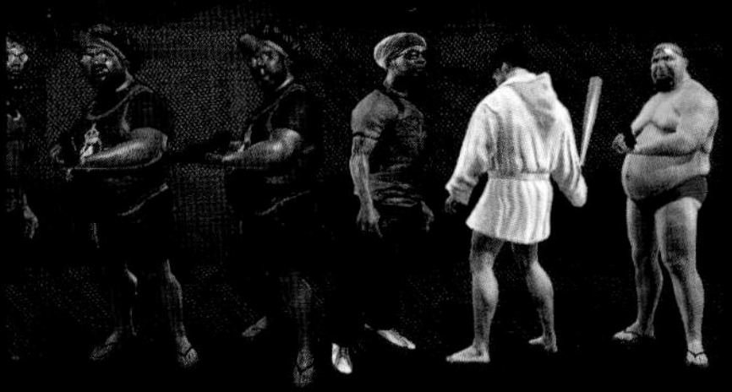

It wouldn't be a true male fantasy of a gangster world without their version of the women that inhabit it. Here is the better half of humanity as envisioned by the villains of our story.

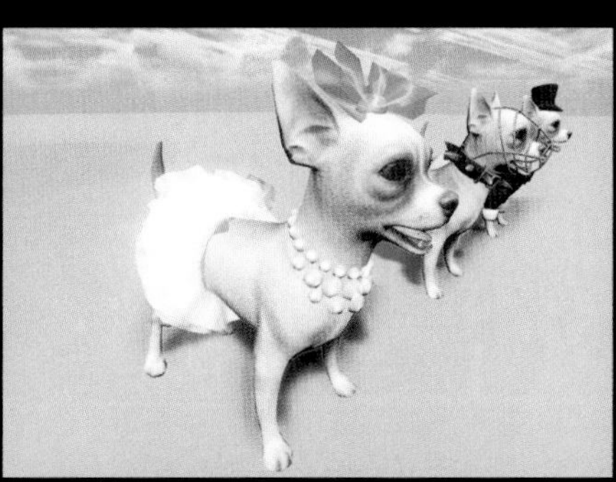

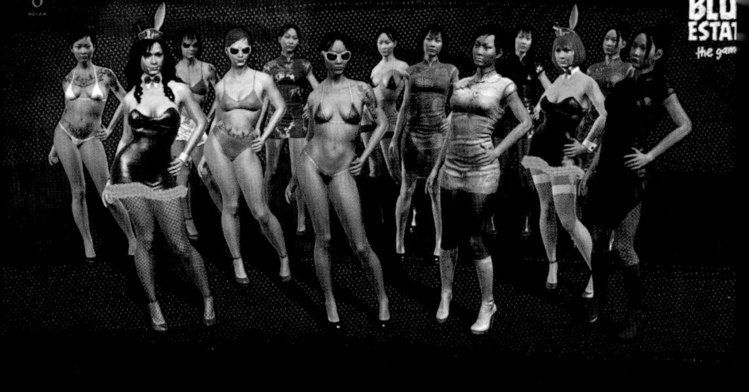

HESAW

# BLUE ESTATE THE GAME CREDITS

Blue Estate® created by Viktor Kalvachev & Kosta Yanev

## HESAW

Producer - Samuel Jacques
Creative Director & Art Director - Viktor Kalvachev
Associate producer - Jérémie Skornik
Technical Director - Arnaud Carré
Lead Technical Artist - Hervé "BirO" Vazeilles
Co-creative Director - Emmanuel Guardiola
Lead Programmer - François Karr
Senior Gameplay Programmer - Cyrille "YeDo" Combes
Programmer - Trung Nguyen
3D art design - Franck Chipouka
Senior Environment Artist - Eddy Neveu
Lead Character Artist & additional motion design
Christophe Dur
Senior Animator - Antonin Delboy
Additional Animator - Stéphane Fradet
Visual FX Artist - Orson Favrel
Audio director - Nicolas Bredin
Music - Eric Los
Game Designer - Amandine Lacomme
Senior Level Designer - Julian Lemonnier
Level Designer - Pierre Moret
Additional level design - Mathieu Lagadec
Game Design Trainee - Rémi Boutin

President - Oskar Guilbert
Managing Director - Samuel Jacques
Marketing Manager - Abrial Da Costa
Office Manager - Aurélie Savre

## CONTRACTORS

Scriptwriter - Ivan Brandon
Additional writing - Andrew Osborne
Motion Designer - François-Côme du Boistesselin
Additional 3D character models - BonArt Studio

## 2D Cinematic Artists:

Alexander Vachkov
Andrew Robinson
Bruno (NoX) Gore
Dan Brereton
Dan Panosian
Dustin Nguyen
Evgenii (Otto) Schmidt
Igor-Alban (The Black Frog) Chevalier
Jason Felix
John Hoffman
Juanjo Guarnido
Justin (Coro) Caufman
Lelio Bonaccorso
Mike Huddleston
Nathan Fox
Peter Nguyen
Pierre Alary
Robert Valley
Ted Mathot
Tomm Coker
Viktor Kalvachev
Colors - Viktor Kalvachev

## VOICE TALENTS

ROY DEVINE JR. - Doug Rand
TONY LUCIANO; LINO; DON LUCIANO - Ernesto Brandon
CLARENCE - Barry Johnson
MAURO - David Coburn
CHERRY POPZ - Nicole Poole
TENIU THE GRAVE; the SIK Brothers; BLOODSHOT -
Nicolas Parry-Jones
KOSTA KOKOSHKOV; ALYOSHA - Viktor Kalvachev
VARIOUS GANGSTERS - Doug Rand; Nicolas Parry-Jones;
David Coburn
MERMAID and VARIOUS GIRLS - Ann-Christine Herstadt

**This game could not have been made without the constant and unfailing support of Claudie Hawes; Douglas Hawes; Mariana Yanev and Kosta Yanev.**

www.BlueEstateTheGame.com